Animal Cruelty

Animal Cruelty

A Multidisciplinary Approach to Understanding

THIRD EDITION

Edited by

Cassandra L. Reyes
Associate Professor of Criminal Justice
West Chester University of Pennsylvania

Mary P. Brewster
Professor of Criminal Justice
Graduate Program Coordinator
West Chester University of Pennsylvania

Carolina Academic Press
Durham, North Carolina

Library of Congress Cataloging-in-Publication Data

Names: Reyes, Cassandra, editor. | Brewster, Mary P., editor.
Title: Animal cruelty : a multidisciplinary approach to understanding / [edited] by Cassandra L. Reyes, Mary P. Brewster.
Description: Third Edition. | Durham, North Carolina : Carolina Academic Press, LLC, [2022] | Revised edition of Animal cruelty, [2016] | Includes bibliographical references and index.
Identifiers: LCCN 2022036369 (print) | LCCN 2022036370 (ebook) | ISBN 9781531022327 (paperback) | ISBN 9781531022334 (ebook)
Subjects: LCSH: Animal welfare—United States. | Animal welfare—Law and legislation—United States.
Classification: LCC HV4764 .A635 2022 (print) | LCC HV4764 (ebook) | DDC 179/.3—dc23/eng/20220909
LC record available at https://lccn.loc.gov/2022036369
LC ebook record available at https://lccn.loc.gov/2022036370

Carolina Academic Press
700 Kent Street
Durham, North Carolina 27701
Telephone (919) 489-7486
Fax (919) 493-5668
www.cap-press.com

Printed in the United States of America

Contents

Section V • Current and Controversial Topics

Acknowledgments

We would like to thank Beth Hall and the entire Carolina Academic Press family for providing a forum for the third edition of this much-needed text on animal cruelty. We would like to extend our sincere gratitude to all of contributors to the book for sharing the expertise that they have attained through their research and field experience, and to Kitty Block, President and Chief Executive Officer of the Humane Society of the United States and Chief Executive Officer of Humane Society International, for her willingness to write the foreword for this manuscript.

We are also grateful to our graduate assistant, Miriam van der Spek, for her work on the instructor's manual.

—CLR and MPB

My heartfelt appreciation goes to my husband, Jaime: through his undying love and support, I have been able to continue bringing the topic of animal cruelty to the forefront, especially in areas where it is often overlooked. I also would like to thank our "furry kids," Diablo, Bastet, and Incognito, who remind me every day of the passion I have toward fighting the victimization of nonhuman animals.

—CLR

Special thanks go to my family, Ryan, Michael, Elle, Jade, Jet, and June for putting up with my absence from the dinner table on many occasions throughout this past year. Your patience, love, and support have sustained me throughout this project.

—MPB

Foreword

When it first appeared a decade ago, this anthology amply met emerging demand for a focused, multidisciplinary discussion of the social, cultural, historical, legal, psychological, political and other dimensions of animal cruelty. In this third edition, it remains a valuable resource for students and scholars working across many disciplines, and for many of us involved in organized animal protection. The recognition of cruelty to animals as a problem deserving of sustained study is now more common, but it is still remarkable to see the weight of contemporary scholarship and thought on the subject come together so well in one volume.

Human cruelty to animals takes many forms, both individual and institutional. Some of that cruelty we as a society prohibit and criminalize, some of it we try to inhibit and discourage, and some of it we accept, authorize or sanction. There is often disagreement about what practices are cruel, and in cases where people do agree, they may differ on what should be done to address the issue. But the inspiring thing about the current moment is that there are few human practices involving animals that are not the subject of sustained moral and practical scrutiny. That is a sign not only of real progress but of a more thoughtful and engaged society overall—one that increasingly values animals, takes account of the importance of the human-animal bond, and seeks to reinforce such connectedness through positive action across the range of social, cultural and political institutions. It is also one that extends its ethical consideration beyond a few privileged species, and grounds its public policy solutions on empirical evidence as well as a compassionate spirit.

In recent years, this deeper understanding of animal cruelty as a complex problem has enabled us to build a public policy framework for addressing certain activities harmful to animals. This has resulted, for example, in the designation of animal fighting and many other acts of animal cruelty as felony-level crimes across the country over the last few decades. As a society we are also far more engaged in examination of the connecting threads between bullying, harassment, exploitation of power and the different forms that abuse—including the abuse of animals—may take. We are also more inclined to recognize the sentinel status of acts of cruelty to animals and their co-occurrence with other forms of violence.

The criminal justice dimension is important, but it also raises challenges for a society engaged in substantive and highly charged debates over policing, sentencing, and the challenges of the justice system as a whole. Those who study animal protection and those who seek to advance it must come to terms with those challenges. I believe it is feasible—and imperative—that we do our best to balance the goal of accountability with an understanding that punitive approaches have their limits.

It is also true, as the contributions in this work make clear, that law is only one frame of reference. We are going to need others as we try to center cruelty to animals in broader discussions of violence and how to address it as a social problem. This will require thinking clearly about the kind of society we would like to see, one that acknowledges animals as deserving not only of our consideration but of greater inclusion and protection within our social contract. This goal does not and should not rely on punishment alone but on building out new practices, services and infrastructure that recognize and serve to address issues of unequal resources, to the benefit of animals and those who love and protect them. These features of a more humane society are rooted in the human capacity for kindness and an appreciation for the human-animal bond. And we can promote these values through affirmative laws and other positive approaches that focus not on human punishment but on the cultivation of a kind regard for animals within our families, communities and social institutions.

As this volume demonstrates, scholarship has taught us much about human kindness and cruelty during the last quarter century. But it is also clear that there is much more to learn. We need more research and more resources to support further inquiry. Does punishment deter cruelty to animals? Is mandated counseling for offenders effective? What is the value of humane education, prosocial learning and related early intervention in the lives of children? What training would most benefit humane society agents, law enforcement officers, social workers, psychologists and veterinarians? What might restorative justice mean when the cruelty involved is institutional rather than individual? How can future scholarship contribute to the goal of building a more inclusive animal protection movement? In pursuit of the answers to these and other questions, we must encourage and build upon the work that the contributors to this book have set out to do.

Kitty Block, President and Chief Executive Officer
The Humane Society of the United States, and
Chief Executive Officer of Humane Society International

Section I

Animal Cruelty

History, Legislation, and Prevalence

Chapter 1

Definitions of Animal Cruelty, Abuse, and Neglect

Phil Arkow and Randall Lockwood

Introduction

An ongoing, and perhaps unresolvable, challenge facing humane and law enforcement investigators, prosecutors, defense attorneys, judges, and juries is how to define such an abstract concept as animal cruelty. All human (and many non-human) societies attempt to identify actions that threaten to disrupt a stable, efficient, and harmonious group and take action against offenders. Cultural norms, laws, or other forces seek to restore balance by changing the behavior of those who transgress, or by removing them from society either temporarily or permanently. Even after two centuries of statutory language updates and case law precedents, the criminal justice system still faces a morass of conflicting legal, academic, cultural, and public perceptions in seeking to define animal cruelty, abuse and neglect.

Law and culture interact. The social norms of a particular culture give rise to the political actions that result in laws. The laws of a region (city, state, country) codify those norms and define a desired standard of behavior for all citizens. Certain elements of these laws are viewed as immutable by most people (e.g., prohibition of murder), while other provisions may change rapidly with changing social norms, sensitivities and situations (e.g., murder is acceptable in warfare). This kind of evolution of attitudes and legal standards has been particularly true for laws addressing animal cruelty which have undergone major changes in recent decades (Favre & Tsang, 1993; Frasch, 2008).

Historically, concern about animal cruelty initially reflected human-centered concerns either about the loss of use of animals as property, or consideration of what additional harm the perpetrators of such acts might do to humans. Early writings on duties to animals did not consider the impact of cruelty toward animal victims. In *Summa Contra Gentiles,* St. Thomas Aquinas reflected this prevailing view:

> ... if any passages of Holy Writ seem to forbid us to be cruel to dumb animals, for instance to kill a bird with its young, this is ... to remove man's thoughts from being cruel to other men, and lest through being cruel to other animals one becomes cruel to human beings.... (St. Thomas Aquinas, as cited in Regan & Singer, 1976, p. 59).

Some five centuries later, Immanuel Kant echoed this notion of reasons for concern about animal cruelty in his essay *Metaphysical Principles of the Doctrine of Virtue*:

> ... Our duties towards animals are merely indirect duties towards humanity. Animal nature has analogies to human nature, and by doing our duties to animals in respect of manifestations of human nature, we indirectly do our duties to humanity ... cruelty to animals is contrary to man's duty to himself, because it deadens in him the feeling of sympathy for their suffering, and thus a natural tendency that is very useful to morality in relation to other human beings is weakened (Kant, as cited in Regan & Singer, 1976, p. 125).

The idea that animal cruelty was an intrinsic, moral evil based on its impact on the animal itself is a relatively recent concept, first gaining a foothold in the late eighteenth century. This view was expressed quite clearly by Reverend Humphry Primatt in *The Duty of Mercy* (1776): "Pain is pain, whether it be inflicted on man or on beast; and the creature that suffers it, whether man or beast, being sensible of the misery of it while it lasts, suffers evil" (p. 21).

One of the most influential ideas concerning animal cruelty was buried in a footnote to *Introduction to the Principals of Morals and Legislation* by Jeremy Bentham (1789) entitled "Interests of the inferior animals improperly neglected in legislation." Bentham argued that the capacity for suffering is the vital characteristic that gives a being the right to legal consideration. The final sentence of the footnote is often used today as a foundation for those seeking to promote the cause of animals: "The question is not, Can they *reason?* nor, Can they *talk?* but *Can they suffer?*" (p. 130).

These writings stressed the contemporary concept that the definition and assessment of acts of animal cruelty must include consideration of the impact of these acts on the life, health, and well-being of the animal victim. This concept became popular in the 18th and 19th Centuries as part of what Moyn (2021) described as "a Christianity of good works," which evolved into a secular enlightenment ethic of empathetic identification with the pain of others manifesting in social justice movements including the abolition of slavery, prison reform, caring for wounded soldiers, and animal protection (Arkow, 2021).

Despite concerns about the effects of cruelty on the animals themselves, today, as in the 18th Century, animals are legally viewed as property and animal cruelty is a crime against the property owner. The status of animals as a special category of property that is capable of pain, suffering, and death, and to which we can form unique attachments, is rarely recognized in legislation or case law, but has increasingly attracted the attention of legal scholars who argue for the recognition of a new category of "living property" or "sentient property" (Favre, 2009; Matlack, 2006).

Similarly, courts wary of weighing in on the unresolved dilemmas of whether animal well-being is a matter of moral concern or a result of their alleged inalienable rights may be persuaded by growing evidence that animal abusers pose potential concurrent or future risks for child maltreatment, domestic violence, elder abuse, and other criminal offenses (Arkow, 2021). Keeley (2020) suggested that a more comprehensive examination of the prosecution of animal cruelty would be to follow the abovementioned statement by Bentham with another question: "Who else could be suffering at the same hands?" Turgoose and McKie (2020) suggested the criminal justice system should see the interconnected nature of human and animal abuse as "inclusive victimology." These considerations often lead the courts to take animal cruelty more seriously in consideration of what the act tells us about the perpetrator and the risks he or she poses to society.

The core purpose of most Western legal systems is to achieve what the National District Attorneys Association refers to as balanced and restorative justice or BARJ (Harp, 2002). Under the BARJ model, criminal justice systems should strive to achieve three goals:

1. hold offenders accountable for their actions;
2. protect the public from those who would bring harm to people or property; and
3. restore or rehabilitate offenders who can be returned to society.

With respect to animal cruelty, the challenge is in defining acts that cannot be socially tolerated and which identify those who threaten further harm to people and property. This process must involve attempts at classification of acts of abuse and neglect and their significance in meeting these objectives.

Defining cruelty to animals (the most common legal term), animal abuse (a preferred operational term that has not yet been as widely adopted in the legislative lexicon), or neglect is a daunting challenge. Each individual has their own definitions of animal maltreatment, based upon personal experiences, upbringing, cultural standards, spiritual beliefs, and other variables. These definitions are organic, and change based on time, experience, and situational contexts (Sinclair, Merck, & Lockwood, 2006). Individual concerns for the welfare of animals that result in reports of suspected cruelty may not meet the legal definitions of maltreatment in a specific jurisdiction, and the interpretation and enforcement of animal cruelty may vary widely from agency to agency (Arkow, 2003).

Consequently, recognizing animal cruelty, abuse, or neglect—and building a successful criminal case against it—is not always easy, particularly in a society that condones and institutionalizes such accepted practices as hunting and intensive livestock production while simultaneously revering its companion animals. If beauty is in the eye of the beholder, then its antithetical construct of cruelty is equally subjective as well. What an outraged member of the public perceives to be abusive treatment of animals may differ greatly from the bottom-line economic perspective of the animal's owner, the formal language of state statutes, an academic interpretation, and ultimately what a jury decides. In the end, the best one can say about defining cruelty is that it is like trying to define pornography: you can't define it, but you think you know it when you see it (Arkow, 2006).

Definitions of Terms

All 50 states have enacted criminal laws designed to punish individuals who commit acts of cruelty against animals. Most state anti-cruelty statutes are comprised of six elements:

1. the types of animals protected;
2. the types of acts prohibited, or duties of care required;
3. the mental culpability required to meet a standard of liability;
4. the defenses to criminal liability;
5. certain activities exempted from the law; and
6. penalties for each offense.

Underlying the application of these elements are additional dimensions that can affect whether the community or the legal system will take action in response to an act. These include: the intrinsic and extrinsic value of the animal victim; the deviant nature of the act itself (e.g., its level of depravity); public and professional recognition of the victims' capacity for stress, pain, fear or suffering; and financial cost to society to address the consequences of the act.

While the concept behind these provisions may seem straightforward, the devil is in the details and the definitions underlying them can be particularly problematic. A majority of states define cruelty with such vague and ambiguous language that, unless the alleged act or omission is extreme and outrageous, it is unlikely to be perceived to violate the statute (Lacroix, 1999).

In common usage, the terms cruelty to animals, abuse, and neglect may appear interchangeable in some contexts, and more narrowly defined in others. They encompass a range of behaviors harmful to animals, from unintentional neglect to malicious killing, with tremendous differences in the underlying motivations and outcomes of these acts. Some incidents may be individualized (an owner leaving a dog without adequate food and water, a juvenile tying a firecracker to a cat) or institutionalized (abuses in puppy mills, dogfighting rings, factory farms or biomedical research enterprises). Attempting to use any one word such as "cruelty," which can describe such a broad range of behaviors and motivational states, is highly challenging at best, and runs the risk of overuse and weakened impact (Rowan, 1999). It is difficult to arrange so many divergent acts of commission and omission along a continuum of care that is universally acceptable across a variety of cultures.

The most spectacular, egregious, and publicized cruelty cases may be rooted in psychopathological behavior or indicative of other forms of family and community violence. However, the vast majority of cases that are reported to humane law enforcement agencies represent instances of neglect, animal maltreatment that may often be unintentional due to lack of education or temporary lapses in care from an otherwise responsible owner. Some neglect may be incidental, short-term, and easily resolved through educational or social services interventions; other neglect may be long-term, large-scale, and chronic (Crook, 2000). Legislators are coming to recognize that highly charged cruelty cases may not reflect the vast majority of animal maltreatment instances, and consequently are expanding the purview of animal welfare legislation. For example, the Hawaii legislature in 1998 noted that the existing statute identified only those acts which were the most heinous and extreme, such as beating, mutilation, poisoning, starvation, and torture. However, on a daily basis, other less overt acts such as daily neglect also resulted in the inhumane treatment of animals. Thus, the legislature agreed that pet animals deserved a minimum level of care including adequate food, water, and shelter (Hawaii State Legislature, 1998).

Perhaps the simplest and most effective definition may be one suggested in a British veterinary medical dictionary. Blood and Studdert (1999) defined cruelty as the infliction of pain or distress unnecessarily. However, even here, the authors noted that the "definition of unnecessary varies between countries and from time to time in one country. Determination of the prevailing standard of cruelty can only be decided by the courts" (p. 295). The worst cases, they noted, should be pursued under the classification of aggravated cruelty.

Black's Law Dictionary (2021) provides a somewhat more detailed definition of animal cruelty that addresses the issue of necessity. It defines it as:

> The infliction of physical pain, suffering, or death upon an animal, when not necessary for purposes of training or discipline or (in the case of death) to procure food or to release the animal from incurable suffering, but done wantonly, for mere sport, for the indulgence of a cruel and vindictive temper, or with reckless indifference to its pain.

Perspectives on Definitions

Numerous interest groups have attempted to craft specific definitions of animal maltreatment.

Researchers

Academic attempts to standardize a definition of animal maltreatment have been largely unsuccessful and have generally not been reflected in legal standards. Felthous and Kellert (1987) defined "substantial" cruelty to animals as a "pattern of deliberately, repeatedly, and unnecessarily hurting vertebrate animals in a manner likely to cause serious injury" (p. 1715).

Note the interpretational problems with such definitions: is an individual or unrepeated act of heinous physical torture that is not part of a pattern cruel? If the perpetrator is not aware of possible painful outcomes of his act, is it cruel? Given growing discussion of sentience and welfare in invertebrates (e.g., Broom, 2020), should only vertebrates be afforded this protection?

Ascione (1993) said developing a widely acceptable definition of animal cruelty would be as difficult as defining interpersonal aggression. He believed that achieving consistency would prove more daunting than in the parallel child welfare field where federal definitions and specific categories of physical abuse, sexual abuse, emotional abuse, and neglect are extant. Nevertheless, he attempted to contrive a working definition of animal cruelty that captured the most common features of 50 state statutes: "Socially unacceptable behavior that intentionally causes unnecessary pain, suffering, or distress to and/or death of an animal" (Ascione, 1993, p. 228).

Parsing this working definition uncovers a range of challenging issues. "Socially unacceptable" requires subjective sensitivity to cultural variations, economic realities, and political pressures in judgments of what a community values. This definition, widely cited over the years, excludes socially approved practices related to the treatment or use of animals in veterinary practices and livestock production, animal husbandry, hunting, and laboratory research. "Behavior" is meant to include acts of omission and commission. What does Ascione (1993) mean by "unnecessary"? "Pain, suffering and distress" are described as physical conditions as distinguished from emotional or psychological suffering, the latter being more subjective, if not impossible, to verify. Although not specifically included in his definition, bestiality may be considered cruel even when proving physical harm to the animal cannot be accomplished.

As the definition was considered in a rapidly evolving corpus of literature, Ascione and Shapiro subsequently (2009) refined the original definition and called the condition animal abuse: "Nonaccidental, socially unacceptable behavior that causes pain, suffering or distress to and/or the death of an animal" (p. 570).

Note the subtle change from "cruelty" (which implies malicious intent on the part of the perpetrator) to "abuse" (which mirrors child protection systems terminology and which describes maltreatment that occurs regardless of the perpetrator's intentionality). Also note the addition of "nonaccidental," to capture new veterinary forensics terminology describing "Non-Accidental Injury" (NAI) and implying a certain measure of causality. Most importantly, note the elimination of "intentionally" from the earlier definition. Animal cruelty, abuse, and neglect cases should be able to stand on their own merits regarding the facts and evidence of the case without having to overcome a nearly impossible hurdle of proving the perpetrator's intent.

Government Panels

One of the most comprehensive attempts to address animal suffering began in 1965, when the United Kingdom government commissioned an investigation, led by Professor Roger Brambell, into the welfare of intensively farmed animals. This was driven in part, by concerns raised in the book, *Animal Machines* (Harrison, 1964). The goal of the Brambell Commission was not to offer a critique of the agricultural industry, but rather to define practices that would maximize the quality of life for animals in confinement. As a result of the Commission's initial report, the Farm Animal Welfare Advisory Committee was created to monitor the livestock production sector. In 1979, this was replaced by the Farm Animal Welfare Council, and that year, they codified what has come to be known as the **Five Freedoms**:

1. **Freedom from hunger and thirst**, by ready access to water and a diet to maintain health and vigor;
2. **Freedom from discomfort**, by providing an appropriate environment;
3. **Freedom from pain, injury, and disease**, by prevention or rapid diagnosis and treatment;
4. **Freedom to express normal behaviour**, by providing sufficient space, proper facilities, appropriate company of the animal's own kind; and
5. **Freedom from fear and distress**, by ensuring conditions and treatment which avoid mental suffering.

The Five Freedoms have achieved worldwide recognition and are a component of national legislation, marketing, and farm assurance schemes. They have withstood much criticism and, within Great Britain, are the cornerstone of government and industry policy and the Codes of Recommendations for the Welfare of Livestock (Farm Animal Welfare Council, 2009).

Although the intent of the concept of the Five Freedoms is to set goals for promoting welfare, animal advocates have argued that these definitions can be used to help define levels of animal cruelty by noting which of these freedoms are not being met in specific circumstances. Patronek and Weiss (2011) use the concept of the Five Freedoms to illustrate how failing to meet the conditions of many of the freedoms can indicate conditions under which animal cruelty laws can be applied. They specifically apply this analysis to cases of animal hoarding in which many animals may be kept under conditions which they identify as "A life not worth living" (*see* Chapter 9).

Similarly, Wathes (2010), a member of the Farm Animal Welfare Council, notes that the Council's most recent analysis builds on Bentham's foundations and proposes that acceptable welfare should move beyond the current test of whether the animal suffers to a new standard of whether the animal has a life worth living, from the animal's point of view.

Recently, the role of sentience in assessing farm animal welfare has attracted greater attention. Nawroth et al. (2019) review the welfare implications of current farm animal cognition research, particularly focusing on cattle, horses, pigs, and small ruminants. They identify a variety of cognitive capacities they argue should be taken into consideration when assessing welfare or the absence of welfare. These include physical cognition (categorization, numerical ability, object permanence, reasoning, and tool use) and social cognition (individual discrimination and recognition, communication with humans, social learning, attribution of attention, prosociality, and fairness). In the past, such concerns focused on species that were obviously cognitively complex such as great apes, elephants, and cetaceans. Jones (2013) argues that even the most progressive current welfare policies lag behind, are ignorant of, or arbitrarily disregard the science on sentience and cognition. Future research into animal sentience and cognition in a wider variety of species is likely to present new challenges to the assessment and legal definition of animal suffering and cruelty.

Public Opinion

Definitions in statutes are written and negotiated by attorneys and legislators responding to public demands for change. What varying stakeholders in any jurisdiction seek to change can be highly contentious, particularly in such an emotionally charged environment as animal protection. Building a consensus depends upon achieving wide public agreement: as Abraham Lincoln said, "Public sentiment is everything. With public sentiment, nothing can fail; without it nothing can succeed" (Basler, 2001, p. 458).

But the constituents interested in issues facing animals represent a fractious element of society with highly divergent interests. Morgan (1983) first described a continuum of public attitudes toward animals ranging from radical Animal Liberation and activist Animal Rights through more centrist Animal Welfare and Animal Control to more conservative Animal Use and Animal Exploitation. Animal activists frequently define any act in which an animal is perceived to suffer as a violation of the animal's alleged inherent rights, although such rights have never been established in a legal context in a system where animals are defined as property and are lacking in legal standing. Such attitudes can vary widely within and across communities as a function of economy, population demographics, education, and other variables. The criminal justice field is continually challenged by disconnects between varying professional, personal, public, and legal standards regarding alleged animal maltreatment (Arkow & Munro, 2008).

Legislation, Law Enforcement, Prosecutors, and Judges

While law enforcement, prosecutors, and jurists may take comfort in a "just the facts" approach that minimizes their need to make ethically challenging decisions, the framework for animal cruelty law is fraught with inherent ethical debates. Anti-cruelty statutes are most often found among offenses against public morals, order, and decency, with little or no recognition of the crime's effect upon the victim. Meanwhile, these laws come from a historical tradition in which animals are firmly established as property without inherent legal standing. Some constituents may prefer to resolve the problem rather than prosecute the defendant, while others seek maximum prosecution and punishment. These forces often result in a lack of clear consensus on what defines an incident worthy of prosecution. These problems are further complicated by the fact that some forms of animal maltreatment, (e.g., animal hoarding), are associated with recognized mental disorders rather than malicious intent. In such cases prosecution is often not in the best interests of balanced and restorative justice (Lockwood, 2018).

The criminal justice system is necessarily bound by the statutes imposed by the jurisdiction and the case law underpinning each judgment. However, animal welfare laws vary inconsistently from state to state, and are continually being amended. There may be separate laws on how companion, wild, and livestock animals ought to be treated, often catering to powerful political and economic interests and cultural and religious traditions. Some incidents are considered petty offenses, while others are misdemeanors or felonies.

Despite recent advances, many state laws still incorporate the original and now antiquated anti-cruelty language first enshrined in code when these statutes were enacted over a century and a half ago. During that era, the welfare of draft horses was of prime concern and many state statutes still prohibit overdriving, overloading, and overworking as the primary targets of law enforcement interest (Donley et al., 1999).

Some of these older statutes are impossibly convoluted, such as Connecticut's 209-word sentence in §53.247:

> **Cruelty to animals.** Any person who overdrives, drives when overloaded, overworks, tortures, deprives of necessary sustenance, mutilates or cruelly beats or kills or unjustifiably injures any animal, or who, having impounded or confined any animal, fails to give such animal proper care or neglects to cage or restrain any such animal from doing injury to itself or to another animal or fails to supply any such animal with wholesome air, food and water, or unjustifiably administers any poisonous or noxious drug or substance to any domestic animal or unjustifiably exposes any such drug or substance, with intent that the same shall be taken by an animal, or causes it to be done, or, having charge or custody of any animal, inflicts cruelty upon it or fails to provide it with proper food, drink or protection from the weather or abandons it or carries it or causes it to be carried in a cruel manner, or fights with or baits, harasses or worries any animal for the purpose of making it perform for amusement, diversion or exhibition, shall, for a first offense, be fined not more than one thousand dollars or imprisoned not more than one year or both, and for each subsequent offense, shall be guilty of a Class D felony.

Connecticut, like many other states, has added separate statutes covering more specific instances of cruelty, such as "maliciously and intentionally" maiming, mutilating, torturing, wounding or killing an animal, or knowingly being involved with animals fighting for amusement or gain, or intentionally injuring a working law enforcement animal.

Some statutes are remarkably simple, such as Wisconsin's §951.02:

> **Mistreating animals.** No person may treat any animal, whether belonging to the person or another, in a cruel manner.

States vary widely in their inclusion of specific harmful acts within the definition of cruelty. All states, with the exception of Alaska, include desertion or abandonment of animals in their cruelty codes. As of 2011, 38 states specifically include "poisoning" under cruelty. Hanging, a common presentation in cruelty cases, is specifically mentioned only in New Jersey law [N.J. Stat Ann. §4:22-15-26]. Burning or scalding is only included in definitions used by Nebraska [Neb. Rev. Stat. §28-1008] and Tennessee [Tenn. Code Ann. §39-14-201 to 212], although burning of animals has often been charged as arson if the owner of the burned "property" has been identified. Drowning, another common form of cruelty, is specifically mentioned only in Arkansas state law [Ark. Code Ann. §5-62-102 to 118].

Forms of Animal Abuse

The mistreatment of animals takes many forms and is generally codified statutorily under one catch-all term of cruelty to animals that may include acts of physical abuse, abandonment, neglect, or torture. More specialized subsets of animal harm, such as bestiality or animal fighting, are often codified in separate statutes or sections. While alleged emotional or mental abuse of animals is considered by many to be an inherent problem in animal well-being, documenting that an animal has suffered emotionally or mentally is difficult, if not impossible, especially if no other signs of abuse are present (Kurst-Swanger, 2007). Consequently, emotional abuse has not yet been included in statutory definitions within the United States.

The legal definitions of the following terms (and even the statutory definition of "animal") vary from jurisdiction to jurisdiction, and clinical descriptions and public perceptions may vary from statutory terminology. Nevertheless, the following terms are commonly used to describe the types of animal maltreatment seen in law enforcement investigations:

Animal cruelty: The most prevalent term used in animal anti-cruelty statutes, rooted in history and societies for the prevention of cruelty to animals (synonymous in the U.S. with humane societies). Cruelty implies a deliberate infliction of pain on an animal from which the abuser derives enjoyment or amusement (King, 1998).

Animal abuse: A newer and more neutral term to describe animal maltreatment, modeled after the nomenclature of the child protection system. "Abuse" describes willful failure to provide care and harmful behaviors that result in maltreatment regardless of the intent, motivation or mental condition of the perpetrator, whereas "cruelty" connotes more deliberate intention (Arkow, 2005, p. 2).

Neglect: An act, often of omission, signifying a lack of care. Neglect may often result from ignorance regarding appropriate animal husbandry or from extenuating circumstances such as poverty, family crises or substance abuse. Neglected animals endure physical injury and deprivation from careless behavior on the part of the animal's owner or caretaker, such as failure to provide adequate levels of food, water, shelter, veterinary care, grooming, or sanitation. The vast majority of cases investigated by animal protection authorities and brought to the court system involve neglect rather than physical cruelty. Of particular concern are individuals, often called collectors or hoarders, who accumulate large numbers of neglected animals (Kurst-Swanger, 2007).

Animal Hoarding: Animal hoarding is animal neglect on a significant scale involving large numbers of animals. Initially described as "multiple animal ownership" by

Worth and Beck (1981) and later as "animal collectors" by Lockwood and Cassidy (1988), Patronek (1999) introduced the term "animal hoarding" and brought what was often thought to be purely an animal welfare concern into the public health arena by recognizing the phenomenon as a potential sentinel for mental health problems which merit serious assessment and prompt intervention. While the underlying psychosocial causes for animal hoarding behaviors are indeterminate, the crime generally means failure to provide minimal standards of nutrition, sanitation, and veterinary care, combined with a failure to act on the deteriorating conditions of the animals and the environment. The specific number of animals kept is not as determinative as how this number overwhelms the ability of the owner to provide acceptable care (Patronek, 1999). Animals in hoarding situations are not only at great risk of neglectful care, but also pose public health problems in the home and surrounding community. Illinois became the first state in the U.S. to specifically define animal hoarding (as distinguished from general animal neglect or cruelty) in 2001 [§510 ILCS 70/2.10] in the context of a criminal act (Patronek, 2008). Hawaii's penal code [§711.1109.6] defines hoarding as the intentional, knowing or reckless possession of more than 20 dogs or cats, the failure to provide necessary sustenance for each one, and failure to correct conditions injurious to the health of the animals' or owner's health and well being. Rhode Island attempted to enact a law in 2017 which would have added "animal hoarding" to the list of animal cruelty offenses in GenLaws §4-1-1. After opposition from mental health associations, the American Civil Liberties Union and the state chapter of the National Association of Social Workers that such language would criminalize what is essentially a mental health disorder, "animal hoarding" was stricken and replaced with a "hazardous accumulation of animals" by a person unable to provide '"adequate living conditions." Livestock are specifically excluded (Lockwood, 2018). As of 2021, no other states are believed to have specific statutes defining animal hoarding.

Animal physical abuse: The physical abuse of animals can involve a wide range of injurious acts requiring an active engagement. Injuries may be caused by hitting, kicking, throwing, beating, shaking, poisoning, burning, scalding, suffocation, and many other actions. Institutional or commercial incidents of physical animal abuse include socially sanctioned situations where the intention is not to harm the animal specifically, but rather to use the animal for economic benefit, often with little regard to the animal's welfare. Individual motivations for physically abusing an animal vary greatly and may manifest in inappropriate disciplinary procedures or training methods, punishment, psychopathic behavior, or assaultive behaviors meant to control or intimidate a human member of the family. Currently (as of 2022), Alaska, Arizona, Colorado, Indiana, Kentucky, Maine, Nebraska, Nevada, New Hampshire, Tennessee, Utah, and Puerto Rico identify a special category of animal cruelty used to frighten, intimidate or coerce others or include such acts of intimidation within statutory definitions of domestic violence or elder abuse. Arkansas includes the harming of a spouse's pet within the statutory definition of emotional abuse. Michigan makes it illegal to kill, harm or threaten an animal with the intent to cause mental suffering or distress to a person or to exert control over a person. Minnesota allows courts to impose double penalties for felony animal torture or cruelty when the act is done to threaten, intimidate or terrorize another person. Threats to animals which instill fear in another individual are included in the definitions of stalking in Texas, Missouri, and the Navajo Nation, and in the crime of coercion in Oregon.

Non-accidental injury (NAI): A term borrowed from the British child protection field. NAI is a synonym for physical abuse, the clinical presentation of various injuries to the skeleton, soft tissues or organs of a child sustained as a result of beating or repeated mistreatment, usually by an individual responsible for its care. Munro and Thrusfield (2001a, 2001b, 2001c, 2001d) first applied this term as a synonym for physical abuse of animals.

Animal sexual abuse: Any abusive act with an animal involving the rectum, anus or genitalia; or sexual contact with animals which may or may not result in physical injury to the animal. While as of this writing all states except New Mexico and West Virginia have outlawed sex with animals, the legal terminologies used to describe these crimes are often euphemisms rooted in Biblical antecedents and the admittedly uncomfortable nature of discussing them. While 11 states refer to bestiality as "sexual assault or misconduct," at least 15 states use the archaic term "bestiality" (Edwards, 2019). Several states link sex with animals with homosexuality: Idaho §18-6605 prohibits "The infamous crime against nature, committed with mankind or any animal"; Massachusetts §34-272 and Oklahoma §21.886 prohibit "the abominable and detestable crime against nature, either with mankind or with a beast"; Michigan's Penal Code §750.158 prohibits "the abominable and detestable crime against nature either with mankind or with any animal"; South Carolina is even more archaic with §16-15-120 prohibiting "the abominable crime of buggery, whether with mankind or with beast." Other states use such terms as "indecency with an animal" (Nebraska), "sexual contact with an animal or creature" (New Jersey), "sexual activity with an animal" (Tennessee), or "act of sexual gratification with an animal" (Wisconsin). Standardizing these definitions with a more contemporary terminology such as "animal sexual abuse" would model definitions used in sex crimes against humans, replace archaic terms in which sexual intercourse or penetration would have to take place, and counter the arguments of those who favor zoophilia (a strong, erotic preference for animals), neither of which take into account the potential deleterious effects on the animal (Beetz, 2008; Beetz & Podberscek, 2005; Beirne, 1997).

An offshoot of sex crimes linked with animals was the passage in 2010 of the federal Animal Crush Video Prohibition Act banning the distribution of animal "crush" videos that show the torture and killing of animals. Crush videos often feature a provocatively dressed woman crushing, stomping or impaling small animals for the sexual pleasure of the viewers. However, the act did not outlaw the underlying cruelty itself. This changed in November 2019 with the Preventing Animal Cruelty and Torture (PACT)

Act that prohibits the purposeful crushing, burning, drowning, suffocation, impalement, or other violent acts committed against animals, allowing the prosecution of crimes that affect interstate commerce or occur under federal jurisdictions. This is the first federal animal cruelty law giving law enforcement another tool to stop brutality by building upon the existing animal cruelty laws available at the state level (Robinson & Clausen, 2021).

Emotional abuse: Although emotional abuse, bullying, excessive teasing, intimidation, exploitation, or coercion that leads to a fragile emotional state in humans are specified in numerous criminal statutes, such terminology is currently lacking from animal cruelty laws. Persistent threatening behavior to animals or a failure to provide them with basic emotional and companionship needs is considered by some to constitute emotional abuse. However, this has not been recognized clinically or in statutory language in the U.S., U.K., or Canada (Arkow et al., 2011).

A potential simplification of these diverse terms may evolve over time through a typology defined by the Federal Bureau of Investigation's (FBI) National Incident Based Reporting System (NIBRS). Released in 2016, NIBRS enables participating law enforcement agencies to enter investigated incidents into a national database (which incidentally offers the first opportunity to quantify the number of animal cruelty incidents and case outcomes). NIBRS defines animal cruelty as: "Intentionally, knowingly, or recklessly taking an action that mistreats or kills any animal without just cause, such as torturing, tormenting, mutilation, maiming, poisoning, or abandonment" (Federal Bureau of Investigation, 2016).

Included in the NIBRS definition are instances of duty to provide care (e.g., shelter, food, water, care if sick or injured), transporting or confining an animal in a manner likely to cause injury or death, causing an animal to fight with another, and inflicting excessive or repeated unnecessary pain or suffering (e.g., using objects to beat or injure an animal). The NIBRS definition does not include proper maintenance of animals for show or sport, or use of animals for food, lawful hunting, fishing, or trapping. NIBRS incidents are logged in a typology of four main categories:

- **Simple/gross neglect:** the failure of a person to provide for the needs of an animal (lack of food, water, shelter, grooming or veterinary care). Gross neglect pertains to an excess number of animals such as in a hoarding situation;
- **Intentional abuse and torture:** the intentional act of harming an animal;
- **Organized abuse:** dog fighting and cockfighting; and
- **Animal sexual abuse.**

The FBI's definition is meant to encompass all state animal cruelty statutes, which, of course, vary in what they cover; what constitutes abuse and neglect will differ from jurisdiction to jurisdiction (DeSousa, 2017).

Challenges in Definitions

Vague, Ambiguous, and Archaic Language

Throughout all state anti-cruelty statutes, animal cruelty is commonly referred to in qualified terms designed to permit investigators some flexibility and to exempt socially accepted practices. The net effect, however, is to create ambiguity that can frustrate courts. Most states, for example, define cruelty with such qualifying adjectives as *needless* mutilation (so as to exempt acceptable mutilations such as neutering a cat or docking a dog's ears), the infliction of *unnecessary* pain and suffering (to keep veterinarians from being charged with cruelty for administering inoculations), or failure to provide *proper* sustenance (so a cat owner will not be charged for putting her overweight feline on a diet). Qualifications such as these beg the question: what is "proper"? "Unnecessary"? "Needless"?

Some statutes have attempted to address this confusion with carefully crafted explanations. Missouri, for example, defines "adequate" care as "normal and prudent attention to the needs of an animal, including wholesome food, clean water, shelter, and health care as necessary to maintain good health in a specific species of animal" [§578.005]. Maine defines "necessary" sustenance as food "of sufficient quantity and quality to maintain all animals in good health" [§7-4013]. Washington goes further to define "food" as "food or feed appropriate to the species for which it is intended" [§16.52.011]. Michigan feels compelled to define "'water'" as potable water that is suitable for the age and species of animal and that is made regularly available unless otherwise directed by a licensed veterinarian" [§750.50].

An example of ambiguity may be found in the concept of ritual killing of animals. Many states, such as Illinois [§510 ILCS 75/2] require livestock to be slaughtered by a humane method, with a variety of acceptable techniques identified including the ritual Kosher slaughter, which is required by some Jews but condemned by many animal activists. However, ritual killing of animals in cult, occult, sacrificial or satanic religious practices is not similarly delineated. While a 1993 U.S. Supreme Court decision (Lukumi Babalu Aye v. City of Hialeah, 113 Ct. 2217) ruled that a municipal law prohibiting Santeria animal sacrifices was too specific in its restrictions on a specific religious organization, the court unanimously held that governments have the right to enforce more broadly based prohibitions against cruelty. However, the case created a climate in which some prosecutors, unfamiliar with the full court decision, may be reluctant to take action against animal abuse occurring within the context of a religious practice (Sinclair et al., 2006).

To further confound matters, many statutory definitions are rooted in archaic language highly appropriate for the 19th century, but patently outmoded for the 21st. Many states still prohibit *overdriving, overworking*, and *overloading* animals, which were significant concerns when horses were the primary form of transport but rarely enforced today; should a humane investigator even wish to cite a farmer for improperly using his horse to pull a wagon, there are no absolute standards defining how much weight for this particular horse would constitute overloading.

Similarly, many states combine many offenses under the single, archaic crime of *cruelty* to animals. In recent years, several states have begun to differentiate among the various offenses comprising cruelty, recognizing that these different manifestations have differing motivations and degrees of seriousness. Penalties for offenses are now often differentiated between felony and misdemeanor categories, or by sub-categories, depending on the culpability of the offender and the intensity, duration or ultimate outcome of the act. Upgrading more serious crimes to felonies increases the gravity of the crime in the eyes of the judges and juries and enables more law enforcement and prosecutorial resources to be brought to bear in working a case through the criminal justice system.

For example, several state statutes now define a new category of "aggravated" cruelty (e.g., Montana §45-8-217 for a person who "purposely or knowingly kills or inflicts cruelty to an animal with the purpose of terrifying, torturing, or mutilating the animal," or inflicts cruelty on 10 or more animals). Some states, such as Illinois [§510 ILCS 70/3.03] consider animal "torture" a separate classification. All states consider dog fighting a separate felony offense. Many regard bestiality and inhumane transport of animals in a vehicle (e.g., Nevada §574.190 which prohibits "inhuman" transport) as separately defined and codified offenses.

Some statutes provide elaborate and comprehensive definitions of *neglect*. For example, Indiana §35-46-3-0.5 prohibits endangering an animal's health by failing to provide or arrange for food or drink for a dependent animal, restraining an animal for more than a brief time on a chain or tether that is too heavy or too short, failing to provide veterinary care, and leaving a dog or cat outside and exposed to excessive heat or cold.

Finding animal cruelty laws and their definitions can be a challenge. Some states (e.g., Maine) have both civil and criminal prohibitions against cruelty. Some states have separate cruelty laws for livestock and for other animals (e.g., Texas §42.09 and 42.092, or Iowa §717.1A and 717.B1). Some have differing provisions if the victim is a dog or cat (e.g., Maine §17-1031 or Alabama §13A-11-240) or a bird (e.g., Minnesota §343.30). Relatively few states have replaced animal "cruelty" with the more objective term "abuse" (e.g., Missouri §578.012).

Phrases such as *unnecessary suffering* or *unnecessarily kill* may be broad, but the presence of the modifier presumes that some forms of suffering (e.g., those believed to result in societal benefit) are acceptable. The ambiguity lies in determining how much suffering is acceptable, often requiring the courts to attempt to determine legislative intent (Ibrahim, 2006).

Despite the proliferation of laws and humane issues now addressed by legislation, many statutes remain ill-defined. The use of such imprecise and outdated terminology with little additional statutory guidance has left investigators, prosecutors, and the courts confused as to what acts fall within the confines of the statute. As a result, the formidable evidentiary and procedural challenges incurred in bringing a case to court are exacerbated by language-induced inconsistency and unpredictability. Redefining what constitutes cruelty is essential: before animal cruelty charges or convictions can be widely considered evidence of maltreatment, statutory language must reflect a clear and current understanding of what is meant by abusive treatment (Lacroix, 1999).

Absence of a Universal Standard of Cruelty

The child protection movement, whose origins lie in the animal protection movement (Unti, 2008), achieved significant progress following the development of medical profiles identifying child abuse and neglect (Arkow & Munro, 2008). The development of veterinary forensics as a sub-specialty, and training for veterinarians and investigators to recognize clinical symptoms of NAI, offer potential for the animal protection field to replicate the statutory objectivity of child protection. Literature from veterinary forensics is providing useful guidelines for practitioners and prosecutors to implement in cases of suspected NAI in order to confidentially differentiate accidental injuries from instances of NAI (Intarapanich et al., 2016; Smith-Blackmore & Bethard, 2021). Clarification and amplification of the conditions inherent in a "battered pet" syndrome (Munro & Thrusfield, 2001a, 2001b, 2001c, 2001d) would help to distinguish accidental from non-accidental injuries in the animal and degrees of malice and intent in the perpetrator.

In the absence of such universal clinical profiles, prevailing cultural standards frequently determine what is perceived to be acceptable animal treatment. Many states for years resisted efforts to outlaw cockfighting on grounds that this was part of the cultural heritage of politically powerful Latino constituencies. California once had to enact legislation prohibiting Cambodian immigrants from humanely killing and eating their own dogs, an acceptable cultural practice in Southeast Asia but highly objectionable in the U.S. Surgically docking a Doberman pinscher's ears is considered a legitimate (albeit controversial) practice in the U.S., but is defined as illegal in the U.K.

Even animal protection officials have widely varying animal husbandry standards. For example, one of this chapter's authors (Arkow) once observed an animal shelter in Austin, Texas, that had installed an elaborate and expensive kennel heating system to respond to public criticism that the dogs might be cold when the ambient temperature occasionally dipped below 60 degrees. Meanwhile, at another shelter in Fairbanks, Alaska, officials routinely housed huskies and malamutes outdoors in unheated doghouses in sub-zero winters because it was felt to be inhumane to subject these cold-acclimated dogs to warmer indoor temperatures. To address such inconsistencies, the Association of Shelter Veterinarians issued comprehensive *Guidelines for Standards of Care in Animal Shelters* (2010) to set clear and consistent standards for meeting animals' needs. This document has been referenced in court proceedings against large scale animal hoarding situations to document how these facilities fail to meet acceptable standards of animal care in group housing conditions.

Objectivity vs. Subjectivity

Many decisions whether to pursue an investigation or a prosecution by necessity involve highly subjective decisions based upon the evidence, availability and credibility of witnesses, the likelihood of obtaining a conviction, whether prosecution is the most appropriate response, and whether the animals' condition fits within the vague statutory definitions. To compensate for the lack of a universal definition of cruelty, there have been attempts to introduce objective, quantifiable metrics to elucidate the subjective reports of witnesses and investigators.

The equine welfare field was the first to develop standardized assessment tools to describe horse welfare. The Henneke body condition system was first developed to evaluate fertility in mares on the basis of body fat percentage (Henneke et al., 1983). It has subsequently been widely employed in assisting in documenting equine neglect (Corey, 2012). Later, Patronek (1998) devised the Tufts Animal Care and Condition scales to assist law enforcement officials and veterinarians by quantifying objectively the adequacy or inadequacy of dog care. These scales assess body condition, weather and environmental conditions, and physical care in animals to help objectify incidents of abuse and neglect for use in cruelty prosecutions. It should be noted that the criteria in these scales focus on the consequences for the animal and are independent of human intent. Several Body Condition Score scales for dogs, cats, and other animals have been developed (Laflamme, 1997; Mawby et al., 2004) and are widely used in animal cruelty investigations.

Concerns about possible pain and suffering in laboratory animals has recently led to the development of "grimace" scales that go beyond body condition issues to attempt to document facial expressions that can be indicative of unrelieved pain or suffering. Such scales have been developed for rats and mice (Miller & Leach, 2015; Whittaker & Howarth, 2014), horses (Van Rysewyk, 2016), rabbits (Hampshire & Robertson, 2015), cats (Evangelista et al., 2019) and other species. This reflects a significant shift in the recognition that these and other species experience pain in ways paralleling that of humans, whose comparable "grimace" scales were first documented by Darwin (1872).

More specificity in the definitions and documentation of cruelty would enhance prosecutions. Veterinarians seeking guidance in presenting expert witness testimony, and investigators and prosecutors leading cruelty cases, have been stymied by the absence of universally accepted standards to make informed clinical diagnoses of animal maltreatment. Munro and Thrusfield (2001a, 2001b, 2001c, 2001d) proposed a list of risk factors for abuse and neglect that could achieve mutual understanding among animal health professionals. These factors include client behaviors, such as presenting discrepant medical and care histories or clients' use of multiple animal hospitals to avoid detection; clinical conditions, such as injuries that do not match the client's explanation or multiple fractures of varying age in the same animal; and environmental concerns, such as histories of unexplained deaths or injuries to multiple animals in the household. Munro and Thrusfield (2001a, 2001b, 2001c, 2001d) noted that no one single diagnostic pointer is necessarily indicative of animal cruelty, abuse, or neglect, and that there may be any number of explanations for the presenting signs.

Borrowing from these ideas, Arkow (2003) published guidelines to sensitize veterinarians to conditions that are highly suggestive of animal abuse. These include:

1. Animal welfare concerns (e.g., poor physical condition, absence of food, abandonment, collar too tight, lack of medical care, dehydration, excessive hair matting, parasitic infestation);
2. Environmental concerns (e.g., general lack of sanitation, overcrowding, presence of dead animals, inadequate ventilation or lighting, excessive numbers of animals, presence of feces or urine);
3. Human welfare concerns (e.g., owner unable to afford human or animal food; owner lives in isolation; evidence of animal fighting, bestiality, or ritualistic sacrifice);
4. Physical injuries to animal (e.g., bruising, fractures, repetitive injuries, lesions, burns or scalds, ocular injuries, internal injuries, administration of recreational drugs, poison, gunshot wounds, malnutrition, drowning, asphyxiation, untreated diseases); and
5. Sexual abuse of animals.

However, none of these or subsequent guidelines has been universally accepted or codified into standard veterinary practice or legal terminology.

Another approach to objectify vague definitions has been to propose a typology—a categorization of types of companion animal abuse based along a spectrum of maltreatment. Vermuelen and Odendaal (1993) first proposed such a typology that categorized companion animal abuse. They observed that the lack of a standardized definition of companion animal abuse leads to a wide range of definitions in usage, increases confusion, discourages reporting, and causes discrepant research findings. To comply with standards for uniformity that encourage meaningful, universal, measurable, complete and pragmatic terminologies, type of victimization was chosen to identify the different abuses. They cautioned that additional classification systems would be required in cases where multiple or secondary forms of abuse occur (see Table 1 on next page).

Building on this foundation, Rowan (1999) proposed another typology that defined the act of maltreatment according to the perpetrator's motivations (see Table 2 on next page). Note that in this proposed typology, the term *cruelty* is restricted to a relatively small subset of cases. In order to qualify as "cruel," the act must not involve only a deliberate act to cause harm but also the perpetrator's desire to gain satisfaction from the infliction of pain or suffering. One would need to distinguish between motivations for power and control, curiosity, and sadism and other psychopathic behaviors to achieve an effective response that will not waste the time of law enforcement and the courts.

Table 1. Typology of Companion Animal Abuse

Physical Abuse (intentional or unintentional	**Active Maltreatment**	Assault Burning Poisoning Shooting Mutilation Drowning Suffocation Abandonment Restriction of movement Incorrect training methods Inbreeding Trapping Abusive transportation Fireworks Bestiality
	Passive Neglect or Ignorance	Lack of food, water, or shelter Lack of veterinary care Lack of sanitation General neglect
	Commercial Exploitation	Labor (draft animal) Animal fighting Overbreeding Sport Experimentation
Mental Abuse (intentional or unintentional)*	**Active Maltreatment**	Instilling fear and anxiety Isolation
	Passive Neglect	Deprivation of love and affection Lack of recreational stimuli

* Note: this typology was described for use in South Africa. The category of "mental abuse" is not specifically recognized in any anti-cruelty statutes in the United States.

Table 2. Categories of Human Behavior and Motivation Associated with Animal Use That Sometimes Causes Distress

Term	Agent's Motivation	Animal Suffering	Societal Attitude
I. Cruel	Takes satisfaction from suffering	Always	Condemnation
II(a). Abuse	Satisfaction derived	Usually	Condemnation
II(b). Neglect	No satisfaction derived	Usually	Condemnation
III. Use	Justified by claims to personal societal gains	Sometimes	Approval when are attempts to minimize suffering

For the animal cruelty investigator, the absence of universally accepted definitions is a two-edged sword. On the one hand, a certain amount of discretion must be applied when evaluating the circumstances of a case and whether "cruelty" occurred. A uniform standard, for example, of acceptable ambient temperature for outdoor housing of dogs might not work equally well for a Chihuahua as for a St. Bernard; acceptable winter housing conditions for pets in San Diego might not be appropriate at Lake Tahoe. On the other hand, without highly specific definitions, a good defense attorney can argue that while animal care circumstances might not have been ideal, absent the defendant's malicious motive and intention, a case of cruelty cannot be proven.

Establishing a Motive, Intent, or State of Mind

American criminal law is predicated upon the concept of *mens rea,* or guilty state of mind. The system of crime and punishment is based upon the premise that people have the ability and free will to choose between right and wrong behaviors. In order to be considered criminal, an unlawful act or omission must be accompanied by a criminal state of mind (LaRene, 1987).

A major legalistic problem in enforcing and prosecuting anti-cruelty statutes is that it is very hard to prove the necessary *mens rea* in the case of a defendant whose actions are cruel, but also customary and acceptable (Francione, 1995).

Meanwhile, it is widely acknowledged that the overwhelming majority of cruelty cases investigated by humane authorities constitute unintentional neglect and crimes of omission, rather than deliberate, premeditated acts of physical harm, that can best be resolved through education (Humane Society of the U.S., 2004), Most cases of animal maltreatment seen in veterinary practice are the result of client ignorance and accidents rather than intention, and it has been suggested that most animal abuse occurs as isolated acts influenced heavily by opportunity, impulse, or aggravating social factors rather than by individual psychopathological behavior (Patterson-Kane & Piper, 2009).

Most state statutes have attempted to clarify this situation through the insertion of qualifying adjectives, defining cruelty solely as *intentional, willful,* or *reckless* acts. The unintended consequence of this strategy, however, is to force prosecutors to prove that the alleged perpetrator intended to harm the animal, or was knowingly reckless, as opposed to merely having to prove that the abuse occurred under the perpetrator's control without regard for his or her motivations.

Further complicating matters in prosecutorial efforts to establish intent are two parallel philosophies in psychology as to whether acts of animal cruelty are part of a graduation hypothesis (in which animal abuse is a dress rehearsal for violence that escalates against humans in range and severity as offenders need greater thrills) or a pattern of general deviance (in which the abuse is part of a broader constellation of antisocial behaviors) (Balkin et al., 2019). Research indicates that while childhood animal abuse is one of the earliest indicators of conduct disorder (Frick et al., 1993), the majority of youths who abuse animals do not go on to commit extreme violence against humans (Levin & Arluke, 2009), and that hands-on abuse of companion animals for entertainment may be a statistically significant predictor for extreme violence (Arluke & Madfis, 2014).

"Intentionally" and "willfully" are often used interchangeably and mean that the illegal act was committed consciously and with the idea of doing the act or causing the harm. The person had to have a conscious objective. It is not an essential element to the crime of cruelty to intend that the animal suffer: it can be argued that the person exercised general intent by committing acts or omissions which can foreseeably cause pain and suffering. But the party must be proven to have knowingly caused the act or omission without just cause or excuse (LaRene, 1987).

The majority of states consider *malicious harm* or *torture* to be grounds for felony-level charges of animal cruelty. Such a designation usually requires the assertion of a particular *mens rea.* New York [N.Y. Agric. & Mkts. Law §353], Kentucky [Ky. Rev. Stat. Ann. §525.135], and Tennessee [Tenn. Code Ann. §39-14-202] define such acts as those "done or carried out in an especially depraved or sadistic manner." Oregon [O.R.S. §167.322] and the US Virgin Islands [14 V.I. Code Ann. §181] define "maliciously" as "acting with a depravity of mind and wanton disregard of life" while North Carolina [N.C. Gen. Stat. §14.360(b)] defines it as "committed intentionally and with malice or bad motive."

Several states define *torture* in terms of its intended and ultimate effect on the victim. Illinois [510 Ill. Comp. Stat. Ann. 70/3.03] defines it as acts "motivated by an intent to increase or prolong the pain, suffering or agony of the animal." Similarly, Indiana [Ind. Code §35-46-3-12(b), (c)] defines it as acts that "inflict upon the animal severe physical pain with a depraved or sadistic intent to cause prolonged suffering or death." Florida [Fla. Stat. Ann. §828.12], Ohio [Ohio Rev. Code Ann. §1717.01] and Wyoming [Wyo. Stat. Ann. §181] all describe torture in terms of pain or suffering that is "allowed to continue when there is reasonable remedy or relief."

In general, definitions that are based more on objective documented medical evaluations of physical harm and suffering are easier to communicate to the triers of fact in a criminal case than attempts to determine the underlying mindset of a suspect. However, the nature of the injuries that are documented, such as mutilations, burning, multiple types of injuries, etc., can be used to strengthen the assertion that such harm is the result of excessive, repeated or prolonged mistreatment (Lockwood & Arkow, 2016; Touroo et al., 2018).

What is an "Animal"?

Among the many definitional challenges facing investigators and prosecutors, perhaps the most unusual is the most basic: what is an *animal*? The supposedly simple task of determining which animals are protected by law is often open to question and adds to the many significant challenges in prosecuting crimes against animals (Lockwood, 2006; Patronek, 1997).

Some states provide no definition of what an animal is, leaving the definition open to the courts. Others go to great lengths to include or exclude animals subject to anti-cruelty laws. For example, Iowa denies legal protection to many species by excluding game, fur-bearing animals, fish, reptiles, and amphibians. Alaska's statutes apply to any vertebrate living creature not a human being or fish. Maryland's laws apply to "any living creature except a human being." Delaware excludes fish, crustaceans, and mollusks. Arkansas and Mississippi include "every living creature." Colorado statutes apply to "any living dumb creature." New Jersey animals are "the whole brute creation." Connecticut's definition applies to "all brute creatures and birds." Georgia excludes fish and pests "that might be exterminated or removed from a business, residence or other structure."

Wisconsin's statutes pertain to reptiles, amphibians, and warm-blooded creatures besides man. Wyoming's statutes (in the "Offenses Against Property" chapter) do not define "animal," but do define "household pet" cruelty as affecting "any privately owned dog, cat, rabbit, guinea pig, hamster, mouse, gerbil, ferret, bird, fish, reptile, amphibian, invertebrate or any other species of domesticated animal sold, transferred or retained for the purpose of being kept as a pet in or near a house."

Louisiana defines "cruel," "abandon," "proper food," "proper water," "proper shelter," and "proper veterinary care," but fails to define "animal." Likewise, Kentucky's criminal code (in the chapter for "Riot, Disorderly Conduct and Related Offenses"), and West Virginia's law (in the "Crimes Against Chastity, Morality and Decency" section), provide no definitions.

Some definitions offer intriguing statutory contradictions. In one section of its criminal code [§47-1-10], South Carolina defines an animal as "a living vertebrate creature except a homo sapien" but a later section [§47-1-40c] states, "This section does not apply to fowl." However, cockfighting was recently made a misdemeanor offense under §16-17-650 (2010). The Texas criminal code defines an animal as "a domesticated living creature and wild living creature previously captured," unless that capture was accomplished by cruel means. These distinctions may seem trivial, but the ability to pursue a case may hinge on whether an animal alleged to have been mistreated is defined as an "animal." For example, in a celebrated Texas case a number of years ago, a jury acquitted two Baylor University students who shot and mutilated a stray cat because state law did not include feral cats as being owned and domesticated, and consequently not covered by the statute.

However, even in the absence of appropriate definitions, prosecutions may succeed. Marquis (1996) described the case of a man who killed Victor, a 26-pound lobster, while stealing him from an aquarium in Oregon whose cruelty statute defines an animal as "any nonhuman mammal, bird, reptile, amphibian or fish." Even though crustaceans are not specifically included, prosecutors were able to obtain a conviction for theft and cruelty to animals.

What/Who is a Victim of Cruelty?

If animals are considered chattel property lacking legal standing, can they be classified as victims? This fundamental question has never been adequately answered, but two Oregon cases offer an intriguing approach. In *Oregon v. Nix* (2012), the defendant had been indicted on 23 separate counts of first-degree animal neglect and 70 counts of second-degree animal neglect involving emaciated horses and goats. The jury convicted him on 20 counts of second-degree animal neglect. However, the trial court concluded that, because only people can be victims, the defendant had committed only one punishable offense involving 20 animals and merged the 20 counts into a single conviction. The Court of Appeals concluded that animals can be victims and reversed and remanded the case back to the trial court for a judgment of conviction and resentencing on each of the 20 original counts. The Oregon Supreme Court affirmed the Court of Appeals' decision.

Although the defendant argued that the term "victim" does not include non-human animals and that animals are property, the appeals court reasoned that under Oregon's criminal statute ORS 167.325 addressing animal neglect, although animals are usually considered the property of persons the statute reflects a broader public interest in protecting individual animals as sentient beings by ensuring that such animals receive minimum care and are not abused or neglected. The Supreme Court concluded:

> Although early animal cruelty legislation may have been directed at protecting animals as property of their owners or as a means of promoting public morality, Oregon's animal cruelty laws have been rooted—for nearly a century—in a different legislative tradition of protecting individual animals themselves from suffering. Indeed, the modern animal cruelty statute was designed to broaden the state's earlier law to encompass abandonment, as well as neglect and abuse, and to graduate punishment in accordance with the severity of the harm to the animals.... [The] defendant is incorrect that the real "victim" of the crime of second-degree animal neglect is either the public or the animal owner.... Nor is there in any indication that the legislature regarded the "victim" of animal neglect to be the owner of the animal (*Oregon v. Nix*, 2014).

After *Nix* was decided by the Oregon Supreme Court, the appellate attorney realized that she technically was not allowed to appeal because the state cannot appeal misdemeanor sentencing decisions. She pointed out the jurisdictional error to the Supreme Court, who vacated their previous decision. A year later, *Oregon v. Hess* (2015) was based on a similar fact pattern: the defendant was convicted on 45 counts of first- and second-degree animal neglect. The defendant argued that all of the guilty verdicts should be merged into a single conviction because the cats were her property and, thus, not victims, leaving only one victim of her crimes—the public. The trial court disagreed, reasoning that Oregon's animal neglect statutes were enacted to protect animals, thus making each cat a victim. The Court of Appeals denied her argument, citing the *Nix* decision which, even though it was vacated on purely jurisdictional grounds, was still persuasive on the question of merging sentences. The defendant in *Hess* then appealed again to the Oregon Supreme Court, who denied review. Therefore, the reasoning behind *Nix* still stands.

Courts are beginning to consider regarding animals as legal victims of cruelty in another way. The concept of having courts appoint volunteer lawyers or law students to serve as advocates for the interests of animals (or "justice") in civil and criminal proceedings has attracted growing interest. The first such program was initiated in Connecticut in 2016 with the passage of "Desmond's Law", named after a New Haven pit bull that was beaten, starved, strangled, and killed by his owner, who was upset that his wife had left him. The man received accelerated rehabilitation, which means the charges would be erased from his record after he served a period of probation and met certain conditions. Outrage over the leniency of this penalty prompted interest in passing legislation that would allow the appointment of advocates who could represent the interests of the animal victim in court (Rubin, 2018, 2021). As of 2021, Maine has enacted a similar law and at least seven other states have considered such legislation.

Defenses and Exemptions

Bowing to political and public pressures, legislatures frequently exempt certain acts that are perceived to be justifiable based upon their potential to improve public health, safety, and often the economy. The political and economic influence of the agribusiness sector and the hunting lobby, combined with clashing cultural constructs of whether animals are property or autonomous beings, have often succeeded in getting agricultural operations exempted from many animal cruelty provisions (Arkow, 2021). Arizona's criminal code, for example, exempts from the criminal statutes activities involving the possession, training, exhibition, or use of an animal in the otherwise lawful pursuits of hunting, ranching, farming, rodeos, shows, and security services [§13.2910.05]. Wyoming's law exempts rodeos and industry-accepted agricultural and livestock practices [§6-3-203]. South Carolina specifically exempts accepted animal husbandry practices of farm operations, the training of animals, the practice of veterinary medicine, agricultural practices, forestry, and silvacultural practices, wildlife management practices, and training dogs for hunting [§47-1-10]. A law enacted in Florida in 2021 requiring veterinarians to report suspected animal abuse to law enforcement authorities specifically exempts such reports if the alleged incident occurred at a commercial food-producing animal operation.

Some exemptions seem appropriate: Kansas, like many states, exempts a person from charges of cruelty for killing in self-defense any animal found outside of the property of its owner or custodian which is injuring or posing a threat to any person, farm animal, or property [§21-4310]. Similarly, Georgia's statutes do not pertain to a person defending his or her person, property, livestock or poultry, or that of another, from injury or damage being caused by an animal, provided that "the method used to injure or kill such animal shall be designed to be as humane as is possible under the circumstances" [§16-12-4]. Other exemptions, however, appear somewhat more frivolous. Alabama §13A-11-246 exempts a person who shoots a dog or cat with a BB gun not capable of inflicting serious injury when the dog or cat is defecating or urinating on the person's property.

It has been argued that anti-cruelty statutes, while noble in theory, are ineffective in practice because they exempt the majority of modern practices that allegedly exploit the most numerically significant number of animals. Broad exemptions for customary practices of intensive animal agriculture, bona fide laboratory experimentation, hunting, and other institutional or socially sanctioned activities are said to weaken the intent of the laws (Ibrahim, 2006).

Conclusion

The animal welfare field has made considerable strides in recent years to enhance the ability to investigate and prosecute cases of animal maltreatment. According to the Animal Legal Defense Fund (aldf.org), as of 2022, 167 law schools in the U.S. and Canada, and 11 in Australia and New Zealand, have offered curriculum courses in animal law. Currently, all 50 states have enacted statutes categorizing certain acts of animal maltreatment as felonies. Many police departments have humane law investigators, and a growing number of prosecutors' offices have assigned assistant district attorneys to handle the increasing caseload of animal cruelty cases (Benetato, 2011).

Despite such notable advances, however, the field continues to be hampered by nomenclature rooted in 19th century perspectives that reflected the property status and commercial value of animals, and that required establishing that perpetrators committed cruel acts with willful or malicious intent. The definitional limitations of state statutes, coupled with a lack of training of law enforcement and veterinary professionals in documenting animal cruelty, make the prosecution of animal cruelty cases difficult, with relatively few investigated cases taken to trial and resulting in convictions (Sinclair, 2006).

Effective response to animal abuse and neglect requires a community-wide, holistic approach. Greater efforts should be made to strengthen and standardize definitions of animal cruelty. The public must be better informed about what constitutes animal cruelty and how to report it; the National Link Coalition has published an online directory of animal cruelty investigation agencies in over 6,500 cities and counties (National Link Coalition, 2021). Police need to be better trained about existing laws protecting animals and the tools for effectively processing crime scenes in which animals are both victims and evidence. Veterinarians need better training in forensics, recognition, and documentation of cruelty, and the presentation of such evidence in court. As of 2022, 42 states either mandate or permit veterinarians to report suspected animal abuse to appropriate investigators; 35 of these states grant limited or absolute immunity from civil and/or criminal liability for making such reports in good faith. They should have universal exemption from civil and criminal liability when providing good-faith testimony in animal cruelty cases. Prosecutors need training and assistance in building strong animal cruelty cases and making proper use of testimony from veterinarians and humane law enforcement. Finally, judges need additional training about the importance of animal cruelty as a serious and often violent crime and the appropriateness of the strong public concern that is often voiced in these cases. Fortunately, many national animal protection and law enforcement organizations have increased efforts to address all of these concerns. Such efforts will play an important role in protecting animals and people alike.

References

Arkow, P. (2021). "Humane criminology": An inclusive victimology protecting animals and people. *Social Sciences, 10*, 335.

Arkow, P. (2006). "Old wine in a new bottle": New strategies for humane education. In A.H. Fine (Ed.), *Handbook on animal-assisted therapy: Theoretical foundations and guidelines for practice* (2nd Ed., pp. 425–452). Academic Press.

Arkow, P. (2005). Multidisciplinary prevention and interventions: Animal abuse and family violence. *Animal Anti-Cruelty League Newsletter,* (Johannesburg, South Africa) No. 2, 1–6.

Arkow, P. (2003). *Breaking the cycles of violence: A guide to multi-disciplinary interventions. A handbook for child protection, domestic violence and animal protection agencies.* Latham Foundation.

Arkow, P., Boyden, P., & Patterson-Kane, E. (2011). *Practical guidance for the effective response by veterinarians to suspected animal cruelty, abuse and neglect.* American Veterinary Medical Association.

Arkow, P., & Munro, H. (2008). The veterinary profession's roles in recognizing and preventing family violence: The experiences of the human medicine field and the development of diagnostic indicators of Non-Accidental Injury. In F.R. Ascione (Ed.), *International handbook of animal abuse and cruelty: Theory, research, and application* (pp. 31–58). Purdue University Press.

Arluke, A., & Madfis, E. (2014). Animal abuse as a warning sign of school massacres: A critique and refinement. *Homicide Studies, 18*(1), 7–22.

Ascione, F. R. (1993). Children who are cruel to animals: A review of research and implications for developmental psychopathology. *Anthrozoös, 6*(4), 226–247.

Ascione, F. R., & Shapiro, K. (2009). People and animals, kindness and cruelty: Research directions and policy implications. *Journal of Social Issues, 65*(3), 569–587.

Association of Shelter Veterinarians. (2010). *Guidelines for Standards of Care in Animal Shelters.* Accessed 9/15/21 at https://www.sheltervet.org/assets/docs/shelter-standards-oct2011-wforward.pdf.

Balkin, D., Blomquist, M., Bowman, S., Chitwood, H. L., & Dunn, L., et al. (2019). *Animal cruelty issues: What juvenile and family court judges need to know.* National Council of Juvenile and Family Court Judges.

Basler, R. P. (Ed.). (2001). *Abraham Lincoln: His speeches and writings.* Da Capo Press.

Beetz, A. M. (2008). Bestiality and zoophilia: A discussion of sexual contact with animals. In F. R. Ascione, (Ed.), *International handbook of animal abuse and cruelty: Theory, research, and application* (pp. 201–220). Purdue University Press.

Beetz, A. M., & Podberscek, A. L. (Eds.) (2005). *Bestiality and zoophilia: Sexual relations with animals.* Purdue University Press.

Beirne, P. (1997). Rethinking Bestiality: Towards a concept of interspecies sexual assault. *Theoretical Criminology, 1*(3), 317–340.

Benetato, M.A., Reisman, R., & McCobb, E. (2011). The veterinarian's role in animal cruelty cases. *Journal of the American Veterinary Medical Association, 238*(1), 31–34.

Bentham, J. (1789). *The principles of morals and legislation.* Reprinted in T. Regan & P. Singer (Eds.) (1976), *Animal rights and human obligations* (pp. 129–130). Prentice Hall.

Black's Law Dictionary. (2021). Cruelty to animals. *Black's Law Dictionary Free Online* (2nd Ed.). Retrieved September 15, 2021, from https://thelawdictionary.org/cruelty-to-animals/.

Blood, D. C., & Studdert, V. P. (1999). *Saunders comprehensive veterinary dictionary* (2nd Ed.). W.B. Saunders.

Broom, D. M. (2020). Brain complexity, sentience and welfare. *Animal Sentience, 5*(29), 27.

Corey, P. (2012). Equine Cruelty. *Shelter Medicine for Veterinarians and Staff,* 453–460.

Crook, A. (2000). The CVMA animal abuse position—how we got here. *Canadian Veterinary Journal, 41,* 631–633.

Darwin, C. (1965). *The expression of the emotions in man and animals* (1872). University of Chicago Press.

DeSousa, D. (2017). *NIBRS user manual for animal control officers and humane law enforcement.* Alexandria, Va.: National Coalition on Violence Against Animals.

Donley, L., Patronek, G. J. & Luke, C. (1999). Animal abuse in Massachusetts: A summary of case reports at the MSPCA and attitudes of Massachusetts veterinarians. *Journal of Applied Animal Welfare Science, 2*(1), 59–73.

Edwards, M. J. (2019). Arrest and prosecution of animal sex abuse (bestiality) offenders in the United States, 1975–2015. *Journal of the American Academy of Psychiatry and the Law, 47*(3), 1–12.

Evangelista, M. C., Watanabe, R., Leung, V. S., Monteiro, B. P., O'Toole, E., Pang, D. S., & Steagall, P. V. (2019). Facial expressions of pain in cats: the development and validation of a Feline Grimace Scale. *Scientific Reports, 9*(1), 1–11.

Farm Animal Welfare Council. (2009) *Farm animal welfare in Great Britain: Past, present and future.* Retrieved on September 15, 2021, from https://www.gov.uk/government

/publications/fawc-report-on-farm-animal-welfare-in-great-britain-past-present-and-future.

Favre, D. (2009). Living property: A new status for animals within the legal system. *Marquette Law Review, 93*, 1021.

Favre, D., & Tsang, V. (1993). The development of anti-cruelty laws during the 1800s. *Detroit College of Law Review, 1,* 1–35.

Federal Bureau of Investigation. (2016). *New to NIBRS.* Retrieved December 20, 2021, from https://ucr.fbi.gov/nibrs/2016/resource-pages/nibrs-2016-homepage_alt.pdf.

Felthous, A. R., & Kellert, S. R. (1987). Psychosocial aspects of selecting animal species for physical abuse. *Journal of Forensic Science, 32,* 1713–1723.

Francione, G.L. (1995). *Animals, property and the law.* Temple University Press.

Frasch, P. D. (2008). The impact of improved American anti-cruelty laws in the investigation, prosecution, and sentencing of abusers. In F.R. Ascione (Ed.), *International handbook of animal abuse and cruelty: Theory, research, and application* (pp. 59–86). Purdue University Press.

Frick, P. J., Lahey, B. B., Loeber, R., Tannenbaum, L., Van Horn, Y., Christ, M. A. G., Hart, E. A., & Hanson, K. (1993). Oppositional defiant disorder and conduct disorder: A meta-analytic review of factor analyses and cross-validation in a clinic sample. *Clinical Psychology Review, 13*(4), 319–340.

Hampshire, V., & Robertson, S. (2015). Using the facial grimace scale to evaluate rabbit wellness in post-procedural monitoring. *Lab animal, 44*(7), 259–260.

Harp, C. (2002). *Bringing balance to juvenile justice.* American Prosecutors Research Institute.

Harrison, R. (1964). *Animal machines: The factory farming industry.* Vincent Stuart.

Hawaii State Legislature (1998). Senate Standing Committee Report No. 3222, Conference Committee Report No. 87.

Henneke, D. R., Potter, G. D., Kreider, J. L., & Yeates, B. F. (1983). Relationship between condition score, physical measurements and body fat percentage in mares. *Equine Veterinary Journal, 15*(4), 371–372.

Humane Society of the United States (2004). *Making the connection: What veterinary professionals need to know.* Author [brochure].

Ibrahim, D. M. (2006). The anti-cruelty statute: A study in animal welfare. *Journal of Animal Law and Ethics, 1,* 175–203.

Intarapanich, N. P., McCobb, E. C., Reisman, R. W., Rozanski, E. A., & Intarapanich, P. P. (2016). Characterization and comparison of injuries caused by accidental and non-accidental blunt force trauma in dogs and cats. *Journal of Forensic Sciences, 61*(4), 993–999.

Jones, R. C. (2013). Science, sentience, and animal welfare. *Biology & Philosophy, 28*(1), 1–30.

Keeley, J. (2020). The link between animal abuse and crimes against humans. *Journal of Animal and Environmental Law, 12*(1), 1–25.

King, M. (1998). Red flag: Signs of animal abuse. *Veterinary Product News, 10*(1), 18–21.

Kurst-Swanger, K. (2007). Animal abuse: The link to family violence. In, N. A. Jackson (Ed.), *Encyclopedia of domestic violence*, (pp. 22–29). Routledge.

Lacroix, C. A. (1999). Another weapon for combating family violence: Prevention of animal abuse. In F. R. Ascione & P. Arkow, (Eds.), *Child abuse, domestic violence, and animal abuse: Linking the circles of compassion for prevention and intervention* (pp. 62–80*)*. Purdue University Press.

Laflamme, D. P. (1997, July/August). Development and validation of a body condition score system of dogs. *Canine Practice, 22,* 10–15.

LaRene, S. (1987). *Handbook of animal cruelty law* (3rd Ed. Rev.) Michigan Humane Society.

Levin, J., & Arluke, A. (2009). The link between animal abuse and human violence: Reducing the link's false positive problem (pp. 163–171). Sussex Academic Press.

Lockwood, R. (2018). Animal hoarding: The challenge for mental health, law enforcement, and animal welfare professionals. *Behavioral Sciences & the Law, 36,* 698–716.

Lockwood, R. (2006). *Animal cruelty prosecution: Opportunities for early response to crime and interpersonal violence.* American Prosecutors Research Institute.

Lockwood, R. & Arkow, P. (2016). Animal abuse and interpersonal violence: The cruelty connection and its implications for veterinary pathology. *Veterinary Pathology,* 53(5), 910–918

Lockwood, R., & Cassidy, B. (1988, Summer). Killing with kindness? *The Humane Society News,* 14–18.

Marquis, J. (1996). The Kittles case and its aftermath. *Animal Law, 2,* 197–201.

Matlack, C. B. (2006). *We've Got Feelings Too!: Presenting the Sentient Property Solution.* Log Cabin Press.

Mawby, D., Bartges, J. W., & Mayers, T., et al. (2001). Comparison of body fat estimates by dual-energy x-ray absorptimotery and deuterium oxide dilusion in client owned dogs. *Compendium, 23*(9A), 70.

Miller, A. L., & Leach, M. C. (2015). The mouse grimace scale: a clinically useful tool?. *PloS one, 10*(9), e0136000

Morgan, K. (1983). An overview of animal-related organizations with some guidelines for recognizing patterns. *Community Animal Control, 2*(2), 18–19.

Moyn, S. (2021). *Humane: How the United States abandoned peace and reinvented war.* Farrar, Straus & Giroux.

Munro, H. M. C., & Thrusfield, M. V. (2001a). Battered pets: features that raise suspicion of non-accidental injury. *Journal of Small Animal Practice, 42,* 218–226.

Munro, H.M.C., & Thrusfield, M.V. (2001b). Battered pets: non-accidental physical injuries found in dogs and cats. *Journal of Small Animal Practice, 42,* 279–290.

Munro, H.M.C., & Thrusfield, M.V. (2001c). Battered pets: sexual abuse. *Journal of Small Animal Practice, 42,* 333–337.

Munro, H.M.C., & Thrusfield, M.V. (2001d). Battered pets: Munchausen syndrome by proxy. *Journal of Small Animal Practice, 42,* 385–389.

Nawroth, C., Langbein, J., Coulon, M., Gabor, V., Oesterwind, S., Benz-Schwarzburg, J., & von Borell, E. (2019). Farm animal cognition-linking behavior, welfare and ethics. *Frontiers in Veterinary Science*, 6, 24.

National Link Coalition (2021). How do I report suspected abuse? Retrieved September 15, 2021, from https://nationallinkcoalition.org/how-do-i-report-suspected-abuse.

Patronek, G. (2008). Animal hoarding: A third dimension of animal abuse. In F. R. Ascione (Ed.), *International handbook of animal abuse and cruelty: Theory, research, and application* (pp. 221–246). Purdue University Press.

Patronek, G. (1999). Hoarding of animals: An under-recognized public health problem in a difficult-to-study population. *Public Health Reports, 114*, 81–87.

Patronek, G. (1998). Issues and guidelines for veterinarians in recognizing, reporting and assessing animal neglect and abuse. In, P. Olson (Ed.), *Recognizing & reporting animal abuse: A veterinarian's guide* (pp. 25–39). American Humane Association.

Patronek, G. (1997). Issues for veterinarians in recognizing and reporting animal neglect and abuse. *Society and Animals, 5*, 267–280.

Patronek, G. J. & Weiss, K. J. (2011). *Animal hoarding: A neglected problem at the intersection of psychiatry, veterinary medicine, and law.* Report on Findings from the Henderson House Interdisciplinary Workgroup, Weston, MA, July 26, 2011.

Patterson-Kane, E. G., & Piper, H. (2009). Animal abuse as a sentinel for human violence: A critique. *Journal of Social Issues, 65*(3), 589–614.

Primatt, H. (1776). *The duty of mercy*. Reprinted in R. D. Ryder (Ed.) (1992). Centaur Press.

Regan, T., & Singer, P. (Eds.) (1976). *Animal rights and human obligations.* Prentice Hall.

Robinson, C., & Clausen, V. (2021, Aug. 10). The Link between animal cruelty and human violence. *FBI Law Enforcement Bulletin.*

Rowan, A. N. (1999). Cruelty and abuse to animals: A typology. In F. R. Ascione & P. Arkow (Eds.), *Child abuse, domestic violence, and animal abuse: Linking the circles of compassion for prevention and intervention* (pp. 328–334). Purdue University Press.

Rubin, J. (2018). Desmond's Law: A novel approach to animal advocacy. *Animal Law, 24*, 243.

Rubin, J. (2021). Desmond's Law: Early impressions of Connecticut's court advocate program for animal cruelty cases. *Harvard Law Review, 134,* 263.

Sinclair, L., Merck, M., & Lockwood, R. (2006). *Forensic investigation of animal cruelty: A guide for veterinary and law enforcement professionals.* Humane Society of the U.S.

Smith-Blackmore, M., & Bethard, J. D. (2021). A multidisciplinary investigation of chronic animal abuse: Collaboration between veterinary forensics and forensic anthropology. *Journal of Forensic Sciences, 22,* 389–392.

Touroo, R. T., Brooks, J. W., Lockwood, R. & Reisman, R. (2018). Medicolegal investigation. In J. W. Brooks (Ed.) *Veterinary Forensic Pathology* (pp. 1–8*)*. Springer.

Turgoose, D., & McKie, R. (2020, Dec. 7). *Pet victimology and coercive control* [Video]. YouTube. https://www.youtube.com/watch?v=c_aEfJyqMXE.

Unti, B. (2008). Cruelty indivisible: Historical perspectives on the link between cruelty to animals and interpersonal violence. In F.R. Ascione (Ed.), *International handbook of animal abuse and cruelty: Theory, research, and application* (pp. 7–30). Purdue University Press.

Van Rysewyk, S. (2016). Nonverbal indicators of pain. *Animal Sentience, 1*(3), 30.

Vermeulen, H., & Odendaal, J. S.J. (1993). Proposed typology of companion animal abuse. *Anthrozoös, 6,* 248–257.

Wathes, C. (2010, April 10). Lives worth living? *Veterinary Record*, p. 468.

Whittaker, A. L., & Howarth, G. S. (2014). Use of spontaneous behaviour measures to assess pain in laboratory rats and mice: How are we progressing? *Applied Animal Behaviour Science, 151*, 1–12.

Worth, D., & Beck, A.M. (1981). Multiple ownership of animals in New York City. *Transactions & Studies of the College of Physicians of Philadelphia,* 3(4), 280–300.

Chapter 2

The History of Anti-Cruelty Laws

Concepts of Animal Welfare and Animal Rights

David Favre

Laws reflect both social awareness and social concern at the time of their adoption. When laws are enacted, a threshold of political consideration has been passed and society has new expectations about a topic. This is certainly the case with the issue of how our society considers and treats the animals that live among us. The history of the anti-cruelty laws shows a conceptual breakthrough in social thinking in the United States, beginning with the adoption of the 1867 New York cruelty law. This law, which was replicated in other states in the following decades, remains as a statement of social contract between humans and animals: we humans may use animals, but in so doing, we shall not inflict unnecessary pain and suffering. This basic contract remains the cornerstone of the law, but there has been a shift of what constitutes *unnecessary* in favor of at least some animals.

The unfolding of this story provides a full context for the exploration of the concepts of animal welfare and cruelty. Having developed the concept of animal welfare, the concept of animal rights, as a new social contract, will also be considered. This view asserts that animals deserve a more robust and visible presence in the legal system, not otherwise supported under animal welfare concepts.

In the Beginnings, Just Property

Prior to 1800 in both the United States and England, economically useful animals, such as horses or sheep, had the legal status of being property, while others, like dogs, did not exist in the eyes of the law and had no legal status. If a person possessed a dog, and a stranger harmed the dog, the possessor could do nothing about it in a court of law. If the dog was not property, then no legal action could be filed concerning the dog. The possessor had no legal rights concerning the dog. If, on the other hand, a person possessed a sheep or a horse, the animals were considered of value, were bought and sold, and therefore were considered personal property in the eyes of the law. As personal property, the possessor/owner could sue another individual for the value of his animal if the animal were harmed or killed. The human could also sue for the return of the animal if it were stolen. Additionally, the government could bring criminal charges against the human who harmed or stole the horse or sheep (but not for a dog).

One case under the Minnesota law shows the different outcomes under the law for different species. A defendant was indicted for the shooting of a dog under the criminal statute providing penalties for "[e]very person who shall wilfully and maliciously kill, maim or disfigure any horses, cattle or other beasts of another person."[1] The court directed that the charges be dismissed, holding that no crime had been committed as a dog could not be considered a beast.

> [I]t seems to me, that all [animals] such as have, in law, no value, were not intended to be included in that general term.... The term beasts may well be intended to include asses, mules, sheep and swine and perhaps, some other domesticated animals, but it would be going quite too far to hold that dogs were intended.[2]

Thus, only animals of social/economic value, those used in the production and movement of goods, were acknowledged to exist in the eyes of the law. The quoted law above was passed not for the benefit of the animals, but for the benefit of the owner of the animal. It would not be appropriate to consider this an anti-cruelty law or a reflection of the idea of animal welfare.

While moving into the category of property was a good thing for these limited numbers of animals, as some negative human conduct might be restrained, the law really did not see these special animals any differently than the wagons they pulled. Both were simply personal property. That the horse was alive and the wagon was not alive was not particularly noticed by the law. Additionally, the rights of the human owner were not distinguished if the property in question was a wagon or a horse. The owner might take good care of both or he might not. He might chop up the wagon or the horse; the law was mute. The lawmakers, reflecting the views of their citizens, did not think it appropriate to interfere with a man's use of his property. (At this time the law also had almost nothing to say about a man's use of his children or his slaves, where they were allowed.)

Before considering the transformation of law in the United States, it is informative to review the corresponding evolution of law in Britain.

1. United States v. Gideon, 1 Minn. 292, 296 (1856).
2. *Id.*

The British Set the Stage

Notwithstanding the political independence that the United States obtained from Great Britain during the late 1700s and 1800s, there was still a considerable transfer of ideas from the intellectually mature mother country to the newly formed, and basically frontier, United States. Early articulations of concern for the moral and legal status of animals appeared in British writing.[3] Reverend Humphrey Primatt in *A Dissertation on the Duty of Mercy and Sin of Cruelty to Brute Animals,* written in 1776, pleaded for the care of animals.

> See that no brute of any kind ... whether intrusted to thy care, or coming in thy way, suffer thy neglect or abuse. Let no views of profit, no compliance with custom, and no fear of ridicule of the world, ever tempt thee to the least act of cruelty or injustice to any creature whatsoever. But let this be your invariable rule, everywhere, and at all times, to do unto others as, in their condition, you would be done unto.[4]

Jeremy Bentham, an English barrister, was one of the few legal writers who addressed the issue of animals and the legal system. His *Introduction to the Principles of Morals and Legislation*[5] (1781) was closely studied at the time by a large number of individuals, some of whom went on to propose legislation for the protection of animals. Bentham argued that there was no reason why animals should not be accorded protection under the law. Bentham pointed out that animals, "on account of their interests having been neglected by the insensibility of the ancient jurists, stand degraded into the class of *things*."[6] Within a footnote entitled "Interests of the inferior animals improperly neglected in legislation," as noted in Chapter 1 of this text, Bentham argued that the capacity for suffering is the vital characteristic that gives a being the right to legal consideration. The final sentence of the footnote is often used today as a rallying cry for those seeking to promote the cause of animal rights. "The question is not, Can they *reason*? nor, Can they *talk*? But, *Can they suffer*?"[7]

Having made the intellectual arguments for concern about animals, the British followed up with changes to the legal system. On May 15, 1809, Lord Erskine addressed Parliament in support of the bill he had introduced for the protection of animals.[8] This

---

3. For a fuller discussion of the English debate about duty toward animals, see Roderick F. Nash, The Rights of Nature 16–25 (Madison Wisconsin: University of Wisconsin Press 1989); James Turner, Reckoning with the Beast: Animals, Pain and Humanity in the Victorian Mind (Baltimore: John Hopkins Press 1980).

4. Sydney H. Coleman, Humane Society Leaders in America 18 (Albany NY: The American Humane Society 1924) (quoting Rev. Humphrey Primatt, A Dissertation on the Duty of Mercy and Sin of Cruelty to Brute Animals (London 1776)).

5. Jeremy Bentham, An Introduction to the Principles of Morals and Legislation (Oxford: Clarendon Press 1781).

6. Bentham, *supra* note 5, at 311 (emphasis in original).

7. *Id.*

8. Coleman, *supra* note 4, at 20–21.

may represent the first time animal protection was seriously debated by a full legislative body. In his address, Lord Erskine stated:

> They (animals) are created, indeed, for our use, but not for our abuse. Their freedom and enjoyment, when they cease to be consistent with our just dominions and enjoyment, can be no part of their natures; but whilst they are consistent I say their rights, subservient as they are, ought to be as sacred as our own ... the bill I propose to you, if it shall receive the sanction of Parliament, will not only be an honor to the country, but an era in the history of the world.[9]

The bill passed in the House of Lords, but was defeated in the House of Commons.

Some thirteen years later the battle was taken up again, this time by Richard Martin.[10] On June 10, 1822, he succeeded in obtaining passage of a law known as "Dick Martin's Act.... An Act to Prevent the Cruel and Improper Treatment of Cattle." As compromise was necessary for its passage, the law protected only animals "of another"; it was a limited first step. It was made illegal for any person to "wantonly and cruelly beat or ill-treat [any] horse, mare, gelding, mule, ass, ox, cow, heifer, steer, sheep or other cattle...." The law imposed a "fine of not more than five pounds or less than ten shillings, or imprisonment not exceeding three months."[11] From the language of the law, it is clear that the purpose of the law is to protect the listed animals from being "cruelly beat or ill-treated," rather than protecting the property interests of the owner. In the decades following the adoption of this law, an organization was formed in London that would become the Royal Society for the Protection of Animals and be an inspiration for animal advocate Henry Bergh several decades later.

New Concerns in America

Representative of the first wave of anti-cruelty laws in the United States was the New York law of 1829:

> §26 Every person who [part one] shall maliciously kill, maim or wound any horse, ox or other cattle, or any sheep, belonging to another, or [part two] shall maliciously and cruelly beat or torture any such animals, whether belonging to himself or another, shall, upon conviction, be adjudged guilty of a misdemeanor.[12]

The criminal prohibitions consist of two distinct aspects. The first part is qualified with the phrase "belonging to another" while the second is qualified "belonging to

9. *Id.* at 21–22 (quoting LORD ERSKINE, ADDRESS TO PARLIAMENT (1809)). For a few more details see RICHARD D. RYDER, ANIMAL REVOLUTION 81–88 (Oxford, Basil Blackwell, 1989).

10. Richard Martin was a flamboyant duelist who served in the British House of Commons for 25 years. He would go on to be a co-founder of a humane society which in time would become the present day Royal Society for the Protection of Animals. Ryder, *supra* note 9, at 84–92.

11. *Id.* For a full discussion of the English law with quotes and references, see Davis v. American Soc'y for the Prevention of Cruelty to Animals, 75 N.Y. 362 (1873).

12. N.Y. REV. STAT. tit. 6, §26 (1829).

himself or another." The purpose of the first part is to provide protection for private property, while the second deals with cruelty to the animal regardless of ownership. The two parts prohibit very different actions. In the first part, the legislature has made criminal those actions which would most likely interfere with the commercial value of the animal: killing, maiming, or wounding. In the second part, the legislature has focused upon that which might be perceived as causing pain and suffering to the animal: beatings and torture.

The level of concern for the welfare of animals expressed by this legislation was modest and can be thought of as a small conceptual box. Consider this animal welfare box to have three dimensions. The first dimension is the number of species included in the protection of the statute. The second is the actions (or inactions) of the human that are made illegal. The third is the extent of the punishment that might be imposed under the criminal law. The above New York law has a very short list of species. It was not yet illegal to torture a dog or a bear. The dog is not the right species; a bear is not only not a listed species, but is not owned by a human. The legislature had not yet made the conceptual bridge that, if it is wrong to cruelly torture a cow, it should also be wrong to torture a cat or dog. The only acts made illegal are cruel beatings and torture. This is an early use of that critical word "cruel." This will be focused upon later in the chapter, but note that there is no definition of the term in this statute; it is used as a qualifier of the action "beat." A jury would have the responsibility to decide if a fact pattern was or was not a cruel beating.

The grading of the crime is a misdemeanor.[13] While the legislature decided that their concern for animals would only result in minor punishment, some additional insight on legislative attitude can be obtained from reviewing other criminal laws of that time period and the level of punishments that were set by the legislature. For instance, under a Pennsylvania statute of 1860, it was a misdemeanor, with a maximum fine of two hundred dollars, to cruelly beat a horse.[14] In the same state code, to expose and abandon one's own child under the age of seven was also a misdemeanor, but with a maximum fine of one hundred dollars.

---

13. The gradings of crimes are divided into two categories, felonies and misdemeanors. Felonies represent the potential for a sentence of more than a year in a state prison and have consequences afterward, such as limitations on the right to vote. Misdemeanors are commonly punished by less than one year in a local jail, and usually have no long term consequences beyond the punishment itself.

14. Pa. Laws tit. IV, §46 (1860).

The Bergh Era Begins

The life of Henry Bergh is set out elsewhere and will not be repeated here.[15] Bergh's impact on the legal world began in 1866. After his return from a trip to Europe, where he observed both the cruelty inflicted upon animals and the efforts of the Royal Society for the Protection of Animals on behalf of animals, he became focused upon animal cruelty issues in New York City. Because of his social and political connections, it was not difficult for him to approach the New York legislature with proposed legislation.

While not a lawyer, Henry Bergh was able to direct the drafting of legislation. He understood that the mere passage of animal welfare legislation would be insufficient. Without dedicated enforcement, the laws would never actually reach out and touch the lives of the animals about which he was concerned. Therefore, beside the drafting and passage of new criminal laws, he sought the charter of an organization which, like the Royal Society in London, would be dedicated to the implementation of the law. He asked the New York Legislature for a state-wide charter for the American Society for the Prevention of Cruelty to Animals (ASPCA), whose purpose, as set forth in its by-laws, was

> ... [t]o provide effective means for the prevention of cruelty to animals throughout the United States, to enforce all laws which are now, or may hereafter be, enacted for the protection of animals and to secure, by lawful means, the arrest and conviction of all persons violating such laws.[16]

This was granted on April 10, 1866. Henry Bergh was unanimously elected as the ASPCA's first president, a position he continued to hold until his death in 1888. In 1866, a new anti-cruelty law was also passed by the state legislature with the urging of Henry Bergh, but this was just a stepping stone to the milestone law that was passed the next year. This law of 1867 will be the focus of consideration.[17] The 1867 Act is relatively short, and is provided in Appendix A to this chapter. A summary of some of the key provisions follows.

A significant expansion of our animal welfare box is realized with this law as two of the three dimensions increased in their dimension. Section 1 defined animal as "any living creature." This marvelously sweeping statement finally eliminated the restriction that legal protection was only for animals of commercial value. One might rightly ask: did they really mean any living creature? The answer is no. While not having direct evidence of what they were thinking, it is most likely that the legislature, without much deep thought about what they were doing, was thinking mammals. The ASPCA itself, in the decades afterwards, sought to use the law primarily when mammals were at issue. The most unexpected animal they brought an action about were sea turtles that

15. Materials on the early events of Bergh's life are set out in Coleman, *supra* note 4, at 33–35; Clara Morris, *Riddle of the Nineteenth Century: Mr. Henry Bergh*, in 18 McClure 414, 422 (1902).

16. American Society for the Prevention of Cruelty to Animals, 1905 Annual Report 144 (New York, 1906).

17. N.Y. Rev. Stat. §§375.2-.9 (1867).

were tied to the deck of a ship, on their backs, being shipped from Florida. Additionally, note that all provisions of this law applied regardless of the ownership status of the animal.

The list of illegal acts greatly expanded upon prior laws to include: overdriving, overloading, torturing, tormenting, depriving of necessary sustenance, unnecessarily or cruelly beating, and needlessly mutilating or killing. However, the punishment remained a misdemeanor. So, two of the three dimensions were significantly expanded.

This law was much more comprehensive than prior laws. Whereas prior laws were usually just one section, this law had ten sections. These additional sections went beyond the general language of the first section, and addressed specific issues. To address the ongoing problems of animals being forced to fight each other, often to their death, Section 2 of the 1867 New York Act made animal fighting illegal. While specifically identifying bull, bear, dog and cock fighting, it applied to any animal fight. The ownership and keeping of fighting animals, as well as the management of the fights themselves, was illegal. This may well have been the first state law to prohibit animal fighting. Note that for this issue it is not a jury question as to whether such an action is cruel. The legislature made the judgment itself, prohibiting all animal fighting. The jury would only have to decide if animal fighting were present, not whether it was cruel.

Also for the first time, Section 4 of this law imposed a duty to provide "sufficient quality of good and wholesome food and water" upon anyone who kept (impounded) an animal. More than likely the common sight of starving horses in the alleys of New York provided political support for the adoption of this provision. Note that this is fundamentally different from the other provisions of the law, in that it requires a human to act rather than requiring a human to not act in a particular way. As will be seen below, it will be over a century before this provision is expanded under modern duty to provide care provisions as we see today in animal welfare laws. Just as important from a practical enforcement perspective, the new law allowed any persons, even the ASPCA, to enter private premises and care for the animal's needs. This was a very practical provision which allowed immediate help to the animals regardless of whether criminal charges were later brought against the owner or keeper.

Another first for this legislation was its concern about the transportation of animals. Section 5 made it illegal to transport "any creature in a cruel or inhuman manner." Besides making the act a crime, it empowered the taking away by officials, such as ASPCA officers, any animal being transported cruelly.

Section 6 is a curious provision requiring the registration of dogs used by businesses for the pulling of loads. The registration number was to be placed on the vehicle being pulled by the dog.[18] Perhaps this was to make identification of owners easier. Large dogs were the poor man's horse at this time.

Section 7 of the 1867 Act made illegal the abandonment of any "maimed, sick, infirm or disabled creature." Under the previous law it was not at all clear what could be done

18. *Id.* §6.

with an abandoned animal. Given that there was almost no such thing as veterinarian care at this time, an abandoned animal such as a horse in an alley of New York, would simply be in pain and suffer until death came. Under this law, a magistrate, or the captain of the police, could authorize the destruction of such a creature, providing the most humane option available at the time.

Focusing on the issue of enforcement, Mr. Bergh must have realized that the normal police forces could not be counted upon to seriously and vigorously enforce this new law. Therefore, Section 8 specifically provided that agents of the ASPCA with appointment by the sheriff had the power to arrest violators of the adopted law. This delegation of state criminal authority to a private organization was, and is, truly extraordinary. This, more than any other aspect of the 1867 Act, reflected the political power and trust that Bergh must have had within the city of New York and in the state capital. Another unusual provision was the requirement that all collected fines would be given to the ASPCA, the pragmatic Bergh again at work.[19] For the first twelve months of the society's existence, 66 convictions were secured out of 119 prosecutions, and more than $296 from criminal fines went to the operation of the society.[20] So while violations of the law remained misdemeanors, the likelihood of actual enforcement was greatly enhanced under this law.

With the threat of actual enforcement of meaningful anti-cruelty statutes came the first lobbying for an exemption from the law. Section 10 of the Act provided an exemption for "properly conducted scientific experiments or investigations," at a medical college or the University of the State of New York. Thus, one of the more heated debates about animal use of today must have been carried out over 120 years ago in the New York Legislature. Note that there is not an exception for hunting and trapping. Most likely it was not even conceivable to the legislature that anyone could suggest there was illegality in such acts; indeed, there is no sign from the annual reports of the ASPCA that they had any concern about the issue of hunting or trapping.

With this 1867 Act, an ethical concern for the plight of animals was transformed for the first time into comprehensive legislation. The focus of social concern was on the animals themselves. While it is not known who drafted the specific words used, the language was visionary in scope while addressing a number of specific, pragmatic points.

---

19. American Society for the Prevention of Cruelty to Animals, 1867 Annual Report 47–54 (1867) [hereinafter Report 1867].

20. *Id.*, 47–54.

Enforcement on the Streets of New York

A law is meaningless unless it directs or controls the conduct of individuals. For this to happen the laws must be enforced. This is normally the responsibility of the police and prosecutors, but Henry Bergh realized early on that if the law were to have any meaning in the streets of New York, where the animals lived and suffered, it was up to him and his newly formed ASPCA. He had the power to arrest lawbreakers, normally reserved for the police, and was appointed a prosecutor in New York so that he could also argue for the conviction of the criminals before a judge. It is a testament to the character of Henry Bergh that this extraordinary power of the state, vested in one private individual, was apparently never abused or wrongly used. It was, however, aggressively used.

The first case for which Mr. Bergh obtained a successful prosecution under the new statute dealt with the method by which sheep and calves were transported to the "shambles" (slaughter houses). In this case, the animals had their four feet tied together and were put into carts on top of one another like so many sacks for transportation. The ASPCA brought charges, obtaining a conviction and a ten dollar fine.[21]

A landmark case which brought the ASPCA and Mr. Bergh to the attention of the general public in the first year was focused upon sea turtles.[22] As described by Sydney Coleman:

> But the general public was still apathetic and Mr. Bergh longed for some case that would turn the spotlight on the society and give it space on the front page of the newspapers. The discovery of a boatload of live turtles that had been shipped from Florida on their backs, with their flippers pierced and tied together with strings, offered this opportunity. When the captain of the vessel refused to turn the turtles over, Mr. Bergh caused his arrest, together with the members of his crew. They were taken to the Tombs, but were later acquitted of cruelty by the court.... The judge, before whom the case was tried, told Bergh to go home and mind his own business. Some of the newspapers charged him with being overzealous and many abused him roundly. A lengthy satire in the *New York Herald*, a few days later, set all New York talking. For a time, James Gordon Bennett continued to systematically ridicule Bergh and his society, but later the two men became personal friends and the *Herald* one of the staunchest supporters of the movement. The final outcome of the turtle case was to greatly increase the number of supporters and friends of the new society.[23]

During the first year, a number of different types of cruelty situations were addressed by Mr. Bergh. One of the most abusive dealt with the horses used to pull the omnibuses

---

21. REPORT 1867, *supra* note 18, at 4, 47; *See* COLEMAN, *supra* note 4, at 42.
22. REPORT 1867, *supra* note 18, at 5.
23. COLEMAN, *supra* note 4, at 42–43.

and street railways of the time.[24] Other topics included concern about adulterated food for horses and cattle and transportation of cattle by railroad. Bergh also fought to eliminate dog and cock fights. Bergh opened a vigorous fight against these cruelties, even instigating raids.

The Ripple Effect

The New York law would not have happened but for the energy and drive of Henry Bergh, and his actions clearly struck a responsive chord in a number of individuals around the country. Evidence of the societal readiness for animal protection laws is found in the rapid adoption of the legislation and the creation of animal protection societies around the country (indeed around the world) over the next 25 years. Bergh was the initial catalyst, but the actions in many other states required the work and support of others outside the political power and influence of Bergh. Besides the drafting of the laws, Bergh's other major contribution was the generation of publicity about the issues. Because of the force of his personality and the visible way in which he ran his campaigns against animal cruelty, he was able to generate a large volume of newspaper coverage, first in New York and then around the country.

Within a few years Massachusetts,[25] Pennsylvania,[26] Illinois,[27] New Hampshire,[28] and New Jersey[29] had adopted the same pattern of legislation as that in New York with both new criminal laws and the chartered creations of state Societies for the Prevention of Cruelty to Animals (SPCA). As of 1890, thirty-one states had some level of organized Society for the Prevention of Cruelty to Animals.[30] One exception to the pattern is Maryland, which did not adopt any statute until 1890. It then adopted a very short provision which clearly was not based on New York's statute.[31] One legally significant addition to the New York model was a clause used by a number of states which imposed a specific duty on the owner or keeper of an animal to provide it appropriate shelter or protection from the weather.[32] These statutes also tended to use slightly different terminology. While the New York statute consistently referred to "any living creature," other states would use the term "animal" and then would go on to define the term "animal" to include "all brute creatures."[33] Levels of punishment also varied between the states.

24. People v. Tinsdale, 10 Abb. Pr. (n.s.) 374 (N.Y. 1868).

25. "An Act for the More Effectual Prevention of Cruelty to Animals," Mass. Gen. L., ch. 344 (1869).

26. XXIV Pa. Stat. §§7770–7783 (1920).

27. "Prevention of Cruelty to Animals Act," 1869 Ill. Laws §3.

28. 1878 N.H. Laws §281.

29. N.J. Rev. Stat. §§64–82 (1873).

30. American Society for the Prevention of Cruelty to Animals, 1890 Annual Report 36. *See generally*, Ryder, *supra* note 8, 171–75 (1989).

31. 1890 Md. Laws 198.

32. Mass. Gen. L., ch. 344, §1 (1869).

33. New Hampshire defined animals as "all brute creatures and birds." N.H. Rev. Stat. 281.31 (1878).

While New Hampshire and Massachusetts both provided penalties of up to one year in jail and a $250 fine, Michigan provided a maximum of three months in jail and a $100 fine;[34] Illinois had no jail time and a fine of $50 to $100;[35] and Nebraska, whose law protected only domestic animals, had a fine of $5 to $50.[36] Note that the penalty decreased the further west the law traveled; perhaps this reflected a decreasing level of social concern.

Apparently, the legislation was lost on the wagon trains heading for California. In 1872, the California Legislature adopted a law similar to the 1829 New York legislation.[37] It was not until 1900 that California passed the more comprehensive legislation which had been adopted thirty years earlier in New York.[38]

Development of the Concept of Animal Welfare

Twenty years after Bergh started his efforts in New York, Judge Arnold of the Supreme Court of Mississippi provided eloquent words on how the legal system now viewed animals, especially after decades of significant change.

> This statute is for the benefit of animals, as creatures capable of feeling and suffering, and it was intended to protect them from cruelty, without reference to their being property, or to the damages which might thereby be occasioned to their owners....
>
> ... [L]aws, and the enforcement or observance of laws for the protection of dumb brutes from cruelty, are, in my judgment, among the best evidences of the justice and benevolence of men. Such statutes were not intended to interfere, and do not interfere, with the necessary discipline and government of such animals, or place any unreasonable restriction on their use or the enjoyment to be derived from their possession. The common law recognized no rights in such animals, and punished no cruelty to them, except in so far as it affected the right of individuals to such property. Such statutes remedy this defect.... To disregard the rights and feelings of equals, is unjust and ungenerous, but to willfully or wantonly injure or oppress the weak and helpless is mean and cowardly. Human beings have at least some means of protecting themselves against the inhumanity of man,—that inhumanity which 'makes countless thousands mourn,'—but dumb brutes have none. Cruelty to them manifests a vicious and degraded nature, and it tends inevitably to cruelty to men. Animals whose lives are devoted to our use and pleasure, and which are capable, perhaps, of feeling as great physical pain or pleasure as ourselves,

---

34. Mich. Comp. Laws §285.1 (1929).
35. Ill. Stat. §§5*a*.6-.7 (1869).
36. Neb. Stat. §67*d* (1887).
37. Cal. Penal Code §597 (1872).
38. 1900 Cal. Stat. §154 (amending Cal. Penal Code §597 (1872)).

> deserve, for these considerations alone, kindly treatment. The dominion of man over them, if not a moral trust, has a better significance than the development of malignant passions and cruel instincts. Often their beauty, gentleness and fidelity suggest the reflection that it may have been one of the purposes of their creation and subordination to enlarge the sympathies and expand the better feelings of our race. But, however this may be, human beings should be kind and just to dumb brutes; if for no other reason than to learn how to be kind and just to each other.[39]

This judge's statement reflects the perspective of many. There is a duty to animals beyond the status of property, and the law needs to restrain uncivilized human conduct towards animals.

Judge Shea in a trial opinion of the New York Marine Court from 1873 showed more emphasis on the latter aspect.

> It is not correct to assert that the policy of this kind of legislation, especially that which has for its purpose the prevention of cruelty to brutes, is a regulation of the dominion of the private citizen over his own private property merely. It truly has its origin in the intent to save a just standard of humane feeling from being debased by pernicious effects of bad example—the human heart from being hardened by public and frequent exhibitions of cruelty to dumb creatures, committed to the care and which were created for the beneficial use of man.[40]

Terminology and Scope of Animal Welfare

Court opinions give shape and scope to the words of the legislature. They place the issues in the broader social and legal context. Judges, like legislators, usually reflect the attitudes of the times and bring their personal attitudes and beliefs with them when they make decisions. We will move from one state court opinion to another without pause because the laws are so similar in nature, and the issues so fundamental, that there is very little variation in judicial outlook around the country.

One of the functions of the court is to simply confirm the language of the legislature. The courts agreed that the language of the new statutes imposed liability without regard to the issue of ownership; the provisions applied to one's own animals, to those owned by others, and to animals with unknown or no owners. In *State v. Bruner*,[41] where a man poured turpentine on a live goose and set it afire, the court clarified that under the statute, "a man may be guilty of cruelty to his own animal, or to an animal without any known owner, or to an animal which has in fact no owner." The court also

39. Stephens v. State, 3 So. 458–59 (Miss. 1887).

40. Christie v. Bergh, 15 Abb. Pr. (n.s.) 51 (N.Y. 1873) (this case has been referred to as *The Stage Horse Cases*), available at www.animallaw.info/historical/cases/cahus/15Abbott51.htm.

41. 104 N.E. 103 (Ind. 1887).

had to clarify that the list of protected animals was, in fact, as broad as the legislature stated. In *Grise v. State*,[42] the court provided one of the first opinions which discussed the cruelty statute with a view toward assessing the types of animals to be afforded protection by the law: animal statutes "embrace all living creatures" and the "abstract rights in all animal creation ... from the largest and noblest to the smallest and most insignificant."

Another function of the courts is to provide key definitions of words used in statutes, but left undefined by the legislature. An obviously important term is "cruelty." Although used frequently in every day conversation, its definition, particularly for criminal law purposes, is not so obvious. Combining the opinions of a number of cases, one useful definition of cruelty is: (1) human conduct, by act or omission; (2) which inflicts pain and suffering on a nonhuman animal; and (3) which occurs without legally acceptable justification (by legislative language or socially acceptable custom). It should be remembered that at this time there was very little understanding of the science of pain, or of suffering.

Both at common law and under the statutes adopted, the mere killing of an animal, without more, is not "cruelty." Before the killing of an animal can support a conviction under a cruelty statute, it must be found that the killing was done in a cruel manner.[43] The court in *Horton v. State*[44] held: the mere act of killing an animal, without more, is not cruelty, otherwise one could not slaughter a pig or ox for the market, and man could eat no more meat. Thus, the court held that shooting and almost instantly killing a dog was not a violation of the statute that criminalized the cruel killing of any domestic animal. The court said that the purpose of the statute was not to punish for an offense against property, but to prevent cruelty to animals. To them the word "cruelty," when taken in connection with other offenses proscribed by the statute (torturing, tormenting, mutilating, or cruelly beating), evidently meant something more than to kill. The court in *State v. Neal*[45] defined cruelty to "include every act, etc., whereby unjustifiable physical pain, suffering, or death is caused." The focus should be on the method of death. Did the method impose unnecessary pain or suffering? While it might not be cruel to use a gunshot to obtain death, burning a dog alive would certainly be judged cruel. The death can be acceptable, while the method is not.

Courts have construed "cruelty" to include beating horses;[46] burning a goose;[47] pouring acid on hooves;[48] overworking;[49] starving or depriving a horse of proper shelter;[50] freeing a captive fox in the presence of a pack of hounds and allowing the

---

42. 37 Ark. 456 (1881).
43. *See* Horton v. State, 27 So. 468 (Ala. 1900); State v. Neal, 27 S.E. 81 (N.C. 1897).
44. 27 So. 468 (Ala. 1900).
45. 27 S.E. 81 (N.C. 1897).
46. State v. Allison, 90 N.C. 734 (1884).
47. State v. Bruner, 104 N.E. 103 (Ind. 1887).
48. Commonwealth v. Brown, 66 Pa. Super. 519 (1917).
49. State v. Browning, 50 S.E. 185 (S.C. 1905) (hiring out unfit mules).
50. Griffith v. State, 43 S.E. 251 (Ga. 1903).

hounds to tear the fox apart;[51] and passively permitting a dog to attack or kill other dogs.[52] In most criminal cases that are brought to trial, the actions of the defendant (hitting the horse, shooting the cat, etc.) are easily proven. The more difficult question then becomes whether the actions proven in the court violate the existing standards of anti-cruelty. Was the hitting of the horse or shooting of the cat cruel and/or did it cause unnecessary pain, suffering or death? It is also the case that, generally, the courts accept that the animal experiences pain or suffering. Many cases revolve around the third part of the definition, whether or not the action is nevertheless justifiable. Under certain circumstances, cruelty and even torture, are not considered "cruelty" in the legal sense because the activity is "necessary" or "useful." For example, sport hunting, commercial trapping of wildlife, and the use of animals in scientific research are usually allowed to exist, although they clearly inflict pain and suffering.

It is generally recognized that in addition to the need to obtain food or the need for medical experimentation, there are certain other situations in which the infliction of discomfort may, as a practical matter, be accepted by the courts as "necessary." Thus, for example, it may be "necessary" to inflict pain to discipline an animal, or to train it. Discipline and training are proper and lawful ends. Therefore, the infliction of pain or suffering which can be categorized as either of these will usually be excused. In *State v. Avery*,[53] the court held that if the beating of young horses was for the purpose of training, however severe it might be, it would not be considered malicious and would be no offense under the statute. However, if the beating was aggravated by the influence of any evil motive, cruel disposition, violent passions, spirit of revenge, or reckless indifference to the sufferings, the excess pain and suffering caused would be deemed malicious and a violation of the law.

Where the defense is necessity, the defendant bears the burden of proving the necessity. Defense of one's self, or of other persons, would appear to excuse at least some degree of assault upon the offending animal, and there are a multitude of statutes and cases which justify shooting or killing animals, especially dogs, which are attacking the defendant's livestock. The court in *Hodge v. State*[54] held that a cruelty statute was not intended to deprive a man of the right to protect himself, his premises and property, against the intrusions of worthless, mischievous, or vicious animals by such means as are reasonably necessary for that purpose.

As in Henry Bergh's New York statute, sometimes a legislature provides specific exemptions. The first annual report of the ASPCA considered in some detail the pain and suffering of dogs and other animals in medical teaching facilities.[55] But for the most part, Bergh was unable to do much about this because of the specific exemption

51. Commonwealth v. Turner, 14 N.E. 130 (Mass. 1887).

52. Commonwealth v. Thorton, 113 Mass. 457 (1873).

53. 44 N.H. 393 (1862).

54. 79 Tenn. 528 (1883).

55. Report 1867, *supra* note 18, at 19–22.

given them in Section 10 of the New York statute. This kind of blanket exemption continues in many of today's anti-cruelty statutes.

In addition to the term "cruelty," the courts have had to decide the meaning of many other terms. The words "overdrive," "override," or "overload," reflect a historical concern for those animals most closely associated with humans (beasts of burden) during a period when motorized transportation was unavailable. No standard is given to determine a violation. The number of possible variables, such as age, strength, and health of the animal, duration of load, degree of effort or weight of load, etc., make it impossible to be more precise in legislation. The riding, driving, or loading becomes cruel when more is being demanded of the animal than could reasonably be expected under all circumstances.[56] Remember this holistic judgment will be made by a jury, not trained in the law, but by using their life experiences to provide a judgment context.

Other terms the court had to define were "torture" and "torment." Again the focus is not on the pain of the animal, but on the justification for the infliction of the pain. In *State v. Allison*,[57] the court found the defendant had unlawfully tortured or tormented a cow by beating her and twisting off her tail. Sometimes the act itself suggested no possible justification. In one court, the pouring of turpentine on a goose, and then burning it, was found to be an unjustifiable act of torture.[58] In *Commonwealth v. Brown*,[59] the defendant applied a solution of nitric and sulfuric acid to the hoofs of two horses. This was found to be a violation of the law. Note that this law requires only the general intention to do the act (pour the acid), not the specific intention to do torture. The general intention can be proven by objective witness testimony. If specific intention were required, then the prosecution would need to know what the defendant was actually thinking at the time, something very difficult to prove.

Modern Animal Welfare Laws

It is not possible to review the present status of all the different anti-cruelty laws around the United States. While the focus of this chapter is on the general criminal statutes, there are many more animal focused laws today, such as dangerous dog statutes or restrictions on exotic animals, in each state. Also, the concepts of animal welfare can be found in the federal Animal Welfare Act[60] which focuses upon animal breeding, animal fighting, and the use of animals in exhibits and scientific research. But the most important set of laws continue to be found at the state level.

A quick review of the state of Virginia's current laws will provide a sense of the present picture. First, the core language from the 1867 act can still be found in present day laws. Consider the Virginia statute (Va. §3.2-6570(A)): "Any person who (i) overrides,

---

56. *See* State v. Browning, 50 S.E. 185 (S.C. 1905) (defendant's mule with his knowledge and permission, was cruelly worked when it was unfit for labor).

57. 90 N.C. 733 (1884).

58. State v. Bruner, 104 N.E. 103 (Ind. 1887).

59. 66 Pa. Super. 519 (1917).

60. 7 U.S.C. §§2131–2159.

overdrives, overloads, tortures, ill-treats, abandons, willfully inflicts inhumane injury or pain not connected with bona fide scientific or medical experimentation, or cruelly or unnecessarily beats, maims, mutilates, or kills any animal...." "Overrides" remains the first illegal act identified. But, with the disappearance of horses from the streets of the cities, clearly it is no longer the most import aspect of the law. Other terms from the 1867 legislation that continue to be used in the Virginia statute include "inhumane injury or pain" and "cruelly or unnecessarily beats." Our society has not changed that fundamental idea of animal welfare as articulated in the New York law. Violation of the Virginia language above, as with the 1876 law, results in just the punishment level of a misdemeanor. However, the next subpart of the section quotes many of the same words but adds the qualifier "malicious" to the language. If the actions of a defendant are malicious, then the penalty is a felony. This suggests that it is the attitude of the human and not the degree of suffering by the animal which is being punished.

Virginia's statute redefines the term "animal" to mean "any nonhuman vertebrate species except fish." No longer does the term refer to "all of creation" or "dumb brutes." Most states that have imposed more serious punishments for violations of animal welfare laws have also become more precise about which animals are covered under the law. The strong majority of states now use vertebrates as the dividing line. Virginia is a bit unusual in excluding fish. The focus of the legislature's policy concern is that if the crime is to be a felony, there must be more certainty that the animal in question can perceive pain as we understand it and be capable of suffering as the term is generally understood. As a matter of public policy, most legislatures really are not interested in protecting insects, jelly fish, or lobsters.

While the historical language continues to exist, Virginia's laws are considerably more extensive at this point in time. The section quoted above has six parts, and there are dozens of sections that are now part of the title on animal welfare law. The definition section of the animal law article defines over 50 different words and terms, a sign of good and comprehensive drafting.

The two major areas of development in the law are the extensive expansion of the provisions against animal fighting and the requirement imposed upon an owner for the well-being of the animal in his or her care. While the 1867 law had the phrase "Any person who shall keep or use, or in any way be connected with, or interested in the management of, or shall receive money for the admission of any person to any place kept or used for the purpose of fighting or baiting any bull, bear, dog, cock, or other creature," Virginia's law is now much more precise:

> §3.2-6571. A. No person shall knowingly:
>
> 1. Promote, prepare for, engage in, or be employed in, the fighting of animals for amusement, sport or gain;
> 2. Attend an exhibition of the fighting of animals;

3. Authorize or allow any person to undertake any act described in this section on any premises under his charge or control; or
4. Aid or abet any such acts.

Violations of portions of this section can result in felony convictions.

The 1867 Act which had only the phrase "deprived of necessary sustenance," created a positive duty for the owner. Again the Virginia law has expanded this duty under their present law:

> §3.2-6503. A. Each owner shall provide for each of his companion animals:
>
> 1. Adequate feed;
> 2. Adequate water;
> 3. Adequate shelter that is properly cleaned;
> 4. Adequate space in the primary enclosure for the particular type of animal depending upon its age, size, species, and weight;
> 5. Adequate exercise;
> 6. Adequate care, treatment, and transportation; and
> 7. Veterinary care when needed to prevent suffering or disease transmission.
>
> The provisions of this section shall also apply to every pound, animal shelter, or other releasing agency, and every foster care provider, dealer, pet shop, exhibitor, kennel, groomer, and boarding establishment. This section shall not require that animals used as food for other animals be euthanized [(e.g., live mice for feeding pet snakes)].
>
> B. Violation of this section is a Class 4 misdemeanor.

Under the above, it is a crime to not provide one's cat with adequate exercise. While the list of obligations is very broad, note that it is limited to companion animals and that violations of the law are only misdemeanors.

The box representative of animal welfare laws today is much larger and more complex. While the newer definitions of animals appear to be narrower than the old definition, practically it is about the same as how the old law was implemented. The scope of the actions covered by the law is clearly more extensive and comprehensive than the 1867 law. The penalties are more varied. Many laws are now felony violations with jail time of two or three years. Penalties can often include forfeiture of the animal, fines in the thousands of dollars, public service and required counseling.

The social contract for animal well-being has grown in strength and supports the larger and more complex box reflected in present legislation.

A Consideration of Animal Rights

All of the above discussion of the law was accomplished without the use of the term "animal rights." This is not a surprise, as the existing law is representative of the social contract based upon a perspective of animal welfare. That is, humans have an obligation to those animals, which are used by humans, to make sure the use of the animal does not result in "unnecessary pain and suffering." Humans have a moral or ethical duty to acknowledge the welfare needs of animals. In stating this, it is not necessary to say that animals are legal entities or have legal personality.

During the development of legal protection for animals under ideas of animal welfare, domestic animals have always been considered personal property. (The other long-existing categories of property are real property and intellectual property.) Thus the law puts dogs and lizards into the same category as tables and computers. This is not a comfortable fit. Society has acknowledged the difference between tables and dogs with the adoption of anti-cruelty laws for the protection of dogs but not tables. A key concern of many who advocate animal rights is the removal of domestic animals from any status of property. The nature of the philosophical arguments seeking this change is diverse and complex.[61] Many arguments resolve into the point that animals as living beings, like humans in many ways, deserve respect and status within the legal system, and that a key aspect of showing respect is their removal from the status of being personal property.[62]

If animal welfare law is represented by a three dimensional box, then animal rights adds a fourth dimension: the categories of entities of who may assert the interests of the animals within the legal system. Consider it the dimension of time; who can move the box forward? The pure form of animal rights seeks to have the animals themselves assert their own, as yet undefined, legal rights. A number of books have been written on this topic, and this chapter can only hint at some of the complexities that are involved with the fourth dimension. This chapter is also too short to review the writers of animal rights in the realm of philosophy.

Consider the following: Roger, an eight-year-old cat owned by Mary, is shot with three arrows by Sam, a 19-year-old human male, out having some "fun." Under pres-

---

61. For a full discussion of the moral and legal status of animals, *see generally* Animal Rights (Clare Palmer ed., 2008). This book is a collection of thirty-one reprinted essays from the major authors in this area. *See also* Martha C. Nussbaum, *Animal Rights: The Need for a Theoretical Basis*, 114 *Harv. L. Rev.* 1506 (2001) (reviewing Steven M. Wise, Rattling the Cage: Toward Legal Rights for Animals (2000); Gary L. Francione, *Animals—Property or Persons?, in* Animal Rights: Current Debates and New Directions 108, 134 (Cass R. Sunstein & Martha C. Nussbaum eds.; Oxford, New York: Oxford Press, 2004). Professor Francione is one vocal advocate of the abolitionist perspective: "And if the treatment of animals as resources cannot be justified, then we should abolish the institutionalized exploitation of animals. We should care for domestic animals presently alive, but we should bring no more into existence.").

62. This author has suggested an new category of property which would acknowledge their special status. A fourth category would be designated "Living Property"; David Favre, Living Property; A New Status for Animals Within the Legal System, 93 Marquette Law Review 1021 (2010).

ent legal concepts, the significant physical injury to Roger is acknowledged as harm to Mary's property. The measure of the harm is not the amount of suffering and pain endured by the cat, but the degree to which Mary's interests in the cat, primarily financial, have been harmed by the event. Financial harm is measured by determining the fair market value for property before the events in question, and then subtracting the value of the goods after the events. Roger, the cat, is not a recognized legal person and therefore cannot sue Sam for his pain and suffering. The other possible legal actor is a local prosecuting attorney of the government who may file criminal law charges against Sam for the legally recognized harm (the cruel and unjustified infliction of pain and suffering). Under existing law, the bad actor will never have to compensate the cat for the pain and suffering intentionally caused by the arrows. Concepts of animal rights would allow Roger visibility in the legal system so as to pursue the wrong inflicted by Sam, in the same way that if the victim of the onslaught of arrows were a two-year-old human, Maud. Today Maud could sue the actor Sam. Note that Maud does not have to be aware of her legal right in order to receive its benefits. Our legal system allows for the appointment of a legal guardian to assert the right of the child and could likewise do so for an animal.

It is relatively easy to conceptualize the application of animal rights concepts in the context of wild animals such as gorillas, elephants, chimpanzee and dolphins. Many of these species already are known as individuals with names and identification. The needs and interests of such animals are ascertainable in an objective way. The legal system could be structured so to allow a court to appoint an attorney to represent a particular animal, or perhaps a group of animals, when they have been harmed or are threatened with harm. This would allow the animal to be the plaintiff, for the court to consider the harm to the plaintiff animal directly and if the harm is real, to fashion a remedy to the benefit of the plaintiff animal, perhaps in the form of an injunction to stop harmful human actions. This author has suggested such a frame of reference in another article.[63] The path forward is more difficult when the animal is domestic, as in such a case there are human owners of the animals.

Before it is possible to move to more consideration of the possible legal rights of domestic animals, their personal property status needs to be considered more closely. Historically, if something is considered property, then it is difficult to conceptualize the property as a holder of legal rights. Rather, it is conceived as the subject of legal rights. Therefore, it is often asserted that the first step in the obtaining of legal rights for animals will be the removal of their property status, and making them like wildlife, self-owned.

Intertwined with having the status of property is the reason that they are personal property, they are to be used by humans for some purpose. Indeed, before the law can find full focus on this difficult issue of property status, there has to be more full agreement on the issue of whether it is ethically permissible for humans to use animals

63. David Favre, Wildlife Jurisprudence, 25(2) Journal of Environmental Law and Litigation 459 (2010).

in any circumstance. One side of the argument is that animals, as living beings on this planet, deserve equal ethical status as human and, therefore, should not be owned or used by humans. This argument would seem to require that domestic animals no longer exist in our society (e.g., no hens to lay eggs for human consumption, no horses to pull the wagon or run the races). Such a future world seems to be defined by the *negative*, animals shall *not* be property, without the *positive* vision of what *would* be acceptable. If they are not property, or a new variation of property that makes some human responsible for them, can domestic animals be a part of our daily lives? If not property, then what? This is not answered with any positive pictures by those who oppose the status of animals as property.

The other side of the discussion would point out that some uses are mutually beneficial to animals and their humans, with millions of companion animals being the primary example. Perhaps the better context for rights development would be to say that the ethical use of animals should be allowed only in the context of respectful use. This would allow the disrespectful use of an animal to give rise to a legal action, forcing the stopping of such an abuse.

Some would suggest that it is not possible to give personal property legal rights of its own. But, this is simply a failure of legal imagination. For example, a fairly recent development of law in the United States is the allowing of trusts to be created for the benefit of animals and providing for lawsuits to be filed by court appointed guardians to make sure the trustees carry out their legal duties toward the animals who are beneficiaries of the trust.[64] If Ms. Jones wishes to create a Cat Trust for her cat Zoe and fund it at $25,000, it is now permissible in all states. This makes Zoe a beneficiary of the trust having the same status as a human child for this limited purpose. If her friend Ms. Heath receives the cat and the money at Ms. Jones' death, she must use the money for the benefit of the cat. If it appears that the money is being spent on gambling trips to Las Vegas, a court action can be filed against Ms. Heath on behalf of the cat to correct this breach of duty. Thus, under existing laws, animals can have a legal personality within a narrow legal context. This is a limited legal right; the cat would have visibility in the courtroom. The needs of the cat would be the focus of concern and the outcome or remedy of the case would run directly to the cat's benefit. This is an example of how a legal right for an animal can exist.

A second area of the law which is changing the status of animals is that of divorce law. First in Alaska, and then in four other states, the divorce laws have been modified, such that the strict status of animal as personal property has been modified to allow a court to consider an animal caught within a divorce more like a child.[65] Under these new laws a court has the power to take into account the "well-being of the animal" in deciding which of the divorcing couple should have custody of the animal. As in trust

---

64. Uniform Trust Code §408.

65. Alaska Stat. §25.24.160(a)(5). See, David Favre, The Future of Animal Law, p. 91–93, Elgar Publishing (2021)

law, this gives legal visibility to a specific animal, where the needs of the animal are balanced in the decision of the court.

The arguments for and against animal rights do not directly change the debate about what acts are cruel, or ought to be cruel and therefore illegal. Animal rights are about that fourth dimension of the box, about who can be a plaintiff and be allowed to file the lawsuit. In 2012, PETA filed a lawsuit in the name of several orca whales being held by Sea World, but the court rejected the argument of the lawsuit saying that the whales were not slaves under the 13th Amendment of the US Constitution and therefore there was no cause of action and no standing for the whales.[66]

In 2014, a series of cases were filed in New York state courts by the Nonhuman Rights Project in an attempt to establish legal personality for some privately-owned chimpanzees. The vehicle for this was an assertion by the organization that chimpanzees should be considered legal "persons" under a New York statutes against the keeping of persons against their will (be seeking a writ of habeas corpus on behalf of the chimpanzees). There were hearings in three different trial courts, all of which denied the motion of the Nonhuman Rights Project. These denials were appealed to the next higher court. This level of court also has denied the plaintiff's motion. One of the court opinions directly addressed the claims of the plaintiff and rejected the concept that chimpanzee should be considered a legal person.[67] Since 2015, the Nonhuman Rights Project has filed a number of additional cases, both outside of New York and cases that have elephants as their focus.[68]

Within the world of law the concept and promotion of legal status for animals to have their own rights is just in the initial stages of development. The results of these efforts may not be known for decades.

Appendix A

The 1867 New York Anti-Cruelty Law

Section 1. Penalty for Overdriving, Cruelly Treating Animals, etc.

If any person shall overdrive, overload, torture, torment, deprive of necessary sustenance, or unnecessarily or cruelly beat, or needlessly mutilate or kill. or cause or procure to be overdrive, overloaded, tortured, tormented or deprived of necessary sustenance, or to be unnecessarily or cruelly beaten, or needlessly mutilated, or killed

66. Tilikum ex rel. People for the Ethical Treatment of Animals, Inc. v. Sea World Parks & Entertainment, Inc. ___ F.Supp.2d ___, 2012 WL 399214 (S.D.Cal.,2012).

67. The People of the State of New York Ex Rel. The Nonhuman Rights Project, Inc., on Behalf of Tommy, Appellant v. Lavery, Respondent, 998 N.Y.S.2d 248 (2014).

68. The website of the organization has all the legal documents about these cases posted on its site and keeps an update of its legal activities. See, http://www.nonhumanrightsproject.org/.

as aforesaid any living creature, every such offender shall, for every such offence, be guilty of a misdemeanor.

Section 2. For Keeping a Place for Cock Fighting, Bull Baiting, Dog Fighting, etc.

Any person who shall keep or use, or in any way be connected with, or interested in the management of, or shall receive money for the admission of any person to any place kept or used for the purpose of fighting or baiting any bull, bear, dog, cock, or other creature, and every person who shall encourage, aid or assist therein, or who shall permit or suffer any place to be so kept or used, shall, upon conviction thereof, be adjudged guilty of a misdemeanor.

Section 3. For Impounding Animals without Giving Sufficient Food and Water

Any person who shall impound, or cause to be impounded in any pound, any creature, shall supply to the same, during such confinement, a sufficient quantity of good and wholesome food and water, and in default thereof, shall, upon conviction, be adjudged guilty of a misdemeanor.

Section 4. In What Case Any Person May Feed, etc. Impounded Animal

In case any creature shall be at any time impounded as aforesaid, and shall continue to be without necessary food and water for more than twelve successive hours, it shall be lawful for any person, from time to time, and as often as it shall be necessary, to enter into and upon any pound in which any such creature shall be so confined, and to supply it with necessary food and water, so long as it shall remain so confined; such person shall not be liable to any action for such entry, and the reasonable cost of such food and water may be collected by him of the owner of such creature, and the said creature shall not be exempt from levy and sale upon execution issued at upon judgment therefor.

Section 5. Penalty for Carrying Animals in a Cruel Manner

If any person shall carry, or cause to be carried, in or upon any vehicle or otherwise, any creature, in a cruel or inhuman manner, he shall be guilty of a misdemeanor, and whenever he shall be taken into custody and therefor by any officer, such officer may take charge of such vehicle and its contents, and deposit the same in some safe place of custody; and any necessary expenses which may be incurred for taking charge of and keeping and sustaining the same, shall be a lien thereon, to be paid before the same can lawfully be recovered. Or the said expenses or any part thereof remaining unpaid, may be recovered by the person incurring the same, of the owner of said creature, in any action therefor.

Section 6. License for Using Dogs before Vehicles

Every person who shall hereafter use any dog or dogs, for the purpose of drawing or helping to draw any cart, carriage, truck, barrow, or other vehicle, in any city or incorporated village, for business purposes, shall be required to take out a license for that purpose, from the mayor or president thereof, respectively, and shall have the number of said license and the residence of the owner distinctly painted thereon; and for each violation of this section shall forfeit and pay a fine of one dollar for the first offence, and a fine of ten dollars for each subsequent offence.

Section 7. Penalty for Abandoning Infirm Animals in Public Place

If any maimed, sick, infirm or disabled creature shall be abandoned to die, by any person, in any public place, such person shall be guilty of a misdemeanor, and it shall be lawful for any magistrate or captain of police in this state, to appoint suitable persons to destroy such creature if unfit for further use.

Section 8. When Agent of Society May Arrest for Violations of This Act

Any agent of the American society for the Prevention of Cruelty to Animals, upon being designated thereto by the sheriff of any county in this state, may, within such county, make arrests and bring before any court or magistrate thereof, having jurisdiction, offenders found violating the provisions of this act, and all fines imposed and collected in any such county, under the provisions of this act, shall inure to said society, in aid of the benevolent objects for which it was incorporated.

Section 9. Who Shall Publish This Act, and When Shall It Be Published

This act shall take effect on the first day of May next. And the said American Society for the Prevention of Cruelty to Animals shall cause the same to be published once in each week for three weeks, in four daily papers published in New York City, or in default thereof shall forfeit the right to receive the penalties and fines as provided.

Section 10. Proviso

Nothing in this act contained shall be construed to prohibit or interfere with any properly conducted scientific experiments or investigations, which experiments shall be performed only under the authority of the faculty of some regularly incorporated medical college or university of the state of New York.

References

Bentham, J. (1781). *An introduction to the principles of morals and legislation.* Oxford: Clarendon Press.

Coleman, S. (1924). *Humane Society leaders in America.* Albany NY: The American Humane Society.

Favre, D. (2010, spring). Living property: A new status for animals within the legal system. *Marquette Law Review, 93,* 1022–1071.

Favre, D., & Tsang, V. (1993). The development of anti-cruelty laws during the 1800s. *Detroit College of Law Review, 1, 1–35.*

Nash, R. F. (1989). *The rights of nature.* Madison, WI: University of Wisconsin Press.

Palmer, C. (Ed.). (2008). *Animal rights.* Aldershot, England; Burlington, VT: Ashgate.

Ryder, R. (1989). *Animal revolution.* Oxford: Basil Blackwell.

Sapontzis, S. F. (1987). *Morals, reason, and animals,* Philadelphia: Temple University Press.

Sunstein, C. R., & Nussbaum, M. C. (Eds.). (2004). *Animal rights: Current debates and new directions.* Oxford, New York: Oxford Press.

Turner, J. (1980). *Reckoning with the beast: Animals, pain and humanity in the Victorian mind.* Baltimore, MD: John Hopkins Press.

Wise, S. (2000). *Rattling the cage: Toward legal rights for animals.* Cambridge, MA.: Perseus Books.

Wise, S. (2002). *Drawing the line: Science and the case for animal rights.* Cambridge, MA: Perseus Books.

Chapter 3

Animal Cruelty and the Law

Prohibited Conduct

Yolanda Eisenstein

Introduction

In its most general sense, animal law is the set of legal rules and cases that involve or relate to animals. The field is diverse, cutting across every substantive area of the law including property, tort, contract, criminal, environmental, and administrative, as well as across all jurisdictions—local, state, federal, and international. But not all animal laws are animal protection laws. For example, those regulating hunting, animals used for food, and dangerous dogs are primarily about human concerns. Nonetheless, laws exist whose primary purpose is animal safety and well-being, and most lawyers who consider themselves animal lawyers focus on legal protection.

Anti-cruelty laws are animal protection laws. Their central purpose is to protect animals from abuse and neglect at the hands of humans. They prohibit certain conduct, establish penalties for violators, and work to prevent cruelty by setting standards for humane treatment. However, this general belief—that society should protect animals from suffering—is relatively new. In the not-too-distant past, the "wrongness" of cruelty to animals was about human interests and morality. When people had a more direct connection to animals for food and income, prohibitions on cruelty were intended to protect that owner's rights. The killing of a person's cow or pig wrongly deprived that person of a valuable resource.

Additionally, there was a moral basis for the proscription on cruelty. German philosopher Immanuel Kant (1724–1804) expressed it when he stated that "[one] must practice kindness towards animals, for he who is cruel to animals becomes hard also in his dealings with men."[1] Thus, Kant's, and society's, objection to animal cruelty was based on its impact on humans.

1. Immanuel Kant, "Duties to Animals and Spirits," in *Lectures on Ethics*, trans. Louis Infield (New York: Harper and Row, 1963), pp 239–241.

Animals as Property

In the United States, animals are legally classified as property. Their property status is key to understanding animal cruelty and our overall treatment of animals. They are owned by humans and have no inherent legal rights. Individuals and agricultural conglomerates own companion animals and those used for food. Wildlife is considered the property of the "common" and held in trust by federal or state governments with jurisdiction over the land on which the wildlife live. Ownership of property comes with a "bundle" of legal rights, but the law has placed limits on those rights as it relates to animals. Owners may no longer abuse their animals simply by way of ownership. Moreover, more states are providing judges with the option of banning the ownership or possession of companion animals if the person has a previous cruelty conviction or the act is particularly heinous.

It seems awkward to view our companion animals, sentient creatures many consider family members, as property. However, the property status has provided courts with a way to monetize animals when they are harmed or killed. Today, that system remains in place but has failed to keep pace with today's evolving views on animals. Attempts to change their status as property or enhance their value have been slow and largely unsuccessful.

Nonetheless, some efforts have been made to advance the legal and societal views of animals beyond property. For example, in most states, it is now legal to provide financially for the care of companion animals through a pet trust when their owner dies. This type of trust designates a companion animal as a beneficiary, a status not accorded any other type of property. Also, states such as Rhode Island have legally changed the word "owner" to "guardian" in an effort to change society's thinking about our relationship with animals. Finally, family laws are beginning to include provisions that allow courts to consider the "best interest" of the animal when there is a custody dispute in a divorce or breakup of a relationship. This analysis mirrors that used by judges in child custody cases. New York's law states that "in awarding the possession of a companion animal, the court shall consider the best interest of such animal [and] any other factor which the court shall expressly find to be just and proper."[2] None of these laws have changed the property status of animals, New York's law is about the distribution of property, but they have started to change human perceptions.

The future of animals' legal status as property is unpredictable. Influential stakeholders in animal industries are committed to retaining the property status, so it is not likely to be resolved any time soon.

Despite their property status, certain animals are protected from conduct that imposes greater pain and suffering than is deemed necessary under the circumstances or is inflicted outside the bounds of accepted human values. This chapter focuses on

2. NY Dom Rel §236 (McKinney, 2021).

conduct that is legally prohibited to protect animals from abuse and to punish or rehabilitate those who commit acts of cruelty.

The Laws against Cruelty

Lawmakers, with input from various stakeholders, decide which acts constitute animal cruelty. The laws are a patchwork of federal, state, and local laws, some dating back to the early nineteenth century. While certain laws endure and maintain their relevance over time, it is less so with animal laws as they rarely reflect current science on animal intelligence and sensitivity to pain. Moreover, laws that were adequate, even at the turn of the 21st century, may now be obsolete due to the fact that knowledge is changing rapidly in the field of animal science as are shifts in public sentiment toward our treatment of animals.

The crime of animal cruelty can be a misdemeanor or felony. A misdemeanor is a minor crime and usually results in a fine. The more serious crimes are felonies. There was a time in our history when no acts of animal abuse rose to the level of a felony. Today, all states include felony-level animal cruelty statutes, although the type of acts that make them felonies and the associated penalties may vary. While most people believe that animal cruelty should be a crime punished by strict laws, states have finite resources, and crimes against humans will take precedence. However, some jurisdictions have prioritized fighting animal abuse, forming cruelty task forces, and hiring dedicated prosecutors.

Contrary to the principle that all people are equal under the law, animals are unequal under anti-cruelty laws. Lawmakers carve out exceptions and exemptions for certain animals, entities, and practices, often leaving few animals covered. If the person who commits an act of cruelty is a scientific researcher, they will likely be exempt from state anti-cruelty laws, but may fall under federal laws and regulations, or be exempt, subject only to the company's policies. Hunters and trappers will be exempt from prosecution if the conduct is related to the activities of hunting and trapping. For example, a person who maliciously kills a neighbor's family cat with a bow and arrow would likely violate a state's anti-cruelty law, while a hunter who kills a deer with a bow and arrow would be exempt, so long as the hunter had complied with the state's licensing laws. Understandably, veterinarians may be required to inflict pain on animals to treat them and are granted various legal exceptions. Veterinarians also fall under the regulatory and disciplinary rules of their professional association.

Agricultural entities receive high levels of protection, with their activities falling under "traditional animal husbandry," regardless of whether those practices are considered illegal under the state's anti-cruelty statute. Some states have gone to great lengths to protect the agriculture industry when its cruel practices have been exposed publicly by undercover humane advocates. Several states have passed "Ag-Gag" laws that criminalize the exposure of abuse by undercover workers. However, there have been legal challenges and the courts have struck down several of these laws as unconstitutional infringements on free speech and other rights.

In all states, defenses exist for anyone who commits an act of cruelty against an animal in self-defense or in defense of others. Furthermore, in certain states, a person would not be charged with cruelty in killing a dog if the dog were attacking the owner's livestock.

The United States Legal Regime in Animal Protection

As discussed in other chapters, today's animal protection movement started in the United States in 1866 with Henry Bergh. He was greatly distressed by the animal cruelty he saw and was responsible for the passage of New York's progressive anti-cruelty laws, as well as their enforcement and prosecution.

Fast forward about 100 years, and we find the more recent creation of an organized and coordinated legal effort to protect animals. Beginning with the first lawsuit, which challenged kosher slaughter, legal protection for animals grew into a movement, and society became aware of the horrible cruelty imposed on animals. One of the major catalysts for action was the Utilitarian philosopher Peter Singer, whose 1975 book, *Animal Liberation*, shocked many in its revelations of untenable and unchecked cruelty occurring in scientific research and farming. Since then, Peter Singer has written a number of books, but none has impacted the legal and societal landscapes like *Animal Liberation*.

Those initial laws, and the lawsuits that followed, comprise the basis of today's legal regime of criminalizing, reporting, investigating, charging, prosecuting, and punishing acts of animal cruelty. At the heart of laws are the prohibited acts and the related processes that support the use of those laws to convict and punish a person for an illegal act of cruelty.

The United States legal system is based on English law, otherwise known as common law, that is the "body of law derived from judicial decisions, rather than from statutes or constitutions."[3] The common law is most apparent to the public when the U.S. Supreme Court rules on a case based on precedent, the court's previous decision on a similar case. However, there is also a significant body of statutory law, codified laws enacted by state and federal lawmakers. Statutory laws are also the subject of judicial decisions if constitutional or other legal challenges arise.

Federal animal cruelty statutes exist, but generally the states occupy the field. These laws continue to evolve as states learn from their own prosecutions and observe the challenges and successes in other jurisdictions. Additional factors that drive the scope and content of statutes include economic and social environments, the tenor of state and local politics, the enforcement mechanisms in place, the influence of any local animal-based businesses, and the citizens' attitudes toward animal protection.

---

3. Common Law Definition, Black's Law Dictionary (11th ed. 2019), Westlaw.

Economics plays a crucial role in a state's legislative priorities. A state that benefits financially from animal agriculture or other animal-use businesses will be more likely to protect those industries before the animals. For example, Missouri had numerous commercial dog breeding operations exposed for their inhumane treatment of their breeding animals. This public exposure led the state to become known as the "puppy mill capital" of the U.S., an undesirable designation. As a result, voters passed a ballot initiative that reigned in some of the practices of the "puppy mills." Unhappy with this outcome, commercial dog breeders went to their legislators, who overrode the voters and repealed and replaced the law, which was supported and signed by the governor.[4] As seen in this example, businesses have significant political influence with legislators, to the point of overriding the voters in this state.

Special Treatment for Companion Animals

Notwithstanding the political, economic, and social differences, one point upon which most people agree is that they love their companion animals. The American Pet Products Association announced for the year 2021, pet supplies, food, treats, vet care, and products saw the largest increase in the industry's history.[5] The North American Pet Health Insurance Association reported double-digit growth for 2021, exceeding $2.17 billion.[6]

So not surprisingly, companion animals are the focus of state anti-cruelty laws, as well as that of many humane organizations. Such laws reflect the inconsistency that we consider dogs and cats part of our families, while animals such as pigs, whose intelligence equals that of dogs, are considered breakfast. Thus, acts of cruelty deemed illegal when inflicted on the family dog may be perfectly legal when carried out on a cow on a farm.

Anatomy of a Cruelty Law

The law categorizes two basic levels of animal abuse: 1) negligent, which is unintentional and could be the result of a lack of humane education, economic resources, or lack of concern; and 2) intentional, which requires a specific mental state—reckless, intentional, knowing, malicious, etc. The laws are constructed around these two types of abuse.

---

4. *See* Pamela M. Prah, *The Seattle Times*, "Missouri's Puppy-Mill Politics: Dog Breeders Outmaneuver Animal-Right Movement," at https://www.seattletimes.com/life/lifestyle/missouris-puppy-mill-politics-dog-breeders-outmaneuver-animal-rights-movement.

5. The American Pet Products Association, "National Pet Industry Exceeds Over $123 Billion in Sales for the First Time in Industry History," at https://www.americanpetproducts.org/press_release-detail.asp?id=1254.

6. North American Pet Health Insurance Association, "Pet Insurance Market Continued Double-digit Growth," at https://naphia.org/news/naphia-news/pet-insurance-market-continued-double-digit-growth.

A statute generally consists of the following:

- *Definitions—what is an animal, which animals are covered, and what constitutes abuse. A state may include "all animals" and leave it to the courts to define if challenged; or exclude animals such as insects, reptiles, or birds. At the federal level, the Animal Welfare Act excludes rats, mice, and birds from the definition of animal.*[7]
- *Prohibited Acts—may include depriving of food, water, or shelter or direct acts such as torture, overworking, or killing. These acts determine the seriousness of the crime and elements the prosecution has to prove to obtain a conviction.*
- *Defenses—Anyone charged with a crime may present certain defenses, and acts of cruelty are no different. Acts of self-defense, or in defense of others, and the protection of livestock are common examples.*
- *Exemptions—unlike defenses, exemptions prevent arrest or charges being filed against a person for cruelty. Usually, they include hunters, the agriculture industry and its workers, and those involved in scientific research.*
- *Penalties—may include monetary fines, probation or community service, state jail or prison time, forfeiture of the animal(s), and, permanent or limited bans on possession of animals. Rehabilitation efforts may include a psychological evaluation, counseling, and/or humane education. Courts determine penalties based on the severity of the acts, and past cruelty convictions, among other factors.*

Legislative Trends

All states have felony-level animal cruelty laws, but they are far from consistent, and animal advocates continue to push for more expansive laws and greater clarification of those that contain vague language that can hamper prosecution. Below are current trends in animal protection legislation.

- *Shoring up existing laws—states are revisiting their laws to close loopholes, provide education and counseling, mandate veterinarian reporting (with immunity from liability), strengthen penalties, and add provisions that assist prosecutors in proving their cases.*
- *Adding sexual assault laws—while usually covered under animal cruelty statutes or the common law, states are adding specific laws against bestiality.*
- *Expanding the types of animals covered by the laws—states are expanding the reach of their laws to include acts of cruelty to wildlife and animals used for food, such as the confinement of infant cows in veal crates.*

7. 7 U.S.C. §2132 (g).

- *Mandating police training—The U.S. Department of Justice estimates 25–30 dogs are killed by police daily with some shootings as high as 10,000.*[8] *Police officer training has been shown to help de-escalate encounters and reduce the number of companion animals killed needlessly by police.*
- *Assigning courtroom advocates—Connecticut became the first state in 2016 to pass a law allowing the appointment of a legal advocate for a cat or a dog in a custody case.*[9] *Maine passed a similar law in 2020.*[10] *The advocate may monitor the proceedings, attend hearings, and present information or recommendations relevant to the case.*
- *Banning retail sales—since the enactment of puppy mill laws, it has become clear that enforcement is a challenge. Some states are even eliminating the law altogether. In an alternative effort to prevent abuse in these large-scale commercial dog-breeding operations, states and cities are enacting total bans on retail sales.*
- *Instituting animal abuse registries—some states have introduced legislation or passed laws creating an animal abuse registry, similar to those for child abusers and sex offenders. However, these registries are controversial, among the public and animal advocacy groups.*[11]

It should be noted that not all legislative trends favor animal protection, although the attitudes toward cruelty have generally remained consistent.

In the Courts

While judges do not make law as legislators do, they do so indirectly through interpreting existing laws in the cases brought before them. Judges may strike down laws as unconstitutional, forcing lawmakers to redraft and pass the law within the parameters expressed in the judicial opinion. In common law cases, judicial decisions become legal precedent, which determines how future cases are decided. Precedent requires judges in the same jurisdiction to consider, and follow, the decisions in a prior case if the case is the same or similar. The legal doctrine of *stare decisis* is Latin for "to stand by things decided."[12] It is the cornerstone of our common law judicial system. Unlike statutory laws that can be changed every legislative session, judges are reluctant to overturn precedent.

---

8. Criminal Legal News, "DOJ: Police Shooting Family Dogs has Become 'Epidemic,'" at https://www.criminallegalnews.org/news/2018/jun/16/doj-police-shooting-family-dogs-has-become-epidemic.

9. Conn. Gen. Stat. §54-86n (West 2021).

10. Me Rev. Stat. Ann. 7 §4016 (West 2021).

11. *See* ASPCA, "Position Statement on Animal Abuse Registry," at https://www.aspca.org/about-us/aspca-policy-and-position-statements/position-statement-animal-abuser-registries.

12. *Stare Decisis* Definition, Black's Law Dictionary (11th ed. 2019), Westlaw.

In addition to the court's role in establishing and preserving precedent, it serves as a check on legislative action. A statute may violate the Constitution through vagueness, overbreadth, or the infringement on fundamental rights such as freedom of speech or religion. The cases below demonstrate the commitment to upholding constitutional rights and following legal precedent.

Case Study: Upholding the Constitution and Invalidating a Statute

In a federal case, *U.S. v. Stevens* (2010), defendant Robert J. Stevens was convicted of violating a statute that prohibited animal cruelty depictions in crush videos (18 U.S.C. §48). Crush videos cater to those with a sexual fetish for seeing animals crushed. The videos show small, and at times larger, animals being crushed, typically by women in stiletto heels. To stop the distribution of crush videos, which were openly sold via the internet, Congress passed a federal law making it a crime to knowingly create, sell, or possess depictions of animal cruelty with the intent to place those depictions in interstate commerce. Stevens was the first person to be prosecuted under the law, testing its validity. The U.S. Supreme Court overturned the conviction, finding the law unconstitutional on several fronts.

This case is an example of the judiciary overturning legislative action. It shows that the enactment of a statute may not be the end of the story. Irrespective of the depravity of the acts in crush videos, or the law's support by the public, the court overturned a law that it found infringed on our constitutional rights. This holding freed the defendant and sent Congress back to the drawing board to draft new legislation that did not infringe on the Constitution, which they did in 2010. The new law was again tested when a Houston man and a co-defendant were charged with producing and distributing a crush video depicting the torture and killing of puppies, chickens, and kittens.[13] This time the revised law withstood the Supreme Court's analysis and remains in force today.

Case Study: Bound to 19th Century Legal Precedent

In the 1891 Texas case, *Heiligmann v. Rose*, Heiligmann had "wickedly and maliciously" poisoned Rose's three dogs. There was no question of guilt, but in determining the level of damages awarded to Rose, the Supreme Court of Texas established the "true rule in determining the value of dogs."[14] The court stated that the value was either the market value or "some special or pecuniary value to the owner, that may be ascertained by reference to the usefulness and services of the dog."[15] The judge found that although

13. *See* United States Department of Justice, "Supreme Court Denies Petition in Animal Crush Video Case—Case Returns to Houston Federal Court," at https://www.justice.gov/usao-sdtx/pr/supreme-court-denies-petition-animal-crush-video-case-case-returns-houston-federal.

14. *Heiligmann v. Rose*, 16 S.W. 931, at 932.

15. *Id.*

the dogs did not have a market value, they were of particular value to the owner and affirmed the trial court's award of $75.00 in damages.

The ruling in *Heiligmann* has been legal precedent for 130 years in the State of Texas. While subsequent cases have found that inanimate objects such as heirlooms and trees have intrinsic or sentimental value, the courts have continued to rule that dogs, although sentient beings, have no sentimental value based on *Heiligmann*. Consequently, Texas plaintiffs have never been awarded non-economic damages for the wrongful deaths of their dogs.

On November 3, 2011, in *Medlen v. Strickland* (2011, p. 576), the Court of Appeals of Fort Worth, Texas, issued a landmark decision, finding that the *Heiligmann* case never ruled out sentimental or intrinsic value. The court challenged the longstanding interpretation of *Heiligmann* in light of later Texas Supreme Court decisions that "acknowledge that the special value of 'man's best friend' should be protected" (*Medlen v. Strickland,* 2011, pp. 580–581).

However, in April 2013, the Supreme Court of Texas reversed the Court of Appeals decision, upholding *Heiligmann*. Today, that 19th century law remains in place in Texas. Much has changed since then, but the *Medlen* case illustrates the effectiveness of the efforts by those who argued in favor of maintaining the property status of dogs and the reluctance of the courts to overturn legal precedent, such as *Heiligmann*, even when the world has moved past it.

Companion Animal Defined

Surprisingly, there is no consistent legal definition of what constitutes a companion animal. Most anti-cruelty laws specifically protect companion animals, but the definitions vary. Listed below are excerpts from various statutes that show the different ways that lawmakers define companion animals.

A "companion animal" is:

- *[A]ny dog, cat or other domesticated animal possessed by a person for purposes of companionship, security, hunting, herding or providing assistance in relation to a physical disability but shall exclude any animal raised on a farm or ranch and used or intended for use as food.*[16] *(Note: the dog or cat must be "possessed by a person.")*
- *[A] a domesticated dog or cat that is normally kept in or near the household of its owner or keeper and is dependent on a person for food, shelter and veterinary care, but does not include a dog or cat kept for farming or biomedical research practices.*[17] *(Note: the court will be required to interpret "domesticated" and "near the household.")*

16. Kan. Stat. Ann §47-816(c) (West 2021).
17. Conn. Gen. Stat. §22-351a(a) (West 2021).

- *Companion animal means domestic dogs, domestic cats, small pet birds, and other nonlivestock species.*[18] *(Note: What is a "small" bird?)*
- *[A]n animal that is commonly considered to be, or is considered by the owner to be, a pet. Companion animal includes, but is not limited to, canines, felines, and equines.*[19] *(Note: the owner can decide whether the animal is defined as a "pet," hence a companion animal.)*

These examples show the complexity of characterizations of a companion animal. Lawmakers in the various states have different ideas regarding the criteria used to determine the definition of an animal. For example, Kansas considers the purpose, while Connecticut views the animals' locations and dependence on humans. Colorado includes all species other than livestock and Illinois considers whether society or the owner considers the animal a pet.

While some of these differences seem minor, they can be significant when prosecuting animal cruelty. As seen in the domestic violence case below, the statutory definition of companion animal was a deciding factor in a felony animal cruelty conviction.

Case Study: A Companion Animal with Fins

In the case of *People v. Garcia* (2006), Michael Garcia was angry with his live-in girlfriend and threw her young son Juan's fish tank into the television and shattered it. When Juan started crying, Garcia looked at him and said, "You want to see something awesome?" and then viciously stomped the goldfish, killing them. Garcia was arrested on several charges, including felony animal cruelty. He argued to the court that goldfish were not companion animals and "stomping" was not aggravated cruelty. However, the judge disagreed, in part, based on New York State's legal definition of companion animal, which includes "any other domesticated animal normally maintained in or near the household...."[20] This broad statutory definition allowed the court to consider whether Juan's pet goldfish could be classified as companion animals under the law. The court found the statute's language and legislative intent to be clear and ruled that Juan's goldfish were companion animals. Hence, the court convicted Garcia of aggravated animal cruelty.

The Victims of Animal Cruelty

A victim is one harmed by a criminal act, typically a person. For example, property such as a car can be stolen or damaged, but it cannot be a "victim" of a crime. In contrast, animal abuse is an area of the law that recognizes animals as victims, distinct from other property. An animal feels pain and suffers or dies from an act of cruelty. Owners are harmed by the damage to or loss of their "property" in both situations. However,

---

18. Colo. Rev. Stat. §35-42-103(5) (West 2021).
19. 510 Ill. Comp. Stat. 70/2.01a (West 2021).
20. N.Y. Agric. & Mkts. §350(5) (McKinney 2021).

the cruelty laws are specific in that they protect the *animal* from abuse, including acts that may be committed by the owner.

In most animal cruelty cases, multiple violations, such as the often hundreds of animals in puppy mills, generally constitute a single act of cruelty under the law. However, in the following situation the court held that each abused animal is an individual victim.

Case Study: Twenty Victims

In *State of Oregon v. Nix*,[21] a jury convicted the defendant of 20 counts of second-degree cruelty (neglect) of animals. At sentencing, the state asked the court to impose 20 separate sentences based on the abuse of 20 different victims, in compliance with the state's "anti-merger" statute. The defendant objected, arguing that animals were not victims, meaning that the state's "anti-merger" statute did not apply. The trial court agreed with the defendant, holding that only people could be victims, sentencing the defendant to 90 days in jail and three years of bench probation for one count of animal cruelty. The court then suspended the jail sentence. The state appealed.

The Oregon Court of Appeals reversed the trial court, ruling that animals, as well as people, could be victims, and the Supreme Court of Oregon affirmed. The Supreme Court agreed with the state's position that the law's intent was to protect more than a "general public interest in animal welfare," it was to protect individual animals from suffering.

The Oregon court's ruling is significant in that the court recognized that animals can be victims. While the case is only applicable in Oregon, judges monitor, and can be influenced by, the decisions in other jurisdictions making the reach of this ruling influential beyond the state of Oregon.

When a crime is committed, there is a victim beyond the one injured—the public. A crime is seen as an infringement on public order and safety; society itself is a victim that is harmed. In the past, animal cruelty was seen as a victimless crime, one in which there was no impact on society. That view is no longer valid, as demonstrated throughout this book. Moreover, it is incumbent on the law to keep pace with society's concerns.

There are others who maybe not be legal victims, yet pay an emotional price related to animal cruelty. People who witness the suffering of their neighbor's dog chained to a tree day in and day out may unknowingly grow insensitive to the animal's suffering. Victims of domestic violence suffer when their abusers take out their wrath on the beloved family cat. Shelter workers, animal control officers, and rescue volunteers who care about animals are victims when they repeatedly see the cruelty humans can inflict on animals.

21. *State of Oregon v. Nix*, 355 Or. 777.

Society is beginning to acknowledge and address these nameless victims of animal cruelty. More than 50 percent of states have "pet protection" laws that allow judges to include the family pet in protective orders along with the children. Law enforcement, social service agencies, and animal welfare organizations are working together and sharing information to prevent domestic violence and animal cruelty. And shelters are looking at counseling and other ways to alleviate the stress of employees who care for, and then are required to euthanize, the often-large numbers of animals thoughtlessly abandoned and abused.

Cruel Acts and Omissions

Various terms are used to define the acts and omissions that constitute cruelty. Standard terms include torture, injure, overwork, and torment. These are broad terms that may include any number of actions, sometimes making it difficult for prosecutors to prove their cases. Some laws are specific, such as Colorado's:

> A person commits cruelty to animals if he or she knowingly, recklessly, or with criminal negligence overdrives, overloads, overworks, torments, deprives of necessary sustenance, unnecessarily or cruelly beats, allows to be housed in a manner that results in chronic or repeated severe physical harm, carries or confines in or upon any vehicles in a cruel or reckless manner, engages in a sexual act with an animal, or otherwise mistreats or neglects any animal, or causes or procures it to be done, or, having the charge or custody of any animal, fails to provide it with proper food, drink, or protection from the weather consistent with the species, breed, and type of animal involved, or abandons an animal.[22]

Courts look to legal definitions and legislative intent for guidance in their decisions and will also consider the ordinary meaning of words found in dictionaries. Thus, some judges take a narrow view, while others, a broad one.

There may be a distinction by animal, such as laws that impose harsher sentences on abusive acts committed on a service dog as opposed to those committed on a dog that is considered a companion. The reverse may be true, such as laws that impose lesser sentences for cruelty to livestock. For example, Texas has two separate laws, one for cruelty to livestock and another for non-livestock animals.[23] Certain acts, such as dogfighting or cockfighting, may include additional charges, such as gambling, resulting in harsher sentences.[24] The reasons for these differences are usually related to the impact on human lives and society, not the animals.

---

22. Colo. Rev. Stat. §18-9-202(1)(A) (West 2021).

23. Texas. Penal Code Ann. §42.09 (West 2021); Texas Penal Code Ann. §42.092 (West 2021).

24. In the Michael Vick dogfighting case, because interstate gambling was involved, Vick and the other defendants faced the possibility of federal charges under the Racketeer Influenced and Corrupt Organizations Act (R.I.C.O.).

An act may be a misdemeanor or a felony, the level of which is determined by a number of factors. One factor is the intent, or mindset, of the abuser. In criminal law, that intent is called *mens rea*, a Latin phrase meaning "guilty mind." *Mens rea* is characterized by words such as intentionally, negligently, knowingly, maliciously, or recklessly. The prosecutor is usually only required to prove one intent, although some states will require a combined standard, such as "knowingly and maliciously."[25]

Acts that are committed knowingly are those where the person knows and is aware that their conduct will cause a specific result. Intentional has the common meaning, that the actor intends that their acts will have a certain result. Some of the other language that may be found includes willfully, maliciously, and cruelly. Willful and malicious are sometimes used together. Willful simply means a voluntary act, one committed purposefully but not maliciously. Malice is the "intent, without justification or excuse, to commit a wrongful act [with a] reckless disregard of the law or a person's legal rights."[26] Cruelly is another way to describe "willfully and maliciously," but is usually specific to animal or human physical abuse. Other factors that can affect the severity of the crime and the punishment include prior convictions, the use of dangerous weapons, concurrent crimes, or threats to people.

An act committed negligently will be a lesser offense. Negligence is the "failure to exercise the standard of care that a reasonably prudent person would have exercised in a similar situation ... a culpable carelessness."[27] The definition means that negligence is not typically a criminal act in that the perpetrator did not have a guilty mind. The harmful acts or omissions simply failed to live up to the standard of the "reasonable person."[28] An omission or failure to act can include failure to provide food, water, veterinary medical care, and adequate shelter.

The Broad Spectrum of Abusers

Acts of cruelty and those who commit them cover a broad spectrum. It is difficult to classify abusers without considering the context of the abuse. For example, agricultural workers only commit abuse if they go beyond accepted animal husbandry practices. And poachers actually kill the elephants for their ivory, but one cannot leave out those who pay the poachers and the end purchasers, without whom there would be no poaching.

For companion animals, owners may be charged with cruelty from their omissions as well as their affirmative acts. They have a special responsibility to provide proper care for their animals, such as adequate food and shelter. Owners also have the right to end the lives of their sick animals as long as they do it humanely. Most owners choose to

25. *See* Kan. Stat. Ann. §21-6412(1) (West 2012).

26. Malice Definition, Black's Law Dictionary (11th ed. 2019), Westlaw.

27. Negligence Definition, Black's Law Dictionary (11th ed. 2019), Westlaw.

28. The reasonable person is a hypothetical person used in the law to exemplify the proper or standard behavior. *See* 57A Am. Jur. 2d. Negligence §133 (2021). The defendant's acts are measured against the reasonable person, who always acts prudently and carefully. *Id.*

euthanize their animals to end their suffering, an act that is considered kind, not cruel. However, the euthanasia of healthy animals for trivial reasons is morally controversial, and veterinarians may refuse on ethical grounds.

Angry neighbors may turn up in cruelty and abuse cases as either the abusers or the eyewitnesses. Poisoning, shooting, and trapping/relocating are all acts of cruelty committed by people who are unhappy with the behavior of their neighbors' animals. Defenses are available in some situations, such as when dogs kill or threaten livestock or other property.[29]

Irresponsible breeders who operate large-scale commercial breeding facilities may be charged with cruelty when their operations cross the line from acceptable practices to cruelty. Their motivation is money, and their crime is often the cruelty of indifference, an insensitivity to their breeding animals' suffering and quality of life. In contrast, hoarding is a medical disorder that involves a "persistent difficulty discarding or parting with possessions because of a perceived need to save them."[30] People who hoard animals may collect so many animals that they cannot care for them properly, creating health risks for the animals and people. Although hoarding is a mental health disorder, states have previously prosecuted them under traditional cruelty laws. However, that situation is changing as courts increasingly have the option of psychological counseling.

The police are regularly confronted with situations involving dogs. Dogs may interfere with law enforcement's efforts to settle domestic violence disputes, make arrests, and issue warrants. When a police officer kills an owner's dog, it constitutes "state action," triggering constitutional issues. The officer will usually claim, and is often granted, "qualified immunity," meaning that the officer is immune from liability because their actions in killing the animal were reasonable and therefore constitutional. However, where the killing is not reasonable, it can violate the owner's rights under the Constitution, such as the Fourth Amendment prohibition of unreasonable searches and seizures. The owner may file a lawsuit based on a provision of the Civil Rights Act of 1871, 42 U.S.C. 1983, generally referred to as a "1983 lawsuit."

Case Study: A Limit to Police Immunity

In *San Jose Charter of Hells Angels v. City of San Jose* (2003), the Hells Angels brought a civil rights action under 42 U.S.C. §1983 against seven San Jose, California, police officers and Deputy Sheriff Linderman. The Hells Angels claimed that the San Jose police violated their Fourth Amendment rights against unreasonable search and seizure when they searched the residences of two group members, killing three dogs. The officers argued that they were entitled to qualified immunity because their conduct was reasonable and did not violate the owners' Constitutional rights.

---

29. *See* Tex. Penal Code Ann. §42.092(e)(1) (West 2021).

30. Mayo Clinic, "Hoarding Disorder," at https://www.mayoclinic.org/diseases-conditions/hoarding-disorder/symptoms-causes/syc-20356056.

The court disagreed with the police. In addition to finding an unreasonable execution of the search warrants in violation of the Hells Angels' Fourth Amendment rights, the court found that the officers did not have qualified immunity in the shooting of the three dogs. The officers knew the dogs would be at the homes and made no provisions for dealing with them in a nonviolent manner. The judge stated that the "emotional attachment to a family's dog is not comparable to a possessory interest in furniture" (*San Jose Charter of Hells Angels v. City of San Jose,* 2003, pp. 977–978) and that the intrusion was severe. He recited past cases that should have "alerted any reasonable officer that the Fourth Amendment forbids the unnecessary [destruction of property], i.e., when less intrusive, or less destructive, alternatives exist." (*San Jose Charter of Hells Angels v. City of San Jose,* 2003, p. 977–978). Under the circumstances, the court summed up that a "reasonable officer would have known that the killing of the dogs ... was unlawful" (*San Jose Charter of Hells Angels v. City of San Jose*, 2003, pp. 977–978). The Supreme Court refused to take the case and the city of San Jose settled with the Hell's Angels.[31]

This case shows that qualified immunity is not absolute, even in a case brought by a notorious plaintiff. It also illustrates how the property status of animals resulted in an unconstitutional taking by the state.

Additional research is needed on the causes of abuse and the demographics of abusers. In some situations, men are more likely to be the abuser, and in some, such as hoarding, it is women. Before 2016, when the Federal Bureau of Investigation (FBI) began classifying animal cruelty as a separate crime, animal cruelty was simply classified as an "other offense." Hopefully, with a distinct categorization, more research can be done on the specific causes and profiles of abusers.

Who Reports and Investigates Animal Cruelty?

Anyone can report a case of animal cruelty. Most cities allow anonymous reporting to encourage people to report without concern of retaliation by a neighbor or family member. Also, many humane organizations have cruelty hotlines for reporting. Some states mandate reporting by veterinarians and waive civil liability if the veterinarian is sued.

The responsibility for investigating animal cruelty may be assigned to law enforcement, animal control officers, the county sheriff, or humane society, depending on the size and legal structure of the city or county government. Rural areas and small towns do not usually have the resources to staff an animal control department, and the sheriff will have the job of investigation and enforcement. In cities where animal control departments exist, staffing will be dictated by the city's budget, and the officers' authority will vary. Some officers may have the authority to immediately seize

---

31. *See The Daily*, "San Jose/City Pays Hells Angels $797,500 to Settle Suit, at https://www.sfgate.com/bayarea/article/SAN-JOSE-City-pays-Hells-Angels-797-500-to-2513273.php.

animals based on their assessment of the situation, but others may be required to obtain a warrant.

Some cities have enlisted the services of animal welfare organizations, such as humane societies, to assist in the investigation of animal cruelty. The choice to employ humane organizations can be controversial. Opponents of this approach argue that humane societies are biased in favor of the animal; therefore, cruelty situations will not be investigated fairly. They claim that animal cruelty is a serious charge that can result in incarceration and the deprivation of property and should be investigated by law enforcement or other governmental entities. Nonetheless, humane societies often play significant roles in cruelty cases even without the authority to investigate or take any legal action. Specifically, they may house and care for seized animals, often at a high cost; they may be called on to give expert opinions as to the extent and severity of the cruelty; and they may provide veterinary services to animals who are seized. If the animals are ultimately forfeited, it falls on the humane organizations to continue to care for the animals and adopt them out to permanent homes.

Investigations do not always result in warrants, seizures, and prosecutions. Officers have several options to consider based on their assessment of the situation. In neglect situations, investigators may seek to educate the person or call on charities to provide support in financial hardship cases. Numerous humane organizations will step in to provide food, spay/neuter, and other services, such as building fences, to help persons care adequately for their animals. Officers may also start with citations and warnings before taking more drastic steps. In severe cases of cruelty, officers will usually attempt to persuade the owner to immediately relinquish the animal. Transferring ownership frees the investigators to immediately take possession of the animals and provide veterinary medical care. The alternative is to forcibly take the animals through a warrant or legal exceptions to a warrant.

The Commitment to Enforcement and Prosecution

The level of commitment to the enforcement of animal cruelty laws depends on several factors. First, if a city is not handling human crimes to the citizens' satisfaction, animal abuse will be a lower priority. Second, cities and counties may be low on funds and short-staffed, making them unable and unwilling to devote the necessary time and effort to prosecutions. Finally, there may be an attitude that animal cruelty is "only about animals," and therefore, cases of abuse do not warrant the city's time or resources.

However, empirical evidence supports what many have believed anecdotally, that animal cruelty is connected to human violence. Furthermore, cockfighting and dogfighting are associated with other serious crimes such as gambling, drugs, and the illegal gun trade. Because of mounting evidence of the human costs of animal cruelty, an increasing number of jurisdictions are taking a more proactive stance against cruelty. As noted earlier, in 2016 the FBI began tracking animal cruelty as a separate crime in its National Incident-Based Reporting System (NIBRS). Previously, animal abuse was categorized as an "other offense," making it difficult to obtain a clear picture of animal cruelty and its consequences.[32] As cases of animal abuse are investigated, related instances of domestic violence and child abuse have been discovered. Convictions of animal cruelty have been found to prevent other related crimes.

The prosecution of animal cruelty is generally the same as the prosecution of any other criminal case. While a crime may have been committed, prosecutors must determine whether they have sufficient evidence to prove guilt. In civil cases, the burden of proof is a "preponderance of the evidence," which means there is a greater than 50 percent chance that the proposition is true. In criminal cases, the burden is much higher and requires the prosecution to prove "beyond a reasonable doubt" that the defendant is guilty. It means that no reasonable doubt exists as to the defendant's guilt.

Prosecutors are granted what is called "prosecutorial discretion" in that they may choose not to prosecute. The prosecutor will look at the alleged abuser's criminal record and the circumstances surrounding the act. The proper handling of the animal, witnesses, and the crime scene can make the difference as to whether the case goes forward or not. In animal cases, the victim, the animal, can never say what happened. It makes the evidence even more critical to proving the case. If an animal has died, a necropsy has to be performed quickly to determine the cause of death. Mishandling the body, such as freezing, can destroy valuable evidence. A veterinarian should be on the scene to assess the situation and advise officers regarding how the animal should be handled.

One of the challenges in cruelty cases is that they may involve seizing large numbers of animals. There may be a seizure of 500–700 dogs in commercial dog breeder raids, with many needing veterinary medical care. The financial burden to cities and humane organizations in such cases can be significant and will impact many decisions. The following animal seizure required an extraordinary effort from the city and the animal welfare organization.

Case Study: Seizing and Caring for 27,000 Animals

In December 2010, the city of Arlington, Texas, was involved in what was at the time the largest cruelty seizure of animals in the U.S. The defendant owned a company that imported and exported exotic animals, primarily reptiles.[33] An employee's tip to the Arlington police led to the search, which revealed a large number of dead and malnourished animals. The police seized 27,000 animals, more than 500 species, including hedgehogs, turtles, three-toed sloths, wallabies, and tarantulas.

---

32. *See* "Tracking Animal Cruelty: F.B.I. Collecting Data on Crimes Against Animals," at https://www.fbi.gov/news/stories/-tracking-animal-cruelty.

33. *See* PETA, "Behind the Scenes in the Pet Trade," at https://investigations.peta.org/us-global-exotics-exposed.

The police requested the assistance of the Society for the Prevention of Cruelty to Animals (SPCA) of Texas. They had been notified in advance of the raid and were at the scene when the search and seizure occurred. They collected and transported the animals over 16 hours in freezing weather to a space at the SPCA facility that had been specifically modified to accommodate animals from the tropics. Seized animals cannot be permanently relocated until the case is complete and the defendant is divested of ownership. The care of these animals during the defendant's three-month trial involved the work of 12 animal-related agencies and veterinary experts. After the trial, the City of Arlington transferred ownership to the SPCA, which then permanently relocated all of the animals to rescue organizations, zoos, and sanctuaries. Because of their long-time captivity, none of the animals could have survived in the wild.

The cost of caring for these animals during the prosecution was substantial and was not collected from the defendant. The care and placement of the animals could not have been successful without the help of the SPCA and other donors, individuals, and organizations.

On Trial

If the evidence warrants moving forward with a case, the prosecuting attorney will decide whether to file felony or misdemeanor charges and start the proceedings. Of the cases that are filed, some will not go to trial as a result of a plea bargain with the defendant.

For those that do go to trial, the preparation is the same for animal cruelty as for any other criminal case. Defendants are entitled to jury trials, although some may choose a bench, or judge only, trial, particularly if the cruelty is gruesome. Many lawyers will advise their clients not to expose a jury to horrific cases of animal abuse, in part, because these cases can attract media attention and large numbers of animal advocates.

If the defendant is found guilty, the judge has several options for punishment depending on the law in that jurisdiction. As discussed earlier, trends show that lawmakers are looking not only at increasing the incarceration time for cruelty offenses but at providing rehabilitation and education. Judges may require restitution, ordering abusers to repay society for expenses incurred in caring for sick or injured animals, or may include restitution in the form of community service. Community service to animal welfare organizations is controversial, given the nature of the crime, although some animal advocates support it. In addition, the defendant may be required to go through counseling, which can be especially important in hoarding cases. Judges also may have the discretion to prohibit, temporarily or permanently, the person from owning another animal as a condition of probation or a component of the sentence.

Animal cruelty cases can be complex and do not fit within one category. Hoarding, family violence-related harm to animals, dogfighting, and neglect are all animal cruelty but are unique, requiring different approaches by the criminal justice system. Hoarding is a psychological problem with an almost 100 percent recidivism rate. Jail time is rarely an effective punishment. Animal abuse related to family violence is usually more about hurting the animals to harm the spouse, partner, or children and less about the animal. Dogfighting is usually about illegal gambling and making money. Animal abuse is a consequence of the sport and not the only crime. It is easy to see how a "one size fits all" approach to animal cruelty is not practical. These distinct issues are beginning to be realized and addressed by the legal system.

Fines vary, from a minimal amount, such as $25.00, to Arizona's potential fine of up to $150,000 (see also Arizona Supreme Court, 2012).[34] Enhanced punishments of 10 or more years may also be handed down in some jurisdictions for repeat offenders or situations where dangerous weapons are used.

Conclusion

This chapter has focused on acts of animal abuse that are prohibited by law in the United States. The kinds of acts that are prohibited vary widely by state, as well as by actors and animals. Admittedly, progress has been made in the protection of companion animals. Society has become more conscious of and concerned with animal suffering and the moral issues surrounding animal cruelty and its link to human violence. Stronger and broader laws have been passed, but much work remains to be done in the enforcement of existing laws and public education focused on the human and nonhuman costs of animal abuse.

The story for wildlife and animals used for food is less sanguine than that for companion animals. The same acts prohibited against the family dog are allowed legally, and socially accepted, when carried out on a pig destined for the breakfast table. And although numerous sources point to the fact that hunting in the United States has declined for years, lawmakers continue to focus on this small segment of society and exempt hunters from cruelty laws.

Recently, harsher criminal penalties for animal cruelty have been met with questions regarding their effectiveness and impact on society. Does incarceration reliably serve to advance the status of animals and change attitudes? Is the animal protection movement at odds with other social justice movements that refute the value to society of incarceration? Is justice served when human lives are forever damaged by becoming a convicted felon? These are questions that are beginning to appear and are being discussed among a wide variety of social justice and animal advocates.

Beyond the border of the United States, the story is much the same—a patchwork of laws based on each country's cultural, economic, and political environment. From Japan's whaling to ivory poaching in sub-Saharan Africa, acts of cruelty against animals—legal and illegal—continue, with animals losing the struggle for survival. Animals in the wild are losing competition with humans for food and habitat, creating

34. Ariz. Rev. Stat. Ann. §13-801 (West, 2021).

what many scientists call the greatest level of extinction since the dinosaurs. But the current extinction, unlike that of the dinosaurs, will be a human legacy.

References

American Pet Products Association (2021). *National pet industry exceeds over $123 billion in sales for the first time.* Retrieved September 9 2022, from https://www.americanpetproducts.org/press_releasedetail.asp?id=1254.

Garner, B. A. (2019). *Black's Law Dictionary* (11th ed.). Westlaw.

Kant, I. (1963). *Lectures on ethics,* trans. Louis Infield. Harper and Row.

North American Pet Health Insurance Association. (n.d.). *Pet insurance market continued double-digit growth.* Retrieved from https://naphia.org/news/naphia-news/pet-insurance-market-continued-double-digit-growth.

Singer, P. (1975). *Animal liberation.* HarperCollins Publishers.

Wagman, B. A., & Liebman, M. (2011). *A worldview of animal law.* Carolina Academic Press.

Chapter 4

Animal Cruelty and the Law

Permitted Conduct

Joan Schaffner

Introduction

As discussed in Chapter 3, state anti-cruelty laws are the primary laws protecting animals from abuse and neglect. However, these laws often exempt certain animals, for example wildlife and animals used for research or food. Thus, these animals can be subjected to treatment that violates the anti-cruelty law provisions but are nevertheless legal. This chapter will focus on the laws that govern these animals.

The law allows for many different uses of animals—for example for research, entertainment, sport, breeding, food or clothing—and for some of these uses the law imposes standards that govern the animals' treatment during such use in an effort to protect the animals from pain and suffering. The standards differ depending upon the specific use of the animal. Thus, the same animal, for example a rabbit, will be treated very differently under the law depending upon whether the rabbit is someone's companion,[1] bred to be a companion, used in research, exhibition or entertainment, raised for food or fur, or lives in the wild. Of the rabbits just described, only the "companion" rabbit is protected under the state anti-cruelty laws. Every other rabbit will be subjected to a different legal regime depending upon the human use of the rabbit.

This chapter is organized around the human use of the animal and the permitted conduct under U.S. law. Since most human uses of animals may involve interstate commerce, the federal government may regulate such use under the Commerce Clause of the U.S. Constitution.[2] However, generally federal law does not preempt state regulation, and thus state law may govern the regulation of the same animals as well. This chapter will focus primarily on federal law with some mention of state law when of particular note. This chapter will discuss how the law regulates the various

1. Terminology shapes perceptions. Many people and the law refer to animal companions as "pets." While there is nothing particularly demeaning about the use of the term "pet;" it is less descriptive and arguably less ethically sensitive than using the term "companion" when referring to animals with whom we share companionship. Thus, this chapter will use ethically sensitive language to refer to and describe animals unless quoting the law directly.

2. *See e.g.*, 7 U.S.C. §2131.

permissible uses and treatment of animals and explore how effective the law is in preventing cruelty, in other words, whether the law provides for the animals' well-being or merely sanctions their abuse for human purposes.

Animals Bred as Companions and Animals Used in Research or Exhibition

Federal Animal Welfare Act

The law allows for animals to be used as property by humans in a variety of ways. Permissible uses of animals allegedly necessary to achieve legitimate human goals often inflict pain and suffering on the animal. Animal welfare laws define the legitimate uses of animals and set standards for their treatment in an attempt to avoid inflicting "unnecessary" pain. The World Organisation for Animal Health (OIE)[3] defines "animal welfare" to mean "how an animal is coping with the conditions in which it lives."[4] The Five Freedoms, developed in 1965, guide the standards established under the law to protect them from unnecessary pain or suffering. The Five Freedoms are: "freedom from hunger, malnutrition and thirst, freedom from fear and distress, freedom from heat stress or physical discomfort, freedom from pain, injury and disease; and freedom to express normal patterns of behaviour."[5] In recent years, animal welfare science has moved towards replacing the Five Freedoms with the Five Provisions to address two disadvantages of the Five Freedoms. First, the Five Freedoms suggest it is possible for the animals to be free from these negative experiences, when in fact, we can only minimize the negative experiences they suffer from our use. And second, the Five Freedoms focus on preventing negative experiences rather than promoting positive experiences for the animal. The Five Provisions for promoting animal welfare are: "providing ready access to fresh water and a diet to maintain full health and vigour, providing an appropriate environment including shelter and a comfortable resting area, prevention or rapid diagnosis [of pain injury or disease] and treatment, ensuring conditions and treatment which avoid mental suffering, and providing sufficient space, proper facilities and company of the animal's own kind."[6] The standards set under the law should reflect the Five Provisions if we are to provide animals with good welfare.

While there are over 90 U.S. federal statutes that affect animals,[7] the leading federal statute that regulates humans' uses of animals is the Animal Welfare Act (AWA).[8] The

3. The World Organisation for Animal Health is known by the acronym OIE for the French "Office International des Epizooties."

4. OIE, World Organisation for Animal Health, *Animal Welfare,* Retrieved from https://www.oie.int/en/what-we-do/animal-health-and-welfare/animal-welfare/ (last visited July 29, 2021).

5. *Id.*

6. Mellor, D. J. (2016). Moving Beyond the "Five Freedoms" by Updating the "Five Provisions" and Introducing Aligned "Animal Welfare Aims," *Animals 6,* 59–65.

7. Chu, V. S. (2010, Feb. 1). *Brief summaries of federal animal protection statutes.* CRS 7-5700, 94–731 (noting that many "concern animals but are not necessarily animal protection statutes").

8. 7 U.S.C. §2131–2159; Cowan, T. (2016, Jan. 5). *The Animal Welfare Act: Background and selected animal welfare legislation.* CRS 7-5700, RS22493.

AWA is enforced by the United States Department of Agriculture (USDA) Animal and Plant Health Inspection Service (APHIS). The AWA is designed to set humane standards for animals bred for sale as companions, used in research, exhibited to the public, or transported commercially.[9] All animals so used, however, are not covered by the law. The AWA defines "animal" to mean "any live or dead dog, cat, monkey (nonhuman primate mammal), guinea pig, hamster, rabbit, or such other warm-blooded animal."[10] Birds, rats, and mice, bred for use in research, horses not used for research, other farm animals used for food, and cold-blooded animals are excluded from protection under the AWA.[11]

Under the AWA, animal dealers and exhibitors must be licensed, and animal research facilities and carriers must be registered. "Dealer" is defined as anyone who in commerce and for compensation in excess of $500 annually buys or sells an animal, *except* a "retail pet store."[12] "Exhibitors" specifically include carnivals, circuses, and zoos but *exclude* retail pet stores, livestock and other agricultural shows or fairs, rodeos, and purebred dog and cat shows.[13] "'Research facility'" means any school (except an elementary or secondary school), institution, organization, or person that uses or intends to use live animals in research, tests, or experiments, and that (1) purchases or transports live animals in commerce, or (2) receives funds under a grant, award, loan, or contract from a department, agency, or instrumentality of the United States for the purpose of carrying out research, tests, or experiments."[14] However, the Secretary may *exempt* all such entities that do not use live dogs or cats and whose principal function is not biomedical research. All general carriers including airlines, railroads, motor carriers, and shipping lines, are covered as "carriers."[15]

Note the exemptions from both the animals covered and the entities regulated under the AWA. The animals affected by these exemptions have no legal protection and thus they may be, and often are, subject to cruel treatment. The rationale underlying these exclusions generally is based on a utilitarian balancing that the cost to protect these animals, whose intrinsic interests are not valued, is outweighed by the benefit they provide to humans. A classic example of this is the exclusion of birds, mice, and rats bred for research who[16] represent 90% of all animals in research labs.[17] They are excluded from protection under the AWA because the researchers and government argued that their inclusion would require significant resources both to com-

9. 7 U.S.C. §2131 (only animals or activities in interstate or foreign commerce or those that substantially affect such commerce are subject to these regulations).

10. *Id.* §2132(g).

11. *Id.*

12. *Id.* §2132(f).

13. *Id.* §2132(h).

14. *Id.* §2132(e).

15. *Id.* §2132(j).

16. As in Chapter 3, this chapter uses the word "who" rather than "it" to refer to animals. Animals are not things, but sentient beings who show emotion, feel pain, and communicate. The word "who" is a more appropriate reference and serves to promote their rightful place in society.

17. Cohen, H. (2006). The Animal Welfare Act. *J. Animal Law* 2, 13–24.

ply with and enforce the law. Additionally, horses,[18] when not used for research, and animals on the farm, get no protection under the AWA. Similarly, retail pet stores are excluded from the definition of dealers and rodeos, agricultural fairs, and purebred dog and cat show are excluded from the definition of "exhibitors". Arguably, some of these activities, for example rodeos, would be prohibited outright if the participants were forced to meet minimal requirements of humane treatment because the activities are inherently inhumane.

Case Study: Redefining "Retail Pet Store"

When the AWA was first enacted, the traditional "retail pet store" was a brick-and-mortar store where customers would go to purchase animals as companions. Because these retailers sold the animals to the public in-person, the public was able to view the condition of the animals at the store providing public oversight of these establishments. Since the customers could help ensure that the animals were being treated well, the AWA exempted the "retail pet store" from regulation.

With the advent of the internet, many animal breeders are able to sell directly from their breeding facility to the general public, sight-unseen, without being regulated under the AWA because they met the definition of "retail pet store," one who sold directly to the public. As a result, over the years, APHIS began receiving numerous complaints from the public about the lack of oversight of these facilities and the resulting harm to the animals under their care. In late 2013, APHIS amended the AWA altering the definition of "retail pet store" and thus closing the loophole that allowed internet sellers of animals to bypass regulation under the AWA.[19] Now the definition expressly provides that a "retail pet store" is a place "at which the seller, buyer and the animal available for sale are physically present so that every buyer may observe the animal available for sale prior to purchasing and/or taking custody of that animal after purchase."[20] This amendment has provided greater protection for many animals bred for sale as companions.

For those animals and entities covered under the AWA, the statute requires that the Secretary of Agriculture "promulgate standards to govern the humane handling, care, treatment, and transportation of animals ... [which] shall include minimum require-

---

18. Thus, for example, racing horses are not protected under the AWA even though they may be subject to cruel treatment, doping, and death. The Horse Racing Integrity Act of 2020, H.R. 1754 (116th Cong. 2019–2020), passed by the House, requires a national uniform anti-doping and medication control program but does not address other forms of animal abuse. The Horse Protection Act (HPA) prohibits horses subjected to soring, the process of intentionally causing pain to a horse's front legs and hoofs to enhance his or her gait, from participating in exhibitions, sales, shows, or auctions. 15 U.S.C. §§1821–1831. However, it has not been effectively enforced. In 2021, the Animal Cruelty Enforcement Act, H.R. 1016 (117th Cong. 2021–2023), was introduced in the House to provide greater enforcement of this and other federal animal cruelty laws, including the 2019 Preventing Animal Cruelty and Torture (PACT) Act, Pub. L. 116-72. See Chapter 3 for discussion of animal cruelty laws.

19. Animal Welfare; Retail Pet Stores and Licensing Exemptions, 78 Fed. Reg. 57227 (Sept. 18, 2013).

20. *Id.* at 57228.

ments for handling, housing, feeding, watering, sanitation, ventilation, shelter from extremes of weather and temperatures, adequate veterinary care, and separation by species."[21] Dealers and exhibitors must handle animals "in a manner that does not cause trauma ... behavioral stress, physical harm, or unnecessary discomfort"[22] and physical abuse may not be used to train, work, or handle an animal.[23] Notably, the standards focus on the avoidance of pain and suffering, per the Five Freedoms, rather than on providing quality care to ensure good animal welfare, a state in which the animal is physically and psychologically healthy, comfortable, well-nourished, and able to express innate behavior per the Five Provisions.

Two species are provided added protection. The AWA requires the Secretary to provide "for exercise of dogs ... and for a physical environment adequate to promote the psychological well-being of primates."[24] Interestingly, the two species granted special protections are dogs, "man's best friend," and who, in the United States, are often considered members of the family, and primates who are clearly very intelligent and emotional social beings and arguably most "human-like".[25] Of course, all animals are in need of some form of exercise and psychological stimulation but the government only provides these specific protections for dogs and primates.

AWA standards provide only minimal protections for the animals. For example, puppy mills—commercial dog breeding operations that keep dogs in crowded, dirty, and unhealthy conditions—exist, even though they are regulated under the AWA.[26] The dogs are kept confined in stacked wire cages, 14 inches tall and 20 inches wide, leaving only six inches of space above the dog's head and in front of their nose. They live solely to breed approximately two million puppies annually for the pet trade. The puppies sold are often sick and/or suffer from congenital disorders, and the breeding dogs are often killed or abandoned when they can no longer breed. In 2015, several animal welfare organizations petitioned the USDA to amend their regulations to improve their standards, including: "banning the use of stacked cages and harmful wire flooring; providing annual hands-on veterinary examinations and preventive care for breeding dogs; requiring that breeding dogs be given an opportunity for daily exercise[27] and positive human interaction; requiring that dogs have continual access to potable water; protecting dogs from extreme temperatures; and doubling the minimum required cage

---

21. 7 U.S.C §2143 (a) (1)-(2)(A).

22. *Handling of Animals*, 9 C.F.R. 2.131.

23. *Id.*

24. 7 U.S.C §2143 (a) (2) (B).

25. This statement is not to suggest that other species are not intelligent, emotional, and social, only that because the great apes are humans' closest relative, humans recognize these qualities in the great apes more readily.

26. Puppy Mills and the Animal Welfare Act. (n.d.). *Humane Society of the United States*, https://www.humanesociety.org/sites/default/files/docs/puppy-mills-awa-booklet-lores_0.pdf.

27. Note that while the AWA specifically requires exercise for dogs, the exercise regulations exempt "bitches with litters, housed, held, or maintained by any dealer, exhibitor, or research facility." 9 C.F.R. §3.8.

space."[28] In 2020, five years later, the USDA finalized a rule that addressed only two of the requested amendments—"requiring continual water and annual hands-on veterinary examinations and vaccinations for breeding dogs."

Case Study: Agency Action to Establish Bird-Specific Welfare Standards Unreasonably Delayed

The AWA was enacted in 1966 and until 2002 the USDA excluded all birds from the definition of "animal."[29] In 2002 Congress amended the AWA to exclude only birds bred for use in research, leaving all other birds otherwise used by the entities regulated by the AWA subject to protection. In 2004, the USDA concluded that its general animal welfare standards would not be appropriate for birds and proposed rulemaking to establish standards for birds. To date, no such standards exist. The American Anti-Vivisection Society and the Avian Welfare Coalition filed suit to compel the USDA to either issue bird-specific standards or apply the general animal welfare standards to birds arguing that the USDA's failure to apply any standards for the protection of birds not bred for use in research is "arbitrary and capricious"[30] agency action and/or agency action "unlawfully withheld [and] unreasonably delayed."[31] The district court dismissed the case but on appeal the D.C. Circuit reversed and remanded.

On the first argument, that the USDA's actions are "arbitrary and capricious," the appellate court held that parties may only challenge "final" agency actions under this standard. "To be final, an action must (1) mark the consummation of the agency's decision-making process and (2) be one by which rights or obligations have been determined, or from which legal consequences will flow."[32] Here, although it has been almost 18 years since the USDA initiated rulemaking, "it has repeatedly reiterated its intention to issue such standards."[33] Thus the first requirement is not met and there is no final agency action. However, to state an "unreasonably delayed" claim, the court explained that plaintiffs must assert that the USDA failed to take discrete action that it is required to take, which they have done. The court held that the 2002 amendments to the AWA require the USDA to issue standards governing the humane treatment of birds not bred for research.[34] Since the USDA has stated that the general welfare standards are inappropriate and they have failed to issue bird-specific standards, the USDA has failed to take discrete action that it is required to take. The only issue that remains is whether 18 years constitutes "unreasonably delayed." The appellate court

---

28. Puppy Mills and the Animal Welfare Act. (n.d.). *Humane Society of the United States*, https://www.humanesociety.org/sites/default/files/docs/puppy-mills-awa-booklet-lores_0.pdf.

29. American Anti-Vivisection Society v. USDA, 946 F.3d 615, 617 (D.C. Cir. 2020).

30. 5 U.S.C. §706(2)(A).

31. 5 U.S.C. §706(1).

32. *American Anti-Vivisection Society*, 946 F.3d at 620 (internal quotes and citations omitted).

33. *Id.*

34. *Id.*

remanded this issue to the district court.[35] Soon thereafter, USDA APHIS initiated a process to develop bird-specific welfare standards. Hopefully it will not take another 18 years before the standards are promulgated.

Regarding animals used in research, while the AWA states that researchers shall "ensure that animal pain and distress are minimized"[36] including the "appropriate use of anesthetic, analgesic, tranquilizing drugs, or euthanasia"[37] and "consider ... alternatives to any procedure likely to produce pain to or distress in an experimental animal,"[38] the Secretary of Agriculture has no authority to alter research protocol. Thus, if the researcher believes that it is "necessary" to inflict pain on the animals and that anesthetic will interfere with the experiment, it is lawful.

Allowing the use of any live animal in research is controversial but allowing the use of live primates, and especially Great Apes,[39] in research is highly controversial. In fact, several countries have recognized that no amount of regulation providing for the welfare of primates can justify subjecting them to invasive research and have either banned or imposed very strict limits on their use. These countries include the United Kingdom, New Zealand, the Netherlands, Sweden, Austria, Belgium, Australia, and Japan.[40] In the United States, the Great Ape Protection and Cost Savings Act was reintroduced to Congress in 2011 and would end invasive research on great apes and retire them to a suitable sanctuary.[41] The Act was never enacted. However, in June 2013, the National Institutes of Health announced that it would significantly reduce the number of chimpanzees it used for research and retire to a sanctuary most of the chimpanzees it then currently owned.[42] In 2015, "NIH announced it would no longer fund such studies" and "pledged to retire all of the approximately 300 chimps it owned or supported to Chimp Haven."[43] Experts expected the approximately 340 privately owned chimps would also be retired. In October 2019, NIH announced it would not retire all of its chimps claiming several are too old or sick to move. At that time 178 government-owned or supported chimps and 190 privately-owned chimps remained in research facilities.

---

35. *Id.* at 621.

36. 7 U.S.C §2143 (a)(3)(A).

37. *Id.* §2143 (a)(3)(A).

38. *Id.* §2143 (a)(3)(B).

39. Great apes include chimpanzees, bonobos, gorillas, orangutans, and gibbons. Great Ape Protection and Cost Savings Act, H.R. 1513 Sec. 3(2), 112th Cong. (2011).

40. Schrengohst, K. (2011). Animal law—Cultivating compassionate law: Unlocking the laboratory door and shining light on the inadequacies & contradictions of the Animal Welfare Act. *Western New England Law Review, 33*, 855–900.

41. Great Ape Protection and Cost Savings Act, H.R. 1513, 112th Cong. (2011), S. 810, 112th Cong. (2011).

42. NIH to reduce significantly the use of chimpanzees in research. (2013, June 26). *National Institutes of Health*. Retrieved from http://www.nih.gov/news/health/jun2013/od-26.htm.

43. Grimm, D. (2019, Oct. 24). Some of NIH's chimpanzees will not retire to a sanctuary as planned. *Science.* Retrieved from https://www.sciencemag.org/news/2019/10/some-nih-s-chimpanzees-will-not-retire-sanctuary-planned.

In 1959, authors Russell and Burch, proposed the Three Rs—Reduction, Refinement, and Replacement—as the ethical principles that should inform all animal research.[44] In other words, all researchers should work to reduce the number of animals used in research, to refine the techniques as applied to animals to minimize the pain and distress experienced by the animals, and to replace animals as research subjects with alternative methodologies. Moreover, in 1993, Congress called for NIH to "conduct or support research into ... methods of biomedical research and experimentation that do not require the use of animals and methods of such research and experimentation that reduce the number of animals used in such research."[45] In 2021, estimates of animals used in research range from "17 million to 100 million" despite the "dramatically rising costs and extremely high failure rates in drug development" using animal methods and with "effective alternatives to animals ... available and growing." Nevertheless, 70 percent of all NIH grant applications relate to studies using mice. Recognizing more must be done to replace animals used in research, the Humane Research and Testing Act of 2021[46] was introduced in the House. The bill directs the Secretary to establish a National Center for Alternatives to Animals in Research and Testing within the NIH that will develop, promote and fund alternatives and establish a plan for reducing the number of animals used in federally funded research. If passed, this law could signal the end to the suffering of millions of animals used in research and testing.

Enforcement of the AWA is important to ensure that the regulated entities are in fact meeting the standards set to protect the animals. The Secretary, through APHIS, is given broad discretion "to make such investigations or inspections *as he deems necessary*"[47] to determine if a covered entity has violated any regulation. If a violation is found, the Secretary "*may*" suspend or revoke a license,[48] assess a civil penalty "of not more than $10,000,"[49] issue a cease-and-desist order,[50] or file criminal prosecution against the violator for knowing violations of the statute.[51] Note that the Secretary has unfettered discretion in determining whether to investigate and what, if any, sanction to impose if violations are found. The Government Accountability Office has reported that the Secretary has failed to adequately enforce the AWA, allowing the inhumane treatment of animals by covered entities.[52]

---

44. Russell W.M.S. and Burch R.L. (1959). *The Principles of Humane Experimental Technique*. London (UK): Methuen & Co. Ltd.

45. 42 U.S.C. 283e.

46. H.R. 1744 (117th Cong. 2021–2023).

47. 7 U.S.C §2146(a) (emphasis added).

48. *Id.* §2149(a) (emphasis added).

49. *Id.* §2149 (b).

50. *Id.* §2149 (b).

51. *Id.* §2149 (d).

52. Government Accountability Office. (2010, Sept.). USDA's oversight of dealers of random source dogs and cats would benefit from additional management information and analysis. *GAO-10-945*.

Case Study: Lolita's Inhumane Treatment under the AWA

Lolita is an orca whale who has spent over 50 years in captivity for public display at the Miami Seaquarium. Lolita was captured off the coast of Washington state in 1970, ripped from her mother and pod at the age of four. The captors bombed the pod trying to separate the calves from the adults, resulting in the drowning death of four calves and one adult. Although Lolita made it out alive, she now lives alone with no orca companionship since Hugo, her tank mate, died in 1980 after repeatedly ramming his head into the walls of the tank. Miami Seaquarium has been licensed under the AWA for decades although the conditions under which they maintain Lolita fail to meet AWA standards. First, although Lolita's tank is to have a minimum horizontal dimension of at least 48 feet, it is only 35 feet. Second, although she is to be housed in a tank that is protected from direct sunlight, she is exposed to the mid-day Florida sun, when it is the hottest. Third, although she is to have appropriate social interaction with animals of the same or a biologically-related species, Lolita lives with white-sided dolphins who are not sufficiently biologically related to Lolita to provide proper social interaction for her.[53]

In August 2012, advocates filed a complaint against the USDA challenging their renewal of Miami Seaquarium's AWA license in light of these violations.[54] The USDA did not dispute the violations but rather supported their renewal of the license under their regulations stating that violation of AWA standards are **not grounds** for denying the renewal of an AWA license and the trial court agreed! The court first found that Congress did not speak to the specific issue of "whether the AWA requires that a licensee demonstrate compliance with the statute prior to renewal."[55] Thus, if the USDA's regulations governing renewal procedure is "based on a permissible construction of the statute"[56] it must be upheld. The court then found the regulations met this requirement. The court noted that the statute does not require a renewal of an issued license and only allows for cessation of a license in an enforcement proceeding. Thus, since the USDA "ensures compliance with the AWA (1) prior to issuing a license, and (2) through enforcement proceedings, it does not, and need not, ensure the same (or require demonstration of the same) prior to renewals."[57] Moreover, the USDA "has discretion with respect to how and when non-research licensees are subject to compliance inspections."[58] The result is that Lolita is destined to remain in inhumane conditions

53. Animal Legal Defense Fund, et al. v. USDA, Case3:12-cv-04407-SC, Complaint for Declaratory and Injunctive Relief (N.D. Cal. Aug. 22, 2012).

54. Note that the AWA does not allow for private enforcement thus the only challenges plaintiffs may bring are under the Administrative Procedure Act, 5 U.S.C. §551 et seq., that allows for judicial review if a person has been adversely affected by agency action. See *infra*, Private enforcement of animal welfare laws, for more detailed discussion of private enforcement.

55. Animal Legal Defense Fund, et al. v. USDA, et al., 2014 WL 11444100 at *4 (S.D. Fl. Mar. 25, 2014), aff'd, Animal Legal Defense Fund v. USDA, 789 F.3d 1206 (11th Cir. 2015).

56. Chevron, USA, Inc. v. Natural Resources Defense Council, Inc., 467 U.S. 837, 843 (1984).

57. *Animal Legal Defense Fund, et al.*, 2014 WL at *7.

58. *Id.*

that fail to meet the minimal standards of the AWA until the USDA decides to enforce their own standards against Miami Seaquarium.

In 2015, NMFS recognized Lolita as covered under the Endangered Species Act (ESA), as a captive member of the protected SRKW species.[59] Recognizing a new opportunity to seek a remedy for her, PETA filed suit against Miami Seaquarium claiming they are "actively 'harming' and 'harassing' Lolita by keeping her in an undersized tank, without adequate shade, and with incompatible animals"[60] and thus are "taking" Lolita in violation of the ESA.[61] Plaintiffs identified thirteen injuries to Lolita caused by her confinement, including skin abrasions, blisters, surfer's eye, and abnormal behaviors she exhibits that indicate psychological distress. The 11th Circuit ultimately determined that "'harm' or 'harass[ment]' is actionable [only] if it poses a threat of **serious** harm"[62] and Lolita's injuries do not rise to such a level. The court explained that this interpretation is required to provide "captive endangered animals with an additional layer of protection from harmful conditions of captivity without abrogating the complex regulatory scheme crafted and administered by APHIS."[63] In other words, keeping Lolita captive clearly "harms" Lolita but the AWA allows for such captivity (and relatedly such harm) and Congress did not intend for the ESA to "nullify the AWA's regime of administrative enforcement."[64] In September 2020, members of the Lummi Nation travelled to Miami to honor Lolita, then 54 years old, on the 50th anniversary of her capture although they and others have no legal recourse to help her. In June 2021, the USDA issued an inspection report noting dozens of "critical" issues with the pools and enclosures for Lolita and the other animals, including poor water quality and inadequate shade. In March 2022, with Lolita's health at risk, Miami Seaquarium agreed it would no longer exhibit Lolita under its new license with the USDA. Advocates are hoping that she may be retired to a seaside sanctuary although as of fall 2022 she remains in the Seaquarium.[65]

Although PETA was not successful in freeing Lolita, some advocates have been successful in proving owners of animals listed as endangered and held in zoos violated the ESA. For example, the plaintiffs in *Kuehl v. Sellner*,[66] sued the owners and operators of the Cricket Hollow Zoo in Iowa housing some 300 animals, including endangered lemurs and tigers, arguing they were "harming and/or harassing" these animals. On appeal the court upheld the district court's findings that "defendants had harassed the lemurs by keeping them in social isolation; by not developing, docu-

59. Captive killer whale included in endangered listing (2015, Feb. 4). *National Oceanic and Atmospheric Administration*. Retrieved from https://www.noaa.gov/media-release/captive-killer-whale-included-in-endangered-listing.

60. PETA v. Miami Seaquarium, 189 F.Supp.3d 1327, 1342 (S.D. Fla. 2016).

61. *See infra*, Endangered Species Act, for additional details on the ESA.

62. PETA v. Miami Seaquarium, 879 F.3d 1142, 1150 (11th Cir. 2018).

63. *Id.*

64. *Id.*

65. Allen, Greg. (2021, Oct. 30). For 51 years this killer whale has lived in a tiny tank. Now her health is at risk. NPR. Retrieved from https://www.npr.org/2021/10/30/1049297157/killer-whale-lolita-miami-seaquarium.

66. 887 F.3d 845 (8th Cir. 2021).

menting, and following an appropriate plan for environmental enhancement; and by not providing clean water and sanitary conditions" and "defendants had injured, and thereby harmed, the tigers by 'fail[ing] to provide timely and appropriate veterinary care … and had harassed the tigers by not providing them with sanitary conditions.'"[67] Notably, although the plaintiffs won the case, the court ordered the animals transferred to the facility proposed by the defendants that had been cited by the USDA for noncompliant behavior in the past rather than the plaintiff's proposed sanctuary with significantly more resources and better able to meet the animals' needs.[68] Moreover, the court denied the plaintiffs' request for attorney's fees even though successful private attorneys enforcing important Congressional objectives should recover such fees unless there are "special circumstances that render such an award unjust."[69] The court found such special circumstances here stating that plaintiffs were seeking to use the ESA "as a vehicle to close Cricket Hollow."[70] The court was concerned about the defendants' inability to pay plaintiffs' attorney fees and the effect such an award would have on "private animal owners" forced "to defend lawsuits brought by well-financed national organizations."[71]

Lolita and the lemurs and tigers held in Cricket Hollow are just a few of many wild animals used in exhibition. As the above discussion demonstrates—the AWA standards are minimal and often do not provide for the five provisions necessary for the wild animal to live a good life; the AWA it is not effectively enforced; and often judges are more concerned with the interests of the animal owners who are not adequately providing for their animals rather than the interests of the animals. For some wild animals, such as Lolita, no captive space can provide her with a good life. Some countries, and a few U.S. states, have realized this and have banned orcas in captivity[72] with some jurisdictions including dolphins as well.[73] India was among the first countries to ban all dolphinaria in their country finding that: "cetaceans … are highly intelligent and sensitive, and various scientists who have researched dolphin behavior have suggested that the unusually high intelligence as compared to other animals means that dolphin[s] should be seen as 'non-human persons' and as such should have their own specific rights and [it] is morally unacceptable to keep them captive for entertainment purposes."[74] Nevertheless, as of 2019, there were 59 orcas in

---

67. *Id.* at 852, 853.

68. *Id.* at 854–55.

69. *Id.* at 855.

70. *Id.*

71. *Id.* at 856.

72. Kirby, David. (2014, Apr. 10). Here's all the places around the world that ban orca captivity. *Takepart*. Retrieved from http://www.takepart.com/article/2014/04/10/all-states-countries-and-cities-ban-orcas-captivity.

73. *See e.g.*, Held, Amy. (2019, June 11). Canada bans keeping Whales and dolphins in captivity. *NPR*. Retrieved from https://www.npr.org/2019/06/11/731570415/canada-bans-keeping-whales-and-dolphins-in-captivity.

74. Government of India, Ministry of Environment & Forests, Central Zoo Authority. (2013, May 17). Circular, Policy on establishment of dolphinarium, F. No. 20-1/2010-CZA(M).

captivity world-wide, with a third of them in the United States, and all of them, except Lolita, living in Sea World Parks.[75] This is despite the California Orca Protection Act[76] as it grandfathered all captive orcas in California as of June 1, 2017.

State Law

Although the AWA is the primary law regulating research facilities, dealers, and exhibitors, the AWA does not preempt state law and thus individual states may enact laws that regulate these entities and/or affect the animals they use. For example, regarding animals in research, several states, including California, Connecticut, Delaware, Illinois, Maryland, Minnesota, Nevada, New York, Oregon, Rhode Island, and Washington,[77] now require research facilities to attempt to adopt certain retired research animals before killing them.[78] Additionally, several states, including California, Illinois, and Nevada[79] have enacted Cruelty-Free Cosmetics laws that ban the sale of cosmetics tested on animals or that contain ingredients that have been tested on animals.[80] With respect to commercial breeders, 25 states have laws that govern commercial dog breeders that set minimum standards of care that may exceed those set by APHIS and a few states limit the maximum number of dogs a breeder may have at one time.[81] And, in recent years, recognizing the harms from puppy mills (and similar large-scale commercial breeders of other animals for the pet trade) and the many "homeless" animals in need of adoption, several localities and a few states, including California and Maryland,[82] have passed laws banning the sale of certain commercially-bred ani-

---

75. Day, Natasha. (2019, Mar. 25). Orcas don't do well in captivity. Here's why. *National Geographic.* Retrieved from https://www.nationalgeographic.com/animals/article/orcas-captivity-welfare.

76. Cal. AB 1453 (2015–2016). Retrieved from https://leginfo.legislature.ca.gov/faces/billTextClient.xhtml?bill_id=201520160AB1453. This legislation was triggered by the tragic death of a Sea World trainer by Tilikum, an orca at Sea World in San Diego, whose own tragic life was told in the documentary *Blackfish.* Tilikum died in 2017 and was survived by 10 of his 21 offspring. Howard, Brian. (2017, Jan. 6). Why Tilikum, Sea World's killer orca, was infamous. *National Geographic.* Retrieved from https://www.nationalgeographic.com/animals/article/tilikum-seaworld-orca-killer-whale-dies.

77. *See* Cal. Ed. Code §66017.7; Conn. Gen. Stat. §10a-150e; 2018 Del. ALS 272; 2017 Ill. ALS 323; 2018 Md. ALS 236; Minn. Stat. §135A.191; Nev. Rev. Stat. Ann. §574.205; N.Y. Educ. Law §239-b; 2019 Enrolled Bill Text Or. S.B. 638; R.I. Gen. Laws §4-27-2; Wash. Rev. Code Ann. §18.92.0001.

78. In 2021, Senator Susan Collins introduced a similar bill in the Senate—the Animal Freedom from Testing, Experiments and Research (AFTER) Act, S. 1378 (117th Cong. 2021–2023).

79. Cal. Civ. Code §1834.9.5(a), Nev. SB 197; 410 Ill. Comp. Stat. 620/17.2.

80. The EU and several countries, including the UK, Austria, Belgium, Israel, India, New Zealand and Australia, ban testing cosmetics on animals including. Animal Testing: Models for Improvement, *Animal Legal Defense Fund.* Retrieved from https://aldf.org/article/animal-testing-models-for-improvement/ (last visited Aug. 3, 2021).

81. Wisch, Rebecca. (2017). Table of state commercial pet breeders laws. *Animal Legal & Historical Center.* Retrieved from https://www.animallaw.info/topic/table-state-commercial-pet-breeders-laws.

82. *See e.g.* Cal. Health & Safety Code §122354.5; Md. Code Ann. Bus. Reg §19-703 (pet stores may collaborate with animal welfare organizations to provide space to showcase animals for adoption).

mals in retail pet stores.[83] And for animals in exhibits, some states have adopted laws that "set out more specific requirements for ownership, possession, and exhibition of certain wildlife."[84] Arguably, one of the most publicized events in recent years, was the closing of the so-called "Greatest Show on Earth" Ringling Brothers Circus. Their demise arguably was ultimately the result of states banning the use of bull hooks used by the circus to train and control the elephants because of the serious trauma and injury they cause.[85]

Animals on Farms

Federal Humane Methods of Slaughter Act

Animals on farms and/or used for food are excluded from protection under most state anti-cruelty laws and the federal AWA. Two federal statutes govern animals used for food during their transport and slaughter but neither addresses their treatment while on the farm. Congress has chosen to preempt the field in the area of transport and slaughter and thus the federal law sets not only a floor but a ceiling on the protection that may be afforded animals in these contexts. In other words, states may not set more protective standards for animals during transport or slaughter.[86]

The Humane Methods of Slaughter Act (HMSA) defines slaughter to be "humane" if livestock is rendered insensible to pain by a rapid and effective means "before being shackled, hoisted, thrown, cast or cut"[87] or if slaughtered in accordance with religious ritual requirements whereby "the animal suffers loss of consciousness by anemia of the brain caused by the simultaneous and instantaneous severance of the carotid arteries with a sharp instrument."[88] The law is enforced by the Food Safety and Inspection Service of the Department of Agriculture (FSIS) pursuant to the Federal Meat Inspection Act (FMIA) incorporating the HMSA standards.[89]

---

83. Operators of Maryland pet stores and out-of-state commercial breeders challenged the Maryland law, known as the No More Puppy-Mill Pups Act, arguing, inter alia, it was unconstitutional in violation of the Dormant Commerce Clause and the Equal Protection Clause, and preempted by the AWA. The trial court dismissed the complaint holding plaintiffs failed to state a claim under any of their theories. Just Puppies, Inc. v. Frosh, 457 F.Supp.3d 497 (D. Md. 2020).

84. Tala DiBenedetto. (2020). Overview of welfare standards for animals used in zoos and exhibition. *Animal Legal & Historical Center*. Retrieved from https://www.animallaw.info/article/overview-welfare-standards-animals-used-zoos-and-exhibition.

85. *See e.g.* Cal. S.B. 1062 (2015–2016). Retrieved from https://leginfo.legislature.ca.gov/faces/billNavClient.xhtml?bill_id=201520160SB1062.

86. National Meat Assoc. v. Harris, 132 S. Ct. 965 (2012) (finding the FMIA expressly exempted California law prohibiting sale of federally inspected meat of "nonambulatory" animals for human consumption and requiring immediate euthanization of nonambulatory animals).

87. 7 U.S.C. §1902 (a).

88. *Id.* §1902 (b).

89. 21 U.S.C. §§603(b), 610(b); Fact sheet: Production and inspection. (2012). *U.S. Department of Agriculture, Food Safety & Inspection Service*. Retrieved from http://www.fsis.usda.gov/Factsheets/Key_Facts_Humane_Slaughter/index.asp.

Case Study: Who are Livestock?

Notably, poultry, who represent 95–98% of all animals slaughtered for food,[90] are **excluded** from protection under the HMSA because they are not included within the term "livestock." The HMSA covers "cattle, calves, horses, mules, sheep, swine, and other livestock."[91] The Secretary of the USDA interprets the term "livestock" to exclude birds. That interpretation was challenged in court by poultry slaughterhouse workers[92] arguing that such interpretation is inconsistent with the language and purpose of the statute and the intent of the legislature.[93] The court, in an exhaustive exercise in statutory interpretation, upheld the Secretary's interpretation.

First, the court noted that the term "livestock" was ambiguous, and dictionaries differed as to whether it encompassed all animals "kept or raised on a farm" or impliedly limited such animals to "quadrupeds" only.[94] Second, a review of the legislative debate showed that some members of Congress intended that birds be included while others did not. Moreover, there is a separate statute that governs poultry, although it does not provide for humane slaughter, suggesting birds were not intended for coverage under the HMSA.[95] Turning then to the traditional canon of construction that the ambiguous term must be interpreted in light of the other enumerated terms, the court held that since the enumerated animals were all quadrupeds, and goats, also quadrupeds, were not enumerated, the term "other livestock" should be limited to quadrupeds only.[96] Finally, in response to the poultry workers' argument that exempting 98% of all slaughtered animals from the HMSA is inconsistent with the overall intent of the statute of providing for humane slaughter, the court stated that had Congress intended to cover such a large portion of slaughtered animals, they would have expressly included poultry in the list of enumerated animals.[97] On appeal, this case was reversed and remanded for lack of standing. The appellate court found that the poultry workers were not proper plaintiffs to file this suit as their alleged injuries were not redressable through the lawsuit.[98]

This case exemplifies the Secretary's narrow reading of laws designed to protect animals and the court's literal approach to the interpretation of the statute and reluctance to invalidate the Secretary's findings. Note that, like the AWA, the HMSA exempts

90. Thornton, Alex. (2019, Feb. 8). This is how many animals we eat each year. *World Economic Forum*. Retrieved from https://www.weforum.org/agenda/2019/02/chart-of-the-day-this-is-how-many-animals-we-eat-each-year/.

91. 7 U.S.C. §1902.

92. Note the plaintiffs are poultry workers challenging the law for their own interests, not on behalf of the birds.

93. Levine v. Connor, 540 F. Supp. 2d 1113 (N.D. Cal. 2008), *vacated and remanded*, Levine v. Vilsack, 587 F.3d 986 (9th Cir. 2009).

94. *Id.* at 1115–16.

95. *Id.* at 1117–18.

96. *Id.* at 1120–21.

97. *Id.* at 1116 n.4.

98. Levine v. Vilsack, 587 F.3d 986, 997 (9th Cir. 2009); *see infra*, Private Enforcement of Animal Welfare Laws, for a discussion of standing.

from protection over 95% of the animals affected. This is quite disturbing and suggests that perhaps Congress' purpose in enacting these laws is to mislead the public into believing the animals are treated humanely when, in fact, over 95% of them are not.

Americans find especially cruel the slaughter of horses for human consumption often because many Americans consider horses to be "companions" rather than animals used for food. However, the slaughter of horses in fact inflicts greater pain and suffering than the slaughter of other animals because it is very difficult to slaughter horses in compliance with the HMSA. The reason is that horses are flight animals and, instinctively, when afraid, they panic and try to escape. The chutes used by most slaughterhouses are built for cattle, thus the stalls are too wide, and the captive-bolt stun gun method used for cattle is ill-suited for horses. The result is that horses will thrash their heads in the stalls making it difficult to effectively stun them before slaughter.

In 2005, Congress effectively ended the slaughter of horses on American soil by defunding USDA inspections at horse slaughterhouses.[99] However, tens of thousands of horses are still transported for slaughter to Mexico and Canada where the HMSA does not apply. This arguably results in a greater infliction of suffering by adding a long and often inhumane transport preceding the inhumane slaughter.[100] In December 2011, Congress reinstituted funding for USDA inspections of horse slaughter facilities in the U.S. In January 2014, before plants were able to reopen, President Obama signed a budget measure withholding money required for federal inspections. In an effort to permanently end horse slaughter in the United States, members of Congress introduced the Save America's Forgotten Equines (SAFE) Act in May 2021.[101] And, in July 2021, the House voted "to ban the transportation of horses across state lines or to Canada or Mexico to slaughterhouses for human consumption."[102] Time will tell if these laws will be adopted.

The FSIS has been criticized by the GAO for inadequate enforcement of the humane slaughter provisions citing no comprehensive enforcement strategy and inadequate training of inspectors.[103] The failure of government to properly enforce the humane

99. Pub. L. 109-97 (2006). *Agriculture, Rural Development, Food and Drug Administration, and Related Agencies Appropriations Act.* Retrieved from http://www.gpo.gov/fdsys/pkg/PLAW-109publ97/pdf/PLAW-109publ97.pdf.

100. Arguably, even if slaughterhouses in the United States did not have the proper equipment for horses, they are at least subject to the HMSA, while slaughterhouses in Mexico and Canada obviously are not. Sulzberger, A. G. (2011, Oct. 23). Slaughter of horses goes on: Just not in U.S. *N.Y. Times.* Retrieved from http://www.nytimes.com/2011/10/24/us/Horse-Slaughter-Stopped-in-United-States-Moves-Across-Borders.html?pagewanted=all.

101. H.R. 3355 (117th Cong. 2021–2023), https://www.govtrack.us/congress/bills/117/hr3355.

102. Caldwell, Emily. (2021, Jul. 2). House votes to halt export of horses to supply horsemeat industry in Canada and Mexico. *Dallas Morning News.* Retrieved from https://www.dallasnews.com/news/politics/2021/07/02/us-house-passes-amendment-to-ban-transporting-of-horses-to-canada-or-mexico-for-slaughter/.

103. GAO. (2010, Feb.). Humane methods of slaughter act: Actions are needed to strengthen enforcement. *GAO-10-203.*

slaughter law is due to inadequate funding and lack of incentive. Arguably this may change as scientists study the effect of these practices on human workers in factory farms and slaughterhouses. Researchers have begun to study the correlation between acts of slaughtering animals and increased crime rates in surrounding communities. One study from 2009 found that "slaughterhouse employment is a significant predictor of both arrest and report rate scales ... [and] has significant effects on arrests for rape and arrests for sex offenses."[104] This study is an important first step to understanding the link between institutionalized cruelty and violence against humans. Like the way that studies linking traditional animal cruelty with human violence affected the enforcement and sanctions afforded under state anti-cruelty laws, such research may justify a dramatic shift away from the currently socially accepted institutionalized cruelty against animals slaughtered for food.

In 2020, the COVID-19 pandemic forced slaughterhouses to shut down temporarily and backlogs occurred at production facilities. This resulted in the "depopulation"—the mass extermination—of hundreds of thousands of pigs and chickens in the most inhumane of methods—ventilation shutdown—"when heat, steam, and/or gas are injected into the building" housing the animals and effectively "baking the animals alive".[105] Clearly the existence of the HMSA provided no protection for these animals, nor did any other law. In fact, far from being outlawed, the AVMA currently classifies ventilation shutdown as "'permitted in constrained circumstances' for pigs and chickens in situations of acute urgency involving an animal disease outbreak.'"[106] Although several federally-funded projects are underway to identify more "humane" depopulation methods,[107] "convenience and cost should never be prioritized over the most basic standards of animal welfare."[108]

Federal Twenty-Eight Hour Law

The Twenty-Eight Hour Law prohibits transporting any animal (including those used for food) for more than twenty-eight consecutive hours (or thirty-six consecutive hours at the request of the owner) without being unloaded for five hours for rest, food,

---

104. Fitzgerald, A. J., Kalof, L., & Dietz, T. (2009, June). Slaughterhouses and increased crime rates: An empirical analysis of the spillover from the "jungle" into the surrounding community. *Organization & Environment 22(2),* 158–84.

105. Block, K. (2021, Aug. 3) Why some veterinarians keep fighting to end one of the worst factory farm practices. *A Humane World.* Retrieved from https://blog.humanesociety.org/2021/08/why-some-veterinarians-keep-fighting-to-end-one-of-the-worst-factory-farm-practices.html?credit=blog_em_080321_id12431.

106. *Id.* (quoting AVMA guidelines for the depopulation of animals 2019 edition. *AVMA.* Retrieved from https://www.avma.org/sites/default/files/resources/AVMA-Guidelines-for-the-Depopulation-of-Animals.pdf).

107. *Id.* (citing National Animal Disease Preparedness and Response Program (NADPRP) 2020 Projects. Retrieved from https://www.aphis.usda.gov/animal_health/farmbill/nadprp-2020-projects.pdf).

108. *Id.*

and water.[109] This law is enforced by the U.S. Attorney General who may impose a civil fine of between $100 and $500 for each knowing and willful violation.[110] The law was enacted in 1906 and, despite the tremendous changes in transportation methods, the standards have remained the same. Moreover, the law is rarely, if ever, enforced.[111]

In comparison, the European Union sets terms for journey times depending on the type of animal and imposes greater restrictions on the transporters. For example, cattle, sheep, and goats may only travel for fourteen consecutive hours, followed by one hour's rest to enable the animals to drink, followed by a further fourteen hours of travel. This may be repeated provided the cattle, sheep, and goats are "unloaded, fed, watered and rested for at least 24 hours at an approved control post."[112] These laws are significantly more protective of the animals than the Twenty-Eight Hour Law.

State Law

As discussed, at the federal level only 5% of all animals used for food have any legal protection and such protection is afforded only when being transported and at the moment of death. As such, intensive farming practices that include over-crowding of livestock and poultry; housing gestating sows and veal calves in tiny crates and chickens in battery cages with insufficient space to turn around or perform natural behaviors; and docking pig tails, dehorning cattle, and trimming poultry beaks with no anesthesia; although arguably "cruel," are legal in most states. In 2002, Florida became the first state to prohibit some of the worst abuses, with a ballot measure that phased out gestation crates by 2008. In 2008, California passed Proposition 2 that required that "veal calves, pregnant pigs and egg-laying hens be given enough space to lie down, stand up, fully extend their limbs, and turn around freely" by 2015 with "misdemeanor penalties of up to $1500 and/or 180 days in jail" for violations.[113] The law not only required that California egg producers comply but it banned the sale of all eggs laid by hens who are kept in cages that fail to meet the requirements.

---

109. 49 U.S.C. §80502(a).

110. *Id.* §80502(d).

111. Legal Protections for Farm Animals During Transport. (2010). *Animal Welfare Institute.* Retrieved from https://awionline.org/sites/default/files/uploads/legacy-uploads/documents/FA-LegalProtectionsDuringTransport-081910-1282577406-document-23621.pdf ("Lacking a mechanism under the auspices of either the USDA or the Department of Justice for monitoring truck transport, for all intents and purposes, there is no federal transport law in the United States.").

112. The entire provision states: "unweaned animals, i.e. animals still drinking milk (nine hours of travel, followed by one hour's rest to enable the animals to drink, followed by a further nine hours of travel), pigs (24 hours of travel, provided there is continuous access to water), horses (24 hours of travel, with access to water every eight hours), cattle, sheep and goats (14 hours of travel, followed by one hour's rest to enable the animals to drink, followed by a further 14 hours of travel). The above sequences may be repeated provided the animals are unloaded, fed, watered and rested for at least 24 hours at an approved control post." Animal welfare during transport—EU Rules. (2005). *Eur-Lex.* Retrieved from http://europa.eu/legislation_summaries/food_safety/animal_welfare/f83007_en.htm.

113. Cowan, T. (2010, Sept. 13). Humane treatment of farm animals: Overview and issues. *CRS 7-5700, RS21978.*

In 2018, Californians voted to approve Proposition 12 that set improved cage and crate-free standards for laying hens, mother pigs, and veal calves, and expanded its sales ban to include pork products and veal products. Soon thereafter, two lawsuits were filed by the North American Meat Institute[114] and the National Pork Producers Council,[115] respectively, challenging Proposition 12 as unconstitutional under the dormant Commerce Clause. Both cases were dismissed with the Ninth Circuit holding that plaintiffs failed to demonstrate a violation of the dormant Commerce Clause.[116] The Supreme Court accepted certiorari and will hear the case in fall 2022. As of summer 2021, 14 states have banned some forms of extreme confinement methods for farmed animals.[117] Meanwhile, in July 2021, the European Commission announced plans to phase out the use of all cages for farmed animals by 2027.

In 2009, voters in Ohio elected for an alternative approach to provide more humane conditions for animals on the farm. The voters, backed by the agricultural community, elected to create an Ohio Livestock Care Standards Board of 13 members representing veterinarians, farmers, experts in food safety, and consumer groups tasked with setting animal welfare standards for animals on the farm. In adopting rules, the following factors are among those considered by the Board: "best management practices for the care and well-being of livestock, food safety, prevention of disease, protection of local, affordable, food supplies for consumers, and generally accepted veterinary medical and livestock practices."[118]

Arguably, California's approach is superior to Ohio's for reducing cruelty against animals on the farm. California expressly sought to "prohibit the cruel confinement of farm animals"[119] and set specific parameters for accomplishing that goal. In contrast, Ohio created a Board with members drawn primarily from the agricultural community to establish standards "governing the care and well-being of livestock."[120]

---

114. North American Meat Institute v. Becerra, 825 Fed. Appx 518 (9th Cir. 2020).

115. National Pork Producers Council v. Ross, 2021 WL 3179247 (9th Cir. 2021).

116. *North American Meat Institute*, 825 Fed. Appx at 519–20 (The district court did not abuse its discretion in concluding that Proposition 12 does not—"have a discriminatory purpose given the lack of evidence that the state had a protectionist intent", "have a discriminatory effect because it treats in-state meat producers the same as out-of-state meat producers", "directly regulate extraterritorial conduct because it is not a price control or price affirmation statute", "impact an industry that is inherently national or requires a uniform system of regulation", nor "create a substantial burden because the law precludes sales of meat products produced by a specified method, rather than imposing a burden on producers based on their geographical origin."); *National Pork Producers Council*, 2021 WL 3179247 at *8 ("Under our precedent, unless a state law facially discriminates against out-of-state activities, directly regulates transactions that are conducted entirely out of state, substantially impedes the flow of interstate commerce, or interferes with a national regime, a plaintiff's complaint is unlikely to survive a motion to dismiss.").

117. Farm Animal Confinement Bans by State. *ASPCA*. https://www.aspca.org/improving-laws-animals/public-policy/farm-animal-confinement-bans (last visited Aug. 3, 2021).

118. OH Rev. Code §904.03.

119. California Proposition 2. (2008). Standards for Confining Farm Animals. Retrieved from https://vigarchive.sos.ca.gov/2008/general/title-sum/prop2-title-sum.htm.

120. OH Rev. Code §904.03(A).

There is no assurance that the goal of prohibiting cruel treatment of animals will be accomplished. In fact, it is probable that the standards established will merely replicate so-called "standard agricultural practices," many of which are cruel. The Ohio Livestock Care Standards enacted in 2011 demonstrate this. For example, the standards provide for a minimum of 67 square inches per hen layer, the same standard that exists under conventional battery cage systems.[121] Thus, the standard failed to improve the lives of egg-laying hens. The same standards remain in effect as of summer 2021. The following case study presents a real-life example of the issues that arise in trying to protect animals' interests when the agency that is tasked with setting animal welfare standards has the primary mission to promote the interests of the industry that uses and abuses the animals.

Case Study: Humane or Cruel?

In 1996, the New Jersey Legislature added a new section to the state's cruelty statute that directed the New Jersey Department of Agriculture (Agency), within six months of its enactment, to develop standards for the humane treatment of livestock. Further, the law directed that any treatment of livestock in accordance with such standards would be presumed not to constitute animal cruelty.[122]

In 2005, **nine years later**, the Agency adopted regulations to establish "humane" standards for livestock. The regulations defined "humane" as "marked by compassion, sympathy, and consideration for the welfare of animals"[123] and "animal welfare" as "a state or condition of physical and psychological harmony between the animal and its surroundings characterized by an absence of deprivation, aversive stimulation, over stimulation or any other imposed condition that adversely affects health and productivity of the animal."[124] Although "animal welfare" focused on the absence of deprivation, the regulations also defined "well-being" as "good health and welfare."[125] However, the Agency chose specifically to establish only "the minimum level of care that can be considered humane"[126] in consideration of the agency's overarching mission to "preserve our farms, fight for our farmers, and ensure that our agricultural industry is profitable and strong, innovative and poised for a bright future."[127] Most notably, the regulations provided a safe harbor for all "routine husbandry practices," many of which are not "humane," and expressly allowed for a variety of inhumane practices including:

121. Ohio Livestock Care Standards §901:12-9-03(F).

122. N.J. Soc'y for the Prevention of Cruelty to Animals v. N.J. Dep't of Ag., 196 N.J. 366 (N.J. 2008).

123. N.J.A.C. 2:8-1.2(a).

124. *Id.*

125. *Id.*

126. *N.J. Soc'y for the Prevention of Cruelty to Animals*, 196 N.J. at 375.

127. *Id.*

tail docking,[128] castration, dehorning,[129] and debeaking[130] animals without anesthesia so long as the practices are performed by "knowledgeable individuals in a sanitary manner in a way to minimize pain," and the confinement of calves and pigs in veal and sow gestation crates[131] (the very practices targeted by California Prop 2).

A number of organizations, including the New Jersey Society for the Prevention of Cruelty to Animals (New Jersey SPCA), and concerned citizens filed suit against the Agency asking the court to invalidate the regulations as arbitrary, unreasonable, and inconsistent with the legislative mandate to create "humane" standards.[132] The trial court, noting the highly deferential review standard of agency actions, held that the regulations were not arbitrary, unreasonable, or in derogation of the statutory mandate and thus were valid. The plaintiffs appealed and the New Jersey Supreme Court struck several of the provisions as inconsistent with the statutory mandate to establish "humane" standards.

The New Jersey Supreme Court set the focus for its decision as follows:

> The dispute before this Court has nothing to do with anyone's love for animals, or with the way in which any of us treats our pets; rather, it requires a balancing of the interests of people and organizations who would zealously safeguard the well-being of all animals, including those born and bred for eventual slaughter, with the equally significant interests of those who make their living in animal husbandry and who contribute, through their effort, to our food supply.[133]

The Court first addressed the provision that defined all "routine husbandry practices" as "humane." The Court noted that the legislature sought to exempt only "humane" practices from prosecution as compared to other states that exempt "routine, common, or accepted practices" from their cruelty statute and that to interpret "humane" as "routine" would "abuse the interpretative process and ... frustrate the announced will of the people."[134] Next, the Court struck "tail docking" from the regulations finding a "consensus among scientists that tail docking is without any apparent health, welfare, or human health justification, ... causes acute pain, and interferes with the ability of the affected animals to perform natural behaviors, including slicking their tails to chase

---

128. A "procedure that involves 'the amputation of the lower portion of a dairy cow's tail.' Lawrence J. Hutchinson, *Tail Docking for Cattle* (1997)." *Id.* at 403.

129. A procedure that involves removing the horns from, or preventing the growth of the horns of, an animal as by cauterization. *The Free Dictionary*. Retrieved from http://www.thefreedictionary.com/dehorn.

130. A procedure that involves removing the "tip of the upper mandible" of a bird, such as a chicken. *Merriam-Webster Dictionary.* Retrieved from http://www.merriam-webster.com/dictionary/debeak.

131. *N.J. Soc'y for the Prevention of Cruelty to Animals*, 196 N.J. at 378.

132. N.J. Soc'y for the Prevention of Cruelty to Animals v. N.J. Dep't of Ag., 2007 WL 486764 (N.J. Super. A.D.).

133. *N.J. Soc'y for the Prevention of Cruelty to Animals*, 196 N.J. at 371. The court found humans' interest in profits "equally significant" to animals' interest in welfare and life.

134. *Id.* at 396–403.

away flies in the summer."[135] The Court stated that the Agency failed to adhere to the Legislative mandate that the Agency "permit only those practices that it finds to be humane (as opposed to not inhumane)" and held the regulation allowing tail docking arbitrary and capricious.[136]

Note the court observed the difference between defining a practice as "humane" as compared to "not inhumane." The varied treatment of animals by humans may fall along a broad spectrum of conduct. At one extreme are our beloved family companions who many people pamper and treat quite well. At the opposite extreme is the heinous torture of animals that is clearly inhumane and cruel. Arguably, "humane" treatment, "marked by compassion" would be easily distinguished from "inhumane" or cruel treatment.

The third set of so-called "humane" provisions allowed for a variety of mutilations, such as castration and debeaking so long as performed by "knowledgeable individuals in a sanitary manner in a way to minimize pain."[137] These mutilations are only necessary because the animals are so intensively confined that they climb upon and peck one another and can become aggressive and cannibalistic. However, the Court refused to opine on the controversial debate over whether intensive confinement of animals is itself appropriate stating it was not addressed in the statute.[138] Nevertheless, the Court did find that because the regulation is so vague, it provides no objective criteria and is entirely "circular in its logic, for it bases the definition of humane solely on the identity of the person performing the task, while creating the definition of that identity by using an undefined category of individuals of no discernible skill or experience."[139] Thus, the Court found the regulations failed to set a standard to ensure that the practices are humane or enforceable and thus were invalid.

Finally, the Court turned to the intensive confinement of calves and pigs in crates so small that they prohibit the animals from moving freely or even turning around, causing significant distress in the animals. The Court held that although controversial, the Agency must account for the "interests of the farmers whose livelihood depends on such techniques and whose existence would be threatened were they to be banned"[140] and thus the determination to allow such confinement was within the Agency's expertise and discretion.

In closing, the Court emphasized that by striking the provisions of the regulations, the Court was not banning the practices. These practices merely are not exempt from the anti-cruelty statute and thus may be found cruel if challenged by the enforcing authority with the burden of proving the practice cruel on the enforcer.[141] Interestingly,

135. *Id.* at 403–04.

136. *Id.* at 405.

137. N.J.A.C. 2:8-2:6(f).

138. *N.J. Soc'y for the Prevention of Cruelty to Animals*, 196 N.J. at 406–07.

139. *Id.* at 411.

140. *Id.* at 415.

141. *Id.* at 417–18.

at the time, the New Jersey SPCA, one of the plaintiffs in this case, enforced the New Jersey anti-cruelty laws. In 2018, enforcement powers related to animal cruelty cases was transferred to the individual municipalities.

This case exemplifies the difficulty with institutional uses of animals for profit and the struggles of animal protection lawyers to seek even the most minimal standards of care for the animals' treatment. First, the agency that is tasked with drafting laws to protect the animals is the same agency whose mission is to promote the regulated industry. As a result, the agency has little incentive to impose regulations that would dramatically change the industry's production methods or reduce their profits. Second, the same agency typically enforces the regulations and often does not adequately oversee implementation or enforcement of the laws. Third, judicial review of agency findings is highly deferential. A court may invalidate the agency's regulations only if it finds that they are arbitrary, unreasonable, or contrary to the legislative mandate. Moreover, the challenger has the burden of proof. As a result, judges often rubber stamp agency action, as the trial judge did in this case. Fourth, on appeal the court struck the most egregious aspects of the regulations; however, the effect is that they are not deemed "humane" under the law. The practices are not banned; they merely are not exempt from coverage under the anti-cruelty law. Given the practical problems of enforcement, they likely remain in wide practice throughout the state. Finally, private oversight is difficult and expensive, if not impossible. As we will see, it is difficult to find persons having standing to file suit, especially at the federal level. Moreover, since much of the abuse takes place behind closed doors, discovering, documenting, and proving the abuse is very difficult. In fact, some states have enacted laws, typically called "ag-gag" laws, that prohibit the making of unauthorized videos and sound recordings, or the taking of unauthorized photographs by activists, journalists, and even employees of the company.[142] Ag-gag laws are designed to censor efforts by animal advocates who are working to raise public awareness of the horrific plight of animals on farms, to hold those who inflict cruelty on these animals accountable, and to improve farmed animal welfare. Thus, instead of prosecuting persons who inflict animal cruelty these states are prosecuting those investigating animal cruelty! Animal advocates have successfully challenged several state ag-gag laws as unconstitutional—violating First Amendment rights.[143]

Other animals, for example mink, foxes, rabbits, and raccoon dogs, are farmed for their fur. About 85% of all fur is from farmed animals, with the remainder from wild animals trapped and killed for their fur.[144] Their situation is perhaps even worse than the animals farmed for food. On the federal level, no law regulates their treatment on

---

142. *See e.g.* Ala. Code 1975 §13A-11-150-158; Ark. H.B 1665 (2017). As of 2021, five states have ag-gag laws—Alabama, Arkansas, Missouri, Montana, and North Dakota. What is ag-gag legislation? *ASPCA*. Retrieved from https://www.aspca.org/improving-laws-animals/public-policy/ (last visited Aug. 7, 2021).

143. Ag-Gag Laws. *ALDF.* Retrieved from https://aldf.org/issue/ag-gag/ (last visited Aug. 4, 2021), *see e.g.* Animal Legal Defense Fund v. Wasden, 878 F.3d 1184 (9th Cir. 2018).

144. Peterson, L. (2010). Detailed discussion of fur animals and fur production. *Animal Legal & Historical Center*. Retrieved from https://www.animallaw.info/article/detailed-discussion-fur-

the farm. The federal Fur Products Labelling Act mandates that garments be properly labelled, the Fur Seal Act which addresses North Pacific fur seals, does apply to farmed animals, and the Dog and Cat Fur Protection Act prohibits dog and cat fur trade in the U.S.[145] Because most fur animals are wild species, they are not afforded protection under the AWA or the HMSA.[146] Moreover, because they are wild species, their captivity is especially difficult physically and emotionally for the animals.[147] On the state level, the laws vary significantly with some states designating fur farming as a "agricultural pursuit" and the animals considered "domestic" animals, while others consider them "livestock."[148] However, no matter their classification by the state, the fur farming industry is largely unregulated.[149] As such, fur farming is an especially cruel industry in the U.S. and internationally, with the animals bred and confined in tiny and often filthy cages, then often inhumanely killed, often gassed, poisoned, or electrocuted.[150]

In recent years, the fur industry has come under attack for its cruelty and environmentally destructive processes,[151] merely to cater to human's desire for fashion that can be replicated by faux fur. Many top designers, including Versace, Ralph Lauren, and Chanel, have dropped fur from their collections and many retailers, including Macy's, Bloomindale's and Nordstrom's, have discontinued sales of fur products. In 2020, amid the COVID-19 pandemic, mink farming demonstrated the close link between human mistreatment of animals and the spread of zoonotic disease with the outbreak of COVID-19 on mink fur farms in 10 nations. The devastation was staggering, with Denmark, the largest producer of mink with more than one thousand farms, culling some 17 million mink and banning the industry until 2022.[152] The Danish government

animals-and-fur-production. See *infra,* Wildlife: State Law, for a brief description of laws governing trapping.

145. *Id.*

146. A call to phase out mink farms. (2021). *AWI Quarterly*. Retrieved from https://awionline.org/awi-quarterly/spring-2021/call-phase-out-mink-farms.

147. Kenner, J. (2020). Think about mink: Examining the gap in legal protection for fur-farmed animals through the lens of mink farming, *Animal & Natural Res. L. Rev. (16)* 81, 87–88 (noting that mink are "highly active and inquisitive animals," instinctively nomadic with home ranges in the U.S. of three to six miles and also, as semi-aquatic animals, "they are physiologically hardwired to seek large bodies of water for diving, hygiene, and food").

148. Peterson, L. (2010). Detailed discussion of fur animals and fur production. *Animal Legal & Historical Center.* Retrieved from https://www.animallaw.info/article/detailed-discussion-fur-animals-and-fur-production.

149. Kenner, J. (2020). Think about mink: Examining the gap in legal protection for fur-farmed animals through the lens of mink farming, *Animal & Natural Res. L. Rev. 16* 81, 82–83 (noting the lack of regulation over fur farming in the United States).

150. Bale, R. (2016, Aug. 17). Fur farms still unfashionably cruel, *National Geographic*. Retrieved from https://www.nationalgeographic.com/news/2016/08/wildlife-china-fur-farming-welfare/.

151. Wakefield, Isaac. (2011). Drop dead stylish: Mitigating environmental impact of fur production through consumer protection in the truth in fur labelling act of 2010, *Penn. St. Envt'l L. Rev. 19* 267, 270–71 (2011).

152. Denmark to cull up to 17 million mink amid coronavirus fears. (2020, Nov. 5). *BBC*. Retrieved from https://www.bbc.com/news/world-europe-54818615; SARS-CoV-2 mink-associated variant strain—Denmark. (2020, Dec. 3). *World Health Organization.* Retrieved from https://www.who.int/csr/don/03-december-2020-mink-associated-sars-cov2-denmark/en/.

extended the ban until 2023 and it appears in fall 2022 that few mink breeders will return to mink farming.[153] The Netherlands and France announced they would join other countries, including the U.K., Austria, and Germany, and phase out fur farming. And Israel became the first nation to announce its intention to ban the fur trade with the Israeli environmental protection minister explaining: "The fur industry causes the killing of hundreds of millions of animals around the world, and involves indescribable cruelty and suffering.... Utilizing the skin and fur of wildlife for the fashion industry is immoral."[154] In the U.S., several cities and the state of California, have banned the sale of fur, with similar legislation introduced in other states. Moreover, in 2020 San Francisco's fur trade ban was upheld as constitutional.[155] With U.S. mink fur production at an all-time low,[156] the end of this cruel industry in the U.S. and worldwide may be close at hand.

Wildlife

Federal Endangered Species Act

The Convention on International Trade in Endangered Species of Wild Fauna and Flora (CITES)[157] is an international agreement among countries designed to ensure that international trade in wild animals and plants does not threaten their survival. It was entered in force in 1975 and now boasts 183 Parties—countries agreed to be bound by the Convention.[158] All import and export of species covered under CITES by Parties must be authorized through a licensing system. The United States was an original Party to CITES and implemented CITES through enactment of the Endangered Species Act (ESA). CITES is a trade-related treaty and not focused on animal welfare. Nevertheless, CITES does require that "any living specimen will be so prepared and shipped as to minimize the risk of injury, damage to health or cruel treatment."[159] However, the provision governs only international travel and the parties have never defined "cruel treatment."

---

153. Kevany, Sophie. (2022, May 13). Danish farmers turn their backs on mink after Covid mutation cull. *Guardian*. Retrieved from https://www.theguardian.com/environment/2022/may/13/danish-farmers-turn-their-backs-on-mink-after-covid-mutation-cull.

154. Reich, Aaron. (2020, Oct. 5). Israel set to be first nation to ban the fur trade. *Jerusalem Post*. Retrieved from https://www.jpost.com/israel-news/israel-set-to-be-first-nation-to-ban-the-fur-trade-644590.

155. IFTF v. San Francisco, 2020 WL 4459123 (July 16, 2020).

156. Mink pelt production down 49 percent. (2021). *USDA*. Retrieved from https://downloads.usda.library.cornell.edu/usda-esmis/files/2227mp65f/8c97mm649/hd76sx594/mink0721.pdf.

157. Convention on International Trade in Endangered Species of Wild Fauna and Flora (Mar. 3, 1973), 27 U.S.T. 1087, 993 U.N.T.S. 243, https://cites.org/eng/disc/text.php (last visited Aug. 6, 2021) (also known as the Washington Convention).

158. *See generally* What is CITES. *CITES*. Retrieved from http://www.cites.org/eng/disc/what.php (last visited Aug. 6, 2021).

159. Convention on International Trade in Endangered Species of Wild Fauna and Flora (Mar. 3, 1973), 27 U.S.T. 1087, 993 U.N.T.S. 243, art. III, P 2(c), art. IV, P 2(c).

The ESA authorizes the Secretary of the Interior (or Commerce for marine mammals) to promulgate lists of species who are endangered—"in danger of extinction throughout all or a portion of its significant range"[160] or threatened—"likely to become endangered within the foreseeable future,"[161] and to designate critical habitat for them.[162] Congress in enacting the ESA declared that animal species had become extinct as a "consequence of economic growth and development untempered by adequate concern and conservation" and that such species are of "aesthetic, ecological, educational, historical, recreational, and scientific value to the Nation and its people."[163] Note that the rationale behind the ESA is to protect human interests in preserving ecological diversity rather than to protect animals from cruelty and death.

To protect endangered species from extinction, the ESA prohibits importing, exporting, selling, purchasing, or taking any member of an endangered species.[164] The ESA defines "take" to mean "harass, harm, pursue, hunt, shoot, wound, kill, trap, capture, or collect, or to attempt to engage in any such conduct."[165] The Secretary may issue permits authorizing a take to "enhance the propagation or survival of the affected species"[166] or when "incidental to, and not the purpose of, carrying out an otherwise lawful activity."[167] Such protections generally extend to endangered species held in captivity.[168] The Secretary of the Interior or Commerce may assess civil penalties that range from $500 to $25,000,[169] as well as criminal penalties not to exceed $50,000 or imprisonment for more than one year for violation of the statute.[170] In addition, and unlike the other federal statutes discussed, the ESA allows private citizens to file suit to enforce certain provisions of the statute.[171] Congress provided for such private attorney general enforcement of the ESA in order to encourage and enhance enforcement of its provisions because they feared that regulators "may work out 'agreements' [with the regulated entities] that are not necessarily true to the spirit of the environmental law in question."[172]

160. 16 U.S.C. §1532(6).

161. *Id.* §1532(20).

162. *Id.* §1533.

163. *Id.* §1531(a).

164. *Id.* §1538(a).

165. *Id.* §1532(19).

166. *Id.* §1539(a)(1)(A).

167. *Id.* §1539(a)(1)(B).

168. *Id.* §1538(b)(1).

169. *Id.* §1540(a).

170. *Id.* §1540(b).

171. *Id.* §1540(g). Citizens may not enforce the permit provisions of the ESA. Am. Soc'y for the Prevention of Cruelty to Animals v. Ringling Bros. & Barnum & Bailey Circus, 502 F. Supp. 2d 103, 111–12 (D.C.C. 2001).

172. Beverage, E. (2010). Arise under the big top: Seeking legal protection for circus elephants after ASPCA v. Ringling Brothers. *Vanderbilt Journal of Entertainment & Technology Law 43,* 155–84 (citing Wald, P.M. (1992). The role of the judiciary in environmental protection. *Boston College Environmental Affairs Law Review 19,* 519–46).

The killing of Cecil the lion in Zimbabwe by an American dentist went viral calling international attention to trophy hunting—"the killing of animals for recreation with the purpose of collecting trophies such as horns, antlers, skulls, skins, tusks, or teeth for display."[173] Trophy hunting is a multi-million dollar industry and highly controversial. Proponents claim the practice provides revenue for the conservation of species and a means of income for some impoverished areas in range countries while critics argue it is unethical, contributes to the decline and extinction of species, and often linked to corruption.[174] Because the killing of the animal is performed in the range country, the laws of the range country generally govern its legality. However, the U.S regulates the import of trophies into the U.S. under the ESA. For import trophies of ESA-listed species an enhancement-of-survival permit is needed. Such a permit presumably means that the import of the endangered animal provides "incentives to increase the survival of the species in its native habitat."[175] Arguably, since the U.S. is "the largest importer of sport-hunted trophies in the world" and for CITES-listed species[176] and between 2017 and 2018, 150 lion trophies we legally imported into the U.S.,[177] the regulations do little to protect wild animals killed for their horns, antlers, or tusks. In 2019, the Prohibiting Threatened and Endangered Creature Trophies (ProTECT) Act was introduced in the House "To amend the Endangered Species Act of 1973 to prohibit the taking for a trophy of any endangered or threatened species of fish or wildlife in the United States and the importation of endangered and threatened species trophies into the United States, and for other purposes."[178]

Federal Marine Mammal Protection Act

Wildlife not designated as endangered or threatened generally have few protections although Congress has provided for some protection for certain animals such as migratory birds,[179] bald and golden eagles,[180] and marine mammals.[181] The Marine Mammal Protection Act (MMPA) has received greater publicity in recent years since the tragic death of a Sea World trainer at the jaws of Tilikum, the largest orca held in captivity. The event demonstrated the terrible effects of captivity on these magnificent, social, and intelligent creatures after decades of confinement. Nevertheless, the MMPA allows permits to take wild marine mammals for public display and human pleasure.

---

173. International Trophy Hunting. (2019, Mar. 20). *Cong. Res. Serv.* Retrieved from https://crsreports.congress.gov/product/pdf/R/R45615.

174. *Id.*

175. *Id.* at 11.

176. *Id.*

177. Block, K., Amundson, S. (2020, June 29). Putting an end to lion trophy hunting in the memory of Cecil. *A Humane World.* Retrieved at https://blog.humanesociety.org/2020/06/putting-an-end-to-lion-trophy-hunting-in-memory-of-cecil.html?credit=blog_post_062920_id11486_blog_em_070121_id12374.

178. H.R. 4804 (116th Cong. 2019–2020).

179. Migratory Bird Treaty Act, 16 U.S.C. §§703–712.

180. Bald and Golden Eagle Protection Act, 16 U.S.C. §§668–668(d).

181. Marine Mammal Protection Act, 16 U.S.C. §§1361–1407.

Congress enacted the MMPA in 1972, soon after the horrific capture of Lolita (discussed earlier). Congress acknowledged that

> ... man's impact upon marine mammals has ranged from ... malign neglect to virtual genocide. These animals, including whales, porpoises, seals, sea otters, polar bears, manatees, and others, have only rarely benefitted [sic] from our interest; they have been shot, blown up, clubbed to death, run down by boats, poisoned, and exposed to a multitude of indignities, all in the interests of profit or recreation, with little or no consideration of the potential impact of these activities on the animal populations involved.[182]

The MMPA sets limits on the take of marine mammals and allows permits for takes only when consistent with the purpose of the MMPA—to maintain the optimum sustainable population of marine mammal species and population stocks in order to maintain the health and stability of the marine ecosystem. Congress directed the Secretary of Commerce via the National Oceanic and Atmospheric Administration's (NOAA), National Marine Fisheries Service (NMFS) for cetaceans and seals, and the Secretary of the Interior, for all other marine mammals, to implement and enforce the MMPA.

The MMPA allows permits for "scientific research, public display, or enhancing the survival or recovery of a marine mammal species of stock."[183] Generally wildlife laws do not focus on the welfare of the animals but permits for public display under the MMPA are subject to certain limitations that arguably are designed to protect the welfare of the marine mammal during capture. Specifically, no permit may issue for public display if the marine mammal was "(1) pregnant at the time of taking; (2) nursing at the time of taking, or less than eight months old, whichever occurs later; ... or (4) taken in a manner deemed *inhumane* by the Secretary."[184] Additionally, the applicant for a public display permit must show they offer a program of education or conservation based on professionally recognized standards, have a license to exhibit under the Animal Welfare Act (AWA), and maintain facilities open to the public on a regularly scheduled basis.[185]

Case Study: The MMPA and "Inhumane" Capture

In 2012, in the wake of the tragedy at Sea World when Tilikum killed his trainer, the Georgia Aquarium submitted a permit request to NMFS to import eighteen wild-caught beluga whales from Russia for public display. This request sparked a tremendous response from animal advocates as it was the first request in some 20 years for the import of wild-caught marine mammals for public display, a highly controversial use of these intelligent and social wild animals. NMFS received over 9,000 public com-

---

182. House Report (Merchant Marine and Fisheries Committee) No. 92-707, Marine Mammal Protection Act of 1972, 1972 U.S.C.C.A.N. 4144, 92nd Cong. 2nd Sess. 1972.

183. 16 U.S.C. §§1371(a)(1); 1374(c).

184. *Id.* §1372 (b) (emphasis added).

185. *Id.* §1374(c).

ments, most in opposition to the permit request on several grounds including that the proposed capture and transport of the animals was inhumane. NMFS ultimately denied the permit, the first time in the history of the MMPA that a permit request for public display was denied.

While this was a victory for marine mammal advocates,[186] the reasoning of NMFS for denying the permit was the effect of the take on the wild population, not concern for the welfare of the individual animals.[187] NMFS rejected the arguments that their capture was, or their transport would be, inhumane. The reasoning lies in how the MMPA defines "humane." While most animal biologists recognize that the term "humane" identifies an objective standard that is either met or is not, the MMPA does not. Instead, the MMPA defines "[h]umane in the context of taking a marine mammal [as] that method of taking which involves the least possible degree of pain and suffering practicable to the mammal involved."[188] Thus the take will occur no matter how objectively "inhumane" the capture technique may be, so long as the technique used is the "best" available. That standard sets no objective standard at all. After reviewing video of a similar capture of belugas in Alaska several years earlier, NMFS found no violation stating, "Although some may argue that capture techniques are per se inhumane, the captures were accomplished in a manner with as minimal a degree of pain and suffering to the animals involved as possible, consistent with the statutory definition of humane."[189]

Regarding transport, transporting the belugas from Russia to Atlanta, Georgia would have required flights of approximately thirty hours in duration through Liege, Belgium to Atlanta, Georgia, USA. NMFS noted that the legal standard demands that the transport "not present any unnecessary risks to the health and welfare of the marine mammals."[190] Thus NMFS determined that so long as the proposed method of transport was the best available option, it would be deemed "humane." Under such an analysis, there is no per se inhumane methods of capture or transport, even if the best available methods impose great pain and suffering upon the animals.

---

186. Sadly, the eighteen beluga whales had been captured over the course of six years and were being held in a dolphinarium in Russia and are likely being held in captivity somewhere, just not the U.S. Thus, the case was hardly a victory for them.

187. Many comments raised the more general concern that whales should not be on public display at all because there is no humane way of holding these animals in captivity. NMFS summarily dismissed these comments stating that the statute provides for permits for public display and the AWA provides standards to ensure the animals' welfare. Lolita's captivity demonstrates that the AWA often fails to protect marine mammals on display.

188. 16 U.S.C. §1362(4).

189. Payne, M. P. (2013, Aug. 5). Report on the Application for a Public Display Permit (File No. 17324): Recommendation for Denial, Memorandum to Donna S. Weiting, Director, Office of Protected Resources, NMFS, 12.

190. *Id.* at 14.

State Law

Wildlife protection from cruelty at the state level is quite minimal. Many states either exempt the hunting and trapping of wildlife or exempt all wildlife from their anti-cruelty laws, leaving the state's game laws as the only law governing these animals. The game laws generally set hunting periods for a variety of wildlife species and may impose limits on the kill without any provisions to protect the animals from cruelty. However, in recent years, some states have banned certain cruel hunting and trapping methods. Such methods include leg-hold traps, comprised of two jaws powered by high strength springs that slam shut on an animal's paw causing injury and severe pain, but not death,[191] and bear baiting, placing materials out to attract a bear and then shooting the bear from a blind spot.[192] Bowhunting, although illegal in the United Kingdom and in several other European countries, is legal in most states even though a report on bowhunting summarizing twenty-four studies across the United States concluded that bow hunting is inhumane and wasteful. The report stated:

> The possibility of a deer being impaled by a broadhead arrow and then dying instantaneously is extremely slight. Wounding and crippling losses are inevitable. Every one of these studies has concluded that for every deer legally killed by bowhunters, at least one or more is struck by a broadhead arrow, wounded, and not recovered. The studies indicate an average bowhunting wounding rate of 54%, with the shots per kill averaging 14.[193]

In general, animals in the wild have very little protection from cruelty.

Private Enforcement of Animal Welfare Laws

A statute or regulation can provide for the protection for certain animals, but if the provision is not enforced it is meaningless. The under-enforcement of laws designed to protect animals is a serious problem in the United States resulting from inadequate funding and lack of incentive. Moreover, private citizens often are unable to access the courts to seek enforcement.

The doctrine of "standing" must be met to file suit in federal court. Animals do not have "standing" thus a private (human) citizen or organization must file suit to enforce

191. Zuardo, T. (2017). How the United States was able to dodge international reforms designed to make wildlife trapping less cruel. *J. Int'l Wildlife L & Policy 20*, 73. In July 2021, the Refuge from Cruel Trapping Act was again introduced in the House which would prohibit the use of cruel body-gripping traps on federal public protected lands. Press release, Nadler & Blumenauer Introduce the Refuge from Cruel Trapping Act (July 27, 2021).

192. *E.g.* RCW 77.15.245. Bear baiting is legal in 9 states: Alaska, Idaho, Maine, Michigan, Minnesota, New Hampshire, Utah, Wisconsin, and Wyoming. BearBaitingTips.com. States allowing bear baiting USA. *BearBatingTips.com.* Retrieved from https://bearbaitingtips.com/states-allowing-bear-baiting-usa/ (last visited Aug. 6, 2021).

193. Report on bowhunting. *Animal Rights Coalition*. Retrieved from http://animalrightscoalition.com/doc/bowhunting_report.pdf (last visited Aug. 7, 2021).

the law. Federal standing has both a constitutional requirement and a "prudential" statutory requirement.[194] Article III of the U.S. Constitution grants courts the authority to hear "cases or controversies." This means that any person filing suit must establish that they have suffered injury to a "legally cognizable interest" that is (1) concrete and particularized, (2) actual or imminent, (3) fairly traceable to the defendant's actions, and (4) redressable by the relief requested.[195] Note, since animals do not have standing, the human plaintiffs must show injury to themselves, not to the animals. Legally cognizable interests include aesthetic, environmental, and economic interests as they are "important ingredients of the quality of life in our society."[196] Plaintiffs seeking to enforce animal welfare laws generally allege injury to their aesthetic interests because of agency action that fails to properly protect endangered species from extinction or animals from abuse.

Prudential standing, that which allows a party to sue under a given statute, requires that the plaintiff fall within the "zone of interests" to be protected under a statute that itself provides for a private right of action.[197] Although the AWA does not grant citizens a private cause of action, the Administrative Procedures Act (APA) provides that a "person suffering legal wrong because of any agency action, or adversely affected ... by agency action within the meaning of the relevant statute, is entitled to judicial review thereof."[198] Animal advocates have used the APA as the procedural hook to challenge agency actions implementing the AWA. Nevertheless, it is very difficult to find a "person" who falls within the "zone of interests" of the AWA, since arguably the AWA was intended to protect animals, who are not recognized for purposes of standing, not humans. However, the ESA grants standing to "any person" and thus advocates are able to enforce it so long as they meet the constitutional standing requirements. The following case provides a unique and interesting view into the current animal welfare legal regime in the United States and the ability of private citizens to enforce the law in an attempt to protect animals from cruelty.

Case Study: Who May Seek Enforcement of the Law?

In July 2000, plaintiffs filed suit to protect endangered Asian elephants from abuse by Feld Entertainment, owners of Ringling Brothers circus. On December 30, 2009, after almost ten years of litigation and six weeks of trial, the federal district court judge issued an opinion finding that plaintiffs failed to establish standing under the Constitution and, without reaching the merits of the case, found for Ringling Brothers.[199]

194. Lujan v. Defenders of Wildlife, 504 U.S. 555, 559 (1992).

195. *Id.* at 560–61.

196. Sierra Club v. Morton, 405 U.S. 727, 734 (1972).

197. Bennett v. Spear, 520 U.S. 154, 162–64 (1997).

198. 5 U.S.C. §702.

199. Am. Soc'y for the Prevention of Cruelty to Animals v. Feld Entertainment, 677 F. Supp. 2d 55 (D.D.C. 2009).

Thomas Rider worked as a "handler" tending the elephant barns for Ringling.[200] He witnessed Ringling employees beat the elephants with sharp bull hooks, chain them for long periods of time, and forcibly remove baby elephants from their mothers before they were ready to be weaned. These actions caused the animals pain and suffering exemplified by the lesions and rope burns on the elephants and their stereotypic behavior.[201]

Ringling was licensed under the AWA as an exhibitor and thus subject to AWA regulations detailing the proper handling of animals under their care. This treatment of the elephants, if proven, clearly violated the requirements that "physical abuse shall not be used to train, work or otherwise handle animals," that "handling of all animals shall be done ... in a manner that does not cause trauma ... behavioral stress, physical harm, or unnecessary discomfort," and that "young or immature animals shall not be exposed to rough or excessive public handling."[202] In fact, USDA investigators routinely documented these and other violations of the AWA by Ringling but failed to impose serious fines and thus the abusive treatment continued.[203]

After two years, Rider left Ringling because of this mistreatment and joined with several animal welfare organizations to enjoin Ringling from abusing the elephants. The most obvious legal channel would be to file suit to compel enforcement of the AWA. Unfortunately, this channel was not available because agency enforcement decisions are presumptively unreviewable by courts[204] and the plaintiffs lacked prudential standing to enforce the AWA directly.

However, the Asian elephants are listed as endangered under the ESA. Under the ESA, no one may "take" a member of an endangered species unless they have a permit and such permits are only granted to promote the propagation or survival of the species.[205] Moreover, the permits require that wildlife "be maintained under humane and healthful conditions"[206] and in accordance with all applicable laws, including the AWA. Ringling had a permit for twenty-one of the twenty-eight elephants under their care. Thus, the plaintiffs filed suit under the ESA to enforce the permit requirements for the twenty-one elephants subject to the permit, and for violation of the "take" provision

---

200. Am. Soc'y for the Prevention of Cruelty to Animals v. Ringling Bros. Barnum & Bailey Circus, 317 F.3d 334, 335 (D.C. Cir. 2003).

201. *Id.*

202. 9 C.F.R. §2.131(a),(b).

203. *See generally* Beverage, E. (2010). Arise under the big top: Seeking legal protection for circus elephants after ASPCA v. Ringling Brothers. *Vanderbilt Journal of Entertainment & Technology Law 43,* 155–84.

204. To rebut the presumption the statute must provide guidelines for agency enforcement discretion and the agency must consciously and expressly adopt a policy that abdicates its statutory responsibilities. Heckler v. Cheney, 470 U.S. 821, 831–32 (1985). Because the AWA grants the Secretary broad discretion, the presumption is virtually impossible to overcome. Animal Legal Defense Fund v. Glickman, 943 F. Supp. 44, 63 (D.D.C 1996), *rev'd,* 204 F. 3d 229 (D.C. Cir. 2000).

205. 16 U.S.C. §1539(a)(1)(A).

206. 50 C.F.R. §13.41.

for the seven elephants not subject to the permit. The court ultimately held that the plaintiffs lacked standing to enforce both.

For the 21 elephants held subject to the permit, the court held that, although the ESA allows for citizen enforcement of violations of the ESA under section 11(g), only sections 11(a), (b), and (e) specifically reference permits. As such, the court found the statute contemplates only **government** enforcement of issued permits.[207]

For the remaining seven elephants, the trial judge held that plaintiffs lacked constitutional standing to file suit to enforce the "take" provision and dismissed the case.[208] Plaintiffs appealed this decision to the U.S. Court of Appeals for the District of Columbia. In 2003, the appeals court held that based on the allegations of the complaint, if proven at trial, Tom Rider would have standing to sue as he met each element of constitutional standing. First, the court explained that if the animals continued to be mistreated by Ringling, Rider would suffer both aesthetic and emotional injury. As a matter of first impression, the court held that "emotional attachment to a particular animal ... could form the predicate of a claim of injury."[209] Second, the injury was sufficiently concrete, particularized, and imminent because, although Rider no longer worked for Ringling, Rider alleged that he would attend the circus and see the effects of the mistreatment. Finally, Ringling's mistreatment of the elephants is the source of Rider's injuries and if Rider won the case and Ringling was enjoined from mistreating the elephants, his injuries would be redressed.[210] This was a huge victory for animal advocates because the court recognized that not only aesthetic injury but emotional injury based on an emotional attachment to the animal was cognizable under the standing doctrine.

Unfortunately, after years of litigation and six weeks of trial, the plaintiffs ultimately lost the case on standing grounds. Although the plaintiffs introduced extensive evidence of Ringling's use of bull hooks and chains to train and work the elephants, as well as expert testimony on the emotional and physical injury it caused the elephants, the trial court, upheld on appeal, ultimately found that "Rider failed to prove that he had a 'personal and emotional attachment' to the seven elephants with whom he worked sufficient to establish injury in fact."[211] The primary lesson of this case is that

207. Am. Soc'y for the Prevention of Cruelty to Animals v. Ringling Bros. Barnum & Bailey Circus, 502 F. Supp. 2d 103, 112 (D.D.C. 2007).

208. *Am. Soc'y for the Prevention of Cruelty to Animals*, 317 F. 3d at 336 (district court held that Rider's "exposure to the mistreatment of the elephants in the past did not cause him any present injury or threaten to cause any injury in the near future").

209. *Id.* at 337.

210. *Id.* at 337–38.

211. Am. Soc'y for the Prevention of Cruelty to Animals v. Feld Entertainment, 659 F.3d 13, 20 (D.C. Cir. 2011) (quoting Am. Soc'y for the Prevention of Cruelty to Animals v. Feld Entertainment, 677 F. Supp. 2d 55, 89 (D.C.C. 2009)). Regarding the standing of the organizational plaintiffs, the court held they lacked "informational standing" because the "take" provision of the ESA under which they filed suit does not require disclosure of information. Finally, if injury to the organizational plaintiffs' advocacy and educational work may be cognizable, they failed to prove that Ringling's unlawful prac-

private enforcement of animal protection laws is extremely limited, even when abuse is proven.

Ironically, exactly one month after the D.C. Circuit released its decision the USDA reached a settlement agreement in which Feld Entertainment paid a civil penalty of $250,000 for alleged violations of the AWA, the largest ever assessed against an exhibitor. Of course, for a company that in 2004 made $800 Million in revenue, it is a miniscule cost of doing business. That same month, November 2011, U.S. Representative Jim Moran of Virginia introduced a bill to amend to the AWA that would "restrict the use of exotic and non-domesticated animals in traveling circuses and exhibitions."[212] This bill died in Committee.[213] A few months later, in March 2012, the United Kingdom Department for Environment Food and Rural Affairs announced that legislation will be introduced to ban all wild animals in traveling circuses. The U.K. Animal Welfare Minister Lord Taylor said, "There is no place in today's society for wild animals being used for our entertainment in travelling circuses. Wild animals deserve our respect."[214] Until the ban takes effect, any circus that uses a performing wild animal must "be licensed, meet strict welfare standards, prepare and follow plans for caring for every animal and have a retirement plan for each animal."[215] The U.K. Wild Animals in Circuses Act was finally enacted in 2019.[216] These legislative efforts support animal advocates' claims that no regulations can provide for the proper welfare of wild animals forced to travel chained or in cages for many hours. Moreover, subjecting these animals to such conditions for mere human entertainment is unjustified and thus must be banned.

Conclusion

The laws protecting animals from cruelty and providing for their welfare are often illogical and inconsistent. The very same act of abuse directed toward the same animal, for example a pig, may be prosecuted as a felony, if the pig is a companion to a human, and yet be codified as "humane," if the pig is used for food. The pig feels the same pain and suffers regardless of where or with whom he or she lives. The law follows societal attitudes and until society respects the intrinsic interests of animals, independent of the owners' use of the animal, this paradox will remain in the law.

---

tices harm their efforts by creating the public impression that such conduct is humane even because Ringling conceals such conduct from the public. *Id.* at 27–28.

212. Traveling Exotic Animal Protection Act, H.R. 3359, 112th Cong. (2011). The most recent bills introduced in 2019 are the Traveling Exotic Animal and Public Safety Act, H.R. 2863 (116th Cong. 2019–2020), S. 2121 (11th Cong. 2019–2020).

213. In 2019 the Traveling Exotic Animal and Public Safety Act, H.R. 2863 (116th Cong. 2019–2020), S. 2121 (11th Cong. 2019–2020) were introduced.

214. Circuses to be banned from using wild animals, government announces. (2012, Mar. 14). *Guardian*. Retrieved from https://www.theguardian.com/world/2012/mar/01/circuses-wild-animals-ban-government.

215. *Id.*

216. U.K. Public General Acts, 2019 c.24. Retrieved from https://www.legislation.gov.uk/ukpga/2019/24/contents/enacted.

As societal attitudes change and humans recognize the true nature of nonhuman animals, legal protections for animals will follow. We must decide whether the serious harm inflicted on other sentient beings to satisfy human interests is ever justified. Moreover, even if some uses may be considered important enough to justify the use, can the law effectively regulate and enforce standards to adequately protect the animals?

The COVID-19 pandemic killed millions of people, crippled economies, and unmasked inherent inequities in our society. It has also demonstrated how human health is intricately linked with the health and welfare of other animals.[217] In the early months of the pandemic, after realizing the disease may have originated in a wet market in Wuhan China, authorities warned that wildlife trade and trafficking and human encroachment and destruction of natural habitat has "increased interactions between us and wild animals" thus increasing the potential for the spread of zoonotic diseases.[218] This link between human health and animal health, directly affect by our treatment of animals, is recognized under the One Health approach[219] embraced by the United Nations and the US Center for Disease Control and Prevention. Although a tragedy of immense proportions, there may be a silver-lining to the pandemic, as the pandemic has focused attention and provided increased incentives to address our mistreatment of animals and our destruction of the environment,[220] in an effort to protect all beings—human and non-human alike.

In recent years, advocates have been attempting to seek "personhood" for certain animals. In 2015, a court in Argentina granted personhood to Sandra, a 28-year-old orangutan held captive her entire life and living in the Buenos Aires zoo. The court found she was being illegally detained under writ of habeas corpus and ordered her moved to a sanctuary.[221] In 2019, Sandra finally arrived at her new home in Florida at the Center for Great Apes. In the U.S., the Nonhuman Rights Project has filed several suits in New York using the writ of habeas corpus to establish the "fundamental right to bodily liberty for great apes, elephants, dolphins and whales held in captivity across

---

217. Preventing the Next Pandemic: Zoonotic Diseases and How to Break the Chain of Transmission (2020). Joint Report of the UNEP, ILRI, COVID-19 Response, and CGIAR. Retrieved from https://wedocs.unep.org/bitstream/handle/20.500.11822/32316/ZP.pdf?sequence=1&isAllowed=y.

218. Brigs, Helen. (2020, May 5).Coronavirus: Calls to shut down 'dirty fur trade.' *BBC*. Retrieved from https://www.bbc.com/news/science-environment-52535075.

219. One Health Basics. *Centers for Disease Control and Prevention*. Retrieved from https://www.cdc.gov/onehealth/basics/index.html ("One Health is an approach that recognizes that the health of people is closely connected to the health of animals and our shared environment.") (last visited Aug. 8, 2021).

220. *See e.g.* American Bar Association Resolution101C adopted in February 2021 urging all nations to negotiate an international convention for the protection of animals that establishes standards for the proper care and treatment of all animals to protect public health, the environment, and animal wellbeing. 21M 101C. Retrieved from https://www.americanbar.org/content/dam/aba/directories/policy/midyear-2021/101c-midyear-2021.pdf.

221. Court in Argentina grants basic rights to orangutan. (2014, Dec. 21). *BBC News*. Retrieved from https://www.bbc.com/news/world-latin-america-30571577.

the U.S."[222] In June 2022, New York's highest court held "the writ of habeas corpus in intended to protect the liberty right of *human beings* to be free of unlawful confinement, it has no applicability to Happy, a nonhuman animal who is not a 'person' subjected to illegal detention."[223] Nevertheless, the two dissenting justices provided well-reasoned arguments for extending the availability of habeas corpus relief to Happy which may provide persuasive authority in future cases.

One federal law not discussed in this chapter is the U.S. Constitution, the legal document that establishes fundamental principles and protections for all in this country. The reason it is absent from this chapter is because animals are absent from the U.S. Constitution; it only recognizes "people."

In contrast, for over 100 years Switzerland has granted,

> ... constitutional protection to the 'dignity of creature,' explicitly according esteem to all non-human living beings, namely animals, at the highest legal level. The principle encompasses all legal aspects of human/animal interrelations and is supposed to restrict in particular the kind of treatment of animals that, although not necessarily associated with pain, suffering or damage, nevertheless affects other animal interests that must be respected by humans. Central features in this regard are the protection of animals from humiliation, from excessive instrumentalisation, and from intervention in their appearance.[224]

In 2002, Article 20a of the German Constitution, was amended to include "and the animals" and now states: "The state, aware of its responsibility for present and future generations, shall protect the natural resources of life and the animals within the framework of the constitutional order through the legislature and, in accordance with the law and principles of justice, the executive and judiciary."

In 2008, the European Union ratified the Lisbon Treaty, the "equivalent" of a constitutional text that states:

> In formulating and implementing the Union's agriculture, fisheries, transport, internal market, research and technological development and space policies, the Union and the Member States *shall, since animals are sentient beings, pay full regard to the welfare requirements of animals*, while respecting the legislative or administrative provisions and customs of the Member States relating in particular to religious rites, cultural traditions and regional heritage.[225]

---

222. Litigation: Challenging the legal thinghood of autonomous nonhuman animals. *Nonhuman Rights Project.* Retrieved at https://www.nonhumanrights.org/litigation/ (last visited Aug. 7, 2021).

223. In the Matter of Nonhuman Rights Project, Inc. v. Breheny, No. 52 (N.Y. June 14, 2022). Retrieved from https://www.nycourts.gov/ctapps/Decisions/2022/Jun22/52opn22-Decision.pdf.

224. Bolliger, G. (2007). Constitutional and Legislative Aspects of Animal Welfare in Europe. Retrieved from https://www.tierimrecht.org/documents/1358/Abstract_Bruessel_TIR_Papier.pdf.

225. Treaty of Lisbon amending the Treaty on European Union and the Treaty establishing the European Community, signed at Lisbon, 13 December 2007, art. 6(b).

The explicit recognition of animals as sentient beings and the requirement that their welfare be regarded when formulating and implementing public policy is a monumental step towards greater legal protections for animals' inherent interests. It is hoped that Americans also may formally recognize animals as sentient beings and provide them fundamental protections in the highest law of our land, the U.S. Constitution.

Chapter 5

Animal Cruelty and the Legislative Process

Sarah Speed Gabel, Emily Spivak and Kristen Tullo

How Does a Bill Become Law?

A certain famous cartoon with a really catchy theme song really did sum up the process very well (Frishberg et al., 1976). State or federal, everything starts with a bill.

What is a Bill?

Generally speaking, a legislative bill is a document, whose form varies depending on the jurisdiction, which changes an existing law or creates an entirely new law. The vast majority of bills are changes to current laws, addressing updates to technology, realities of implementation, and oversights, and creating new processes. Most states have extensive bodies of law that can be adapted to cover emergent issues. However, there are times when something new must be created out of thin air because no program currently in existence can be adapted to fill the need. That is when either an entirely new chapter to a law or a free-standing act is created (e.g., medical marijuana, for example, in recent years).

Types of Legislative Bodies

There are several kinds of legislatures in the United States. Most model themselves after the United States Congress with a House of Representatives whose number of members varies based on population and a Senate with a static number of members who work in conjunction with the Governor. Nebraska is the only state with a nonpartisan unicameral legislature. Each state's session length varies, from full-time legislatures like Pennsylvania's which is in session several days a month nearly every month and whose members are generally full-time elected officials, to Oregon's which meets for two months of the year and whose members do not rely on their position for their living (State of Oregon, n.d.).

Introduction

A bill always begins as an idea for some kind of change. A legislator accepts the idea and has the language drafted generally by a legislative attorney or other staff member, occasionally by an outside party such as a professor, advocate, or an interest group with expertise. Next, the legislator asks for the support of colleagues. This is often in the form of a co-sponsorship memo which lays out the basic changes the bill is seeking to make and occasionally the actual language is included for review. Those who support the concept may choose to add their names to the bill (cosponsoring it) which is, among other things, a public statement that, if the bill's sponsor was unable to carry the bill, they (the cosponsor) would introduce it personally. Many advocacy organizations work hard to ensure that priority bills are introduced with at least as many members cosponsoring as are needed to pass the bill should it come to a vote. This sends a strong signal of support for the bill which can be advantageous later in the process. After a reasonable time, the legislation is finalized and introduced with the name of all sponsors listed.

Committees

All legislatures have a committee structure through which bills are vetted by members and staff who have experience with the subject matter. This ensures that educated eyes are the first to review bills within the context of existing law, ensuring that they work harmoniously. This is the first stop for all bills introduced and the first place to which advocates for that bill must turn their attention. In some states, such as California, all bills introduced are guaranteed a hearing in their assigned committee. Therefore, the advocate's role is to prepare the best case possible in conjunction with the sponsor for why the bill deserves the support of the committee. In most states, the majority (that political party with the most elected members) Chair of the committee exclusively decides whether and when the bill will come for a vote. Some committees meet frequently and others very rarely. It is up to the sponsor and those supporting the bill to determine the best course of action to advance the movement of the bill, taking into account the political realities of the moment in that particular legislature.

Floor Votes

After a bill has been voted on in committee, it generally proceeds to the entire body for the next vote of all members. All legislatures have rules around how many times members must be given notice of an intent to call the bill for a vote. In Pennsylvania, for example, a bill must be read aloud on the floor three times over at least 48 hours before it is eligible for a final vote of the members. There are also rules around amendments or suggested changes to the bills, including when and in what form and with how much notice they may be offered. At this point, advocates for the bill must first focus on getting the bill added to the calendar. In some states, that happens automatically; in others, it is at done at the discretion of the majority leader. After the date is secured, advocates' attention must turn to the members themselves. It is a good idea to speak with the Chairs of the committee from where the bill originated as their colleagues will likely ask their opinion on the merits of the bill and the likely number of champions and cosponsors. It is important that advocates monitor closely attacks on the bill or negative feedback from other members or interest groups because behind-the-scenes-mischief or, in a worst-case scenario, open controversy can often delay or derail a final vote.

Appropriations or Rules Committees

Most states require an additional stop between the standing committee with subject matter expertise and the final floor vote. This will often be a stop in the Appropriations or Rules Committee. These pass-through committees are generally simply checkboxes where bills are moved through the process. The Appropriations committee will review for financial impact (if any) whereas the Rules committee serves as more of a final review step and is generally made up of members of party leadership. While generally just a routine procedural stop, sometimes these committees are the scenes of power plays where amendments are added in a more friendly setting than the standing committee or floor, so votes of these committees on key bills must be watched carefully.

Do It All Over Again

After a successful vote on final passage, the process begins all over again in the opposite chamber (unless you're in Nebraska). The cycle is generally the same, however. If changes are made in one chamber that have not been voted on in the other, a game of ping pong may ensue in which a bill will go through several floor votes in each chamber before submission to the Governor. Often, unless the bill is a major priority of a powerful legislator, this will cause the bill to lose momentum and be sidelined in favor of less complicated bills.

Governor

Once a favorable vote is achieved in both legislative chambers, the bill is submitted to the Governor who will have a proscribed time period in which sign the legislation. Popular or important bills may be the subject of a signing ceremony with an invitation to the media. These are opportunities to thank all the people who supported the legislation throughout the process.

Media Management

Media coverage drives a lot of what the legislature does. A well-timed article or exposé can spark new ideas to combat old problems or help a bill which has stagnated to get moving. However, it can also do the opposite, for greater attention may do just as much to motivate new opposition. So, media outreach must be carefully managed.

Messaging Matters

People who work in this space understand the issues and while most can explain themselves thoroughly, very few are able to do so in a 60 second soundbite. From the start, it is important to frame the quick message bites that are easy for legislators and the public to pick up and understand. The message will be competing for those few seconds of a legislator's attention on a busy day with local and national news stories that are pressing, and with the heartstrings of supporters who may make the constituent phone call that gets the bill that floor vote. Most legislative offices have a communications professional, so it is important that advocates find out who those people are and take the time to educate them on what the advocates are trying to accomplish. This ensures that the communications professional will be ready with a capable answer and not caught off guard by the media. But the advocate will benefit also; the communications professional does this for a living, so they can help the advocate to come up with the strategy.

The message is important, and it must be quick.

The goal will always be to earn more time, to have the opportunity for the sit-down interview or the closed-door meeting, but the reality is that to even get considered for that opportunity, the advocate must have a quick pitch developed ahead of time that can capture people's interest and attention.

Pennsylvania is no place for puppy mills.

The follow up messaging for this example covers how Pennsylvania was the "Puppy Mill Capitol of the East" (Hurdle, 2009) with more kennels keeping dogs in squalor than any state east of Missouri and how hundreds of Pennsylvania pet stores sold thousands of dogs bought in lots at auction from disreputable sources.

But the advocate must start with capturing the public's and legislators' interest to know more.

Using and Finding Earned Media

Animal protection issues are popular with the press. Stories on animals get more pickup and sharing than nearly any other category of local news story. Sarah Speed, then the Pennsylvania State Director for the Humane Society of the United States, was absolutely shocked when the first story she participated in which received national attention was about porcupines. The Pennsylvania Game Commission opened an unlimited hunting season on porcupines at the request of one man who thought they were a pest and with no scientific evidence of overpopulation, population density across the state, or information on mating habits or impact on our ecosystem. Speed warned the Commission that this would generate a lot of negative attention and then Speed set about making sure it did. Within 24 hours, an Associated Press story had made national news and the Commission got a collective shaming from the rest of the country and quickly modified the regulation.

If you work regularly with animal issues, you can develop relationships with friendly reporters. Reporters are increasingly required to handle multiple jobs in news, sometimes even operating their own cameras and editing their own stories. The more advocates can do to take the burden off them to find, research, and produce stories, the more amenable they will be to covering an issue. Having those talking points short and sweet and ready for editing, simple and straightforward background materials with links to reputable information and approved quotes from legislators and experts is the key to getting your issue quickly featured in resulting stories. Keep an eye on the news as well and if you can find a way to tie your story into something else that is happening locally that's another way to build relationships and get attention. For example, if a county provides a grant award to a shelter to build additional space, contact the reporter and offer some statistics on shelter intakes and how your bill to create a new funding stream for shelters that take in strays could help. Make sure the reporter contacts or quotes your bill sponsor and you have just strengthened your relationship with the legislator as well.

Social Media

We have covered it before, but it is also relevant in this context. Follow local reporters and especially your capitol press corps on social media. Make sure you take note of any interests that can overlap with your bills and then use those connections to raise their awareness of what you are working on. If you have a "hot topic" posted to your page that you think that they should be aware of, tag them. If you think that they should cover some questions that have come up in a thread, ask their opinion. It's another way to engage and build a relationship, plus, they are looking for reach as well, so if they know that their stories on animals will receive social media attention, that is another incentive to give them coverage.

Libre's Law: A Case Study

This case study is based on the personal experience of the current Pennsylvania State Director for The Humane Society of the United States, Kristen Tullo, and her involvement with the passage of HB 1238, the Animal Abuse Statute Overhaul (Libre's Law) in Pennsylvania. The passage of Libre's Law was a bellwether event in the history of modern animal protection, ushering in one of the most comprehensive revisions of a state's animal cruelty law in recent decades. The law did more than strengthen penalties for cruelty, however. It also expanded the Pennsylvania anti-cruelty statute so that it would better align with the rest of the state's criminal code, simplifying interpretation and application of its provisions by law enforcement agencies and specifying grades of cruelty and differentiated penalties based on the degree of the perpetrator's misconduct and the number of prior offenses. Libre's Law included provisions for protection of all animals by way of act-based rulings rather than species-specific safeguards. In addition, Libre's Law extended the reach of the animal protection statute to new or previously untouched dimensions of neglect, such as inclement weather and tethering regulations, forfeiture of abused animals, and civil immunity for humane society police officers and veterinarians. The adoption of this precedent-setting measure was not happenstance, but rather the result of a well-conceived and tightly managed legislative campaign led by humane advocates and stakeholder allies in law enforcement and other sectors. The hallmarks of this campaign centered on relationships, coalition building, and effective communication, the essential elements of success in campaigning for animal protection legislation in the 21st century.

Our nation is divided, which means our movement is divided, too. So if your favored candidate wins, accept victory with humility. If your favored candidate loses, don't give up. Dust yourself off and get back to the business of making change for animals. Public officials look to you as a voice for animals. We must be rational, cohesive, strong, and willing to embrace diversity on issues that are so close to our hearts. We rely on people of all political inclinations to join us in fighting cruelty and providing care for animals. If you take to social media once results come in, feeling either joy or despair, choose your words carefully, be diplomatic. The animals need us to continue to build bridges and relationships to protect them. Libre's Law was the most significant strengthening of anti-cruelty legislation in Pennsylvania in 30 years, and it began not with politicians but with produce delivery driver Dextin Orme, who saw a dying dog on a farm and asked if he could take the puppy to get medical care. Libre was septic, hairless, and near death with ulcers in his eyes and maggots embedded in his skin. His rescue and recovery involved a long journey for Libre, and for others who helped him, like Humane Society Police Officer Jennifer Nields, Janine Guido at Speranza Animal Rescue, and the team at Dillsburg Vet Center, where Dr. Ivan Pryor saved Libre's life over the course of many weeks of treatment. Senator Richard Alloway stopped by to see Libre, too. At the time, Pennsylvania was one of three states without a law that specified animal torture as a first-offense felony. After seeing all the little Boston terrier had suffered and survived, we (this chapter's authors) decided to push for one.

Libre, with fur regrown and a healthy, happy grin, started visiting the state Capitol to lobby for stiffer penalties for animal cruelty. Nearly every lawmaker around took a picture with him. He quickly became the most loved lobbyist in Harrisburg, and he proved to be a tireless worker. Advocates, local groups, and animal rescue leagues visited the Capitol, too, meeting with their legislators (many for the first time) and attending rallies. Scores of supporters called and emailed their legislators, posted support for the bill on social media, and gathered in a parking lot to film a campaign video led by journalist Lucy Noland urging passage of Libre's Law. People brought their rescued pets, along with before and after photos.

> "I am the voice of Riker. I saved him from abandonment."
>
> "I am the voice of Maynard. Someone took out his eye. He had teeth missing."
>
> "I am the voice of Jimbo. He came to us; he hardly had any hair."
>
> "I am the voice of BD. He was smashed in the skull during a domestic dispute."

Organizations and advocacy groups such as the Fraternal Order of Police, District Attorneys Association, and Center for Children's Justice supported this bill because they wisely recognized the high correlation between animal abuse and human violence. Together, the Pennsylvania Veterinary Medical Association, Pennsylvania SPCA, Federated Humane Societies of Pennsylvania, Justice for Libre, Facebook animal advocacy action group, and an army of advocates in partnership with the Humane Society of the United States and Humane PA PAC formed a united effort to effect positive change for animals.

Libre's Law in bill form evolved to incorporate additional animal protections for horses. Omega Horse Rescue and Rehabilitation and the Pennsylvania Equine Rescue and Retirement Foundation took in Penn and Penny, our horse protection mascots who became key to raise awareness for the need to add protection for equines in this animal abuse statute overhaul. Aladdin, a nationally loved canine ambassador, appeared at rallies and events representing countless amazing animal heroes throughout the state and nation. During the course of the lobbying effort, unofficial coalitions of various kinds ultimately were instrumental in the passage of Libre's Law. Local media outlets also played a critical role in reporting on Libre's story and related advocacy events to help keep the public informed.

> Grassroots made an enormous difference—in my humble opinion, all the difference. In 2016, with critical legislation on the line, we kept track of potential roadblocks in real time—be they from lawmakers or interest groups. When something popped up on our radar, I'd let advocates know immediately via social media what they could do to help, such as email, call or even talk in person with lawmakers. They were the driving force to finally putting some teeth into animal welfare legislation in the commonwealth. In the summer of 2016, we asked advocates to show up for a campaign rally and show up they did, spending the afternoon and evening with us as we shot a video for stronger animal protection laws. Their voices are powerful. Their stories are powerful. Their compassion is powerful. And that made one powerful video (Lucy Noland, n.d.).

In Pennsylvania, we executed on a program to promote Libre's Law and subsequent iterations of the bill using multiple communication mediums, and we sustained our efforts during all phases of the legislative process. Our campaign was successful not merely because of our numbers, but because of unity, passion, and perseverance, consistent with the advice of Anita Sardo, one of the advocates involved and the Administration Volunteer Leader of the Humane Society of the United States: "be ever mindful of the endgame throughout the entire legislative process" (Sample Libre's Law Communications Program—Appendix A in this chapter).

The Law as a Vehicle for Change

Governor Tom Wolf understood that Libre's Law was the most comprehensive animal protection bill in the history of Pennsylvania, and he was ready to sign this bill into law. More than 30,000+ concerned citizens signed a petition to express support. Animal protection billboards went up in the Harrisburg area. Media kept this issue in the public's eye. Phone calls, emails, use of social media, and in-person meetings with legislators continued. Shortly after our first rally for Libre's Law, Senator Alloway added an amendment to state Representative Ryan Bizzarro's HB 869; and because of our collective advocacy, that bill passed the Senate unanimously in November 2016. Our efforts were making a difference! Despite a majority of support in the House, opposition from the NRA prevented a vote on the bill. The next chance to get a vote would be in January 2017. We were delayed, but not defeated. We took the disappointment and used it as an opportunity to grow our cause by encouraging other concerned citizens and coalition partners to add their legislative voices to Libre's Law. Our numbers and coalitions and voices became stronger and mightier, and they were our strength. But why did people continue to show up and help to grow the visibility of our cause after this loss?

> What kept the momentum going for Libre's Law is that Libre's case, as well as that of other animal ambassadors representing different components of the bill, raised the profile of animal protection issues in our state. We banded together knowing if we didn't get a vote, we wouldn't give up. No matter how long or difficult, we stayed positive by continuing to build bridges and relationships with legislators.—Kristi Powell Rhine

On June 20, 2017, Representative Todd Stephens' HB 1238, incorporating Senator Alloway's Libre's Law and Representative Ryan Bizzarro's Mandatory Forfeiture, passed with no amendments in the House and unanimously in the Senate. Powered by relationships, coalitions, and effective communication to protect animals, HB 1238 reached the Governor's desk. As promised, with pen and paw in hand at a public event, Governor Wolf signed this bill into law on June 28, 2017, complete with Libre's paw print!

The Legislation

This section describes the five key components of Act 10 of 2017 (Pennsylvania Act 10, 2017). Representative stories relevant to each of the components of the law reflect case studies used to illustrate the imperative need for updated statutes. These contemporary case studies of real animals being abused and neglected in Pennsylvania were integral to the process of advocating for the bill to become law. Bringing these stories to the public generated the awareness, interest, support, and momentum to pass the legislation. The animal ambassadors from each case study inspired advocates, coalition partners, and legislators to join together and to stand together in this endeavor.

First, Mandatory Forfeiture

As the law stood, a perpetrator of animal cruelty could retain custody of the very animal for which they were convicted of abusing. HB 1238 required that upon conviction of felony animal cruelty, the abused animals be forfeited to an animal shelter.

The ANNA Shelter in Erie, Pennsylvania took in Biscuit, a horribly abused dog and the victim of a domestic violence dispute. The perpetrator broke his jaw and extinguished 13 cigarettes on his body. Charges were not filed against the person who did this to Biscuit, while the shelter paid $4,000 in medical costs. Biscuit was adopted by the Executive Director of the ANNA Shelter, and he continues to appear at the state Capitol as an ambassador for the abused and neglected.

Second, Libre's Law

This comprehensive overhaul of animal protection legislation in Pennsylvania increased penalties for egregious acts of cruelty. Inspired by Libre and the suffering he endured, and his miraculous recovery, an army of advocates persisted through opposition, setbacks, and reintroductions to shepherd the law to passage. Now animal abusers face tougher penalties for their crimes; and in cases like Libre's, felony charges can be filed.

Since Libre was brought to Speranza in Mechanicsburg, he has healed and still lives at the animal rescue, in the private residence that overlooks the farm.

Third, Inclement Weather and Tethering Regulations

This part of Libre's Law instituted reasonable limitations for tethering a dog outside during inclement weather. It was a step in the right direction to prevent dogs from suffering in the extreme cold. A list of Q&A's which clarify and simplify legal provisions established by the law is included at Appendix B.

Tanner presented to the Animal Care Sanctuary in East Smithfield, PA in dire condition. Spending ten years at the end of a chain, he was emaciated with no muscle mass and barely able to walk. Tanner literally embodied the urgent need for clearly defined anti-tethering guidelines.

Fourth, Added Protection for Equines

This part of the law added protections for horses similar to those for dogs and cats. It came to be known as Cordelia's Law, named after a horse who was held in an auto salvage yard with no shelter, food, or water. Upon her rescue from shockingly cruel conditions, Cordelia received intensive foster care and veterinary medical treatment. Unfortunately, she soon died due to the permanent damage caused by severe starvation. The perpetrator paid a mere fine because misdemeanor level charges only applied to dogs and cats. Under the new law, misdemeanor or felony charges can be filed.

Omega Horse Rescue, Pennsylvania Equine Rescue and Retirement Foundation, and the Humane Society of the United States Humane Policy Volunteer Leaders banded together to save Penn (mentioned earlier in this chapter) from an at-risk slaughter situation. Penn's noble nature raised awareness for equine protection issues in Pennsylvania, and ultimately helped pass Libre's Law. On top of "Cordelia's Law" being enacted, Penn continues raising awareness for the "Safeguard American Food Exports (SAFE) Act," which would ban the slaughter and export for slaughter of America's horses.

Fifth, Civil Immunity

This portion of the law provides civil immunity to veterinarians, veterinary technicians, and Humane Society Police Officers to prevent frivolous lawsuits against professionals when they are reporting animal cruelty. These professionals, like Libre's rescue and recovery heroes, Dr. Pryor and Jen Nields, need legal protection in order to properly do their job and protect animals without fear of retribution.

The above cases make clear why so many stakeholders concluded that Pennsylvania needed stronger, updated legislation to protect animals. According to the PA Courts, since Act 10 went into effect in August 2017, over 25,000 animal abuse offenses have been filed statewide—54% of which were for neglect of an animal. Act 10 quickly influenced the prosecution and outcome of many cases. From requiring that abused animals be forfeited to a shelter upon felony convictions to tethering stipulations that limit the continuous chaining of dogs to granting civil immunity for veterinarians and humane officers, and increasing penalties for heinous animal abuse, Act 10 ensures that Pennsylvania's cruelty laws are no longer species-specific, but rather act-based. Because of Act 10, more serious charges are being brought against the perpetrators of cruelty.

> Under the prior law, animal cruelty was largely a summary offense, so offenders received penalties that were the legal equivalent of a traffic violation. Even egregious acts of cruelty were not penalized commensurate to the severity of the crime. Penalties are greatly enhanced under the new law. For instance, aggravated cruelty is a felony which is the first time that felony charges can and have been rendered in cases that are not related to animal fighting or harming an endangered species.—Elissa B. Katz, Esquire, Co-Chair, Animal Law Committee of the Pennsylvania Bar Association; President, Humane PA PAC

The Work Left to Do

Pennsylvania has steadily risen in the ranks of American states in the passage and implementation of upgraded and ground-breaking animal protection measures, as measured in such instruments as the HSUS Humane State Index and the Animal Legal Defense Fund's Animal Protection Laws Rankings Report. Pennsylvania is now within reach of the top ten states in our nation for the best animal protection laws (Humane Society of the United States, 2018). In 2018, Pennsylvania became the most-improved state with the effectiveness of Act 10 (Animal Legal Defense Fund, 2018).

There are a few areas for obvious future action when it comes to animal protection in the Commonwealth of Pennsylvania. High on the list would be ending the sales of puppies in Pennsylvania pet stores. The Pet Retail Sales bill (a.k.a. Victoria's Law) would prohibit Pennsylvania pet stores from selling dogs, cats, and rabbits. In lieu of these sales, this legislation would promote partnerships between Pennsylvania pet stores and nonprofit rescue groups and municipal shelters for the adoption of dogs, cats, and rabbits from pet shop locations. Driving the pet market to humane sources would help to protect pets and consumers. Along these same lines, there would be value in securing legislation to stop the predatory deceptive financing of companion animals. All too often, pet stores have taken advantage of consumers by offering financed purchases at exorbitant interest rates and hidden fees. Predatory lending by pet stores with financing at high interest rates and hidden fees is bad for both animals and people, and financing is not the right way to acquire a family member. Ending live pigeon shoots remains a long-standing problem in the Commonwealth and would be a natural goal for advocates in the future. Banning cruel wildlife trafficking as Pennsylvania continues to be the top sellers of ivory in the United States (Biologists without Borders, 2021) would also be deserving of legislative intervention, as would policy action to increase access to veterinary telemedicine to address gaps in service and better serve pets and their people more equitably. According to the Humane Society of the United States and other wildlife protection groups, Pennsylvania hosts more wildlife killing contests than any other state east of the Mississippi River (Lange, 2018) and whether by initiation of a Pennsylvania Game Commission rule to ban cruel, unsporting, and scientifically unsound killing contests, as other state wildlife commissions have done, or by other means, a prohibition would likely attract strong public support.

How to Replicate in Your State

Based on first-hand experience, there are three fundamental ways to contribute to animal welfare campaigns:

1. **Build Relationships:** Establish and maintain respectful relationships with your legislators. Know that your voice counts. Communicate with them and their staff on issues important to you. They want to hear from you, their constituents; and they will listen, as evidenced by the passing of the most historic animal protection package in Pennsylvania state history. When talking to legislators and their office staff, be prepared to explain and defend your position on political concerns and proposed legislation. This includes being aware of potential opposing views with a readiness to refute those claims. Desired outcomes are more likely if the relationship involves consistent communication and multiple instances of exchanging information and ideas during the introduction and consideration of specific legislative priorities. Citizens working together with their legislators can construct a more humane state and nation for animals and the people who love them.

   Former Pennsylvania State Senator Roy Afflerbach (n.d.) once offered a short but striking observation about public policy:

   > The question is not "*What* is happening in city hall or in the capitol?"; but rather, "*Who* is making what happen?" If you are not visiting, telephoning, writing to, or otherwise becoming a friend of your public officials, you can bet that someone else is. And that someone else may be advocating public policy beliefs completely contrary to yours. While the legislative process can

be daunting, success requires patience and perseverance and is most often measured by incremental compromise.

2. **Develop partnerships:** Partnering with other people and organizations brings additional knowledge and experience, perspectives, and expertise, and supplies and resources. Allied partners collaborating toward a common goal can achieve measurable success greater than individuals working independently.

   The long process of winning passage of HB 1238 generated exponential growth in advocate involvement, ongoing media coverage, and public support. In the ensuing years, the HSUS and other humane organizations have partnered with Humane Society Police Officers, state and local law enforcement agencies, and legal authorities to provide training on the meaning, interpretation, and enforcement of Act 10. The impact of the new law and training programs can be assessed through an examination of prosecutions and trials for misdemeanor and felony charges and sentences with more appropriate penalties.

   Research has drawn a clear link time and again between animal cruelty and acts of human violence (e.g. Ascione et al., 2007; Bright et al., 2018; Campbell et al., 2021; Kavanaugh et al., 2013; Merz-Perez et al., 2001; Trentam et al., 2018). That's why organizations in Pennsylvania, including the State's Center for Children's Justice, the Pennsylvania Coalition Against Domestic Violence and the Pennsylvania Coalition Against Rape are now asking prosecutors to consider mental health evaluations and counseling for cases involving egregious animal cruelty.

   One of the strongest examples of cooperative partnership was the establishment of the Animal Protection Caucus within the Pennsylvania General Assembly. In the aftermath of the Libre campaign, like-minded legislators assembled to form an official caucus to improve conditions for animals in the state.

3. **Practice Effective Legislative Communications:** The following tips came from Pennsylvania legislators about the best ways to communicate with them.

   - Maintain a polite, respectful, and calm demeanor. Common courtesy and mature behavior pave the path to obtain and retain their attention.
   - Be straightforward and clear with your ask. Be specific about what you want them to do. This is, in part, a matter of time management for them, and you should be sure to make good use of their time and yours.
   - When writing, use bullet points to explain why you want them to co-sponsor a bill. Also, use bullet points to present and rebut possible opposition arguments.
   - If possible, tell them which legislators are likely to be against the bill and the reasons why. Referencing their views will help to qualify a rationale toward contradiction of their opinions.

- Legislators like briefing packets, one-pagers, and leave-behinds as reference materials when discussing issues with other people.
- If you are unable to keep a scheduled appointment, notify the relevant office staff as soon as possible. "No shows" are discourteous and a waste of other people's time.
- For follow-up, they appreciate thank you notes to their staff in addition to themselves.

The passing of Act 10 stands as a benchmark of Pennsylvania's animal advocacy. What started with Libre's Law certainly does not have to end there, and it won't. In the words of another advocate, Marianne Weaver, "Now that we've finally arrived, the journey has truly just begun." And in the wise words of Margaret Mead (1978), "Never doubt that a small group of thoughtful, committed citizens can change the world. Indeed, it is the only thing that ever has."

Animal Protection as a Social Movement

Strategically focused social movements have driven society's progress toward protecting the most vulnerable populations, including animals, who are unable to advocate for themselves. The movement to protect animals is a natural extension of our ethics and compassion toward members of our own species. A cornerstone of this movement's philosophy of is that people from all backgrounds share a kinship with animals. In a day and age when the majority of socio/political issues appear contentious and polarizing, animal protection stands out as one of the few issues that is bipartisan in nature. On its behalf, advocates are able to consistently reach across the aisle, and call upon folks of all political stripes to feel empathy for these sentient beings who are literally at our mercy. From the extreme confinement of farm animals to the inhumane conditions in puppy mills, from unsporting and ineffective wildlife killing contests and the endless cycles of overpopulation that unmanaged community cats endure, to the transport and slaughter of American horses—animals everywhere are in dire need of our help.

Thankfully, the inclination to help animals is innate for most people and as children, we are captivated by the magic of these beings. As a child, Emily Spivak made the connection between her cat Lily and pigs, realizing that it didn't make sense to care about one animal with whom she had a relationship, while consuming the other. Though she had not yet met a pig, she reasoned that this species also must have preferences, enjoy affection, and be able to experience pain. Spivak was captivated by all beings that we share our world with, and her admiration only grew as she matured.

Our first-hand experience with pets, familiarity with observing wildlife in our own backyard, and fascination with majestic species such as elephants and lions, captivates and nurtures a vested interest in the protection of animals. Over 67% of households have companion animals (American Veterinary Medical Association, n.d.) and as of 2017, there were 86 million wildlife-watching participants in the United States (U.S.

Department of the Interior, 2017). Federal bills such as the Big Cat Public Safety Act (which prohibits the possession of big cats by unaccredited individuals/exhibitors and bans physical contact between the public and big cats) and the Puppy Protection Act (which protects dogs from enduring atrocious conditions such as wire flooring and freezing temperatures in puppy mills), have bill sponsors from both the Democratic and Republican parties, as well as strong numbers of cosponsors from each.

The Importance of Legislative Advocacy in the Animal Protection Movement

To address the root cause of animal cruelty, it is imperative that we work towards prevention. It is simply not practical or possible to rescue all animals from the grievous situations they are in. Therefore, one of the most impactful ways to prevent the systemic abuse of animals is to pass legislation phasing out egregious practices, behaviors, and industries—to stop the cruelty before it even begins. The solution to reducing animal suffering en masse lies in our tenacity to strategically steward the successful passage of legislation at the federal, state, and local levels. Using the Big Cat Public Safety Act as an example, by making it illegal to privately own and have physical contact with big cats, the vicious cycle of immense cruelty from America's cub petting industry would be stopped; the number of big cats living in highly unsuitable conditions would drastically decrease, thereby preventing the suffering of countless animals. That's the power of legislation to move the needle forward for animals in society.

The Importance of Developing Relationships with Your Elected Officials

One of the most effective ways to advance animal protection legislation—and stop legislation that would be harmful for animals—is by cultivating professional and durable relationships with your elected officials and their staff at all three levels of government: federal, state, and local. Legislators are in a position of authority to institute tangible, lasting change to address and rectify inhumane practices, so informing and educating them about the issues is key. Policy makers at all levels of government have incredibly full plates; they do not have the bandwidth to be well-versed in all issues. Constituents can enhance their own influence with legislators by initiating contact, maintaining communication to discuss ongoing concerns, and serving as a reliable resource by providing current, accurate information. It is important to share your position on issues with legislators and to contradict the individuals and interest groups expressing opposing views. Unfortunately, they too are seeking to develop relationships with legislators. By consistently engaging with those who represent us, we can overcome the influence of those interests and further strengthen the inclination of those in power to take the welfare of animals seriously.

Politicians take an interest in what their voting constituency prioritizes. As constituents, we can lobby for a variety of issues such as tax reform, but there is something uniquely special and compelling about advocating for those who will never be able to pay you back. They will never know what you did for them, and they will never be able to express appreciation. Representing the interests of defenseless creatures is one of the most selfless actions we can take as human beings. It is a practice that aids in our own introspection and helps us further develop our own moral compass, discovering goodwill and joy in one of the noblest of pursuits. Working through the political system to advance humane public policies also provides us with the opportunity to attain valuable real-world experiences with the policy process and political landscape, develop a deeper knowledge of key animal protection issues, practice transferable skillsets such as relationship-development and strategic thinking, and serve as leaders in our communities and a trusted contact for elected officials. Above all, this work presents an opportunity to create lasting societal change, which elevates both animals and humankind. Every person we have worked with who has connected with their legislators' offices on behalf of animals has valued the time and effort spent, no matter the outcome. There is one thing that unites all champions for animals: working to better the animal condition is certainly its own reward, but in the process, they learn more about themselves.

Key Steps to Relationship-Building

Scheduling a Meeting

Sitting down with your elected officials and their staff members either at their office or through a virtual platform provides the opportunity for them to get to know you, and you them. As their constituent, you have their attention and the platform to communicate with them about crucial animal protection issues. To gain and foster this legislative advocacy for the animal protection movement, this section provides information from the Humane Society of the United States' (HSUS) 2022 Humane Policy Volunteer Leader Toolkit, by Spivak et al. (2022).

At the federal level, Spivak suggests developing relationships with your U.S. Representative and both U.S. Senators, via their staff members who work on animal issues. At the state level, you can also forge connections with your State Senator and State Representative and their staff. Note that most federal and state legislators have district offices, which are right in your community. Staff in district offices are much more accessible and there is great value in developing relationships with them as a constituent. Finally, at the local level, get to know who represents you on your City Council and County Board of Supervisors. Building relationships with local elected officials now can help even more animals in the future; today's county council member could be tomorrow's State Representative (HSUS & Sprivak et al., 2022)!

Visit your legislators' websites to gain insight about their background, interests, positions, and the issues they care about most to better understand their frame of reference. Some legislators will even include information about their pets in their biographies, which is helpful information to have in your back pocket. Look for common ground to help you identify mutual areas of interest (HSUS, 2022).

As you prepare for your meetings, review the basics of the issue and/or the bill(s) you would like to speak about with your elected officials. Remember that you do not need to be an expert on the issue—what truly matters is that you are a voting constituent who cares about animals (HSUS, 2022).

If possible, form a partnership with community members and organizations in the legislator's district who may have the same positions as you, even if for reasons other than animal protection. Examples include parents who are concerned about the safety of their children, leaders of a religious congregation who are morally opposed to a specific practice, business owners who are worried about how their tax dollars are being spent, etc. Remember to encourage your family, friends, and community members to register to vote, and to become more engaged too (HSUS, 2022).

As generally indicated in the Toolkit (HSUS, 2022), to set up a virtual appointment, call the number of the main office and ask to speak with a staff member who works on animal issues. If you are meeting in person, set up an appointment in the district office closest to you. Provide your name and let the staff member know that you are a voting constituent, identify the city you are from, and the purpose of the meeting (to discuss animal protection issues and/or legislation). You will likely meet with a staff member—and that's wonderful! Staff members are the eyes and ears of lawmakers, and they can have tremendous influence over issues and policy decisions. Establishing a positive relationship with staff members is vital. Invite community members to participate with you and let the office know if you will be including additional voting constituents. Remember that there is power in numbers—lawmakers pay more attention when more people show an interest in the issue. Note that you should *only* contact the offices of elected officials who represent your congressional district, state legislative district, city, or county (HSUS, 2022).

Crafting the Ask

When relaying your ask (the primary reason for your meeting), it is important to be a respectful professional who is clear and concise about what you would like them to pay attention to and what action you'd like them to take. Examples include asking that the elected official cosponsor a piece of legislation or that they support/oppose a bill. Legislators and their staff are apprised of numerous bills in many issue areas, so it is helpful to iterate the bill number, name, and a brief description. At the beginning of your meeting, provide any relevant fact sheets and letters to the editor that support your position; it is also helpful to relay any news story emerging from current events that further highlight the timeliness of the issue (HSUS, 2022).

Explain why you feel this issue or bill is important by sharing personal stories that are related to your community, if possible. Consider making a pitch for the issue based on a public safety, economic or consumer protection argument. It is important to consider the legislators' background and frame of reference when making your case so that it will resonate with your audience, draw on their interests, and help them to be more open to your message (HSUS, 2022).

During the Meeting

The animals are counting on you to speak on their behalf in the most effective way possible—so it is important to keep these points in mind (HSUS, 2022):

- *Start on time and at the beginning of your meeting, introduce yourself and anyone in your group as voting constituents.*
- *Wear business attire, as legislative offices are more open to hearing what you have to say if you dress professionally.*
- *Make eye contact and state your views in a personable manner. Imparting a positive attitude goes a long way!*
- *Remember that animals have friends in all political parties and being politically divisive does not serve the animals' best interests.*
- *After communicating the information and your ask, provide the opportunity for the legislator or their staff member to respond. Their comments will allow you to determine the best path forward for the rest of your conversation and ascertain what additional information might be helpful.*
- *Inform the legislator or staff member of the possible sources of opposing views and be prepared to help them understand the flaws in those rationales.*
- *If you don't know the answer to a question, let them know you will find out and circle back to them. Getting back to your legislator's office with the answer provides a valuable opportunity to further build your professional relationship.*
- *Legislators and their staff appreciate short, concise meetings because they are so busy; keep them to 20 minutes maximum.*
- *Thank the legislator or their staff member for taking the time to meet with you and/or your group.*
- *If you are unable to keep your appointment, contact the office as soon as possible to let them know and reschedule.*

After the Meeting—The Art of Thanking

Relaying your sincere appreciation is crucial. Within the next couple of days after your meeting, call, email, or send a hand-written thank you card to your legislator and their staff for taking the time to meet with you. Don't forget to follow up with any additional information they may have requested. As a former intern for both federal and state lawmakers, Spivak discovered that many people contacted their legislators when they are unhappy about something, but far too few take the time to express their appreciation. You can help animal protection issues stand out from the crowd by consistently letting your legislators and their staff members know that you appreciate their time and animal protection efforts. In your follow-up, offer to be a resource for them on animal issues and keep in touch—remember that well-founded relationships take time to develop (HSUS, 2022).

Avenues for Continuous Engagement

Through her years of experience with the HSUS, Emily Spivak has found that in addition to meeting with your legislators' offices, there are several additional ways to raise awareness about an animal protection issue, garner support for a piece of legislation, and ultimately improve animals' lives.

Letters to the Editor

Having a well-written letter to the editor (LTE) published in your local newspaper can make an incredible difference in shifting public opinion and influencing policy. Many elected officials' offices read published LTEs to keep their finger on the pulse of issues that their constituents are focused on. Here are a few tips for writing effective LTEs (HSUS, 2022):

- *Review the newspaper's letter to the editor submission guidelines on their website, which will likely include word limits and requirements for the author's identifying information.*
- *Open your letter with a statement that will catch the reader's attention and indicate what actions readers can take to help. Examples include "Please take action to protect cats from painful declawing procedures" or "Don't allow legislators to roll back protections for farm animals."*
- *Focus on an overarching message that briefly explains the issue to the readers and provide one or two key supporting points. Strengthen your position with cited facts and statistics and convey the effect this issue has on your community.*
- *If your LTE is about legislation, reference the bill by number and name, clearly express your support or opposition and why, then indicate what actions readers can take to help.*
- *Editors prefer to publish concise letters that are timed alongside current events; note that they may modify your letter as they see fit.*
- *It's helpful to ask a peer to review your draft letter prior to submitting to ensure you are getting your point across effectively.*

Phone Call or Email

A polite phone call or friendly email can go a long way in maintaining contact with your elected official's office and encouraging them to take the pro-animal position on an issue. In your correspondence, be sure to provide the home address where you are registered to vote, thank them for their service, and mention any recent positive action they have taken for your community. Then, highlight the animal protection issue and/or legislation you would like them to focus on and briefly state the animal protection position you would like them to take. If you are bringing up a specific bill, provide the bill number, name, and a summary. Convey how the bill affects you and your community. In my experience with the HSUS and as a former intern for federal and state lawmakers, Spivak has seen numerous instances in which a legislator was not a cosponsor on a bill simply because they hadn't been asked and the issue was not on their radar. However, after having been asked and given a chance to learn about the issue and the bill, the legislator signed on as a cosponsor, making a major the difference in the outcome of the bill (HSUS, 2022).

Social Media

Follow and 'like' your elected officials on social media to learn more about the issues and current events they are focused on. A good way to show appreciation is to publicize their animal protection efforts on these platforms. If you meet with your legislator or their staff, snap a photo at the end of your meeting (or take a screenshot if virtual), tag your legislator, and post the photo on social media with a friendly public message. You can also praise legislators on social media when they support animal protection legislation and politely express disappointment when they do not (HSUS, 2022).

Town Halls

Participating in your legislators' town hall meetings and community events can help foster your relationship as a constituent and animal protection advocate. Sign up for their e-newsletters to receive notice of upcoming meetings. Invite community members to attend with you and provide them with brief background information on the legislator and an overview of the issue or legislation you are there to highlight. Town halls normally provide the opportunity to ask the legislator a question, so think of a sample question that demonstrates support for the animal protection issue and/or legislation you are there to highlight (HSUS, 2022).

The Power of Local Ordinances and Resolutions

One of the most effective ways to create and execute meaningful change is to collaborate with your local governing body, such as the city council and/or county board of supervisors, to pass an animal protection ordinance or resolution. An ordinance is an enforceable law at the local level that includes penalties for those who do not comply. A resolution is a non-enforceable public statement by the local government declaring support or opposition to an issue; there are no penalties for those who do not comply (HSUS, 2022).

Working locally is a powerful way to educate the public about the issue and to build a strong base of community support. Amanda Coats, the Co-Founder of Kitten Scoop, a Trap-Neuter-Vaccinate-Return (TNVR) advocacy and rescue group based in southwestern PA, explains: "The best tool we have to combat the problems facing animals is education. There is nothing higher. When you educate the public, you touch across multiple generations reaching the most animals possible."

Local ordinances and resolutions can serve to create a groundswell of support for the introduction and passage of animal protection legislation in your state capital. The more cities and counties that pass these measures, the stronger the foundation for the introduction of a bill that mirrors it at the state level. In addition, it is often easier to get local laws adopted than it is to enact them at the federal and state levels, in part because it is easier to meet and interact with local elected officials and their staff members. They live in your community and have a high stake in the issues in play there. Also, there are fewer competing pieces of legislation at the local level and fewer constituents who embrace a participatory role in local government, giving you a greater platform and better access to the local governing body (HSUS, 2022).

Kristen Moyer, the Director of North Carolina Voters for Animal Welfare and a Humane Policy Volunteer Leader with the Humane Society of the United States, worked with the Charlotte City Council over a period of several years to ban the use of exotic animals in circuses and traveling exhibits. As a result, the Council voted 7–5 to pass this ordinance in December 2021. Moyer offers the following: "I think it is important to work with local officials for the betterment of your community. Obviously, the animals do not have a voice, and if change is going to happen on a grassroots level, it takes members of the community stepping up and raising awareness about the suffering that animals endure in the name of food, clothing, and entertainment. Identifying elected officials who love animals I think is an important factor. Once we identified a member of the council who cared about animal welfare, we knew we had someone who would champion this issue to the rest of the council. So many advocates spoke up on behalf of the animals that it became impossible to ignore us. In the end, perseverance paid off."

Examples of popular measures that have passed in cities and counties nationwide include retail sales ordinances prohibiting the sale of puppy mill dogs/cats/rabbits in pet stores and the sale or manufacture of new fur products, as well as resolutions that publicly endorse pending state/federal animal protection legislation or publicly oppose cruel practices such as wildlife killing contests in which event participants win prizes for killing the most animals within a specified time period (HSUS, n.d.). These local ordinances and resolutions have proven to be instrumental in building the momentum needed to enact game-changing laws for animals at the state and federal levels (HSUS, 2022).

If you would like to work on passing a local ordinance or resolution in your community, Spivak shares the following standard steps you can take in the process (HSUS, 2022):

1. Familiarize yourself with the governing body you would like to work with by attending several of its public meetings. The process of enacting local legislation varies by city and county, so pay attention to the issues this one is focusing on and how it approaches them.
2. Think about what animal protection issues speak to you on a personal level. Spivak likes to describe animal advocacy as our "heart's work"—altruistic acts that bring us pure joy. It is vital to think critically about the needs in your community and focus on an issue area that you care about as you develop a plan.
3. Gather information about the issue, such as if there are any existing related animal protection laws on the books, what community groups could be allies

in this effort, and who may be opposed. Be prepared to make a compelling case as to why this issue is important and requires the local governing body's attention.

4. Contact your Humane Society of the United States (HSUS) State Director. They will be able to support you through the process and provide invaluable resources, as well as let you know if any efforts on this issue are already in progress.
5. Develop a partnership with community members and organizations who may care about passing an ordinance or resolution on the issue; think about those who may have a common goal and would benefit from this work, even if for reasons other than animal protection. The key is to build as much support as you can going into the process.
6. Approach your councilmember's office with your idea for a local ordinance or resolution. If you have several councilmembers who represent you, choose the one you feel would be the most receptive to working with you on this specific animal protection issue.
7. It is helpful to present a sample ordinance or resolution that has passed in other cities/counties to share with your councilmember; connect with your HSUS State Director about this.
8. It is *absolutely* vital that you work with an expert to ensure that the language is legally well-crafted in order to prevent problems that could negate your efforts. Your HSUS State Director will work with you to develop solid ordinance or resolution language and will engage experts in the specific issue area to thoroughly review all language.
9. If your city or county councilmember agrees to sponsor the ordinance or resolution, create a succinct fact sheet with talking points and have a peer review the draft.
10. Plan for how to handle any opposition by providing the ordinance or resolution sponsor with talking points to address their concerns.
11. Mobilize your coalition by asking them to meet with their councilmembers, engage with city/county residents in-person on social media, secure letters of endorsement by local businesses and organizations, submit letters to the editor, and meet with the editorial board of your local newspaper to ask for their public support.
12. During a public hearing in which your proposed ordinance or resolution is being discussed, testify alongside others who have a stake in the outcome. Your HSUS State Director will be able to provide guidance and tips on how to relay your message effectively and professionally. During the hearing, pay careful attention to questions that the legislative body has and what the opposition's arguments are.
13. Keep in close contact with the sponsor and follow up with the Council to address any issues as they arise.

It is important to note that navigating the legislative process at any level of government usually requires compromise on all sides. "Very few pieces of legislation are enacted without bipartisan support," noted Elizabeth Smith, an animal advocate from York, PA. "You need buy-in from both sides of the aisle for your bill to gain real traction. Often that means compromising your ideal bill down to something that Republicans, Democrats, and everyone in between can jump onto. It might not bring you 100% of the way to your goal but compromised legislation that passes has more of an impact on the everyday lives of animals than a messaging bill."

In observing the progression of humane public policies over the years, Spivak has found that oftentimes, it takes several legislative sessions for a proposed federal/state bill or local ordinance/resolution to make it to the finish line—this is completely normal. The legislative achievements for animals that we see today are due to advocates who planted those seeds with federal, state, and local elected officials years ago. As is the case with all social movements, progress is incremental. While occasionally wins for animals are achieved easily in a single legislative session, the vast majority require active participation from constituents over a period of time. When we harness our empathy for animals and utilize our power as voting constituents to advance humane public policies at all levels of government, we are laying the foundation of lasting change for the animals.

References

American Veterinary Medical Association. (n.d.). U.S. pet ownership statistics. Retrieved March 7, 2022, from www.avma.org/resources-tools/reports-statistics/us-pet-ownership-statistics.

Animal Legal Defense Fund. (2018, January 18). Best and worst states for animal protection laws, 2017 report released. Retrieved March 7, 2022, from https://aldf.org/article/best-worst-states-animal-protection-laws-2017-report-released/.

Ascione, F. R., Weber, C. V., Thompson, T. M., Heath, J., Maruyama, M., & Hayashi, K. (2007). Battered pets and domestic violence: Animal abuse reported by woman experiencing intimate violence and by non-abused woman. Violence Against Women, 13(4), 354–373. https://doi.org/10.1177/1077801207299201.

Biologists without Borders. (2021, February). *2020 Online ivory listed for sale in the United States.* Retrieved March 7, 2022, from 2020 Online Ivory Listed for Sale in the United States.pdf.

Bright, M. A., Huq, M. S., Spencer, T. Applebaum, J. W., & Hardt, N. (2018). Animal cruelty as an indicator of family trauma: Using adverse childhood experiences to look beyond child abuse and domestic violence. *Child abuse & Neglect, 76*, 289–296. DOI: 10.1016/j.chiabu.2017.11.011.

Campbell, A. M., Thompson, S. L, Harris, C. L., & Wiehe, S. E. (2021). Intimate partner violence in pet abuse: responding law-enforcement officers' observations and victim reports from the scene. *Journal of Interpersonal Violence, 36*(5–6), 2353–2373. https://doi.org/10.1177/0886260518759653.

Frishberg, D. (Writer), Rushnell, S. D. (Creative Producer), & Dazzo, J. (Animator). (1976). *I'm just a bill.* [Video]. Schoolhouse Rock!

Humane Society of the United States. (2022). *Humane Policy Volunteer Leader Toolkit.* The Humane Society of the United States.

Humane Society of the United States. (2018, January 8). California again ranks as the nation's most humane state, while the Dakotas, Mississippi at bottom of list. *The Humane Society of the United States.* Retrieved March 3, 2022, from https://blog.humanesociety.org/2018/01/california-ranks-nations-humane-state-dakotas-mississippi-bottom-list.html.

Humane Society of the United States. (n.d.). *Facts about wildlife killing contests.* Retrieved March 7, 2022, from www.humanesociety.org/wildlifekillingcontests. The Humane Society of the United States.

Hurdle, J. (2009, August 17). 2008 Law leading to crackdown on Pennsylvania puppy mills. *The New York Times.* Retrieved March 3, 2022, from https://www.nytimes.com/2009/08/18/us/18dogs.html?login=smartlock&auth=login-smartlock.

Kavanagh, P. S., Signal, T. D., & Taylor, N. (2013). The Dark Triad and animal cruelty: Dark personalities, dark attitudes, and dark behaviors. *Personality and Individual Differences, 55*(6), 666–670.

Lange, K. E. (2018, September 1). *Better off alive: Why it's time to end senseless wildlife killing contests.* Retrieved March 7, 2022, from https://www.humanesociety.org/news/better-alive.

Merz-Perez, L., Heide, K. M., & Silverman, I. J. (2001). Childhood cruelty to animals and subsequent violence against humans. *International Journal of Offender Therapy and Comparative Criminology, 45*, 556–573.

State of Oregon (n.d.) Legislative information. Retrieved March 7, 2022, from https://www.oregon.gov/lcd/NN/Pages/Legislative-Updates.aspx#:~:text=The%20Oregon%20State%20Legislature%20convenes,%22short%20session%22%20is%20held.

Pennsylvania Act 10, 18 PA. C.S. Stat. §§5531–5561. (2017). https://www.legis.state.pa.us/cfdocs/legis/li/uconsCheck.cfm?yr=2017&sessInd=0&act=10.

Trentham, C. E., Hensley, C., & Policastro, C. (2018). Recurrent childhood animal cruelty and its link to recurrent adult interpersonal violence. *International Journal of Offender Therapy and Comparative Criminology, 61*(8), 2345–2356.

U.S. Department of the Interior. (2017, September 7). *New 5-year report shows 101.6 million Americans participated in hunting, fishing & wildlife activities.* Retrieved March 7, 2022, from U.S. Department of the Interior. *U.S. Fish and Wildlife Service Survey Preliminary Findings Show Importance of Increasing Access to Public Lands.* "2017, September 7." www.doi.gov/pressreleases/new-5-year-report-shows-1016-million-americans-participated-hunting-fishing-wildlife.

Appendix A

Libre's Law Communication Program

We (this chapter's authors) deployed a program to promote Libre's Law and subsequent iterations of the bill using multiple communication mediums, and we sustained our efforts during all phases of the legislative process.

Our campaign was successful because of our numbers, unity, passion, and perseverance.

Post-Election (January)

- *Sent letters to newly elected senators & representatives describing Libre's Law and proclaiming support for the bill*
    - Attached fact sheet

Pre/Post-Introduction (Senate & House)

- *Sent letters to senators & representatives seeking co-sponsors*
- *Emailed volunteer leadership requesting contact with legislators via phone, email, social media, and district & Capitol complex office visits*
- *Posted on Facebook & Twitter asking advocates to contact legislators*

Post-Introduction/Pre-Committee Vote (Senate & House)

- *Sent letters to committee members urging passage of the bill out of committee*
- *Emailed advocates & shelter representatives requesting contact with legislators to urge passage of the bill out of committee*
    - Used phone, email, social media, and office visits
        - Encouraged group meetings for the in-person office visits
    - Provided sample message language
    - Advised about potential opposition
    - Included links to find legislators & committee members
- *Emailed status updates to advocates & shelter representatives*
- *Posted on Facebook and Twitter asking folks to contact legislators*

Post-Committee Vote/Pre-Full Floor Vote (Senate & House)

- *Reminded folks to thank bill sponsors, co-sponsors, and committee members who voted in our favor*
- *Increased frequency of emails to advocates & shelter representatives*
    - Issued requests for them to engage their own network of supporters
- *Repeatedly posted on Facebook & Twitter asking folks to contact legislators*
- *Encouraged letters to the editor to garner public attention and support*

Post-Full Floor Vote (Senate & House)

- *Sent thanks to legislators who voted for the bill*

It all starts over again in the event re-introduction is required!

Appendix B

Animal Abuse Statute Overhaul (Libre's Law) Q&A File

Libre's Law: A Few Clarifications

Recent cold weather has brought well-deserved attention to the care of dogs who live outdoors. Libre's Law was a huge step in the right direction, enhancing penalties for animal abuse and placing limits on chronic chaining. That said, there are areas for improvement within the law that have been highlighted during the recent extreme weather. The HSUS is working with lawmakers to clarify the extreme weather provision and provide a meaningful definition of adequate shelter but in the meantime, we hope these questions provide clarity.

This Q & A has been reviewed by the Pennsylvania SPCA, Federated Humane Societies of Pennsylvania, Pennsylvania Veterinary Medical Association and Animal Legal Defense Fund.

Q: Who can take action for a dog lacking appropriate shelter/exposed in extreme weather?

A: A humane officer and/or law enforcement officer may enforce the cruelty code and seize an animal and file charges. If you believe that Act 10 is not being enforced, lawfully document the situation as best you can (take photographs, record times and dates) and request to speak with a law enforcement supervisor.

When speaking with a supervisor, cite the section of the law believed to be violated and inform him/her you are requesting an investigation.

Keep in mind that during extreme weather the number of calls increases exponentially and therefore response times are likely to be longer than usual.

Additionally, animals with access to shelter will always be investigated after animals without access to any shelter or having medical conditions needing immediate treatment.

Q: Can dogs be tethered outside in extreme weather?

A: The circumstances and manner in which a dog is tethered for longer than 30 minutes in weather under 32 or over 90 degrees may lead to charges of neglect.

The statute allows an exception to this rule for temporary tasks lasting one hour (for example, while doing yardwork), so if tethering in extreme weather is the only violation, many officers will use that timeframe for determining a violation.

When circumstances are non-life threatening, an officer may provide the owner an opportunity to remedy the issue.

In more serious circumstances when the dog's health and safety are at risk, an officer may choose to file charges and/or obtain a search warrant to remove the dog. These decisions are based on numerous situationally specific factors.

Q: Can a dog be left outdoors in extreme weather?

A: Yes. While the intent of Libre's Law was to protect dogs from severe conditions, current language still allows that a dog can be kept outside in these temperatures as long as s/he is untethered, and s/he has shelter that maintains adequate body temperature and keeps them dry.

There are certainly severe weather conditions under which no outdoor shelter will allow them to maintain their body temperature. Additional penalties may apply if the conditions are so poor that the animal is at imminent risk of severe injury or death.

If you are aware of a dog in immediate danger, continue reporting it to law enforcement until an officer responds.

Q: What about dogs with inadequate shelter?

A: Pennsylvania cruelty code requires 'shelter must be sufficient to permit the animal to retain body heat and keep the animal dry.' An officer is empowered to utilize the cruelty code if, upon responding to a report, he/she finds a dilapidated/damp/uninsulated structure, and/or the dog appears to be in distress (excessive vocalization, limping, panting, shivering, paleness, whimpering, frostbite, stiff limbs, ice on body parts, etc.).

Q: In addition to extreme weather guidelines, what are the new rules for tethering?

A: In order to ensure compliance with the law, dogs should not be tethered for more than 9 cumulative hours in a 24-hour period.

The tether should not be a tow or logging chain and must be at least 7.0 feet long and attached to a well-fitted collar with a swivel (no choke/prong/chain collars allowed).

Tethered dogs should not be surrounded by excess waste or have open sores/wounds.

Tethered dogs should have access to drinkable water and an area of shade.

Note: these conditions can be met, and an officer may still cite for neglect if the officer can prove that the conditions justify it. Similarly, an owner may fail to meet one of these standards and the officer may find insufficient evidence of neglect. The law allows discretion to the officer and the court.

Chapter 6

Veterinary Forensic Sciences in the Response to Animal Cruelty

Randall Lockwood and Rachel Touroo

History

Today we recognize that the response to and prevention of animal cruelty and neglect cannot be effective without the involvement of veterinary professionals. That has not always been recognized. The growth of organized animal protection efforts in America in the 19th century and the development of veterinary medicine as a formal, science-based field occurred in parallel. Therefore, the role of veterinarians in addressing animal cruelty has evolved along with animal protection. Prior to the formation of the American Veterinary Medical Association (AVMA) in 1863 and the American Society for the Prevention of Cruelty to Animals (ASPCA) in 1866, both fields were represented by an assortment of people with a common interest in animals, without formal training and no central focus on effective actions to promote animal welfare or address animal cruelty.

The welfare of working horses was a major concern of ASPCA's founder, Henry Bergh. Much of the care and treatment of horses at the time was in the hands of farriers, self-styled "horse doctors" and quacks (Lane & Zawistowski, 2008). In 1867, the ASPCA introduced horse ambulances and hired veterinary surgeons to provide care for the ambulance horses as well as the animals they aided. Bergh was concerned with the lack of standards for veterinarians and called for legislation in New York to address this. Cornell University opened in 1868 as the first statutory college in New York and incorporated instruction in veterinary medicine from the outset. Dr. James Law, a renowned graduate of the Edinburgh Veterinary College in Scotland, was hired to oversee veterinary training. Cornell set higher requirements for a veterinary degree than any other institution in North America. By 1871, it required four years of study for a Bachelor of Veterinary Science (BVS) degree and an additional two years for a Doctor of Veterinary Medicine (DVM), a degree previously unavailable from any institution in the United States. This eventually lead to the founding of the New York State College of Veterinary Medicine in 1894 (Cornell University College of Veterinary Medicine, 2015). Bergh met frequently with another leading veterinarian, Dr. Alexandre Liautard, a founder of the Veterinary College in New York City in 1875 and one of the first officers of the AVMA who also championed improvements in veterinary education to improve the welfare of animals.

Bergh also recognized the importance of working with law enforcement agencies, as well as veterinarians, in combating animal cruelty. The original patrons of the ASPCA included the Police Board President (the equivalent of the current Police Commissioner) and the District Attorney for New York County. Bergh also succeeded in being appointed to the bar and being given authority to act as an assistant district attorney to help prosecute the cases that came under the ASPCA's authority as the enforcement agency for New York state's animal cruelty statutes that had been passed shortly after the establishment of the ASPCA.

This blending of resources and goals of veterinary medicine, law enforcement, and animal protection continues today and is best reflected in the emerging discipline of veterinary forensic science, defined as "the application of a broad spectrum of sciences, including veterinary medicine, to answer questions of interest to a court of law."

Defining Forensic Veterinary Medicine

The broader term "forensic medicine" is used to encompass all aspects of forensic work of a medical nature. In the past, this term was often used interchangeably with "forensic pathology." Forensic pathology, however, refers to the branch of forensic medicine which deals with death investigations. Nowadays, the term "clinical forensic medicine" is applied to the branch of forensic medicine involving the living.

In some ways, the role of the forensic veterinarian can be compared to that of a human medical examiner. The duties of a forensic veterinarian, however, are often broader, including the triage, examination and treatment of live victims, necropsy of deceased victims, evidence identification, documentation, and assessment, including assessment of the scene and its effects on the victims, and expert witness testimony. Unlike human forensic cases, most animal cruelty investigations typically have not had access to supporting forensic specialists until recent years. Without such expertise, vital evidence may go undetected, may not be properly preserved, processed or analyzed, or may not withstand scrutiny in court.

We will review the qualities that describe the practice of forensic veterinary medicine and give examples of the many ways in which this new field is enhancing the investigation, prosecution, and prevention of animal cruelty. It is a field which has attracted growing academic attention and is still in the process of being defined. The first degree-granting program in Veterinary Forensic Sciences began in 2014 at the University of Florida. In 2021 the ASPCA and Florida International University launched the first phase of a new program in Veterinary Forensic Sciences. The program will include a Professional Science Master's (PSM) degree, graduate and undergraduate certificates, and professional training. The PSM degree will include both a clinical track targeting veterinarians and veterinary technicians, and an investigation track targeting law enforcement and animal control officers, prosecutors, and other field investigators.

The Henry C. Lee College of Criminal Justice and Forensic Science at the University of New Have, Connecticut has also started a four-unit graduate-level certificate program in Animal Cruelty Investigations. In addition, a growing number of veterinary schools are adding electives or other forensic trainings to supplement traditional veterinary instruction. It is a discipline now recognized by the American Academy of Forensic Sciences and is represented by a nascent professional organization—the International Veterinary Forensic Sciences Association, started in 2008.

Several pioneering publications introduced many of the key concepts of the application of veterinary sciences to legal cases (Byard & Boardman, 2011; Cooper, 1998; Green, 1979, 1980; Munro, 1996; Munro & Thrusfield, 2001a, 2001b, 2001c, 2001d; Stroud, 1998) but there was no compilation of this information in a comprehensive way until the last decade with the publication of a handful of textbooks devoted to the subject (Brooks, 2018; Cooper & Cooper, 2007, 2013; Merck, 2007, 2013; Miller & Zawistowski, 2013; Munro & Munro; 2008; Sinclair, Merck, & Lockwood, 2006). In September of 2016, a special focus issue of the journal *Veterinary Pathology* was devoted to Veterinary Forensic Pathology, with 26 papers on the topic.

The practice of forensic veterinary medicine expands the core skill set of practitioners to include activities that allow veterinary facts and opinions to serve the purpose of the law. We consider a forensic veterinarian to be a veterinarian with additional knowledge, training, and experience to include:

- *Applying veterinary medical knowledge to answer questions of interest to the law;*
- *Basic understanding of the local, state, and federal laws that may apply to cases of animal cruelty or neglect;*
- *A thorough understanding of animal welfare concerns, especially animal pain, suffering and distress;*
- *Knowledge of forensic science and medicine;*
- *Experience with treating victims of animal cruelty;*
- *Experience testifying in court and authoring forensic reports;*
- *Acting as a "teacher" to clearly convey what has or has not happened to an animal based in science and fact, in order to assist the judge and/or jury in understanding the evidence;*
- *Acting as an advocate for the truth, putting the pieces of the puzzle of an animal cruelty case together in the most logical and reasonable fashion;*
- *Interacting with other forensic professions—toxicology, pathology, DNA, ballistics, behavior, etc. to become familiar with the contributing advances that these fields can make to forensic veterinary medicine; and*
- *Educating veterinarians on recognizing potential indicators of animal cruelty and the need to report such suspicions to the appropriate authorities.*

Animal victims cannot speak, but careful study of their medical condition and behavior as well as other evidence can create a narrative of what they have experienced. The forensic veterinarian plays a role analogous to that of a medical examiner explaining the death of a human and providing a voice for the voiceless in a court of law or other forum.

Forms of Animal Cruelty

Animal cruelty is defined in many different ways and exists in many forms (see Chapter 1). The most common cases seen by veterinarians include:

- *Simple neglect—failure to provide appropriate food, water, shelter or veterinary care;*
- *Institutional neglect—including "puppy mills," inadequate shelters or rescue groups, farms, exhibitors;*
- *Severe neglect—including starvation, animals in left hot or cold vehicles, embedded collars;*
- *Animal hoarding—the keeping of many animals in substandard conditions in connection with possible mental disorders;*
- *Intentional abuse—non-accidental injury (NAI) including burns, blunt force trauma, sharp force trauma, strangulation, gunshot, poisoning;*
- *Organized abuse—including "bloodsports" such as dogfighting and cockfighting;*
- *Ritualized abuse—animal cruelty in the context of "occult" or other religious rituals; and*
- *Animal sexual abuse.*

There are certain protocols and procedures that will be part of the response in *any* case of suspected animal cruelty or neglect. In addition, there are special considerations unique to each form of cruelty, which will be discussed later. In all cases, the appropriate response begins with recognizing that animal cruelty has or may have occurred and taking suitable action as required or permissible.

Recognizing and Responding to Animal Cruelty

Many authors have noted the importance of having veterinarians recognize and report animal cruelty (Arkow, 1999; Arkow, Boyden, & Patterson-Kane, 2011; Arkow & Munro, 2008; Landau, 1999; Miller & Zawistowski, 2005; Robertson, 2009; Veterinary Council of New Zealand, 2013; Yoffe-Sharp & Loar, 2009). Much of this has been motivated by the growing appreciation of the connections between animal cruelty and interpersonal violence (Ascione, 2008; Ascione & Lockwood, 2001; Linzey, 2009; Lockwood, 2014; Lockwood & Ascione, 1998; Merz-Perez & Heide, 2004; Pickles,

2020). Several reports have emphasized the importance of veterinary professionals in recognizing potential human and animal victims of violence through greater awareness of the common occurrence of animal cruelty within the dynamics of interpersonal violence (Allison et al., 2017; Larkin, 2018; Newland et al., 2019). Other reports have cited how the investigation of companion animals' non-accidental injuries closely models the experience in child abuse investigations (Bartelink et al., 2021).

A growing number of veterinary professionals are acknowledging having encountered animal cruelty in their practice. A 2021 ASPCA survey of 1027 veterinarians and technicians/assistants found that 43% had seen at least one case of suspected animal cruelty in the previous 12 months (Patterson-Kane et al., 2022). The first global survey of veterinarians found that, overall, 60% considered the problem of animal abuse to be "important" or "very important." This included 71.8% of veterinarians in Asia, 61.8% in North America, 56.4% in Europe, 55.1% in Africa, 50% in South America, and 46% in Oceania (Endenburg & Takashima, 2021). Recent surveys of veterinarians in South Korea reported that veterinarians who have a "pro-animal attitude," and a belief in the link between animal and human abuse and a belief in a moral and legal obligation to report are more likely to be willing to intervene in animal abuse cases (Joo et al., 2019; 2020).

Currently (as of February 2022), 21 states have laws that *require* veterinarians to report animal cruelty either by statute, occupational code or codes of professional conduct (Alabama, Arizona, California, Colorado, Hawaii, Illinois, Kansas, Maine, Maryland, Massachusetts, Minnesota, North Dakota, Nebraska, New York, Ohio, Oklahoma, Oregon, Pennsylvania, Virginia, West Virginia, and Wisconsin) and 21 states permit, but do not require reporting.

There continue to be obstacles to the effective involvement of veterinarians in responding to such cases. Veterinarians are not traditionally trained to identify features that raise the index of suspicion of animal cruelty or to recognize signs consistent with or highly suggestive of cruelty. Additionally, veterinarians may fall into the trap of thinking that owners who care enough about their animals to provide veterinary care are unlikely to abuse their animals; however, this is simply not the case. The largest barriers to diagnosing potential cruelty are a lack of training on indicators of cruelty and the existence of emotional blocks in the minds of professionals. These can be so powerful that they prevent the diagnosis from even being considered in quite obvious cases. The most important step in diagnosing potential animal cruelty is to force oneself to think of it in the first place as a potential differential diagnosis.

Veterinarians may become involved with an animal cruelty case in several ways. They may witness suspected abuse in animals presented in their own practice and may be mandated or otherwise permitted to report it to appropriate authorities. They may become involved in a suspected case at the request of local humane, animal control or law enforcement agencies. This can be the most effective route since it can provide the opportunity to be present when animals are first encountered and assess the environment in which they have been maintained. In other cases, the veterinarian may be called in after the fact to assess living or dead animals or to comment on evidence or medical histories provided by law enforcement, serving as an expert witness.

The role of the veterinarian can include:

- *Documenting the physical condition of all animals associated with a cruelty case and documenting changes in their condition in response to care and treatment;*
- *Commenting on reasonably prudent actions and standards of care that could have been taken to prevent disease, injury or death including basic vaccinations and other preventative care;*
- *In the case of deceased animals, determining the cause of death, sequence of injuries and timing of antemortem or postmortem injuries;*
- *Offering expert opinion to distinguish between death and injury resulting from human versus non-human causes (e.g., predation) or intentional vs. accidental injury;*
- *Identifying and preserving physical evidence that may link the injuries to a particular suspect (e.g., projectiles, ligatures, trace evidence); and*
- *Offering opinions regarding the speed of unconsciousness or death, and degree of pain or suffering to evaluate whether the death or killing was humane.*

The primary distinction between conventional veterinary procedures (e.g., examination, treatment, necropsy) and *forensic* or medicolegal veterinary procedures is that forensic efforts require that the practitioner be aware that *every* action taken or omitted may be open to the intense scrutiny of the court (McEwan, 2012). Every step must be carefully documented and all evidence must be handled and preserved in a manner that carefully limits access to the evidence and tracks the chain of custody of such evidence. A veterinary forensic medical examination can be defined as a detailed exam done in order to methodically document physical findings and facilitate the collection of evidence from the patient's body.

Oregon's mandatory veterinary reporting law (2003) is the most specific *statutory* description of the kind of evidence and information that should be gathered in cases of suspected animal cruelty (Miller, 2006, p. A6). It notes:

> Oregon 686.455 Duty to report aggravated animal abuse.
>
> (1) A veterinarian who has reasonable cause to believe that an animal with which the veterinarian has come in contact has suffered aggravated animal abuse, or that any person with whom the veterinarian has come in contact has committed aggravated animal abuse, shall immediately report the suspected aggravated animal abuse in the manner prescribed in subsection (2) of this section.
>
> (2) A report of suspected aggravated animal abuse required under subsection (1) of this section shall be made to a law enforcement agency, either orally or in writing, and shall include, if known:

(a) The name and description of each animal involved;

(b) The address and telephone number of the owner or other person responsible for the care of the animal;

(c) The nature and extent of the suspected aggravated animal abuse;

(d) Any evidence of previous aggravated animal abuse;

(e) Any explanation given for the suspected aggravated animal abuse; and

(f) Any other information that the person making the report believes may be helpful in establishing the cause of the suspected aggravated animal abuse or the identity of the person causing the aggravated animal abuse [2003 c.275 §3].

Guidelines from the Colorado Veterinary Medical Association (2007, p. 5) go into even greater detail in recommending steps veterinarians should take when animal cruelty is known or suspected. They note that the following information should be collected and included in reports that go to law enforcement:

Signalment

- *Date and time of exam*
- *Animal's name, species, gender and reproductive status, age, color, identification or unusual markings, tattoos, microchip, etc.*
- *Name of owner, contact information, how long the owner has had the animal*
- *All veterinary staff members involved with exam*

Verbal Account of Injury

- *Reason for bringing in the animal and chief complaint (by client)*
- *Documentation of what the client tells you when explaining the animal's condition including relationship, behavior, conduct concerning the animal's injury, any changes/inconsistencies of the account, age of suspected abuser (adult, child, etc.)*
- *Timeliness of seeking veterinary care*

Photography

- *Take "before and after" pictures, and full body shots as well as close-ups. Document that all photos came from the same animal.*
- *Take full body shots and close-ups.*
- *Video recording could be used to document an animal's gait or other behavior, if applicable.*

Physical Findings

- *Perform a complete physical exam noting any abnormalities, injuries*
- *Note if these are new or old injuries. A wound diagram using a silhouette drawing for that species may be helpful.*

Guidelines from the American Veterinary Medical Association (Arkow et al., 2011) offer additional suggestions that apply to proper handling of animal evidence that might be part of any criminal investigation or other legal procedure. In addition to the procedures outlined above, they note that attending veterinary professionals should prioritize the collection of evidence. An item of evidence is anything that can prove or disprove a fact in contention. Evidence most likely to be destroyed by time, other people, or environmental conditions should be collected first. In addition, all staff handling the animals should avoid cross contamination of evidence and utilize sterile procedures, as necessary. Additional guidelines and standards for clinical forensic veterinary exams are detailed in Touroo et al., (2020) and in standards proposed by the International Association of Veterinary Forensic Sciences (IVFSA, 2020).

The physical examination of the animal should not just focus on the chief complaint or obvious abnormalities or overlook the unremarkable. If a parameter is normal, that should be stated. The record should include necessary diagnostics such as a complete blood count (CBC), chemistry panel, fecal, urinalysis or whole-body radiographs. The animal and everything associated with it could be evidence and must be preserved and documented, and its integrity maintained. Standard procedure involves a secure evidence storage area and the keeping of an evidence log with details of each item. An evidence receipt should accompany every item of evidence in order to document chain of custody.

Photography is an important aspect of proper evidence documentation. Forensic photography is utilized to:

- *Identify the victim;*
- *Show the condition of evidence or injuries at the time of discovery or examination;*
- *Record and document injuries and evidence that cannot be preserved or left unaltered;*
- *Allow for later review of the evidence;*
- *Document injuries or conditions and record what they looked like before and after medical intervention;*
- *Illustrate and supplement a written medical report;*
- *Demonstrate the absence or presence of alleged injury or findings; and*
- *Present in a court of law, the items of evidence as they were and, in effect, check the testimony being presented.*

In addition to careful record keeping and preservation of chain of custody, forensic veterinary medicine also often involves the application of forensic methods and techniques that are not part of the conventional veterinary clinical toolkit. As we will see, the documentation of suspected cruelty cases may involve use of techniques such as alternative light sources, DNA analysis, toxicology, ballistics, entomology, blood spatter analysis, grave excavation, applied animal behavior, and other forensic methods (Sharma, 2003; Touroo & Fitch, 2016).

Role of the Veterinarian at a Scene

Veterinarians can have the greatest impact on the investigation of an animal cruelty case if they are involved in the planning of the operation and are present at the scene when action is taken. Their role will include triage of live victims, assisting law enforcement with evidence identification, documentation, and preservation including assessment of the scene and its effects on the victims.

Triage

Triage is the rapid sorting of animals on scene for examination and treatment priority based on medical condition. Animals are triaged at two different points on scene. The first is a "field triage," conducted during initial walk through on scene in order to identify red-coded (critical) animals. This is followed by an "intake triage," conducted prior to or during the removal of animals from the scene in order to identify yellow- and green-coded animals. Red-coded animals include animals that are recumbent or unresponsive, are actively hemorrhaging, are reluctant to move, are vocalizing in apparent pain, are actively seizuring, have open fractures, or are in respiratory distress.

Red-coded animals will require immediate medical attention, provided either at an onsite mobile clinic or a nearby veterinary clinic. Yellow-coded animals include animals that have swollen limb(s) or face, non-weight bearing lameness, significant abdominal distension, draining wounds, eyes closed/reluctant to open, or corneal perforation, or are dehydrated. Yellow-coded animals will also require veterinary attention and examination prior to being transported off scene, such accommodations need to be anticipated and planned out prior to being on scene. Green-coded animals are animals that are bright, alert, and responsive. They may have minor medical conditions such as diarrhea or vomiting for which treatment can wait until after transportation off scene. Care should be taken so that transient evidence, such as mild dehydration, is documented on scene.

When possible, it is desirable to have two veterinarians on scene, with one functioning as a "forensic" vet and the other functioning as a "treating" vet. This treatment veterinarian will allow for the forensic veterinarian to concentrate on the collection of evidence on scene, while they focus on patient care.

Evidence Handling

On scene, the veterinarian may need to assist with the identification of evidence and its potential value and the proper preservation of evidence (Touroo & Fitch, 2016). The types of evidence that a veterinarian may assist in identifying and examining could include:

- *Situational evidence—Elements of the scene that may or may not change. For example, lighting conditions, weather conditions, smells, ammonia levels, sounds and temperature*
- *Physical evidence—Any tangible object that can establish that a crime has been committed, or can provide a link between a crime and its victim or a crime and a suspect*

The veterinarian may need to assist in ensuring that some evidence is properly preserved. If a deceased animal is found on site, it typically will not be examined at the scene. The veterinarian must ensure that any physical evidence present on the body is properly preserved by handling the body as little as possible, placing paper bags on all four feet and securing them in place with rubber bands, and wrapping the body in a clean sheet prior to placing it in a body bag.

Assessment of the Scene and Its Relation to Veterinary/Medical Issues

A veterinarian cannot fully interpret exam findings without scene information. This is why it is ideal to have the veterinarian present at the scene. If this is not possible, it is essential to have good photographic and/or video documentation of the conditions available for review and animal examinations should occur as soon as is possible. For example, the veterinarian may observe dehydration due to poor water quality, interdigital dermatitis, or bacterial conjunctivitis due to dirty and wet living conditions. Depending on the ambient temperature, hypothermia may be observed due to the inability to remain dry without the provision of adequate shelter. Scene photographs may also show safety issues such as exposed metal or broken glass or the presence of possible pesticides, toxins, or poisonous plants which may guide the veterinarian in the workup of the animal.

The Forensic Necropsy

General considerations for live animal examinations in suspected cruelty cases are outlined above. In cases in which animals are deceased, a primary role of the veterinarian will be to complete a forensic necropsy. The goals will be to first determine the cause of death, the event that initiated the chain of events that led to the death. The primary cause of death is often identified by the statement "if it weren't for X, this animal would still be alive," where X is the first, earliest injury or disease in the sequence of events that culminated in death. *Causes* of death are in contrast to the *mechanism(s)* of death, the altered physiology and/or biochemistry set into motion by the cause of death. Mechanisms of death are nonspecific and include the common pathophysiologic events and pathways that precede termination of brain, heart, and/or lung function (e.g., septicemia, organ failure) (Gerdin & McDonough, 2013). If an animal has been euthanized due to suffering or non-survivable injuries, it is important to note that the cause of death is the rationale for euthanasia (e.g., spinal injuries, extensive burns). Some defense attorneys may attempt to assert that the veterinarian who performed humane euthanasia, rather than his or her client, was the person responsible for death of the animal; therefore, it is important to make this distinction.

The necropsy report will also usually attempt to clarify the *manner of death*, either natural (disease, age), accidental, non-accidental (which implies an intentional act), or undetermined (Davis & McDonough, 2018). However, there is currently no universally accepted standard for classifying the manner of death in animals as we have established in human forensic pathology. The manner of death explains how the cause of death came about. In many cases, it will be desirable to offer estimates of postmortem interval or time since death. This may be based on physical or physiological measures or entomological evidence based on the life stages of insects found in association with the body. In order to determine the cause and manner of death, the veterinarian will need to consider the crime scene findings, any available history, as well as the necropsy findings.

Veterinary Forensic Considerations in Different Forms of Animal Cruelty

Many of the forensic procedures applied in animal cruelty cases are universal to crime scenes involving human or animal victims. However, the development of a specialized field of veterinary forensics has been necessitated by the fact that many crimes against animals such as dogfighting, cockfighting, illegal hunting, and ritualistic sacrifice have little or no counterpart in human forensic pathology (Gerdin & McDonough, 2013). We will provide an overview of some of the specific veterinary forensic concerns related to several forms of cruelty. This is not intended to serve as a complete guide to investigations. Detailed discussion of these kinds of cases is provided in the texts mentioned previously.

Neglect

The majority of animal cruelty cases investigated by animal care and control and humane law enforcement involve "simple neglect" in the form of failure to provide adequate food, water, shelter, sanitation, or veterinary care which has not resulted in death or prolonged suffering. Such cases usually result in citations or, at most, misdemeanor charges. However, the investigation of these cases still requires good documentation of the living conditions of the animal(s), their overall health and body condition, the quality and quantity of food and water available, and sanitation of the primary enclosure. In addition, notation should be made of signs of pica (ingestion of non-edible items) and the course of weight gain and general recovery when given adequate food and water.

Institutional Neglect

Larger scale neglect cases may involve "puppy mills" or other breeders, pet shops, substandard animal shelters or rescue groups, animal exhibitors and livestock operations. Since these cases may involve a larger number of animals or a longer history of neglect, they are more likely to result in criminal charges. In addition to the information collected in the simple neglect cases described above, veterinarians should also review any available records of past and current veterinary treatments, any drugs found on site (and whether they have been dispensed), and quality, quantity, and appropriateness of food found at the scene. In addition, large scale operations may have resulted in the death and disposal of animals. The investigation should include a search for deceased animals—either buried or concealed on the premises (e.g., in freezers). It can also be helpful to review financial records to see if expenditures for food and veterinary care are reasonable for the number and type of animals on the scene.

Severe Neglect

Severe neglect cases involve serious injury, suffering, or death that may be prosecuted as felony or high-level misdemeanor crimes. This can include cases of starvation/malnutrition, untreated injuries that might necessitate amputation, heavy matting that interferes with normal urination and defecation, overgrown or ingrown hooves and nails, or ingrown collars or chains. In cases of poor body condition, the veterinarian will often be called upon to rule out causes unrelated to cruelty, such as underlying disease processes that are being treated. In some cases, death from starvation may be documented through necropsy and analysis of bone marrow fat. The percentage of bone marrow fat may be quantified for recently deceased (<24 hours) horses, cattle, dogs, pigs, cervids, and sheep by submitting an entire intact femur for analysis to a diagnostic laboratory. This test might also be useful in bovine and equine cases with a postmortem interval (PMI) of 30 to 60 days, but the test has not been validated for other species with PMIs greater than 24 hours (Gerdin & McDonough, 2013).

Cases in which animals have been subjected to extremes of temperature (e.g., left in a hot or extremely cold vehicle) have also been prosecuted, particularly if such neglect has resulted in death. In such instances, veterinary testimony about the pathological chances associated with such stresses help document the cause and mechanism of death (Bruchim, Loeb, Saragust, & Aroch, 2009; Drobatz & Macintire, 1996). This may be supplemented with evidence from the scene, such as evidence of attempted escape.

Animal Hoarding

A special form of severe neglect is animal hoarding, the keeping of large numbers of animals in extreme unsanitary conditions, has received increasing attention from the veterinary, animal protection, law enforcement and mental health communities (Arluke & Patronek, 2013; Berry, Patronek, & Lockwood, 2005; Frost, 2000; Frost, Patronek, & Rosenfield, 2011; Patronek, 1999), potentially affecting hundreds of thousands of animals each year. Veterinary forensics can play an important role in describing the effects of such treatment on the animals involved. This analysis can play an important part in supporting legal actions (i.e., prosecution for animal cruelty) or documenting the need for social service and/or mental health intervention for the people responsible.

Animal hoarding cases can differ from other neglect cases in several ways that necessitate special veterinary forensic considerations. By definition, hoarding cases involve large numbers of animals, often several hundred. Although such cases primarily involve dogs and/or cats, a wide variety of domestic and wild species have been encountered in such cases, necessitating special veterinary knowledge and attention to concerns about potential zoonotic diseases. Hoarders usually lack insight to the severity of problems many of their animals may have developed—or they may have employed their own ineffective remedies to treat serious illnesses. Attending veterinarians should be alert to the need to document ailments that have been untreated or improperly treated.

Hoarders may have animal acquired at different times or have special "companions" within the population. The presence of healthy animals amidst many sick ones should be noted since it helps convey the fact that the person involved knew how to care for animals but *intentionally* chose to deny care to some.

In addition to the conventional documentation needed in neglect cases, veterinarians examining victims of hoarding should also be aware of and document conditions common in hoarding. Animals that spend time in environments with large accumulations of urine and feces commonly show urine scalds on extremities and may show general bleaching of the fur. High levels of ammonia can create or exacerbate upper respiratory ailments. Competition for food can result in cannibalization of other animals, particularly newborn or stillborn animals. Evidence of such problems should be collected and documented.

Intentional Abuse

Cases of intentional abuse are among the most important cruelty cases to require the careful attention of a veterinarian for several reasons. First, such cases usually have the potential for the most serious criminal penalties, often at the felony level, thus defendants in such cases usually seek strong legal defense. In addition, intentional abuse is a form of cruelty most strongly associated with the potential for interpersonal violence, particularly domestic violence and child abuse. Third, such cases are often of high public and media concern and the responsiveness and effectiveness of law enforcement, animal care and control and veterinary professionals involved in the case will be closely scrutinized.

Intentional or "non-accidental" injuries (NAIs) include a variety of presentations described below. Munro (1996, 1998) and Arkow et al. (2011) describe some general principles that should raise the "index of suspicion" that an injury or ailment may be the result of intentional actions or willful neglect of needed treatment. Such indicators include:

- *The client presents an inconsistent history (the story doesn't fit the injuries);*
- *The client presents a discrepant history (the history changes). The client may offer different histories to various staff members, or various family members may present different histories;*
- *Types of injuries. Some of the more common physical injuries that might raise an index of suspicion include old injuries evident on examination, ultrasound or x-ray. Rib injuries (fractures) in particular should raise suspicion;*
- *A history of repetitive injury; and/or*
- *A history of unexplained injuries or deaths in other animals in the household.*

A given case may involve more than one form of injury. We will briefly review some of the specific forensic concerns associated with common forms of NAI.

Blunt Force Trauma

Blunt force trauma can be the result of falls, being hit by a vehicle, or other accidental injuries. However, such injuries from direct beatings, being thrown against a wall or floor, or stomping or crushing are frequently seen in association with interpersonal violence where harm or threats of harm to a pet are part of the dynamic of the exercise of power and control by an abuser (Ascione, 2008a; Gupta, 2008). Animal victims of blunt force trauma should undergo full-body radiographs in order to possibly identify fractures at multiple stages of healing. Certain patterns of injuries may raise additional suspicions, such as injuries that might reflect the dimensions of the instrument used to inflict injury (e.g., boot tip, hammer, rod). In the case of live animals, bruising may not be apparent even if a wound area is shaved to reveal the skin. In the case of deceased animals, the extent and pattern of blunt force trauma may not be revealed until the skin is reflected to show damage to the underlying tissues.

Sharp Force Trauma

Sharp force injuries include incised, stab and chop wounds from knives, axes, or other implements. Bite wounds are unique and tend to be a combination of both blunt and sharp force trauma. (Ressel et al., 2016). In addition to standard information collected in all suspected cruelty cases, the forensic veterinary examination of sharp force trauma should include description of the anatomical location of the injury, the shape and depth of the wound and description of the tissue characteristics and underlying structure. In some cases, it may be possible to match these wound characteristics to the type of instrument that may have been used.

One of the most common cases presented for forensic analysis is the mutilation of small animals, usually cats, where it is suspected that the injuries were inflicted by a person. In the majority of cases, such injuries are ultimately attributed to the actions of predators (dogs, coyotes, foxes) whose bites can produce clean injuries that may appear to, untrained observers, have been caused by a knife. Several characteristics help identify such trauma as having been caused by predation. First, wound edges are usually not as smooth as described, skin has often been torn rather than cut. Second, hairs around the wound show no signs of clean cuts. When blades are used to inflict injury, a portion of the overlying hair is usually cleanly cut. Finally, predator-related deaths usually show signs of bite wounds with associated saliva, which may be revealed by use of alternate light sources and which can be swabbed for DNA that can reveal the species of animal involved or even the specific individual, if reference samples are available. This approach was successful in correctly establishing that foxes, coyotes, and other predators were responsible for a number of cat mutilations in Canada (Nation, 2019) and the United Kingdom (Hull et al., 2021) that had raised widespread concerns about the possibility that they were the acts of a deranged human. In blunt or sharp force trauma cases where there is a human suspect, it is possible that the animal victim may have scratched or bitten the suspect while being restrained or attacked and may have some DNA evidence from the suspect, particularly embedded in claws. The veterinarian should coordinate with other investigators to see if efforts should be made to gather such evidence.

Projectile Injuries

Veterinary forensic analysis of animals that have received projectile injuries from bullets, pellets, BBs, arrows, darts, or other projectiles should include full body radiographs. In some cases, not all injuries will be externally visible, or the animal may have received repeated injuries over time. Any projectiles recovered from the animal should be carefully handled to avoid disturbing other potential evidence such as fingerprints, DNA, or other markings. Efforts should be made to distinguish between entry and exit wounds, path through the body. In the case of deceased victims, the veterinarian may be asked to provide opinions regarding the time between injury and death, the sequence of injuries, and the overall "humaneness" of the killing (Sinclair et al., 2006).

Strangulation

Strangulation and hanging are not uncommon animal cruelty presentations and, like blunt force trauma, are frequently associated with intimate partner violence. In addition to a complete forensic necropsy, careful attention should be paid to any external items or lesions possibly created by such an item used to bind, tie, or hang the animal. Ligatures often contain traces of DNA from a suspect and tape used to bind an animal may have both DNA and fingerprint evidence. All such evidence should be carefully handled, packaged, and turned over to law enforcement for potential processing and analysis. In cases of hanging, one goal of the investigation may be to determine whether the hanging was a direct cause of death or occurred post-mortem following an unrelated cause (e.g., hit by car) or intentional killing by some other means followed by display of the animal to frighten or intimidate a person.

Drowning

Diagnosis of drowning as a cause of death is difficult. It is often a diagnosis by exclusion—no other cause of death is evident and other circumstances support an interpretation of drowning. As with blunt and sharp force trauma, there may be other evidence associated with restraint and struggle and possible injuries to the perpetrator.

Burning

Burns to animals may take the form of thermal injuries (scalding or direct heat/fire) or chemical burns from caustic substances such as lye. As with other forms of injuries, serious burns may be accidental or intentional. Careful documentation of the nature of the injuries (location, pattern, depth) may help distinguish between intentional harm (e.g., pouring or throwing hot or toxic liquid on animal) versus spills. Cases in which animals have been deliberately set on fire are particularly significant given the close connection between firesetting, animal cruelty, and a high risk of perpetrating interpersonal violence (Becker et al., 2004; Heath, Hardesty, & Goldfine, 1984). The pattern of injuries should be carefully documented and photographed. In the case of chemical burns, injury sites should be swabbed to collect samples for further analysis. If an accelerant (e.g., gasoline, kerosene, lighter fluid) were used in connection with burning of an animal, samples should be collected of fur and any other material contaminated by the accelerant. These samples should be stored in an airtight metal container for later analysis. Veterinary testimony regarding the pain and suffering associated with burn injuries could be particularly important at trial.

Poisoning

The ASPCA's National Animal Poison Control Center handles nearly 200,000 calls per year. Intentional exposures comprise less than 1% of all exposures of animals to potentially toxic agents, and malicious poisonings account for less than 0.5% of all poisonings reported (Hansen et al., 2001). Most cases involve ingestion of human prescription drugs or exposure to household pesticides, fertilizers, or other chemicals. When the Center is called to consult on a case, the following information is considered essential for diagnosis (Miller & Zawistowski, 2005):

- *A thorough, detailed history including the presence of any toxins or poisonous plants in the immediate or surrounding environment;*
- *The use of any pesticides, fertilizers or chemicals by the owner, neighbors or local authorities;*
- *A list of both veterinary and human medications that the animal may have had access to or been given, such as Tylenol, in case the poisoning was accidental; and*
- *A history of the animal's diet, including snacks, in case a nutritional deficiency has been confused with a poisoning.*

In suspected cruelty cases, the veterinarian may be asked to:

- *Identify the toxin and possible route of delivery based on medical symptoms;*

- *Estimate the time of exposure based on the progression of symptoms;*
- *Help identify possible evidence based on items in stomach contents or vomitus;*
- *Help exclude possible natural or accidental exposures such as snake or insect bites, toxic plants; and*
- *Provide testimony as to amount of pain and suffering induced by any intentional exposure to toxins.*

Domestic animals can ingest many potentially harmful things, voluntarily or through human maliciousness. The veterinarian can play a key role in trying to provide an accurate account of what an animal was exposed to, what consequences it caused, and how it may have been prevented.

Organized Abuse

Many veterinary forensic investigations focus on animal victims of organized abuse, most commonly in the form of the illegal "blood sports" of dogfighting and cockfighting. Detailed discussion of the role of veterinarians in these investigations is provided elsewhere (Lockwood, 2011; 2013, Touroo & Reisman, 2018). Such investigations usually involve documenting the separate crimes of animal cruelty and animal fighting. Since animal fighting punishments can carry federal and state felony penalties, these charges may take precedence over general animal cruelty charges.

Dogfighting prosecutions are usually based on the preponderance of circumstantial evidence such as the presence of dogfighting paraphernalia and training equipment as well as medical supplies specific to the training and treatment of fighting dogs. Another key form of evidence is the documentation of injuries found in the animals that have been seized. The pattern of injuries on the animals' bodies as well as the presence of wounds in various stages of healing can be strongly indicative of a history of fighting rather than the result of a single "yard accident" fight between two dogs (Intarapanich et al., 2017; Miller et al., 2016). In addition, veterinarians should note other medical conditions consistent with dogfighting such as unprofessional wound closures (suture or staples). These actions may result in additional charges of cruelty or unlicensed practice of veterinary medicine. Veterinarians should familiarize themselves with the range of drugs and supplements commonly encountered in dogfight and cockfight operations and be prepared to discuss how they may be used and which are restricted or otherwise regulated.

Ritualized Abuse

Veterinarians may be asked to examine deceased animals that have allegedly been used in ritualistic sacrifice. Such cases are rare and but involve cats or small animals killed by "self-styled" occult practitioners or other animals associated with the practice of certain forms of "cultural spiritualism" such as Santeria, Palo Mayombe, or Voodoo (Sinclair et al., 2006). In many cases, animals or animal parts have been discovered in public places. As noted above, an important first step in such investigations is to consider the possibility that the remains are the results of predator activity. If there is clear evidence of human involvement, care should be taken to preserve any evidence that might be found in association with the animal. Certain rituals involve placing coins or notes on or in the animal and, in some cases, potentially toxic substances such as mercury may have been involved.

It is often assumed that animal sacrifice cannot be prosecuted as animal cruelty since it is protected by First Amendment religious freedoms. However, such protection does not offer a defense from charges of animal cruelty (Perdue & Lockwood, 2013). The role of the veterinarian in such cases may be to comment on the speed and humaneness of the manner of killing involved—particularly in the case of larger mammals such as sheep or goats. Many animal sacrifice rituals involve chickens or doves. In such cases, veterinarians may also be asked to comment on the humaneness of the method of killing or on possible risks to other livestock posed by avian diseases in unregulated populations kept or sold for sacrifice.

Animal Sexual Abuse

"Animal sexual abuse" is the term more accurately used to describe what had earlier been referred to in laws as "bestiality." This represents a rethinking of both the underlying motivations and impact on the animal victim. Beirne (1997) makes this argument very clearly, noting that sexual abuse of animals parallels that of sexual abuse of women and children and is also problematic because (1) human-animal sexual contact is almost always coercive, (2) such practice often causes pain or death for the animal, and (3) animals are unable to consent or to communicate about their abuse. Likewise, Ascione (1993) notes that bestiality may be considered cruel even in cases when physical harm to an animal does not occur, drawing a parallel to cases of adult sexual activity with a child where consent is presumed to be impossible. As with other forms of animal cruelty, there has been increased attention to animal sexual abuse in part because of evidence of connections to the potential for interpersonal violence (Beetz, 2005; Fleming et al., 2002; Hensley et al., 2010). This has increased the likelihood that suspected cases of animal sexual assault will be reported and prosecuted.

With few exceptions, veterinarians have been slow to recognize occurrences of animal sexual abuse and receive little or no training on how to address such cases (Munro, 2006; Munro & Thrusfield, 2001c). Detailed discussion of appropriate veterinary examination of animal victims of sexual assault is provided elsewhere (Bradley & Rasile, 2014; Merck, 2013, Sinclair et al., 2006; Stern & Smith-Blackmore, 2016). Evidence of any form of injury should be noted, particularly traumatic injury to the anus, rectum, or vulvar/vaginal area. This should include inspection of the entire animal with a UV light source, such as a Woods lamp, which may cause semen stains to fluoresce. In addition, if there is any evidence to suggest that there has been sexual contact between the animal and the abuser or with a human victim of the abuser, care should be taken to collect human or animal semen, seminal fluid, vaginal fluids, epithelial cells, pubic hairs, and any other existing evidence. A standard human Sexual Assault Evidence Kit (often referred to as a "rape kit") can be useful in processing evidence from animal victims as well. It is possible that the animal bit or scratched the perpetrator. The teeth, gums, and lips should be swabbed for possible DNA testing and scrapings of the nails saved. As with other forms of abuse that may involve violent restraint, full body radiographs should be taken to document possible underlying injuries, such as those that might be produced in restraining the animal victim. Animal sexual abuse is rarely prosecuted in the absence of harm to the animal, so detailed veterinary testimony can be essential to moving such cases forward.

The Veterinary Professional in Court

One of the most import roles for a veterinarian is to testify in court to help tell the story of an animal that may have suffered or died. This is a role that few veterinarians receive any formal training in as part of their veterinary education. As a result, they may be hesitant to become involved. Veterinarians are the logical and natural advocates for animals in society. However, in a court of law, the veterinarian's duty is to the court. The lawyer is the advocate for the animal, while veterinarians are the advocate for the truth, which should be their opinion. It can place them in an unfamiliar adversarial relationship with the opposition, one which can call their competence and training into question as a common defense tactic. However, good preparation and communication with retaining counsel can make the process easier. Veterinarians also benefit from the fact that they are among the most trusted of all professionals and are almost universally admired by jurors; thus, their testimony is given great weight and opposing counsel attempts to undermine their efforts can easily backfire.

It is important to remember that the responsibility to "prove" a case does not lie on the veterinarian. It is the duty of the prosecutor to prove a case of animal cruelty. The veterinarian's role is part of a multidisciplinary approach in which veterinary evidence is only part of the case. Additionally, it is not for the veterinarian to decide if neglect or cruelty have occurred, rather the veterinarian assists those involved in the legal process in understanding the medical facts of the particular case by rendering a medical opinion. Ultimately, the judge or jury is the trier of fact and decide guilt or innocence.

Veterinary Forensics and the Response to Common Defenses

As the potential for serious consequences for conviction for animal cruelty has increased, defense attorneys have increased their efforts to vigorously challenge the prosecution of these cases and raise some measure of doubt about their client's guilt. Often veterinary forensic evidence serves as one of the most significant factors in overcoming such challenges. Good animal cruelty case preparation requires anticipating possible defenses even if they seem illogical, inconsistent, or far-fetched. Phillips and Lockwood (2013) review some of the most common defenses.

The animal had an accident.

The defendant may claim the animal was hit by a car, fell off of a high level (bookshelf, stairs, etc.) and broke its leg, or inadvertently got into some poison. As noted earlier, there is information to aid veterinarians and others to distinguish between accidental and non-accidental injury, with well-established guidelines on situations that should raise suspicions of abuse (Phillips & Lockwood, 2013).

Someone else did it!

Forensic evidence specifically linking the defendant or his/her property (e.g., tools or weapons) or residence to the animal victim (e.g., fur, blood, feces, DNA) can help counter this defense. In general, DNA samples should be collected and stored from most animal victims for potential future reference to other evidence (Phillips & Lockwood, 2013).

It was a "mercy killing."

This defense is common in states where the law allows the "humane" killing of one's own animals. In some states, the killing must also be "justified" (e.g., animal was sick, aged, or had attacked someone). However, the methods used (e.g., drowning, blunt force trauma, multiple gunshot, poisoning, suffocation) may fall outside of the definition of a given state statute and the euthanasia guidelines of the American Veterinary Medical Association (AVMA, 2020), and thus can be challenged as being an inhumane killing, particularly if there is veterinary or other evidence that the animal was not killed quickly and painlessly. It should not be assumed that a practice that has been tolerated in the past (e.g., drowning unwanted young animals) meets contemporary societal and veterinary standards for humane killing (Phillips & Lockwood, 2013).

It was self-defense.

This is sometimes seen in cases involving the killing of an animal that allegedly was involved in an attack. In some cases, the age, size and temperament of the animal may contradict this defense (as in the killing of a small cat by a large person). In a shooting situation, veterinarians may be asked to review forensic or ballistics evidence of where the animal was shot to demonstrate whether the animal was acting aggressively or retreating. If the defendant went back into his/her home to retrieve a gun, then that evidence will work against this defense (Phillips & Lockwood, 2013).

The animal is a "picky eater."

This defense may be offered to explain the poor body condition of animals involved. It is important for a veterinary exam to rule out medical problems that might result in failure to maintain weight. The feeding habits of the animal after being seized should be documented closely. Humane agencies often make a video recording of the first time a seized animal is offered food or water to document its response. In addition, data from weekly weighing that show a consistent weight gain with proper access to food can defeat such claims (Phillips & Lockwood, 2013).

The animal was recently rescued and was received in bad condition.

Refuting this defense may require other evidence regarding how long an animal has been in the defendant's care. Evidence that an animal has been at the facility for some time may include testimony from concerned staff or volunteers, testimony from individuals or organizations who may have originally surrendered the animal, or physical evidence such as the accumulation of feces in an unclean cage (Phillips & Lockwood, 2013).

The defendant claims to be an animal hospice provider and says animals are dying from other causes.

Some rescue hoarders will claim that the animals in their care were already diagnosed with a fatal disease and they simply allowed the animals to live out their lives in their care. The difference between a hoarder and a true hospice caregiver is that the hospice caregiver does not deny veterinary care or food, and they provide a clean and safe environment for the animal. For the animals, it is important to obtain prior documentation of the claimed "fatal" disease. If no documentation can be provided, an examination of the surviving or deceased animal(s) may determine whether the animal(s) truly had a fatal disease (Phillips & Lockwood, 2013).

Trends in Veterinary Forensics

The growth of veterinary forensic sciences in addressing animal cruelty is not simply a fad building on popular interest in forensics and "CSI-type" stories. It has become an essential tool in the investigation and prosecution of an increasing number of cases. McEwen (2012) reviewed 1,706 medicolegal cases submitted to the Animal Health Laboratory of the University of Guelph, Ontario, Canada between 1998 and 2010. Criminal cases are the only medicolegal case category that consistently increased over the 12-year period. Based on pathology reports for the 271 criminal cases, 117 (43.1%) were consistent with neglect, 79 (29.2%) were compatible with non-accidental injury (NAI), including two cases of sexual abuse, 13 (4.80%) were poisoning, 29 (10.7%) were deemed to be due to natural disease, and 31 (11.43%) were inconclusive. Of the 79 cases of NAI, the majority (52%) were solely blunt force trauma, which on occasion was accompanied by sharp force injury, gunshot, or asphyxia. A survey of 200 prosecuting attorneys reported that veterinary forensic evidence, including forensic necropsies and detailed medical reports, was viewed as an important factor by a majority of prosecutors in deciding whether to accept a case for prosecution and in achieving a successful outcome, but a need for additional training for investigators was indicated (Lockwood et al., 2019).

The field has also seen the growth of specialty animal forensic laboratories including the ASPCA Veterinary Forensic Science Center in Gainesville, Florida, the Veterinary Genetics Laboratory at the University of California, Davis and major expansion of the Fish and Wildlife Service's Forensic Laboratory in Ashland, Oregon. Most of the efforts of this laboratory involve identifying species that may be the victim of illegal hunting or trafficking and assisting in legal cases involving wildlife by determining the cause of death and assessing factors that contribute to an environment that may be unhealthy or lethal to protected species (Stroud, 1998). As with veterinary forensics in general, the field of wildlife forensics has seen a recent growth in textbooks devoted to the subject (Brooks, 2018; Cooper & Cooper, 2013; Huffman & Wallace, 2011; Linacre & Tobe, 2013).

International attention to the importance of veterinary forensics has also seen growth in the last decade. In June 0f 2021 the 1st International Virtual Meeting of Forensic Animal Sciences, conducted in Spanish, Portuguese, and English, featured over 100 participants and speakers from countries including Spain, Colombia, Argentina, Mexico, Brazil, Portugal, Chile, Turkey, Albania, Kenya, Zambia, Croatia, and Taiwan, as well as the U.S. and U.K. The conference's overall theme was to achieve "better science for better justice" in addressing veterinary forensics investigations of companion and domesticated animal and wildlife.

Several new international studies have described the importance of veterinary forensic sciences in the investigation and prosecution of animal cruelty. Salvagni et al. (2016) describes the necropsy and toxicological findings in the investigation of the killing of 37 dogs and cats by a single person, which resulted in the first conviction for animal cruelty in Brazil. Araujo et al. (2021) describe a study at the Portuguese national pathology laboratory for agrarian and veterinary investigations characterized deaths of dogs and cats by blunt-force trauma, firearms, poisoning, and asphyxiation. Rebollada-Merino et al. (2020) detail forensic cases of dog and cat abuse in Spain and emphasize that veterinarians who can accurately recognize signs of animal abuse may be able to better respond to cases of companion animal cruelty, which in turn, may prevent possible escalation to interpersonal violence. Geraldo and Arias (2020) detail the advances of veterinary forensic science in Chile.

Future Needs

There have been significant improvements in the recognition, reporting, prosecution, and prevention of animal cruelty and neglect in the last decade, and the involvement of veterinarians and forensic scientists has helped produce and sustain these changes. Future progress will benefit from additional advances in various ways.

Improved Tracking of Animal Cruelty Cases

Animal cruelty is defined differently in every state and the responsibility for responding to cruelty is often delegated to a variety of different agencies and organizations, including police, sheriff's departments, health departments, animal care and control, humane societies, and SPCAs. This has made the accurate tabulation of such crimes extremely difficult since no centralized reporting mechanism exists. This in turn hampers attempts to assess the effectiveness of responses to these crimes.

On January 1, 2016, the Federal Bureau of Investigation (FBI) began collecting data on crimes involving animal cruelty from law enforcement agencies that participate in the National Incident-Based Reporting System (NIBRS) in the United States. Data is grouped into four categories of animal crimes: simple/gross neglect; intentional abuse and torture; organized abuse; and animal sexual abuse. Definitions of these crimes would include torturing, tormenting, mutilating, maiming, poisoning, abandoning, and failing to provide shelter, food, water, and veterinary care. Transporting or confining an animal in a manner likely to cause injury or death, causing animals to fight with one another, and inflicting repeated or excessive pain and suffering would also be included. Analysis of the first four years of data from NIBRS (Palais, 2021) identify obstacles remain in implementing these changes, as each state has its own laws and definitions and many states do not participate in the system. However, it is significant that the U.S. Department of Justice now recognizes cruelty to animals as a matter worthy of law enforcement concern. Hopefully, this will inspire state and local law enforcement agencies to initiate better tracking systems for animal cruelty, neglect, and fighting in order to provide valuable information to assist communities in allocating animal care and control resources and training.

Incorporation of Animal Cruelty Reporting and Veterinary Forensics into Veterinary Curricula

As noted above, the University of Florida, Florida International University and the University of New Haven currently have or are developing degree or certificate programs in veterinary forensic sciences. In addition, several schools currently offer electives in the subject or incorporate coverage of the field into shelter medicine programs. It is hoped that this trend will follow that seen with the addition of animal law courses to over 160 law schools in the last decade (Animal Legal Defense Fund, n.d.).

Establish Guidelines and Policies for Reporting Suspected Animal Abuse by Staff in Veterinary Clinics

The 2021 ASPCA survey of veterinary professionals found that 72% of veterinarians and 87% of vet techs/assistants had received no training on the recognition and reporting of animal cruelty. Lack of training or lack of institutional/practice policies on reporting suspected cruelty is a major obstacle to effective veterinary response to the problem. The National Link Coalition (nationallinkcoalition.org) has compiled a collection of known veterinary hospital policies and procedures for reporting suspected animal abuse currently including policies from The Ohio State University Veterinary Medical Center, North Carolina State University Veterinary Health Complex, Colorado State University College of Veterinary Medicine, Veterinary Hospital of the University of Pennsylvania and Animalia Health & Wellness in Franklin, Tennessee.

Incorporation of Animal Cruelty Investigation into the Core of Law Enforcement Training

Growing recognition of the connection between animal cruelty and other serious crimes has attracted the attention of many law enforcement agencies, but inclusion of training on animal cruelty laws, cruelty investigations and the capabilities of veterinary forensic sciences into police academies or state-mandated Police Officer Standards and Training (POST) is still in its infancy. In the past, law enforcement response to intimate partner violence was similarly dependent upon the level of concern about the issue shown by local law enforcement leadership, but societal pressures have resulted in it becoming a core part of all contemporary police training and response. In mid-2013 the ASPCA entered into a four-month pilot partnership with the New York Police Department (NYPD) in the Bronx, NY. The agreement for this partnership identified the responsibilities of the two agencies. The NYPD would:

- *Create an Animal Cruelty Squad of specially trained officers to serve as the primary contact for animal cruelty cases*
- *Provide rapid response to animal cruelty calls to emergency (911) and non-emergency (311) police lines*
- *Use its resources, including forensic teams, to investigate and document animal crimes as needed*
- *Participate in community outreach efforts to encourage the public to report crimes against animals*
- *Provide criminal case data to the ASPCA for analysis of animal-related crimes*

The ASPCA would:

- *Provide animal cruelty response training to all officers and managers*
- *Provide for immediate care of all animals brought by NYPD*
- *Conduct veterinary forensic exams and prepare reports on animals involved in cases where charges might be filed*
- *Provide long-term housing, care, treatment and placement of animals*
- *Work with prosecutors and police to provide legal expertise and assistance for cruelty case management*
- *Assist in public information and awareness campaigns and events*

The pilot project proved to be successful and popular with NYPD officers and leadership and was expanded to the entire NYPD in January of 2014 with the goal of eventually reaching all 34,000 officers of the nation's largest police force. In the first two years of operation, arrests for animal cruelty crimes rose 18% and the number of animals rescued from harm by NYPD rose 58%, to over 1,000 (Lawrence, 2019; Lockwood, 2022). Although most smaller and rural agencies do not have the resources of agencies the size of the ASPCA and the NYPD, it is hoped that many of the elements of this partnership, including the involvement of forensically trained veterinarians, will be transferable to many law enforcement and animal care and control agencies.

Society's response to animal abuse and neglect has become truly interdisciplinary, as evidenced by the diversity of professional viewpoints represented in this volume. It is exciting to add the field of forensic sciences and the specialized discipline of veterinary forensic medicine to the broad base of expertise united in efforts to address violence and cruelty in all its forms.

References

Alleyne, E., Sienauskaite, O., & Ford, J. (2019). To report, or not to report, animal abuse: The role of perceived self-efficacy in veterinarians' decision-making. *The Veterinary Record, 185,* 538.

Allison, M., Satterwhite, C., Ramaswamy, M., Hynek, M.T., & Agnew-Svoboda, Z. (2017). Strategies veterinary practices can use to address the problem of intimate partner violence. *Journal of the American Veterinary Medical Association, 250*(1), 42–45.

American Veterinary Medical Association. (2020). *AVMA guidelines for the euthanasia of animals.* American Veterinary Medical Association.

American Veterinary Medical Association. (2015). Abuse Reporting Requirements by State. Retrieved February 18, 2015, from https://www.avma.org/KB/Resources/Reference/AnimalWelfare/Pages/Abuse-Reporting-requirements-by-State.aspx.

Animal Legal Defense Fund. (n.d.). *Animal Law Courses.* Retrieved March 4, 2022, from http://aldf.org/article/animal-law-courses/.

Arkow, P. (1999). Initiating an animal abuse reporting policy at a veterinary teaching hospital. In F. R. Ascione & P. Arkow (Eds.), *Child abuse, domestic violence, and animal abuse: Linking the circles of compassion for prevention and intervention* (pp. 257–259). Purdue University Press.

Arkow, P., & Munro, H. (2008). The veterinary profession's roles in recognizing and preventing family violence: The experiences of the human medicine field and the development of diagnostic indicators of Non-Accidental Injury. In F. R. Ascione (Ed.), *International handbook of animal abuse and cruelty: Theory, research, and application* (pp. 31–58). Purdue University Press.

Arkow, P., Boyden, P., & Patterson-Kane, E. (2011). *Practical guidance for the effective response by veterinarians to suspected animal cruelty, abuse and neglect.* American Veterinary Medical Association.

Arluke, A., & Patronek, G. (2013). Animal hoarding. In, M. P. Brewster & C. L. Reyes, (Eds.), *Animal cruelty: A multidisciplinary approach to understanding* (pp. 197–214). Carolina Academic Press.

Ascione, F. R. (1993). Children who are cruel to animals: A review of research and implications for developmental psychology. *Anthrozoös, 6*: 226–247.

Ascione, F. R. (Ed.). (2008). *International handbook of animal abuse and cruelty: Theory, research, and application.* West Lafayette, IN: Purdue University Press.

Ascione, F. R. (2008a). Animal/pet abuse. In C. Renzetti & J. Edleson (Eds.). *Encyclopedia of interpersonal violence.* Sage.

Ascione, F. R., & Lockwood, R. (2001). Cruelty to animals: Changing psychological, social, and legislative perspectives. In D. J. Salem & A. N. Rowan (Eds.). *The State of the Animals 2001* (pp. 39–54). Washington, DC: Humane Society of the U.S.

Bartelink, E.J., Clinkinbeard, S., Spessard, C., Kilmartin, A., & Spangler, W.L. (2021). Documenting non-accidental injury patterns in a dog abuse investigation: A collaborative approach between forensic anthropology and veterinary pathology. *Journal of Forensic Sciences,* 00:1-10. https://doi.org/10.1111/1556-4029.14948.

Becker, K., Stuewig, J., Herrera, V., & McCloskey, L. (2004). A study of firesetting and animal cruelty in children: Family influences and adolescent outcomes. *Journal of the American Academy of Child and Adolescent Psychiatry, 43*(7), 905–912.

Beetz, A. M. (2005). Bestiality and zoophilia: Associations with violence and sex offending. In, A.M. Beetz. & A.L. Podberscek (Eds.). *Bestiality and zoophilia: Sexual relations with animals* (pp. 46–70). Purdue University Press.

Berry, C., Patronek, G., & Lockwood, R. (2005). Long-term outcomes in animal hoarding cases. *Animal Law Review, 11,* 167–194.

Bradley N., & Rasile, K. (2014, April). Recognition and management of animal sexual abuse. *Clinician's Brief,* 73–75.

Brooks, J. W. (Ed.). (2018). *Veterinary forensic pathology, Volume 1.* Springer.

Bruchim, Y., Loeb, E. Saragust, J., & Aroch, I. (2009) Pathological findings in dogs with fatal heatstroke. *Journal of Comparative Pathology*, *140*, 97–104.

Byard, R. W., & Boardman, W. (2011). The potential role of forensic pathologists in veterinary forensic medicine. *Forensic Science, Medicine and Pathology*, *7*, 231–232.

Colorado Veterinary Medical Association (2007). *Mandatory Reporting of Cruelty to Animals and Animal Fighting.* Retrieved January 18, 2015 from www.colovma.org/resource/resmgr/imported/Animal%20Cruelty%20Issue%20Brief.pdf.

Cooper. J. E. (1998). What is forensic veterinary medicine? Its relevance to the modern exotic animal practice. *Journal of Exotic Pet Medicine*, *7*(4),161–165.

Cooper, J. E. & Cooper, M. (2007). *Introduction to veterinary and comparative forensic medicine.* Wiley-Blackwell.

Cooper, J. E. & Cooper, M. (2013). *Wildlife forensic investigation: Principles and practice.* Wiley-Blackwell.

Cornell University College of Veterinary Medicine. (2015). History and archives. Retrieved February 12, 2015 from http://vet.cornell.edu/about/history.cfm.

Davis G. J., & McDonough S. P. (2018). Writing the necropsy report. In J. W. Brooks (Ed.). *In Veterinary Forensic Pathology, Volume 2* (139–149). Springer.

Drobatz, K. J., & Macintire, D. K. (1996). Heat-induced illness in dogs: 42 cases (1976–1993). *Journal of the American Veterinary Medical Association, 209*,1894–1899.

Endenburg, N., Takashima, G., van Lith, H. A., Bacon, H., Hazel, S. J., Jouppi, R., Lee, N. Y. P. … & Ryan, S. (2021). Animal welfare worldwide, the opinion of practicing veterinarians. *Journal of Applied Welfare Science, 24*(3), 215–237.

Fleming, W. M., Jory, B., & Burton, D.L. (2002). Characteristics of juvenile offenders admitting to sexual activity with nonhuman animals. *Society & Animals, 10*(1), 31–45.

Frost, R. (2000). People who hoard animals. *Psychiatric Times, 1*(4), 25–29.

Frost, R., Patronek, G., & Rosenfield, E. (2011). Comparison of object and animal hoarding. *Depression and Anxiety, 28*, 885–891.

Geraldo, E., & Arias, F. (2020). Veterinary forensic medicine in Chile: A professional examination. *Journal of Veterinary Forensic Science, 1*(2), 21–23.

Gerdin, J. A., & McDonough, S. P. (2013). Forensic pathology of companion animal abuse and neglect. *Veterinary Pathology Online, 50*(6), 994–1006.

Green, P. D. (1979). Protocols in medicolegal veterinary medicine I. Identification of cases and preparation for court. *Canadian Veterinary Journal, 20*, 8–12.

Green, P. D. (1980). Protocols in medicolegal veterinary medicine II. Cases involving death due to gunshot and arrow wounds. *Canadian Veterinary Journal, 21*, 343–346.

Gupta, M. (2008). Functional links between intimate partner violence and animal abuse: Personality features and representations of aggression. *Society & Animals, 16*(3), 223–242.

Hansen, S. R., Murphy, L. A., Khan, S. A., & Allen, C. (2001). An overview of malicious animal poisonings. *North American Congress of Clinical Toxicology.* October 4–9, 2001. Montreal, Quebec, Canada.

Heath, G. A., Hardesty, V. A., & Goldfine, P.E. (1984). Firesetting, enuresis, and animal cruelty. *Journal of Child and Adolescent Psychotherapy 1*, 97–100.

Hensley, C., Tallichet, S. E., & Dutkiewicz, E. L. (2010). Childhood bestiality: A potential precursor to adult interpersonal violence. *Journal of Interpersonal Violence, 25*(3), 557–567.

Huffman, J. E., & Wallace. J.R. (2011) *Wildlife forensics: Methods and applications.* Wiley-Blackwell.

Hull, K. D., Jeckel, S., Williams, J. M., Ciavaglia, S. A., Webster, L. M., Fitzgerald, E., Chang, Y. & Martineau, H. M. (2021). Fox (Vulpes vulpes) involvement identified in a series of cat carcass mutilations. *Veterinary Pathology (XX)*X, 1–11. http://doi/10.1177/03009858211052661.

Intarapanich N. P., Touroo R. M., Rozanski E. A, Reisman R. W., Intarapanich P. P., & McCobb E. C. (2017). Characterization and comparison of injuries caused by spontaneous versus organized dogfighting. *Journal of the American Veterinary Medical Association, 251*(12), 1424–1431.

International Association of Veterinary Forensic Sciences (2020). Standards Document for the Forensic Live Animal Examination. Available from ivfsa.org. Retrieved February 22, 2022.

Joo, S., Chun, M. S., & Jung, Y. (2019). Survey on the correlation between veterinarians' attitude and intention of intervention in animal abuse. In E. Vinnari & M. Vinnari (Eds.), *Sustainable governance and management of food systems: Ethical perspectives.* (pp. 343–346). Wageningen Academic Publishers.

Joo, S., Jung, Y., & Chun, M. S. (2020). An analysis of veterinary practitioners' intention to intervene in animal abuse cases in South Korea. *Animals, 10*(5), 802.

Landau, R. (1999). The veterinarian's role in recognizing and reporting abuse. In F. R. Ascione & P. Arkow (Eds.), *Child abuse, domestic violence, and animal abuse: Linking the circles of compassion for prevention and intervention* (pp. 241–249). Purdue University Press.

Lane, M. S., & Zawistowski, S. L. (2008). *Heritage of care: The American Society for the Prevention of Cruelty to Animals.* Praeger.

Larkin, M. (2018). When domestic violence arrives at the clinic door: How veterinary staff can respond to abused clients and patients. *Journal of the American Veterinary Medical Association, 253*(6), 656–660.

Lawrence, H. (2019). The ASPCA/NYPD partnership. *Sheriff & Deputy.* Special Issue, 16–17.

Linacre, A., & Tobe, S. (2013). *Wildlife DNA analysis: Applications in forensic science.* Wiley-Blackwell.

Linzey, A. (Ed.). (2009). *The link between animal abuse and human violence.* Sussex Academic Press.

Lockwood, R., & Ascione, F. (Eds.) (1998). *Animal cruelty and interpersonal violence: Readings in research and application.* Purdue University Press.

Lockwood, R. (2011). *Dogfighting toolkit for law enforcement: Addressing dogfighting in your community.* Community Oriented Policing Services, U.S. Department of Justice.

Lockwood, R. (2013). Animal fighting, in L. Miller & S. Zawistowski (Eds.). *Shelter medicine for veterinarians and staff (2nd ed.)* (pp. 441–452). Blackwell.

Lockwood, R. (2014). *Cruelty to animals and interpersonal violence: An update.* Training key #689. International Association of Chiefs of Police.

Lockwood, R. (2018). Animal hoarding: The challenge for mental health, law enforcement, and animal welfare professionals. *Behavioral Science and the Law,36*(6), 698–716.

Lockwood, R., Touroo, R., Olin, J. & Dolan, E. (2019). The influence of evidence of animal cruelty prosecution and case outcomes. *Journal of Forensic Sciences, 64*(6), 1687–1692. https://doi.org/10.1111/1556-4029.14085.

Lockwood, R. (2022). Bringing animal cruelty investigation into mainstream law-enforcement in the United States. in A. Linzey and C. Linzey (Eds.) *Animal Ethics and Animal Law.* (in press).

McEwen, B. J. (2012). Trends in domestic animal medico-legal pathology cases submitted to a veterinary diagnostic laboratory 1998–2010. Journal of Forensic Science, *57*(5), 1231–1233.

Merck, M. (2007). *Veterinary forensics: Animal cruelty investigations.* Wiley-Blackwell.

Merck, M. (2013). *Veterinary forensics: Animal cruelty investigations* (2nd ed.). Wiley-Blackwell.

Merz-Perez, L., & Heide, K. M. (2004). *Animal cruelty: Pathway to violence against people.* AltaMira Press.

Miller, K. A., Touroo, R. Spain, C. V., Jones, K., Reid, P. & Lockwood, R. (2016). Relationship between scarring and dog aggression in pit bull-type dogs involved in organized dogfighting. *Animals, 6*(11), 72–86; doi:10.3390/ani6110072.

Miller, L. (2006). *The recognition and documentation of animal abuse.* Oregon Veterinary Medical Association.

Miller, L., & Zawistowski, S. (2005). A call for veterinary forensics: The preparation and interpretation of physical evidence for cruelty investigation and prosecution. In P. Olson (Ed.), *Recognizing and reporting animal abuse: A veterinarian's guide* (pp. 63–67). American Humane Association.

Miller, L., & Zawistowski, S. (Eds.) (2013): *Shelter medicine for veterinarians and staff.* (2nd ed.). Wiley-Blackwell.

Munro, H. M. C. (1996). Battered pets. *Irish Veterinary Journal, 49,* 712–713.

Munro, H. M. C. (2006). Animal sexual abuse: A veterinary taboo? *The Veterinary Journal, 172*(2), 195–197.

Munro, H. M. C., & Thrusfield, M. V. (2001a). 'Battered pets': Features that raise suspicion of non-accidental injury. *Journal of Small Animal Practice, 42,* 218–226.

Munro, H. M. C., & Thrusfield, M. V. (2001b). 'Battered pets': Non-accidental physical injuries found in dogs and cats. *Journal of Small Animal Practice, 42,* 279–290.

Munro, H. M. C., & Thrusfield, M. V. (2001c). 'Battered pets': Sexual abuse. *Journal of Small Animal Practice, 42,* 333–337.

Munro, H. M. C., & Thrusfield, M. V. (2001d). 'Battered pets': Munchausen Syndrome by Proxy (factitious illness by proxy). *Journal of Small Animal Practice, 42,* 385–389.

Munro, R., & Munro, H. M. C. (2008). *Animal abuse and unlawful killing: Forensic veterinary pathology.* Elsevier/Saunders.

Nation, P. N., & St. Clair, C. C. (2019). A forensic pathology investigation of dismembered domestic cats: coyotes or cults?. *Veterinary Pathology, 56*(3), 444–451.

Newland, X., Boller, M., & Boller, E. (2019, March). Considering the relationship between domestic violence and pet abuse and its significance in the veterinary clinical and educational contexts. *New Zealand Veterinary Journal, 67*(2), 55–65.

Palais, J. M. (2021). Using the National Incident-Based Reporting System (NIBRS) to study animal cruelty: Preliminary results (2016–2019). *Social Sciences, 10*(10), 378. https://doi.org/10.3390/socsci10100378.

Patterson-Kane E. G, Kogan L. R, Gupta M. E, Touroo R., Niestat L.N, & Kennedy-Benson A. (2022). Animal cruelty recognition and response: A survey of veterinary professionals in the United States (in preparation).

Patronek, G. (1999). Hoarding of animals: An under-recognized public health problem in a difficult to study population. *Public Health Reports, 114*, 82–87.

Perdue, A., & Lockwood, R. (2014). *Animal cruelty and freedom of speech: When worlds collide. U.S. v. Stevens and other challenges on public policy and animal protection.* W. Lafayette, IN: Purdue University Press.

Phillips, A., & Lockwood, R. (2013). *Investigating & prosecuting animal abuse: A guidebook on safer communities, safer families & being an effective voice for animal victims.* Alexandria, VA: National District Attorneys Association.

Pickles, S. (2020). Pets at home? Considering animal forensics in the domestic setting. *UK Journal of Animal Law, 4*(1), 37–41.

Rebollada-Merino, A., Bárcena, C., Mayoral-Alegre, F.J., García-Real, I., & Domínguez, L., et al. (2020, Sept. 24). Forensic cases of suspected dog and cat abuse in the Community of Madrid (Spain), 2014–2019. *Forensic Science International, 316,* 1–10. https://doi.org/10.1016/j.forsciint.2020.110522.

Ressel, L., Hetzel, U., & Ricci, E. (2016). Blunt force trauma in veterinary forensic pathology. *Veterinary Pathology. 53*(5), 941–961.

Robertson, I. (2009). A legal duty to report suspected animal abuse—Are veterinarians ready? In A. Linzey (Ed.), *The link between animal abuse and human violence* (pp. 263–272). Sussex Academic Press.

Salvagni, F. A., De Siqueira, A., Fukushima, A. R., Landi, M. F. de A., & Ponge-Ferreira, H., & Maiorka, P. C. (2016). Animal serial killing: The first criminal conviction for animal cruelty in Brazil. *Forensic Science International, 267,* e1–e5.

Sharma, B. R. (2003). Clinical forensic medicine—management of crime victims from trauma to trial. *Journal of Clinical Forensic Medicine. 10*(4), 267–273.

Sinclair, L., Merck, M., & Lockwood, R. (2006). *Forensic investigation of animal cruelty: A guide for veterinary and law enforcement professionals.* Washington, DC: Humane Society of the U.S.

Stern, A. W., & Smith-Blackmore, M. (2016). Veterinary forensic pathology of animal sexual abuse. *Veterinary Pathology, 53*(5), 1057–1066.

Stroud, R. K. 1998. Wildlife forensics and the veterinary practitioner. *Journal of Exotic Pet Medicine. 7*(4),182–192.

Touroo, R., Baucom, K., Kessler, M. & Smith-Blackmore, M. (2020). Minimum standards and best practices for the clinical veterinary forensic examination of the suspected abused animal. *Forensic Science International Reports, 2,* 1–6. https://doi.org/10.1016/j.fsir.2020.100150.

Touroo, R. & Fitch, A. (2016). Identification, collection, and preservation of veterinary forensic evidence: In scene and during the postmortem examination. *Veterinary Pathology, 53*(5), 880–887.

Touroo, R., & Reisman, R. (2018). Animal fighting. In *Veterinary Forensic Pathology, Volume* 2 (pp. 97–119). Springer.

Veterinary Council of New Zealand. (2013). *Guidance for veterinarians dealing with cases of suspected or actual animal abuse and family violence*. Retrieved from http://nationallinkcoalition.org.

Yoffe-Sharp, B. L., & Loar, L. M. (2009). The veterinarian's responsibility to recognize and report animal abuse. *Journal of the American Veterinary Medical Association, 234*(6), 732–737.

Chapter 7

The Human-Animal Bond

Bethanie A. Poe, Elizabeth B. Strand and Christina Risley-Curtiss

Introduction

> "I just don't want to be the bad guy no more ... I *don't* want to be the bad guy no more and the puppies showed me that I don't have to be. It is all right to be a person, it is all right to express myself, it is all right to want to help someone.
>
> —Michael Jenkins, Prison Inmate, Orange County Prison New York ("BBC NEWS|Americas|Prisoners raise puppies in jail," n.d.)

In the Puppies Behind Bars (PBB) program incarcerated inmates are given a chance for rehabilitation instead of simple "warehousing," through raising puppies to be service animals. The trained dogs end up serving the justice department through bomb detection, serving the needs of physically and mentally wounded veterans coming back from war, or serving the needs of people who are blind, deaf, or have other disabilities. In the program, puppies live with prisoners 24 hours a day, seven days a week. These prisoners are responsible for socializing these dogs to become good working companions for the human beings who need them (Cheakalos, 2004). Prison based animal programs (PAPs) are increasing and highlight how attention to the human-animal bond is being recognized and included in the field of criminal justice in practical ways (Furst, 2006).

The human-animal bond (HAB) is a broad concept, however, with the PBB program being just one example of the way people bond with animals. For many of us, animals are considered companions, best friends, and family members. Animals even meet human needs emotionally and socially by providing what is perceived as unconditional love, being part of daily activities and routines, and being a witness to and sharing important life experiences (Toray, 2004). Additionally, animals and people are connected through relationships with working animals such as service dogs, military dogs and horses, or barn cats, as well as through attention to wildlife like watching bird feeders in the yard or going to visit animals at the zoo. For many, relationships with animals go beyond the traditional pet-owner dynamic and are not always beneficial to the non-human animals involved. People are connected to animals as a food source, which may or may not be lethal for the animal depending on the food product in question, and sadly, the human-animal bond between a victim and their companion animal can put that animal in danger in homes where interpersonal violence or abuse is present.

The term "human-animal bond" began appearing internationally in the 1970s and 1980s (Hines, 2003). The American Veterinary Medical Association defines the HAB as "a mutually beneficial and dynamic relationship between people and animals that is influenced by the behaviors essential to the health and wellbeing of both (AVMA, n.d.)." Therefore, in recognition that not all connections between humans and animals are mutually beneficial, the HAB is considered to be one aspect of a broader continuum of "human animal relationships" or "human animal interactions", and is used to describe the positive, mutually beneficial connections between people and animals.

With attention to this breadth of the HAB, this chapter reviews four main areas: 1) theories that help explain how and why people bond with animals, 2) the different types of HABs that can occur, 3) what is known about cultural influences and animals, and 4) the criminal justice implications of the HAB.

Theories of the HAB

While there are many theories that explain aspects of the HAB we will briefly discuss the biophilia hypothesis, the anthropomorphic-chattel continuum, attachment theory, and social support theory. Also, given there are other chapters dedicated to the issue of theories of violence to animals in this volume, we will focus here more on the general theories that describe these relationships.

The Biophilia Hypothesis

"It should come as no great surprise to find that *Homo sapiens* at least still feels an innate preference for the natural environment that cradled us," (Wilson, 2001, p. 241) Developed by evolutionary biologist E. O. Wilson, the biophilia hypothesis posits that human beings are genetically predisposed to pay attention to nature. Hunting and locating food through paying attention to the natural world meant survivability to early humans (Beck & Katcher, 2003). This means that, from an evolutionary perspective, attending to the natural world was not simply a pleasurable activity, like walking in the park or enjoying the birds singing, but rather a habit that was directly related to one's ability to maintain life (Kellert & Wilson, 1993). Frumkin (2001) defines the domains within the biophilia hypothesis to be animals, plants, landscapes, and wilderness experiences. Given the fact that animals are a main focus point in people's experience of nature, this theory has been used to describe the HAB.

Gullone (2000) notes the biophilia hypothesis is exhibited in three main ways. From an animal-related human experience (ARHE) perspective, *adaptive approach behaviors* are when a situation is deemed to be safe and secure because animals in the environment are calm and engaging in normal behaviors. One example of this would be people bringing Emotional Support Animals (ESAs) with them for comfort on airplanes.

Seeing the animal looking calm and relaxed helps the person to feel safe while flying. This experience gives the message that one can "approach" a situation safely. *Avoidance behaviors,* alternatively, are when animals show signs of stress or are fleeing, giving the message that a situation is unsafe and must be avoided. For example, horses or cattle that are disturbed may alert a person that potential danger is near. Therefore, from an evolutionary perspective, paying attention to animals helps a humans make life and death decisions. Moreover, Gullone (2000) describes a third category of survival behaviors called *restoration and stress recovery*. This explains how the presence of animals can help a person overcome challenging circumstances, such as the benefits of service animals for war veterans or even birds for prison inmates (Furst, 2006). Even people suffering from dementia benefit from the presence of animals. Using a pre-test post-test design, Edwards, Beck, and Lim (2014) found that Alzheimer's patients in a nursing facility improved on scales of uncooperative, irrational, sleep, and inappropriate behaviors after the addition of a fish tank. When individuals are in environments lacking contact with nature, the biophilia hypothesis may suggest that absence of contact with the natural world thwarts appropriate development leading to problems with mental health, violence, and substance abuse (Besthorn, 2002; Frumkin, 2001; Gullone, 2000).

Barbiero and Berto (2021) suggest that biophilia should be seen as an evolutionary process, and that as the human world becomes more urbanized, there is a need to incorporate *biophilic design,* a way of creating artificial environments that appear as close to the natural world as possible to benefit people's health and well-being. Animals are not included in Barbiero and Berto's (2021) list of important features for biophilic design, but keeping animals as pets may be one way human beings seek to satisfy the need to have nature around on a consistent basis (Beck, 2014). However, because the scope of the biophilia theory is so broad, encompassing animals, plants, and the environment as well as all of the human genetic code, it does not easily lend itself to precisely researching and understanding the factors that underlie the HAB (Joye, 2011).

Anthropomorphic-Integrated-Chattel Orientation Continuum

Myrna Milani, DVM has written extensively on the HAB in veterinary medical practice (Milani, 1991;1995; 2011) and has identified a continuum of the way people themselves relate to animals. The continuum goes from an anthropomorphized view of animals to a view that considers animals as chattel.

In the anthropomorphized view, people see their animals as having human qualities. Milani acknowledges that, to a certain extent, we have no choice but to anthropomorphize animals because the only perspective we can ultimately take is our own—that of the human being. Anthropomorphizing animals has the benefit of allowing people to form deep emotional connections with animals and to express care and concern through that connection. However, there are limitations to this view as well such as when an animal is so anthropomorphized, they are no longer treated as animals, but as human beings, causing the animal's species specific needs to go unseen and unmet.

This may occur when instead of giving an animal prescribed medications the person gives his own medication because he feels it will work for his dog like it works for him. It can also manifest in a deep and unhealthy emotional dependency on an animal that prevents the animal from living a life natural to its species, such as in animal hoarding situations (Nathanson, 2009). This can also be true when a person uses an animal to get human attention. An extreme example is when a person intentionally harms an animal in order to get attention from the veterinarian as in Munchausen syndrome by proxy (Milani, 2006; Munro & Thrusfield, 2001).

On the other end of the continuum is the chattel orientation that is characterized by emotional detachment from an animal, seeing them more like machines to be utilized than as beings with whom one can emotionally connect. This may be the case in situations where animals serve a utilitarian purpose such as food animals or animals that are for show. In these relationships, the animal is utilized by people as tools for income, entertainment, and perhaps work. On the positive side of a chattel orientation is the willingness of the person who is responsible for decisions regarding the animal to accept scientific and health related recommendations without placing irrelevant or excessive emotional content into decision-making. Additionally, sometimes having a chattel orientation can be protective for the emotions of a person who may be in a situation such as caring for large numbers of unwanted animals that must be euthanized (Baran et al. 2009; Chur-Hansen, 2010). On the negative side of the chattel orientation is the possibility of a person using an animal as a tool to harm another human being as in domestic and family violence situations (Faver & Strand, 2007). Moreover, separating oneself emotionally from animals, which is required in the chattel orientation, may result in abusive behaviors in the food animal industry (Porcher, 2010).

Milani (1995) writes, "people who maintain an integrated approach relate to animals neither as people or [nor] as objects, but rather as separate, animate beings who become incomprehensible beyond a certain limit" (pp. 25–26). Because the human experience of the animal is incomprehensible at a certain point, it becomes necessary for the human to set limits that may seem arbitrary to others but meaningful to them. These relationships can be emotional and connected but may also come to an end because the person in the relationship makes decisions based on their needs, instead of the needs of an animal which are deemed "incomprehensible." This is a difficult area to define because the point at which a person makes a decision about an animal varies according to their own culture, previous experience with animals, and available resources, not from seeing the animal as either human (anthropomorphized) or inanimate (chattel).

Attachment Theory

Similar to the biophilic idea that attention to animals is an evolutionary instinct, is the concept of attachment theory for humans developed by a 20th century British psychiatrist and psychoanalyst, John Bowlby. Attachment theory holds that proximity seeking of the infant to the caregiver (attachment figure) is an evolutionary survival tool to ensure protection and eventual growth of the infant into adulthood. His perspectives on attachment were significantly influenced by research in the field of ethology—namely the imprinting instincts of goslings studied by Konrad Lorenz and his collaboration with many other well-known ethologists such as Robert Hinde and Harry Harlow (Horst, LeRoy, & Veer, 2008). Of particular influence to Bowlby was Harlow's research with rhesus monkeys demonstrating that "contact comfort" (in a clinical laboratory setting) was more important to the infant rhesus monkey, than food. Given the ethological influences that contributed to attachment theory, it is logical that researchers would look to the attachment model as a theoretical explanation for how animals and human beings bond.

There are four behaviors that are inherent in the development of an attachment relationship—1) *proximity maintenance* with the attachment figure, 2) experiencing the attachment figure as a *safe haven* from discomfort and stress, 3) using the attachment figure as a *secure base* from which exploration and risk taking can occur, and 4) experiencing *separation distress* when not with the attachment figure (Zilcha-Mano, Mikulincer, & Shaver, 2011). Mary Ainsworth and Silvia Bell (1970) contributed "attachment styles" to the theory, using a test called "The Strange Situation." Ainsworth observed the behaviors of young children (12 to 18 months) interacting with their attachment figure through periods of separation and reunification. She differentiated between *secure attachments* and *insecure attachments*. Ainsworth identified two types of insecure attachments: resistant/ambivalent and avoidant. Later Main, Kaplan, and Cassidy (1985) added the disorganized insecure attachment style.

In the past two decades, research has supported the relevance of attachment theory to describe the HAB. Peacock, Chur-Hansen, and Winefield (2012) explored the mental health implications of the HAB using attachment theory. Zilcha-Mano et al. (2011) developed an assessment tool, the "Pet Attachment Questionnaire" (PAQ) to explore the human-animal relationship in terms of anxious and avoidant attachments. Additionally, Palmer & Custance (2008), utilized attachment theory to demonstrate the human-animal attachment through the application of a modified version of Ainsworth's Strange Situation test.

Peacock et al. (2012) measured the HAB by assessing proximity maintenance with the animal, the owner's experience of emotional reciprocity in the relationship, and level of commitment to the animal (i.e., would the animal be relinquished if it posed health threats to the owner). The researchers found that level of attachment was a significant predictor of somatoform (physical) symptoms, depression, and anxiety for the owners. However, the researchers found that level of human social support was not a moderating factor between level of human-animal attachment and psychological distress. In other words, if there was poor social support people reported poor psychological wellbeing regardless of attachment to their pets. This finding was in opposition to some studies indicating that the presence of animals is associated with better psychological wellbeing (Garrity, Stallones, Marx, & Johnson, 1989).

Zilcha-Mano, Mikulincer, and Shaver (2011) explored attachment and human-animal relationships, through the development PAQ as well as human-animal attachment and mental health, attachment styles in human relationships, and human experiences of animal loss. The PAQ assesses the insecure attachment styles of anxious attachment and avoidant attachment. Findings of the study indicate attachment insecurities in human-animal relationships *match* more than they *compensate* for attachment insecurities in human-human relationships. In other words, anxious human-animal attachments were associated with being sensitive and insecure in human relationships and that avoidant human-animal attachments were related with being more solitary in human-human relationships. They also found that anxious human-animal attachments were related to psychological distress.

It seems as if attachment behaviors in the HAB are reciprocal across species. For instance, Palmer and Custance (2008) randomly assigned 38 dog owner pairs into one of two conditions in the Ainsworth's Strange Situation Test: Condition 1 allowed the dog and owner to enter the new setting together first and Condition 2 placed the dog with a stranger in the new setting first. Findings indicated that the owner did serve as a *secure base* for the dog as evidenced by the dog exploring its surroundings more in the presence of the owner and less when the dog was with a stranger or alone. Although the dogs were willing to engage the stranger in both conditions, (unlike with human infants), those dogs who met the stranger with the owner present more quickly engaged the stranger. Independent play was also depressed in dogs when they were with the stranger only or alone. Therefore, there is evidence that supports that owners can serve as a secure base in canine-human connections.

Scholars have indicated that the application of attachment theory to human-animal relationships is perhaps weak because, a) many of the instruments used do not actually adhere to the attachment theory itself (Collis & McNicholas, 1998; Crawford, Worsham, and Swinehart, 2006), and b) more research indicates that social support theory may be a more appropriate representation of the human-animal relationship (Collis & McNicholas, 1998). However, there has been progress in the measures used to explore attachment theory to understand the human-animal connection (Palmer & Custance, 2008; Zilcha-Mano et al., 2011), as well as applying both social support theory and attachment theory to this relationship (Peacock et al., 2012).

Social Support Theory

Sidney Cobb, a seminal leader in the field of social support theory held that there are three main ways social support occurs: "1) information leading the subject to believe that he is cared for and loved, 2) information leading the subject to believe that he is esteemed and valued, and 3) information leading the subject to believe that he belongs to a network of communication and mutual obligation" (Cobb, 1976, p. 300). As the theory developed, additional factors were added to these three including: tangible/practical/instrumental support and the opportunity to provide nurturance (Collis & McNicholas, 1998). Moreover, the way in which social support is most effective has also been explored (Lakey & Orehek, 2011; McConnell, Brown, Shoda, Stayton, and Martin, 2011).

Social support generally is understood to operate in two ways: direct effects and buffering effects. Direct effects mean that the presence of social support is life enhancing even when things are calm. Buffering effects mean that social support helps buffer the negative health and well-being consequences that may occur when things are stressful. People who live in communities that have a great deal of mutual aid and enjoy a lot of support may be experiencing the direct effects described in social support theory, whereas those people who have been in a tornado and are surrounded by a church or other community reinforcements may be experiencing the buffering effects described in social support theory. Moreover, there is a difference between perceived social support (how a recipient feels about their level of social support) and enacted social support (concrete resources or intervention for the recipient), with perceived social support sometimes being experienced as more helpful than enacted social support (Lakey & Orehek, 2011).

Lakey and Orehek (2011) argue that relational social support (providing and receiving emotional, behavioral, and cognitive regulation through human contact) and quasi-relational support (interacting with or just thinking about animals, special activities, objects, or ideas, and symbolic people such as revered religious leaders) are important factors in how social support functions. The more people share the same preferences in communication style and quasi-relational support, the more beneficial are the emotional, behavioral, and cognitive regulation. This theory may explain why animals are sometimes called social lubricants (Messent, 1985). According to this model, the presence of an animal may become a shared quasi-relational focus between people, making their connection feel more supportive. The ways animals "lubricate" social connections between people has been observed with children (Friedmann et al., 1983), people receiving some form of medical treatment (Wesley, Minatrea, & Watson, 2009) as well as for people with disabilities (Eddy, Hart, & Boltz, 1988).

McConnell, Brown, Shoda, Stayton, and Martin (2011) conducted three studies to explore how animals provide social support for people. Their findings suggested that people who felt their animals provided them with good social support had better well-being than non-animal owners. They also found that animals provide a *complementary* as opposed to a *compensatory* form of social support. In other words, people who felt more supported by their animals also felt more supported by the people in their lives. People low on human social support did not compensate with higher levels of social support from their animals. These two studies provide evidence for the main effects method of social support theory. McConnell and colleagues' third study explored if social support offered by companion animals served as a buffer for stress. The researchers placed people into groups where they wrote about a humiliating story and then either, a) wrote about their animals, b) wrote about a best friend, or c) drew a map of campus. Findings suggested that those who wrote about their animals or their friends after the humiliating story reported significantly higher levels of social support than those individuals who drew a map after the humiliating story. These findings support a buffering hypothesis for social support provided by animals as well as suggest that the quasi-relationships offered by remembering important people and animals has an effect of perception of social fulfillment.

In another stress buffering social support study, Duvall Antonacopoulos and Pychyl (2010) conducted an on-line survey of 132 cat and dog owners to explore levels of human social support, attachment to companion animals, depression, and loneliness. They found that for those individuals living alone level of attachment to a companion animal had no effect on levels of depression or loneliness. However, dog owners with high human social support were significantly less lonely than non-companion animal owners with high levels of human social support. For owners with high attachment to companion animals and low human social support, depression and loneliness were also significantly higher than for owners with low levels of attachment to their animals. Therefore, in this study support was again found for the *complementary* more than *compensatory* hypothesis of animals as social supports.

As mentioned in the previous section, attachment theory and social support theory alone may not be enough to explain the human-animal bond. Instead, it may require a combination of both. Meehan, Massavelli, and Pachana (2017) surveyed a convenience sample of 161 pet owning university students to determine if companion animals are perceived to be sources of social support, the relationship between attachment and that perception of social support, and if participants include their pets on their attachment hierarchy. An attachment hierarchy can be used to understand a person's multiple attachment bonds to others such as friends, siblings, romantic partners, and in the case of this study, companion animals. The authors found that respondents did find their pets to be a source of social support, and that those who scored higher on pet attachment were more likely to rank their pets as important providers of particular support behaviors. Pets were also included on respondents' attachment hierarchies, ranking fifth in order of importance behind romantic partners, mothers, best friends, and fathers, but ahead of siblings.

Thus far, attention has been given to general theories that may describe the HAB including biophilia, the anthropomorphic-chattel continuum, attachment theory, and social support theory. Additionally, findings from the research studies shared thus far indicate how the HAB benefits people as well as mimics human-to-human bonds. Some evidence has also pointed to increased levels of depression and loneliness for people highly attached to companion animals.

Sadly, there is also a negative side to the HAB that includes violence to animals, and the co-occurrence of violence to animals with other forms of interpersonal violence. While the theories and research that underlie these negative relationships are discussed at length in other chapters, it is appropriate to acknowledge that being part of the family can make animals victims of violence as well. Attention to some of the research in this area will be briefly covered later in this chapter as well as some of the innovative ways animals are being integrated into programs to rehabilitate individuals who have exhibited aggressive and anti-social behaviors as well as depression and substance abuse.

Attention will now turn to some of the different types of relationships people have with animals. The following section will cover companion animals, assistance animals, farm animals, wildlife, and HABs among animal-related professionals such as animal control and police officers, research laboratory and animal shelter workers.

Kinds of HABs

Much of the attention in the previously cited studies have focused on companion animals, such as dogs and cats (Peacock et al., 2012), and sometimes horses or small reptiles (McConnell et al., 2011), however the breadth of HABs is far greater than these relationships. In fact, the HAB occurs within sub-cultures according to species and/ or function.

Companion Animals

The human-companion animal bond has been shown to serve a familial function for many, with these animals often being described as children or at least a "member of the family" (Cohen, 2002; C. Risley-Curtiss et al., 2006; Risley-Curtiss, Holley, & Kodiene, 2011). Even though most laws categorize them this way, very few people consider their companion animals to be property (American Veterinary Medicine Association, 2007), but rather close friends or family who both give and receive care and nurturance (Cohen, 2002). The research attention given to the companion HAB has had varying foci and varying results. Some findings suggest that pet ownership is beneficial and associated with emotional and physical health and wellbeing (McConnell et al., 2011). For instance, Sugawara et al. (2012) explored the biological and psychological benefits of a familiar companion dog on healthy owners using heart rate variability, brain activity, and a measure of psychological stress. Measures were completed in two conditions: one while in the presence of a companion dog and one without the dog. Results showed responses in regions of the brain associated with relaxed states when the dog was present. Findings also showed significant decreases in participants' subjective experience of stress, although there were no differences between conditions in heart rate variability.

On the other hand, some research suggests that companion animal ownership is not associated with these things (Winefield, Black, & Chur-Hansen, 2008), and that intense relationships with animals can sometimes be associated with negative mental health and personality characteristics (Zilcha-Mano et al., 2011). For instance, Miltiades & Shearer (2011) conducted a study of older adults living in a rural environment to explore attachment to companion animals and depression. Results indicated that older adults who were more attached to their companion animals had higher levels of depression than those older adults who had lower levels of attachment to their companion animal. However, being able to meet the needs of the companion animal and having a social network were associated with lower levels of depression.

For those individuals who fall into the category of being seriously and persistently mentally ill (SPMI), however, there seems to be some reliable benefits of having a companion animal. For instance, Wisdom, Saedi, and Green (2009), found that 57% (101 of 177) of individuals diagnosed with schizophrenia, schizoaffective disorder, bipolar disorder, or affective psychosis who were living in the community owned companion animals. Through both quantitative and qualitative methods, the researchers discovered that animal owners: a) were more likely to be diagnosed with bipolar disorder or affective psychosis than a schizophrenia related disorder, b) were more likely to have a co-occurring addiction, c) were more likely to live with another person than by themselves, and d) were less likely to have been hospitalized. Almost 75% reported that their animal companions were "very important to them" and 67% of non-animal owners wished they had an animal but could not due to residential restriction and other reasons. Wisdom et al. (2009) also found four qualitative themes about how animals helped participants heal from mental illness. Participants felt their animals: 1) provided them with empathy and non-judgmentally "sensed" their emotions, 2) helped them stay connected to something outside the isolation of mental illness and gain social support with other people, 3) filled the role of family members who were either absent or with whom the relationship was strained, and 4) provided participants with a sense of self-worth and self-efficacy in their care of the companion animal.

Likewise, Zimolag and Krupa (2009) also studied animal ownership among people with SPMI living in the community through the help of around the clock mental health and case management support teams. Surveys were sent to 60 program participants (20 animal owners and 40 non-animal owners). Findings indicated that more women than men owned animals, and animal owners had higher Global Assessment of Functioning (GAF) scores than non-animal owners. Animal owners also had higher levels of perceived meaningful activities as well as social and psychological integration into the community. As found in Wisdom et al. (2009), people with schizophrenia were less likely to own pets and 68% of non-pet owners wished to own a pet but did not because of cost and housing policies. Participants reported that the main reason they owned an animal was the companionship offered and having someone to love.

Another element of the HAB manifests in the grief many people feel when their animals become ill and die, or if they have to be separated from their animal companions due to illness or even deployment at wartime. This form of grief can be considered a disenfranchised grief since not everyone immediately understands the intensity of feelings that arise for people who are deeply attached to their animal companions. There are books that have been written about the topic (Allen, 2007), emotional and clinical support for people in animal-related bereavement such as The University of Tennessee's Veterinary Social Work Program (for more information see http://vetsocialwork.utk.edu) and increasing attention to the experience in the scholarly world (Packman, Field, Carmack, & Ronen, 2011; Toray, 2004).

For instance, Packman, Field, Carmack, and Ronen (2011) conducted a survey of 33 individuals whose dog or cat died within the past year and measured psychosocial adjustment to the loss using the Continuing Bonds (CB) theory. This theory posits that people maintain continuing bonds with others who have died and that this process is healthy in grieving the loss. Findings suggested that death of a companion animal is experienced similarly to human loss and that attachment to the animal continues after death just as occurs in human loss. Some people report that the loss of their companion animal has even been more difficult than the loss of other important people in their lives (Weisman, 1990). Factors associated with more intense animal-related grief include strength of the HAB (Planchon, Templer, Stokes, & Keller, 2002), and whether the owner is socially isolated (living with one other person or less) (Planchon & Templer, 1996), and/or experiencing co-occurring social stressors (Gosse & Barnes, 1994).

Farm Animals

One of the most varied types of human-animal relationships is that between human beings and animals raised for food and fiber. The domestication of wild animals by humans began thousands of years ago and would change the future for both. For the animals, it meant the selective breeding over time of animals that were morphologically and temperamentally different. Bred to be less dangerous and easy to handle, domestic breeds are more docile and generally have finer bone structure including shortened skulls, and therefore smaller brains, as well as smaller teeth than their wild counterparts. By cultivating domestic plants and animals, people were able to have consistent food source in one location meaning people no longer had to lead a nomadic existence to survive. The population increased, agriculture became the norm, and eventually urban societies developed (Magee, MacHugh, & Edwards, 2014). Today, 661 out of every 1,000 households have livestock animals according to the AVMA 2012 *U.S. Pet Ownership & Demographics Sourcebook.*

In contemporary society, farmers must balance the seemingly contradictory needs of animal welfare against being able to make money in a market that demands inexpensive food. Much of the literature on livestock refers to "production animals" and "animal husbandry", and "human-animal interactions." These terms are often utilized by animal activists in their campaigns against industrialized farming to emphasize that the animals are seen as commodities (Croney, 2014). However, AHBs occur between farm animals and people. Although the function of that bond *may* fall more on the chattel side of the spectrum as described by Milani (1995), the evidence of the relationship is clear, ranging from the everyday interactions between a farmer and his or her herd (Porcher & Schmitt, 2012) to the relationship between the abattoir worker and the animals "going to market" (Coleman, McGregor, Hemsworth, Boyce, & Dowling, 2003).

For example, Porcher, Cousson-Gélie, and Dantzer (2004), explored farmers' affective relationships with their animals and found four relevant factors: 1) the status farmers gave to the animals, 2) the status farmers gave to the farming profession, 3) self-perception of behavior toward the animals personally as well other farmers' behavior toward their animals, and 4) how the affective bond was demonstrated with the animal. They found two orthogonal dimensions: Friendship and Power relationships with animals. Friendship was associated with emotional difficulty at time of slaughter and preferring the company of animals over the company of people. Power was associated with increased distance from animals such as thinking it ridiculous to talk with animals or show feelings at work. Women seemed to be higher on the Friendship factor than were men, and the older the stock person, the higher the Power scores, indicating greater emotional distance. Findings also suggested that the more animals on the farm, the higher the scores on the Power dimension.

Zasloff (2010), through surveys exploring relationships between people and their goats, donkeys, and chickens, also found strong bonds on the farm. For goat owners, 55.4% of respondents considered all their goats "pets," 9.8% considered none of their goats "pets," and 34.7% reported that some in the herd were considered "pets" and some were not. Respondents indicated various reasons for owning goats such a hobby activity, for milk and cheese production, to participate in 4-H activities, to clear brush around the property, and for their meat. Individuals who had goats for their meat reported challenging experiences at times of slaughter. Many would limit time spent with their meat goats and if names were given, the names were more food oriented such as "Taco" or "Burger Boy." Zasloff also found that more and more people are having "backyard chickens" that serve both as pets as well as working animals. These chickens provide eggs for their owners and many respondents indicated they would continue to care for the chickens beyond their egg laying years. These backyard chickens are serving the roles as pets more and more as evidenced by some owners even putting diapers of their chickens and playing them classical music. Of the donkey owners surveyed, 89% had donkeys for human companionship, but also reported some working functions such as breeding, guarding livestock, carrying packs, and participating in sporting events (Zasloff, 2010). The quality of the human-animal relationship can vary greatly across and within farms with some animals experiencing gentle, consistent care while others receive infrequent or rough handling. Overall, having a positive AHB would be beneficial for all of the creatures involved. For the animals, in addition to receiving adequate care, having a positive experience with people reduces fear and stress responses such as bolting or trying to escape which can lead to injury, illness and death. For the farmers, having positive associations with the farm animals means that they are going to be more likely to enjoy their work in addition to reaping the economic and public health benefits of having more healthy and productive animals (Waiblinger et al., 2006).

Assistance Animals

Given the strong bonds that people often develop with animals, animals have the potential to help people in many ways. One such way is an assistance animal. Assistance animals can be defined in three ways: 1) Animal Assisted Therapy (AAT) or Animal Assisted Activity (AAA) animals, 2) Emotional Support Animals (ESAs), and 3) service animals.

AAT and AAA animals participate in animal assisted interventions (AAI) with special populations such as the elderly, disabled children, or people with cancer. AAI animals are companion animals that have been behaviorally and medically screened and deemed good candidates for AAI. This usually means they are healthy, well behaved, and appear to enjoy affectionate interactions with specific populations such as the elderly or children. Unlike ESAs and service animals that focus on an individual, AAI animals need to be social and comfortable interacting with a variety of different people. There are also animals that reside in settings such as farms or in the water that people interact with for AAI. (Breitenbach, Stumpft, Fersen, & Ebert, 2009; Pedersen, Martinsen, Berget, & Braastad, 2012).

ESAs and service animals are often thought to be the same thing, but there are significant differences between the two. An ESA is a companion animal that provides comfort and support to a person suffering from a mental illness. Unlike a typical "pet", the animal owner's mental health professional has determined the animal to be a necessary therapeutic agent and as such, the mental health professional has written a letter designating the animal as an ESA which will allow the companion animal to live in housing where pets are prohibited (Hoy-Gerlach, Vincent, & Hector, 2019). Prior to 2021, ESA letter also allowed owners to bring a companion animal into the cabin of an airplane at no additional cost. The U.S. Department of Transportation changed its rules at the end of 2020, leaving the decision about ESA policy in the hands of each particular airline. The rule changes were likely in response to an increasing number of incidents in which people tried to bring unusual animals onto airplanes, such as an "emotional support pig" (CNN, 2014, Dec 1) and an "emotional support peacock" (BBC, 2018, Jan 31), as well as incidents of other passengers being attacked by emotional support dogs (BBC, 2019, May 30).

In the United States, service animals are defined by the Americans with Disabilities Act (ADA) as dogs that are individually trained to do work or perform tasks for people with disabilities. Service dogs, unlike companion animals or ESAs, are traditionally trained from an early age to provide task-based *service* for an individual with a disability, or they can be owned by an occupational therapy service that has one or two handlers who oversee their care (Wenthold & Savage, 2007). Examples of service include guiding people who are blind, alerting someone to a seizure or drop in blood sugar, retrieving objects, opening and closing doors, cabinets, or drawers, or calming someone suffering from PTSD during an anxiety attack. As they are a necessary accommodation for someone with a disability, these dogs are allowed access anywhere the general public is allowed. This points to an important distinction between ESAs and service dogs. An ESA is for support and comfort for someone with a mental illness, but they are not trained to do any particular task and as such, they are not given access to all public spaces like service dogs. While an ESA may provide comfort that will make life easier for an individual, a service dog makes the person's environment accessible. While the potential benefits of a service dog to someone with a disability are numerous, the welfare of the dog must also be taken into consideration. Instruments to help appropriately match people with service dogs have been developed, (Zapf & Rough, 2002) and the ethical issues of maintaining proper animal welfare for these animals is important and has received attention (Wenthold & Savage, 2007).

People who benefit from relationships with service animals report strong attachment to their helpers. Kwong and Bartholomew (2011) conducted a qualitative study, interviewing 25 individuals who lost an assistance dog to retirement or death. Using an attachment theory framework, they explored the presence for "*secure base,*" "*safe haven,*" and "*separation anxiety*" in the human-service dog bond. They also explored the "role of caregiving" and "grief experiences" present in these relationships. They found evidence for both *safe haven* and *secure base* for the humans in the human-service dog attachment experience. Caregiving was also an intense emotional experience for the human being as was the loss of the service dog.

People report that service animals help them be more connected to others and the world around them as well. For instance, Solomon (2010), in an ethnographic study of service dogs with children and families affected by autism, found that "child-dog interactions afford an experience of emotional connection between an autistic child and family members, as well as between the child and the dogs," (p. 161). This is also true for veterans with combat related disabilities and post-traumatic stress that were paired with service dogs. The National Education for Assistance Dog Services (NEADS) Canines for Combat Veterans and the Trauma Alert Dog Program provides these services for veterans. NEADS is a leader in the field of service dogs training for people with sight and hearing disabilities and developed the Prison PUP Program to help in the socialization and training for their canines (Foreman & Crosson, 2012). Anecdotal evidence to date suggests that the use of service dogs for veterans results in improved emotional regulation and engagement, decrease in startle response as well as pain medication use, and that the presence of these service dogs has had beneficial effects for the families as well as the staff who are caring for the veterans (Yount, Olmert, & Lee, 2012).

Wildlife

The National Survey of Fishing, Hunting, and Wildlife-Associated Recreation reported that in 2016, 103.7 million people in the United States engage in wildlife associated recreation—including hunting and fishing (39.6 million) and wildlife watching (86 million). For the wildlife watchers, 81.1 million watch wildlife around their home, 23.7 million take special trips away from home to watch wildlife, and 18.8 million do both (U.S. Fish and Wildlife Service, 2016). According to the World Association of Zoos and Aquariums, over 700 million people visit zoos and aquariums worldwide each year.

Though the HAB with wildlife can be both biophilic (pleasant) as well as biophobic (fearful or unpleasant) (Gullone, 2000), clearly humans have a natural interest in wildlife. Bird feeding in backyards, family trips to the zoo, natural fears of spiders, snakes, or sharks as well as the annoyances of mice in the house, raccoons in the garbage, or even bears in the backyard (Harker & Bates, 2007) all point to the ways people pay attention to wildlife.

Researchers in the HAB field have also explored this connection. For instance, Smith, Ham, and Weiler (2011) conducted a qualitative study with 18 individuals about their "profound" experiences interacting with wildlife. They found that these experiences were pleasurable, incited a desire for more connections with wildlife as well as an impulse to help wildlife. Bjerke and Ostdahl (2004) in an exploration of how urban adult residents felt about wildlife found that small birds, squirrels, butterflies and hedgehogs were well-liked animals, and that rats, mosquitos, and mice were the least liked animals. In this study gender also affected positive attitudes towards wild animals with females liking animals such as cats, crows, seagulls, and grasshoppers, and men preferring birds of prey, bumblebees, bats, beetles, and snails (Bjerke & Ostdahl, 2004). There is also evidence that having a companion animal is associated with more positive attitudes towards wild animals unless the companion animal owner had had a problem with a wild animal, like an opossum in the house.

Researchers have also explored HABs at the zoo both for visitors and for zookeepers. For instance, Sakagami and Ohta (2010) found that zoo visitor's blood pressure and quality of life scores were lower and better after a zoo visit than before. Phillips and Peck (2007) explored how the personalities of zookeepers and tigers affected the zookeeper-tiger bond. They found that zookeepers who had a higher propensity for anger gave fewer "pats" to the tigers and conscientious and more neurotic zookeepers interacted with the tigers less. Findings also suggested that the tigers' personalities did not greatly influence the zookeeper tiger interactions (Phillips & Peck, 2007). The impact of the relationship between zoo animals and their keepers can even be detected in the blood. Carlstead, Paris, and Brown (2018) found in their study of 427 zoo keeper-elephant pairings that positive interactions with the elephants, and stronger keeper-elephant bonds resulted in lower levels of the stress hormone cortisol.

Animals Used by Animal-Related Professionals

Like zookeeper-tiger bonds, many other animal-related professionals also experience bonds with the animals in their care. These animal-related professionals may include animal control officers, police officers affiliated with canine units or mounted horsemen, veterinary professionals, people who work with animals in research laboratories and animal shelter workers to name only a few. Very often, people who "love animals" pursue employment where they can work with animals. These types of jobs may require dealing with animals that are sick, abused, unwanted, or used in research settings. It also may mean watching an animal, in the line of duty, come into harm's way (Hart, Zasloff, Bryson, & Christensen, 2000; Sanders, 2006). For many animal-related professionals the affection felt for animals naturally results in the development of bonds with the animals they interact and care for (Arluke, 1999; Black, Winefield, & Chur-Hansen, 2011; Chur-Hansen, 2010; Frommer & Arluke, 1999). These professionals often suffer from what is referred to as 'compassion fatigue' and may need help to maintain their professionalism and resiliency.

In the criminal justice system, the HAB within professional services occurs for animal control officers and police officers. Animal control officers can feel a great deal of stress addressing animal-related conflicts between neighbors, enforcing animal cruelty laws, and witnessing the warehousing of animals caught in animal cruelty legal cases. These experiences take an emotional toll on these professionals (Leinberger, 2009). Innovative programs like Maricopa County Sheriff Office's Animal Safe House Program (for more information, see https://mcsomash.org/) can help. MASH is a limited-intake shelter that was created to house the 'evidence' of animal crimes—the abused and neglected animals.

Police officers can experience ambivalence about the bonds with their working animals seeing them as "tools" for conducting their work as well as sentient beings whom they love (Sanders, 2006). Of the 265 police officer canine teams surveyed by Hart et al. (2000), 75% indicated that their dogs were important members of the family who helped the police officer with stress and maintaining good health. One-third reported that the dog had even saved their lives. Where the dog slept was indicative of attachment to the dog with those officers who let their dogs sleep inside (38%) being more likely to express that they loved their dogs than those whose dogs slept outside. The bond between police and their canine officers can also be seen in how the dogs are honored in death. Police dogs have been buried with full police honors after being killed in the line of duty (Kuruvilla, 2014) and K9 monuments have been erected across the country.

It has been confirmed that professionals who care for animals used for research also experience HABs (Arluke, 1999; Chang & Hart, 2002; Rohlf & Bennett, 2005; Russow, 2002). The animals under these professionals' care can even show preference for a particular human caregiver as well (Chang & Hart, 2002). Research veterinary technicians may feel uneasy and conflicted between the bond they feel with the research animals and the scientific manipulations they must perform for the research protocol (Arluke, 1999). Caregivers of research animals report being rewarded when they actively enrich the lives of the research animals under their care (Chang & Hart, 2002) and also grieve when the animals die (Chang & Hart, 2002; Rohlf & Bennett, 2005). Because of these emotional experiences attention has been given to the ethical implications of HABs in laboratory settings (Herzog, 2002; Russow, 2002) and placing an emphasis more on supporting an "ethic of care" than a "utilitarian" relationship in the laboratory environment (Russow, 2002). Recommendations also include ensuring direct care providers have a "voice" on the Institutional Animal Care and Use Committee (IACUC) (Herzog, 2002).

The problem of companion animal over-population and unwanted and homeless animals is a very difficult one (Kass, John Jr, Scarlett, & Salman, 2001). People who feel a strong affinity towards animals generally and unwanted animals in particular, very often engage in efforts to care for and rescue these animals (Neumann, 2010).

The sickness and death of these animals can be very difficult for these animal-related professionals and volunteers (Baran et al., 2009).

Violence and the HAB

Although hard to understand, there is a dark side to the AHB that results in violence to animals. One commonly accepted definition of animal abuse is: "socially unacceptable behavior that intentionally causes unnecessary pain, suffering, or distress to and/or death of an animal" (Ascione, 1993, p. 28). This unnecessary violence to animals can occur in the form of "bruises, fractures, ... burns and scalds, stab and incised wounds, poisoning, asphyxiation, ... drowning, sexual abuse and injuries specifically caused by firearms" (Munro & Thrusfield, 2001a, p. 279). Violence to animals can also come in the form of neglect such as in animal hoarding situations (Lockwood, 2018), as well as animal fighting (Humane Society of the United States, 2003).

Since the 1980s, there has been increasing scholarly attention to the link between violence to animals and violence to people (Flynn, 2001). The presence of violence to animals has been associated with bullying, (Gullone & Robertson, 2008) family violence situations (Ascione et al., 2007), and life histories of incarcerated felons (Merz-Perez et al., 2001). Violence towards animals can occur for pleasure and entertainment such as in blood sports, better known as animal fighting. While animal fighting may occur on a small scale, such as between gang members meeting on the street corner, there is also an entire black market industry for breeding fighting animals, training instruments, and spectator events. The pride a person takes in their fighting animals is deep and there are strong social networks that center around animal fighting. These social networks are male-dominated and include criminal behaviors like illegal gambling, drug and weapon offenses, and animal theft (Kalof & Taylor, 2007). Violence to animals, however, can also be associated with neglect instead of active harm, such as in cases of animal hoarding. Animal hoarding is the excessive collection of, and retention of, animals far beyond an individual's capacity to humanely house and care for them. Scholarly attention has begun to focus on the motivations for animal hoarding behavior; for instance, Steketee et al. (2011) found that the animal hoarders had more childhood stressful life events, anthropomorphized animals more, and demonstrated more negative attachment style. Moreover, some people have sexual impulses towards, and therefore engage in, sexual acts with animals (Edwards, 2019; Hensley, Tallichet, & Dutkiewucz, 2010; Zequi et al., 2012;), a practice termed as zoophilia, bestiality, or animal sexual abuse.

Thorough attention to the theoretical concepts and research findings on the link between violence towards animals and people is paid in later chapters in this volume (e.g., family violence, see Chapter 13; animal hoarding, see Chapter 10; blood sports, see Chapter 9; bestiality, see chapter 11). Here, it is simply important to note that some people's attachment histories and own pathology influence the negative bonds they establish with animals, in both active and passive forms of cruelty.

Cultural Influences in the HAB

Attention will now turn to the ways in which cultural influences affect the HAB. Since the criminal justice system touches the lives of people from a wide variety of cultural, racial, and ethnic backgrounds, putting effort toward understanding how these backgrounds might affect the HAB is important. Unfortunately, there is relatively little research that examines how culture, ethnicity or race may impact the HAB. Most of what research there is examines differences between racial/ethnic groups, with a smaller number of studies looking at within-group attitudes, beliefs, and practices. For example, Marx, Stallones, Garrity, and Johnson (1988) examined demographics of companion animal ownership among U.S. adults age 21–64 and found that Whites were statistically more likely than people of color to have such animals. There was, however, no exploration of this finding. Applebaum, Peek, and Zsembik (2020) found similar results using data from the 2018 General Social Survey. They found the overall pet ownership rate in the United States to be 60.9%, with significant differences in pet ownership by race and ethnicity with 70.4% of Whites reporting owning pets, 29.0% among African Americans, and Latinxs being very close the national average at 60.0%. The authors also found significant differences in the relationships between pet ownership and age, population density, household composition, and housing type, but they did not explore any connections between those factors, pet ownership, and race and ethnicity.

In a study that yielded more information regarding differences between racial and ethnic groups, Siegel (1995) interviewed 877 urban non-Latina/o White, Latina/o, African American, Asian, and "other" adolescents between the ages of 12 and 17. She found distinct racial/ethnic differences in companion animal ownership and attachment. African Americans were least likely to have companion animals in their homes while Whites were most likely to, followed by Latino/as and Asians. White youth also rated their companion animals as significantly more important to them than did Latina/o youth while African American and Asian youth reported intermediate levels of attachment but were not significantly different from any of the other groups. Having sole responsibility for the care of one's companion animal was also related to race/ethnicity with African American youth most likely to have sole responsibility, followed by Latina/o, White, and Asian youth.

Brown (2011) examined racial variations in attachment to companion animals among 76 African American and 57 White veterinary students. Among her findings were that more White students had companion animals (100% versus 86%); they had a larger number of such animals, and were more likely to sleep with their animals than were African American students (70% versus 53%). Additionally, Whites had significantly higher scores on an animal attachment scale than did African Americans. There were differences in responses to attachment statements such as "no family is complete without a pet," and to questions about taking animals to visit friends and relatives. Brown concluded that how attachment to animals is shown may vary from culture to culture. She also noted that differences in housing, socio-economic factors, and urban-rural background may help in explaining the differences she found.

Schoenfeld-Tacher, Kogan, and Wright (2010) interviewed 419 Hispanic and non-Hispanics with companion animals, who presented at three veterinarian clinics and found that the majority considered companionship as a major benefit of having companion animals. Differences in sterilization rates were found but no differences were found in how Hispanics and non-Hispanics viewed their companion animals. They did, however, challenge the validity of the animal attachment instrument (Lexington Attachment to Pets Scale) being used for Hispanic populations. Risley-Curtiss et al. (2006), in their study of women of color and their relationships with companion animals, also questioned the validity of such scales based on their findings that what "family" means when people say they consider their animals to be family may differ based on race/ethnicity as well as other factors.

Risley-Curtiss, Holley, and Wolf (2006) examined the relationship of race/ethnicity to companion animal beliefs and practices in a random sample telephone survey of 587 adults in a southwestern metropolitan area. They found that Whites and Indigenous people were most likely to have companion animals and Asians were least likely; Latina/os were less likely to have cats (similar finding by Schoenfeld-Tacher et al., 2010) and birds than other animals, and were also less likely than other groups to have their animals sterilized. Asians were most likely to agree that "Animals do not feel pain." Almost 97% of those with companion animals agreed with the statement that "My pet is a member of my family."

More recently Risley-Curtiss, Holley, and Kodiene (2011) found in a qualitative study of 12 men (9 were men of color) and their relationships with animals that the majority of men in the sample engaged in physical activities such as playing, walking, or running with their pets. However, the four men who did not talk about play were either Indigenous or immigrants, suggesting the influence of ethnic and national cultures on men's interactions with animals. Additionally, all four immigrants and two of the three Indigenous men raised the issue of cultural differences in the treatment of animals. This reflects one of the effects of living as a person of color in a majority white culture—that "outsiders" might be better able to identify characteristics of the "insider" culture. Two Indigenous men who raised the topic of animals as a source of food described the cultural traditions related to killing animals for food. Recognizing the contrast between their own cultures and that of the dominant U.S. culture, some men came to consider their own culture's treatment of animals as better than that of the larger U.S culture, while others changed the way they treat animals as they learned what one of the participants called the "cultural rules" of the U.S. The authors concluded that the men's relationships were influenced—though not determined—by individual perceptions and experiences, family perceptions and experiences, perceptions and experiences of peers at the intersection of ethnicity, national origin, social class, urban/suburban/rural setting, and U.S. white, middle class culture.

In a study of within-group similarities and differences Johnson and Meadows (2002) examined 24 dog owning Latina/os over age 50 with regard to their relationships with their dogs and whether attachment to a dog was related to self-perceived health and functional ability. The majority of participants viewed their dogs as equals (54%) and as members of their family (79%). Sixty-seven percent stated their dog was the reason they got up in the morning and 62% stated their dog comforts them. Although the study results did not support any relationship between animal companion relationship and a participant's health or functional ability, the authors concluded that for these Latino/as, dogs were as important as they have been reported to be among Whites and that dogs are considered, among these elderly Latina/os, to be valued members of their families.

In addition, Faver and Cavazos (2008) surveyed Latina/o university students and found that of the 69.2% (of 208) who had companion animals, most had dogs and 92% of the dog and cat guardians regarded their companion animals as family. Over 80% stated they received companionship and unconditional love as benefits of animal guardianship and 86% of those with dogs also specified protection as a benefit. In the first study of the co-occurrence of animal abuse and domestic violence specifying Hispanic participants, Faver and Cavazos (2007) also found that animal abuse is a component of domestic violence in Hispanic families similar to non-Hispanic families. Finally, Vaughn et al. (2011) reported on what appears to be the first national assessment of the prevalence of animal cruelty in the U.S. and included race/ethnicity. They found animal cruelty to be more common among males, those born in the U.S., and African-Americans, and less likely among Latina/os; however, it is unclear why certain racial/ethnic categories were grouped together (e.g., Indian/Alaskan/Asian).

As evidenced above there has been some research on ethnic/racial populations and the HAB. In particular the research on Hispanics and Latina/os seems to be increasing though not on African, Asian, or Middle Eastern Americans, nor on Indigenous populations. Nonetheless, two major national HAB studies periodically done by American Pet Products Manufactures Association and the American Veterinary Medical Association have begun to include ethnicity/race in their demographics. Unfortunately, there continues to be relatively little attention in the broad professional literature to the impact of ethnic/racial culture on the HAB in the U.S. (Hoy-Gerlach & Wehman, 2017; Risley-Curtiss, Holley & Wolf, 2006; Schoenfeld-Tacher et al., 2010). In discussing the relevance of culture to the link between animal abuse and family violence, Kaufman (1999) noted that "rarely has animal protection in general, and the violence link specifically, been discussed in the context of a multicultural society" (p. 260), and that statement is still relevant today. The non-professional *Best Friends* magazine in 2004 published a planned series of articles on the lack of people of color in the animal welfare field. The first report was on African Americans and was anecdotal, but it made an important observation regarding the lack of people of color in animal welfare work: "white people often believe that minority communities simply don't care about animals..." (Richard, 2004, p.14), which the research that is present shows is not the case.

This lack of attention to race or ethnicity applies across virtually all areas of HAB research, including the animal abuse and interpersonal violence research, other areas of research on the HAB as well as the research on AAI. This translates into a lack of knowledge to apply to practice; for example, how might the race/ethnicity of clients influence their reception to and the effectiveness of AAI?

More research is needed on the influence of racial or ethnic culture on the HAB in order to better understand how it functions, how it impacts those touched by the criminal justice system, and how it might be utilized in AAI programs. For example, just as the meaning of *"family"* may vary for different racial/ethnic groups, so too may the meaning of attachment to companion animals. Psychometric qualities should also be considered as current animal attachment scales require norming for populations of color, or new measures are created for evaluating animal-related programs. Research also needs to examine differences in the therapeutic effects of AAI across different ethnic/racial groups. Given the research that suggests the benefits of animal companionship, can companion animals provide emotional, psychological, physical, and spiritual support for racial/ethnic groups facing adverse circumstances, such as racism, family violence, abuse, and/or incarceration?

We do know from completed studies that companion animals have meaning for people of color and that culture, among other factors, influences the HAB. Most people of color see their companion animals as family and receive comfort, companionship, and a sense of safety from them.

HAB and Criminal Justice: Practice Implications

There are three main implications of the HAB within the criminal justice system. The first is in the thorough assessment and response to HABs that exist for those touched by or entering the system. The second is the legal response and psychological treatment of perpetrators of animal cruelty. The third is the utilization of AAI for rehabilitation and prevention.

Assessment and Response to the HAB

A thorough psychosocial assessment for people touched by or entering into the criminal justice system must include questions about animals. This not only gives important information about violence to animals in people's lives, but also about attachments that people may have to animals that affect treatment planning and interventions. For instance, many victims of domestic violence will delay leaving an abusive situation because of concern for the safety of their animals (Strand & Faver, 2005). Thus, when a victim of domestic violence is seeking services, such as an order of protection, asking about animals is essential in finding out about any barriers that may prevent seeking safety. Moreover, victims of domestic violence, especially those without children, worry and grieve over their animals when they have to leave them behind (Strand & Faver, 2005). This grief and worry may also be true for people who must leave animals behind when they are incarcerated. Risley-Curtiss, one of this chapter's co-authors, supervised social work students working with female inmates caring for the cats and dogs at the MCSO MASH unit. Anecdotally, the students related stories from some of the inmates about how much they worried about the animals they had to leave behind when they entered jail. The grief people feel over the loss of attachments to animals is a real form of loss (Packman et al., 2011), and this may affect how children and adults cope with losing animals they have cared for in AAI such as Humans and Animal Learning Together (for more information, see www.haltdogs.org) or Puppies Behind Bars (for more information see http://www.puppiesbehindbars.com). Finally, a thorough psychosocial assessment may also show that a person has committed violence to animals, which may affect what type of treatment or legal response is needed.

Preventing and Treating Violence to Animals

Given the co-occurrence of violence to animals and violence to people, it is beneficial that as of March 2014 all 50 states have felony levels laws to convict animal cruelty (Animal Legal Defense Fund, 2014), 32 states have mandated counseling for people convicted of animal cruelty, and 36 states as well as Washington D.C., and Puerto Rico allow victims of domestic violence to include their companion animals on orders of protection (National Link Coalition, 2021a). The Pets and Women's Safety (PAWS) Act was enacted on December 20, 2018 to increase federal protections to include pets of domestic violence survivors. In addition to creating funding for pet housing options in domestic violence cases, the PAWS Act also adds veterinary care to potential restitution costs that can be recovered by survivors. Additionally, 16 states now have cross-reporting laws which mandate or at least encourage animal and human welfare government professionals to report to the other when evidence of violence to animals or people is occurring (National Link Coalition, 2021b).

Although there is some progress in the ways in which violence to animals is detected and addressed, much work still needs to be done in how it is treated. In a survey of 174 therapists about their experiences with violence to animals in their counseling practices Schaefer, Hays, and Steiner (2007) found that 87% of respondents agree that violence to animals is a mental health issue. Sixty-seven percent of the mental health professionals indicated that they inquire about the safety of animals with clients, and 49% indicated they would be supportive of a voluntary reporting law, but only 29% said they would support a mandatory reporting law of violence to animals. Most respondents cited the reason against mandatory reporting was concern about breaking client confidentiality. Currently, the only cohesive treatment protocols that are widely known is The AniCare Approach developed by what is now known as the Animals & Society Institute (see http://www.animalsandsociety.org). With one handbook for adults and another for children, the AniCare Approach provides mental health providers with guidance about how to identify, assess, and treat those who have done acts of animal abuse.

In animal hoarding situations, it has become increasingly clear that intervention must be interdisciplinary in nature. The professionals who must come together to intervene in such situations are law enforcement, public health professionals, animal welfare professionals, psychological services, the legal system, as well as public housing and human medical professionals. Without a comprehensive intervention such as these, it has been estimated that there will be a 100% recidivism rate (Lockwood, 2018; Patronek, 1999). Hoarding disorder included in the Fifth Edition of the Diagnostic and Statistical Manual of Mental Disorders (DSM-5) in 2013, including animal hoarding as a special manifestation. If the only intervention includes removing animals and animal cruelty conviction, which may or may not carry jail time, with no mental health intervention or social support engaged, perpetrators will again begin their hoarding behavior in another location given that the underlying problems contributing to the behavior have not been resolved (Lockwood, 2018; Patronek, 1999).

Humane education programs could also be utilized to detect the presence of violence to animals among school-aged children and their families, as well as increase empathy these children have toward both animals and people (Arbour, Signal, & Taylor, 2009; Ascione, 1997; Faver, 2010). Currently, humane education programs are not utilized on a broad basis in schools even though more and more attention has been given toward anti-bullying programs (Faver, 2010). There has been a call for human services to take the lead in integrating humane education programs as a prevention effort to reduce aggressive behavior among children and increase empathy (Faver, 2010). Given the evidence that violence to animals and childhood bullying behavior can co-occur (Gullone & Robertson, 2008; Henry & Sanders, 2007), it seems fitting that humane education should be incorporated into anti-bullying programs utilized in school systems today. Even though not widespread, there are a few examples where anti-bullying and animal-assisted humane education programs are paired that are demonstrating positive results (Sprinkle, 2008).

Animal-Assisted Interventions

Integrating AAI into the criminal justice system may serve both preventative and rehabilitative functions. The same humane education programs mentioned above that incorporate animals as a form of teaching empathy and promoting self-esteem, as well as reducing anti-social youth behaviors such as bullying and aggression (Dupper, 2013), can serve both functions. Results from a study of one such program, Healing Species, indicate that empathy increased, out of school suspensions due to violent behavior decreased, as did aggressive behaviors for the 4th, 5th, and 6th graders who participated in the program. Healing Species incorporates animal shelter dogs as "teachers" in each of the 12 sessions in the curriculum. Another program that incorporates animals as topics for teaching humane attitudes and reducing bullying and violence is Mutt-i-grees® which now includes 5,000 schools libraries, and after-school programs and 100 animal shelters across all 50 states and in Canada (for more information, https://education.muttigrees.org/). This program allows visits to the animal shelter as service learning or visits from a "therapy dog" enhance its sessions, and routinely includes animal related experiences through representations in stories, photos, and videos.

While few diversion programs exist for juveniles or adults who abuse animals. there are many animal-related intervention programs in both juvenile and adult correctional facilities. Examples in juvenile facilities include Project Pooch—an animal centered correctional vocational program (see www.pooch.org) and Project Second Chance in Michigan and New Mexico.

AAI is increasingly happening for incarcerated adults through animal-related programs. Through the TRF Second Chances Program, inmates provide supervised care to retired racehorses as a part of vocational training (see https://www.trfinc.org/trf-second-chances-program/). In the Larch Corrections Center in Yacolt, Washington, cats labeled as "unadoptable" are diverted to the Larch Cat Adoption Program where prisoners socialize and care for the cats until they can be adopted. North Carolina has a program called "A New Leash on Life" in several of their correctional facilities in which dogs from local animal welfare agencies are trained by prisoners, under the guidance of a professional dog trainer, to increase the odds of the dogs getting adopted (North Carolina Department of Public Safety, 2021). In addition to helping the animals find forever homes, the inmates in the program learn marketable skills which they can use after their release.

Furst (2006), in a national survey of adult Prison Based Animal Programs (PAPs), found that animal visitation programs, wildlife rehabilitation programs, livestock care programs, pet adoption programs, service animal socialization programs, vocational programs, community service programs, and multimodal programs were represented in 36 states. Males were more likely to participate in such programs, and the most commonly used animal was the dog. Community service programs that help animals become more adoptable or are actually adopted by inmates were the most common types of programs. Ninety-eight percent of wardens reported that they felt the programs were beneficial noting such positive results for the prisoners as sense of responsibility, anger management, patience, empathy, self-esteem, communication skills, and self-control. Organizational benefits also cited were humanizing and calming the facility. Moreover, many programs offer vocational certificates such as grooming, animal care assistant, and farm animal management. It is important to note, however, there has been some concern that utilizing animals in such facilities may cause harm to the animals. Given that so many incarcerated felons have a history of animal abuse (Merz-Perez et al., 2001), this seems like a valid concern. To address this, 71.8% of programs have a pre-participation interview and assessment process to determine if an inmate is appropriate for the program. This pre-assessment may include review of the inmate's psychological evaluation, administration of standardized measures, and review of disciplinary history. Some program administrators make decisions about participation in PAPs based on the nature of the crime, excluding those convicted of such offenses as animal abuse, sexual perpetration, and child abuse, while some program administrators do not exclude any inmates from participating (Furst, 2006). Moreover, Hennessy, Morris, and Linden (2006), through an intervention-control group design, found that shelter dogs who participated in a prison-based socialization program were better behaved at post-test than were those dogs who remained in the shelter. Evaluation for the well-being of other animals utilized in PAPs is warranted.

People who are involved with the criminal justice system very often have mental health and substance abuse problems as well. Therefore, the efficacy of AAI for adults with mental health and substance abuse problems is also salient in developing rehabilitative programs for people touched by the criminal justice system. There is some evidence to support the potential benefits of AAI for these issues. For instance, Pedersen, Martinsen, Berget, and Braastad (2012) investigated the application of an AAI utilizing farm animals with a population of individuals who had been diagnosed with major depression. Participants were randomly assigned into intervention (n = 16) and wait-list control (n = 13) groups; those in the intervention group went to work alongside dairy farmers twice a week for 12 weeks for up to 3 hours at a time. Intervention group participants were able to choose to engage in physical contact with the cows, feeding, taking care of calves, mucking stalls, milking, and grooming activities. Researchers administered the Beck Depression Inventory (BDI), the State-Trait Anxiety Inventory-State Subscale, and the Generalized Self-Efficacy Scale. Results indicated that participants in the intervention had significant reductions in depression and significant improvement in self-efficacy at the end of the intervention, and that these gains were maintained at a 6-month follow up. Qualitative results suggest that not only did the animals have a calming and positive influence on participants, but the collegial relationship with the farmer was also beneficial. Given that 14% of Prison based Animal Programs (PAPs) (Furst, 2006) are livestock programs, further research is warranted to explore the mental health benefits of such programs.

In many prisons, group counseling is a form of rehabilitation. The integration of an animal in these groups may have positive effects on group cohesion. For instance, Wesley, Minatrea, and Watson (2009), in an experimental study utilizing a therapy dog for in patient substance abuse group counseling, found that the members of the group with a dog reported more positive feelings about the group than did the control group members without a dog.

Conclusion

This chapter has provided evidence to show that the HAB is real, broad, complex, and powerful. Whether it involves a cat or a bird, whether it occurs in a home environment or in an institutional setting, attention to the HAB provides insights into human functioning as well as support and therapy for people in need. Incorporating the HAB into the criminal justice system can occur in a multitude of ways, and the results of such integration must be meticulously studied to ensure that people as well as animals are supported in the chance to live a good life.

References

Ainsworth, M. D., & Bell, S. M. (1970). Attachment, exploration, and separation: Illustrated by the behavior of one-year-olds in a strange situation. *Child Development, 41* (1), 49–67. http://dx.doi.org/10.2307/1127388.

Allen, M. A. (2007). *Coping with Sorrow on the Loss of Your Pet* (20 Anv Exp.). Dog Ear Publishing, LLC.

American Veterinary Medical Association (n.d.). Human-animal bond. Retrieved November 21, 2021, from: https://www.avma.org/one-health/human-animal-bond.

American Veterinary Medicine Association. (2012). *U.S. Pet Ownership & Demographics Sourcebook 2012*. Amer Veterinary Medical Assn.

Animal Legal Defense Fund. (2014, March 14) All 50 states now have felony animal cruelty provisions! Retrieved March 23, 2015 from: http://aldf.org/blog/50-states-now-have-felony-animal-cruelty-provisions/.

Applebaum, J. W., Peek, C. W., & Zsembik, B. A. (2020). Examining U.S. pet ownership using the General Social Survey. *The Social Science Journal* (Fort Collins), 1–10. https://doi.org/10.1080/03623319.2020.1728507.

Arbour, R., Signal, T., & Taylor, N. (2009). Teaching kindness: The promise of humane education. *Society & Animals, 17*, 136–148.

Arkow, P. (2011, July). The Link Letter. *The National Link Coalition*. Retrieved from http://www.nationallinkcoalition.org.

Arluke, A. (1999). Uneasiness among laboratory technicians. *Occupational medicine (Philadelphia, Pa.), 14*(2), 305–316.

Ascione, F. (1997). Humane education research: Evaluating efforts to encourage children's kindness and caring toward animals. *Genetic Social and General Psychology Monographs, 123*(1), 59–77.

Ascione, F. (1993). Children who are cruel to animals—A review of the research and implications for developmental psychopathology. *Anthrozoos, 6*, 226–247.

Baran, B., Allen, J., Rogelberg, S., Spitzmuller, C., DiGiacomo, N., Webb, J., Carter, N., et al. (2009). Euthanasia-related strain and coping strategies in animal shelter employees. *Journal of the American Veterinary Medical Association, 235*(1) 83–88.

BBC NEWS|Americas|Prisoners raise puppies in jail. (n.d.). Retrieved May 11, 2012, from http://news.bbc.co.uk/2/hi/americas/8280726.stm.

BBC NEWS (2018, January 31). 'Emotional support peacock' barred from United Airlines plane. Retrieved November 22, 2021, from: https://www.bbc.com/news/world-us-canada-42880690.

BBC NEWS (2019, May 30). 'Emotional support dog attack' on plane sparks US lawsuit. Retrieved November 22, 2021, from: https://www.bbc.com/news/world-us-canada-48458271.

Beck, A., & Katcher, A. (2003). Future directions inhuman-animal bond research. *American Behavioral Scientist, 47*, 79–93.

Besthorn, F. H. (2002). Natural environment and the practice of psychotherapy. *Annals of the American Psychotherapy Assn, 5*(5), 19–20.

Bjerke, T., & Ostdahl, T. (2004). Animal-related attitudes and activities in an urban population. *Anthrozoös, 17*(2), 109–129.

Black, A. F., Winefield, H. R., & Chur-Hansen, A. (2011). Occupational stress in veterinary nurses: Roles of the work environment and own companion animal. *Anthrozoös, 24*, 191–202. doi:10.2752/175303711X12998632257503.

Breitenbach, E., Stumpft, E., Fersen, L., & Ebert, H. (2009). Dolphin-assisted therapy: changes in interaction and Communication between children with severe disabilities and their caregivers. *Anthrozoos, 22*, 277–289.

Brown, S. E. (2011). Theoretical concepts from self psychology applied to animal hoarding. *Society & Animals, 19*, 175–193. doi:10.1163/156853011x563006.

Carlstead, Paris, S., & Brown, J. L. (2019). Good keeper-elephant relationships in North American zoos are mutually beneficial to welfare. *Applied Animal Behaviour Science*, 211, 103–111. https://doi.org/10.1016/j.applanim.2018.11.003.

Chang, F. T., & Hart, L. A. (2002). Human-animal bonds in the laboratory: how animal behavior affects the perspectives of caregivers. *ILAR JOURNAL, 43*(1), 10–18.

Cheakalos, C. (2004). New Leash on Life. *Smithsonian, 35*(5), 62–68.

Chur-Hansen, A. (2010). Grief and bereavement issues and the loss of a companion animal: People living with a companion animal, owners of livestock, and animal support workers. *Clinical Psychologist, 14*(1), 14–21. doi:10.1080/13284201003662800.

CNN. (2014, December 1). Airline: 'Emotional support" pig kicked off flight for being disruptive. Retrieved November 22, 2021 from: https://www.cnn.com/2014/11/30/travel/emotional-support-pig-booted-flight/index.html.

Cobb, S. (1976). Presidential Address--1976. Social support as a moderator of life stress. *Psychosomatic Medicine, 38*(5), 300–314.

Cohen, S. P. (2002). Can pets function as family members? *Western Journal of Nursing Research, 24*(6), 621–638. doi:10.1177/019394502320555386.

Coleman, G., McGregor, M., Hemsworth, P., Boyce, J., & Dowling, S. (2003). The relationship between beliefs, attitudes and observed behaviours of abattoir personnel in the pig industry. *Applied Animal Behaviour Science, 82*, 189–200.

Collis, G. M., & McNicholas, J. (1998). A theoretical basis for health benefits of pet ownership: Attachment versus psychological support. *Companion animals in human health.* (pp. 105–122). Sage Publications, Inc.

Crawford, E. K., Worsham, N. L., & Swinehart, E. R. (2006). Benefits derived from companion animals, and the use of the term "attachment." *Anthrozoös, 19*(2), 98–112. doi:10.2752/089279306785593757.

Croney, C. (2014). Bonding with commodities: Social constructions and implications of human-animal relationships in contemporary livestock production. *Animal Frontiers, 4(3),* 59–64. doi:10.2527/af.2014-0023. https://www.animalsciencepublications.org/publications/af/pdfs/4/3/59.

Dupper, D. R. (2013). *School bullying: New perspectives on a growing problem.* Oxford University Press.

Duvall Antonacopoulos, N. M., & Pychyl, T. A. (2010). An examination of the potential role of pet ownership, human social support and pet attachment in the psychological health of individuals living alone. *Anthrozoös, 23*(1), 37–54.

Eddy, J., Hart, L. A., & Boltz, R. P. (1988). The effects of service dogs on social acknowledgments of people in wheelchairs. *Journal of Psychology: Interdisciplinary and Applied, 122*(1), 39–45.

Edwards NE, Beck AM, Lim E. Influence of aquariums on resident behavior and staff satisfaction in dementia units. West J Nurs Res. 2014 Nov;36(10):1309-22. doi: 10.1177/0193945914526647. Epub 2014 Mar 17. PMID: 24643090.

Faver, C. (2010). School-based humane education as a strategy to prevent violence: Review and recommendations. *Children and Youth Services Review, 32,* 365–370.

Faver, C. A., & Strand, E. B. (2007). Fear, guilt, and grief: Harm to pets and the emotional abuse of women. *Journal of Emotional Abuse, 7*(1), 51–70. doi:10.1300/J135v07n01_04.

Faver, C. A., & Cavazos, A. M. (2007). Animal abuse and domestic violence: A view from the border. *Journal of Emotional Abuse, 7*(3), 59–81.

Faver, C. A., & Cavazos, A. M. (2008). Love, safety, and companionship: The human-animal bond and Latino families. *Journal of Family Social Work, 11*(3), 254–271.

Flynn, C. P. (2000). Battered women and their animal companions: Symbolic interaction between human and nonhuman animals. *Society & Animals, 8*(2), 99–127. doi:10.1163/156853000511032.

Flynn, C. P. (2001). Acknowledging the "Zoological connection": A sociological analysis of animal cruelty. *Society & Animals, 9*(1), 71–87. doi:10.1163/156853001300109008.

Foreman, K., & Crosson, M. D. (2012). Canines for Combat Veterans: The National Education for Assistance Dog Services. *The United States Military Medical Journal,* Canine Assisted Therapy in Military Medicine, *April-June,* 63–64.

Friedmann, E., Katcher, A., Thomas, S., Lynch, J., & Messent, P. (1983). Social-interaction and blood-pressure-influence of animal companions. *Journal of Nervous and Mental Disease, 171*(8), 461–465. doi:10.1097/00005053-198308000-00002.

Frommer, S. S., & Arluke, A. (1999). Loving them to death: Blame-displacing strategies of animal shelter workers and surrenderers. *Society and Animals, 7*(1), 1–16.

Frumkin, H. (2001). Beyond toxicity: Human health and the natural environment. *American Journal of Preventive Medicine, 20*(3), 234–240.

Furst, G. (2006). Prison-Based Animal Programs: A National Survey. *The Prison Journal, 86*(4), 407–430. doi:10.1177/0032885506293242.

Garrity, T. F., Stallones, L., Marx, M. B., & Johnson, T. P. (1989). Pet ownership and attachment as supportive factors in the health of the elderly. *Anthrozoös, 3*(1), 35–44. doi:10.2752/089279390787057829.

Gosse, G. H., & Barnes, M. J. (1994). Human grief resulting from the death of a pet. *Anthrozoös, 7*(2), 103–112. doi:10.2752/089279394787001970.

Gullone, E. (2000). The biophilia hypothesis and life in the 21st century: Increasing mental health or increasing pathology? *Journal of Happiness Studies, 1*(3), 293–322.

Gullone, E., & Robertson, N. (2008). The relationship between bullying and animal abuse behaviors in adolescents: The importance of witnessing animal abuse. *Journal of Applied Developmental Psychology, 29*, 371–379.

Harker, D., & Bates, D. C. (2007). The black bear hunt in New Jersey: A constructionist analysis of an intractable conflict. *Society & Animals, 15*(4), 329–352.

Hart, L. A., Zasloff, R. L., Bryson, S., & Christensen, S. L. (2000). The role of police dogs as companions and working partners. *Psychological Reports, 86*(1), 190–202.

Hennessy, M. B., Morris, A., & Linden, F. (2006). Evaluation of the effects of a socialization program in a prison on behavior and pituitary—adrenal hormone levels of shelter dogs. *Applied Animal Behaviour Science, 99*(1), 157–171.

Henry, B., & Sanders, C. (2007). Bullying and animal abuse: Is there a connection? *Society & Animals, 15*, 107–126.

Hensley C, Tallichet SE, Dutkiewicz EL. *Childhood bestiality: a potential precursor to adult interpersonal violence.* J Interpers Violence. 2010 Mar;25(3):557-67. doi: 10.1177/0886260509360988. PMID: 20124030.

Herzog, H. (2002). Ethical aspects of relationships between humans and research animals. *ILAR Journal, 43*(1), 27–32.

Horst, F. C. P., LeRoy, H. A., & Veer, R. (2008). "When Strangers Meet": John Bowlby and Harry Harlow on attachment behavior. *Integrative Psychological and Behavioral Science, 42*(4), 370–388. doi:10.1007/s12124--008--9079--2.

Hosey, G., & Melfi, V. (2014). Human-animal interactions, relationships, and bonds: A review and analysis of the literature. *International Journal of Comparative Psychology, 27*(1), 117–142. http://escholarship.org/uc/item/6955n8kd.

Hoy-Gerlach, J., Vincent, A., & Lory Hector, B., (2019). Emotional support animals in the United States: Emergent Guidelines for Mental Health Clinicians. *Journal of Psychosocial Rehabilitation and Mental Health, 6*, 199–208. https://doi.org/10.1007/s40737-019-00146-8.

Hoy-Gerlach, J., & Wehman, S., (2017). *Human-Animal Interactions: A social work guide.* NASW Press.

Humane Society of the United States. (2003). *2003 Animal Cruelty Report.*

Johnson, R. A., & Meadows, R. L. (2002). Older Latinos, Pets, and Health. *Western Journal of Nursing Research, 24*(6), 609–620. doi:10.1177/019394502320555377.

Joye, Y. (2011). Biophilia in animal-assisted interventions—Fad or fact? *Anthrozoös, 24*(1), 5–15. doi:10.2752/175303711X12923300467249.

Kalof, L., & Taylor, C. (2007). The discourse of dog fighting. *Humanity & Society, 31*(4), 319–333.

Kass, P. H., John Jr, C., Scarlett, J. M., & Salman, M. D. (2001). Understanding animal companion surplus in the United States: Relinquishment of nonadoptables to animal shelters for euthanasia. *Journal of Applied Animal Welfare Science, 4*(4), 237–248.

Kellert, S. R., & Wilson, E. O. (1993). *The Biophilia Hypothesis*. Island Press.

Kuruvilla, C (2014, August 28). Kye the K-9 police dog is buried with full honors; cops investigate handler who shot animal's killer. *New York Daily News*. Retrieved June 10. 2015, from: http://www.nydailynews.com/news/national/kye-k-9-police-dog-laid-rest-full-honorsarticle-1.1920699.

Kwong, M., & Bartholomew, K. (2011). "Not just a dog": An attachment perspective on relationships with assistance dogs. *Attachment & Human Development, 13*(5), 421–436. doi:10.1080/14616734.2011.584410.

Lakey, B., & Orehek, E. (2011). Relational regulation theory: A new approach to explain the link between perceived social support and mental health. *Psychological Review, 118*(3), 482–495. doi:10.1037/a0023477.

Leinberger, Jr., R. C. (2009). *The Emotional Impact of the Animal Control Profession*. [Thesis, University of Richmond School of Continuing Studies].

Lockwood. (2018). Animal hoarding: The challenge for mental health, law enforcement, and animal welfare professionals. *Behavioral Sciences & the Law, 36*(6), 698–716. https://doi.org/10.1002/bsl.2373.

Magee, D. A., MacHugh, D. E., & Edwards, C. J. (2014). Interrogation of modern and ancient genomes reveals the complex domestic history of cattle. *Animal Frontiers, 4(3)*, 7–22. doi:10.2527/af.2014-0017.

Main, M., Kaplan, N., & Cassidy, J. (1985). Security in infancy, childhood, and adulthood: A move to the level of representation. *Monographs of the Society for Research in Child Development*, 66–104.

Marx, M. B., Stallones, L., Garrity, T. F., & Johnson, T. P. (1988). Demographics of Pet Ownership Among U.S. Adults 21 to 64 Years of Age. *Anthrozoös, 2*(1), 33–37.

McConnell, A. R., Brown, C. M., Shoda, T. M., Stayton, L. E., & Martin, C. E. (2011). Friends with benefits: On the positive consequences of pet ownership. *Journal of Personality and Social Psychology, 101*(6), 1239–1252. doi:10.1037/a0024506.

Meehan, M., Massavelli, B., & Pachana, N. (2017). Using attachment theory and social support theory to examine and measure pets as sources of social support and attachment figures. *Anthrozoös, 30*(2), 273–289. https://doi.org/10.1080/08927936.2017.1311050.

Merz-Perez, L., Heide, K., & Silverman, I. (2001). Childhood cruelty to animals and subsequent violence against humans. *International Journal of Offender Therapy and Comparative Criminology, 45*(5), 556–573. doi:10.1177/0306624X01455003.

Messent, P. (1985). Pets as social facilitators. *Veterinary Clinics of North America-Small Animal Practice, 15(2),* 387–393.

Milani, M. (1991). Considering the human/animal bond. *Journal of the American Veterinary Medical Association, 198*(10), 1706–1707.

Milani, M. (1995). *The art of veterinary practice: A guide to client communication.* University of Pennsylvania Press.

Milani, M. (2006). Problematic client-animal relationships: Munchausen by proxy. *The Canadian Veterinary Journal. La revue Vétérinaire Canadienne, 47*(12), 1161–1164.

Milani, M. (2011). The art of private veterinary practice: intellectual communication. *The Canadian Veterinary Journal. La revue Vétérinaire Canadienne, 52*(8), 897–898.

Miltiades, H., & Shearer, J. (2011). Attachment to pet dogs and depression in rural older adults. *Anthrozoös, 24*(2), 147–154. doi:10.2752/175303711X12998632257585.

Munro, H. M. C., & Thrusfield, M. V. (2001). Battered pets: Non-accidental physical injuries found in dogs and cats. *Journal of Small Animal Practice, 42*(6), 279–290.

Munro, H. M., & Thrusfield, M. V. (2001). "Battered pets": Munchausen syndrome by Proxy (factitious illness by proxy). *The Journal of Small Animal Practice, 42*(8), 385–389.

Nathanson, J. N. (2009). Animal hoarding: Slipping into the darkness of comorbid animal and self-Neglect. *Journal of Elder Abuse & Neglect, 21*(4), 307–324. doi:10.1080/08946560903004839.

National Link Coalition (2015, March). *The Link Letter, 8*(3), p.7.

National Link Coalition (2021, June 30). Pets in protection orders by state. Retrieved on November 22, 2021, from: https://nationallinkcoalition.org/resources/articles-research.

National Link Coalition (2021, June 30). Cross reporting by reporter. Retrieved on November 21, 2021, from: https://nationallinkcoalition.org/resources/articles-research.

Neumann, S. L. (2010). Animal welfare volunteers: Who are they and why do they do what they do? *Anthrozoös, 23*(4), 351–364. doi:10.2752/175303710X12750451259372.

North Carolina Department of Public Safety (2021). "New Leash on Life Dog Training Program." Retrieved on November 21, 2021, from: https://www.ncdps.gov/adult-corrections/prisons/programs/leash-facilities.

Packman, W., Field, N. P., Carmack, B. J., & Ronen, R. (2011). Continuing bonds and psychosocial adjustment in pet loss. *Journal of Loss and Trauma, 16,* 341–357. doi: 10.1080/15325024.2011.57204.

Palmer, R., & Custance, D. (2008). A counterbalanced version of Ainsworth's strange situation procedure reveals secure-base effects in dog-human relationships. *Applied Animal Behaviour Science, 109*(2–4), 306–319. doi:10.1016/j.applanim.2007.04.002.

Patronek, G. J. (1999). Hoarding of animals: An under-recognized public health problem in a difficult-to-study population. *Public Health Reports, 114*, 81–87. doi:10.1093/phr/114.1.81.

Patronek, G. J. (2006). Animal hoarding: Its roots and recognition. *Veterinary Medicine, 101*(8), 520.

Patronek, G. J., & Nathanson, J. N. (2009). A theoretical perspective to inform assessment and treatment strategies for animal hoarders. *Clinical Psychology Review, 29*, 274–281. doi:10.1016/j.cpr.2009.01.006.

Peacock, J., Chur-Hansen, A., & Winefield, H. (2012). Mental Health Implications of Human Attachment to Companion Animals. *Journal of Clinical Psychology, 68*(3), 292–303.

Pedersen, I., Martinsen, E. W., Berget, B., & Braastad, B. O. (2012). Farm animal-assisted intervention for people with clinical depression: A randomized controlled trial. *Anthrozoös, 25*(2), 149–160. doi:10.2752/175303712X13316289505260.

Pet-abuse.com (2015). Illegal Animal Fighting. Retrieved March 25, 2015, from http://www.pet-abuse.com/pages/animal_cruelty/animal_fighting.php.

Peters,S.(2011,September9).Dogshelpschoolslickbullies.USATODAY.COM.Retrieved June10,2012,fromhttp://yourlife.usatoday.com/parenting-family/story/2011-09-28/Dogs-help-schools-lick-bullies/50592574/1.

Phillips, C., & Peck, D. (2007). The effects of personality of keepers and tigers (Panthera tigris tigris) on their behaviour in an interactive zoo exhibit. *Applied Animal Behaviour Science, 106*(4), 244–258.

Planchon, L. A., Templer, D. I., Stokes, S., & Keller, J. (2002). Death of a companion cat or dog and human bereavement: Psychosocial variables. *Society and Animals, 10*(1), 93–105.

Planchon, Lynn A., & Templer, D. I. (1996). The correlates of grief after death of pet. *Anthrozoös, 9*(2–3), 107–113. doi:10.2752/089279396787001491.

Porcher, J. (2010). The relationship between workers and animals in the pork industry: A shared suffering. *Journal of Agricultural and Environmental Ethics, 24*(1), 3–17. doi:10.1007/s10806-010-9232-z.

Porcher, J., Cousson-Gelie, F., & Dantzer, R. (2004). Affective components of the human animal relationship in animal husbandry: Development and validation of a questionnaire 1. *Psychological reports, 95(1)*, 275–290.

Porcher, J., & Schmitt, T. (2012). Dairy cows: Workers in the shadows? *Society & Animals, 20*(1), 39–60. doi:10.1163/156853012X614350.

Risley-Curtiss, C, Holley, L., & Wolf, S. (2006). The human-animal bond and ethnic diversity. *Social Work, 51*, 257–268.

Risley-Curtiss, C., Holley, L. C., Cruickshank, T., Porcelli, J., Rhoads, C., Bacchus, D. N. A., Nyakoe, S., & Murphy, S. B. (2006). "She was family": Women of color and human-animal connections. *Affilia, 21*(4), 433–447. doi:10.1177/0886109906292314.

Risley-Curtiss, Christina, Holley, L. C., & Kodiene, S. (2011). "They're there for you": Men's relationships with companion animals. *Families in Society,* 92(4), 412–418.

Rohlf, V., & Bennett, P. (2005). Perpetration-induced traumatic stress in persons who euthanize nonhuman animals in surgeries, animal shelters, and laboratories. *Society & Animals, 13*(3), 201–220.

Russow, L. M. (2002). Ethical implications of the human-animal bond in the laboratory. *ILAR Journal, 43*(1), 33–37.

Sakagami, T., & Ohota, M. (2010). The effect of visiting zoos on human health and quality of life. *Animal Science Journal, 81*(1), 129–134.

Sanders, C. R. (2006). "The dog you deserve": Ambivalence in the K-9 officer/patrol dog relationship. *Journal of Contemporary Ethnography, 35*(2), 148–172. doi:10.1177/0891241605283456.

Schaefer, K., Hays, K., & Steiner, R. (2007). Animal abuse issues in therapy: A survey of therapists' attitudes. *Professional Psychology-Research and Practice, 38*, 530–537.

Schoenfeld-Tacher, R., Kogan, L. R., & Wright, M. L. (2010). Comparison of strength of the human-animal bond between Hispanic and non-Hispanic owners of pet dogs and cats. *Journal of the American Veterinary Medical Association, 236*(5), 529–534.

Siegel, J. M. (1995). Pet ownership and the importance of pets among adolescents. *Anthrozoös, 8(4), 217–223.*

Signal, T., Ghea,V., Taylor, N., & Acutt, D.(2103). When do psychologists pay attention to children harming animals? *Human-Animal Interaction Bulletin, 2,* 82–97.

Smith, L. D. G., Ham, S. H., & Weiler, B. V. (2011). The impacts of profound wildlife experiences. *Anthrozoös, 24*(1), 51–64. doi:10.2752/175303711X12923300467366.

Solomon, O. (2010). What a dog can do: Children with autism and therapy dogs in social interaction. *Ethos, 38*, 143–166.

Sprinkle, J. E. (2008). Animals, empathy, and violence: Can animals be used to convey principles of prosocial behavior to children? *Youth Violence and Juvenile Justice, 6*(1), 47–58. doi:10.1177/1541204007305525.

Steketee, G., Gibson, A., Frost, R. O., Alabiso, J., Arluke, A., & Patronek, G. (2011). Characteristics and antecedents of people who hoard animals: An exploratory comparative interview study. *Review of General Psychology, 15*, 114–124. doi:10.1037/a0023484.

Strand, E. B., & Faver, C. A. (2005). Battered women's concern for their pets: A closer look. *Journal of Family Social Work, 9*(4), 39–58. doi:10.1300/J039v09n04_04.

Sugawara, A., Masud, M. M., Yokoyama, A., Mizutani, W., Watanuki, S., Yanai, K., Itoh, M., & Tashiro, M. (2012). Effects of presence of a familiar pet dog on regional cerebral activity in healthy volunteers: A positron emission tomography study. *Anthrozoös, 25*(1), 25–34. doi:10.2752/175303712X1324047242731.

Toray, T. (2004). The human-animal bond and loss: Providing support for grieving clients. *Journal of Mental Health Counseling, 26*(3), 244–259.

U.S. Fish and Wildlife Service. (2016). *2016 National Survey of Fishing, Hunting, and Wildlife-Associated Recreation.*

Vaughn, M. G., Fu, Q., Beaver, K. M., DeLisi, M., Perron, B. E., & Howard, M. O. (2011). Effects of childhood adversity on bullying and cruelty to animals in the United States: Findings from a national sample. *Journal of Interpersonal Violence, 26*(17), 3509–3525. doi:10.1177/0886260511403763.

Waiblinger, S., Boivin, X., Pedersen, V., Tosi, M. V., Janczak, A. M., Visser, E. K., & Jones, R. B. (2006). Assessing the human-animal relationship in farmed species: A critical review. *Applied Animal Behaviour Science, 101(3),* 185–242.

Weisman, A. D. (1990). Bereavement and companion animals. *Omega: Journal of Death and Dying, 22*(4), 241–248. doi:10.2190/C54Y--UGMH--QGR4--CWTL.

Wenthold, N., & Savage, T. A. (2007). Ethical issues with service animals. *Topics in Stroke Rehabilitation, 14*(2), 68–74. doi:10.1310/tsr1402--68.

Wesley, M. C., Minatrea, N. B., & Watson, J. C. (2009). Animal-assisted therapy in the treatment of substance dependence. *Anthrozoös, 22,* 137–148. doi:10.2752/175 303709X434167.

Wilson, E. O. (2001). Nature matters. *American Journal of Preventive Medicine, 20*(3), 241–242. doi:10.1016/S0749--3797(00)00318--4.

Winefield, H. R., Black, A., & Chur-Hansen, A. (2008). Health effects of ownership of and attachment to companion animals in an older population. *International Journal of Behavioral Medicine, 15*(4), 303–310. doi:10.1080/10705500802365532.

Wisdom, J., Saedi, G., & Green, C. (2009). Another breed of "service" animals: STARS study findings about pet ownership and recovery from serious mental illness. *American Journal of Orthopsychiatry, 79,* 430–436.

World Association of Zoos and Aquariums (2021). Retrieved November 22, 2022, from: http://waza.org.

Yount, R. A., Olmert, M. D., & Lee, M. R. (2012). Service dog training program for the treatment of posttraumatic stress in service members. *The United States Military Medical Journal, Canine Assisted Therapy in Military Medicine, April-June,* 63–69.

Zapf, S. A., & Rough, R. B. (2002). The development of an instrument to match individuals with disabilities and service animals. *Disability & Rehabilitation*, *24*(1–3), 47–58.

Zasloff, L. (2010, May). *Chickens and donkeys and goats— Oh my! Exploring relationships with other kinds of pets.* Presented at the University of Tennessee Veterinary Social Work Summit.

Zequi SC, Guimarães GC, da Fonseca FP, Ferreira U, de Matheus WE, Reis LO, Aita GA, Glina S, Fanni VSS, Perez MDC, Guidoni LRM, Ortiz V, Nogueira L, Rocha LCA, Cuck G, da Costa WH, Moniz RR, Dantas Jr. JH, Soares FA, and Lopes A. *Sex with animals (SWA): Behavioral characteristics and possible association with penile cancer.* A multicenter study. J Sex Med 2012;9:1877–1884.

Zilcha-Mano, S., Mikulincer, M., & Shaver, P. (2011). An attachment perspective on human-pet relationships: Conceptualization and assessment of pet attachment orientations. *Journal of Research in Personality*, *45*, 345–357.

Zimolag, U., & Krupa, T. (2009). Pet ownership as a meaningful community occupation for people with serious mental illness. *American Journal of Occupational Therapy*, *63*, 126–137.

Chapter 8

Statistics and Measurement of Animal Cruelty

Cassandra L. Reyes and Orlando Hernandez

Introduction

The primary focus of the chapters in this text is on animal cruelty through both prohibited and permitted human conduct. Previous chapters have defined many kinds of animal cruelty (see Chapters 1, 3, and 4). To provide the foundation for further in-depth discussion about different types of animal cruelty (e.g., profit-related, sports-related, other active cruelty, hoarding), its prevalence will be presented in this chapter through available statistical data. First, prohibited animal cruelty offense statistics will be examined through available through the Federal Bureau of Investigation's (FBI) Uniform Crime Reporting (UCR) Program National Incident-Based Reporting System (NIBRS) and the Wildlife Reports for 2016 and 2020 based on the Convention on International Trade in Endangered Species (CITES) of Wild Fauna and Flora. This chapter will conclude with the second section that focuses on the prevalence of permitted animal cruelty. This information will include hunting (trophy hunting, game hunting, fur trapping), farming (fur farming, fisheries, food), and mills (puppy, kitty, and rabbit).

Prohibited Animal Cruelty

Prohibited animal cruelty was discussed in Chapter 3 and includes negligent and intentional actions such as not providing food, water, or shelter; torturing; overworking; and killing a non-human animal. As mentioned previously, the review of the prohibited animal cruelty statistics will begin with the National Incident-Based Reporting System (NIBRS) data.

National Incident-Based Reporting System (NIBRS) Data

In the United States, tracking the prevalence of animal cruelty on a nationwide level can prove to be a daunting task. Previously, a non-profit organization, Pet-Abuse.com, provided fairly up-to-date statistics that were gleaned from court documents, police records, and news reports (Reyes, 2016); however, current Pet-Abuse.com statistics are no longer available. Excluding Pet-Abuse.com, up until 2016, there was no other known database that provided animal cruelty-specific information. Collecting voluntarily-submitted data from law enforcement agencies (LEA), the Federal Bureau of Investigation's (FBI) Uniform Crime Reporting (UCR) Program National Incident-Based Reporting System (NIBRS) provides information on animal cruelty cases (FBI, 2017; FBI, 2018a; FBI, 2019a; FBI, 2020b; FBI, 2021). Nevertheless, prior to 2016, these cases were included in the "all other offenses" category, making any assessment of animal cruelty-specific offenses difficult (Palais, 2021). As mentioned previously in Chapter 3, on January 1, 2016, NIBRS began amassing yearly data on animal cruelty as a standalone offense under the "Crimes Against Society" category (FBI, 2016a). Crimes Against Society is one of the three NIBRS categories of offenses; the other two are "Crimes Against Persons" and Crimes Against Property" (FBI, 2017; FBI, 2018a; FBI, 2019a; FBI, 2020b; FBI, 2021). The other offenses in the Crimes Against Society category are drug/narcotic offenses, gambling offenses, pornography/obscene material, prostitution offenses, and weapon law violations. The FBI (2018c) defines animal cruelty as

> Intentionally, knowingly, or recklessly taking an action that mistreats or kills any animal without just cause, such as torturing, tormenting, mutilation, maiming, poisoning, or abandonment. Included are instances of duty to provide care, e.g., shelter, food, water, care if sick or injured; transporting or confining an animal in a manner likely to cause injury or death; causing an animal to fight with another; inflicting excessive or repeated unnecessary pain or suffering, e.g., uses objects to beat or injure an animal. This definition does not include proper maintenance of animals for show or sport; use of animals for food, lawful hunting, fishing or trapping.

The yearly NIBRS data are presented in publicly available tables (FBI, 2017; FBI, 2018a; FBI, 2019a; FBI, 2020b; FBI, 2021), but, unfortunately, do not include details regarding the types of animal cruelty being committed, nor the types of animals who are the victims of these acts. The data concentrate on the offenders' and arrestees' characteristics, and the location and time of the offenses.

The NIBRS animal cruelty data from 2016 to 2020 are available under "Tables with All Offenses," which include 13 sets of tables that provide information for the offenses within the three categories mentioned previously (FBI, 2017; FBI, 2018a; FBI, 2019a; FBI, 2020b; FBI, 2021). The first table set is "Participation," which focuses on the "Number of agencies and population covered by population group." The next table set,

"Incidents" comprises the "incidents, offenses, victims, and known offenders by offense category." It is important to note how "victims'" data are gathered for the NIBRS. According to the FBI (2016b),

> Through the Uniform Crime Reporting (UCR) Program's National Incident-Based Reporting System (NIBRS), law enforcement agencies report a separate set of victim data for each victim (up to 99) involved in an incident. Depending upon the offense type, the associated victim type may be an individual (including a law enforcement officer in some instances), a business, a financial institution, a government agency/entity, a religious organization, society/public, other, or unknown. Regardless of the victim type, however, at least one set of victim data must be connected to each specific offense in a crime incident.

The NIBRS's third table set is "Victims;" however, because the data in this set depict interpersonal offenses, it is excluded from this chapter. The fourth table set is "Offenders," and it provides the offender characteristics of "age category by offense category, age by offense category, sex by offense category, and race by offense category" (FBI, 2017; FBI, 2018a; FBI, 2019a; FBI, 2020b; FBI, 2021). The fifth table set is "Arrestees," which contains the "age category by arrest offense category, age by arrest offense category, sex by arrest offense category, and race by arrest offense category" of those who were arrested for known and reported animal cruelty offenses. The NIBRS's sixth table set is "Relationship," which also involves human victims and is therefore excluded from this chapter. The seventh table set, "Location," presents the "offense category by (the) location" at which the offense occurred. As these tables are specific to each of the three aforementioned categories, the Crimes Against Society table was selected for the purposes of this chapter. Another category-specific table set, "Time of Day" lists the "offense category by (the) time of day" during which the offense occurred. The NIBRS's next two table sets, "Type of Weapon/Force" and "Circumstances" only consist of interpersonal offenses and are also excluded from this chapter. The last category-specific table set, "State" is next, which provides data for the number of participating agencies, population covered, and state-level offenses. Due to space constraints, only the number of participating agencies and animal cruelty offenses will be included here. The penultimate table set is "Completed and Attempted," which is the "number of offenses completed and attempted by offense category." Finally, the last table set, "Clearances" provides data from "incidents cleared by offense category" (FBI, 2017; FBI, 2018a; FBI, 2019a; FBI, 2020b; FBI, 2021).

Because the data provided by the NIBRS are reliant on the voluntary participation of LEA, the review of the available NIBRS data will begin with a brief discussion regarding how two organizations, the FBI and the National Council on Violence against Animals' (NCOVAA) NIBRS Implementation Committee, have advised LEA, Animal Control Officers (ACO), and Humane Law Enforcement (HLE) Officers about collecting and submitting the said data. Next, an overview of the LEA that collect and submit the offense information, along with the populations they cover will follow.

Law Enforcement Agency Data and Populations Covered

The FBI is an organization that provides guidance to LEA regarding the collection of and how to report the data to NIBRS. For example, in August 2018, the FBI (2018d) published a document entitled "NIBRS Readiness Assessment for Law Enforcement Agencies." This document includes the following sections (FBI, 2018d):

> Overview: This section asks about the name of the system being assessed and the primary functions and users of the system (p. 3);
>
> NIBRS-Specific Requirements: This section asks about specific elements of the NIBRS data standard and the ability of the system to collect and store data according to this standard (p. 3); and
>
> Staffing/Resources: The purpose of this section is to understand how data is entered into the system and the extent to which staff members in your department can work within the system (p. 19).

In addition, on December 21, 2018, the FBI (2018b) posted a YouTube video entitled "NIBRS 101" that presents the background and creation of the UCR and the NIBRS. It then encourages LEA to participate in NIBRS by stating that the International Association of Chiefs of Police, Major Cities Chiefs Association, National Sheriff's Association, the Major County Sheriff's Association, and the FBI's Criminal Justice Information Services Division Advisory Policy Board joined with the FBI to transition to the NIBRS as the only crime statistics collection system (FBI, 2018b). Furthermore, the video indicates that the NIBRS will increase statistical reliability, accuracy, accessibility, and timeliness (FBI, 2018b). The FBI (2019b) also published "A Guide to Understanding NIBRS" in July of 2019 that covered the topics of "Reporting Procedures and Units of Count," "Editing Procedures and Data Validity," "Availability of NIBRS Data," and links for more information. This document additionally provides graphics on the "NIBRS Group A Incident Report and Associated Data Elements" and the "NIBRS Group B Arrest Report and Associated Data Elements" (FBI, 2019b).

As a part of their duties, ACO and HLE are often the first on the scene in animal cruelty cases; however, the FBI does not consider them as LEA (NCOVAA's NIBRS Implementation Committee, n.d., p. 2). Therefore, the NCOVAA's NIBRS Implementation Committee is an organization that provides ACO and HLE thorough information regarding how to collect NIBRS-compliant data and submit them to the ACO's and HLE's LEA partners in its "NIBRS User Manual for Animal Control Officers and Humane Law Enforcement (NCOVAA's NIBRS Implementation Committee, n.d.). The Manual covers the following topics: "Introduction to the NIBRS Animal Cruelty Incident Report," "Administrative," "Offense," "Property," "Offender/Arrestee," "Victim," "Narrative," "Frequently Asked Questions," "Current NIBRS Participation States," "NIBRS Incident Reporting Template," and "Draft MOU (memorandum of understanding) between ACO/HLE and LEA." In the introduction of this manual, the

NIBRS's definition of animal cruelty is provided and further specified (NCOVAA's NIBRS Implementation Committee, n.d., p. 2):

A → simple/gross neglect: the failure of a person to provide for the needs of an animal (lack of food, water, shelter, grooming or veterinary care);

I → intentional abuse and torture: the intentional act of harming an animal;

F → organized abuse: dog fighting and cockfighting; and

S → animal sexual abuse.

Although NIBRS has a specific definition for animal cruelty, as discussed in Chapters 1, 2, 3, and 4 of this book, animal cruelty laws vary from state to state, which could present a challenge for the ACO and HLE reporting of these offenses. As a result, the manual advises ACO and HLE how to address this issue. It states that "(t)he FBI's definition is meant to encompass all state statutes ... if the reported incident meets your state's or agency's definitions, then the incident should be submitted to NIBRS" (NCOVAA's NIBRS Implementation Committee, n.d., p. 2). The manual also provides the ACO and HLE with step-by-step directions on how they should fill out the NIBRS-compliant incident report and submit it to the LEA with which they have an MOU. With regard to reporting, if utilized as written in the Manual, the MOU would require that the LEA accept the said ACO/HS (Humane Society)/HLE's data submissions and provide them to NIBRS no less than once a year (NCOVAA's NIBRS Implementation Committee, n.d., p. 27). With the inclusion of this MOU as the final appendix, this Manual has provided ACO and HLE with a comprehensive start-to-finish guide with regard to reporting animal cruelty cases indirectly to NIBRS.

This has provided some understanding regarding how the FBI and the NCOVAA's NIBRS Implementation Committee provide guidance to LEA, ACO, and HLE on the collection and submission of animal cruelty data to NIBRS. Next, the focus will be on the LEA that submit these data to NIBRS.

In order to fully comprehend the number of animal cruelty cases that have been provided by the NIBRS since 2016, it is important to first take into account the number of participants (LEA) that have provided their data for all offenses, the size of the population they cover, and the methodology under which their data were presented in the NIBRS. These LEA consist of local, state, tribal, college and university, and other types of agencies across the United States (FBI, 2017; FBI, 2018a; FBI, 2019a; FBI, 2020b; FBI, 2021). With regard to the first year that these data were collected, according to the NIBRS (FBI, 2017),

> The number of law enforcement agencies eligible to participate in the UCR Program under the column for Crime in the United States, 2016, represents LEAs that reported their UCR data through either the Summary Reporting System (SRS) or the NIBRS and whose data were reflected in that publication, as well as law enforcement agencies that had an active originating agency identifier. (NIBRS data were converted to summary data using the SRS Hierarchy Rule, which counts only the most serious crime in multiple-offense incidents.)

Beginning in 2017, the submitted NIBRS data were no longer converted via the Hierarchy Rule, thus allowing for a clearer view of the types of offenses committed (FBI, 2018a). Therefore,

> Figures under the column headed Actively Enrolled in the UCR Program represent those agencies that reported their UCR data through either the NIBRS or SRS as well as those LEAs that had an active originating agency identifier but did not contribute data to UCR in ... Figures under the column headed Total Participants Submitting Data includes those LEAs that reported data through either the NIBRS or SRS and excludes those agencies that did not submit data. The number of submitting agencies in the column headed Submitted Data via National Incident-Based Reporting System, includes those LEAs that reported at least one Group A Offense, Group B Arrest Report, or Zero Report via the NIBRS for one or more months of the ... calendar year. Finally, the column headed Submitted Data via Summary Reporting System submitted at least one Return A Record Card to the UCR Program for one or more months of the ... calendar year (FBI, 2018a; FBI, 2019a; FBI, 2020b; FBI, 2021).

The following table, Table 1, shows the number of LEA enrolled, their participation status, method of data submission, and population covered by year from 2016 to 2020, the most recent year available (FBI, 2017; FBI, 2018a; FBI, 2019a; FBI, 2020b; FBI, 2021).

Table 1. Number of LEA and Population Covered

Crime in the US		**Actively Enrolled in UCR Program**			
Year	2016	2017	2018	2019	2020
# of LEA[1]	18,481	18,547	18,586	18,667	18,619
Pop. Covered	323,127,513	325,719,178	327,167,434	328,239,523	329,484,123
		Total Participants Submitting Data			
Year	–	2017	2018	2019	2020
# of LEA	–	16,655	16,659	16,551	15,901
Pop. Covered	–	318,873,991	320,040,056	318,245,527	313,609,388
NIBRS/SRS		**NIBRS**			
Year	2016	2017	2018	2019	2020
# of LEA	6,849	6,988	7,283	8,497	9,880
Pop. Covered	100,900,768	105,672,974	117,181,606	146,562,042	177,522,400
		SRS			
Year	–	2017	2018	2019	2020
# of LEA	–	9,672	9,376	8,054	6,021
Pop. Covered	–	213,322,696	202,858,450	171,683,485	136,086,988

1. # of LEA eligible to participate in the UCR Program (2016 only).

As shown in Table 1, the number of LEA that were either eligible to participate or actively enrolled in the UCR Program fluctuated between 18,481 in 2016 and 18,619 in 2020 (FBI, 2017; FBI, 2018a; FBI, 2019a; FBI, 2020b; FBI, 2021). The population that they covered grew from 323,127,513 people in 2016 to 329,484,123 people in 2020, which is an average increase of 1,589,152.5 people per year. With regard to the LEA that submitted data, the number was fairly stable from 2017 to 2019 with an average of 16,621; however, the number decreased slightly to 15,901 in 2020. The population that these LEA covered increased between 2017 and 2018 to 320,040,056 people, but there was a decline through 2020, ending at 313,609,388, a difference of 6,430,668 people (FBI, 2017; FBI, 2018a; FBI, 2019a; FBI, 2020b; FBI, 2021). This decrease in the population could stem from a number of causes including the beginning of the COVID-19 pandemic in 2020.

As mentioned previously and shown in Table 1, the method in which the data were submitted changed from its initial year of 2016 to 2017. Thus, the main difference between the first two years was the separate data submissions to the NIBRS and the SRS, which then remained the same through the most recent year available (FBI, 2019a; FBI, 2020b; FBI, 2021). Even though the LEA data were submitted to the NIBRS and converted via the SRS Hierarchy Rule in 2016 (FBI, 2017), there was a marked increase from the said year of 6,849 agencies providing data to 9,880 agencies submitting data solely to the NIBRS in 2020. However, the number of LEA submitting data solely via SRS from 2017 to 2020 decreased from 9,672 to 6,021 (FBI, 2017; FBI, 2018a; FBI, 2019a; FBI, 2020b; FBI, 2021).

Regardless of the manner via which the data were submitted, it appears that the NIBRS may be a growing venue where the prevalence of animal cruelty cases can be assessed superficially. However, as will be shown in the following sections, the NIBRS data do not provide the non-human animals' demographics (i.e., type of animal, age, relationship to the alleged perpetrator) who were the victims of the cruelty nor the types of offenses (i.e., violent offenses, active cruelty, passive cruelty, neglect) that were committed. Instead, the primary focus of the data in the following sections is on the offender and arrestee characteristics, as well as the location and time of the offense.

Incidents, Offenses, Victims, and Known Offenders by Offense Category

The next set of data in the NIBRS to be discussed is the "Incidents, Offenses, Victims, and Known Offenders by Offense Category" (FBI, 2017; FBI, 2018a; FBI, 2019a; FBI, 2020b; FBI, 2021). Of specific interest here are the statistics for the total number of incidents, offenses, victims, and known offenders, as well as the number of incidents, offenses, victims, and known offenders in the reported animal cruelty cases. When reviewing the statistics in their totality, it is important to note the NIBRS clarification regarding the data (FBI, 2017; FBI, 2018a; FBI, 2019a; FBI, 2020b; FBI, 2021),

> To arrive at the totals provided for each column of data, the UCR Program used the following counting rules: Incidents—one for each offense type identified within each incident, aggregated by offense category. In multiple-offense incidents, incidents were counted two or more times when there were two or more offense types in the incident ... Offenses Categories: Crime Against Society—one for each unique offense type.... The term Known Offender does not imply the identity of the suspect is known, but only that an attribute of the suspect has been identified which distinguishes him/her from an unknown offender. Therefore, the figures in this column do not account for the ... incidents with unknown offenders.

The total and animal cruelty data from 2016 to 2020 are presented in the following table, Table 2 (FBI, 2017; FBI, 2018a; FBI, 2019a; FBI, 2020b; FBI, 2021).

Table 2. Incidents, Offenses, Victims, and Known Offenders

		Incidents			
Offense Category	2016	2017	2018	2019	2020
Total	5,237,106	5,369,204	5,617,945	6,572,870	7,560,867
Animal Cruelty	1,126	3,228	5,201	9,956	11,566
		Offenses			
Offense Category	2016	2017	2018	2019	2020
Total	6,101,034	6,290,042	6,586,140	7,688,645	8,879,728
Animal Cruelty	1,126	3,228	5,201	9,956	11,566
		Victims			
Offense Category	2016	2017	2018	2019	2020
Total	6,437,018	6,631,461	6,944,242	8,116,849	9,362,709
Animal Cruelty	1,126	3,228	5,201	9,956	11,566
		Known Offenders			
Offense Category	2016	2017	2018	2019	2020
Total	4,963,644	5,266,175	5,652,156	6,543,257	7,173,072
Animal Cruelty	1,057	3,115	4,999	9,453	10,414

As noted in Table 2, according to the NIBRS (FBI, 2017; FBI, 2018a; FBI, 2019a; FBI, 2020b; FBI, 2021), in 2016, there were 5,237,106 total incidents reported, which included 1,126 animal cruelty offenses (approximately .02% of all reported incidents). From 2017 to 2020, the total number of incidents grew from 5,369,204 to 7,560,867. During this same time period, the reported animal cruelty incidents increased approximately 3.6 times from 3,228 incidents (approximately 1% of the total number of incidents) in 2017 to 11,566 incidents (approximately 1.5% of the total number of incidents) in 2020 (FBI, 2017; FBI, 2018a; FBI, 2019a; FBI, 2020b; FBI, 2021).

With regard to the number of offenses, as shown in Table 2, according to the NIBRS (FBI, 2017; FBI, 2018a; FBI, 2019a; FBI, 2020b; FBI, 2021), in 2016, there were 6,101,034 total offenses reported; animal cruelty offenses accounted for 1,126 (approximately .02%) of them. From 2017 to 2020, the total number of offenses grew from 6,631,461 to 9,362,709. During this same time frame, the reported animal cruelty offenses increased approximately 3.6 times from 3,228 offenses (approximately .05% of the total number of offenses) in 2017 to 11,566 offenses (approximately 1% of the total number of offenses) in 2020 (FBI, 2017; FBI, 2018a; FBI, 2019a; FBI, 2020b; FBI, 2021).

Next, as noted in Table 2, according to the NIBRS (FBI, 2017; FBI, 2018a; FBI, 2019a; FBI, 2020b; FBI, 2021), in 2016, there were 6,437,018 total victims reported, which included 1,126 animal victims (approximately .02% of total victims). During this same time period, the reported animal cruelty victims increased approximately 3.6 times from 3,228 victims in 2017 (approximately .04% of the total number of victims) to 11,566 victims (approximately 1% of the total number of victims) in 2020 (FBI, 2017; FBI, 2018a; FBI, 2019a; FBI, 2020b; FBI, 2021).

Finally, regarding the known offenders data, as noted in Table 2, according to the NIBRS (FBI, 2017; FBI, 2018a; FBI, 2019a; FBI, 2020b; FBI, 2021), in 2016, there were 4,963,644 total known offenders reported, including 1,057 known animal cruelty offenders (approximately .02% of the total known offenders). From 2017 to 2020, the total number of known offenders grew from 5,266,175 to 7,173,072. During this same time, the number of reported known offenders in animal cruelty cases increased approximately 3.3 times from 3,115 known offenders (approximately .05% of all known offenders) in 2017 to 10,414 known offenders (approximately .1% of all known offenders) in 2020 (FBI, 2017; FBI, 2018a; FBI, 2019a; FBI, 2020b; FBI, 2021).

Upon review of the total and animal cruelty case data with regard to the number of incidents, offenses, victims, and known offenders that have been submitted to the NIBRS by the LEA, it would appear that the number of said cases has increased since 2016. However, one needs to be critical in their assessment of these data. As stated earlier, for example, the number of incidents could be counted more than once. In addition, although the NIBRS began including animal cruelty in 2016, it is considered a less serious offense compared to more serious UCR Part I offenses (i.e., criminal homicide; rape; robbery; aggravated assault; burglary; motor vehicle theft; arson; human trafficking, commercial sex acts) (FBI, 2020a). Therefore, due to the Hierarchy Rule, it would have been eclipsed by those offenses and not as readily depicted in the NIBRS data for the first year. As a result, this along with other factors [i.e., lack of knowledge about animal cruelty offenses, lack of resources to enforce and prosecute animal cruelty offenses (see Chapters 1, 3, and 4 in this book), voluntary agency reporting, human error in data entry, the COVID-19 pandemic (see Chapter 4 in this book)] could have had an impact on the number of animal cruelty cases listed in the NIBRS data for 2016 as well as the other years.

Offender Characteristics

The examination of the available NIBRS information regarding animal cruelty cases will continue with the offender characteristics. When assessing the offender statistics in their totality, it is important to note the NIBRS clarification regarding the data (FBI, 2017; FBI, 2018a; FBI, 2019a; FBI, 2020b; FBI, 2021),

> The UCR Program counted one offender for each offense type to which they were connected, with the exception of unknown offenders. In a multiple-offense incident, each offender (for which data was submitted) was counted more than once. The offender data were aggregated by the age categories presented and broken down by their associated offense categories. For this table, an adult is an offender who is age 18 or older, and a juvenile is an offender who is under 18 years of age. The Unknown column represents the number of offenders whose age was unknown. Note: Data for the … incidents reported with unknown offenders are not included in this table because nothing is known about the offender(s).

This review will begin with the offenders' age, followed by age range, sex, and conclude with their race.

Offenders' Age Category by Offense Category

The total offenders, adult, juvenile, and unknown age for the total offense categories and animal cruelty data from 2016 to 2020 are presented in the following table, Table 3 (FBI, 2017; FBI, 2018a; FBI, 2019a; FBI, 2020b; FBI, 2021).

Table 3. Offenders' Age Category by Offense Category

Total Offense Categories					
Age Category	2016	2017	2018	2019	2020
Total Offenders	5,237,106	5,266,175	5,652,156	6,543,257	7,173,072
Adult	3,714,387	3,901,203	4,200,429	4,824,667	5,350,030
Juvenile	481,006	501,503	490,649	584,732	494,379
Unknown	768,251	863,469	961,258	1,133,858	1,328,663
Animal Cruelty					
Age Category	2016	2017	2018	2019	2020
Total Offenders	1,057	3,115	4,999	9,453	10,414
Adult	884	2,620	4,276	7,916	8,834
Juvenile	25	116	186	270	335
Unknown	148	379	537	1,267	1,245

As noted in Table 3, according to the NIBRS (FBI, 2017; FBI, 2018a; FBI, 2019a; FBI, 2020b; FBI, 2021), in 2016, there were 5,237,106 total offenders reported and

1,057 animal cruelty offenders (approximately .02% of total offenders) listed for that year. From 2017 to 2020, the total number of total offenders grew from 5,266,175 to 7,173,072. During this same time period, the reported number of animal cruelty offenders increased approximately 3.3 times from 3,115 incidents (approximately .05% of the total number of offenders) in 2017 to 10,414 offenders (approximately 1.4% of the total number of offenders) in 2020 (FBI, 2017; FBI, 2018a; FBI, 2019a; FBI, 2020b; FBI, 2021).

With regard to the number of adult offenders, as shown in Table 3, according to the NIBRS (FBI, 2017; FBI, 2018a; FBI, 2019a; FBI, 2020b; FBI, 2021), in 2016, there were 3,714,387 adult offenders reported; adult animal cruelty offenders accounted for 884 (approximately .02%) of them. From 2017 to 2020, the total number of adult offenders grew from 3,901,203 to 5,350,030. During this same time frame, the reported number of adult animal cruelty offenders increased approximately 3.4 times from 2,620 offenders in 2017 (approximately .07% of the total number of adult offenders) to 8,834 offenders in 2020 (approximately 2% of the total number of adult offenders) in 2020 (FBI, 2017; FBI, 2018a; FBI, 2019a; FBI, 2020b; FBI, 2021).

Next, as noted in Table 3, according to the NIBRS (FBI, 2017; FBI, 2018a; FBI, 2019a; FBI, 2020b; FBI, 2021), in 2016, there were 481,006 total juvenile offenders reported, which included 25 juvenile animal offenders (approximately .01% of total juvenile offenders). In 2017, there were 501,503 total juvenile offenders reported. This number decreased to 494,379 in 2020. Conversely, during this same time period, the reported number of juvenile animal cruelty offenders increased approximately 2.9 times from 116 juvenile animal cruelty offenders in 2017 (approximately .05% of the total number of juvenile offenders) to 335 juvenile animal cruelty offenders (approximately .06% of the total number of juvenile offenders) in 2020 (FBI, 2017; FBI, 2018a; FBI, 2019a; FBI, 2020b; FBI, 2021).

Finally, in regard to the unknown offenders data, as noted in Table 3, according to the NIBRS (FBI, 2017; FBI, 2018a; FBI, 2019a; FBI, 2020b; FBI, 2021), in 2016, there were 768,251 total unknown offenders reported, including 148 unknown animal cruelty offenders (approximately .02% of the total unknown offenders). From 2017 to 2020, the total number of unknown offenders grew from 863,469 to 1,328,663. During this same time, the number of reported unknown offenders in animal cruelty cases increased approximately 3.3 times from 379 unknown offenders (approximately .04% of all unknown offenders) in 2017 to 1,245 unknown offenders (approximately .1% of all unknown offenders) in 2020 (FBI, 2017; FBI, 2018a; FBI, 2019a; FBI, 2020b; FBI, 2021).

Upon review of the total and animal cruelty offender case data with regard to their age that have been submitted to the NIBRS by the LEA, it would appear that the number of said cases has generally increased since 2016, with the exception of the total juvenile offender number. However, one needs to be critical in their assessment of these data. As stated earlier, for example, the number of offenders could be counted more than once when there is a multiple-offense incident. One would need to consider the same issues with the data as mentioned with the previous category.

The next offender-focused category of data to be reviewed is the offenders' age range. Although these data are presented in the total, unknown, and 13 separate age ranges, due to space considerations, the age ranges will be consolidated for the purpose of this examination.

Offenders' Age Range by Offense Category

Unlike the other offender age-related data, no data were available for 2016 via the NIBRS for the age-range data. The total offender and unknown age (addressed in the previous category), 13 age ranges, and unknown age categories; and animal cruelty offender age-range data from 2017 to 2020 are presented in the following table, Table 4 (FBI, 2018a; FBI, 2019a; FBI, 2020b; FBI, 2021).

Table 4. Offenders' Age Range by Offense Category (in Years)

Total Offense Categories				
Age Range	2017	2018	2019	2020
Total Offenders	5,266,175	5,652,156	6,543,257	7,173,072
10 and Under	19,883	19,241	26,797	18,067
11–15	235,948	234,056	293,955	230,476
16–20	729,517	721,308	793,885	792,384
21–25	760,583	774,591	840,697	917,511
26–30	717,700	774,517	878,697	972,769
31–35	578,470	635,078	735,126	850,807
36–40	449,190	505,818	605,748	685,825
41–45	287,144	319,449	384,170	452,126
46–50	240,794	265,329	303,480	331,436
51–55	174,441	189,610	217,419	234,695
56–60	115,436	143,079	192,143	202,295
61–65	48,954	58,523	74,349	84,548
66 and over	44,646	50,299	63,292	72,470
Unknown Age	863,469	961,258	1,133,858	1,328,663
Animal Cruelty				
Age Range	2017	2018	2019	2020
Total Offenders	3,115	4,999	9,453	10,414
10 and Under	8	34	34	41
11–15	74	87	104	159
16–20	170	290	603	672
21–25	330	506	1,017	1,092
26–30	390	619	1,133	1,285
31–35	323	557	1,038	1,227
36–40	342	553	901	1,073
41–45	237	425	712	793
46–50	211	345	663	642
51–55	190	298	586	587
56–60	161	278	511	590
61–65	137	195	359	401
66 and over	163	275	525	607
Unknown Age	379	537	1,267	1,245

As stated, there are 13 age ranges and an unknown age group listed in Table 4; therefore, to consolidate the information and save space in this book, it will be presented as 10 years old and under, 11–20 years old, 21–30 years old, 31–40 years old, 41–50 years old, 51–60 years old, and 61 years old and over, for the total offense categories and animal cruelty cases. These selected age groups are based primarily on decades of years. The total number of offenders, total numbers of animal cruelty offenders by age and the unknown age of offenders of all offenses and of animal cruelty offenses were addressed in Table 3, they will not be discussed again here.

As noted in Table 4, according to the NIBRS (FBI, 2018a; FBI, 2019a; FBI, 2020b; FBI, 2021), from 2017 to 2020, the number of offenders aged 10 years old and under declined from 19,883 to 18,067. During this same time period, the reported number of animal cruelty offenders aged 10 and under increased approximately 5.1 times from eight offenders (approximately .04% of the total number of offenders in that age range) in 2017 to 41 offenders (approximately .2% of the total number of offenders in that age range) in 2020 (FBI, 2018a; FBI, 2019a; FBI, 2020b; FBI, 2021).

As observed in Table 4, according to the NIBRS (FBI, 2018a; FBI, 2019a; FBI, 2020b; FBI, 2021), from 2017 to 2020, the number of offenders aged 11–20 years old increased from 965,465 to 1,022,860. During this same time period, the reported number of animal cruelty offenders aged 11–20 years old increased approximately 3.4 times from 244 offenders (approximately .02% of the total number of offenders in that age range) in 2017 to 831 offenders (approximately .1% of the total number of offenders in that age range) in 2020 (FBI, 2018a; FBI, 2019a; FBI, 2020b; FBI, 2021).

As shown in Table 4, according to the NIBRS (FBI, 2018a; FBI, 2019a; FBI, 2020b; FBI, 2021), from 2017 to 2020, the number of offenders aged 21–30 years old increased from 1,478,283 to 1,890,280. During this same time period, the reported number of animal cruelty offenders aged 21–30 years old increased approximately 3.3 times from 720 offenders (approximately .05% of the total number of offenders in that age range) in 2017 to 2,377 offenders (approximately .1% of the total number of offenders in that age range) in 2020 (FBI, 2018a; FBI, 2019a; FBI, 2020b; FBI, 2021).

As demonstrated in Table 4, according to the NIBRS (FBI, 2018a; FBI, 2019a; FBI, 2020b; FBI, 2021), from 2017 to 2020, the number of offenders aged 31–40 years old increased from 1,027,660 to 1,536,632. During this same time period, the reported number of animal cruelty offenders aged 31–40 years old increased approximately 3.5 times from 665 offenders (approximately .06% of the total number of offenders in that age range) in 2017 to 2,300 offenders (approximately .1% of the total number of offenders in that age range) in 2020 (FBI, 2018a; FBI, 2019a; FBI, 2020b; FBI, 2021).

As displayed in Table 4, according to the NIBRS (FBI, 2018a; FBI, 2019a; FBI, 2020b; FBI, 2021), from 2017 to 2020, the number of offenders aged 41–50 years old increased from 527,938 to 783,562. During this same time period, the reported number of animal cruelty offenders aged 41–50 years old increased approximately 3.2 times from 448 offenders (approximately .1% of the total number of offenders in that age range) in 2017 to 1,435 offenders (approximately .2% of the total number of offenders in that age range) in 2020 (FBI, 2018a; FBI, 2019a; FBI, 2020b; FBI, 2021).

As exhibited in Table 4, according to the NIBRS (FBI, 2018a; FBI, 2019a; FBI, 2020b; FBI, 2021), from 2017 to 2020, the number of offenders aged 51–60 years old increased from 289,877 to 436,990. During this same time period, the reported number of animal cruelty offenders aged 51–60 years old increased approximately 3.4 times from 351 offenders (approximately .1% of the total number of offenders in that age range) in 2017 to 1,177 offenders (approximately .3% of the total number of offenders in that age range) in 2020 (FBI, 2018a; FBI, 2019a; FBI, 2020b; FBI, 2021).

As evidenced in Table 4, according to the NIBRS (FBI, 2018a; FBI, 2019a; FBI, 2020b; FBI, 2021), from 2017 to 2020, the number of offenders aged 61 years old and over increased from 93,600 to 157,018. During this same time period, the reported number of animal cruelty offenders aged 61 years old and over increased approximately 3.4 times from 300 offenders (approximately .3% of the total number of offenders in that age range) in 2017 to 1,008 offenders (approximately .6% of the total number of offenders in that age range) in 2020 (FBI, 2018a; FBI, 2019a; FBI, 2020b; FBI, 2021).

The number of animal cruelty offenders by age range for 2017 and 2020 are provided in Chart 1 as a visual presentation of the data. The increase in the number of offenders in each age-range category is clear between the two years is clear; however, it should be noted that as previously stated, there have been more LEA participating in NIBRS during this time frame.

As demonstrated in Chart 1, it would appear that animal cruelty offenders are committing the said offenses more often between the ages of 21–40 years old. This information seems to contradict age-based criminological theories, such as the developmental theories, which posit that offenders generally peak in their delinquent and criminal activity during a younger age range, usually in their late teens to late 20s (see Hirschi

Chart 1. Animal Cruelty Offenders' Age Range by Offense Category (in Years)

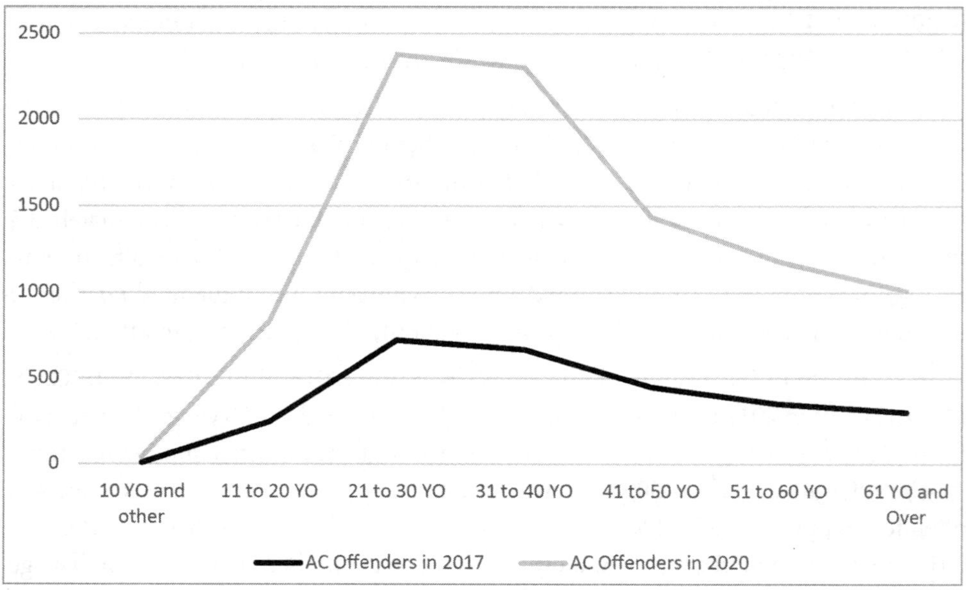

& Gottfredson, 1983; Kressler & Reinecke, 2021; Laub & Sampson, 1993; McGee & Farrington, 2019; McGee et al., 2021; Moffitt, 1993; Rosa et al., 2020; Sampson & Laub, 2005). Additional theories that attempt to explain why animal cruelty is committed are addressed in Chapters 7, 13, 15, and 16. However, as stated with regard to the rest of the offender-based information, one needs to be critical in their assessment of these data. The same issues with these data exist as mentioned with the previous category.

The review of the offender demographics now shifts from age to sex in the next section. The available NIBRS offender sex-based data are divided by the total number of offenders, male, female, and unknown sex. The data on the animal cruelty offenders are divided in the same manner.

Offenders' Sex by Offense Category

The data for the offenders' sex are available from 2016 to 2020 via the NIBRS. These data are presented in the following table, Table 5 (FBI, 2017; FBI, 2018a; FBI, 2019a; FBI, 2020b; FBI, 2021).

Table 5. Offenders' Sex by Offense Category

Total Offense Categories					
Offenders' Sex	2016	2017	2018	2019	2020
Total Offenders	4,963,644	5,266,175	5,652,156	6,543,257	7,173,072
Male	3,127,609	3,285,814	3,475,860	4,034,643	4,451,194
Female	1,268,880	1,343,303	1,439,981	1,662,913	1,737,987
Unknown	567,155	637,058	736,315	845,701	983,891
Animal Cruelty					
Offenders' Sex	2016	2017	2018	2019	2020
Total Offenders	1,057	3,115	4,999	9,453	10,414
Male	569	1,758	2,831	5,173	5,964
Female	407	1,113	1,818	3,480	3,609
Unknown	81	244	350	800	841

As stated, there are four groupings for the total offense categories and animal cruelty cases in Table 5, the total offenders, male, female, and unknown sex. Each group will be discussed separately.

As observed in Table 5, according to the NIBRS (FBI, 2017; FBI, 2018a; FBI, 2019a; FBI, 2020b; FBI, 2021), in 2016, there were 3,127,609 male offenders, of whom were 569 animal cruelty offenders (approximately .02% of male offenders). From 2017 to 2020, the number of male offenders for all offenses increased from 3,285,814 to 4,451,194. During this same time period, the reported number of male animal cruelty offenders increased approximately 3.4 times from 1,758 offenders (approximately .05%

of the total number of male offenders) in 2017 to 5,964 offenders (approximately .1% of the total number of male offenders) in 2020 (FBI, 2017; FBI, 2018a; FBI, 2019a; FBI, 2020b; FBI, 2021).

As shown in Table 5, according to the NIBRS (FBI, 2017; FBI, 2018a; FBI, 2019a; FBI, 2020b; FBI, 2021), in 2016, there were 1,268,880 female offenders for all offenses, of whom were 407 animal cruelty offenders (approximately .03% of female offenders). From 2017 to 2020, the number of female offenders for all offenses increased from 1,343,303 to 1,737,987. During this same time period, the reported number of female animal cruelty offenders increased approximately 3.2 times from 1,113 offenders (approximately .1% of the total number of female offenders) in 2017 to 3,609 offenders (approximately .2% of the total number of female offenders) in 2020 (FBI, 2017; FBI, 2018a; FBI, 2019a; FBI, 2020b; FBI, 2021).

As demonstrated in Table 5, according to the NIBRS (FBI, 2017; FBI, 2018a; FBI, 2019a; FBI, 2020b; FBI, 2021), in 2016, there were 567,155 offenders of unknown sex, of whom were 81 animal cruelty offenders (approximately .02% of the offenders of unknown sex). From 2017 to 2020, the number of offenders of unknown sex increased from 637,058 to 983,891. During this same time period, the reported number of animal cruelty offenders of unknown sex increased approximately 3.4 times from 244 offenders (approximately .03% of the total number of offenders of unknown sex) in 2017 to 841 offenders (approximately .1% of the total number of offenders of unknown sex) in 2020 (FBI, 2017; FBI, 2018a; FBI, 2019a; FBI, 2020b; FBI, 2021).

Although these data provide some information on the sex of the total offenders and of animal cruelty offenders, as stated with regard to the rest of the offender-based information, one needs to be critical in their assessment of these data. The same issues with these data exist as mentioned with the previous categories.

The review of the offender demographics will now focus on race in the next section. The available NIBRS offender race-based data are divided by the total number of offenders, White offenders, Black or African American offenders, American Indian or Alaska Native offenders, Asian, Native Hawaiian or Other Pacific Islander offenders, and offenders of an unknown race. The data on the animal cruelty offenders are divided in the same manner.

Offenders' Race by Offense Category

The data for the offenders' race are available from 2016 to 2020 via the NIBRS. These data are presented in the following table, Table 5 (FBI, 2017; FBI, 2018a; FBI, 2019a; FBI, 2020b; FBI, 2021).

Table 6. Offenders' Race by Offense Category

Total Offense Categories					
Offenders' Race	2016	2017	2018	2019	2020
Total Offenders	4,963,644	5,266,175	5,652,156	6,543,257	7,173,072
White	2,810,115	2,931,373	3,045,089	3,397,715	3,642,932
Black or African American	1,339,227	1,4393	1,549,315	1,929,001	2,122,038
American Indian or Alaska Native	55,792	60,688	64,925	71,615	83,161
Asian	33,941	37,147	46,766	54,502	58,063
Native Hawaiian or Other Pacific Islander	1,388	1,913	13,830	19,959	15,391
Unknown Race	723,181	805,661	932,231	1,070,465	1,251,487
Animal Cruelty					
Offenders' Race	2016	2017	2018	2019	2020
Total Offenders	1,057	3,115	4,999	9,453	10,414
White	642	2,023	3,303	5,917	6,442
Black or African American	265	653	1,014	2,134	2,468
American Indian or Alaska Native	5	32	41	45	76
Asian	6	29	47	104	117
Native Hawaiian or Other Pacific Islander	0	2	18	31	25
Unknown Race	139	376	576	1,222	1,286

As stated, there are eight groupings for the total offense categories and animal cruelty cases in Table 6, the total offenders, White offenders, Black or African American offenders, American Indian or Alaska Native offenders, Asian offenders, Native Hawaiian or Other Pacific Islander offenders, and offenders of an unknown race. Each group will be discussed separately.

As demonstrated in Table 6, according to the NIBRS (FBI, 2017; FBI, 2018a; FBI, 2019a; FBI, 2020b; FBI, 2021), in 2016, there were 2,810,644 White offenders, of whom 642 were animal cruelty offenders (approximately .02% of the White offenders). From 2017 to 2020, the number of White offenders for all offenses increased from 2,810,115 to 3,642,932. During this same time period, the reported number of White animal cruelty offenders increased approximately 10 times from 642 offenders (approximately

.02% of the total number of White offenders) in 2017 to 6,442 offenders (approximately .2% of the total number of White offenders) in 2020 (FBI, 2017; FBI, 2018a; FBI, 2019a; FBI, 2020b; FBI, 2021).

As observed in Table 6, according to the NIBRS (FBI, 2017; FBI, 2018a; FBI, 2019a; FBI, 2020b; FBI, 2021), in 2016, there were 1,339,227 Black or African American offenders, of whom 265 were animal cruelty offenders (approximately .02% of the Black or African American offenders). From 2017 to 2020, the number of Black or African American offenders for all offenses increased from 1,339,227 to 2,122,038. During this same time period, the reported number of Black or African American animal cruelty offenders increased approximately 10.7 times from 265 offenders (approximately .02% of the total number of Black or African American offenders) in 2017 to 2,468 offenders (approximately .1% of the total number of Black or African American offenders) in 2020 (FBI, 2017; FBI, 2018a; FBI, 2019a; FBI, 2020b; FBI, 2021).

As recorded in Table 6, according to the NIBRS (FBI, 2017; FBI, 2018a; FBI, 2019a; FBI, 2020b; FBI, 2021), in 2016, there were 55,792 American Indian or Alaska Native offenders, of whom five were animal cruelty offenders (approximately .01% of the American Indian or Alaska Native offenders). From 2017 to 2020, the number of American Indian or Alaska Native offenders for all offenses increased from 155,792 to 83,161. During this same time period, the reported number of American Indian or Alaska Native animal cruelty offenders increased approximately 15.2 times from five offenders (approximately .003% of the total number of American Indian or Alaska Native offenders) in 2017 to 76 offenders (approximately .1% of the total number of American Indian or Alaska Native offenders) in 2020 (FBI, 2017; FBI, 2018a; FBI, 2019a; FBI, 2020b; FBI, 2021).

As documented in Table 6, according to the NIBRS (FBI, 2017; FBI, 2018a; FBI, 2019a; FBI, 2020b; FBI, 2021), in 2016, there were 33,941 Asian offenders, of whom six were animal cruelty offenders (approximately .02% of the Asian offenders). From 2017 to 2020, the number of Asian offenders for all offenses increased from 33,941 to 58,063. During this same time period, the reported number of Asian animal cruelty offenders increased approximately 19.5 times from six offenders (approximately .02% of the total number of Asian offenders) in 2017 to 117 offenders (approximately .2% of the total number of Asian offenders) in 2020 (FBI, 2017; FBI, 2018a; FBI, 2019a; FBI, 2020b; FBI, 2021).

As revealed in Table 6, according to the NIBRS (FBI, 2017; FBI, 2018a; FBI, 2019a; FBI, 2020b; FBI, 2021), in 2016, there were 1,388 Native Hawaiian or Other Pacific Islander offenders, of whom zero were animal cruelty offenders. From 2017 to 2020, the number of Native Hawaiian or Other Pacific Islander offenders for all offenses increased from 1,388 to 15,391. During this same time period, the reported number of Native Hawaiian or Other Pacific Islander animal cruelty offenders increased approximately 25 times from zero offenders in 2017 to 25 offenders (approximately .2% of the total number of Native Hawaiian or Other Pacific Islander offenders) in 2020 (FBI, 2017; FBI, 2018a; FBI, 2019a; FBI, 2020b; FBI, 2021).

As exhibited in Table 5, according to the NIBRS (FBI, 2017; FBI, 2018a; FBI, 2019a; FBI, 2020b; FBI, 2021), in 2016, there were 723,181 offenders of unknown race, of whom 139 were animal cruelty offenders (approximately .02% of the offenders of unknown race). From 2017 to 2020, the number of offenders of unknown race increased from 723,181 to 1,251,487. During this same time period, the reported number of animal cruelty offenders of unknown race increased approximately 9.3 times from 139 offenders (approximately .01% of the total number of offenders of unknown race) in 2017 to 1,286 offenders (approximately .1% of the total number of offenders of unknown race) in 2020 (FBI, 2017; FBI, 2018a; FBI, 2019a; FBI, 2020b; FBI, 2021).

Although these data provide some information on the race of the total offenders and of animal cruelty offenders, as stated with regard to the rest of the offender-based information, one again needs to be critical in their assessment of these data. The same issues with these data exist as mentioned with the previous offender categories.

This concludes the review of the offenders' characteristics. Next, the arrestees' characteristics will be evaluated in the same manner.

Arrestees' Characteristics

When evaluating the arrestee statistics in their totality, it is important to note the NIBRS clarification regarding the data (FBI, 2017; FBI, 2018a; FBI, 2019a; FBI, 2020b; FBI, 2021),

> The UCR Program counted each arrestee associated with an incident. In addition, ... the UCR Program counted each arrestee reported through only an arrest report. The arrestee data were aggregated by the age categories presented and broken down by their associated arrest offense categories. For this table, an adult is an offender who is age 18 or older, and a juvenile is an offender who is under 18 years of age. Figures in the Unknown Age column represent the number of arrestees whose age was unknown. Arrest offense categories include the offense types for which agencies arrested individuals, but they are not necessarily the same offense types as were initially reported in the incidents. Therefore, users should exercise caution when comparing data for offenders by offense category in other tables with data for arrestees by arrest offense category in this table. This table does not include duplicate data for arrestees who were reported to have been involved in more than one incident and, therefore, had arrestee reports submitted with multiple incident reports.

As with the offenders, the evaluation of the arrestee data will begin with the arrestees' age, followed by age range, sex, and conclude with their race.

Arrestees' Age Category by Offense Category

The total arrestees, adult, juvenile, and unknown age for the total offense categories and animal cruelty data from 2016 to 2020 are presented in the following table, Table 7 (FBI, 2017; FBI, 2018a; FBI, 2019a; FBI, 2020b; FBI, 2021).

Table 7. Arrestees' Age by Offense Category

Total Offense Categories					
Age Category	2016	2017	2018	2019	2020
Total Arrestees	3,261,521	3,361,416	3,480,625	3,931,924	3,621,299
Adult	2,996,751	3,093,602	3,219,774	3,636,714	3,399,164
Juvenile	260,735	264,672	257,356	291,786	220,877
Unknown	4,035	3,142	3,456	3,424	1,258
Animal Cruelty					
Age Category	2016	2017	2018	2019	2020
Total Arrestees	237	756	1,052	1,852	1,884
Adult	230	726	1,021	1,795	1,817
Juvenile	7	30	31	57	67
Unknown	0	0	0	0	0

As noted in Table 7, according to the NIBRS (FBI, 2017; FBI, 2018a; FBI, 2019a; FBI, 2020b; FBI, 2021), in 2016, there were 3,261,521 total arrestees reported and 237 animal cruelty arrestees (approximately .01% of total arrestees) listed for that year. From 2017 to 2020, the total number of total arrestees grew from 3,361,416 to 3,621,299. During this same time period, the reported number of animal cruelty arrestees increased approximately 2.5 times from 756 arrestees (approximately .02% of the total number of arrestees) in 2017 to 1,884 arrestees (approximately .5% of the total number of arrestees) in 2020 (FBI, 2017; FBI, 2018a; FBI, 2019a; FBI, 2020b; FBI, 2021).

With regard to the number of adult arrestees, as shown in Table 7, according to the NIBRS (FBI, 2017; FBI, 2018a; FBI, 2019a; FBI, 2020b; FBI, 2021), in 2016, there were 2,996,521 adult arrestees reported; adult animal cruelty arrestees accounted for 230 (approximately .02%) of them. From 2017 to 2020, the total number of adult arrestees grew from 3,093,602 to 3,399,164. During this same time frame, the reported number of adult animal cruelty arrestees increased approximately 2.5 times from 726 arrestees in 2017 (approximately .02% of the total number of adult arrestees) to 1,884 arrestees in 2020 (approximately .06% of the total number of adult arrestees) in 2020 (FBI, 2017; FBI, 2018a; FBI, 2019a; FBI, 2020b; FBI, 2021).

Next, as shown in Table 7, according to the NIBRS (FBI, 2017; FBI, 2018a; FBI, 2019a; FBI, 2020b; FBI, 2021), in 2016, there were 260,735 total juvenile arrestees reported, which included seven juvenile animal arrestees (approximately .002% of total juvenile arrestees). In 2017, there were 264,672 total juvenile arrestees reported. This number decreased to 220,877 in 2020. Conversely, during this same time period, the reported number of juvenile animal cruelty arrestees increased approximately 2.2 times from 30 juvenile animal cruelty arrestees in 2017 (approximately .01% of the total number of juvenile arrestees) to 67 juvenile animal cruelty arrestees (approximately .03% of the total number of juvenile arrestees) in 2020 (FBI, 2017; FBI, 2018a; FBI, 2019a; FBI, 2020b; FBI, 2021).

Finally, in regard to the unknown arrestees data, as displayed in Table 7, according to the NIBRS (FBI, 2017; FBI, 2018a; FBI, 2019a; FBI, 2020b; FBI, 2021), in 2016, there were 4,035 total unknown arrestees reported, including 0 unknown animal cruelty arrestees (0% of the total unknown arrestees). From 2017 to 2020, the total number of unknown arrestees decreased from 3,142 to 1,258. During this same time, the number of reported unknown arrestees in animal cruelty cases remained at zero across all years in the data from 2017 to 2020 (0% of all unknown arrestees) (FBI, 2017; FBI, 2018a; FBI, 2019a; FBI, 2020b; FBI, 2021).

Upon review of the total and animal cruelty arrestee case data with regard to their age that have been submitted to the NIBRS by the LEA, only the total number of animal cruelty arrestees and adult animal cruelty arrestees increased between 2016 and 2020. The number of juvenile animal cruelty arrestees decreased during that time and the number of animal cruelty arrestees whose age was unknown remained zero during that time frame. However, one needs to be critical in their assessment of these data. As stated earlier, for example, the number of arrestees could be counted more than once when there is a multiple-offense incident. One would need to consider the same issues with the data as mentioned with the previous categories.

The next arrestee-focused category of data to be reviewed is the arrestees' age range. Although these data are presented in the total, unknown, and 13 separate age ranges, due to space considerations, the age ranges will be consolidated for the purpose of this examination.

Arrestees' Age Range (in Years) by Offense Category

The total arrestees, adult, juvenile, and unknown age for the total offense categories and animal cruelty data from 2016 to 2020 are presented in the following table, Table 8 (FBI, 2017; FBI, 2018a; FBI, 2019a; FBI, 2020b; FBI, 2021).

Table 8. Arrestees' Age Range (in Years) by Offense Category

Total Offense Categories					
Age Range	2016	2017	2018	2019	2020
Total Arrestees	3,261,521	3,361,416	3,480,625	3,931,924	7,173,072
10 and Under	2,838	2,924	2,696	3,259	18,067
11–15	119,263	122,979	123,324	147,389	230,476
16–20	470,459	466,909	440,160	467,760	792,384
21–25	580,068	561,759	546,990	583,813	917,511
26–30	530,621	554,382	583,098	654,379	972,769
31–35	439,646	465,352	495,356	569,306	850,807
36–40	331,157	365,598	404,737	478,509	685,825
41–45	241,543	249,407	269,222	320,144	452,126
46–50	200,636	209,627	222,411	251,710	331,436
51–55	164,834	168,401	174,366	195,543	234,695
56–60	98,935	107,155	119,267	140,567	202,295
61–65	45,294	49,670	57,160	69,369	84,548
66 and over	32,192	34,471	38,343	46,752	72,470
Unknown Age	4,035	3,142	3,495	3,424	1,328,663
Animal Cruelty					
Age Range	2016	2017	2018	2019	2020
Total Arrestees	237	756	1,052	1,852	1,884
10 and Under	0	0	0	1	3
11–15	3	20	16	23	39
16–20	16	51	81	153	138
21–25	21	101	122	230	204
26–30	33	108	142	263	295
31–35	36	97	123	236	258
36–40	28	94	132	202	207
41–45	17	60	103	168	187
46–50	22	55	78	150	120
51–55	22	57	87	123	117
56–60	13	37	60	127	116
61–65	10	34	40	77	86
66 and over	16	42	68	99	114
Unknown Age	0	0	0	0	0

As stated, there are 13 age ranges and an unknown age group listed in Table 8; therefore, as with the offenders, to consolidate the information and save space in this book, it will be presented as 10 years old and under, 11–20 years old, 21–30 years old, 31–40 years old, 41–50 years old, 51–60 years old, and 61 years old and over, for the total offense categories and animal cruelty cases, based primarily on decades of years. The total number of arrestees, total number of animal cruelty arrestees by age, and the unknown age of arrestees of all offenses and of animal cruelty offenses were addressed in Table 7 and will not be discussed again here.

As observed in Table 8, according to the NIBRS (FBI, 2017; FBI, 2018a; FBI, 2019a; FBI, 2020b; FBI, 2021), in 2016, there were 2,838 arrestees aged 10 years old and younger for all offenses, of which zero were animal cruelty arrestees. From 2017 to 2020, the number of arrestees aged 10 years old and under increased from 2,924 to 18,067. During this same time period, the reported number of animal cruelty arrestees aged 10 years old and under increased approximately 3 times from zero arrestees (0% of the total number of arrestees in that age range) in 2017 to three arrestees (approximately .02% of the total number of arrestees in that age range) in 2020 (FBI, 2017; FBI, 2018a; FBI, 2019a; FBI, 2020b; FBI, 2021).

As shown in Table 8, according to the NIBRS (FBI, 2017; FBI, 2018a; FBI, 2019a; FBI, 2020b; FBI, 2021), in 2016, there were 589,722 arrestees for all offenses aged 11–20 years old, of which there 19 animal cruelty arrestees (approximately .003% of all arrestees in that age range). From 2017 to 2020, the number of arrestees aged 11–20 years old increased from 589,888 to 1,259,293. During this same time period, the reported number of animal cruelty arrestees aged 11–20 years old increased approximately 2.5 times from 71 arrestees (approximately .01% of the total number of arrestees in that age range) in 2017 to 177 arrestees (approximately .01% of the total number of arrestees in that age range) in 2020 (FBI, 2017; FBI, 2018a; FBI, 2019a; FBI, 2020b; FBI, 2021).

As demonstrated in Table 8, according to the NIBRS (FBI, 2017; FBI, 2018a; FBI, 2019a; FBI, 2020b; FBI, 2021), in 2016, there were 1,110,689 total offense arrestees aged 21–30 years old, including 54 animal cruelty arrestees. From 2017 to 2020, the number of arrestees aged 21–30 years old increased from 1,116,141 to 1,890,280. During this same time period, the reported number of animal cruelty arrestees aged 21–30 years old increased approximately 3.4 times from 209 arrestees (approximately .02% of the total number of arrestees in that age range) in 2017 to 499 arrestees (approximately .03% of the total number of arrestees in that age range) in 2020 (FBI, 2017; FBI, 2018a; FBI, 2019a; FBI, 2020b; FBI, 2021).

As recorded in Table 8, according to the NIBRS (FBI, 2017; FBI, 2018a; FBI, 2019a; FBI, 2020b; FBI, 2021), in 2016, there were 770,803 total offense arrestees aged 31–40 years old, including 64 animal cruelty arrestees. From 2017 to 2020, the number of arrestees aged 31–40 years old increased from 830,950 to 1,536,632. During this same time period, the reported number of animal cruelty arrestees aged 31–40 years old increased approximately 2.4 times from 191 arrestees (approximately .02% of the total number of arrestees in that age range) in 2017 to 465 arrestees (approximately .03% of the total number of arrestees in that age range) in 2020 (FBI, 2017; FBI, 2018a; FBI, 2019a; FBI, 2020b; FBI, 2021).

As documented in Table 8, according to the NIBRS (FBI, 2017; FBI, 2018a; FBI, 2019a; FBI, 2020b; FBI, 2021), in 2016, there were 442,179 total offense arrestees aged 41–50 years old, including 39 animal cruelty arrestees. From 2017 to 2020, the number of arrestees aged 41–50 years old increased from 459,034 to 783,562. During this same time period, the reported number of animal cruelty arrestees aged 41–50 years old increased approximately 2.7 times from 115 arrestees (approximately .02% of the total number of arrestees in that age range) in 2017 to 307 arrestees (approximately .03% of the total number of arrestees in that age range) in 2020 (FBI, 2017; FBI, 2018a; FBI, 2019a; FBI, 2020b; FBI, 2021).

As written in Table 8, according to the NIBRS (FBI, 2017; FBI, 2018a; FBI, 2019a; FBI, 2020b; FBI, 2021), in 2016, there were 263,769 total arrestees aged 51–60 years old, including 35 animal cruelty arrestees. From 2017 to 2020, the number of arrestees aged 51–60 years old increased from 275,556 to 436,990. During this same time period, the reported number of animal cruelty arrestees aged 51–60 years old increased approximately 2.5 times from 94 arrestees (approximately .03% of the total number of arrestees in that age range) in 2017 to 233 arrestees (approximately .05% of the total number of arrestees in that age range) in 2020 (FBI, 2017; FBI, 2018a; FBI, 2019a; FBI, 2020b; FBI, 2021).

As exhibited in Table 8, according to the NIBRS (FBI, 2017; FBI, 2018a; FBI, 2019a; FBI, 2020b; FBI, 2021), in 2016, there were 77,486 total arrestees between the aged 61 years old and over, including 26 animal cruelty arrestees. From 2017 to 2020, the number of arrestees aged 61 years old and over increased from 84,141 to 157,018. During this same time period, the reported number of animal cruelty arrestees aged 61 years old and over increased approximately 2.6 times from 76 arrestees (approximately .1% of the total number of arrestees in that age range) in 2017 to 200 arrestees (approximately .1% of the total number of arrestees in that age range) in 2020 (FBI, 2017; FBI, 2018a; FBI, 2019a; FBI, 2020b; FBI, 2021).

The number of animal cruelty arrestees by age range for 2017 and 2020 are provided in Chart 2 as a visual presentation of the data. The increase in the number of arrestees in each age-range category is clear between the two years is clear; however, it should be noted that as previously stated, there have been more LEA participating in NIBRS during this time frame.

As demonstrated in Chart 2, as with Chart 1, it would appear that animal cruelty arrestees are being arrested more often between the ages of 21–40 years old. Like the animal cruelty offenders, this information seems to contradict age-based criminological theories, such as the developmental theories, which posit that offenders generally peak in their delinquent and criminal activity during a younger age range, usually in their late teens to late 20s (see Hirschi & Gottfredson, 1983; Kressler & Reinecke, 2021; Laub & Sampson, 1993; McGee & Farrington, 2019; McGee et al., 2021; Moffitt, 1993; Rosa et al., 2020; Sampson & Laub, 2005). Additional theories that attempt to explain why animal cruelty is committed are addressed in Chapters 7, 13, 15, and 16. However, as stated with regard to the rest of the arrestee-based information, one needs to be critical in their assessment of these data. The same issues with these data exist as mentioned with the previous category.

Chart 2. Animal Cruelty Arrestees' Age Range by Offense Category (in Years)

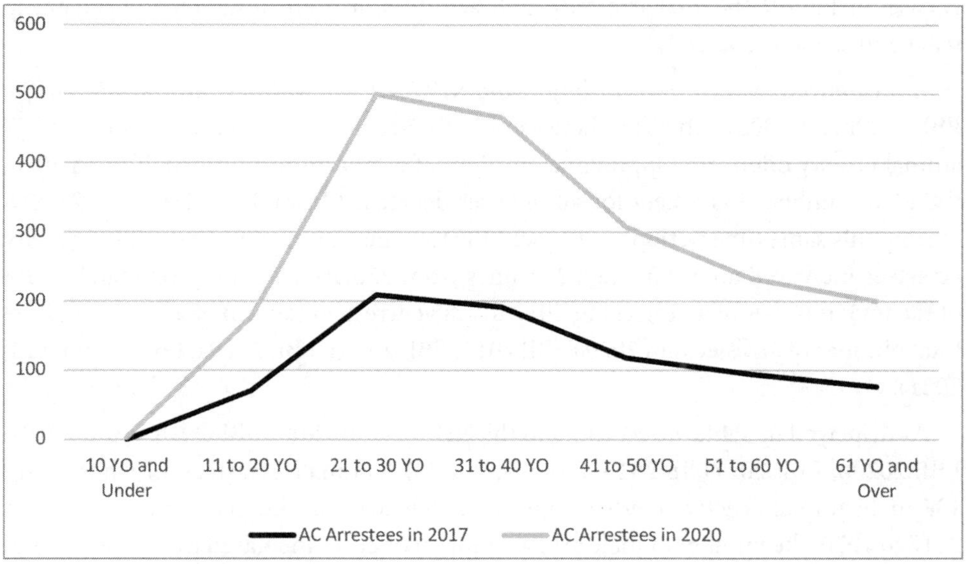

The review of the arrestee demographics now shifts from age to sex in the next section.

Unlike the available NIBRS offender sex-based data that include information on individuals of unknown sex, these data are divided by the total number of arrestees, male arrestees, and female arrestees. The data on the animal cruelty arrestees are divided in the same manner.

Arrestees' Sex by Offense Category

The data for the arrestees' sex are available from 2016 to 2020 via the NIBRS. These data are presented in the following table, Table 9 (FBI, 2017; FBI, 2018a; FBI, 2019a; FBI, 2020b; FBI, 2021).

Table 9. Arrestees' Sex by Offense Category

Total Offense Categories					
Arrestees' Sex	2016	2017	2018	2019	2020
Total Arrestees	3,261,521	3,361,416	3,480,625	3,931,924	3,621,299
Male	2,337,544	2,405,418	2,485,050	2,810,332	2,629,119
Female	923,977	955,998	995,575	1,121,592	992,180
Animal Cruelty					
Arrestees' Sex	2016	2017	2018	2019	2020
Total Arrestees	237	756	1,052	1,852	1,884
Male	137	459	642	1,114	1,172
Female	100	297	410	738	712

As stated, there are three groupings for the total offense categories and animal cruelty cases in Table 9, the total arrestees, male arrestees, and female arrestees. Each group will be discussed separately.

As evidenced in Table 9, according to the NIBRS (FBI, 2017; FBI, 2018a; FBI, 2019a; FBI, 2020b; FBI, 2021), in 2016, there were 3,261,521 total arrestees, of whom were 237 animal cruelty offenders (approximately .01% of total arrestees). From 2017 to 2020, the total number of arrestees for all offenses decreased from 3,361,416 to 3,621,299. During this same time period, conversely, the total number of reported animal cruelty arrestees increased approximately 2.5 times from 756 arrestees (approximately .02% of the total number of arrestees) in 2017 to 1,884 arrestees (approximately .05% of the total number of arrestees) in 2020 (FBI, 2017; FBI, 2018a; FBI, 2019a; FBI, 2020b; FBI, 2021).

As displayed in Table 9, according to the NIBRS (FBI, 2017; FBI, 2018a; FBI, 2019a; FBI, 2020b; FBI, 2021), in 2016, there were 2,337,544 male arrestees, of whom were 137 male animal cruelty arrestees (approximately .01% of the male arrestees). From 2017 to 2020, the number of male arrestees for all offenses increased from 2,405,418 to 2,629,119. During this same time period, the reported number of male animal cruelty arrestees increased approximately 2.6 times from 459 male arrestees (approximately .02% of the total number of the male arrestees) in 2017 to 1,172 male arrestees (approximately .04% of the total number of the male arrestees) in 2020 (FBI, 2017; FBI, 2018a; FBI, 2019a; FBI, 2020b; FBI, 2021).

As recorded in Table 9, according to the NIBRS (FBI, 2017; FBI, 2018a; FBI, 2019a; FBI, 2020b; FBI, 2021), in 2016, there were 923,977 female arrestees, of whom were 100 animal cruelty offenders (approximately .01% of the female arrestees) From 2017 to 2020, the number of female arrestees for all offenses decreased from 955,998 to 992,180. During this same time period, conversely, the reported number of female animal cruelty arrestees increased approximately 2.4 times from 297 female arrestees (approximately .03% of the total number of female arrestees) in 2017 to 712 female arrestees (approximately .07% of the total number of female arrestees in 2020 (FBI, 2017; FBI, 2018a; FBI, 2019a; FBI, 2020b; FBI, 2021).

Although these data provide some information on the sex of the total arrestees and of animal cruelty arrestees, as stated with regard to the rest of the arrestee-based information, one needs to be critical in their assessment of these data. The same issues with these data exist as mentioned with the previous category.

The review of the arrestee demographics will now focus on race in the next section. The available NIBRS arrestee race-based data are divided by the total number of arrestees, White, Black or African American arrestees, American Indian or Alaska Native arrestees, Asian arrestees, Native Hawaiian or Other Pacific Islander arrestees, and arrestees of an unknown race. The data on the animal cruelty arrestees are divided in the same manner.

Arrestees' Race by Offense Category

The data for the arrestees' race are available from 2016 to 2020 via the NIBRS. These data are presented in the following table, Table 10 (FBI, 2017; FBI, 2018a; FBI, 2019a; FBI, 2020b; FBI, 2021).

Table 10. Arrestees' Race by Offense Category

Total Offense Categories					
Arrestees' Race	2016	2017	2018	2019	2020
Total Arrestees	3,261,521	3,361,416	3,480,625	3,931,924	3,621,299
White	2,342,345	2,377,649	2,422,377	2,676,427	2,452,623
Black or African American	781,707	823,023	858,445	1,039,897	982,010
American Indian or Alaska Native	53,904	58,238	60,083	65,364	65,330
Asian	28,694	30,385	33,541	37,016	33,147
Native Hawaiian or Other Pacific Islander	1,087	1,422	8,504	11,598	8,259
Unknown Race	53,774	70,699	97,677	101,622	79,930
Animal Cruelty					
Arrestees' Race	2016	2017	2018	2019	2020
Total Arrestees	237	756	1,052	1,852	1,884
White	182	610	844	1,404	1,384
Black or African American	48	122	162	375	420
American Indian or Alaska Native	2	6	12	13	25
Asian	0	8	10	27	23
Native Hawaiian or Other Pacific Islander	0	1	3	5	3
Unknown Race	5	9	21	28	29

As stated, there are eight groupings for the total offense categories and animal cruelty cases in Table 10, the total arrestees, White arrestees, Black or African American arrestees, American Indian or Alaska Native arrestees, Asian arrestees, Native Hawaiian or Other Pacific Islander arrestees, and arrestees of an unknown race. Each group will be discussed separately.

As exhibited in Table 10, according to the NIBRS (FBI, 2017; FBI, 2018a; FBI, 2019a; FBI, 2020b; FBI, 2021), in 2016, there were 2,342,345 White arrestees, of whom 182 were animal cruelty arrestees (approximately .01% of the White arrestees). From 2017 to 2020, the number of White arrestees for all offenses increased from 2,377,649 to 2,452,623. During this same time period, the reported number of White animal cruelty arrestees increased approximately 2.3 times from 610 arrestees (approximately .02% of the total number of White arrestees) in 2017 to 1,384 arrestees (approximately .05% of the total number of White arrestees) in 2020 (FBI, 2017; FBI, 2018a; FBI, 2019a; FBI, 2020b; FBI, 2021).

As shown in Table 10, according to the NIBRS (FBI, 2017; FBI, 2018a; FBI, 2019a; FBI, 2020b; FBI, 2021), in 2016, there were 781,707 Black or African American arrestees, of whom 48 were animal cruelty arrestees (approximately .01% of the Black or African American arrestees). From 2017 to 2020, the number of Black or African American arrestees for all offenses increased from 823,023 to 982,010. During this same time period, the reported number of Black or African American animal cruelty arrestees increased approximately 3.4 times from 122 arrestees (approximately .02% of the total number of Black or African American arrestees) in 2017 to 420 arrestees (approximately .04% of the total number of Black or African American arrestees) in 2020 (FBI, 2017; FBI, 2018a; FBI, 2019a; FBI, 2020b; FBI, 2021).

As demonstrated in Table 10, according to the NIBRS (FBI, 2017; FBI, 2018a; FBI, 2019a; FBI, 2020b; FBI, 2021), in 2016, there were 53,904 American Indian or Alaska Native arrestees, of whom two were animal cruelty arrestees (approximately .004% of the American Indian or Alaska Native arrestees). From 2017 to 2020, the number of American Indian or Alaska Native arrestees for all offenses increased from 58,238 to 65,330. During this same time period, the reported number of American Indian or Alaska Native animal cruelty arrestees increased approximately 4.2 times from six arrestees (approximately .01% of the total number of American Indian or Alaska Native arrestees) in 2017 to 25 arrestees (approximately .04% of the total number of American Indian or Alaska Native arrestees) in 2020 (FBI, 2017; FBI, 2018a; FBI, 2019a; FBI, 2020b; FBI, 2021).

As observed in Table 10, according to the NIBRS (FBI, 2017; FBI, 2018a; FBI, 2019a; FBI, 2020b; FBI, 2021), in 2016, there were 28,694 Asian arrestees, of whom zero were animal cruelty arrestees. From 2017 to 2020, the number of Asian arrestees for all offenses increased from 30,385 to 33,147. During this same time period, the reported number of Asian animal cruelty arrestees increased approximately 2.9 times from eight arrestees (approximately .03% of the total number of Asian arrestees) in 2017 to 23 arrestees (approximately .07% of the total number of Asian arrestees) in 2020 (FBI, 2017; FBI, 2018a; FBI, 2019a; FBI, 2020b; FBI, 2021).

As documented in Table 10, according to the NIBRS (FBI, 2017; FBI, 2018a; FBI, 2019a; FBI, 2020b; FBI, 2021), in 2016, there were 1,087 Native Hawaiian or Other

Pacific Islander offenders, of whom zero were animal cruelty. From 2017 to 2020, the number of Native Hawaiian or Other Pacific Islander arrestees for all offenses increased from 1,422 to 8,259. During this same time period, the reported number of Native Hawaiian or Other Pacific Islander animal cruelty arrestees increased approximately 3.0 times from one arrestee (.07% of the total number of Native Hawaiian or Other Pacific Islander arrestees) in 2017 to three offenders (approximately .03% of the total number of Native Hawaiian or Other Pacific Islander arrestees) in 2020 (FBI, 2017; FBI, 2018a; FBI, 2019a; FBI, 2020b; FBI, 2021).

As evidenced in Table 10, according to the NIBRS (FBI, 2017; FBI, 2018a; FBI, 2019a; FBI, 2020b; FBI, 2021), in 2016, there were 53,774 arrestees of unknown race, of whom five were animal cruelty arrestees (approximately .01% of the arrestees of unknown race). From 2017 to 2020, the number of arrestees of unknown race increased from 70,699 to 79,930. During this same time period, the reported number of animal cruelty arrestees of unknown race increased approximately 3.2 times from nine arrestees (approximately .01% of the total number of arrestees of unknown race) in 2017 to 29 arrestees (approximately .04% of the total number of arrestees of unknown race) in 2020 (FBI, 2017; FBI, 2018a; FBI, 2019a; FBI, 2020b; FBI, 2021).

Although these data provide some information on the race of the total arrestees and of animal cruelty arrestees, as stated with regard to the rest of the arrestee-based information, one again needs to be critical in their assessment of these data. The same issues with these data exist as mentioned with the previous arrestee categories.

This concludes the review of the arrestee characteristics. Next, the animal cruelty offense data will be assessed by the location and time of day of the occurrence.

Animal Cruelty Offenses by Location and Time of Day

Animal Cruelty Offenses by Location

When reviewing the animal cruelty offenses by location statistics in their totality, it is important to note the NIBRS clarification regarding the data (FBI, 2017; FBI, 2018a; FBI, 2019a; FBI, 2020b; FBI, 2021),

> To arrive at the offense totals provided for each table, the UCR Program used the following counting rules: ... Crime Against Society—one for each unique offense type. In a multiple-offense incident, an offense was counted for each offense type in the incident. The UCR Program aggregated the data by offense category and location within each table.

The data for the animal cruelty offenses by location are available from 2016 to 2020 via the NIBRS. These data are presented in the following table, Table 11 (FBI, 2017; FBI, 2018a; FBI, 2019a; FBI, 2020b; FBI, 2021).

Table 11. Animal Cruelty Offenses by Location

Location	2016	2017	2018	2019	2020
Total	1,126	3,228	5,201	9,956	11,566
Abandoned/Condemned Structure	0	2	7	14	11
Air/Bus/Train Terminal	0	0	3	9	13
Amusement Park	0	1	4	2	0
Arena/Stadium/Fairgrounds/Coliseum	0	1	4	5	3
ATM Separate from Bank	0	0	0	0	1
Auto Dealership New/Used	0	2	2	4	4
Bank/Savings and Loan	0	0	2	1	1
Bar/Nightclub	0	3	5	7	5
Camp/Campground	1	8	4	10	9
Church/Synagogue/Temple/Mosque	1	5	4	14	4
Commercial/Office Building	8	28	32	77	94
Community Center	0	1	0	2	1
Construction Site	0	1	2	2	3
Convenience Store	3	10	13	22	41
Cyberspace	0	0	0	0	0
Daycare Facility	0	1	0	2	1
Department/Discount Store	8	29	45	79	77
Dock/Wharf/Freight/Modal Terminal	0	1	2	1	0
Drug Store/Doctor's Office/Hospital	7	10	14	48	41
Farm Facility	6	28	55	95	92
Field/Woods	23	100	149	292	357
Gambling Facility/Casino/Race Track [sic]	0	0	2	4	2
Government/Public Building	4	16	36	61	55
Grocery/Supermarket	4	17	21	55	67
Highway/Road/Alley/Street/Sidewalk	78	211	533	834	900
Hotel/Motel/Etc.	3	19	31	59	101
Industrial Site	1	2	0	6	2
Jail/Prison/Penitentiary/Corrections Facility	1	1	2	4	1
Lake/Waterway/Beach	0	3	10	19	30
Liquor Store	0	0	0	2	1
Military Installation	0	0	0	3	1
Park/Playground	11	31	36	94	118

Location	2016	2017	2018	2019	2020
Parking/Drop Lot/Garage	60	209	399	664	640
Rental Storage Facility	3	8	5	16	20
Residence/Home	849	2,326	3,513	6,898	8,160
Rest Area	3	0	0	2	0
Restaurant	1	15	17	31	36
School/College	1	1	2	0	5
School—College/University	1	4	12	10	10
School—Elementary/Secondary	3	11	8	22	13
Service/Gas Station	1	0	5	13	20
Shelter—Mission/Homeless	0	0	2	6	8
Shopping Mall	4	10	9	20	26
Specialty Store	4	19	14	34	43
Tribal Lands	0	0	2	1	0
Other/Unknown	37	94	195	412	549

As demonstrated in Table 11, there are 46 locations listed including "other/unknown" where the reported animal cruelty offenses occurred. In the interest of saving time and space, the five locations with the highest number of animal cruelty cases in 2020 will be discussed here. The data for 2016 and the comparison between 2017 and 2020 will be evaluated. The total number of animal cases for the said years will also be included in this analysis. Each location will be discussed in descending order from the highest number of cases to the lowest.

As noted in Table 11, according to the NIBRS (FBI, 2017), in 2016, there were 1,126 animal cruelty cases, 849 of those cases occurred in a residence/home (approximately 75%). Next, 78 of those cases occurred on a highway/road/alley/street/sidewalk, which accounts for approximately 7% of the total cases for that year. Sixty cases occurred in a parking/drop lot/garage, which is approximately 5% of the total cases. Additionally, 37 animal cruelty cases occurred at other/unknown locations, which is approximately 3% of the total number of cases. Finally, 23 of the cases occurred in the field/woods, accounting for approximately 2% of the animal cruelty cases in 2016 (FBI, 2017).

As shown in Table 11, according to the NIBRS in 2017 (FBI, 2018a), there were 3,228 animal cruelty cases reported of which 2,326 occurred in a residence/home (approximately 72%). Next, 211 of those cases occurred on a highway/road/alley/street/sidewalk, which accounts for approximately 6.5% of the total cases for that year. Two-hundred-nine cases occurred in a parking/drop lot/garage, which is approximately 6.5% of the total cases. Additionally, 94 animal cruelty cases occurred at other/unknown locations, which is approximately 3% of the total number of cases. Finally,

100 of the cases occurred in the field/woods, accounting for approximately 3% of the animal cruelty cases in 2017 (FBI, 2018a).

As displayed in Table 11, according to the NIBRS in 2020 (FBI, 2021), there were 11,566 animal cruelty cases reported of which 8,160 occurred in a residence/home (approximately 71%). Next, 900 of those cases occurred on a highway/road/alley/street/sidewalk, which accounts for approximately 8% of the total cases for that year. Six-hundred-forty cases occurred in a parking/drop lot/garage, which is approximately 5.5% of the total cases. Additionally, 549 animal cruelty cases occurred at other/unknown locations, which is approximately 5% of the total number of cases. Finally, 357 of the cases occurred in the field/woods, accounting for approximately 3% of the animal cruelty cases in 2020 (FBI, 2021).

As presented in Table 11, between 2017 to 2020, the total number of reported animal cruelty offenses increased 3.6 times from 3,228 cases to 11,566 cases (FBI, 2018a; FBI, 2019a; FBI, 2020b; FBI, 2021). Within this time frame the number of animal cruelty cases that occurred within a residence/home increased approximately 3.5 times from 2,326 in 2017 to 8,160 in 2020. Next, the number of cases that occurred on a highway/road/alley/street/sidewalk increased approximately 4.3 times, from 211 in 2017 to 900 in 2020. The number of animal cruelty offenses in a parking/drop lot/garage also increased approximately 3.0 times from 209 in 2017 to 640 in 2020. Additionally, the number of animal cruelty cases that occurred at other/unknown locations in 2017 was 94, which increased approximately 5.8 times to 549 in 2020. Finally, there were 100 animal cruelty cases occurred in the field/woods in 2017 and that number increased approximately 3.6 times to 357 cases in 2020 (FBI, 2018a; FBI, 2019a; FBI, 2020b; FBI, 2021).

The number of animal cruelty offenses by location for 2017 and 2020 is provided in Chart 3 as a visual presentation of the data. The increase in the number of offenses for the top five locations is clear between the two years is clear; however, it should be noted that as previously stated, there have been more LEA participating in NIBRS during this time frame.

As depicted in Chart 3, it would appear that the majority of animal cruelty offenses in 2017 and 2020 (FBI 2018a, FBI 2021) were occurring in the residence/home. This would confirm Levinthal's (2010) and Monsalve et al.'s (2018) research, which came to the same conclusion. In addition, these data are consistent with the information presented in Chapters 10, 12, and 13 in this book.

Chart 3. Animal Cruelty Offenses by Location

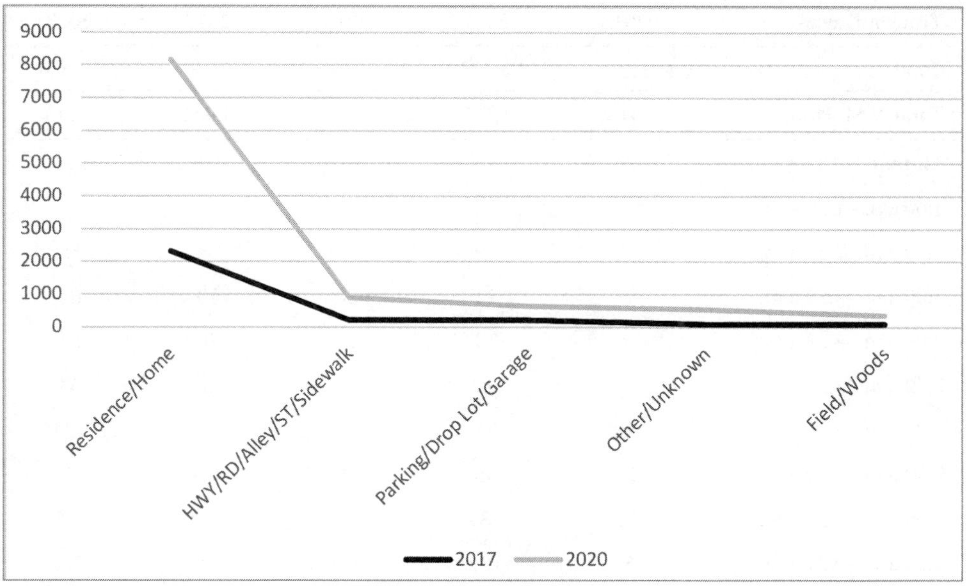

The examination of the animal cruelty offenses now moves from the location to the time of day during which these offenses occur in the next section. The data on the animal cruelty offenses by time of day are divided by one-hour segments beginning from midnight to 12:59 a.m.

Animal Cruelty Offenses by Time of Day

When reviewing the animal cruelty offenses by time of day statistics in their totality, it is important to note the NIBRS clarification regarding the data (FBI, 2017; FBI, 2018a; FBI, 2019a; FBI, 2020b; FBI, 2021),

> In NIBRS, the time of day is collected at the incident level, not at the offense level.... To arrive at the totals provided for each column of data, the UCR Program counted one incident for each offense type identified within each NIBRS incident. In a multiple-offense incident, one incident was counted for each offense type in order to attribute the incident to each associated offense category. The UCR Program aggregated the incident data by offense category and the incidents' time of day for each table.

The data for the animal cruelty offenses by time of day are available from 2016 to 2020 via the NIBRS. These data are presented in the following table, Table 12 (FBI, 2017; FBI, 2018a; FBI, 2019a; FBI, 2020b; FBI, 2021).

Table 12. Animal Cruelty Offenses by Time of Day

Time of Day	2016	2017	2018	2019	2020
Total	1,126	3,228	5,201	9,956	11,566
Total A.M. Hours	416	1,125	1,784	3,604	4,213
Midnight–12:59 a.m.	36	96	167	489	573
1:00 a.m.–1:59 a.m.	8	23	31	68	98
2:00 a.m.–2:59 a.m.	5	29	35	66	85
3:00 a.m.–3:59 a.m.	3	14	26	50	65
4:00 a.m.–4:59 a.m.	3	10	15	40	54
5:00 a.m.–5:59 a.m.	11	21	21	42	64
6:00 a.m.–6:59 a.m.	10	26	42	88	120
7:00 a.m.–7:59 a.m.	21	58	108	239	247
8:00 a.m.–8:59 a.m.	83	184	284	489	525
9:00 a.m.–9:59 a.m.	67	189	284	565	710
10:00 a.m.–10:59 a.m.	76	253	378	718	830
11:00 a.m.–11:59 a.m.	93	232	393	750	842
Total P.M. Hours	649	2,000	3,288	6,158	7,167
Noon–12:59 p.m.	116	313	516	894	1,004
1:00 p.m.–1:59 p.m.	75	242	401	772	887
2:00 p.m.–2:59 p.m.	76	235	409	788	948
3:00 p.m.–3:59 p.m.	87	228	437	793	842
4:00 p.m.–4:59 p.m.	68	226	358	703	757
5:00 p.m.–5:59 p.m.	64	221	308	592	676
6:00 p.m.–6:59 p.m.	51	145	248	470	578
7:00 p.m.–7:59 p.m.	34	120	207	380	465
8:00 p.m.–8:59 p.m.	29	98	138	274	357
9:00 p.m.–9:59 p.m.	17	67	120	216	292
10:59 p.m.–10:59 p.m.	20	58	87	148	212
11:00–11:59 p.m.	12	47	59	128	149
Unknown Time of Day	61	103	129	194	186

As demonstrated in Table 12, there are 25 time frames listed including "unknown time of day" when the reported animal cruelty offenses occurred. In addition, the total "A.M." and total "P.M." hours are listed. Like with the location data, in the interest of saving time and space, the five time frames with the highest number of animal cruelty cases in 2020 will be discussed here. In addition, the data for 2016 and the comparison between 2017 and 2020 will be evaluated as they were with the location data. The total number of animal cases for the said years will also be included in this analysis. Each time frame will be discussed in descending order from the highest number of cases to the lowest, again according to the 2020 figures.

As noted in Table 12, according to the NIBRS (FBI, 2017), in 2016[2], there were 1,126 animal cruelty cases, 116 of those cases occurred between noon and 12:59 p.m. (approximately 10%). Next, 75 of those cases occurred 1:00 p.m. and 1:59 p.m., which accounts for approximately 6.7% of the total cases for that year. Seventy-six cases occurred between 2:00 p.m. and 2:59 p.m., which is approximately 6.7% of the total cases. According to the 2020 statistics, there are two time frames in 2020 that are tied, 11:00 a.m. to 11:59 a.m. and 3:00 p.m. to 3:59 p.m. (FBI, 2021). Therefore, they will be discussed here as well. In 2016, 93 animal cruelty cases occurred between 11:00 a.m. and 11:59 a.m., which is approximately 8.3% of the total number of cases and 87 cases of animal cruelty occurred between 3:00 p.m. and 3:59 p.m. (approximately 8% of the total number of cases). Finally, 76 of the cases occurred between 2:00 p.m. and 2:59 p.m., accounting for approximately 7% of the animal cruelty cases in 2016 (FBI, 2017).

As shown in Table 12, according to the NIBRS in 2017 (FBI, 2018a), there were 3,228 animal cruelty cases reported of which 313 occurred between 12:00 p.m. and 12:59 p.m. (approximately 10%). Next, 235 of those cases occurred between 2:00 p.m. and 2:59 p.m., which accounts for approximately 7.3% of the total cases for that year. Two-hundred-forty-two cases occurred between 1:00 p.m. and 1:59 p.m., which is approximately 7.5% of the total cases. As mentioned with the 2016 statistics, the number of cases between 11;00 a.m. to 11:59 a.m. and 3:00 p.m. to 3:59 p.m. are tied in 2020 (FBI, 2021). Therefore in 2017, between 11:00 a.m. and 11:59 a.m., there were 232 cases of animal cruelty (approximately 7.2% of the total number) and between 3:00 p.m. and 3:59 p.m., there were 228 cases, which account for approximately 1.4% of the total number of cases (FBI, 2018b). Finally, 253 of the cases occurred between 10:00 a.m. and 10:59 a.m., accounting for approximately 8% of the animal cruelty cases in 2017 (FBI, 2018a).

As displayed in Table 12, according to the NIBRS in 2020 (FBI, 2021), there were 11,566 animal cruelty cases reported of which 1,004 occurred between 12:00 p.m. and 12:59 p.m. (approximately 9%). Next, 948 of those cases occurred between 2:00 p.m. and 2:59 p.m., which accounts for approximately 8.2% of the total cases for that year. Eight-hundred-eighty-seven cases occurred between 1:00 p.m. and 1:59 p.m., which is approximately 8% of the total cases. Additionally, 842 animal cruelty cases occurred between 11:00 a.m. to 11:59 a.m. and 3:00 p.m. to 3:59 p.m., which is approximately 7.3% of the total number of cases. Finally, 830 of the cases occurred between 10:00 a.m. and 10:59 a.m., accounting for approximately 7.3% of the animal cruelty cases in 2020 (FBI, 2021).

---

2. Because the number of animal cruelty offenses by time frame were selected in descending order based on the 2020 data, they will not appear to be in order for other years assessed.

As presented in Table 12, between 2017 to 2020, the total number of reported animal cruelty offenses increased 3.6 times from 3,228 cases to 11,566 cases (FBI, 2018a; FBI, 2019a; FBI, 2020b; FBI, 2021). Within this time frame the number of animal cruelty cases that occurred between12:00 p.m. and 12:59 p.m. increased approximately 3.2 times from 313 in 2017 to 1,004 in 2020. Next, the number of cases that occurred between 1:00 p.m. to 1:59 p.m. increased approximately 4 times, from 235 in 2017 to 948 in 2020. The number of animal cruelty offenses between 2:00 p.m. to 2:59 p.m. also increased approximately 3.7 times from 242 in 2017 to 887 in 2020. Additionally, the number of animal cruelty cases that occurred between 11:00 a.m. and 11:59 a.m. in 2017 was 232, which increased approximately 2.8 times to 842 in 2020. Likewise, the number of animal cruelty cases that transpired between 3:00 p.m. and 3:59 p.m. increased by approximately 3.7 times from 228 in 2017 to 842 cases in 2020. Finally, there were 253 animal cruelty cases occurred between 10:00 a.m. and 10:59 a.m. in 2017 and that number increased approximately 3.3 times to 830 cases in 2020 (FBI, 2018a; FBI, 2019a; FBI, 2020b; FBI, 2021).

The number of animal cruelty offenses by time of day for 2017 and 2020 are provided in Chart 4 as a visual presentation of the data. The increase in the number of offenses for the top five time frames is clear, especially for 2020; however, this peak is less noticeable in 2017. It should be noted that as previously stated, there have been more LEA participating in NIBRS in 2020 than in 2017, which could be a factor in the number of animal cruelty offenses reported.

As depicted in Chart 4, it would appear that the time frame with the highest number of animal cruelty offenses in 2020 (FBI 2018a, FBI 2021) was 12:00 p.m. to 12:59 p.m. This finding is similar to Yang et al.'s (2021) research with regard to the number of theft and fraud cases in Chicago from February to June 2020. In addition, Yang et al. (2021) found that other crimes such as assault and battery were fairly high during the same time frame. Furthermore, Yang et al. (2021) found that the second highest time frame for the number of robbery offenses is the same as for the number of animal cruelty offenses, 2:00 p.m. to 2:59 p.m. during the said months.

Chart 4. Animal Cruelty Offenses by Time of Day

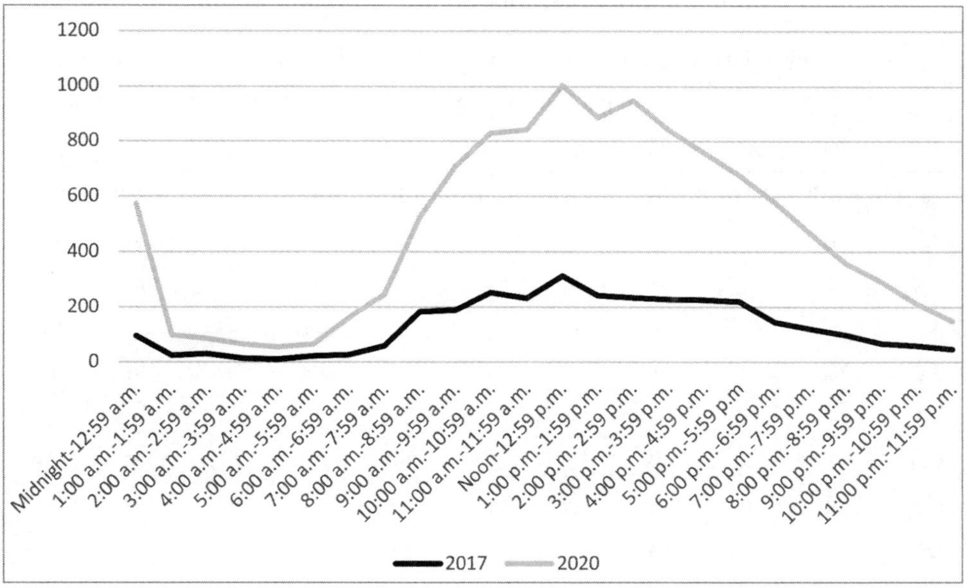

Animal Cruelty Offenses by State

When reviewing the age statistics in their totality, it is important to note the NIBRS clarification regarding the data (FBI, 2017; FBI, 2018a; FBI, 2019a; FBI, 2020b; FBI, 2021),

> In addition, each of these tables show the number of law enforcement agencies (LEAs) in each state that contributed their UCR data via NIBRS, as well as the aggregate population figures for those agencies' jurisdictions.... Figures in the column for the number of participating agencies include those LEAs in each state that reported at least one Group A Offense Report, Group B Arrest Report, or Zero Report via NIBRS for one or more months of the ... calendar year.

The data for the animal cruelty by state and the District of Columbia are available from 2016 to 2020 via the NIBRS. These data are presented in the following table, Table 13 (FBI, 2017; FBI, 2018a; FBI, 2019a; FBI, 2020b; FBI, 2021).

Table 13. Animal Cruelty Offenses by State (within the Crimes against Society Offenses category)

Number of Participating Agencies (PA) and Animal Cruelty (AC) Offenses										
State	2016		2017		2018		2019		2020	
	PA	AC	PA	AC	PA	AC	PA	AC	PA	AC
Total	6,849	1,126	6,998	3,228	7,283	5,201	8,497	9,956	9,880	11,566
AL	1	0	1	0	1	2	1	2	131	43
AK	–	–	–	–	–	–	–	–	–	–
AZ	5	0	5	0	5	2	11	43	22	182
AR	288	0	292	0	286	0	278	6	281	11
CA	–	–	–	–	–	–	–	–	–	–
CO	226	8	219	526	216	782	221	755	225	759
CT	91	0	94	18	96	74	100	131	105	85
DE	63	494	63	923	63	1,097	63	1,294	62	1,154
DC[3]	1	0	1	0	1	0	1	0	1	1
FL	–	–	–	–	–	–	–	–	–	–
GA	–	–	–	–	12	0	276	260	401	885
HI	–	–	–	–	1	0	1	51	1	46
ID	109	-0	105	3	105	50	106	34	107	52
IL	1	0	1	0	1	0	1	0	7	1
IN	93	0	105	2	112	0	185	311	160	437
IA	240	0	240	0	228	0	246	0	251	0
KS	339	0	362	0	361	0	372	0	356	1
KY	427	0	437	45	411	186	410	266	423	178
LA	33	0	33	0	33	0	30	0	70	2
ME	25	2	25	3	28	13	39	8	68	26
MD	–	–	1	3	1	0	2	8	3	5
MA	298	130	300	13	302	44	317	89	342	115
MI	624	8	629	277	631	398	637	520	627	487
MN	1	1	26	4	72	61	157	272	401	260
MS	30	0	5	0	12	47	30	193	83	209
MO	19	15	25	43	41	43	80	68	321	214
MT	103	0	104	83	101	1	97	104	100	100

3. Data were reported to the Metro Transit Police. This agency has no population associated with it.

State	2016		2017		2018		2019		2020	
	PA	AC	PA	AC	PA	AC	PA	AC	PA	AC
NE	85	0	89	0	95	1	116	6	121	53
NV	–	–	–	–	–	–	5	1	28	44
NH	174	0	178	81	184	173	188	191	193	188
NJ	–	–	–	–	–	–	–	–	–	–
NM	–	–	–	–	2	11	4	32	17	62
NY	–	–	–	–	–	–	–	–	56	0
NC	–	–	–	–	–	–	331	420	377	481
ND	108	7	107	46	105	81	106	100	106	88
OH	530	0	544	23	520	102	530	100	560	218
OK	294	0	356	0	372	0	386	164	404	102
OR	176	150	195	134	220	421	202	446	207	407
PA	31	0	29	0	28	0	25	0	22	1
RI	47	0	47	0	47	5	47	23	47	35
SC	446	0	445	200	436	295	405	321	398	313
SD	112	10	111	12	122	24	121	33	121	21
TN	467	219	468	476	463	463	463	473	463	423
TX	106	0	161	69	336	393	621	1,394	806	2,137
UT	71	0	71	0	75	0	88	6	114	64
VT	94	0	90	21	88	41	88	39	88	33
VA	421	0	413	0	415	0	415	1,372	416	1,164
WA	233	85	228	114	236	128	235	188	232	200
WV	329	13	246	18	251	11	240	11	251	9
WI	135	37	147	97	168	154	215	237	282	241
WY	–	–	–	–	–	–	5	368	23	29

As demonstrated in Table 13, there are 50 states and the District of Columbia where the reported animal cruelty offenses occurred. In addition, the total number of Participating Agencies (PA) and the total number of Animal Cruelty (AC) offenses are listed. Like with the other lengthy tables, in the interest of saving time and space, the states with the highest number of animal cruelty cases in 2020 will be discussed here: Texas, Virginia, Delaware, Georgia, and Colorado. In addition, the data for 2016 and the comparison between 2017 and 2020 will be evaluated as they were with the location and time of day data. The total number of animal cases for the said years will also be included in this analysis. Each state will be discussed in descending order from the highest number of cases to the lowest, again according to the 2020 figures.

As noted in Table 13, according to the NIBRS (FBI, 2017), in 2016[4], there were 1,126 animal cruelty cases, none of those cases occurred in Texas (0%). Next, none of those cases occurred in Virginia which accounts for 0% of the total cases for that year. Four-hundred-ninety-four cases occurred in Delaware which is approximately 44% of the total cases. Next, Georgia did not participate in 2016; therefore, no animal cruelty cases were gathered in 2016. Finally, eight of the cases occurred in Colorado accounting for approximately .7% of the animal cruelty cases in 2016 (FBI, 2017).

As shown in Table 13, according to the NIBRS in 2017 (FBI, 2018a), there were 3,228 animal cruelty cases reported of which 69 occurred in Texas (approximately 2%). Next, none of those cases occurred in Virginia which accounts for 0% of the total cases for that year. Nine-hundred-twenty-three cases occurred in Delaware, which is approximately 29% of the total cases. Like in 2016, Georgia did not participate in 2017; therefore, there were no animal cruelty cases reported. Finally, 526 of the cases occurred in Colorado, accounting for approximately 16% of the animal cruelty cases in 2017 (FBI, 2018a).

As displayed in Table 13, according to the NIBRS in 2020 (FBI, 2021), there were 11,566 animal cruelty cases reported of which 2,137 occurred in Texas (approximately 18%). Next, 1,164 of those cases occurred in Virginia which accounts for approximately 10% of the total cases for that year. One-thousand-one-hundred-fifty-four cases occurred in Delaware, which is approximately 10% of the total cases. Additionally, 885 of the cases occurred in Georgia, accounting for approximately 8% of the animal cruelty cases in 2020. Finally, 759 animal cruelty cases were reported in Colorado in 2020, accounting for approximately 7% of the total number (FBI, 2021).

As presented in Table 13, between 2017 to 2020, the total number of reported animal cruelty offenses increased 3.6 times from 3,228 cases to 11,566 cases (FBI, 2018a; FBI, 2019a; FBI, 2020b; FBI, 2021). Within this time frame the number of animal cruelty cases that occurred in Texas increased approximately 31 times from 69 in 2017 to 2,137 in 2020. Next, the number of cases that occurred in Virginia increased by 1,164 cases, from 0 in 2017 to 1,164 in 2020. The number of animal cruelty offenses in Delaware also increased approximately 1.25 times from 923 in 2017 to 1,154 in 2020. Additionally, the number of animal cruelty cases that occurred in Georgia was non-existent in 2017; however, as mentioned previously, there were 885 cases in the said state in 2020. Finally, there were 536 animal cruelty cases occurred in Colorado in 2017 and that number increased approximately 1.4 times to 759 cases in 2020 (FBI, 2018a; FBI, 2019a; FBI, 2020b; FBI, 2021).

Number of Offenses Completed and Attempted

The data for the total offense categories and animal cruelty offenses completed and attempted are available from 2016 to 2020 via the NIBRS. These data are presented in the following table, Table 14 (FBI, 2017; FBI, 2018a; FBI, 2019a; FBI, 2020b; FBI, 2021).

4. Because the number of animal cruelty offenses by state were selected in descending order based on the 2020 data, they will not appear to be in order for other years assessed.

Table 14. Number of Offenses Completed and Attempted

Total Offense Categories					
	2016	2017	2018	2019	2020
Total Offenses	6,101,034	6,290,042	6,586,140	7,688,645	8,879,728
Number Completed	5,979,409	6,166,637	6,450,575	7,525,711	8,674,010
Number Attempted	121,625	123,405	135,565	162,934	205,718
Animal Cruelty					
	2016	2017	2018	2019	2020
Total Offenses	1,126	3,228	5,201	9,956	11,566
Number Completed	1,110	3,200	5,118	9,691	11,182
Number Attempted	16	28	83	265	384

As stated, there are three groupings for the total offense categories and animal cruelty cases in Table 14, the total offenses, number completed, and number attempted. Each group will be discussed separately.

As evidenced in Table 14, according to the NIBRS (FBI, 2017; FBI, 2018a; FBI, 2019a; FBI, 2020b; FBI, 2021), in 2016, there were 6,101,034 total offenses, of which were 1,126 animal cruelty offenses (approximately .01% of total offenses). From 2017 to 2020, the total number of total offenses increased from 6,290,042 to 8,879,728. During this same time period, the total number of reported animal cruelty offenses increased approximately 3.6 times from 3,228 (approximately .05% of the total number of offenses) in 2017 to 11,566 offenses (approximately .1% of the total number of arrestees) in 2020 (FBI, 2017; FBI, 2018a; FBI, 2019a; FBI, 2020b; FBI, 2021).

As displayed in Table 14, according to the NIBRS (FBI, 2017; FBI, 2018a; FBI, 2019a; FBI, 2020b; FBI, 2021), in 2016, there were 5,979,409 offenses completed, of which were 1,110 completed animal cruelty offenses (approximately .01% of the completed offenses). From 2017 to 2020, the number of all completed offenses from increased from 6,166,637 to 8,674,010. During this same time period, the reported number of completed animal cruelty offenses increased approximately 3.5 times from 3,200 completed offenses (approximately .05% of the total number of the completed offenses) in 2017 to 11,182 completed offenses (approximately .1% of the total number of the completed offenses) in 2020 (FBI, 2017; FBI, 2018a; FBI, 2019a; FBI, 2020b; FBI, 2021).

As recorded in Table 14, according to the NIBRS (FBI, 2017; FBI, 2018a; FBI, 2019a; FBI, 2020b; FBI, 2021), in 2016, there were 121,625 attempted offenses, of which were 16 attempted animal cruelty offenses (approximately .01% of the attempted offenses). From 2017 to 2020, the number of attempted offenses for all offenses increased from 123,405 to 205,718. During this same time period, the reported number of attempted animal cruelty offenses increased approximately 14 times from 28 attempted offenses (approximately .02% of the total number of attempted offenses) in 2017 to 384 attempted offenses (approximately .2% of the total number of attempted offenses in 2020 (FBI, 2017; FBI, 2018a; FBI, 2019a; FBI, 2020b; FBI, 2021).

Although these data provide some information on the completed and attempted total offenses and of the animal cruelty offenses, as stated with regard to the rest of the offense-based information, one needs to be critical in their assessment of these data. The same issues with these data exist as mentioned with the previous categories.

The review of the available NIBRS data will now focus the cleared incidents in the next section. The data are divided by the total number of incidents, total number of incidents cleared, number of incidents cleared by arrest, and number of incidents cleared by exceptional means. The data on the animal cruelty incidents are divided in the same manner.

Number of Incidents Cleared

When reviewing the number of incidents cleared statistics in their totality, it is important to note the NIBRS clarification regarding the data (FBI, 2017; FBI, 2018a; FBI, 2019a; FBI, 2020b; FBI, 2021),

> To arrive at the totals provided for each column of data, the UCR Program used the following counting rules: Incidents—one for each offense type identified within each incident, aggregated by offense category. In multiple-offense incidents, incidents were counted two or more times when there were two or more offense types in the incident. (For example, if an incident involved both a rape and a robbery, the incident was counted only once in the total. However, the incident is reflected twice in the breakdown because it was counted in both the sex offenses category [rape] and the robbery offense category.) Cleared by Arrest—one for each offense type in an incident containing at least one arrestee. Cleared by Exceptional Means—one for each offense type in an incident reported as cleared exceptionally. Note: There is no direct correlation between the numbers in the Total Incidents column and those in the Total Incidents Cleared column. The numbers in the Total Incidents column are included only for informational purposes.

The data for the total and animal cruelty incident categories, which are divided into for groupings: total incidents, total incidents cleared, number of incidents cleared by arrest, and number of incidents cleared by exceptional means. These data are available from 2016 to 2020 via the NIBRS. These data are presented in the following table, Table 15 (FBI, 2017; FBI, 2018a; FBI, 2019a; FBI, 2020b; FBI, 2021).

Table 15. Number of Incidents Cleared

Total Offense Categories					
	2016	2017	2018	2019	2020
Total Incidents	5,237,106	5,369,204	5,617,945	6,572,870	7,560,867
Total Incidents Cleared	1,969,162	1,884,833	2,138,931	2,477,614	2,544,763
by Arrest	1,781,373	195,833	1,942,452	2,230,215	2,278,469
by Exceptional Means	187,789	195,414	196,479	247,399	266,294

Animal Cruelty					
	2016	2017	2018	2019	2020
Total Incidents	1,126	3,228	5,201	9,956	11,566
Total Incidents Cleared	307	973	1,406	2,604	2,625
by Arrest	280	909	1,302	2,376	2,433
by Exceptional Means	27	64	104	228	192

As stated, there are four groupings for the total incident categories and animal cruelty cases in Table 15, the total incidents, total incidents cleared, number of incidents cleared by arrest, and number of incidents cleared by exceptional means. Each group will be discussed separately.

As evidenced in Table 15, according to the NIBRS (FBI, 2017; FBI, 2018a; FBI, 2019a; FBI, 2020b; FBI, 2021), in 2016, there were 5,237,106 total incidents, of which were 1,126 animal cruelty incidents (approximately .02% of total incidents). From 2017 to 2020, the number of total incidents increased from 5,369,204 to 7,560,867. During this same time period, the total number of reported animal cruelty incidents increased approximately 3.6 times from 3,228 (approximately .06% of the total number of incidents) in 2017 to 11,566 offenses (approximately .2% of the total number of incidents) in 2020 (FBI, 2017; FBI, 2018a; FBI, 2019a; FBI, 2020b; FBI, 2021).

As displayed in Table 15, according to the NIBRS (FBI, 2017; FBI, 2018a; FBI, 2019a; FBI, 2020b; FBI, 2021), in 2016, there were 1,969,162 total incidents cleared, of which were 1,126 animal cruelty cleared incidents (approximately .06% of the cleared incidents). From 2017 to 2020, the number of all cleared incidents increased from 1,884,833 to 2,544,763. During this same time period, the reported number of cleared animal cruelty incidents increased approximately 2.7 times from 973 (approximately .05% of the total number of the cleared incidents) in 2017 to 2,625 cleared incidents (approximately .1% of the total number of the cleared incidents) in 2020 (FBI, 2017; FBI, 2018a; FBI, 2019a; FBI, 2020b; FBI, 2021).

As recorded in Table 15, according to the NIBRS (FBI, 2017; FBI, 2018a; FBI, 2019a; FBI, 2020b; FBI, 2021), in 2016, there were 1,781,373 incidents cleared by arrest, of which were 280 animal cruelty incidents (approximately .02% of the incidents cleared by arrest). From 2017 to 2020, the total number of incidents cleared by arrest increased from 195,833 to 2,278,469. During this same time period, the reported number of animal cruelty incidents that were cleared by arrest increased approximately 2.7 times from 909 (approximately .05% of the total number of incidents cleared by arrest) in 2017 to 2,433 incidents cleared by arrest (approximately .1% of the total number of incidents cleared by arrest) in 2020 (FBI, 2017; FBI, 2018a; FBI, 2019a; FBI, 2020b; FBI, 2021).

As revealed in Table 15, according to the NIBRS (FBI, 2017; FBI, 2018a; FBI, 2019a; FBI, 2020b; FBI, 2021), in 2016, there were 187,789 incidents cleared by exceptional means, of which were 27 animal cruelty incidents (approximately .01% of the incidents cleared by exceptional means). From 2017 to 2020, the total number of incidents cleared by exceptional means increased from 195,414 to 266,294. During this same time period, the reported number of animal cruelty incidents that were cleared by exceptional means increased 3 times from 64 (approximately .03% of the total number of incidents cleared by exceptional means) in 2017 to 192 incidents cleared by exceptional means (approximately .1% of the total number of incidents cleared by exceptional means) in 2020 (FBI, 2017; FBI, 2018a; FBI, 2019a; FBI, 2020b; FBI, 2021).

Although these data provide some information on the total and animal cruelty incidents, as stated with regard to the offense-based information, one needs to be critical in their assessment of these data. The same issues with these data exist as mentioned with the other categories.

The final review of the available NIBRS data will include offenses involving the offender's suspected use of drugs/narcotics and alcohol in the next section. The data are divided by the total number of offenses, drugs/narcotics, the percentage of the total offenses in which the offender's drugs/narcotic usage was suspected, alcohol, and the percentage of the total offenses in which the offender's alcohol usage was suspected. The data on the animal cruelty offenses are divided in the same manner. Please note that these data were not available in the available 2016 NIBRS information.

Offenses Involving Offender's Suspected Use (Drugs/Narcotics and Alcohol)

When reviewing the offenses involving the offender's suspected use (drugs/narcotics and alcohol) statistics in their totality, it is important to note the NIBRS clarification regarding the data (FBI, 2018a; FBI, 2019a; FBI, 2020b; FBI, 2021),

> This table uses the following rules and then distributes the data by whether law enforcement suspected that the offender used drugs/narcotics and/or alcohol during or shortly before perpetrating the crime by the number of offenses per offense category: Crime Against Society—one for each unique offense type. Offenses Involving Offender's Suspected Use—one in each involvement category for each offense type where the Offender Suspected of Using contains Drugs/Narcotics or Alcohol, respectively. Percent—percentage of offenses associated with the offender's use of Drugs/Narcotics and/or Alcohol Involvement in an offense by offense category. Percentage = Type of Involvement/Total Offenses (round to tenths/round up) Note: Drugs/Narcotics and Alcohol Involvement will not add to Total Offenses because the offender may have used both in the incident and/or this table only shows two aspects of the Offender Suspected of Using.

The data for the offenses involving the offender's suspected use of drugs/narcotics and alcohol with regard to the total and animal cruelty offenses categories are divided into five groupings. These groups are the total number of offenses, drugs/narcotics, the percentage of the total offenses in which the offender's drugs/narcotic usage was suspected, alcohol, and the percentage of the total offenses in which the offender's alcohol usage was suspected. These data are available from 2017 to 2020 via the NIBRS. These data are presented in the following table, Table 16 (FBI, 2018a; FBI, 2019a; FBI, 2020b; FBI, 2021).

Table 16. Offenses Involving Offender's Suspected Use (Drugs/Narcotics and Alcohol) [5]

Total Offense Categories				
	2017	2018	2019	2020
Total Offenses	6,290,042	6,586,140	7,688,645	8,879,554
Drugs/Narcotics	576,160	611,207	653,205	668,274
% of Total Offenses	9.2%	9.3%	8.5%	7.5%
Alcohol	241,876	256,016	287,522	326,319
% of Total Offenses	3.8%	3.9%	3.7%	3.7%
Animal Cruelty				
	2017	2018	2019	2020
Number of Offenses	3,228	5,201	9,956	11,565
Drugs/Narcotics	25	49	94	115
% of Offenses	.8%	.9%	.9%	1%
Alcohol	63	114	154	229
% of Offenses	2%	2.2	1.5%	2%

As stated, there are five groupings for the total categories and animal cruelty offenses involving the offender's suspected use (drugs/narcotics and alcohol) in Table 16, are the total number of offenses, drugs/narcotics, percentage of the total offenses in which the offender's drugs/narcotic usage was suspected, alcohol, and the percentage of the total offenses in which the offender's alcohol usage was suspected. Each group will be discussed separately.

As evidenced in Table 16 and mentioned previously, according to the NIBRS (FBI, 2018a; FBI, 2019a; FBI, 2020b; FBI, 2021), from 2017 to 2020, the number of total offenses increased from 6,290,042 to 8,879,554. During this same time period, the total number of reported animal cruelty offenses increased approximately 3.6 times from 3,228 (approximately .05% of the total number of offenses) in 2017 to 11,566 offenses (approximately .1% of the total number of incidents) in 2020 (FBI, 2018a; FBI, 2019a; FBI, 2020b; FBI, 2021).

As displayed in Table 16, according to the NIBRS (FBI, 2018a; FBI, 2019a; FBI, 2020b; FBI, 2021), from 2017 to 2020, the number of all offenses involving the offender's suspected use of drugs/narcotics increased from 576,160 to 668,274. During this same

5. These data were not included in the NIBRS 2016 statistics

time period, the reported number of animal cruelty offenses involving the offender's suspected use of drugs/narcotics increased approximately 4.6 times from 25 (approximately .004% of all offenses involving the offender's suspected use of drugs/narcotics) in 2017 to 115 (approximately .02% of all offenses involving the offender's suspected use of drugs/narcotics) in 2020 (FBI, 2018a; FBI, 2019a; FBI, 2020b; FBI, 2021).

As presented in Table 16, according to the NIBRS (FBI, 2018a; FBI, 2019a; FBI, 2020b; FBI, 2021), in 2017 to 2020, the percentage of the total number of offenses involving the offender's suspected use of drugs/narcotics decreased from 9.2% to 7.5%. Conversely, during this same time period, the percentage of reported number of animal cruelty involving the offender's suspected use of drugs/narcotics increased .8% in 2017 to 1% in 2020 (FBI, 2018a; FBI, 2019a; FBI, 2020b; FBI, 2021).

As recorded in Table 16, according to the NIBRS (FBI, 2018a; FBI, 2019a; FBI, 2020b; FBI, 2021), from 2017 to 2020, the total number of offenses involving the offender's suspected use of alcohol increased from 241,876 to 326,319. During this same time period, the reported number of animal cruelty offenses involving the offender's suspected use of alcohol increased approximately 3.6 times from 63 (approximately .02% of all offenses involving the offender's suspected use of alcohol) in 2017 to 229 involving the offender's suspected use of alcohol (approximately .1% of all offenses involving the offender's suspected use of alcohol) in 2020 (FBI, 2018a; FBI, 2019a; FBI, 2020b; FBI, 2021).

As demonstrated in Table 16, according to the NIBRS (FBI, 2018a; FBI, 2019a; FBI, 2020b; FBI, 2021), in 2017 to 2020, the percentage of the total number of offenses involving the offender's suspected use of alcohol decreased from 3.8% to 3.7%. However, during this same time period, the percentage of reported number of animal cruelty involving the offender's suspected use of alcohol remained the same at 2% in 2017 and in 2020 (FBI, 2018a; FBI, 2019a; FBI, 2020b; FBI, 2021).

Chart 5. Animal Cruelty Offenses Involving the Offender's Suspected Use

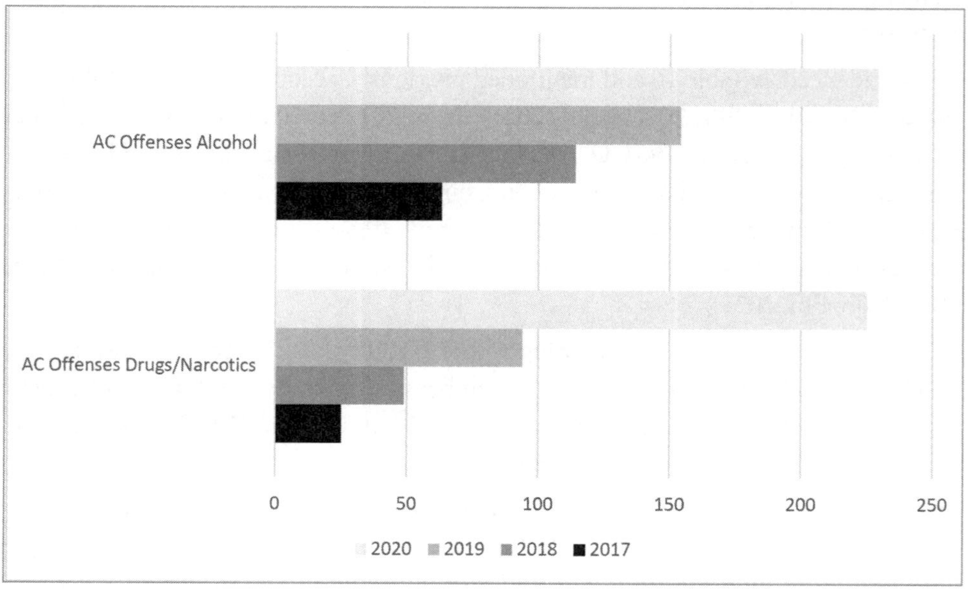

The number of animal cruelty offenses involving the offender's suspected use (drugs/narcotics and alcohol) for 2017, 2018, 2019 and 2020 are provided in Chart 5 as a visual presentation of the data (FBI, 2018a; FBI, 2019a; FBI, 2020b; FBI, 2021).

As depicted in Chart 5, it would appear that the numbers of animal cruelty offenses involving the offender's suspected use of drugs/narcotics and alcohol have increased each year from 2017 to 2020 (FBI, 2018a; FBI, 2019a; FBI, 2020b; FBI, 2021). This information is contradictory to recent research findings that substance-related crime rates have generally declined, especially when stay-at-home/lockdown orders were issued at the beginning of the COVID-19 pandemic closing bars and restaurants (i.e., Abrams, 2021; Klick & MacDonald, 2020).

Although these data provide some information on the total and animal cruelty offenses involving the offender's suspected use of drugs/narcotics and alcohol, as stated with regard to the offense-based information, one needs to be critical in their assessment of these data. The same issues with these data exist as mentioned with the other categories.

This concludes the examination of the available NIBRS data. The review of the prohibited animal cruelty statistics will continue in the next section with the Wildlife Reports 2016 and 2020 based upon the Convention on International Trade in Endangered Species (CITES) of Wild Fauna and Flora.

Wildlife Reports 2016 and 2020 (Convention on International Trade in Endangered Species of Wild Fauna and Flora)

The World Wildlife Crime Report is a publication released by the United Nations Office on Drugs and Crime (UNODC). The report provides data on the illicit trafficking of protected species across national borders. Details of the illicit market include figures for wildlife species seized, the sources of the trafficked species, financial estimates, and the penalties given to offenders. The report additionally provides in-depth case studies of the illicit trade of rosewood, ivory and rhino horn, pangolin scales, live reptiles, big cats, and eels.

The primary source of data for the World Wildlife Crime Report is the World Wildlife Seizure (World WISE) database. The World WISE is a collection of reports by States party to the Convention on International Trade (CITES) in Endangered Species of Wild Fauna and Flora, an international agreement meant to protect wildlife species endangered by international trade. Entering force in 1975, CITES provides a framework for domestic legislation on trade and enforcement against wildlife crime for 184 member parties.

Data collected by CITES provides a sizable pool of cooperating nations, creating a more robust assessment of international wildlife crime. However, the World Wildlife Report identifies noteworthy limitations to being based on World WISE data. First, CITES-oriented data sources apply to only 35,000 species out of millions of possible flora and fauna species that may be illegally harvested and traded. Second, the scope of

CITES-oriented data is limited to international trade. The result is that illegal harvesting within a single nation, such as localized poaching of non-human animal species, is not represented in the data. Lastly, the framework and definitions provided by CITES do not pertain to domestic markets. Just as CITES data cannot provide information on localized illicit harvesting, the market data is limited to wildlife and goods that cross-national borders.

Despite these limitations, the use of CITES data provides insight into international wildlife crime from 1999 to 2018. The World Wildlife Crime Report has two editions, released first in 2016 and second in 2020. The reports operate with a definition of wildlife crime as "harvesting and trade contrary to national law, particularly, but not exclusively, the national laws implemented in fulfillment of CITES obligations" (United Nations Office on Drugs and Crime, 2020). It is important to note that while the offenses described in the report do violate the international agreement, they may not necessarily violate the local or national law in each region where the wildlife is harvested, transported, or traded.

2016

The first World Wildlife Crime Report was released in 2016. The report details seizure records from 1999 to October of 2015. Included in the report are 164,000 seizures from 120 reporting countries (United Nations Office on Drugs and Crime, 2016). The report additionally consists of several case studies following animal and plant products illicitly traded worldwide.

The 2016 report provided insight into the illegal trade of wildlife in both legal and illicit retail markets. According to the report, trade is not nationally regulated for millions of species, with some being harvested or exported from a nation illegally but traded legally in international markets (United Nations Office on Drugs and Crime, 2016). By violating international agreements or trade laws, the animal product may be illegally harvested and transported but not violate any national laws within the market. When the illegally traded wildlife product enters legal markets, criminal traders gain access to greater demand than can be found in the black market alone.

The report likens the international trade of protected wildlife to that of firearms, of pharmaceuticals, and in antiquities. The illegal wildlife "goods" are traded using forged or legitimate documents. Most reported efforts against trafficking, measured through seizures, take place at ports of entry, with customs agents playing a more significant role than domestic enforcement agencies (United Nations Office on Drugs and Crime, 2016). CITES requires observing parties penalize offenders. The offense can range from a fine to more than four years in prison. Of the 131 parties with available data, 31% had a maximum penalty of a fine only, 43% limited penalties to less than four years of imprisonment, and 26% allowed for penalties beyond four years of imprisonment (United Nations Office on Drugs and Crime, 2016). Efforts to deter illicit harvesting and trade are complicated by the speculative trading involved in some markets. As wildlife products are harvested and transported in an effort to predict upcoming trends, national campaigns to reduce demand are limited in impact (World Wildlife Report, 2016).

Among the trends explored in the 2016 World Wildlife Report are those pertaining to the countries and regions shipping and seizing the illicit wildlife products. The report found that no single country was the source of more than 15% of the shipments seized (United Nations Office on Drugs and Crime, 2016). Also compiled were the regional origins of the seizures reported. North American countries made of 46% of seizures reported, 24% were reported from Asian and Pacific nations, 15% from Latin American nations, 14 % from Europe, and 1% from Africa (United Nations Office on Drugs and Crime, 2016). Regions were also associated with particular wildlife. South and Central America were primarily associated with the seizure of birds, Africa and Asia were associated with mammals, Europe and North America with reptiles, and Oceania with corals (World Wildlife Report, 2016).

Trends pertaining to wildlife species were also explored. The 2016 report counted approximately 7,000 species seized in violation, with no single species being responsible for more than 6% of reported seizures (United Nations Office on Drugs and Crime, 2016). The report explored the types of wildlife species seized from 2005 to 2014. Rosewood species consisted of 35% of wildlife among the seizures, 18% were elephant species, 9% were reptile species, 6% agarwood, 5% pangolin, 3% rhinoceros, 3% marine turtles, 2% parrots, 2% big cats, 2% raptor birds, 2% tortoise and freshwater turtle species, 1% each of coral and sturgeon, and a remaining 11% categorized as "other" (United Nations Office on Drugs and Crime, 2016). Pangolins provided a notable case study in the report. Between 2007 and 2013, 1,467 pangolins were legally traded as opposed to 107,060 that were seized in illicit shipments (United Nations Office on Drugs and Crime, 2016). The trafficking markets of the different species overall were found to be highly specialized. Most shipments seized involved only a single species (World Wildlife Report, 2016).

2020

The second World Wildlife Crime Report was published in 2020. The report utilized seizure data reported from 1999–2017. Partial data from 2018 was also included in the analysis. The dataset was expanded to approximately 180,000 seizures from 149 countries (United Nations Office on Drugs and Crime, 2020). The data since 2017 featured the effects of a significant policy change. CITES parties were required to submit data on all seizures of wildlife over the previous year. One objective identified in the report was to begin comparing new data to the past report (United Nations Office on Drugs and Crime, 2020).

The mandatory reporting appeared to have a notable impact on the number of reported seizures. The greatest number of seizures occurred in 2017, more than in any single year with 20,762 recorded seizures (United Nations Office on Drugs and Crime, 2020). A similar sharp increase was also recorded in 2016. No single country was identified as the source of more than 9% of seized shipments (United Nations Office on

Drugs and Crime, 2020). This appeared to be even greater diversity of national origins than found in the 2016 report. It is uncertain to what degree this is due to mandatory reporting policy.

The 2020 World Wildlife Crime Report continued to explore trends pertaining to the species seized in shipments. Nearly 6,000 different species were reported as being seized, with no single species being responsible for more than 5% of seizures (United Nations Office on Drugs and Crime, 2020). The report also explored the seizures by types of wildlife species as was done in the 2016 report. The share of types of wildlife seized was from 2014 to 2019 was examined with following results: 31.7% rosewood, 30.6% elephants, 13.9% pangolins, 11.8% rhinos, 3.6% assorted reptiles, 1.7% sturgeon, 0.8% big cats, 0.6% corals, 0.6% parrots, 0.6% agarwood, 0.4% raptors (United Nations Office on Drugs and Crime, 2020). The 2020 report additionally reviewed the seizures from 1999–2018, reporting the share of seizure incidents in the World WISE database by taxonomic category. The taxonomic category breakdown was 23% mammals, 21.3% reptiles, 14.6% corals, 14.3% plants, 8.5% birds, 7.9% mollusks, 4.7% bony fish, and 5.7% other (United Nations Office on Drugs and Crime, 2020).

Permitted Animal Cruelty

Permitted animal cruelty was discussed in Chapter 4 and includes those forms of cruelty that are exempted by the law. The review of the permitted animal cruelty statistics will begin with the hunting data gathered from various state agencies. This section of Chapter 8 will also address statistics pertaining to farming and mills.

Hunting

One form of permitted animal cruelty is hunting. Hunting can serve several different purposes such as recreation, population control, the harvesting of food, and harvesting of animal parts for other commercial products. This chapter provides collected data on hunting within states and the importation and exportation of wildlife hunting trophies.

The U.S. Fish and Wildlife and the United States Census Bureau estimated that there were 11.5 million people who hunted in the United States in 2016. This was below the 13.7 million estimated to have hunted in the prior 2011 report (U.S. Fish and Wildlife Service & U.S. Census Bureau, 2018, p. 24). While these reports provide data on the people engaged in wildlife recreation activities every five years; wildlife hunting regulations, licensing, and harvest reporting is largely administrated by each individual state's department.

Table 17. Deer and Turkey Harvests by State 2018–2019[6]

State	Deer	Turkey
Total	5,854,037	609,692
AL	203,040	25,750
AK	17,610	-
AZ	13,894	1,228
AR	210,065	8,217
CA	28,043	-
CO	36,389	4,535
CT	10,908	1,435
DE	-	565
FL	73,123	14,000
GA	278, 403	17,073
HI	-	-
ID	37,182	-
IL	151,709	15,190
IN	114,882	12,552
IA	99,999	11,840
KS	81,769	-
KY	148,395	31,247
LA	120,800	6,200
ME	28,323	8,592
MD	77,382	4,172
MA	13,891	2,740
MI	370,948	33,980
MN	183,637	11,533
MS	197,157	12,399
MO	290,224	40,608
MT	96,140	5,897
NE	60,308	20,984
NV	6,454	-
NH	12,306	5,422
NJ	50,861	2,739
NM	10,701	2,876

6. These references provide data for Table 17.

State	Deer	Turkey
NY	224,190	18,627
NC	143,529	18,730
ND	50,000	5,640
OH	172,049	20,142
OK	109,260	25,742
OR	34,350	6,473
PA	387,940	46,342
RI	2,125	270
SC	193,073	17,374
SD	50,000	5,640
TN	136,660	31,620
TX	896,503	30,982
UT	27,663	4,745
VT	16,550	5,851
VA	205,000	2,018
WA	27,187	8,915
WV	99,437	12,000
WI	290,220	42,368
WY	42,161	4,439

Table 17 details the harvest data reported by each different state's department for the 2018–2019 hunting seasons. The harvest data are collected from the harvest reports of 49 individual states. The 2018–2019 seasons were selected to maximize the number of states with data available from their respective agency webpages while representing the interest to report recent statistics at the time of this publication. Deer and wild turkey harvests were selected due to their prominence in hunting across the majority of states.

Table 17 provides data on deer harvests first. Individual states hold differing seasons that allow for the hunting of deer within the state. The states that reported the highest number of deer harvested in the 2018–2019 season were Texas, Pennsylvania, Michigan, Missouri, and Wisconsin. Texas reported a deer harvest of 895,503 (Purvis, 2019a). In Pennsylvania, 387,940 deer were harvested (Pennsylvania Game Commission, n.d.). The Michigan Department of Resources reported that 370,948 deer were harvested (n.d.). The Missouri Department of Conservation reported harvesting 290,224 deer (n.d.). The Wisconsin Department of Natural Resources reported 290,220 deer harvested (2020). The combined total of reported deer harvested in each report is 5,854,037. Table 17 omits two states: Delaware and Hawaii.

Table 17 also provides data on wild turkey harvests reported in 2019. Just as with deer hunting, details of permitted hunting seasons are decided within individual states. The states that reported the highest number of turkeys harvested in the 2018–2019 season were Pennsylvania, Wisconsin, Missouri, Michigan, and Tennessee. The Pennsylvania Game Commission reported a harvest of 46,342 wild turkeys (n.d.). The Wisconsin Department of Natural Resources reported 42,368 harvested turkeys (2020). The Missouri Department of Conservation reported 40,608 wild turkey harvested (n.d.). The Michigan Department of Resources reported that 33,980 wild turkeys were harvested (n.d.). The Tennessee Wildlife Resources Agency reported 31,620 wild turkeys were harvested (n.d.). The combined total of wild turkeys harvested in each report is 609,692. Table 17 omits six states: Alaska, California, Hawaii, Idaho, Kansas, and Nevada.

While hunting can serve numerous purposes, one specific classification is trophy hunting. For the purposes of their analysis, the Humane Society International (2016, p. 2) defined trophy hunting as "killing wild animals for their body parts, such as head and hide, for display but not primarily for food or sustenance." The trophies in question include distinctive animal products, parts of the animal's body, or the full body posed and preserved by a taxidermist. Common examples reported are elephant tusks, rhino horns, and deer antlers (Humane Society International, 2016, p. 3). Trophies in any form are typically displayed in decorative fashion.

The role of the United States, as the largest global importer of hunting trophies, was explored in a 2016 report by the Humane Society. The report analyzed trophy importation in the United States across a 10-year period from 2005 to 2014. In the 10-year period, the United States imported approximately 1,260,000 wildlife trophies (Humane Society International, 2016, p. 2). The annual average number of wildlife trophy imports exceeds 120,000. The origins of imported trophies included numerous countries from across the globe. The top exporters of wildlife trophies to the United States in this 10-year period were Canada, South Africa, Namibia, Mexico, Zimbabwe, New Zealand, Tanzania, Argentina, Zambia, and Botswana (Humane Society International, 2016, p. 4). The majority of the imported wildlife trophies were from the top two exporters: Canada and South Africa. Wildlife trophies from Canada comprised 43% of those imported into the United States and those from South Africa comprised 32% of wildlife trophies brought into the United States from 2005 to 2014 (Humane Society International, 2016, p. 4).

The wildlife trophies imported into the United States were from a variety of different species. The most common types of animals imported as trophies into the United States from 2005 to 2014 were snow geese (111,366), mallards (104,067), Canada geese (70,585), American black bears (69,072), and impalas (70,585) (Humane Society International, 2016, p. 8). Also imported into the United States were coveted African wildlife species that comprise the "African Big Five" (Humane Society International, 2016, p. 12). This group includes African lions, African elephants, African leopards, southern white rhinoceros, and African buffalo. Between 2005 and 2014, 32,453 Africa

Big Five animals were imported to the U.S. (Humane Society International, 2016, p. 12). This number of animals imported in the 10-year period included 17,289 African buffalo, 5,605 African lions, 4,624 African elephants, 4,598 African leopards, and 337 southern white rhinoceros.

The role of European nations in trophy hunting has also been explored. A 2021 Humane Society International analysis reported that from 2014 to 2018 European Union (EU) member states were the world's second largest importer of hunting trophies of internationally protected species, after the US. Between 2014 and 2018, 14,912 trophies were imported into the European Union, placing the EU behind only the United States' reported 72,617 imported trophies in the same time period (Humane Society International, 2021, p. 105). Imported animal trophies were reportedly from 73 different origin species. The most frequently imported were: 21% of the imported trophies from the Hartmann's mountain zebra, 12% from the Chacma baboon, 9% from the American black bear, 7% from brown bears, and 6% from African elephants (Humane Society International, 2021, p. 67).

As a collection of nations, trophy import data are further reported divided by individual member states. The top importers of hunting trophies within the EU from 2014 to 2018 were Germany, Spain, Denmark, Austria, and Sweden (Humane Society International, 2021, p. 106). According to the same report, Germany comprised 27% of imported trophies in the five-year period, bringing in a total of 3,959 trophies for an average of 792 per year. Spain's imports comprised 14% of the EU grand total. Spain imported an average of 424 trophies per year, totaling in 2,117 trophies imported. Denmark's annual average of 334 trophies resulted in a five-tear total 1,670 trophies imported. This comprised 11% of the EU imports. Austria was reported to have imported 1,354 trophies, averaging 271 trophies annually. Austria's imported trophies made up 9% of the EU's five-year grand total. Sweden comprised 6% of the five-year total with 919 imported trophies. This resulted in an average of 184 imported trophies annually (Humane Society International, 2021, p. 106). Consistent with the previous 2016 report that explored U.S. imports from 2005 to 2014, Canada and South Africa continued to comprise over 50% of the global export hunting trophies in the five-year period studied (Humane Society International, 2021, p. 105).

Farming

Another form of permitted animal cruelty is farming. As with hunting, farming involves the harvesting of animals for food and other commercial products. This section outlines statistics on fur farming, fisheries, and animal farming for food.

Table 18. 2018 Fur Farming Statistics Reported by Humane Society International

Origin	Estimated Number of Animals Harvested (Millions)
Canada	1.8
United States	3.1
European Union	37.8
China	50.5

Table 18 details the estimated harvest from fur farming in four regions in 2018. The data are reported by the Humane Society International (n.d.). Canada is estimated to have harvested 1,800,000 animals in fur farming efforts. The majority of these, approximately 1,760,000, were mink and 2,360 were foxes. The United States harvested an estimated 3,100,000 mink. The European Union harvested an estimated 37,800,000 animals. Mink accounted for 34,700,000, 2,700,000 were foxes, 166,000 were raccoon dogs, and 227,000 were chinchilla. Lastly, 50,500,000 animals were reportedly harvested from fur farming efforts in China. Of these animals, 20,700,000 were mink, 17,300,000 were foxes, and 12,300,000 were raccoon dogs.

The National Agriculture Statistics Service (NASS), the Agriculture Statistics Board, and the United States Department of Agriculture (USDA) (2021) published a report on mink production in the United States. As the data retrieved from Humane Society International (n.d.) indicated, mink fur is the product of farming efforts in the United States. The 2021 USDA annual publication reported that 1,410,000 mink pelts were harvested in the United States in 2020. According to the NASS, Agriculture Statistics Board, and USDA report (2021) Wisconsin produced 403,540 pelts in 2020. The other highest producing states in the same year were Utah with 386,880, Idaho with 170,000, Iowa with 61,000, and Minnesota with 42,230. The total mink production in the United States decreased 49% from 2019. This followed the trend of continual annual decrease in mink pelt production since 2014 (NASS, Agriculture Statistics Board, & USDA, 2021).

Another form of farming is through fisheries and aquaculture. The Food and Agriculture Organization of the United Nations (2020) reported that global capture fisheries production reached a new record of 96,400,000 tons. This harvest continues the general upward trend in fisheries production. According to the report, the highest producing nations were China producing 15% of the global total, Indonesia and Peru each producing 7%, India producing 6% of the total, both the Russian Federation and the United States producing 5% of the total each, and Vietnam producing 3% of the global total (Food and Agriculture Organization of the United Nations, 2020). These top seven producers account for almost half of the global production.

The last form of farming discussed is animal farming for the purposes of food production. Table 19 details the USDA-reported inventory of food farming operations in the United States in 2020. The table identifies the five highest producing states for each species farmed as well as total animals produced in the farming efforts.

Table 19. 2021 Cattle, Pig, Chicken, and Turkey Farming in the United States

Cattle Farming Production	
Origin	Produced (heads)
Texas	12,700,000
Nebraska	6,800,000
Kansas	6,500,000
California	5,200,000
Oklahoma	5,200,000
Total	91,901,600
Hog and Pig Farming Production	
Origin	Produced (heads)
Iowa	23,800,000
Minnesota	8,900,000
North Carolina	8,000,000
Illinois	5,350,000
Indiana	4,350,000
Total	74,146,100
Chicken Farming Production	
Origin	Produced (heads)
Georgia	1,298,900,000
Alabama	1,171,600,000
Arkansas	1,051,300,000
North Carolina	971,400,000
Mississippi	707,000,000
Total	9,130,700,000
Turkey Farming production	
Origin	Produced
Minnesota	40,500,000
Arkansas	30,000,000
North Carolina	27,000,000
Indiana	20,500,000
Missouri	17,000,000
Total	216,500,000

The United States Department of Agriculture (2022a) meat animals summary details information about cattle, hogs, and pigs produced in the United States. A total of 91,901,600 cattle and calves were inventoried in the U.S. in 2021. The five highest producing states were Texas with 12,700,000; Nebraska with 6,800,000; Kansas with 6,500,000; and California and Oklahoma both with 5,200,000. A total of 74,146,100 hogs and pigs were inventoried in the United States in 2021. The five highest hog and pig meat producing states were Iowa with 23,800,000; Minnesota with 8,900,000, North Carolina with 8,000,000; Illinois with 5,350,000; and Indiana with 4,350,000 (U.S. Department of Agriculture, 2022a).

Table 19 also details the 2021 production of chicken and turkey farming efforts in the United States. The figures presented are from the United States Department of Agriculture (2022b) poultry summary. The 2021 total of chickens produced in the United States was 9,130,700,000. The five highest broiler producing states were Georgia with the production of 1,298,900,000; Alabama with 1,171,600,000; Arkansas with 1,051,300,000; North Carolina with 971,400,000; and Mississippi with 707,000,000. The total of U.S. turkeys farmed for food production in 2021 was 224,000,000. The states that produced the greatest number of turkeys in 2021 were Minnesota with 40,500,000; North Carolina with 30,000,000; Arkansas with 27,000,000; Indiana with 20,500,000; and Missouri with 17,000,000 (U.S. Department of Agriculture, 2022b).

Mills

The final source of production and potential permitted cruelty of animals is in breeding mills. Unlike with the aforementioned hunting and farming efforts, the purpose of animal mills is producing more animals for ownership rather than harvest for animal products. This section details statistics reported by the Humane Society of the United States in January 2022.

The Humane Society of the United States (2022) reported that there are approximately 10,000 puppy mills in the United States. Among these mills are a mix of those licensed by the USDA and those unlicensed, with the majority, over 75%, belonging to the latter category. Accounting for both the licensed and unlicensed mills, there are an estimated 500,000 dogs kept for breeding (Humane Society of the United States, 2022). Approximately 40% of the dogs kept for breeding purposes are within licensed facilities.

An estimated 1,234,263 puppies are produced in licensed facilities each year, with 2,400,000 sold each year from licensed and unlicensed facilities. The female dogs kept for breeding within either form of mill produce between 9 and 10 puppies each on average annually (Humane Society of the United States, 2022).

Domesticated animals are also kept within shelters. Approximately one quarter of dogs kept in shelters are "purebred," with the majority being of mixed breed (Humane Society of the United States, 2022). Shelters operate on limited budgets. In many shelters, animals that are not placed within new homes are euthanized. The Humane Society of the United States (2022) estimated that approximately 1,500,000 dogs and cats are euthanized by shelters each year.

Conclusion

The reporting of animal cruelty statistics is crucial to the study of the field and the examination of the effectiveness of policy. The recent changes in the reporting of NIBRS data that identifies animal cruelty as a distinct form of offense now allows for more accurate measurement and critical discussion. Furthermore, the annual release of NIBRS data provides reliable resource for the study of trends in animal cruelty in the United States.

Since the release of the last edition of this textbook, the World Wildlife Crime Report now has two publications. Using this resource, as well as other recent published discussed in this chapter, animal cruelty can also be more effectively studied as a global issue. The exploitation of animals for economic means and the role of customs agencies in discovering and reporting such crimes indicates that animal cruelty enforcement is an international effort.

While data pertaining to prohibited animal cruelty is becoming more accessible, it is also important to continue to collect and report information pertaining to permitted animal cruelty as well. Permitted animal cruelty impacts the populations and quality of life of nonhuman animals as well as the health and safety of humans. As with prohibited animal cruelty, increases in the uniformity and accessibility of this data serves to improve the study of animal cruelty and its effects.

References

Abrams, D. S. (2021). COVID and crime: An early empirical look. *Journal of Public Economics, 194,* 1–15. https://doi.org/10.1016/j.jpubeco.2020.104344.

Alaska Department of Fish and Game. (n.d.). *Alaska's game species.* https://www.adfg.alaska.gov/index.cfm?adfg=deerhunting.deerharvest.[6]

Arizona Game and Fish. (n.d.). Survey, harvest & hunt data, draw odds for big & small game. https://www.azgfd.com/hunting/surveydata/.[6]

Arkansas Game & Fish Commission. (n.d.). *Hunting.* https://www.agfc.com/en/hunting/.[6]

California Department of Fish and Wildlife. (n.d.). *Hunting in California.* https://wildlife.ca.gov/Hunting.[6]

Colorado Fish & Wildlife. (n.d.) *Hunting statistics.* https://cpw.state.co.us/thingstodo/Pages/Statistics.aspx.[6]

Connecticut Department of Energy and Environmental Protection. (n.d.). *Wildlife publications and forms: Hunting and trapping publications.* https://portal.ct.gov/DEEP/Wildlife/Wildlife-Publications-and-Forms#wildlife.[6]

Delaware Fish and Wildlife. (n.d.). *Annual turkey harvest data.* https://dnrec.alpha.delaware.gov/fish-wildlife/hunting/wild-turkeys/annual-harvest/.[6]

Federal Bureau of Investigation. (2016a). Animal cruelty. *New to NIBRS.* Retrieved December 9, 2021, from https://ucr.fbi.gov/nibrs/2016/resource-pages/nibrs-2016-homepage_alt.pdf.

Federal Bureau of Investigation. (2016b). *Victims.* Retrieved February 25, 2022, from https://ucr.fbi.gov/nibrs/2016/resource-pages/victims-2016_final.pdf.

Federal Bureau of Investigation. (2017). *2016 National Incident-Based Reporting System Data Tables.* Retrieved December 9, 2021, from https://ucr.fbi.gov/nibrs/2016/tables/data-tables.

Federal Bureau of Investigation. (2018a). *2017 National Incident-Based Reporting System Data Tables.* Retrieved December 9, 2021, from https://ucr.fbi.gov/nibrs/2017/tables/data-tables.

Federal Bureau of Investigation. (2018b, December 21). *NIBRS 101.* [Video]. YouTube. https://www.youtube.com/watch?v=RcR-RwHcsdE.

Federal Bureau of Investigation. (2018c). *NIBRS offense definitions, 2017.* Retrieved February 17, 2022, from https://ucr.fbi.gov/nibrs/2017/resource-pages/nibrs_offense_definitions-2017.pdf.

Federal Bureau of Investigation. (2018d, August). NIBRS readiness assessment for law enforcement agencies. Retrieved February 16, 2022, https://www.fbi.gov/file-repository/ucr/nibrs-readiness-assessment-for-law-enforcement-agencies.pdf/view.

Federal Bureau of Investigation. (2019a). *2018 National Incident-Based Reporting System Data Tables.* Retrieved December 9, 2021, from https://ucr.fbi.gov/nibrs/2018/tables/data-tables.

Federal Bureau of Investigation. (2019b). *A guide to understanding NIBRS.* Retrieved February 16, 2022, from https://www.fbi.gov/file-repository/ucr/a-guide-to-understanding-nibrs.pdf/view.

Federal Bureau of Investigation. (2020a). *2019 Crime in the United States.* Retrieved December 29, 2021, from https://ucr.fbi.gov/crime-in-the-u.s/2019/crime-in-the-u.s.-2019.

Federal Bureau of Investigation. (2020b). *2019 National Incident-Based Reporting System Data Tables.* Retrieved December 9, 2021, from https://ucr.fbi.gov/nibrs/2019/tables/data-tables.

Federal Bureau of Investigation. (2021). *2020 National Incident-Based Reporting System Data Tables.* Retrieved December 9, 2021, from https://crime-data-explorer.app.cloud.gov/pages/downloads.

Florida Fish and Wildlife Conservation Commission. (n.d.). *Hunting in* Florida. https://myfwc.com/hunting/.[6]

Food and Agriculture Organization of the United Nations. (2020). *The state of world fisheries and aquaculture: Sustainability in action.*

Georgia Department of Natural Resources Wildlife Resources Division. (n.d.). *Harvest summaries & population surveys.* https://georgiawildlife.com/harvest-summaries.[6]

Hirschi, T., & Gottfredson, M. (1983). Age and the explanation of crime. *American Journal of Sociology, 89*(3), 552–584.

Humane Society International. (2016). *Trophy hunting by the numbers: The United States' role in global trophy hunting.*

Humane Society International. (n.d.). *The Fur Trade.* https://www.hsi.org/news-media/fur-trade/.

Humane Society of the United States. (2022). *Puppy mills: Facts and figures.*

Idaho Fish & Game. (n.d.). *2019 deer general hunt harvest statistics.* https://fishandgame.idaho.gov/ifwis/huntplanner/stats/?season=general&game=deer&yr=2019.[6]

Illinois Department of Natural Resources. (n.d.). *Hunting and trapping in Illinois.* https://www2.illinois.gov/dnr/hunting/Pages/default.aspx.[6]

Indiana Department of Natural Resources. (n.d.). *Animals.* https://www.in.gov/dnr/fish-and-wildlife/wildlife-resources/animals/.[6]

Iowa Department of Natural Resources. (n.d.). *Deer & turkey harvest report.* https://gooutdoorsiowa.com/RealTimeHarvestReport.aspx.[6]

Kansas Department of Wildlife and Parks. (n.d.). *Wildlife research & surveys.* https://gooutdoorsiowa.com/RealTimeHarvestReport.aspx.[6]

Kentucky Department of Fish & Wildlife Resources. (n.d.). *Harvest Results.* https://fw.ky.gov/Hunt/Pages/Harvest-Results.aspx.[6]

Kessler, G., & Reinecke, J. (2021). Dynamics of the causes of crime: A life-course application of situational action theory for the transition from adolescence to adulthood. *Journal of Developmental and Life-Course Criminology, 7*, 229–252. https://doi.org/10.1007/s40865-021-00161-z.

Klick, J., & MacDonald, J. (2020). Sobering up after the seventh inning: Alcohol and crime around the ballpark (Paper No. 21-14). *University of Pennsylvania Institute for Law & Economic Research.* http://dx.doi.org/10.2139/ssrn.3567418.

Laub, J. H., & Sampson, R. J. (1993). Turning points in the life course: Why change matters to the study of crime, *Criminology, 31*(3), 301–325.

Levinthal, J. (2010) *The community context of animal and human maltreatment: Is there a Relationship between animal maltreatment and human maltreatment: Does neighborhood context matter?* [Doctoral dissertation, University of Pennsylvania]. University of Pennsylvania Digital Archive. https://repository.upenn.edu/cgi/viewcontent.cgi?article=1355&context=edissertations.

Louisiana Department of Wildlife and Fisheries. (2019). *Louisiana big and small game harvest survey for 2018–2019.*[6]

Maine Department of Inland Fisheries and Wildlife. (n.d.). *Harvest information: Historical harvest information.* https://www.maine.gov/ifw/hunting-trapping/harvest-information.html.[6]

Maryland Department of Natural Resources. (n.d.). *Wildlife.* https://dnr.maryland.gov/wildlife/Pages/default.aspx.[6]

Massachusetts Division of Fisheries & Wildlife (n.d.). *Division of Fisheries & Wildlife: Hunting.* https://www.mass.gov/orgs/division-of-fisheries-and-wildlife.[6]

McGee, T. R., & Farrington, D. P. (2019). Developmental and life-course explanations of offending. *Psychology, Crime & Law, 25*(6), 609–625. https://doi.org/10.1080/1068316X.2018.1560446.

McGee, T. R., Whitten, T., Williams, C., Jolliffe, D., & Farrington, D. (2021). Classification of patterns of offending in development and life-course criminology, with special reference to persistence. *Aggression and Violent Behavior, 59,* 1–9. https://doi.org/10.1016/j.avb.2020.101460.

Michigan Department of Resources. (n.d.). *Surveys & reports.* https://www.michigan.gov/dnr/0,4570,7-350-79136_79608_81526---,00.html.[6]

Minnesota Department of Natural Resources. (n.d.). *Minnesota wildlife.* https://www.dnr.state.mn.us/wildlife/index.html.[6]

Mississippi Wildlife, Fisheries, & Parks. (n.d.). *Wildlife & hunting.* https://www.mdwfp.com/wildlife-hunting/.[6]

Missouri Department of Conservation. (n.d.). *Species A-Z hunting & trapping.* https://mdc.mo.gov/hunting-trapping/species.[6]

Moffitt, T. E. (1993). Adolescence-limited and life-course-persistent antisocial behavior: A developmental taxonomy. *Psychological Review, 100,* 674–701.

Monsalve, S., Hammerschmidt, J., Izar, M. L., Marconcin, S., Rizzato, F., Polo, G., & Garcia, R. (2018). Associated factors of companion animal neglect in the family environment in Pinhais, Brazil. *Preventive Veterinary Medicine, 157,* 19–25.

Montana Fish, Wildlife, & Parks. (n.d.). *Harvest estimates search.* https://myfwp.mt.gov/fwpPub/harvestReports.[6]

National Agriculture Statistics Service, Agriculture Statistics Board, & United States Department of Agriculture. (2021). *Mink.*

Nebraska Game and Parks. (n.d.). *Wildlife surveys.* https://outdoornebraska.gov/wildlifesurveys/.[6]

Nevada Department of Wildlife. (2020). *Mule deer 2019 harvest composition by unit group.*[6]

New Hampshire Fish and Game. (n.d.). *NH wildlife harvest summary.* https://www.wildlife.state.nh.us/hunting/harvest-summary.html.[6]

New Jersey Fish & Wildlife. (n.d.). *Hunting in New Jersey*. https://nj.gov/dep/fgw/hunting.htm.[6]

New Mexico Game & Fish. (n.d.). *Harvest Reporting Information*. https://www.wildlife.state.nm.us/hunting/harvest-reporting-information/.[6]

New York Department of Environmental Conservation. (n.d.). *Hunting*. https://www.dec.ny.gov/outdoor/hunting.html.[6]

North Carolina Wildlife Resources Commission. (n.d.). Harvest *Statistics*. https://www.ncwildlife.org/Hunting/Seasons-Limits/Harvest-Statistics.[6]

North Dakota Game and Fish. (2020, March 30). *2019 deer season summarized*. https://gf.nd.gov/news/3733.[6]

Ohio Department of Natural Resources. (n.d.). *Hunting license resources*. https://ohiodnr.gov/buy-and-apply/hunting-fishing-boating/hunting-resources.[6]

Oklahoma Department of Wildlife Conservation. (n.d.). *Hunter Surveys*. https://www.wildlifedepartment.com/hunting/research.[6]

Oregon Department of Fish & Wildlife. (2021, April 30). *Big game hunting harvest statistic*. https://myodfw.com/articles/big-game-hunting-harvest-statistics.[6]

Oregon Department of Fish & Wildlife. (n.d.). *Upland birds harvest information*. https://myodfw.com/articles/upland-birds-harvest-information.[6]

Palais, J. M. (2021). Using the National Incident-Based Reporting System (NIBRS) to study animal cruelty: Preliminary results (2016–2019). *Social Sciences, 10*(10), 378. https://doi.org/10.3390/socsci10100378.

Pennsylvania Game Commission. (n.d.). *Harvest data and maps*. https://www.pgc.pa.gov/HuntTrap/Hunting/HarvestDataandMaps/Pages/default.aspx.[6]

Purvis, J. (2019a). *Big game harvest survey results 2005–06 thru 2018–19*. Texas Parks and Wildlife Department.[6]

Purvis, J. (2019b). *Small game harvest survey results 2005–06 thru 2018–19*. Texas Parks and Wildlife Department.[6]

Responsive Management. (2019). *Alabama Hunter Harvest 2018–2019*.[6]

Reyes, C. L. (2016). Statistics and measurement of animal cruelty. In M. P. Brewster & C. L. Reyes (Eds.), *Animal cruelty: A multidisciplinary approach to understanding* (2nd ed., pp. 141–156). Carolina Academic Press.

Rhode Island Department of Environmental Management. (n.d.). *Reports & publications*. http://www.dem.ri.gov/documents/publications/index.php#wildrep.[6]

Rosa, M., Fox, B., & Jennings, W. G. (2020). Do developmental and life-course theory risk factors equally predict age of onset among juvenile sexual and nonsexual offenders? *Sexual Abuse, 32*(1), 55–78.

Sampson, R. J., & Laub, J. H. (2005). A life-course view of the development of crime. *The ANNALS of the American Academy of Political and Social Science, 605*, 12–45.

South Carolina Department of Natural Resources. (n.d.). *Wildlife Species*. https://www.dnr.sc.gov/wildlife/species.html.[6]

South Dakota Game, Fish & Parks. (n.d.). *Harvest reports and surveys*. https://gfp.sd.gov/hunt-surveys.[6]

Tennessee Wildlife Resources Agency. (n.d.) *Welcome to the TWRA hunter's toolbox*. https://hunterstoolbox.gooutdoorstennessee.com/?reportId=187.[6]

The National Council on Violence Against Animals' NIBRS Implementation Committee. (n.d.). *NIBRS user manual for animal control officers and humane law enforcement*. Retrieved December 9, 2021, from https://awionline.org/sites/default/files/publication/digital_download/AWI-CA-NIBRS-Manual.pdf.

United Nations Office on Drugs and Crime. (2016). *World Wildlife Crime Report: Trafficking in protected species*.

United Nations Office on Drugs and Crime. (2020). *World Wildlife Crime Report: Trafficking in protected species*.

United States Department of Agriculture. (2022a). *Meat animals production, disposition, and income: 2021 summary*.

United States Department of Agriculture. (2022b). *Poultry—production and value: 2021 summary*.

United States Fish and Wildlife Service & U.S. Census Bureau. (2018) *2016 national survey of fishing, hunting, wildlife associated recreation*.

Utah Division of Wildlife Resources. (2021, October 22). *Hunting in Utah*. https://wildlife.utah.gov/hunting/main-hunting-page.html.[6]

Vermont Fish & Wildlife Department. (n.d.). *Hunting and trapping opportunities*. https://vtfishandwildlife.com/hunt/hunting-and-trapping-opportunities.[6]

Virginia Department of Wildlife Resources. (2022, February 11). *Bear, deer, turkey harvest data*. https://dwr.virginia.gov/blog/bear-deer-turkey-harvest-data/.[6]

Washington Department of Fish and Wildlife. (n.d.). *Game harvest reports*. https://wdfw.wa.gov/hunting/management/game-harvest#2019-harvest.[6]

West Virginia Division of Natural Resources. (n.d.). *Hunting*. https://wvdnr.gov/hunting/.[6]

Wisconsin Department of Natural Resources. (2020). *2019 Wisconsin big game and turkey harvest summary*.[6]

Wyoming Game & Fish Department. (n.d.). *Hunting in Wyoming*. https://wgfd.wyo.gov/Hunting/Harvest-Reports/.[6]

Yang, M., Chen, Z., Zhou, M., Liang, X., & Bai, Z. (2021). The impact of COVID-19 on crime: A spatial temporal analysis in Chicago. *International Journal of Geo-Information, 10*(152), 1–20. https://doi.org/10.3390/ijgi10030152.

Section II

Special Types of Animal Cruelty

Chapter 9

Animal Cruelty for Sport and Profit

Jacqueline Privett, Egan Green, John C. Navarro, and Jacqueline L. Schneider

Introduction

This section of this text focuses on specific types of animal cruelty. This chapter will address various types of animal cruelty that are committed for profit and sport, and even entertainment. Although some types of cruelty may be committed purely for sport, purely for profit, or purely for entertainment, these three motives are not always mutually exclusive. For example, some people may consider the illegal pursuit and successful capture of an animal to be sport, and also be willing to sell the animal or its parts, thereby fulfilling both sport and profit motivations. Similarly, blood sports may be motivated by financial gain, but also by the desire to participate in the "sport." Animal abuse may be incorporated into cultural festivals to provide entertainment value, but may also be motivated by financial gain. This chapter encompasses animal cruelty that is related to sport, profit, and entertainment and includes offenses related to factory farming, trading in endangered species, poaching, blood sports, and cultural festivals.

Factory Farming

As societies' populations expand, a paradox emerges. More people have to be fed, but agricultural land is lost to residential and business developments that will house and employ the expanding population. Farmers are tasked with providing food in order to feed the world's people and in order to achieve this goal, new farming methods have to be designed and implemented. In the Western world, agrarian societies have largely disappeared, as have the majority of family farms. In recent years, farming has moved to large-scale operations so that food production could indeed meet world demand.

Industrial animal agriculture, more commonly referred to as factory farming, produces the vast majority of meat for consumption in the U.S. (Safran-Foer, 2010; Zacharias, 2011). In addition to the goal of producing food for human consumption, factory farming also seeks to maximize profits. When profit maximization is the primary goal, some believe that inhumane methods can be utilized, such as, extremely confined spaces, overcrowding, and mutilations (D'Silva, 2006). According to the Human League (2020), there are roughly 1.6 billion animals confined in 25,000 factories across the U.S. Further, the organization claims that approximately 99 percent of animals in the U.S. are raised on factory farms.

There have been improvements in agricultural practices so that many constituents' needs are met. For example, the nutritional value of various crops has increased due to advancements in horticultural science, thus farmers are able to meet global demands for nutritious food. Animal rights and welfare groups have called for more humane treatment of species that provide meat-based protein. Agricultural industries and governments have worked together to improve the living conditions of those animals, as well as those involved in their slaughter. When combined, profit margins have remained healthy for most industrial farms, so they are able to recapitalize profits to further aid advances in agricultural sciences and industry. Advancements are somewhat related to nutrition and management, but most improvements in selective breeding have helped the industry meet its production expectations.

The care and condition of farm livestock remain firmly at the forefront of animal rights and welfare activists, who have always held that animals have emotional capabilities, as well as the ability to feel pain (see Singer, 1990). At the same time, many animal activists hold the belief that farmers, especially factory farmers have little or no concern about animal welfare, which is not the case with the vast majority of farmers in the U.S. Opponents of the perspective that animals have emotional capabilities believe that society is anthropomorphizing animals—meaning that humans are transferring human characteristics, including the ability to feel pain, to their animal counterparts. Regardless, the Treaty of Amsterdam has recognized that animals have the ability to feel pain (D'Silva, 2008). Research has shown that people who believe that animals have lower mental capacities feel more comfortable eating animal products ("Denying mental qualities to animals in order to eat them," 2011).

Temple Grandin, one of the world's more renowned animal scientists, has revolutionized the manner in which livestock are slaughtered for food production. Her designs for more humane slaughtering methods have been implemented in the U.S., Canada, Europe, Mexico, Australia, and New Zealand. Despite, however, her innovative method for humanely preparing animals for death, Grandin (2018) claims that problems persist largely because there is not large enough financial incentive to make farmers stop their harmful practices. She claims that cattle that enter the market via auctions suffer more bruises and injuries than when moved from farm directly to the abattoir (Huertas, Gil, Plaggio, & van Eerdenburg, 2002; Strappini, Frankena, Metz, Gallo, & Kemp, 2011; Weeks, McNally, & Warriss, 2002).

Factory farming is not without its problems. Some farms and their practices are harmful not only to animals, but also to the environment. Research shows that factory farms "cause soil contamination, loss of biodiversity, greenhouse gas emissions, and land, energy and water wastage" (Zacharias, 2011, para. 3). In addition, these animals contain "hormones, antibiotics, pesticides and dioxins" (para. 4) received through injections and/or through their diet, which have been associated with serious human health conditions, such as cancer, heart, and other degenerative diseases. Though this is not an exhaustive list, there are many welfare problems within factory farms, which include overcrowding, unnatural social groupings, confinement, barren environments, mutilations, selective breeding, and feed restriction/inappropriate diet (Pickett, 2003).

Some achievements have been made on the front of discontinuing the use of antibiotics in poultry production. For example, the British Poultry Council's Antibiotic Stewardship reported a reduction in the total use of antibiotics from a high of 94.6 percent in 2013 to 19.7 percent in 2019. That figure is slightly up from an all-time low of 14.4 in 2017 (British Poultry Council, 2020). In the U.S., fast-food restaurant Chick-Fil-A announced in September 2019 that all their raised chickens will be free of routine antibiotic use. They first made this pledged in 2014. Other fast-food restaurants that engage in similar rearing practices include Chipotle, Panera, McDonald's, Subway and KFC (Kar & Brook, 2019).

According to animal rights activists, optimal farming conditions are compromised when farmers try to achieve their role of feeding the world. This, however, is open to debate. Farmers who raise pigs in gestation crates are able to monitor each animal's health, food intake, and veterinary needs, in addition to safeguarding the animals from eating their young, fighting, and committing similar destructive behavior. Animal rights activists, on the other hand, argue that these stalls are too small for the pigs' free movement and too restrictive for "social" interaction and/or play, and that the animals become bored and depressed. Activists would prefer that the animals roam freely. Interestingly, each group actually wants the same end result—well-kept and cared-for animals. Farmers know that sick, malnourished, or stressed animals will not yield profits, in addition to knowing that if they continually present these types of animals at the slaughterhouse, the farmers' reputations will be jeopardized, significantly reducing the likelihood of their animals being purchased in the future.

The farmers' response to these issues is simply—farmers justify their treatment of animals by arguing that the pigs are generally bred in-house and raised from piglets, the restrictive stalls are all they know, so they cannot miss what they have not experienced. Moreover, caring for free-roaming pigs is dangerous to humans as they can seriously hurt, maim, or kill a farmer if he or she is pinned down or trampled. Further, there is no practical way to monitor closely the animal for disease or illness, thus increasing mortality rates among livestock.

Selective Breeding

Going back to the axiom that farmers are tasked with producing quality food in order to feed the world, science can help them become more efficient in completing this objective. For example, through selective breeding, farmers can breed cows whose meat has more protein per ounce than those whose meat is less nutritious. Genetics and genetic engineering play significant roles in improving agricultural animal-based yields.

Selective breeding is defined as the intentional breeding of animals as a way to produce desirable characteristics and to eliminate less desirable ones (Derango, 2012). Most reputable factory farms practice selective breeding practices in order to maximize their animals' marketable traits. According to animal activists, this is done in order to yield results that are beneficial for the company's profits, but according to farmers, this practice is needed to produce the highest quality meat and/or plants for human consumption.

According to animal activists, the process of selective breeding comes at a cost of negatively affecting the animals' skeletal and cardiovascular systems (D'Silva, 2006; Pickett, 2003). According to D'Silva (2006, p. 54), "the time taken for a broiler chicken to reach a weight of 2 kg declined from 57 to 37 days between 1972 and 1999, and that bodyweight gain per day has increased from 34 to 53 g, which is a 54% increase." This rapid body growth has contributed to lameness in these chickens, such as skeletal abnormalities caused by rapid growth, thus making a chicken unable to support itself with its own legs. It is estimated that 27% of chickens suffer from this man-made affliction (Hickman, 2008). The pace of their growth has been increased, but their maturity rate has not changed, which affects their behavioral patterns (D'Silva, 2006; Pickett, 2003).

Cows have similar experiences in factory farms. Cattle farms, according to animal activists, are so focused on their own financial goals that they neglect the well-being of the animal. An HSUS report (2009) discovered that, "from 1987 to 2007, the number of dairy operations declined by 69% and the number of cows decreased by 11%, while the average number of cows per facility increased by 183%" (p. 1). Increases in milk production per cow were also recorded. Further, their research showed that a U.S. dairy cow produced 20,267 pounds of milk in 2007, more than double the per-cow milk yield in 1967 and 47% more than the per-cow milk yield in 1987. The goal in increasing the milk yields versus the concern for the health and welfare of the cow has contributed to cows succumbing to mastitis, which is a painful inflammation of the udder ("An HSUS report," 2009; D'Silva, 2006; Pickett, 2003). Inbreeding is also associated with mastitis ("An HSUS report," 2009).

Confinement and Overcrowding

As is the case with chickens, lameness—physical disorder that affects gait—is another serious affliction associated with current U.S. dairy industry practices ("An HSUS report," 2009). In 2006, 14% of U.S. cows suffered from this affliction, but in Wisconsin and Minnesota, the two states that lead the nation in dairy production, 24.6% of herds experienced lameness. Factors such as concrete flooring, which is also associated with hoof lesions, and insufficient physical exercise, have increased the possibility of lameness. A majority of U.S. dairy operations keep their cows indoors in small spaces that suppress movement. Poor flooring and bedding increases the cows' stress because they cannot lie down or rest. Cows prefer soft surfaces versus the concrete or gravel commonly found in indoor facilities ("An HSUS report," 2009).

As previously mentioned, mastitis is one of the most prevalently reported health problems among dairy cows. Approximately 16.5% of cow deaths in the U.S. dairy industry are due to mastitis. A pathogenic bacterium claims a substantial number of these cases, which is related not only to inbreeding, but also to the small amount of space given and lack of cleanliness of the allotted space. Increased space and hygiene can decrease mastitis cases in cows ("An HSUS report," 2009).

Conditions under which male calves are raised for white veal production have come under scrutiny for decades. These young calves are kept in veal crates, and fed a low-iron reconstituted milk powder once or twice a day (D'Silva, 2006; "An HSUS report," 2009). This meal plan keeps the male calf just above an anemic state—ensuring that its meat will remain extremely pale rather than either pink or red. It is not uncommon for these animals to lick any rusted, metal object in order to obtain more iron. Veal calves gain incredible amounts of weight in relatively short amounts of time. Because of their weight and their limited mobility, when the calves are removed from their crates for slaughter, they can barely walk (D'Silva, 2006; Pickett, 2003).

Swine

Sow stalls, also known as gestation crates, and veal creates have been banned in the U.K. (Pickett, 2003; Safran-Foer, 2010). While the European Union (E.U.) has banned the use of crates that do not permit the calf to turn around, North American nations have not yet restricted their use (D'Silva, 2006). Derango (2012) states that these gestation crates give farmers the ability to individualize and adequately care for their animals and prevent sows from fighting (and thereby injuring each other). However, these pigs, which are bred to be meatier and heavier, develop leg sores from the concrete floors (D'Silva, 2006). The lack of movement also results in other undesirable conditions, like physical discomfort, elevated stress levels, and reduced muscle and bone strength and cardiovascular wellness (Pickett, 2003).

Fowl

Chickens are another type of livestock that have been known to live in extremely crowded conditions. Pickett (2003) reveals that male chicks are killed since they offer no economic value for meat, while the hens are kept in battery cages with four or more birds (D'Silva, 2006; "McDonald's cruelty," n.d.). The small space that hens are allowed disrupts their instincts of pecking for food on the ground or dust-bathing, a process through which chickens clean themselves of parasites by digging into dirt and flipping dust onto their feathers and bodies. Overcrowding results in birds pecking each other—oftentimes causing serious injury. Because the beak is rich with blood vessels and nerve endings, the birds experience immediate pain when the beak is cut off. In 2011, this practice was banned in the U.K., along with forced feeding. In the U.S., this practice is still utilized (Pickett, 2003).

Furthermore, due to the lack of exercise within their battery cages, 35% of hens die from bone fragility-associated illnesses, also known as cage layer osteoporosis. The limited space in these battery cages also does not permit a suitable nest site. Many researchers have agreed that without a nest site, hens become extremely frustrated and display odd behaviors (D'Silva, 2006), such as cannibalism and feather pecking (Pickett, 2003). The lack of care for these hens also includes not replacing old sawdust with new, thus, leading to burns on their legs from walking through each other's urination (Hickman, 2008). Finally, one to four percent of birds die from sudden-death syndrome—a syndrome only related to living in factory farms (Safran-Foer, 2010). Fortunately, the E.U., California, Michigan, Whole Foods, Subway restaurant, and a few other organizations refuse to buy eggs from distributors that operate with battery cages ("McDonald's cruelty," n.d.).

Even though a few organizations refuse to buy from distributors of factory farms that cruelly treat their hens and chickens, there still is no federal law that protects birds at every stage of life—the hatchery, the factory farm, the slaughterhouse ("McDonald's cruelty," n.d.). Unfortunately, the cruelty that chickens face is due to customers requesting cheaper prices. Organic chickens that experience free-ranges and less cruelty are three times more expensive than typical chickens (Hickman, 2011). It is important for the public to understand what free-range means as there may be a misconception that chickens are able to roam around without restriction for the entire 24 hours.

The definition of free-range for poultry according to the USDA is "five minutes of daily open-air access" (Deneen, n.d., para. 2). Further, the door of a coop or stall can be opened for five minutes "and if the animal(s) did not see the open door or choose not to leave ... it could still qualify as 'free range.'" Unfortunately, there is a lack of supervision to ensure this procedure is conducted.

Furthermore, there are varying definitions of free-range. With the E.U. trying to enforce the cage ban, there is a major concern that 12 countries have not complied with the ban's requirements, which was originally slated on January 1, 2012 (Driver, 2014). Currently, Switzerland is leading the E.U. with 82% of their eggs coming from free-range environments, although they have had a cage ban for some time (Deneen, n.d.). Cases such as that of Keith Owen, 44, of Worcestershire in England may have instigated the E.U. cage ban. Owen owned Heart of England Eggs Unlimited that claimed to raise free-range or organic eggs, but he was actually mislabeling his product and therefore abusing public trust. This impacted the largest supermarkets in the U.K. such as Morrison's, Sainsbury's, and Tesco, all of which were victims of Owen's scam. The stores purchased a dozen organic eggs at 90 pence (US$ 1.38) and 70 pence for free-range (US$ 1.07) while Owen's bought them for 35 pence (US$ .54). Owens was forced to relinquish his £3 million (US$ 3,708,990) or face up to six-and-a-half years in prison (Pidd, 2010).

Consumers, who desire to purchase free-range eggs, can buy their eggs at farmers markets or ask supermarkets or food companies how their animals are raised (Deneen, n.d.). In order to ensure that supermarkets are receiving properly labeled free-range eggs, they can, with the correct equipment, differentiate a free-range and a cage-egg with an ultra-violet light. When an egg is laid, it is wet and picks up the marks on the surface. In the case of Keith Owen, investigators used the light, which showed whether the marks were from wires, turf, or straw (Pidd, 2010).

In late 2011, Mercy for Animals exposed Sparboe Egg Farms' animal cruelty in Colorado, Iowa, and Minnesota ("McDonald's cruelty," n.d.; York, 2011). Hidden video camera footage revealed:

> ... rotten hens, decomposed beyond recognization as birds, left in cages with hens still laying eggs for human consumptions; a worker tormenting a bird by swinging her around in the air while her legs were caught in a grabbing device; live chicks thrown into plastic bags to be suffocated" ("McDonald's cruelty," n.d., para. 2).

Sparboe Egg Farms' largest client, McDonald's, came under fire when Sparboe's cruelty was released to the media. McDonald's soon dropped Sparboe as their egg supplier ("McDonald's cruelty," n.d.; York, 2011). Sparboe was then cited for five violations—some including inadequate rodent/fly prevention. If the violations are not corrected, additional violations could be added.

Another case of bird cruelty occurred at a Butterball turkey farm located in North Carolina, which was raided after Mercy for Animals revealed to authorities their video footage of turkeys being abused. Butterball is the U.S.'s largest producer of turkeys, owning 20% of the nation's total turkey manufacturing (Jenkins, 2011; Phillips, 2012; "Police investigates Butterball cruelty cover-up," 2012). The company, in their defense, responded with a statement claiming that they have a "... 'zero tolerance policy for any mistreatment of [their] birds or the failure to immediately report mistreatment of [their] birds by any associates'" (Jenkins, 2011, para. 6). It was later discovered that this particular Butterball facility was aware of Mercy for Animals reporting their cruelty to turkeys, and attempted to conceal their cruel farming practices. Authorities were also notified that a member of the North Carolina Department of Agriculture was complicit in the farm's attempt to cover-up the cruel practices ("Police investigates Butterball cruelty cover-up," 2012).

Mutilations

Pigs have a tendency to bite each other's tails off, which leads to inflammation and infections. In order to prevent this, tails are cut off during infancy—without anesthesia. Pigs that are in an open range do not display this type of biting behavior, due to a more stimulated environment with toys and bedding material (D'Silva, 2006). Derango (2012) refutes this claim by saying that keeping animals in a free-range environment will not give farmers the opportunity to protect their animals from attacks and that pigs in open ranges often do engage in fights that result in worse injuries.

Cows undergo a practice called tail-docking, which is accomplished by placing a rubber ring around the tail, allowing the appendage to atrophy and eventually detach. It is also accomplished by removing it with a sharp instrument. Arguments made for tail-docking included "improved udder and milk hygiene and cleaner milking parlors and holding areas" ("An HSUS report," 2009, p. 6). However, tails are instrumental to a cow's well-being. The tail is a form of defense against fly bites and without it, cows suffer from numerous bites that can result in infestation and infection. In 2001, a USDA survey discovered that 50.5% of U.S. dairy operations perform tail-docking ("An HSUS report," 2009).

Trading in Endangered Species

Schneider (2008, 2012) explains that the illegal trafficking in endangered species has been devoid of attention by the criminological community far too long. Activities, such as poaching protected species and transporting their body parts across national borders, are jeopardizing the survival of some of the most important species on the planet. Many of these animals are apex predators, who help reduce the number of lower order animals, thus ensuring the proper environmental and ecological balance. Hunting, killing, dissecting, transporting, and selling endangered species has been the subject matter of conservation agencies for decades. However, criminality is not the domain for biologists, conservationists, zoologists, and ecologists. These scientists simply do not have the expertise to disrupt, reduce, or eliminate illegal markets, especially when markets transcend global boundaries. Criminologists, if they continue to ignore the subject of trafficking in endangered species, will be complicit in the extinction of various protected species.

There are varying estimates of the monetary size of the illegal market in wild animals and animal parts. The market grew large enough to attract attention in the 1980s although the market had been present for decades prior to that (Amidon, 1968). A consensus of sources agrees that the international illegal wildlife market is growing in terms of scope and profitability. The illegal trade has quickly become one of the most profitable crimes of modern times. Currently, the profits generated from the illicit trade are said to be second only to the illegal international drug trade (Zimmerman, 2003). There are, however, conflicting accounts of just how much profit is generated.

Farnsworth (1980) estimated that the U.S. illegal animal and animal parts market alone is worth approximately US$175 million. The U.S. Fish and Wildlife Service estimated the U.S. market to be US$200 million in 1991 (Poten, 1991). By 1993, the U.S. Fish and Wildlife Service updated the estimate to between US$250 million and US$985 million (Davis, 1993). An estimate for the worldwide trade, which was calculated on the declared import values, was US$159 billion; whereas a figure offered by the United Kingdom's Scotland Yard estimates the profits from illegal activity as being US$5 billion (Schneider, 2012). Because the attention paid to these crimes is relatively new, it is extremely difficult to know how much money is generated from the illegal trading in endangered flora and fauna. By 2007, Interpol (as cited in Cadman, 2007) estimated it to be US$12 billion American dollars. More recent estimates put the maximum figure at between US$23 billion (Nelleman, Henriksen, Raxter, Ash, & Mrema, 2014) and US$33 billion (Wyler & Sheikh, 2013).

Much of the illegal market's demand comes from the Far East (Liddick, 2011; Schneider, 2012; Wyler and Sheikh, 2013). Traditional Asian medicines utilize parts of various terrestrial and marine species in their ingredients. This school of medicine believes that by ingesting parts of animals, the user takes on characteristics such as sexual vitality that are attributed to the animals (Ellis, 2005). Therefore, a segment of the illegal market seeks animal parts like tiger bones and bear gall bladders for the use in these remedies. The belief is that the more ferocious the animal, the more those characteristics will be transferred to the person ingesting dried, ground tiger penis, tiger bone tea, or bear gall bladders. Wildlife traffickers do not ignore the remaining animal parts. A market exists for the other animal parts as novelties, conversation pieces, and decorations. Items such as Walrus penis bones, referred to as oosiks, are on the illegal market along with animal skins, skulls, and claws (Poten, 1991).

This same market has contributed to the rapid decline of elephant and rhinoceros populations in Asia and Africa (Traffic, 2011). Elephants are hunted for their ivory tusks. The illegal ivory market consists of intricate, decorative carvings, as well as raw ivory. Rhinoceros populations have come under great poaching pressure due to a developing market for their horns. Users in the Far East believe that ground rhino horn has medicinal properties that are capable of healing a number of ailments including cancer. Traditional Chinese medicine has long prescribed ground rhino horn for a number of ailments, but the recent belief that it cures cancer has contributed to increased poaching of the animal (WWF, n.d.). Rhino horn is made of keratin, a protein that humans naturally create in the form of hair and fingernails, therefore there is no evidence that rhino horn actually offers medicinal benefits.

Notably, Japan has engaged in the hunting and killing of whales under the guise that such activities were for the purposes of scientific research. For this reason, the International Whaling Commission (IWC) has allowed Japan to continue to kill whales—in the Southern Ocean—even though a global ban was instituted in 1986 toward commercial whaling. Since the establishment of the ban, Japan has killed over 14,000 whales (McCurry, 2013). In 2013, Australia, together with New Zealand pursued to reveal the true intentions of Japan's commercial whaling practices. They were successful in their efforts in that the International Court of Justice (ICJ) decided in March 2014 that Japan's scientific research claims for the commercial hunting of whales were invalid, thus resulted in the termination of the Japanese's whaling program JARPA II (International Court of Justice, 2014). Since ICJ's ruling, Japan responded with a revised whaling program, Newrep-A, in order to continue their commercial hunting of whales for scientific purposes. Even though Japan stipulated a lesser amount of whales to be killed, the IWC rejected their revised whaling program as Japan did not successfully establish a scientific justification for the killing of whales (McCurry, 2015). As of 2014, Norway and Iceland are the only remaining countries that commercially hunt whales, although Greenpeace presumed that Norway's whaling industry will wither due to a lack of demand (France-Presse, 2014).

The law of supply and demand dictates that when there are fewer products for a market, the price increases. As an animal species becomes less common, the animal and/or its parts become more valuable to the black market. Therefore, species are stressed more as their numbers decrease from commercial poaching. Furthermore, because trophy-sized animals are most sought in the black market, the population genetics suffer, resulting in a genetically inferior population of animals in the wild (Poten, 1991). Additionally, because illegal market consumers seek the purest animals, there has been an increase in animal poaching in national parks in the U.S. (Davis, 1993; Lukas, 1999; Milstein, 1989; Poten, 1991). One study concluded that rangers in two-thirds of the U.S. national parks believed poaching in their parks was a major problem. This percentage was higher than other crimes in those parks such as violent crime and drug-related offenses (Lukas, 1999).

Blood Sports: Cock-, Dog-, and Bullfighting

Animal blood sports, specifically cock-, dog-, and bullfighting have a long history of social acceptance in many societies inside and outside of North America, but, in more recent decades have generally fallen out of favor with mainstream U.S. public. Because of the stigma attached to these sports, these practices devolve into secret networks ranging from highly organized international fighting rings to spontaneous street dogfights between the pets of human rivals. To understand the challenges that U.S. police and prosecutors face when dealing with these crimes, it is necessary to understand the background of the participants as well as the deviance.

Cockfighting

This sport, where gamecocks fight to the death, has been extremely popular on a global scale for centuries. This was certainly the case in Colonial America. In fact, it is said that President Abraham Lincoln's nickname, "Honest Abe," was due to his honesty in judging cockfights (Morrow, 1995). In the U.S., fights had no fixed locations, but combatants and locations were advertised in local papers. Conversely, in London, there were specifically constructed fight arenas for fighting birds. Fans of the sport included the wealthiest and most respected people of society, as well as those belonging to the "less desirable" classes. Gambling, most times illegal, occurs simultaneously with the fight itself. Landlords of pubs where fights often took place received payments for allowing the fight to take place on the premise, which provided support for the practice to continue (Crews, n.d).

Existing literature demonstrates a long history of social acceptance of cockfighting from as far back as 528 BCE in Asia Minor (Hawley, 1993) into the Middle Ages in England (Middleton, 2003). However, social acceptance of it began to decline and it was eventually criminalized in England in 1835 (Middleton, 2003). Cockfighting in the U.S. initially took root in the rural South (Hawley, 1982). Maunula (2007) proposes that it is the South's oldest game, and that the peak of cockfighting in England coincided with the establishment and subsequent growth of southern colonies in the New World. Cockfighting was entrenched with the developing southern culture as slaves were imported to establish the plantation economy. It exemplified the culture's emphasis on honor and bravery and seems to have been a bonding experience for males that ignored racial and economic boundaries (Maunula, 2007).

The social acceptance was generally limited to the South as demonstrated by the criminalization of cockfighting in Massachusetts and Pennsylvania prior to the Civil War, yet the southern states kept it legal well into the twentieth century (Maunula, 2007). States gradually strengthened the penalties for involvement in cockfighting, including training, transporting, and attending the events. The penalties were slowly increased, but in some areas this progress was slow as the cockfighters felt enough legitimacy in their actions to hire lobbyists and form political action committees to work in favor of their actions. They won enough legal legitimacy for their sport to occasionally stave off the increasing illegality of cockfighting. For example, they were successful enough in 1987 to have cockfighting legally removed from the threat of enforcement for animal cruelty laws (Hawley, 1993, 1989), and some cockfighters claimed to have had legislators firmly entrenched on their side of the debate. Nevertheless, the growing criminalization of the blood sport continued as penalties increased, and its statutory classification increased from misdemeanors to felonies in some states (Hawley, 1993). Louisiana became the last state to make it illegal in 2008 (Maunula, 2007). Yet despite this criminalization, it remains a popular, though clandestine, blood sport in some southern communities.

This history is helpful for modern participants in cockfighting. They refer to biblical justifications for their sport, refer to the history of its social acceptance, and even note its popularity among significant figures in American history (Hawley, 1993). This also serves to neutralize the illegality of the actions. The cockfighters and trainers, referred to as cockers, note the evolution from a socially acceptable behavior to one that is condemned by members of social classes who have enough social power to label the behavior of others as deviant.

Cockfighting in Modern Times

Modern cockfights occur in pits surrounded by spectators, gamblers, trainers, and owners. Two roosters that are matched by size are placed in the pit to fight (Darden & Worden, 1996). However, there are variations in fight specifics. For example, the cocks sometimes fight with no implements, but they are often equipped with small knife-like blades or pointed spurs that expedite bleeding and death. Roosters fight for several rounds until they are either exhausted or one is killed. When the cocks are exhausted, they are dragged to a secondary pit when a winner is decided by one of them rising to peck at the other thereby demonstrating relentless gameness (Darden & Worden, 1996).

There is a strict, unwritten code of conduct at cockfighting events. It regulates gambling, admission, and behavior (Maunula, 2007). For example, fighting among humans at cockfights is not tolerated and gamblers or spectators who begin or participate in physical confrontations are ejected (Hawley, 1993). Further, the cockfighting events attract small-time capitalists who sell trinkets as well as fighting roosters and cockfighting training aids and spurs (Darden & Worden, 1996). The unwritten rules of this sport require the ironic situation where the groups of people involved in the deviant activity are required to demonstrate trustworthiness and honesty among the participants.

Publications and websites dedicated to cockfighting provide much of the information about schedules and fight results. They also serve to glorify champion roosters and their careers. This leads to the irony of many cockers demonstrating great affection for their roosters, while pitting them in fights to the death with other roosters. Successful trainers and owners are promoted more frequently, and use their roosters in high profile fights that result in bigger purses. This serves to provide some sense of legitimacy to the sport.

Despite the growing illegality of the sport, it retains a following in many communities. This following is almost exclusively male, but cuts across other social boundaries such as race and economic status. The long history of gambling associated with the sport allows traditional barriers to be overlooked while focus is placed exclusively on the gameness of the roosters. Tournament formats allow not only wealthier participation, but also poorer participants to enter roosters. The poorer participants merely enter fewer roosters into the tournament because they have fewer resources to prepare a large group of cocks (Maunula, 2007). Racial boundaries are also overlooked as cockfights include African-Americans, Asians, Hispanics, and Whites. The long, slow decline of cockfighting legality led to decreased participation, but some participants believe that the increasing participation from Hispanic groups has revitalized the sport. This growing involvement, specifically from Hispanics, seems to have increased attendance at cockfighting events and injected new commercial opportunities into the cockfighting subculture (Maunula, 2007).

Support for cockfighting revolves largely around the exemplification of machismo, courage, and honor that participants believe cockfighting demonstrates. They believe cockfighting has historically provided examples of manliness for humans to follow. This ranged from providing examples of how to be a good husband to models for courage and tenacity (Hamill, 2009; Middleton, 2003). The roosters' willingness to fight to the death is thought to provide a metaphor for male preparation for life challenges, and therefore, involvement in the sport builds character. In some southern states, some high school coaches use cockfights to rouse their players to greater efforts. They even extend the derogatory terms of the sport, such as "dunghill roosters," which refers to roosters who do not have the inclination to fight, to student athletes who may not be inclined to put maximum effort into their competitions. In fact, the fighting spirit of a rooster is often viewed as an indicator of the personality of its owner (Hawley, 1993).

The focus on honor in the face of adversity leads some participants to indoctrinate young males into the sport. Men often bring their children to the cockfighting events to teach them the espoused honorable personality characteristics taught by the fights (Hawley, 1993; Maunula, 2007). The boys are told to follow the rooster's lead in protecting family, turf, and honor (Hawley, 1993). Novice cockers are mentored into the sport by more experienced participants once they have been properly accepted into a cockfighting circle. This is considered quite an honor, particularly if the mentor has raised and trained successful fighting roosters over a long period of time (Darden & Worden, 1996; Hawley, 1993). This indoctrination helps insure the continuation of cockfighting. It also serves to demonstrate a hierarchy of cockers ranging from professionals to amateurs who are not given respect until they have proven their worth through their roosters' capabilities.

Dogfighting

In 2007, Michael Vick, a U.S. football star, was arrested for his involvement in a large-scale dogfighting ring. He was later convicted of these crimes at both the state- and federal-levels, and subsequently served time for his involvement. His criminal activities shone considerable light on a form of deviance and criminality that historically drew little attention. The crimes for which Vick was convicted incited an incredible amount of public outrage, which led to several states to revise their dogfighting statues, including stiffer penalties and/or felony classification (Ortiz, 2009).

Historical Accounts

Dogfighting is considered a legitimate sport by those involved in training, organizing, watching, and betting on the fights. The history of dogfighting supports this notion to a degree, but society's evolving sense of decency no longer tolerates it. Dogfighting, and its associated illegal gambling, has an incredibly lengthy history that can be traced back to Roman times. The Romans pitted their dogs against those of the English. The ferocity of England's fighting dogs spread through Europe (Villavincencio, 2007). In the 12th Century, an ancillary sport to emerge from dog-on-dog fights was that of baiting, whereby dogs are pitted against other chained animals, such as bears, badgers or bulls. With regard to bulls, Dogfighting in England derived from the 12th century practice of bull baiting in which dogs were made to attack bulls as a way to tenderize the meat that was to be procured from the bull (Ortiz, 2009). These types of sports were favored by the upper classes, aristocracy, and medieval gentry (Evans, Gauthier, & Forsyth, 1998; Gibson, 2005). After hundreds of years of this sport, British Parliament banned all baiting sports as a result of the concerns over animal cruelty (Villavincencio, 2007).

The Industrial Revolution led to large-scale migrations of citizens to urban areas, which shifted the practice of bull baiting to one in which dogs fought each other. This is because less space was necessary and artificial light allowed the fights to be conducted at night. However, social acceptance of dogfighting decreased, and it was criminalized in 1835 in the U.K. with the Cruelty to Animals Act (Ortiz, 2009).

Modern Times

The English blood sport practices were brought to the New World by immigrants, and the American Pit Bull Terrier was developed for its tenacity and fighting skill. Just as societal standards had developed in England, American states began outlawing dogfighting by the late 1800s (Gibson, 2005; Ortiz, 2009). Despite this, it remained popular in some circles, particularly male subcultures in the Deep South (Evans et al., 1998). Therefore, it moved to clandestine locations and developed into a criminal subculture. This sport is not only cruel, but it also offers participants an opportunity to place bets on the fighters. This form of gambling is not only illegal, but it helps to perpetuate the continuation of the illegal fighting (Villavincencio, 2007).

The state-level criminalization continued and dogfighting eventually became illegal in all fifty states (Evans et al., 1998; Gibson, 2005). Federal legislation did not address it until the AWA was amended in 1976 to forbid animal fighting. Congress again addressed animal fighting in the midst of public outrage about the Michael Vick case with the Animal Fighting Prohibition Enforcement Act of 2007. This Act made violation of its animal fighting prohibitions a felony with a possible incarceration penalty of three years (Ortiz, 2009, Searle, 2008). While the vast majority of countries worldwide have banned this blood sport, Japan does not have a national ban, but, many prefectures have banned the practice (Villavincencio, 2007).

No matter its legal status, organized dogfights continue to take place. The HSUS estimates that there are 40,000 dogfight participants in the U.S. alone (see Gibson, 2005). The sport is a clandestine one so as not to alert authorities. As previously mentioned, this particular blood sport was brought back into the limelight in 2007 by the conviction of American National Football League (NFL) quarterback, Michael Vick (Prah, 2011). Ironically, after his release from prison, Vick formed, what some called an unnatural alliance in the form of a relationship with HSUS as their spokesperson.

Networks and Events

Types of dogfighting events range from an organized circuit to small-scale to amateur operations; with a new type of dogfighting event that has become more common, the unplanned street fight. The major events operate as part of a network of national and international dogfighting rings (Gibson, 2005; Ortiz, 2009; Searle, 2008). These organized events are typically planned for months and only selected spectators and participants are informed. In modern times, this information is transmitted via the Internet as are the locations of the events. Yet even this information is vague; the precise fighting locations remain secretive until shortly before the scheduled fight so as to avoid the attention of law enforcement (Gibson, 2005; Ortiz, 2009). Even then, the participants will sometimes meet at a location where they hand over their cell phones and keys and are bussed to the fight location (Ortiz, 2009).

Once the matches are prepared, they are surprisingly organized with specific rules and expectations for behavior. Participants, handlers, spectators, and referees are expected to abide by a rulebook written in the 1950s entitled *Cajun Rules* (Ortiz, 2009), which dictates the exact rules for conducting an organized dogfight.

The expectation of conformity to a set of rules is odd because of the high number of criminals and other criminal events that take place at the fights (Ortiz, 2009, Searle, 2008). The list of crimes that accompany dogfighting events includes human violence, theft, gambling, gang participation, prostitution, drug intoxication, and drug dealing (Gibson, 2005; Ortiz, 2009). Gibson (2005) states, "[o]rganized dog fights are staged by leaders of the drug trade as forums to distribute narcotics" (p. 7). Additionally, the fighting dogs are used as guard dogs for drug trafficking operations. The deviants will even have their dogs' vocal cords severed so they will not bark before attacking intruders on their illegal trade. Yet, despite all the accompanying criminal activity, the biggest payoff for organized dogfighting is the proceeds from the illegal gambling which is often in the tens of thousands of dollars (Ortiz, 2009), but sometimes reaches the hundreds of thousands of dollars (Gibson, 2005).

Amateurs and dogfighting hobbyists get involved in less organized dogfighting events (Gibson, 2005). They tend to work within a local network and repeatedly use specific dogfighting locations. These types of fights were once considered largely a rural phenomenon (Evans et al., 1998), but now appear to occur in urban areas as well. Gambling obviously takes place at this level of dogfighting as well, but not being part of a national or international circuit of dogfighters, thus the purses are smaller.

The newest evolution of the dogfighting culture is appearing in urban communities. Gangs use fighting dogs to settle disputes, intimidate witnesses and other community members, earn street credibility, overcome boredom, and win gambling proceeds (Ortiz, 2009). This group of dogfighters appears to be the most violent type (Gibson, 2005). The more ferocious their dogs, the more prestige the gang members receive. The dogfights are much more loosely organized than the professional dogfighting circuit, and tend to stay in specific locations. Additionally, some dogfights among this group of dogfighters are rather spontaneous. As potential rivals see or confront each other, they will use their dogs to defend their masculinity and an unplanned dogfight will occur (Searle, 2008). The newest type of street fight involving dogs is called "trunking" (Ortiz, 2009). This type of dogfight involves throwing two canines into the trunk of a vehicle and making bets on which dog will still be alive when the trunk is opened. Participants then drive the car around for a while before returning to the betting location to open the trunk and see which dog survived. Similarly, urban dogfights are sometimes arranged in such a way that multiple dogs will be locked in an abandoned building with a small package of dog food. They are left there until one dog kills the other dogs or survives by keeping the other dogs from eating until they starve (Ortiz, 2009).

The largest dogfighting raid to date occurred in Missouri late 2009, resulting in 26 arrests and 500 dogs rescued from eight states. This was the result of an 18-month investigation involving the Federal Bureau of Investigation (FBI), USDA, U.S. Marshals,

U.S. Attorney General, and Missouri State Highway Patrol. Hundreds of volunteers from 22 organizations throughout the U.S. cared for the dogs rescued (Humane Society of Missouri, 2009). Unfortunately, the future of rescued dogs is somewhat bleak. Due to their violent training and aggressive skills, these dogs are not likely to be placed in caring homes so they can lead normal lives; many are euthanized.

Bullfighting

Bullfighting can be traced back to ancient times and has taken many forms; however, the practice that is more familiar today—a lavishly dressed matador taunting an angry bull with a cape—can roughly be traced back to the 1700s when Francisco Romero of Ronda, Spain brought the estoque (sword) and the muleta (the cape) into the ring ("Bullfighting history," 2012). Typically, three matadors kill up to six bulls in an afternoon of fighting. Fighting bulls are preferred over domesticated bulls, which have to be trained to charge. Training can include starvation and torture in order for the bull to become aggressive. The fight is divided into several parts. The first part of the encounter is with the matador who engages with the bull in a series of graceful and daring maneuvers. The cruelty really begins in the second part where the picadors on horseback enter the ring. It is at this stage that picadors attack the animal with lances all while the banderilleros, who work on foot, attack with barbed sticks. The best location for the attack is at the animal's shoulders. The matador hides his sword under his cape and begins the last part of their fight—the kill—which is accomplished by passing the sword's blade in the small space between the bull's shoulder blades. The animal endures a long, painful, and torturous death—all to the jeers of thousands of spectators while its dying body is dragged around the arena.

In 2012, the first bullfighting ban was enacted in the Catalonia region on the mainland of Spain. The Canary Islands banned bullfighting in 1991 ("Bullfighting in Barcelona ends with Catalonia ban," 2011; Worden, 2011). Lawmakers' decisions were influenced when attendance to these staged fights had dropped significantly, as well as the 180,000 people who had signed a petition in support of the Catalonia ban. Nearly 250,000 bulls are killed annually during the duels between pairs of matadors and bulls in front of spectators (L. E., 2011). Lawmakers in Spain have now listed bullfighting as "an artistic discipline and cultural product" (Worden, 2011) in order to protect other regions from future bullfighting bans. Bullfighters and supporters of bullfighting are stating that the sport is a symbol of Spanish cultural heritage (L. E., 2011; Worden, 2011). A poll conducted by Spain's highest circulated daily newspaper, *El Pais*, discovered that only 40% of Spaniards enjoyed bullfighting (Worden, 2011), thus indicating a decline in enthusiasm and spectator participation.

Emerging Blood Sports

One of the newest blood sports that appears to be increasing is hog-dog fighting, also known as hog-dog rodeos and hog dogging (Ring, 2004). It has been in practice for a number of years, but has not drawn much public attention; therefore, there is no research on this deviance and little is known about it. This much is known: fighting dogs, typically pit bull terriers, are sicked on wild boars in closed pens. Hogs that refuse to fight or try to defend themselves are shocked with a cattle prod. To even the odds, the boar's tusks are sometimes removed. Dogs rip hogs' ears and snouts and typically pin the hogs to the ground in short order. The dogs' jaws are pried apart and the pig is allowed to survive and heal long enough to be the victim of another dog's attack at another public spectacle.

This blood sport shares characteristics with the other blood sports discussed in that the events tend to take place in rural, southern states. Ring (2004) states that this sport derives from hog hunting. This is often done with dogs chasing feral hogs, which rural residents consider nuisance animals.

Though this sport has remained largely unknown to the general public, hog-dog fighting exhibitions have begun drawing law enforcement and media attention. Publicized arrests have been made in South Carolina, Alabama (Ring, 2004), and Florida (Robert, 2006). Laws specifically addressing this practice are rare so animal cruelty laws have been used to limit this blood sport. Bills that would specifically outlaw hog-dogging have begun being introduced in state legislatures (Ring, 2004). With growing public knowledge of this sport, lawmakers are attempting to limit its spread before it becomes as firmly entrenched in some subcultures as cock-, dog-, and bullfighting has done already.

Cultural Festivals

Cultural festivals provide humans a great deal of enjoyment. As previously mentioned, bullfighting, a blood sport that pits man-against-beast, has been an important cultural, and thrilling sporting event in Spain, Mexico, and other Latin countries for hundreds of years. There are other cultural festivals that are oftentimes the highlight of local residents' annual activities. The most popular of these have drawn visitors from all around the globe. Foreigners attend the festivals in order to experience a new culture, and a country's ceremonial and/or ritualistic way of celebrating their heritage. Some of the world's most popular are described here.

Palio Horse Race

In 1581, the first Palio horse race was run in Siena, Italy. The city was divided into 17 distinct neighborhoods (contrade) in 1729, as they remain today. Each contrada has its own colors and emblems, signifying entrance into various sections of the city, but more importantly, signifying allegiance and heritage for a person's entire life ("The Palio in Siena," n.d.). The race is run twice a year; the race, Palio of Provenzano, held on July 2, is in honor of the Madonna of Provenzano. And on August 16, the race of Palio of the Assumption honors the Virgin Mary's Assumption ("The Palio in Siena," n.d.). On the day of the race, a large parade takes place throughout the city, in which nearly 600 citizens wear historical costumes, to celebrate the coming of the race. This event typically brings in 30,000 to 40,000 people a day, many of whom are foreigners. Like auto racing's Le Mans' Grand Prix, the Palio is run on city streets that have been covered in clay. It is an extremely dangerous run for horses and riders. Horses have to navigate through ancient and extremely narrow streets all at the speed of a gallop. This, of course, results in horses running into walls and other horses. At high speeds, horses (and riders) can foster extremely serious injury and even death. The danger to and injury sustained to the animals has resulted in the race's scrutiny.

In 2011, Italy's tourism minister, due to fears of animal cruelty, stopped the race from being nominated for United Nations Educational, Scientific and Cultural Organization (UNESCO) World Heritage status (Squires, 2011). This caused public outcry from the city's residents, as well as from other politicians. Had the race reached UNESCO World Heritage status, it would have been listed as one of the most treasured cultural events globally. Italy has progressed in preventing animal abuse by banning the Palio horse race. Unfortunately, the race has been responsible for 49 or 50 horse deaths, either during the race or through post-race euthanasia since 1970 ("Italian festivals sanctioned for animal cruelty," 2011; Squires, 2011). Animal welfare activists were pleased with the removal of the race from consideration; however, if horses are afforded better protection, it could be submitted for consideration for status in the years to come.

Running with the Bulls

A similar race is the world-wide known event during the Fiesta de San Fermin in Spain known as the running with the bulls in Pamplona (Bils & Gregory, 1995; "Clean start to Pamplona's running of the bulls," 2011; Etxaburu, 2007; Govan, 2009;"Pamplona 'bull runner' killed," 2009). The festival originates from the 16th century (Etxaburu, 2007). Ernest Hemingway popularized the event with his 1926 novel, *The Sun Also Rises* (Etxaburu, 2007; Goodman, 2009; Govan, 2009; Webb, 2009). This event, which is held between July 7 and 14, triples the population of the village of Pamplona of 190,000 with visitors, tourists, and adrenaline junkies (Bils & Gregory, 1995; Goodman, 2009). Pamplona is comprised of eight total runs with each run consisting of six bulls and six steers to guide them through an 850-meter [930 yards] course that usually takes 2.5 minutes to reach the bull ring where they are set to die in a bullfight ("Clean start to

Pamplona's running of the bulls," 2011; Goodman, 2009; "Man gored at Pamplona bull run," 2008). Another purpose for the steers is that they act as a herding dog—without them the bulls would desist charging after 100 meters [109 yards]. ("Clean start to Pamplona's running of the bulls," 2011).

Since record keeping began in 1924 to 2015, there have been 15 reported human deaths due to trampling or goring. The latest fatality occurred in 2009 (Goodman, 2009; Govan, 2009; "Pamplona 'bull runner' killed," 2009) when Daniel Jimeno Romero, 27, of Spain was hit by a bull's horn, puncturing his lung and giving him another severe wound at the neck (Goodman, 2009; Govan, 2009; "Pamplona 'bull runner' killed," 2009; Webb, 2009). Prior to Romero's death, Fermin Etxberri, 63, was trampled to death in 2003 (Govan, 2009). In 1995, the first and only American, Matthew Peter Tassio, 22, of Glen Ellyn, Illinois, was gored to death (Bils & Gregory, 1995; Goodman, 2009; Govan, 2009; "Pamplona 'bull runner' killed," 2009). This University of Illinois engineer graduate received grave wounds to his liver and had his primary abdominal artery severed (Bils & Gregory, 1995).

Pamplona-like events have also occurred in Illinois amongst other states. The American version of running with the bulls began as early as 1998, but such events were intermittent. It was not until two lawyers established their company the Great Bull Run that a consistent schedule of running with the bulls events was formed (Bearak, 2013). Their first official event began in 2012 in the state of Virginia with 12,000 attendees ("The Great Bull Run comes to Florida," 2014) and 4,000 participants that engaged in the Great Bull Run (Bearak, 2013). In 2013, a 10-city schedule would host Great Bull Runs in the states of California, Florida, Illinois, Minnesota, Pennsylvania, and Texas (Martin & Felberbaum, 2013). Later in 2014, a Great Bull Run was cancelled in Los Angeles, California as a permit would not be granted due to public safety standard violations (Franzetta & Backus, 2014). Great Bull Run organizers argued that the American version of the running of the bulls is safer than the Pamplona version. The U.S. running of the bulls events do not kill the bulls afterwards, maintain less harsh terrain onto the bulls' hooves as they run on grass courses (Eltagouri, 2014), and safe zones are found along the course (Martin & Felberbaum, 2013). As of 2015, only Chicago, Illinois, is set for a Great Bull Run, which has since been canceled ("About," 2015), with ticket prices that ranged from US$69 to $89 ("Tickets," 2015).

Zoos and Aquariums

Many of you can recall screaming with joy when our parents told us we were going to spend the day at the zoo. The sight of exotic and strange looking animals from faraway places was truly the things dreams were made of. The traditional benefits of zoos are entertainment and recreation, but in more modern times, these two were simply not enough to justify removing animals from their range state in order to cage them for our delight. Reputable zoos today have added two more purposes—conservation and research in order to justify their continued existence (Gray, 2017). Gray, who served as the president of the World Association of Zoos and Aquariums from 2017 to 2019 and is the current chief executive officer of Zoos Victoria in Australia, states that zoos can be ethical institutions if they align their goals with conservation and run with the interests of individual animals at the core of their operations (Gray, 2017). She further defines zoos in a number of ways:

1. Modern zoos embrace the core philosophy of conservation with outcomes aimed at improving the lives of animals keeping the welfare of individuals at all times while also educating the public;
2. Well-run zoos focus on the professionalism of staff and have a process of caring for animals; and
3. Bad zoos are unprofessional in ways that ignore the physical and mental care of animals, do not provide education to their paying public, do not conduct research and do not include conservation activities as part of their outcomes.

Transitioning from bad to professional zoos takes effort: replacing old cages with modern habitats that resemble their natural range environments; replacing old messages around the facility with conservation information; reducing the number of individuals in a given physical space; and finally, replacing circus-performance type shows aimed to entertain with animal keepers talking to visitors about an animal's behavior in their natural habitats along with characteristics of those natural living spaces.

The animal welfare movement, which began in the mid-1900s, started out recognizing the different ways to protect livestock (Whitham & Wielebnowski, 2013). Preventing animal cruelty was the primary focus of the ethical movement, although it has now blossomed into more, from creating taxon-based manuals for each species to creating the World Association of Zoos and Aquariums (WAZA) and other animal welfare organizations. From the beginning, improving animal welfare and providing the best care for captive animals has been of the highest importance, based on a survey that the European Commission produced (Whitham & Wielebnowski, 2013). This feeling of responsibility to treat animals well has only increased within the last few decades. In addition, the treatment type, how to assess the level of welfare, and more has also been regularly updated.

One tool to assess and monitor animal welfare in zoos is through the resource-based approach (Whitham & Wielebnowski, 2013). This approach contains what and how the zoos provide for their animals, such as the enclosed environment design and the types of enrichment. As stated previously, animal care manuals have been created by the Association of Zoos and Aquariums (AZA) in order to ensure the same species are cared for universally. These manuals contain almost all the information on how to properly care for the animal, listing their diet and items found in their respective habitat. It is important to note that these manuals are based on practices and trial-and-error situations, and not scientific data (Whitham & Wielebnowski, 2013).

From these manuals, the animals physical, psychological, and behavioral health can be measured appropriately. Although these manuals may include similar topics, measures will vary based on different species. Physical health of the animal can be assessed rather easily, compared to the animal's psychological or behavioral health. Simple visits to the veterinary technicians can project how the animal is doing. Some indicators of positive health in an animal include their immunoglobulin-A (IgA) levels, which portrays the animal's immune function, and heart rate (Whitham & Wielebnowski, 2013).

Behavioral health can be rather difficult to assess, on the other hand. A range of behaviors is needed to best assess the welfare of the animal, which can sometimes be difficult to obtain. For example, some animals may avoid showing pain, fear, or stress, as these emotions can weaken them amongst predators in the wild (Hill & Broom, 2009). Exhibiting good sleep habitats, such as the comfortability of the animal in its enclosure, is another indicator of positive behavior. Behavioral health can also be measured through the animal's will to explore the habitat enclosure. If the animal partakes in this behavior, the animal is in need of enrichment, ultimately stating it needs new and exciting stimuli (Hill & Broom, 2009).

These new and exciting stimuli typically come from enriching the animal. Enrichment is given to animals to stimulate natural behaviors they would otherwise show in the wild. Simple enrichment, such as giving a bird a mirror or giving an armadillo a puzzle feeder, are typically what can be seen in wildlife center and zoo settings. If the animal is noticeably becoming bored with their enrichment or not exhibiting excitement with new enrichment, then this is a sign of poor behavioral health. Enrichment manuals are also created for each taxon and set of species. These manuals and programs are based on the animal's biology, and what the animal is expected to produce from the given enrichment item ("The Accreditation Standards and Related Policies," 2020). Like other manuals, the enrichment program manual must be recorded and regularly updated by the institution. Sections of the manual may include goal-setting, planning and approval processes, implementation, record-keeping, evaluation, and reassessment ("Accreditation Basics," 2020). For example, a keeper may record what item(s) was given to the animal, and how the animal reacted to it, ranging from whether it ignored the enrichment altogether or interacted with it.

Other factors that may alter the animal's physical, psychological, and behavioral health, and must be recorded by the institution and that are taken into account by the accreditors, are any significant changes or life events that may occur. These events include construction, unusual weather conditions, noise intrusion, change in housing or habitat, and changes in neighboring animal exhibits ("The Accreditation Standards and Related Policies," 2020).

While it is known what accreditors evaluate of the animal's enclosure and health, other areas and topics surrounding the wildlife center or zoo setting are also taken into consideration. Besides the animal's physiological and behavioral health and the level of enrichment given, the Association of Zoos and Aquariums (AZA) also evaluate the candidate's involvement with conservation and research, and take a look into the educational programs provided by the zoo, which are just few of the core areas of evaluation out of the twelve listed by the accreditation ("The Accreditation Standards and Related Policies," 2020). Each of these topics are further explained in the annual AZA

Accreditation Standards booklet, which can be found on the AZA website, which also list the institutions master plan, governance, finance, staff, guest services, and safety and security as other areas to evaluate (specifically, see https://assets.speakcdn.com/assets/2332/aza-accreditation-standards.pdf for current assessments and updates up to 2022). However, to first begin this process, the association is given a questionnaire and survey to complete. After this, the AZA will visit the zoo or wildlife center to begin assessing the animals and everything surrounding them. At least three experts will visit the zoo together, one veterinarian, one operations expert, and one animal expert ("Accreditation Basics," 2020). Together, these experts and others from the AZA will record their findings on the area, keepers and staff, checking records, and of course, the observation of the animals ("Accreditation Basics," 2021).

Once visited by the AZA experts, the institution may be deemed AZA-accredited. Characteristics of such an institution go hand-in-hand with the twelve core areas of evaluation, listed earlier. These characteristics primarily include a focus in animal care, especially nutrition, environment, physical health, behavior, and psychological well-being. Other characteristics may be exceptional veterinary care, scientific advancement in care and conservation, exhibiting planning and design of habitat enclosures, partnerships within the community, staff training, and more ("The Accreditation Standards and Related Policies," 2020). Institutions listed as this high must regularly keep these standards, plus updating them according to the annual AZA Standards and Related Policies manual.

Animal Tourism

Eco-tourism is a relatively recent innovation whereby humans travel to remote locations with the aim of interacting with some of the most fascinating flora and fauna on earth, many of which are endangered and thus protected. These activities are created under the guise that the tourist activities bring much-needed income to areas of economic deprivation while satisfying the travelers' curiosity. In fact, eco-tourism, while incredibly profitable, can sometimes be detrimental to the very species humans want and need to observe. A long-standing version of eco-tourism are amusement parks that focus on animal performance for the delight of spectators.

Destination Trips

Animal-related tourism can contribute to animal cruelty by participating in events that exploit animals, and place risk toward animals as well as humans. These events include such activities as hiking into the mountains of Rwanda and Uganda in order to see the endangered eastern lowland and Bwindi gorillas ("Mountain gorillas of Uganda," n.d.), diving with various species of shark, riding elephants in India and Thailand, or swimming with dolphins programs, thus debilitating protection efforts worldwide ("Animal friendly tourism," n.d.).

Due to their close genetic-make up and their lack of human interaction, gorillas are susceptible to various human diseases. Eco-tours bring humans and gorillas together in extremely close proximity, thus putting the animals at risk of serious illness or even death from something as simple as the human common cold. While no doubt profitable, these tours offer little or no protection to the endangered species.[1] Tourists tend not to think about the effect their presence in the forests have on the delicate eco-system.

Shark dives, with and without cages are becoming a very popular destination for scuba divers. Dives are offered literally around the globe, with a variety of available types of dives dependent on what species of sharks migrate and swim nearby. No waters are exempt. For example, the once extremely restricted waters of the Galapagos Islands, a UNESCO World Heritage site, even offer not only tourist shark dives, but also shark fishing. The delicate balance in the eco-system is affected once the divers enter the water. The price for cruising and diving the Islands is over US$4,200 per person, and varies by tour company. Diving in open waters carries with it risk on behalf of the diver and the sharks, but at least the sharks have the ability to swim away.

Dives with whale sharks are slightly different. Whale sharks are the largest mammals in the oceans—reaching nearly 30 feet [9 meters] (Schneider, 2012), with the largest known whale shark reaching 40 feet in length (12 meters) ("Whale shark," n.d.). While divers can come across whale sharks in open water, typically, eco-dives are done in large nets where the whale sharks are confined, and therefore not free to leave the vicinity of divers. Studies have not been conducted on the long-term effects of restricting the swimming space of these giant mammals.

Wild elephants have been domesticated for use in the forestry/farming and tourism and industries in Thailand. While revered in Thai culture, these animals have endured cruel conditions and abuse for many decades. There are several potentials for abuse of the elephants in Thailand. The first and most obvious is the killing of elephants for the poaching of their ivory, skin, and even hair (Schneider, 2012). Second, these animals are used in forestry and agriculture practices, road construction, and the commercialization of forest reserves where tourists receive rides from the animals (Lohanan, 2002). The use of elephants in the logging industry has been outlawed for some time in Thailand; however, mahouts[2] still use their elephants illegally in order to haul logs in the forest. Oftentimes, the mahouts give their charges highly addictive drugs, especially amphetamines, to force their elephants to work longer, harder, and more quick-

1. Geographic Expeditions offer tours to in Uganda and Rwanda to see the mountain and Bwindi gorillas. For a ten-day tour, the cost per person is approximately US$11,685, which includes land costs, gorilla permits, and internal airfare. While other companies offer similar trips, this is merely one example. On their website, there are health precautions for American to take before travelling in Africa; however no such warnings are offered about necessary precautions for the gorillas' health and wellbeing.

2. A mahout is the elephant's keeper and one who drives the animal.

ly (Lohanan, 2002). The combination of overwork and drug use always ends poorly for the elephants, with many dying as a result of either the drugs or through work accidents, such as falling off cliffs (Schneider, 2012; Tian, 2012). Many times, illegal operations work the elephants until they literally drop dead from exhaustion. Third, elephants are also used in festivals, and mahouts often will tranquilize the elephants for greater ease of control. Typically, this is not done under the care of veterinarians, thus subjecting the elephants to potential overdose (Cheeran, Panicker, Kaimal, & Girdas, 2002). Fourth, there are approximately 1,000 elephants specifically used in the Thailand tourism industry. Although these animals are primarily used to transport visitors on eco-tours into forest areas; they are also used in elephant shows for the tourists to enjoy (Lohanan, 2002). In order for these unsuspecting tourists to have stories to tell upon return home, these animals are deprived of adequate food, water, and living conditions, which typically are unclean and unsanitary. Captive, domesticated, and/or zoo elephants are subject to other forms of abuse. Living conditions in zoos vary by country and even within a given country—largely due to varying zookeeper expertise and knowledge, funding sources, and available space. Even in zoos with the best intentions, keeping these extremely large animals in confined spaces creates undue stress and anxiety for the elephants. Some elephants have been known to attack their charges after long periods of confinement—even with the best care provided by staff, animal behaviorists, and veterinarians.

Vietnam is another country that has utilized its natural beauty to attract tourists. As a result, the country's animals are exploited for their financial gain with tours and excursions. Animals affected include dogs, monkeys, goats, and bears—all of which are "trained" to perform unusual and bizarre tricks. For example, black bears cycle on tiny bicycles with chains around their neck, muzzles on their mouths, and fez hats on their heads (Probert, 2011). This is hardly the manner in which these magnificent animals were meant to live. Other countries such as Greece and Turkey capture bears as cubs and pierce their lips, nose, or palate in order to attach a chain or rope so that their "trainers" can force them to dance—again a practice neither innate nor dignified (Compassionate traveler, n.d.).

Another popular tourist destination is Santorini, a Greek Island, where tourists are given the option of donkey taxis. These donkeys usually work from 9:00 a.m. to 7:00 p.m., with minimal rest, shelter, and water provided ("Petition to stop the abuse of donkey taxis in Santorini," n.d.). Jordan and Egypt have been facing criticism for their mistreatment of donkeys acting as taxis, but the practice continues. Donkey handlers are locals who live in extreme poverty. They barter with tourists for prices. Because of the high demand and need for the donkeys to be available to tourists with money, the handlers tend to neglect to feed the donkeys and oftentimes place a load that is too heavy for them to handle (Ballinger, 2009).

Nepal is yet another country that exploits animals for tourism purposes. Wild parrots are illegally trapped and subsequently have their wings and tail feathers clipped to prevent flight (i.e., their means of escape). There are high death rates among these parrots due to the cruelty they experience and the unnatural existence in which they are forced to live. Snake charmers are another fascinating tourist attraction that necessitates the mutilation of snakes. Those snakes utilized by snake charmers endure a number of cruel actions, which include having their teeth pulled without painkillers, having their venom ducts pierced with hot needles, and having their mouths sewn shut with only a small gap for food and fluids (Animal friendly tourism in Nepal, n.d.). The tourists who watch in amazement are in awe by the snake charmers' tricks, but live in the bliss of ignorance so they do not have to ponder the cruel sacrifices made by the snakes themselves.

British Columbia is an extremely popular tourist destination where animals are called upon to participate in the tourism industry. In colder seasons, tourists turn to dog sledding as a source of travel, excitement, and amusement. While visitors may never be skilled enough for a run in the Iditarod, they can live out their fantasies with a journey arranged by the local sledding company. Like those who swim with dolphins or ride elephants, the participants remain uninformed of the dogs' living conditions, health care, and/or their fate when business takes a downward trend. For example, in early 2011, a man was ordered to kill 100 of 300 sled dogs owned by a sled dog tour company in Whistler, British Colombia, due to the decline in tourism after the 2010 Winter Olympics in Vancouver ("100 healthy sled dogs slaughtered in Whistler, B.C.," 2011; Lin, 2011). A search to place the unneeded dogs in new homes failed, and as a result, the employee shot, stabbed, and buried these sled dogs in a massive gravesite over a three-day period ("100 healthy sled dogs slaughtered in Whistler, B.C.," 2011). The news of the slaughter was most likely kept relatively quiet so as not to risk of upsetting the next season's potential tourists.

Amusement Parks

The plight of dolphins and porpoises has been highlighted through the award-winning film[3], *The Cove*. *The Cove* is a film that depicts the gruesome practice herding wild dolphins[4] into a hidden cove in Taiji, Japan, where commercial buyers choose the dolphins for use in their aquariums. Those not chosen are immediately slaughtered rather than being returned to open waters. The rationale for the slaughter remains unclear. According to Kageyama (2010), Japanese government officials have come under great scrutiny since the release of the film, but continue to defend the practice at Taiji as tradition. Further, the government allows approximately 20,000 catches each year. They see the slaughter no differently than raising livestock for slaughter. However, in an unusual

3. *The Cove*, directed by Louie Psihoyos, produced by Fisher Stevens and Paula DuPré Pesmen, has won 47 international film awards, including the Academy Award for best documentary; Sundance Film Festival; and best documentary at the Toronto Film Festival, just to name a few.

4. This is also known as driving-fishing.

turn, fishermen in Taiji started turning some of the dolphins loose, which was thought to happen as a result of growing international pressure to stop drives like that in Taiji, Japan. Aqua parks and aquariums outside the U.S. fuel the demand for wild dolphins. Markets, both legal and illegal[5], are driven by the economic law of supply and demand. In this instance, the number of dolphins sought by the various aquariums worldwide will dictate how many dolphins and porpoises are caught, traded, and slaughtered each year. Until the nature of that market changes or international laws change to protect these marine species, the drive-fishing and killings are likely to continue.

Attractions like swimming with dolphins have been available to tourists worldwide, who desire the thrill to interact with these animals in their own environment. Whether available through dolphin drive-fishing or not, these dolphins are taken from their natural habitat of open oceans where they enjoy an active lifestyle of swimming up to 50 miles a day to be placed in cramped quarters (by their standards) where they are forced to swim continuously and unnaturally in circles. Unfortunately, 53% of these dolphins end up dying within three months of their capture due to various reasons, which include suffering from sunburn due to shallow water swimming, chlorine poisoning, and intestinal disease. The popularity of these programs has led to the establishment of many more in the U.S., Mexico, Latin America, and the Caribbean ("Plight of the captive dolphins," n.d.). Another marine attraction includes whale watching, which has recently experienced rapid growth with 10 million people participating, each year—resulting in the industry's profit of US$1.25 billion dollars ("Whale watching," n.d.). The tourists who partake in these types of events unwittingly contribute to the abuse, confinement, and neglect of the animals, which at times can lead to the animals' death ("Plight of the captive dolphins," n.d.; Tian, 2012).

Following the success of *The Cove*, major controversy arose about the treatment of orcas after the release of the critically acclaimed film *Blackfish*. Focus was placed on the commercial exploitation of orcas held in captivity. Specifically, the film documented the life story of a male orca named Tilikum, who has been involved in the death of three people while in captivity (Gallagher, 2013). The first human death occurred at a facility called Sealand, which resulted in Tilikum's transfer to SeaWorld Orlando. At SeaWorld Orlando another death took place that involved a drunk man that climbed into Tilikum's water tank during the night and found the next morning (Brower, 2013). But, the most notable of these three deaths was SeaWorld Orlando's trainer Dawn Brancheau in 2010 (Gallagher, 2013). Tilikum's aggressive behavior was largely attributed to his early capture off the coast of Iceland at two years of age, coupled with the abuse he experienced by female orcas during captivity. *Blackfish* questioned how Tilikum was allowed to continue to engage with humans following each death. Even more troubling, Tilikum has contributed the greatest amount of

5. It should be noted here, that at the time of writing, dolphins and porpoises are not endangered species that are afforded international protections. Therefore, the drive-fishing that takes place in Taiji, Japan, while extremely distasteful and disturbing, is legal.

sperm while held captive, in which half of the orcas at SeaWorld were birthed from Tilikum's sperm (Brower, 2013). SeaWorld have questioned the validity of the claims demonstrated in the film. The company mentioned how the film misrepresented their purpose (Gallagher, 2013), and discussed the lack of focus on their conservation and research efforts (Ahmed, 2013). They also argued that the death of Brancheau was merely horseplay gone wrong (Brower, 2013). The backlash against SeaWorld has been enormous. Bands have canceled tours at SeaWorld (Ahmed, 2013), a 26-year relationship with Southwest Airlines was severed (Stout, 2014), a five percent drop in annual attendance occurred, and the bad publicity extended to affect Busch Gardens' revenue and attendance (Trigaux, 2014)

Like Tilikum, the star of the *Free Willy* trilogy series, Keiko was also captured off the coast of Iceland at a young age. The success of the films resulted in the creation of paraphernalia that was then sold to the general public (Brower, 2013). After the release of the first film interest by the public was generated once it was discovered that Keiko was maintained in unsuitable living conditions. As a result, millions of dollars were invested toward the rehabilitation of Keiko in order to reintroduce him into the wild. Once released into the wild, Keiko joined other orcas to the Norwegian coast where he befriended the community members. Soon after, Keiko beached himself and died in 2003 ("History," 2015).

The exploitation of wildlife animals as tourist attractions has led to habitat loss. It has already led to the extinction of the white-handed gibbon on Thailand's largest island, Phuket. Females were frequently captured and/or killed and have led to a genetic viability problem, where the gibbons are becoming monogamous and mates for life (Waters, 2011). Tourists need to be aware and prepare themselves via knowledge of the abuses of animals that are used for tourist purposes.

Conclusion

Animals and humans have played important, and at times critical, roles in each other's lives. The parameters for our interaction have changed significantly over the centuries. In today's western society, societal expectations mandate that humans treat their animals—be they domesticated or wild—with care and compassion. This chapter has addressed animal cruelty that occurs when humans have. Used animals for the purposes of sport, profit, and entertainment, three motivations that are often inextricably linked. Offenses related to breeding, factory farming, trading in endangered species, poaching, blood sports, and cultural festivals are among the types of crimes often motivated by sport, entertainment and/or profit. Although these activities are garnering increased criticism among animal rights advocates and the general public, these types of offenses are likely to persist until societal views of animals and their treatment have overwhelmingly moved towards a more appropriate and humane perspective. As the public demands change, animals will receive a new standard of care and protection.

References

100 healthy sled dogs slaughtered in Whistler, B.C. (2011, January 31). *CTV News*. Retrieved from http://www.ctv.ca/CTVNews/Canada/20110131/bc-sled-dogs-killed-110131/.

About. (2015). Retrieved from http://www.thegreatbullrun.com/about/.

Ahmed, S. (2013, December 9). Heart cancels SeaWorld show amid 'Blackfish' controversy. *CNN.com*. Retrieved from http://www.cnn.com/2013/12/08/showbiz/seaworld-heart-blackfish/.

An HSUS report: The welfare of cows in the dairy industry. (2009). *The Humane Society of the United States*. Retrieved from http://www.humanesociety.org/assets/pdfs/farm/hsus-the-welfare-of-cows-in-the-dairy-industry.pdf.

Animal friendly tourism in Nepal. (n.d.). Retrieved from http://www.responsibletravel.com/copy/animal-friendly-tourism-in-nepal.

Animal friendly tourism. (n.d.). Retrieved from http://www.wspa-international.org/helping/animalfriendlyliving/travel.aspx.

ASPCA. (n.d.). Dogfighting and cockfighting. *Animal Watch*. Retrieved from http://www.aspca.org/ASPCAKids/Real-Issues/dog-fighting-and-cockfighting.aspx.

Association of Zoos and Aquariums. (2021). *Accreditation Basics*. Retrieved from https://www.aza.org/becoming-accredited?locale=en.

Association of Zoos and Aquariums. (2020). *The Accreditation Standards and Related Policies*. Retrieved from http://assets.speakcdn.com/assets/2332/aza-accreditation-standards.pdf.

Ballinger, L. (2009, May 1). Give the donkeys a rest! Plea to visitors over tourist site cruelty. *Mail Online*. Retrieved from http://www.dailymail.co.uk/news/article-1176270/Give-donkeys-rest-Plea-visitors-tourist-site-cruelty.html.

Barker-Benfield, G. J. (1992). *The culture of sensibility: Sex and society in eighteenth century Britain*. Chicago: The University of Chicago Press.

Bearak, B. (2013, November 14). For thrill seekers, a bull run with a different hook. *The New York Times*. Retrieved from http://www.nytimes.com/2013/11/17/sports/for-thrill-seekers-a-bull-run-with-a-different-hook.html?_r=0.

Bentham, J. (1789/1907). *An introduction to the principles of morals and legislation*. Oxford: Clarendon Press.

Bils, J., & Gregory, T. (1995, July 14). *Chicago Tribune*. Retrieved from http://articles.chicagotribune.com/1995-07-14/news/9507140148_1_san-fermin-pamplona-bulls.

Bittel, J. (2015, March 5). Ringling Bros. to retire its circus elephants. *National Geographic News*. Retrieved from http://news.nationalgeographic.com/news/2015/03/150305-ringling-bros-retires-asian-elephants-barnum-bailey/.

British Poultry Council (2020). *Antibiotics Stewardship Report 2020. Retrieved from* https://acrobat.adobe.com/link/review?uri=urn:aaid:scds:US:5e057ddc-18bf-4fe0-9101-88c09423ae24#pageNum=1.

Brower, K. (2013, August 4). Opinion: SeaWorld vs. the whale that killed its trainer. *National Geographic*. Retrieved from http://news.nationalgeographic.com/news/2013/08/130803-blackfish-orca-killer-whale-keiko-tilikum-sea-world/.

Bullfighting history. (2012). Retrieved from http://www.spanish-fiestas.com/culture/bullfighting-history/.

Bullfighting in Barcelona ends with Catalonia ban. (2011, September 25). *BBC News Europe*. Retrieved from http://www.bbc.co.uk/news/world-europe-15050706.

Cadman, M. (2007). *Consuming wildlife: The illegal exploitation of wild animals in South Africa, Zimbabwe and Zambia. A preliminary report. Prepared for Animal Rights Africa and Xwe African Wildlife*. Retrieved from http://www.nacsa.co.za/Downloads/Consuming_Wild_Life_290307_final.pdf.

Cheeran, J. V., Panicker, K. C., Kaimal, R. K., & Giridas, P. B. (2002). Tranquillization and translocation of captive bulls. *Food and Agriculture Organization of the United Nations, Giants on our hands: Proceedings of the international workshop of the domesticated Asian elephant*. Retrieved from http://www.fao.org/docrep/005/ad031e/ad031e0o.htm.

Clean start to Pamplona's running of the bulls. (2011, July 7). *The Independent*. Retrieved from http://www.independent.co.uk/news/world/europe/clean-start-to-pamplonas-running-of-the-bulls-2308316.html#.

Compassionate traveler. (n.d.). Retrieved from http://www.worldanimalprotection.us.org/take-action/be-compassionate-traveler.

Crews, E. (n.d.). Once popular and socially acceptable: Cockfighting. *The Colonial Williamsburg Foundation*. Retrieved from http://www.history.org/foundation/journal/autumn08/rooster.cfm.

D'Silva, J. (2006). Adverse impact of industrial animal agriculture on the health and welfare of farmed animals. *Integrative Zoology, 1*, 53–58. doi: 10.1111/j.1749-4877.2006.00013.x.

D'Silva, J. (2008). The impact of livestock farming: Solutions for animals, people and the planet. *Compassion in world farming*. Retrieved from http://www.ciwf.org.uk/includes/documents/cm_docs/2008/i/impact_of_livestock_farming.pdf.

Darden, D. K., & Worden, S. K. (1996). Marketing deviance: The selling of cockfighting. *Society & Animals, 4,* 211–231. doi: 10.1163/156853096X00160.

Davis, H. H. (1993, December 19). Plunder from the fields. *The Denver Post*. 16A, 20a.

Deneen, S. (n.d.). Free range foods: Animal welfare for livestock. *The Daily Green*. Retrieved June 18, 2015 from http://preview.www.thedailygreen.com/living-green/definitions/Free-Range-Foods.

Denying mental qualities to animals in order to eat them. (2011, November 27). Retrieved from http://www.sciguru.com/newsitem/11437/Denying-mental-qualities-animals-order-eat-them.

Derango, R. "Agriculture 109." Illinois State University. Normal, Illinois. 20 February 2012.

Driver, A. (2014, April 23). Record egg prices seen on back of battery cage ban. *LA Times*. Retrieved from http://www.latimes.com/opinion/editorials/la-ed-hens-eggs-california-proposition2-ab1437-20141226-story.html.

Ellis, R. (2005). *Tiger bone & rhino horn: The destruction of wildlife for traditional Chinese medicine*. London: Island Press.

Eltagouri, M. (2014, July 11). Cicero re-creates Pamplona bull stampede. *Chicago Tribune*. Retrieved from http://www.chicagotribune.com/news/local/breaking/chi-cicero-recreates-pamplona-bull-stampede-20140711-story.html.

Etxaburu, J. (2007, July 9). 7 crushed in Pamplona bull run. *USATODAY.com*. Retrieved from http://www.usatoday.com/news/world/2007-07-08-bulls-spain_N.htm?csp=34.

Evans, R., Gauthier, D. K., & Forsyth, C. J. (1998). Dogfighting: Symbolic expression and validity of masculinity. *Sex Roles, 39*, 825–838.

Farnsworth, C. L. (1980). *A descriptive analysis of the extent of commercial poaching in the United States* (Unpublished doctoral dissertation). Sam Houston State University, Huntsville, TX.

France-Presse, A. (2014, August 25). Norway whale catch reaches highest number since 1993. *The Guardian*. Retrieved from http://www.theguardian.com/world/2014/aug/25/norway-whale-catch.

Franzetta, L., & Backus, M. (2014, July 31). Canceled: Dangerous and illegal California Great Bull Run. *Animal Legal Defense Fund*. Retrieved from http://aldf.org/press-room/press-releases/canceled-dangerous-and-illegal-california-great-bull-run/.

Gallagher, P. (2013, July 26). Cruelty of the aquarium exposed in killer whale documentary 'Blackfish'. *The Independent*. Retrieved from http://www.independent.co.uk/environment/nature/cruelty-of-the-aquarium-exposed-in-killer-whale-documentary-blackfish-8733758.html.

Grandin, T. (2018). Welfare problems in cattle, pigs, and sheep that persist even though scientific research clearly shows how to prevent them. *Animal, 8*, 7, 124. doi: https://doi.org/10.3390/ani8070124.

Gibson, H. (2005). Detailed discussion of dog fighting. *Animal Legal & Historical Center*. Retrieved from http://www.animallaw.info/articles/ddusdogfighting.htm#s1.

Goodman, A. (2009, July 10). Man killed in Pamplona's running of the bulls. *CNN.com*. Retrieved from http://www.cnn.com/2009/WORLD/europe/07/10/spain.pamplona.bulls.death/index.html.

Govan, F. (2009, July 10). Man gored to death by bull in Pamplona run. *The Telegraph*. Retrieved from http://www.telegraph.co.uk/news/worldnews/europe/spain/5793950/Man-gored-to-death-by-bull-in-Pamplona-run.html.

Gray, J. (2017). *Zoo Ethics: The Challenges of Compassionate Conservation*. Ithaca, NY: Comstock Publishing Associates.

Gruen, L. (2010). The moral status of animals. *The Stanford Encyclopedia of Philosophy*. Retrieved from http://plato.stanford.edu/entries/moral-animal/.

Hamill, T. A. (2009). Cockfighting as cultural allegory in early modern England. *Journal of Medieval and Early Modern Studies, 39*, 375–406.

Hawley, F. (1982). Organized cockfighting: A deviant recreational subculture (Unpublished doctoral dissertation). Florida State University, Tallahassee, FL.

Hawley, F. (1989). Cockfight in the cotton: A moral crusade in microcosm. *Contemporary Crises, 13*, 129–144.

Hawley, F. (1993). The moral and conceptual universe of cockfighters: Symbolism and rationalization. *Society & Animals, 1*, 159–168.

Hickman, M. (2008, January 4). The true cost of cheap chicken. *The Independent*. Retrieved from http://www.independent.co.uk/news/uk/home-news/the-true-cost-of-cheap-chicken-768062.html.

Hill, S.P. and Broom, D.M. (2009). Measuring zoo animal welfare: Theory and practice. *Zoo Biology 28*(6): 531–544.

History. (2015). Retrieved from http://keiko.com/history.html.

Huertas, S.M., Gil, A.D., Piaggio, J.M., & van Eerdenburg, F.J.C.M. (2010). Transportation of beef cattle to slaughterhouses and how this relates to animal welfare and carcass bruising in an extensive production system. *Animal Welfare, 19*, 281–285.

Humane Society of Missouri confirms: Guilty pleas entered in federal court to charges from largest dog fighting raid and rescue in U.S. history. (2009, September 14). Retrieved from http://member.hsmo.org/site/PageServer?pagename=Federal_dog_fighting_case_press_release_9_14.

International Court of Justice. (2014). Whaling in the Antarctic (Australia v. Japan: New Zealand intervening) [Press release]. Retrieved from http://www.icj-cij.org/docket/files/148/18162.pdf.

Italian festivals sanctioned for animal cruelty. (2011, August 10). Retrieved from http://dawn.com/2011/08/10/italian-festivals-sanctioned-for-animal-cruelty/.

Jenkins, C. (2011, December 30). Butterball turkey facility raided for abuse of birds. *The Raw Story*. Retrieved from http://www.rawstory.com/rs/2011/12/30/butterball-turkey-facility-raided-for-abuse-of-birds/.

Kageyama, Y. (2010). 'The Cove' in Taiji, Japan persists with dolphin hunt. *Huffington Post*. Retrieved from http://www.huffingtonpost.com/2010/10/12/the-cove-in-taiji-japan-p_n_759155.html.

Kar, A. & L. Brook (2019, September 12). *Success story: Ending antibiotics overuse in chicken. Retrieved from* https://acrobat.adobe.com/link/review?uri=urn:aaid:scds:US:5e057ddc-18bf-4fe0-9101-88c09423ae24#pageNum=1.

L. E. (2011, August 30). Bullfighting isn't culture, it's cruelty. *Care2 Causes*. Retrieved from http://www.care2.com/causes/bullfighting-isnt-culture-its-cruelty.html.

Liddick, D. R. (2011). *Crimes against nature: Illegal industries and the global environment.* Santa Barbara, CA: Praeger.

Lin, D. (2011, February 2). 100 sled dogs killed in Canada after tourism slump. *About.com.* Retrieved from http://animalrights.about.com/od/animalsinentertainment/a/100-Sled-Dogs-Killed-In-Canada-After-Tourism-Slump.htm.

Lo, S. (2011, December 31). New rules for Feld Entertainment, Inc.: Pay and comply. *Animal Blawg.* Retrieved from http://animalblawg.wordpress.com/2011/12/31/new-rules-for-feld-entertainment-inc-pay-and-comply/.

Lohanan, R. (2002). The elephant situation in Thailand and a plea for co-operation. *Food and Agriculture Organization of the United Nations, Giants on our Hands. Proceedings of the International Workshop on the Domesticated Asian Elephant.* Retrieved from http://www.fao.org/docrep/005/ad031e/ad031e0r.htm.

Lukas, L. (1999). *National park service law enforcement: To conserve and protect.* Incline Village, NV: Copperhouse Publishing Company.

Man gored at Pamplona bull run. (2011, July 8). Retrieved from http://www.guardian.co.uk/world/2011/jul/08/man-gored-pamplona-bull-run.

Martin, J., & Felberbaum, M. (2013, August 3). Inspired by Pamplona, Great Bull Run coming to US. *The Seattle Times.* Retrieved from http://www.seattletimes.com/nation-world/inspired-by-pamplona-great-bull-run-coming-to-us/.

Maunula, M. (2007). Of chickens and men: Cockfighting and equality in the South. *Southern Cultures, 13,* 76–85.

McCurry, J. (2013, June 28). License revoke? Australia takes Japan to court to stop whale hunts. *The Christian Science Monitor.* Retrieved from http://www.csmonitor.com/World/Asia-Pacific/2013/0628/License-revoked-Australia-takes-Japan-to-court-to-stop-whaling-hunts.

McCurry, J. (2015, April, 13). Experts reject Japan's new whaling plan. *The Guardian.* Retrieved from http://www.theguardian.com/environment/2015/apr/14/experts-reject-japans-new-whaling-plan.

McDonald's cruelty: The rotten truth about Egg McMuffins. (n.d.). Retrieved from http://www.mcdonaldscruelty.com/.

Middleton, I. M. (2003). Cockfighting in Yorkshire during the early eighteenth century. *Northern History, XL,* 129–146.

Milstein, M. (1989, May/June). The quiet kill. *National Parks, 1989,* 19–25.

Morrow, L. (1995). History they don't teach you: A tradition of cockfighting. *White River Valley Historical Quarterly, 35.* Retrieved from http://thelibrary.org/lochist/periodicals/wrv/v35/n2/f95d.htm.

Mountain gorillas of Uganda. (n.d.). *Geographic Expeditions Inc.* Retrieved from http://www.geoex.com/adventure-travel/uganda/bwindi-gorilla-safari.asp.

Nellemann, C., Henriksen, R. Raxter, P., Ash, N., & Mrema, E. (Eds). (2014). The environmental crime crisis—Threats to sustainable development from illegal exploitation and trade in wildlife and forest resources. United Nations Environmental Programme. Retrieved June 18, 2015, 2015 from http://www.unep.org/unea/docs/rracrimecrisis.pdf.

O'Connor, J. (2012, January 18). Circus smacked with nearly 3 dozen charges. *People for the Ethical Treatment of Animals.* Retrieved from http://www.peta.org/b/thepetafiles/archive/2012/01/18/circus-smacked-with-almost-three-dozen-charges.aspx.

Ortiz, F. (2009). *Making the dogman heel: Recommendation for improving the effectiveness of dogfighting laws.* Retrieved from http://works.bepress.com/cgi/viewcontent.cgi?article= 1000&context=francesca_ortiz.

Pamplona "bull runner" killed. (2009, July 10). *National Geographic.com.* Retrieved from http://news.nationalgeographic.com/news/2009/07/090710-bullrun-death-video-ap.html.

Petition to stop the abuse of donkey taxis in Santorini. (n.d.). Retrieved from http://drupal.thedonkeysanctuary.org.uk/campaign/santorini.

Phillips, T. (2012, January 2). Butterball's animal abuse comes to light. *Global Animal.* Retrieved from http://www.globalanimal.org/2012/01/02/butterballs-turkey-abuse-comes-to-light-video/62232/.

Pickett, H. (2003). Industrial animal agriculture. *Compassion in World Farming Trust.* Retrieved from http://www.ciwf.org.uk/includes/documents/cm_docs/2008/i/industrial_animal_farming_booklet.pdf.

Pidd, H. (2010, March 11). United Kingdom: Egg boss jailed for 'free range' fraud. *The Guardian.* Retrieved from http://forests.org/shared/reader/welcome.aspx?linkid=154738&keybold=food%20AND%20%20fraud.

Plight of the captive dolphins. (n.d.). Retrieved from http://www.wspa-international.org/helping/animalfriendlyliving/captivedolphins.aspx.

Police investigates Butterball cruelty cover-up. (2012, January 11). Retrieved from http://vegan.com/blog/2012/01/11/police-investigate-butterball-cruelty-coverup/.

Poten, C. J. (1991, September). A shameful harvest: America's illegal wildlife trade. *National Geographic,* 106–132.

Primatt, H. (1776/1992). *The duty of mercy and the sin of cruelty to brute animals.* Sussex, Fontwell: Centaur Press. Reprint Richard Ryder.

Probert, L. (2011, April 12). Vietnam tourism boosted by animal cruelty. *World Tourism and Aviation News.* Retrieved from http://www.travel-news.co.uk/2456/2011/12/vietnam-tourism-boosted-by-animal-cruelty/.

Ring, D. (2004, December 2). Hog-dog fights: Blood "sport" packaged as family entertainment. Retrieved from http://www.humanesociety.org/issues/hogdog_fighting/facts/hog-dog_bloodsport.html.

Robert, J. (2006, February 27). Dog vs. hog fighting club broken up. *Associated Press.* Retrieved from http://www.cbsnews.com/stories/2006/01/27/national/main1245804.shtml.

Safran-Foer, J. (2010, February 22). The truth about factory farming. *The Guardian.* Retrieved from http://www.guardian.co.uk/environment/2010/feb/22/jonathan-safran-foer-factory-farming.

Schneider, J. L. (2008). Reducing the illicit trade in endangered wildlife: The market reduction approach. *Journal of Contemporary Criminal Justice, 24,* 274.

Schneider, J. L. (2012). *Sold into extinction: The global trade in endangered species.* Santa Barbara, CA: Praeger/ABC-CLIO.

Searle, A. M. (2008). *Release the dogs: Creating a social remedy to the dog fighting epidemic.* Retrieved from http://works.bepress.com/amanda_searle/4.

Singer, P. (1990). *Animal Liberation* (2nd ed.). New York: Random House.

Smith, K. (2014, September 6). Descartes' life and works. *The Stanford Encyclopedia of Philosophy.* Retrieved from http://plato.stanford.edu/entries/descartes-works/.

Squires, N. (2011). Palio horse race banned from heritage status because of cruelty claims. *The Telegraph.* Retrieved from http://www.telegraph.co.uk/news/worldnews/europe/italy/8441233/Palio-horse-race-banned-from-heritage-status-because-of-cruelty-claims.html.

Stout, D. M. (2014, August 1). So long, Shamu: Southwest SeaWorld end times. *Time.com.* Retrieved from http://time.com/3069051/so-long-shamu-southwest-seaworld-end-ties/.

Strappini, A.C, Frankena, K., Metz, J.H.M., Gallo, C., & Kemp, B. (2011). Characteristics of bruises in carcasses of cows sourced from farms or from livestock markets. *Animal, 6,* 3, 502–509. doi:10.1017/S1751731111001698.

The Great Bull Run comes to Florida. (2014, February 21). *PR Newswire.* Retrieved from http://www.bizjournals.com/prnewswire/press_releases/2014/02/21/MN69052.

The Human League (2020, November 30). *Factory Farming: What is it and why it's a problem.* Retrieved from https://thehumaneleague.org/article/what-is-factory-farming.

The Humane Society of the United States. (2011, June 21). *New undercover investigation reveals tame and drugged animals shot for trophies at captive hunts.* Retrieved from http://www.humanesociety.org/news/press_releases/2011/06/captive_hunt_undercover_investigation_animal_planet_062111.html.

The Palio in Siena. (n.d.). Retrieved from http://www.discovertuscany.com/siena/palio-siena.html.

Tian, B. (2012, February 11). To entertain tourists, elephants in Thailand face cruelty. *UPIU*. Retrieved from http://next.upi.com/archive/2012/02/11/Giants-in-danger/2621328999087/.

Tickets. (2015). Retrieved from http://thegreatbullrun.com/#rev_slider_5_3.

Traffic. (2011, December 29). 2011: "Annus horribilis" for African elephants, says TRAFFIC. Retrieved from http://www.traffic.org/home/2011/12/29/2011-annus-horribilis-for-african-elephants-says-traffic.html.

Trigaux, R. (2014, November 17). As SeaWorld suffers 'Blackfish' impact, Busch Gardens suffers, too. *Tampa Bay Times*. Retrieved from http://www.tampabay.com/news/business/tourism/as-seaworld-suffers-blackfish-impact-busch-gardens-suffers-too/2206864.

Villavincencio, M. (2007, July 16). A history of dogfighting. *NPR*. Retrieved from http://www.npr.org/templates/story/story.php?storyId=12108421.

Waters, S. (2011, June 11). Wildlife tourism in Thailand: Cruel and exploitative? *The Scavenger*. Retrieved from http://www.thescavenger.net/animals/wildlife-tourism-in-thailand-cruel-and-exploitative-735.html.

Webb, J. (2009, July 10). Bull kills man during Spain's annual Pamplona run. *Reuters.com*. Retrieved from http://www.reuters.com/assets/print?aid=USTRE5691BZ20090710.

Weeks, C.A., McNally, P.W. and Warriss, P.D. (2002), Influence of the design of facilities at auction markets and animal handling procedures on bruising in cattle. *Veterinary Record, 150*, 743–748. https://doi.org/10.1136/vr.150.24.743.

Whale shark: Rhinocodon typus. (n.d.). Retrieved from http://animals.nationalgeographic.com/animals/fish/whale-shark/.

Whale watching: A humane alternative. (n.d.). *World Society for the Protection of Animals*. Retrieved from http://www.wspa-international.org/helping/animalfriendlyliving/whalewatching.aspx.

Whitham, J.C. and Wielebnowski, N. (2013). New directions for zoo animal welfare science. Applied Animal Behavior Science 147(3–4): 247–260.

Worden, T. (2011, July 31). Bullfighting saved from the sword as Spain rules it is an artistic discipline. *The Guardian*. Retrieved from http://www.guardian.co.uk/world/2011/jul/31/bullfighting-saved-spain-artistic-discipline.

WWF (n.d.) *Rhinos*. Retrieved from http://www.worldwildlife.org/species/rhino.

Wyler, L. S., & Sheikh, P. A. (2013). *International illegal trade in wildlife: Threats and U.S. policy.* Washington D.C.: Congressional Research Service.

York, E. (2011, November 18). McDonald's drops egg supplier over animal cruelty report. *Chicago Tribune*. Retrieved from http://articles.chicagotribune.com/2011-11-18

/news/chi-mcdonalds-drops-egg-supplier-over-animal-cruelty-report-20111118_1_egg-farmers-animal-welfare-egg-supplier.

Zacharias, N. (2011, October 19). It's time to end factory farming. *Huffington Post*. Retrieved from http://www.huffingtonpost.com/nil-zacharias/its-time-to-end-factory-f_b_1018840.html.

Zimmerman, M. A. (2003). The black market for wildlife: Combating transnational organized crime in illegal wildlife trade. *Vanderbilt Journal of Transnational Law, 36*, 1657–1689.

Chapter 10

Animal Hoarding

Arnold Arluke and Gary Patronek

For much of the twentieth century, unconventional ownership of large numbers of animals was considered to be an eccentricity. As part of American folklore, neighborhood "cat ladies" were largely tolerated, although not understood, for their excesses. Considered "strange" or "odd," their amassing of animals, although not fully revealed to outsiders, was ignored or tolerated and not seen as an expression of a serious problem for people or animals. If not called "crazy cat ladies," these cases were less stereotypically called "animal collectors," albeit still an imprecise term in need of revision as we see below.

Beginning with Patronek's definition of animal hoarding (1999), members of the Hoarding of Animals Research Consortium (HARC) have built a considerable research base about this behavior. Patronek (1999) and HARC (2002) were the first to note the considerable similarity between the hoarding of objects and the hoarding of animals. In the intervening years, members of HARC have published numerous papers further refining this concept, including a major review comparing features of object hoarding and animal hoarding (Frost, Patronek, & Rosenfield, 2011).

We have also learned a great deal about animal hoarding cases in recent years because humane organizations have been more willing to intervene to stop hoarding and remove animals from harm, generating anecdotal, but useful, reports about how best to manage these cases. Finally, through increasing media coverage of hoarding on the cable networks *Animal Planet* and the *Discovery Channel*, these formerly hidden deviances have been brought out into the open for the general public to see and understand beyond the outdated stereotypes and myths that have surrounded this practice for years.

Characteristics of Animal Hoarding

Although once considered rare, epidemiological estimates suggest that animal hoarding is present in many American communities (Patronek, 1999), a finding paralleled by ethnographic studies of hoarding in other cultures (Svanberg, & Arluke, 2016). A survey of health officers in Massachusetts who were queried about reported cases of all types of hoarding (object and animal) estimated the five-year prevalence rate of 26.3 per 100,000 population, or 5.3 per 100,000 per year (Frost, Steketee, & Williams, 2000). The authors reported that animals were hoarded in roughly a third of these cases, which suggest about 1.75 cases per 100,000 per year that involved animals. The authors also indicated that methodological problems likely resulted in an under-reporting during the first three years of the study. Nevertheless, this figure, if extrapolated to the entire US population, would indicate a minimum of 5,100 reported cases per year. Presuming an average of 50 animals per case, it would not be unreasonable to suggest that nearly a quarter million animals are subjected to this form of abuse each year. Moreover, this rate of 1.75 cases is likely underestimated because the data are just from health officers who responded; not all health officers who were contacted responded. The basic point is that animal hoarding is common and the number of cases appears to climb each year. How much of this is due to increased reporting and how much is attributable to increased incidence is unknown but given the severity of so many of these cases, it seems unlikely that they were previously unrecognized and that the apparent increase is solely due to increased reporting.

Hoarders keep a variety of animals. Cats and dogs are the most commonly hoarded species, but wildlife, dangerous exotic animals and farm animals have been involved, even in urban situations. One study of 71 animal hoarders (HARC, 2002) found that approximately 82% of the cases involved cats, 55% dogs, 17% birds, 6% reptiles, 11% small mammals, 6% horses, and 6% cattle, sheep, or goats.

Animal hoarders come from varied backgrounds, contrary to the stereotype of the neighborhood "cat lady" who is pictured as an older, single female, living alone. As with many stereotypes, there is an element of truth to this image. In one study (Worth & Beck, 1981), 70% of the sample were unmarried women who had cats, while in another study (Patronek, 1999) 76% of the sample were women, 46% were over 60 years of age, most were single, divorced, widowed, and cats were most commonly involved. In another study (HARC, 2002), 83% were women, with a median age of 55 years, and nearly three-quarters of the sample were single, widowed, or divorced.

However, it is not uncommon for hoarders to be living with dependents—children, the disabled, the elderly—as well as husbands, wives, girlfriends and boyfriends. One such example is Barbara Erickson, a hoarder of over 500 dogs[1] who lived with a dependent—her husband, whom she claimed had Alzheimer's disease. In reality this behavior cuts across all demographic and socioeconomic boundaries. As most hoarders are very secretive, many can lead a double life with a successful professional career; hoarding behavior has been discovered among doctors, nurses, public officials, college professors, and veterinarians, as well as among a broad spectrum of socioeconomically disadvantaged individuals (HARC, 2002).

Preliminary research suggests that there are different types of hoarders (Patronek et al., 2006). The most benign is the *overwhelmed caregiver, who* minimizes rather than denies animal care problems that result from economic, social, medical, or domestic changes, such as loss of job or health, but cannot remedy these problems. Despite their strong attachment to animals, the overwhelmed caregivers' compromised situation

1. This chapter draws heavily from Arluke and Killeen's (2009) detailed case study of the Erickson hoarding case because it is the most in-depth study of an animal hoarder to date.

gradually leads to a deterioration of animal care. Although socially isolated, they are less secretive and more cooperative with authorities than are other types of hoarders.

The second type of hoarder, *the rescue hoarder*, has a missionary zeal to save all animals. Not that socially isolated, they may be part of a network of enablers whose offers to take animals are never declined. They also actively seek to acquire animals because they feel that only they can provide adequate care and because they oppose euthanasia. Indeed, this behavior can plague organizations as well as individuals. It was recently suggested that as many as one-quarter of cases now may involve some sort of formal quasi-rescue effort or institutional situation (Manning, 2011).

Finally, the *exploiter* hoarder is the most challenging type to manage. Often showing sociopathic traits and/or evidence of severe personality disorders, their lack of empathy for people or animals contributes to an indifference to the harm they cause. Somewhat charismatic and articulate, they present an appearance that suggests competence to the public, officials, and the media.

Two other types are less well characterized: the incipient hoarder and the breeder hoarder. Although not full-fledged hoarders according to the original operational definition of animal hoarding (Patronek, 1999), some people with a growing collection of animals (*incipient hoarders*) may be headed in that direction. This original definition was based on hoarding cases that came to the attention of law enforcement authorities and could be considered as examples of end-stage cases. But like any psychological disorder, it is reasonable to expect the signs and symptoms of animal hoarding to be expressed on a spectrum of time and severity. Therefore, some people may have all of the intrinsic characteristics predisposing to animal hoarding, but insufficient time has passed for the consequences of that predisposition to be fully expressed when the person's capacity for care is finally exceeded. By contrast, the *breeder-hoarder* at first breeds animals for show or sale and may even be successful at local and national dog or cat shows. Eventually, for whatever reasons, they gradually fail to provide proper care or make the necessary adjustments in the population commensurate with their resources and abilities. The question of insight in these cases raises some interesting questions, because there may still be several favored animals which they maintain in optimal body condition with meticulous grooming, and which they may even continue to enter in competitions.

Although there are different types of animal hoarders, their animals share a similar fate. Those responding to these cases often discover large numbers of animals, sometimes in the hundreds, suffering from malnutrition, various diseases, and untreated physical impairments because they have not received food, water, appropriate shelter, and veterinary care. Furthermore, these cases transcend similar situations of individual animal neglect because of the multiplicative consequences of collective neglect—a situation where the whole indeed becomes much worse than the sum of its parts. Severe crowding compounds whatever suffering is already present through increased noise, aggressive interactions between animals, restriction of movement, and the inability to escape to a safe, clean, quiet location. It also greatly enhances spread of disease and compounds the difficulty of recognizing medical conditions requiring veterinary care.

In some animal-hoarding situations other family members, like minor children, dependent elderly persons, or disabled adults, are present and are also victims of this behavior. Serious unmet human health needs are commonly observed, and the conditions often meet the criteria for adult self-neglect, child neglect, or elder abuse (Nathanson, 2009).

For most hoarders, living spaces are often compromised to the extent that they no longer serve the function for which they were intended. Appliances and basic utilities (heat, plumbing, and electricity) are frequently inoperative. Household functioning is often so impaired that both food preparation and maintaining basic sanitation are impossible. There may be health risk to the occupants from elevated ammonia resulting from the accumulation of urine and feces (Castrodale et al., 2010). From a community health perspective, the clutter can pose a fire hazard, especially when fireplaces and kerosene heaters are used for heat. Rodent and insect infestations, as well as odors, can create a neighborhood nuisance. These public health aspects of animal hoarding should not be ignored as they may provide additional or alternative avenues for intervention.

Causes of Animal Hoarding

Understanding why people hoard animals is complex and any explanation must be tentative. It is complex because it is likely that a number of different psychological, social, and even cultural factors are behind the emergence and recognition of this behavior. It is tentative because the current state of research knowledge about animal hoarding is somewhat limited and still evolving; social science explanations of this behavior are relatively recent, replacing the antiquated, but still expressed, view that it is mere eccentricity or uncontrolled, excessive "love" for animals.

Psychological Disorder

Hoarding was recognized as a specific psychological disorder in the fifth version of the *Diagnostic and Statistic Manual* (*DSM-5*) used by mental health workers to diagnose various disorders (American Psychiatric Association, 2013). Although animal hoarding is mentioned under the DSM-5 hoarding disorder (HD), its clinical place remains unclear (Mataix-Cols, 2014) because the DSM-5 criteria for HD are based on object hoarding. DSM-5, drawing on previously published operational criteria (Patronek, 1999), describes animal hoarding as an associated feature of hoarding disorder defined by

> the accumulation of a large number of animals and a failure to provide minimal standards of nutrition, sanitation, and veterinary care and to act on the deteriorating condition of the animals (including disease, starvation or death) and the environment (e.g., severe overcrowding, extremely unsanitary conditions) (American Psychiatric Association, 2013, p. 249).

This definition has remained essentially unchanged in the DSM-5-TR, released in 2022.

However, the similarities between animal hoarding and object hoarding have been noted (Frost, Patronek, & Rosenfield, 2011). Indeed, the primary observable difference between the two is that animal hoarding is likely to be more severe due to the contribution of accumulated animal waste to the conditions in the home. Object hoarding is known to be associated with multiple psychological co-morbidities, and it is likely that animal hoarding is also a complex disorder from a diagnostic perspective. And elements of numerous known disorders have been previously reported among animal hoarders with each model having some diagnostic validity. These different approaches to understanding animal hoarders should not be viewed as competing with each other but rather as overlapping theories that can share some of the same psychological explanations for this complex behavior.

For example, the delusional aspects of animal hoarding have been noted (HARC, 2000). Like people who hoard inanimate objects (Frost, 2000), animal hoarders lack insight into the problematic nature of their behavior. Most have a persistent and powerful belief that they are providing proper animal care, despite obvious and overwhelming contradictory evidence. And most are equally unable to grasp the extent to which their home environments have become unfit for any living creature, sometimes to the point of needing to be torn down. Further suggestion of delusional disorder in hoarders is evidenced by their paranoia about officials and their belief that they have a special ability to communicate with animals. The delusional model easily fits what we know about Barbara Erickson's adult life (Arluke & Killeen, 2009). She claimed to speak with Federal Bureau of Investigation (FBI) agents, to have graduated with five degrees, and to be a lawyer and a veterinarian. When it came to her animals, she repeatedly turned down offers of help, including taking some of the dogs and relieving her responsibility, because help was not needed, and the dogs' condition was fine. As Celeste Killeen observes, Barbara not only failed to see that her home and animals were deteriorating, she could not see how these conditions adversely affected her husband's and her own health.

When animal hoarding was first recognized as a problem for the animal welfare community, it was noted that parallels with addiction seem to fit the thinking and behavior of many hoarders (Lockwood, 1994). As with substance abusers, hoarders are preoccupied with animals, are in denial over their problems, have many excuses for their situation, are socially isolated, claim to be persecuted, and neglect themselves and their surroundings. Other evidence consistent with the addictions model is the similarity of hoarders with people suffering from impulse control problems, such as compulsive shopping (Frost et al., 1998) and compulsive gambling (Meagher, et al., 1999). Some hoarders report to compulsively collect strays and shelter animals. Flores has noted how addictions can be viewed as rooted in attachment problems, a concept which seems to help weave some of these seemingly disparate features together and overcome some of the issues associated with applying overly simplistic diagnostic labels to a complex problem.

Refining what has been learned, Nathanson and Patronek (2011) and Patronek and Nathanson (2011) have woven these disparate models and approaches together, and rather than applying diagnostic labels to animal hoarders, have suggested that the problem would be better understood by focusing on the thoughts and actions exhibited by hoarders (see Figure 1). From this perspective, animal hoarders often manifest traits such as suspiciousness, mistrust, fear of abandonment leading to unstable and intense interpersonal relationships, feelings of emptiness, difficulty with anger, and occasional paranoia. Those having these traits often come from families where they had a history of unresolved grief due to tragic, untimely deaths or losses and emotional or physical abuse (Cassidy & Mohr, 2001; Lyons-Ruth et al., 2006). This is consistent with what has been observed in other forms of addictive behavior (Flores, 2004). Absence of nurturing relationships in childhood cause these people to have a deep sense of aloneness in adulthood that can never be filled. This leads them to seek a "perfect love" to repair their wounded self and make them feel worthy, only to be constantly disappointed, given the nature of human relationships.

Figure 1. Working Model of How Animal Hoarding Develops[2]

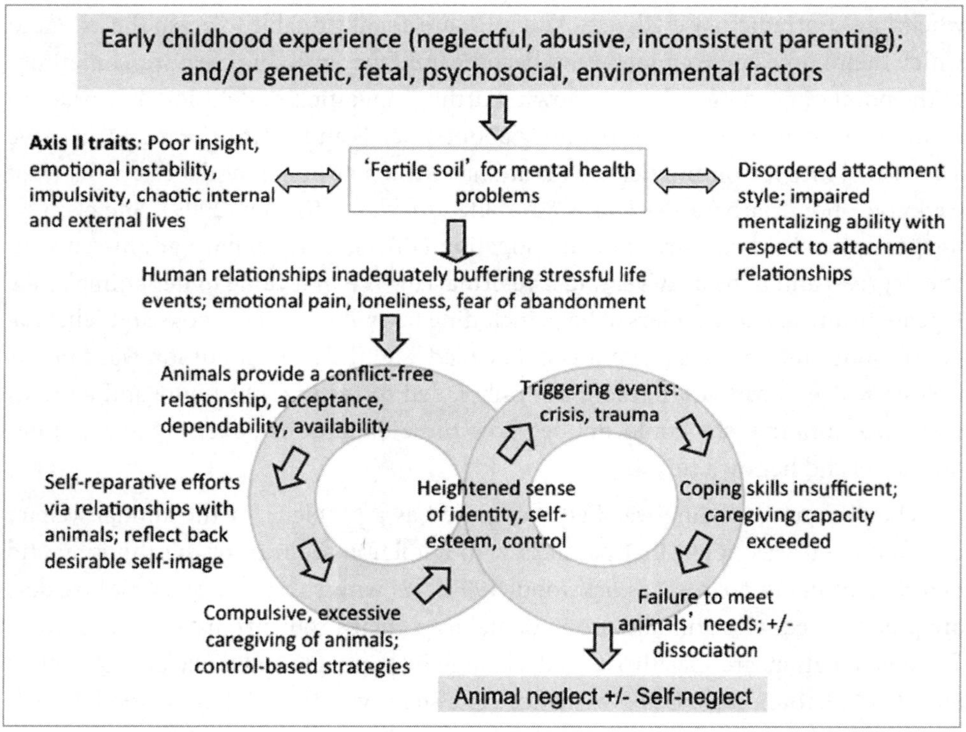

2. Nathanson, J. N., & Patronek, G. J. (2011). Animal hoarding. In B. Oakley, A. Knafo, G. Madhayan, & D. S. Wilson (Eds.), *Pathological altruism* (pp. 107–115). Oxford University Press. Figure 8.1 from (p. 108) (adapted by permission of Oxford University Press).

Animals may provide this perfect, unconditional love, as reported by Worth and Beck (1981). However, just as their own need to be loved was not met by their parents, so too do they neglect the needs of animals dependent on them. As some animals die from lack of care, the hoarder's sense of unworthiness is confirmed, as is their fear of being abandoned, in this case by the dying animals. Nathanson (2009) has suggested that a primary feature of animal hoarding may be less about love than about animals providing a conflict-free relationship to the hoarder, and that features such as control and constancy may be more appropriate ways to characterize the relationship than "love."

In this way, animal hoarding can be viewed as one manifestation of pathological altruism, or the compulsion to devote as much time as possible to giving rather than receiving care (Nathanson & Patronek, 2011). Adult compulsive caregiving has its roots in traumatic losses during childhood that leave children feeling like they need care and help, which parents fail to provide. As these children reach adulthood, they have learned to reverse parenting roles but have lost the ability to express needs or ask for care. They are always trying to help others when deep inside they want care and help. Although it can be argued that hoarders are notorious for not providing care, they adopt a care-giving role by claiming to rescue and save many animals from certain death (Patronek & Nathanson, 2009). Results by Steketee et al. (2011) support this model of hoarding animals.

As a case in point, Barbara Erickson (Arluke & Killeen, 2009) appears to have experienced little if any consistent parental affection, or "love," during her childhood due to significant losses and sexual abuse. To Killeen, these emotional traumas played out in Barbara's adult life as a "search for love" that could never be satisfied. Presumably, she displaced the need for these unfulfilled emotions into perpetual accumulation of dogs as both a source and object of love. Her reluctance to surrender their animals—even to responsible parties who promised to care for them—reflected how seriously and dearly she played the parental role with her animals. This role is also suggested by her emotionality when considering the loss of any one of her many dogs, and by the fact that she allegedly never saw her own baby and had been unsuccessfully searching for it throughout her life. Indeed, Barbara often referred to her dogs as her "children." Seeing the dogs this way meant that they could serve as objects of care and sources of nurturance, allowing her to simultaneously play parent and child roles.

Of course, caution must be exercised when applying these labels or approaches to anyone until individual hoarders are examined by appropriately trained clinicians and more becomes known about the psychology of this behavior. With this caution in mind, a number of these disorders have roots in a chaotic if not traumatic childhood characterized by loss of significant others and abuse. Most hoarders, too, have psychological and social histories beginning in childhood that are chaotic and traumatic. Preliminary research (HARC, 2002) suggests that hoarders grew up in households with inconsistent parenting, in which animals may have been the only stable feature. The vast majority report feelings of insecurity and disruptive and experiences in early life, including frequent relocations, parental separation and divorce, and isolation from peers. For example, Barbara Erickson was reportedly (Arluke & Killian, 2009) raped as a child by her grandfather and father and a farm hand, only to have one of her dogs intervene to stop one rape and another dog to comfort her after those terrifying moments. Barbara also experienced difficult losses as an adolescent, including being abandoned by her mother and having her baby taken from her at birth, never seeing the child again after her father allegedly killed it.

Although those who directly deal with animal hoarders are often convinced that some mental disorder is present, and that some such psychological approach is warranted, it seems unreasonable to lump together all these cases. While some animal hoarders are no doubt plagued by very real psychopathologies, others may not be. The latter subgroup of cases may represent an entirely different ilk of animal hoarding where the problem is due to social breakdown or highly compromised living situations that result from personal, familial, neighborhood or community social problems.

Social Enabling

Those seeking to explain animal hoarding have taken a psychological approach to the problem that sees it as a mental disorder emanating solely from within the individual. While we must continue to explore the psychological roots of animal hoarding, interpersonal and cultural factors must also be considered if our goal is to produce a more complete understanding of the nature and origin of this behavior. Family, friends, neighbors, the wider community, and society at large must be factored into our analysis of why and how hoarding starts and continues. By taking a broader and more complex view of the problem, interventions can address the contextual roots of the problem rather than only focusing on the individual's underlying mental disorder.

For example, some cases of animal hoarding are likely a product of, or at least facilitated by, a dysfunctional society rather than being due solely to the acts of disturbed individuals. If the finger of blame is to be pointed, in such instances, it must be shared with the larger society. In many parts of America, abandoned and stray animals remain a big problem, in part due to irresponsible breeding of pets that produces millions of unwanted animals. Euthanasia practiced by open-admission shelters becomes a way to manage this overpopulation problem, since not all of these unwanted animals could be adopted or kept indefinitely in their cages.

Animal hoarders, and whatever family and emotional support systems they have, become an expedient and injurious dysfunctional system that responds to this societal problem. People in the community, knowing the hoarder's reputation for apparently wanting so many animals, may drop off unwanted pets at the hoarder's home, thereby feeding their ever-growing collection. In this way, the neighborhood "cat lady" or "dog lady serves as a convenient, impromptu shelter where there will be no guilt imparted by staff members for dropping off unwanted animals (Frommer & Arluke, 1999) and no risk of euthanasia. According to Barbara Erickson (Arluke & Killeen, 2009), she played this role in her community when people anonymously left animals at her door rather than abandoning them or taking them to a shelter.

Animal hoarding also can be perpetuated—indeed even started—through social support that provides animals to hoarders as well as food, veterinary care, and other essentials for them. One type of support comes from networks of like-minded or sympathetic people. Friends who identify with the hoarder's feelings and approach to animals may deliberately acquire unwanted animals from various sources, such as veterinary offices or shelters, and to prevent their euthanasia, give them to the hoarder. In the Erickson case (Arluke & Killeen, 2009), after Barbara's dogs were seized in one intervention, her friends tried to get her animals from the shelter by claiming that they were their own, and then presumably to return them to her.

Another type of support comes from misguided people who inadvertently enable hoarders to amass many animals. They can sometimes "pass" as normal appearing people and conceal their private world with animals. One such hoarder, who masked herself as a legitimate breeder, was protected by friends in her community who did not understand the depth of her psychological problem or the way she treated her dogs (Stola Education Group, 2006). She did not allow anyone to visit her home and was charming at public dog events.

Finally, there is an interpersonal component to animal hoarding when other people know about the problem but choose to ignore if not tolerate it. Neighbors, friends, and relatives can be aware that hoarding is taking place but do nothing to intervene or even report it to authorities. Understandably, it is difficult to take such action for fear of alienating personal relationships with the hoarder and for lack of hard evidence to provide authorities. Nevertheless, such inaction allows hoarding to continue unchallenged.

Interventions

Keeping large numbers of animals in inappropriate, inadequate, and over-crowded conditions that cause starvation, disease, behavioral problems, or death seriously challenges relatives, friends, neighbors, and community agencies that want to help hoarders and their animals. However, the complex nature of hoarding cases makes them difficult to investigate and to resolve. The jurisdiction for these cases may cross many state and local agencies and departments, including mental health, police, humane law enforcement, zoning, sanitation, fish and wildlife, child welfare, animal control, public health, building safety, aging, and social services. So, it is the rule rather than the exception that they are procedurally cumbersome, time consuming, and costly to resolve. Although common sense suggests that the accumulation of large numbers of animals in homes can have important public health implications, including placing people at risk due to unsanitary living conditions, facilitating the spread of zoonotic diseases, and endangering the health of vulnerable household members, particularly children or dependent elderly, the potential for these consequences in animal hoarding cases is not widely appreciated by government agencies.

The absence of joint agreements between agencies over their missions and roles in these cases may create more conflict than cooperation. And to date, most communities have not discovered how to bring together available resources, expertise, and authorities to achieve comprehensive solutions. Arluke and Killeen's (2009) description of the community's handling of the Erickson case is more the exception than the rule. In this case, veterinarians, shelters, police, volunteers, and journalists worked together rather seamlessly when they intervened in this case without any formal agreements between county and state agencies. They accomplished this by focusing on the problem and how to solve it, rather than their own jurisdictional issues. This is exemplified in the Idaho Humane Society's offering resources to a case in Oregon, and in the Second Chance Shelter in Fruitland, Idaho which worked closely with an Oregon Sheriff's office prior to the rescue by reporting the problem and organizing the rescue, then offering to house and care for over 500 dogs.

Difficult issues of personal freedom, lifestyle choice, mental competency, and private property rights also confound intervening in these cases. For one, to protect people's civil rights, most laws restrict agencies from intervening unless the person poses a danger to themself or others. Options for intervention are also limited because few hoarders seem to meet the criteria for mental incompetence or immediate danger to self or others. Indeed, hoarders are rarely evaluated psychologically, which is a required step in determining dangerousness. One of the questions that may be raised in the future is whether the concept of dangerousness should be applied to animal victims, and whether a fuller appreciation of the consequences of their actions for people and animals by mental health authorities would lead to improved recognition of the scope of dangerousness often present.

Cases typically come to the attention of authorities because of complaints from neighbors or visitors to the property. The primary problems reported about hoarders are unsanitary conditions, "strong," "obnoxious" odors or "stench," and occasionally nuisance problems such as "barking loudly." Neglect is seldom the initial complaint because animals are usually concealed inside hoarders' homes. So, too, with the Erickson case (Arluke & Killeen, 2009). There, neighbors complained to the Oregon Health Department about smells coming from the farm, leading to an investigation, an order to remove the waste, and a threatened $500 fine that was dropped after the Ericksons removed the waste. Sanitary conditions often deteriorate to the extent that public health authorities condemn dwellings as unfit for human habitation. By the time these situations have deteriorated to the point at which they cannot be ignored, expenses for veterinary care and housing of animals, litigation, and cleanup or demolition of premises can run into the tens of thousands of dollars.

Initial attempts to follow up complaints are usually unsuccessful. Often described as "uncomfortable around people," or as "quiet and somewhat reclusive," hoarders sometimes board up windows, erect tall fences, rarely appear outside, and do not answer phone calls or doorbells, making them notorious for their fortress mentality and hostility toward and suspicion of outsiders. Arluke and Killeen (2009) point out that the Ericksons had a sign posted on the door proclaiming, "This is Private Property. Stay to Hell Out!" If approached, outsiders are almost always turned away before they get into the hoarder's home. The Ericksons also never allowed anyone inside their home; Barbara would intercept anyone before they got to the front door. On more than one occasion she suffered health problems requiring an ambulance but instead of inviting paramedics into the house to treat her, she met them at the street. This isolation makes it difficult, if not impossible, for neighbors to know much about them or their animals. Law enforcement authorities are eventually called to the scene, typically discovering many suffering or dead animals that are taken away from angry or grieving owners who potentially face charges of cruelty and possible conviction and sentencing.

Seizing Animals

Because of the severity of animal suffering and need for expediency, a common scenario is for the hoarder's animals to be removed for their own protection through use of a search warrant, with the hoarder subsequently prosecuted under state anti-cruelty laws. However, seizing animals in hoarding cases is a complicated, expensive, labor intensive, and emotionally upsetting process. Seizing animals may require the coordination of many agencies and organizations. The last and largest "rescue" of the Erickson's dogs required coordination among humane societies in Idaho and Oregon, some of which lacked sufficient funds to pay for all the animal care and staff salaries required in such cases, local veterinarians and animal shelters, law enforcement officials, firefighters, reporters, and volunteers (Arluke & Killeen, 2009). Within the past five years, national animal protection organizations such as the American Society for the Prevention to Cruelty to Animals (ASPCA) and Humane Society of the United States, among others, have come together to coordinate disaster-type responses to the big cases, bringing in teams of people to set up temporary shelters and veterinary teams to evaluate the animals. Some of the big animal-related charitable foundations sponsored by the pet industry provide tractor-trailers full of supplies to help rescuers' efforts. These additional resources and networking allow many more animals to be rehabilitated and rehomed instead of being euthanized. The field of veterinary forensics has also come of age with the establishment of the International Veterinary Forensics Sciences Association, and its members are increasingly playing a role when intervention occurs to collect and present the evidence needed to obtain a criminal conviction.

Emotional costs are high as people venture into disturbingly chaotic homes, deal with hoarders who can be extremely sad or very angry, see animals that are dead, emaciated, very sick, and often living in cramped, inhumane conditions, and end up euthanizing some. Those who intervene often find the experience of carrying out the "rescue" (less often called a "seizure" or even "raid") to be very dramatic and disturbing as they try to help animals or people put in danger by hoarders. A law enforcement presence is usually necessary to manage hoarders and take aggressive steps needed on behalf of animal victims who need to be "taken away" with some urgency. Steps may also be taken to monitor and manage the distress and sadness of hoarders who feel as though their "children" will be taken from them. There have been at least three news reports of people who were being investigated and committed suicide. One woman lit a charcoal grill in her bedroom and died of carbon monoxide poisoning along with her pets.

A study of hoarding cases reported in the news (Arluke et al., 2002) found that rescuers often paint each case as the "worst" or "most horrifying" incident, describing animal neglect in superlative terms. One news article cites a humane official who said, "'You can't imagine people accumulating that sort of filth and garbage.'... Frazier said that it was the most foul scene he had encountered in his six years on the job.'" Another official maintained that a different case involved the "largest number of neglected animals ever seen." Hoarders predictably protest and resist rescues, claiming unlawful and unnecessary seizure of their "children." One is described in a news article as "so belligerent the police were called to help," at which point the hoarder wrestled with police, who sprayed him with pepper spray and finally arrested him. Others have histories of being uncooperative or hostile. It is common for news reports to describe repeated attempts, sometimes spanning years, to take animals away from hoarders who resist these efforts by authorities (Arluke et al., 2002). In one case, an article features the headline, "Notorious Cat Hoarder Jailed" and details the exploits of a "wily and elusive foe." Another article notes that "as is true of most animal hoarders, Becker had a track record," listing her history of being deceptive and difficult with authorities as she chronically acquired animals.

Rescuers also will be confounded by hoarders' paradoxical accounts of their own behavior, sometimes professing great love for animals. Indeed, Arluke and Killeen's (2009) take on Barbara Erickson is that she saw herself as one with a "limitless need to love" that was turned on dogs. Certainly, the thought of losing her dogs seriously disturbed Barbara Erickson and made her cry. It is not clear, however, whether this "love" is a genuine motivation or a dishonest way to appear socially acceptable, if not praiseworthy. Others may claim to be pet rescuers or "no-kill" shelters attempting to help unwanted pets, and some may be professional or hobby animal breeders. All too frequently, these excuses may be used as effective ploys for the media or as defenses in court (Vaca-Guzman & Arluke, 2005). Despite these claims of professionalism and good intentions, hoarders are usually oblivious to the extreme suffering, obvious to the casual observer, of their animals.

Medicolegal Options

By virtue of their animal cruelty statutes, every state at least indirectly mandates that caretakers provide animals with sufficient food and water, a sanitary environment, and necessary veterinary care in case of illness or injury. It is, however, important to recognize that animal cruelty statutes were written with the goal of identifying criminal neglect and punishing offenders, not to ensure optimal or even adequate care for animals. A more recent concept for assessing quality of life across the entire range of potential situations where groups of animals may be kept is to consider the Five Freedoms (Figure 2). (These are briefly described in Chapter 1 in this book.) This concept stems from an effort in 1965 in the United Kingdom to establish relevant and appropriate measures of welfare for agricultural animals. More recently this concept was applied to the care of populations of companion animals (Newbury et al., 2010).

Those who investigate hoarding cases perhaps should be mindful of these considerations, including freedom from hunger, thirst, discomfort, pain, injury, disease, fear, and distress, and freedom to express normal behavior when trying to establish the presence of suffering and deteriorating animal care. Attitudes towards proper treatment of animals are evolving, and while in the past, cruelty was typically prosecuted under a fairly narrow range of criteria (e.g., frank starvation or failure to provide required veterinary care for relief of suffering) it is clear from this diagram that care begins to deteriorate and animals suffer a myriad of detrimental effects to their well-being long before intervention through the criminal justice system occurs.

Figure 2. Relationship of Presence of the Five Freedoms for Animal Welfare to Quality of Life for Animals

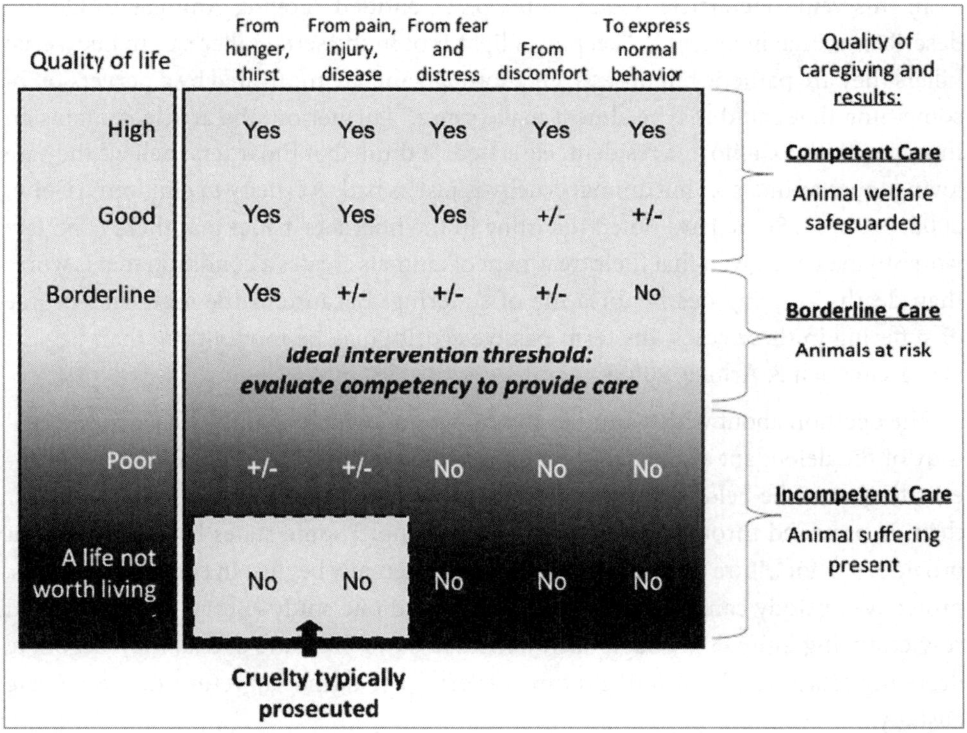

Hoarding cases are often initially investigated and handled by representatives of the local animal shelter, humane society, or other animal protection group. In cases where an animal protection organization does not have jurisdiction, local police officers or municipal animal control officers may be the initial agents to investigate a case.

In some jurisdictions, violations of animal cruelty statutes may be summary offenses prosecuted by local humane agents or animal control officers in front of a magistrate, whereas in others, they may be misdemeanors, or in some cases, felonies, requiring prosecution by the district attorney's office. Penalties in the event of a guilty finding can range from a nominal fine to forfeiture of the animals and jail time (Arluke & Luke,

1997). Although some state statutes provide for the recovery of the costs of boarding and medical care for animals in cruelty cases, the extent to which this is realized in practice is uncertain.

Although their actions are clearly a violation of animal cruelty laws in every state, hoarders can be complicated to prosecute. Cases involving many animals with multiple potential charges for each, are often, for the sake of judicial expediency, reduced to a handful of charges. And in some jurisdictions, successful prosecution requires establishing the abuser's intent to cause harm, particularly for more serious charges. Claims of being a rescue organization with the goal of helping animals can further confound establishing intent. Indeed, decisions by many states to impose more serious penalties on abusers by classifying the intentional harm of animals as a felony crime may have unintentionally downgraded equally egregious cases of neglect with enormous suffering seen in hoarding cases (Patronek et al., 2006).

In this vein, one article (Colin, 2002, p. 2), entitled "Loving Animals to Death," describes animal hoarders as "keeping a light foot in the serial killer camp: Like serial killers they are pathetic but obsessively thorough and are motivated by a perversion of something that could maybe almost make sense." Further on, the article contains an interview with a California resident. He stated: "I think that [hoarders] believe they are loving those animals ... but animal cruelty is just as bad as cruelty to children" (Colin, 2002, pp. 2–3). Some have noted the irony in the hoarders' belief that there is no fate worse than death, given that their treatment of animals creates a condition that is worse than death—a living death—or a life of suffering. Because of the scale and degree of suffering in these cases, the term passive cruelty may be more fitting than neglect (Vaca-Guzman & Arluke, 2005).

The decision about which animals to remove and which, if any, to leave in the custody of the defendant also encumbers prosecution. Because seized animals are property, they must be held in shelters until cases are completed or due process to forfeit them is provided through other means. For example, some states have statutes that provide for a forfeiture hearing long before a trial actually begins. In complicated cases, protective custody can last for years. According to one study (Berry, 2005), to avoid re-victimizing animals through such extended stays, humane agents may negotiate dropping charges and restricting future ownership of animals in return for immediate custody.

According to news reports of hoarding cases (Arluke et al., 2002), guilty verdicts or no contest pleas were rare in the past. If any sentence were passed, hoarders were ordered to give up animals, not get any more either temporarily or permanently, or stop breeding them. Occasionally, they were modestly fined or made to reimburse shelters for the cost of food and veterinary care. Jail time was rarely imposed except for contempt of court, fraud, and violation of probation.

National groups are trying to change this situation. The Animal Legal Defense Fund (ALDF) has made a major effort to provide resources for prosecutors on their website. Also, the Association of Prosecuting Attorneys has created a subsection on prosecuting animal abuse. For hoarding cases that appear motivated by profit, pursuing the financial aspects of a case (e.g., failure to pay taxes, misuse of funds, fraud) may be effective.

There are many reasons for this prior leniency in court, although hoarders think it is stern to impose any limit on their animal ownership. Certainly, hoarding—despite the numbers of animals involved and the extent of their suffering—will be overshadowed in court by the many serious crimes against humans that officials see. Claims of intending to help animals, coupled with the perception that the problems arose from inadvertent neglect rather than intentional abuse, could tilt the proceedings towards more sympathetic as opposed to punitive responses. In addition, the prevailing view of hoarders as eccentric, if not mentally ill, makes criminalization seem inappropriate.

Arluke and Killeen (2009) note that the first time Barbara Erickson appeared in court for animal neglect, charges were dropped against her after she agreed to stop selling dogs, spay and neuter her animals, and allow a veterinarian to make unannounced visits. However, after the final rescue of 552 dogs, the Ericksons were charged with felony criminal mischief (for destruction of their rental house), 134 counts of misdemeanor animal abuse (the euthanized dogs), and 418 counts of misdemeanor animal neglect (the survivors). Barbara was jailed for several weeks, ordered to pay $15,000 in restitution and obtain psychological counseling, sentenced to 60 months supervised probation, and limited to no more than two dogs.

Although there are many challenges in prosecuting animal hoarders, prosecution has an important role to play in how hoarding cases can be approached in the future. Taking a criminal justice approach to these cases may help encourage prosecutors, judges, police, and legislators take them more seriously than they have in the past. Also, a therapeutically-oriented intervention or negotiation may not work with certain types of hoarders who are very irrational and uncooperative. Aggressive prosecution may be the only effective way to deal with hoarders who must be stringently monitored and strictly sanctioned to prevent recidivism. As noted by Patronek et al. (2006), the "broken window approach" to crime (Wilson & Kelling, 1982) may apply to cases of hoarding as well; in other words, the progression to major offenses can be prevented by aggressively intervening when there are early warning signs of social breakdown, whether they are small crimes in the neighborhood or the first stages of animal hoarding. However, current laws make this type of proactive approach difficult (Patronek & Weiss, 2012).

Some states mandate psychological counseling of offenders, whereas others make it an option for the court. Although over 30 states have legislation for evaluation or treatment, no one knows exactly what this involves. However, at least as reflected in press reports of judges' actions, courts have not always viewed hoarders as seriously disturbed (Arluke et al., 2002). Judges in these news stories rarely suggest or require counseling. Indeed, even when they allude to possible mental health problems in hoarders, they may not order or recommend therapy. In one such case, the judge simply commented, "I think it's clear you are fixated on animals. In your obsession, you really are misguided." This reticence to recommend psychological help may seem surprising, given that a number of hoarders' behaviors seem symptomatic of serious mental health problems. Nevertheless, counseling should not be viewed as a panacea in these cases. It is important to note that no psychological treatment program has ever been validated as effective for animal hoarders, nor is it clear what "success" might look like, how long such a process might take (particularly with a treatment-resistant offender who may also be unable to afford or disinclined to pay for such treatment), and most importantly, there does not appear to be any consensus as to the fate of the animals for however long the person is "in treatment."

Even with court-ordered counseling, there can be several problems implementing it. Hoarders in general are very resistant to treatment and few clinicians are trained to work with object hoarders let alone animal hoarders, so they may be hesitant to take on hoarders as patients. If hoarders are on fixed incomes or are unemployed, they will not have funds. Even if they have health insurance, they may only qualify for a limited number of visits to mental health providers and reimbursement rates to these providers can be low. If providers are seen on a fee-for-service basis, it is likely that hoarders will pay them slowly or not all, given their resistance to treatment. Monitoring required counseling, when it comes to matters such as attendance and responsiveness to a counselor's recommendations, will fall in the hands of a probation officer who, in all likelihood, will already be overwhelmed with a very large caseload. Regardless, the probation system is not designed for long-term monitoring of chronic offenders.

Occasionally, there may be prohibitions on future pet ownership, or limitations imposed on the number of animals, along with a requirement of periodic monitoring of the situation by authorities or even formal court-ordered probation. Supervised probation has been recommended over unsupervised probation as a better way to ensure compliance. Prohibitions against future pet ownership are effective only to the extent that monitoring is practical. Probation by contrast, is typically imposed for a fixed, and typically brief, period of time.

Some communities attempt to either prevent or remedy hoarding situations by passing ordinances that limit the number of pets a person can own. There are no data to indicate whether these measures are effective, but what is known is that they are wildly unpopular and difficult to enforce, and likely to be opposed by a broad coalition of pet fanciers, breeders, rescue groups, and animal protection organizations. This is a harsh and probably ineffective remedy that needlessly penalizes responsible pet owners.

The worst situations may be avoided through regulations that stipulate housing densities, sanitation requirements, and veterinary care, and which provide for regular inspections of licensed facilities. For example, Colorado has developed licensing requirements and comprehensive standards for the operation of an animal shelter or pet rescue organization. Such criteria also could help the media and the public, as well as the courts, distinguish between legitimate sheltering efforts and hoarding. Because of the Erickson case discussed throughout this chapter, Oregon's Malheur County enacted a law requiring a shelter license for anyone with 10 or more pets. The license allows for periodic inspections inside the home by officials who could then report neglect or abuse.

Managing these cases is complicated by the fact that hoarders not only have a high recidivism rate, often continuing their behavior after seizures leave them without animals, they move to different towns or states where they are unknown and under the radar screen of local humane and law enforcement authorities. In a typical example, two 50-year-old women and their 73-year-old mother were discovered living with 82 live, and 108 dead, cats. They fled from the investigation, rented a new apartment nearby, and had seven cats and a dog two days later. A hoarder can escape enforcement, even when monitoring is practical, by moving to a new jurisdiction, often only across town or county lines. Indeed, Barbara Erickson abandoned many dogs at her prior rental house in Midvale, Idaho, when moving to another home in Council, Idaho although she returned to feed them after her eviction (Arluke & Killeen, 2009). After a complaint was filed against Erickson for 50 dogs kept in her Council, Idaho, home she moved to Oregon.

Conclusion

Much remains to be learned about the mental health issues involved in animal hoarding. With increased knowledge and understanding of this behavior, mental health professionals will be better prepared to intervene in these cases. Further enhancing the effectiveness of these interventions are new efforts to engage in interdisciplinary cooperation to bring together a broad array of resources and expertise to resolve these cases in a humane and timely fashion. Because the DSM-5 recognizes hoarding as a specific disorder, there should be increased involvement by mental health professionals and researchers in the care and study of this complex disorder. Engagement of forensic psychologists and psychiatrists could also be a consequence of such a designation.

At the same time, advances are underway that will increase the efficacy of interventions by law enforcement and criminal justice authorities in animal hoarding cases. Professional and advocacy organizations like the National District Attorneys Association and the Animal Legal Defense Fund in combination with veterinary forensics are accelerating our ability to successfully prosecute crimes like hoarding once they have occurred. Despite such progress, intervention could be even more effective were it possible to intervene in hoarding cases before they become so severe that a prosecutable crime has occurred, and victims have suffered. An important ethical question is whether the goal is to maximize punishment of the offender OR to expedite rescue and placement of the animals, especially if the two goals are mutually exclusive. At present, humane law enforcement officers are limited in their options to preventively help animals when hoarding behavior is recognized but person refuses help, and the situation has not deteriorated sufficiently that successful prosecution is yet likely. Interestingly, almost half of the states have legislation that provides due process and therefore the possibility of early disposition of the animals through civil, preconviction forfeiture laws long before a criminal trial. These statutes appear to be under-utilized but have the potential to be very helpful in expediting disposition when a person clearly lacks the capacity to provide proper care. Input and collaboration between mental health authorities, members of the criminal justice system, animal advocates, and legislators will be required to bring animal cruelty laws developed in the nineteenth century into alignment with twenty-first century crimes against animals.

References

American Psychiatric Association. (2013). Diagnostic and statistical manual of mental health disorders. American Psychiatric Publishing.

Arluke, A. (2004). *Brute force: Animal police and the challenge of cruelty*. Purdue University Press.

Arluke, A., Frost, R., Steketee, G., Patronek, G., Luke, C., Messner, E., Nathanson J., & Papazian, M. (2002). Press reports of animal hoarding. *Society & Animals, 10*, 113–135.

Arluke, A., & Killeen, C. (2009). *Inside animal hoarding: The case of Barbara Erickson and her 552 dogs*. Purdue University Press.

Arluke, A., & Luke, C. (1997). Physical cruelty toward animals in Massachusetts, 1975–1996. *Society & Animals, 5*,195–204.

Berry, C. (2005). Long-term outcomes in animal cases, *Animal Law, 11*, 167–194.

Cassidy J., & Mohr J. (2001). Unsolvable fear, trauma, psychopathology: Theory, research, and clinical considerations related to disorganized attachment across the lifespan. *Clinical Psychology: Science and Practice, 8*, 275–298.

Castrodale, L., Bellay, Y., Brown, C., Cantor, F., Gibbins, J., Headrick, M., Leslie, M, MacMahon, K., O'Quin, J., Patronek, G., Silva, R., Wright, J, & Yu, D. (2010). General public health considerations for responding to animal hoarding cases. *Journal of Environmental Health, 72*, 14–18.

Colin, C. (2002). Loving animals to death. [Electronic version]. Salon.com. Retrieved June 6, 2002 from http://www.salon.com/people/feature/2002/03/08/hoarders/index.html.

Flores, P. (2004). *Addiction as an attachment disorder.* Jason Aronson Franklin, A. (1999). *Animals and modern cultures: A sociology of human-animal relations in modernity*. Sage.

Frommer, S., & Arluke, A. (1999). Loving them to death: The blame-displacing strategies of animal shelter workers and surrenderers. *Society & Animals, 7*, 1–16.

Frost, R. (1998). Hoarding, compulsive buying and reasons for saving. *Behavioral Research and Therapy, 36*, 657–664.

Frost, R. (2000). People who hoard animals. *Psychiatric Times, 17(4)*, 25–29.

Frost, R., Hartl, T., Christian, R., & Williams, N. (1995). The value of possessions in compulsive hoarding: Patterns of use and attachment. *Behavioral Research and Therapy, 33*, 897–902.

Frost, R., Patronek, G., & Rosenfield, E. (2011). Comparison of object and animal hoarding. *Depression and Anxiety, 28*, 885–891.

HARC. (2002). Health implications of animal hoarding. *Health and Social Work, 27*, 125–131.

Lockwood, R. (1994). The psychology of animal collectors. *American Animal Hospital Association Trends Magazine, 9*, 18–21.

Lockwood, R., & Cassidy, B. (1988). Killing with kindness? *The Humane Society News, Summer*, 1–5.

Lyons-Ruth K., Dutra, L., Schuder, M., & Bianchi, I. (2006). From infant attachment disorganization to adult dissociation: Relational adaptations or traumatic experiences? *Psychiatric Clinics of North America, 29*, 63–86.

Manning S. (2011). When animal rescuers become animal hoarders. Retrieved January 26, 2011 from http://www.msnbc.msn.com/id/38978396/ns/health-pet_health/t/when-animal-rescuers-become-animal-hoarders/#.T5Rxcu2xHaQ.

Mataix-Cols D. (2014). Clinical practice. Hoarding disorder. *New England Journal of Medicine, 370,* 2023–30.

Meagher, E., Frost, R., & Riskind, J. (1999). Compulsive lottery, scratch ticket, and keno gambling: Its relation to OCD, hoarding, impulsivity, and the urge to buy. Paper presented at the annual meeting of the Association for the Advancement of Behavior Therapy, Toronto, November.

Nathanson, J. (2009). Animal hoarding: Slipping into the darkness of comorbid animal and self-neglect. *Journal of Elder Abuse, 21*,307–324.

Nathanson, J., & Patronek, G. (2011). Animal hoarding: How the semblance of a benevolent mission becomes actualized as egoism and cruelty. In B. Oakley, A. Knafo, G. Madhavan, & D. Wilson, (Eds.), *Pathological Altruism*, (pp.107–115). Oxford University Press.

Newbury, S., Blinn, M. K., Bushby, P. A., Barker Cox, C., Dinnage, J. D., Griffin, B., ... Spindel, M. (2010). *Guidelines for standards of care in animal shelters.* Association of Shelter Veterinarians.

Patronek, G. (1999). Hoarding of animals: An under-recognized public health problem in a difficult to study population. *Public Health Reports, 114*, 82–87.

Patronek, G. (2001). The problem of animal hoarding. *Municipal Lawyer, 42*, 6–19.

Patronek, G., Loar, L., & Nathanson, J. (Eds.) (2006). *Animal hoarding: Structuring interdisciplinary responses to help people, animals and communities at risk.* Hoarding of Animals Research Consortium.

Patronek, G., & Nathanson, J. (2009). A theoretical perspective to inform assessment and treatment strategies for animal hoarders. *Clinical Psychology Review, 29*, 274–281.

Patronek G., & Weiss K. (2012). Animal hoarding: A Neglected Problem at the intersection of psychiatry, veterinary medicine, and law. Findings from the Henderson House Workgroup. Poster 117–64; American Psychology Law Conference, San Juan, March 17, 2012. Retrieved from: http://www.tufts.edu/vet/hoarding/index.html.

Steketee, G., Gibson, A., Frost, R., Alabiso, J., Arluke, A., & Patronek, G. (2011). Characteristics and antecedents of people who hoard animals: An exploratory comparative interview study. *Review of General Psychology, 15*,114–124.

Stola Education Group. (2006). Animal hoarding: A hidden danger in the sport of purebred breeding? *IG Times, Spring,* 10–14.

Svanberg, I, & Arluke, A. (2016). The Swedish swan lady: The reaction to an apparent animal hoarding case. *Society & Animals, (24)*1, 63–77.

Vaca-Guzman, M., & Arluke, A. (2005). Normalizing passive cruelty: The excuses and justifications of animal hoarders. *Anthrozoös, 18*, 338–357.

Wilson, J., & Kelling, G. (1982). Broken windows: The police and neighborhood safety. *The Atlantic Monthly, March*, 29–38.

Worth, C., & Beck, A. (1981). Multiple ownership of animals in New York City. *Transactions and Studies of the College of Physicians of Philadelphia, 3*, 280–300.

Chapter 11

Animal Sexual Assault and Human Deviance

Suzanne E. Tallichet, Elizabeth B. Perkins, Christopher Hensley, and Caleb E. Trentham

Animal sexual assault, or bestiality, is an uncomfortable topic that most of the general public, as well as veterinarians, researchers and legislators, usually prefer not to discuss. However, this form of animal cruelty is more common than we want to believe (Maher & Pierpoint, 2020). Too often animals have been deemed the "perfect victims" and unless there is physical harm to the animal or the act becomes exposed to the public, there is little outcry about transspecies sexual assault. We chose to use the term "animal sexual assault," also referred to as animal sexual abuse, in this chapter's title in order to signal the rights of animals to lives without human cruelty and to the link between animal sexual abuse and interpersonal human violence (Beirne, 2009; Holoyda, 2020). We begin our chapter discussing paraphilias, zoophilia, and bestiality. We review studies about the prevalence of bestiality, the characteristics and dynamics associated with it and the potential link between animal sexual abuse and interpersonal violence including related theories. The final two sections provide updates about federal law cases of the relatively recent emerging "crush" videos and state laws against animal sexual abuse.

Paraphilias

The term paraphilia literally means abnormal love. According to a relatively recent edition of the *Diagnostic and Statistical Manual of Mental Disorders* (DSM), a paraphilia is a sexual deviation marked by fantasies, feelings, and behaviors that are necessary for sexual arousal (American Psychiatric Association, 2000). The essential features of a paraphilia involve "recurrent, intense sexually arousing fantasies, urges, or behaviors" that occur over a period of at least six months (American Psychiatric Association, 1994, p. 523). These fantasies and behaviors typically involve non-human objects, the suffering or humiliation of oneself or one's partner, or children or other nonconsenting persons. In addition, paraphilias cause significant damage to social, occupational, and other forms of normal functioning (American Psychiatric Association, 2000). According to the DSM-5, a paraphilia "denotes any intense or persistent sexual interest in other than sexual interest in genital stimulation or preparatory fondling with phenotypically normal, physically mature, consenting human partners" (American Psychiatric Association, 2013, p. 685).

Paraphilic behaviors often hinge on other components, including deviant sexual fantasies, facilitators (drugs, alcohol, and/or pornography), and compulsive masturbation (Hickey, 2010). Deviant sexual fantasies serve to influence and motivate deviant sexual or violent behaviors. Facilitators lower inhibitions, allowing for people to fantasize about or actually engage in aberrant sexual behaviors. Compulsive masturbation, often in conjunction with pornography, serves to reinforce deviant sexual fantasies, as well as deviant sexual behaviors (Hickey, 2010).

Paraphilias exist on a continuum that range from mild to moderate to severe and have the potential to become more extreme over time (Hickey, 2010). What distinguishes those people who have a mild paraphilia from those who suffer from a severe paraphilia is that the former can sexually function without the deviant sexual fantasies, facilitators, and compulsive masturbation that the latter often requires. The behavior is considered severely paraphilic when the individual completely depends on the aberrant fantasy for sexual stimulation and gratification (Hickey, 2010).

The most recent DSM-5 draft adds terminology that distinguishes between those who engage in paraphilias and those who have a paraphiliac disorder, defining a paraphilic disorder as "a paraphilia that causes distress or impairment to the individual or harm to others" (American Psychiatric Association, 2013, p. 685–686). This allows for a clear distinction between a healthy person with a non-normative sexual behavior who requires no psychiatric intervention and a person with a psychopathological non-normative sexual behavior who would need such intervention (American Psychiatric Association, 2013).

History of Paraphilias

Prior to the publication of the DSM-I, paraphilias were classified as cases of psychopathic personality with pathologic sexuality. The DSM-I included sexual deviation as a personality disorder of a sociopathic subtype. The major sexual deviations discussed in the DSM-I included fetishism, homosexuality, pedophilia, sexual sadism (including rape), and transvestism (American Psychiatric Association, 1952).

The DSM-II continued to use the term sexual deviation to describe what would later be termed a paraphilia. These sexual deviations, however, were no longer seen as being attributed to personality disorders, but rather were listed alongside personality disorders in a category described as "personality disorders and certain other nonpsychotic disorders." Such sexual deviations included exhibitionism, fetishism, homosexuality, masochism, pedophilia, sadism, transvestism, voyeurism, and other sexual deviations. However, no examples of sexual deviation were provided for the "other" category (American Psychiatric Association, 1962).

In 1980, the term, paraphilia, was introduced in the DSM-III as a subset of a new category described as "psychosexual disorders." The paraphilias listed included atypical paraphilia, exhibitionism, fetishism, pedophilia, sexual masochism, sexual sadism, transvestism, voyeurism, and zoophilia. Homosexuality was removed from that edition of the DSM-III (American Psychiatric Association, 1980). Seven years later, the DSM-III-R renamed psychosexual disorders to sexual disorders and atypical paraphilia to paraphilia NOS (not otherwise specified). In addition, frotteurism was added to the list of main paraphilias and transvestism was renamed to transvestic fetishism. Zoophilia was relegated to the paraphilia NOS category along with coprophilia, klismaphilia, necrophilia, partialism, telephone scatologia, and urophlilia (American Psychiatric Association, 1987).

The DSM-IV retained the sexual disorders classification, but added a broader category titled, "sexual and gender identity disorders" for paraphilias. It also kept the same paraphilias and the same paraphilia NOS list as the DSM-III-R (American Psychiatric Association, 1994). The DSM-IV-TR provides clinical criteria for only certain paraphilias, including exhibitionism, fetishism, frotteurism, pedophilia, sexual masochism, sexual sadism, transvestic fetishism, and voyeurism. The paraphilia NOS category includes coprophilia, emetophilia, klismaphilia, necrophilia, partialism, telephone scatologia, urophlilia, and zoophilia (American Psychiatric Association, 2000). The DSM-5 also outlines clinical criteria for only certain paraphilic disorders, including voyeuristic disorder, exhibitionistic disorder, frotteuristic disorder, sexual masochism disorder, sexual sadism disorder, pedophilic disorder, fetishistic disorder and transvestic disorder. Examples of the "other specified paraphilic disorders" include, but are not limited to, "recurrent and intense sexual arousal involving telephone scatologia, necrophilia, zoophilia, coprophilia, klismaphilia, urophilia" (American Psychiatric Association, 2013, p. 705).

Zoophilia and Bestiality

One type of paraphilia is zoophilia. As previously mentioned, zoophilia was not introduced to the DSM until 1980 with the publication of the DSM-III. The diagnostic criterion for someone suffering from zoophilia was described with the following language: "the act or fantasy of engaging in sexual activity with animals is repeatedly preferred or the exclusive method of achieving sexual excitement" (American Psychiatric Association, 1980, p. 270). All of the subsequent editions of the DSM placed zoophilia under the paraphilia NOS category with the exception of the current DSM-5 which describes it as an "other specified paraphilic disorder." In addition, anyone who is diagnosed with zoophilia under the DSM must be accompanied by distress or interference with normal functioning (American Psychiatric Association, 2013).

Sexual contact between humans and animals in academic literature has been described using a number of terms, including zoophilia, zoophilism, bestiality, zooerasty, and zoorasty (Aggrawal, 2011). Zoophilia and zoophilism are typically synonymous terms used to describe someone who is both emotionally and sexually attracted to animals. Zoophiles (or zoos) claim to have developed a deep emotional attachment to the animals with which they have sexual contact, often regarding these animals as their lovers. In other words, they feel they truly love the animal (Aggrawal, 2011). Zooerasty and zoorasty are terms that are very similar to bestiality with one notable exception. The zooerast may enjoy sex with an animal even when other normal sexual outlets are available (Aggrawal, 2011). Regardless of the presence of other normal sexual outlets, people who engage in bestiality are most certainly using animals for their own sexual gratification and whether their claim that an emotional bond exists between them and the animal is irrelevant to defining any form of bestiality as anything less than animal abuse.

Aggrawal (2011) identified ten separate classes of zoophiles. Class I zoosexuals include "human-animal role-players." They do not have actual sex with animals; rather, they dress their intimate partners in the likeness of certain animals (i.e., dogs, pandas, foxes, etc.). Such would include members of the "furry fandom." Class II zoosexuals include romantic zoophiles. They keep animals as pets but do not have intimate contact. However, they do achieve some type of mental arousal (i.e., psychosexually stimulated) from having the animal in their proximity. Class III zoosexuals are referred to as zoophilic fantasizers. This group, again, does not have sexual relations with the animals, but rather may masturbate in the presence of their animals. Zoophilic voyeurs and zoophilic exhibitionists are included in this class. Class IV zoosexuals are described as tactile zoophiles. They receive sexual gratification from touching, stroking, or fondling an animal or their genitalia (i.e., frotteurism). Although they receive sexual arousal from the animals, they do not engage in penetration. Class V zoosexuals are also known as fetishistic zoophiles, using animal parts, in particular fur, for sexual aids. In fact, there is a documented case of a woman who used a deer tongue as a masturbatory tool. Aggrawal (2011) believed that individuals in Classes I–V could be treated with behavior modification.

According to Aggrawal (2011), Class VI zoosexuals are characterized as sadistic bestials. This group uses torture (i.e., zoosadism) to receive sexual gratification; however, they do not engage in sexual intercourse with the animals. Class VII zoosexuals comprise opportunistic zoosexuals. They are able to engage in normal sexual relations with people; however, if the opportunity presents itself, they will have sexual relations with animals. They do not develop emotional attachments with animals. Class VIII zoosexuals are referred to as regular zoosexuals. They prefer sex with animals over humans, but can engage in sexual activity with both. Unlike Class VII, they can develop an emotional bond with the animals and sex is a part of the relationship. Class IX zoosexuals are identified as homicidal bestials. People in this class must kill animals to have sex with them (i.e., necrozoophiles). They have the ability to have sexual relations with people but prefer dead animals. Serial killers Jeffrey Dahmer and Henry Lee Lucas would have been included in this category (Hickey 2010). Class X zoosexuals comprise exclusive zoosexuals who only engage in sexual activity with animals to the exclusion of all humans. Aggrawal (2011) argued that those individuals in Classes VI–X must be treated more rigorously and medicated.

Zoophiles may argue that because their preferred sexual animal intimacy is exclusive to adult animals and includes an emotional attachment, it is an alternate sexual orientation that is largely misunderstood and is, therefore, either unacceptable or invisible to most members of society. They believe that their behavior constitutes a sexual preference rather than a form of sexual deviance. Similarly, some researchers may regard bestiality as simply sexual contact between humans and animals or the physical contact humans have with an animal that results in their own sexual arousal (Beetz, 2002, 2004; Miletski, 2002). Such incidents of sexual intimacy include bodily contact, human genital contact with an animal's mouth, masturbation of the animal, and interspecies coitus (Peretti & Rowan, 1982). However, the majority of researchers, such as Ascione (1999), view bestiality as a legitimate form of animal abuse. Furthering this approach, Bierne (1997, 2009) has proposed replacing the term "bestiality" by referring to it as "interspecies sexual assault." Along with animal advocates, these researchers posit that similar to pedophilia, there is an interspecies imbalance of power that makes sexual contact with an animal coercive and that animals are neither able to consent to nor report such an episode (Beirne, 1997, 2009). In addition, sexual activity with an animal often causes pain and sometimes death to that animal.

Using mostly case studies and surveys, the research investigating bestiality has been developing over the past several decades. Generally, the earliest studies focused on the prevalence of bestiality and identified bestialics' demographic characteristics (Hunt, 1974; Kinsey, Pomeroy, & Martin, 1948; Kinsey, Pomeroy, Martin, & Gebhard, 1953), although some of the most recent studies do provide some demographic and prevalence information (Edwards, 2019; Holoyda, Ravipreet, &Welch, 2020; Levitt, Hoffer, & Loper, 2016). Subsequent studies have examined the dynamics of bestiality itself, including perpetrator's abuse and criminal histories, family dynamics, motives for bestiality, and the types of animals involved (Alvarez & Freinhar, 1991; Edwards, 2019; Holoyda, Ravipreet, & Welch, 2020; Hunt, 1974; Kinsey et al., 1948; Levitt, Hoffer, & Loper, 2016; Miletski, 2001; Peretti & Rowan, 1982; Sandnabba, Santtila, Nordling, Beetz, & Alison, 2002; Weigand, Schmidt, & Kleiber, 1999). Many of the most recent studies investigate bestiality as sexual deviance in its relationship with other forms of deviance among institutionalized and non-institutionalized respondents and among juveniles and adults. Specifically, these studies have examined bestiality within the context of animal cruelty and interpersonal violence (Duffield, Hassiotis, & Vizard, 1998; Edwards, 2019; Fleming, Jory, & Burton, 2002; Flynn, 1999; Hensley, Tallichet, & Dutkiewicz, 2010; Hensley, Tallichet, & Singer, 2006; Holoyda, Ravipreet and Welch, 2020; Levitt, Hoffer, & Loper, 2016; Merz-Perez & Heide, 2004; Merz-Perez, Heide, & Silverman, 2001; Ressler, Burgess, Hartman, Douglas, & McCormack, 1986).

Studies of Bestiality Prevalence and Perpetrator Characteristics

In perhaps the earliest study on bestiality, Kinsey et al. (1948) estimated that 8% of the 5,300 white adult American males in their sample had engaged in sexual contact with animals and further suggested that these practices were confined largely to "farm boys" because prevalence rates were much higher among rural males than among their urban counterparts. Specifically, they found that over 40% of adolescent males raised on farms had engaged in bestiality with one-third having started by the age of nine. The most common animals included calves, sheep, donkeys, large fowl (i.e., ducks and geese), dogs, and cats. Males were more likely to engage in vaginal intercourse with the animals and allow the animals to orally stimulate them. In their study of 5,792 women, Kinsey et al. (1953) found that 5% of them reported having sexual contact with an animal. Females in the study reported more involvement with household pets who performed oral sex on them. Twenty-one years later, Hunt (1974) found that only 4.9% of 932 adult men and 1.9% of 1,044 adult women reported having engaged in bestiality. Moreover, Miletski (1999, 2002) found that among 81 bestialic males and 11 bestalic females in her study, only about one-fourth had lived on farms.

Kinsey et al. (1948) found that although frequencies of contact were higher among rural males with lower educational levels, rural males with a college education had a 26% prevalence rate of bestiality compared with a 14% prevalence rate among those who had completed grade school. More recently, Miletski (1999, 2002) also reported that almost half of the men and 45% of the women in her sample who had sexual contact with animals had at least a college education or better. Similarly, Beetz (2002) reported that among the 113 bestialic males in her study, 70% had at least some college education or beyond. However, Flynn (1999) found very low prevalence rates for bestiality among his sample of 267 college students. Specifically, only 2.4% of men and 1.1% of women undergraduate students reported having sexual contact with an animal. Similarly, Holoyda (2017) found that among 84 forensically-committed child sex abusers, just under 4 percent self-reported acts of bestiality. In a later study, Holoyda, Ravipreet, and Welch (2020) found that only 2.6 percent of known sexually violent perpetrators in Virginia between 2003 and 2017 had engaged in bestiality.

However, these percentages are based on limited samples. According to Edwards (2019), 456 adults were arrested in the United States between 1975 and 2015 for bestiality. The number of arrests per year was hardly uniform since there were only one or two arrests each year from 1975 until 2001. Thereafter, the number of bestiality-related arrests noticeably increased in 2004, peaking at 259 between 2011 until 2015. Of the 456 total arrests, just under one-third resulted in convictions. Edwards (2019) notes this may due to the increase in the number of states enacting laws against bestiality, but it could also partially reflect an increase in the behavior itself.

Although more recent studies with limited demographic information show that bestialics tend to be white males between the ages of 18 into their mid-seventies, many were employed and had been or were in intimate relationships, Edwards (2019) found that women accounted for almost 14 percent of offenders in her larger sample. When compared to previous studies using samples of self-reporting animal sex offenders, more women are committing bestiality than was previously known since the number of offenders in her study doubled to a total of 17 between 2012 and 2013. Men also tended to offend later in life than did women with women more often acting with men as a couple.

More recent studies also revealed that animal victims were most often dogs followed by horses, farm animals (chickens, pigs, goats, and cattle), cats, birds, reptiles, and wildlife, such as deer (Edwards, 2019; Holoyda, Ravipreet, & Welch, 2020). In terms of the animal victim-abuser relationship, Leavitt, Hoffer, and Loper (2016) found that the animal victims were abused by either their owners or the current or former owner's intimate partners suggesting the link between animal sexual abuse and domestic violence.

It should be noted that most of the samples in the foregoing studies regarding the prevalence and demographic characteristics of bestialics were non-random and that farm and rural populations have declined dramatically since the Kinsey studies of the late 1940s and 1950s. Indeed, Beirne (2001) has declared that "no valid generalizations can be made about the prevalence of bestiality from the data of Kinsey and colleagues" due to the non-random nature of his sampling and his aggressive interviewing style (p. 47). While later studies attempted to fill more of the void regarding the age, residence, and educational levels of those who engaged in bestiality, relatively little is still known about the prevalence of bestiality and more studies need to be conducted to profile them.

Studies of the Dynamics Associated with Bestiality

Studies examining the dynamics of human/animal sexual contact suggest that bestialic participants may demonstrate a failure to relate to members of their own species. In their case study of an indiscriminant animal and human sex offender since age 15, Wilcox, Foss, and Donathy (2005) found that even in his mid 40s, "Mr. Z" demonstrated cognitive impairment and ungainly social presentation. He admitted to feeling awkward around his potential human sex partners and on occasion had become enraged when rejected by them. Based on interviews, the authors declared him to be socially marginalized, pointing out that at the time of the study, he was often ostracized or "scapegoated" by other members of his treatment group.

Using structured interviews, Peretti and Rowan (1982) investigated the motives of 27 men and 24 women who said they had engaged in habitual acts of bestiality. Men reported that sexual expression was the primary reason for engaging in bestiality (93%), followed by sexual fantasy (81%). Men also indicated that having sex with an animal allowed them to bypass the negotiation process for sex with human partners (74%) or that they could avoid having any human interaction whatsoever (63%). Moreover, the men said that financial reasons contributed to their engagement in bestiality (59%) and that emotional involvement with the animal played an important role

(26%). A majority of the women in the study cited emotional involvement as a reason for engaging in bestiality (88%). Almost as many reported doing so because it did not require human interaction (77%). Not having to negotiate for sex was the reason that over half of the women preferred having sexual contact (58%) followed by desire for sexual expressiveness (46%), sexual fantasy (38%), and financial reasons (21%). Although there were some noteworthy differences between men and women's motivations for engaging in bestiality, foregoing interaction and/or negotiation with other humans were predominant motives for both sexes.

Other researchers have examined the fantasies along with the behaviors of bestialics, and in some cases have found that bestiality may be associated with acts of sadomasochism. In their study of bestiality, Alvarez and Freinhar (1991) surveyed 20 staff members, 20 medical in-patients, and 20 psychiatric in-patients at a single psychiatric institution. From their results, they developed an index indicating overall respondents' fantasies and experiences with bestiality. The scores on this index were significantly higher for male psychiatric patients than for male medical in-patients or male psychiatric staff members. The psychiatric patients were significantly more likely than both medical in-patients and psychiatric staff to have engaged in bestiality or to have fantasized about sexual contact with an animal.

Miletski (1999) found, in a study of 82 bestialic men and 11 bestialic women, that 76% of males and 45% of females reported having sexual fantasies with animals. In addition, the motives that men provided for having sex with an animal included: a sexual attraction to the animal (91%); love and affection for the animal (74%); the animals being accepting and easy to please (67%); no human partners available (12%); and too shy to have sex with humans (7%). Females reported the following reasons for having sex with the animals: a sexual attraction (100%), love and affection (67%), and because the animal wanted it (67%). The majority of the sample preferred sexual activity with the dogs (87% of the males and 100% of the females) and/or horses (81% of the males and 73% of the females). Interestingly, 8% of the male subjects wanted to stop having sex with animals while none of the females did.

Other recent studies also demonstrate that among both juvenile and adult populations, bestiality may be associated with psychological disorders that include aggressive tendencies and behaviors toward humans. Duffield, Hassiotis, and Vizard (1998) found that seven out of 70 youths in their sample who were sent to a psychiatric center for juvenile sexual offenders had engaged in bestiality. These youthful interspecies sex offenders showed a disproportionately higher rate of mental disorders compared with the rest of the sample and were also more likely to have been neglected or abused in their homes. Moreover, their bestiality was almost never an isolated paraphilia. Indeed, many of them planned, targeted, and created situations for abusing both animal and human victims alike. As a result of their findings, these investigators argued that bestiality in the sexual history of a juvenile offender was a warning sign that other sexual paraphilias may be present and that such as individual may be at greater risk for sexually abusing another person in the future.

In their study of 381 youthful offenders from three Midwestern juvenile institutions, Fleming, Jory, and Burton (2002) administered questionnaires inquiring about juvenile offenders' exposure to sexual abuse and childhood trauma, their level of sexual aggression, and the offender's family dynamics. Among their sample, 42.3% reported committing sexual offenses only against humans, while 6.3% reported previous sexual contact with an animal. Moreover, 23 of the 24 individuals who reported previous acts of bestiality also reported committing sexual offenses against humans. The 24 juveniles in the bestiality group were further questioned in detail about the nature of their reported sexual acts with animals. Among them, 16.7% reported having placed their mouth on the genitals of an animal, 58.3% reported having rubbed their genitals against an animal, 41.7% reported having committed penile penetration, 25% reported having penetrated an animal with a finger, and 8.3% reported having inserted an object into an animal's genitalia.

Further analysis of the study participants' family dynamics showed that members of both the bestiality group and the sex offender group reported a higher incidence of negative family communication than did non-sexual offenders, with individuals in the bestiality group indicating significantly less positive family communication than did individuals from the sex offender group. Both bestiality and sex offender group members also reported significantly lower levels of family attachment and family adaptability than the non-sexual offender group. Significant differences in positive family environment were also found between each group, with the bestiality group suffering from the most negative family environment followed by the sex offender group, with the non-sexual offender group indicating the most positive family environment (Fleming et al., 2002). Specifically, as one might expect, members of both the bestiality and sex offender groups suffered from significantly more emotional neglect, and more emotional, physical, and sexual abuse than the non-sexual offender group. Bestiality group members were found to have suffered significantly more emotional neglect and emotional abuse than the sex offender group, but not more physical or sexual abuse. Finally, the authors found that members of the bestiality group reported significantly higher rates of victimization and offending than did members of either the sex offender or the non-sexual offender groups.

Miletski (1999) found that among the 82 bestialic men in her non-random sample, 17% reported having sadomasochist fantasies and one-quarter said they had either forced someone or been forced by someone to perform a sex act that either they or their partner did not want to do. In a later study of bestialic men, Sandnabba et al. (2002) collected data from questionnaires sent to members of two sadomasochistic clubs. They found that of 12 of the 186 respondents (6.4%) reported having sexual contact with an animal during the past year. After further investigation using a matched-groups design due to the small sample size, the authors found that the men's engagement in bestiality most often followed the onset of sadomasochistic sexual practices. Moreover, the bestiality group was significantly more likely to engage in sexual experimentation than their control groups.

Studies of the Potential Link between Bestiality and Later Interpersonal Violence

Ultimately, then, it is possible that bestiality may also be a potentially significant predictor of interpersonal violence. One of the first studies to recognize and explore this potential relationship was conducted by Ressler et al. (1986). They compared the characteristics of 12 sexual killers who had been sexually abused during childhood with 16 sexual killers who had not and found that the sexually abused killers reported higher rates of animal cruelty in general, as well as higher rates of bestiality in particular. Later studies examining the potential bestialics have for committing further violence have found that they have the highest crossover rate for deviant sexual offending (Abel, Becker, Cunningham-Rathner, & Rouleau, 1987; Abel & Rouleau, 1990). More specifically, Abel and his colleagues have declared that individuals convicted of sexual offenses with animals were discovered to be the most indiscriminant and deviant of sexual offenders and that they showed the greatest degree of crossover, meaning that they moved from one type of offending to another, such as abusing animals to abusing humans. This finding has been tempered by Wilcox et al. (2005) who suggest that the risk of crossover may be lower among some bestialics than others. However, they warn that having sexual contact with an animal is not necessarily performed as a substitute for sexual contact with or the sexual assault of another human and that some bestialics may be equally likely to offend against an animal as they would a human.

More recent studies reveal a significant co-occurring relationship between animal and human sexual abuse in the backgrounds of 150 adult men arrested for neglect, physical and sexual abuse of animals between 2004 and 2009 (Levitt, Hoffer, & Loper, 2016). Specifically, among their sample 18 percent had been arrested for sex crimes, such as rape or child molestation, and 41 percent had been arrested for interpersonal violence. Moreover, Edwards (2019) found that 45.6 percent of the sexual animal abusers among their offender sample either sexually exploited or abused children and adults either prior or concurrent to their most recent arrest.

In their study of sexually violent perpetrators in Virginia from 2003 to 2017, Holoyda, Ravipreet, and Welch (2020) found that the bestialics in the sample were more likely to have been victims of child sexual abuse themselves than those who had not sexually abused animals. They noted that "for individuals with significant trauma experience, animals may seem like a safer, less aggressive, and less emotionally distressing outlet for sexual behavior" (Holoyda, Ravipreet, & Welch, 2020: 362). In turn, they also found that bestialics were more likely to report having committed child sexual abuse than nonbestialics. This finding supports previous studies by researchers who have concluded that animal sexual abuse is a good predictor of pedophilia. Moreover, Holoyda, Ravipreet, and Welch (2020) also found that bestialics also are at greater risk for committing other forms of animal cruelty.

Finally, there are several studies that directly test the importance of animal sexual abuse and later interpersonal violence. In their landmark study investigating the relationship between childhood animal abuse and interpersonal violence, Merz-Perez and Heide (2004) and Merz-Perez et al. (2001) discovered the commission of bestiality among members of their inmate sample of violent and nonviolent incarcerated offenders. Using structured interviews with 45 violent and 45 nonviolent inmates to examine the specific acts of animal cruelty, the researchers found three violent offenders (6.6%) reported having engaged in bestiality while no nonviolent offenders reported having engaged in any such behavior. Two of these cases involved pet animals while the third involved a farm animal. In the latter case, this violent subject who was a repeat sex offender had been convicted as an adolescent incarcerated in a reformatory for sodomizing a pig (Merz-Perez & Heide, 2004).

In the first investigation of the association between abusers' demographic characteristics along with self-reported bestiality and later interpersonal violence, Hensley et al. (2006) surveyed a sample of 261 inmates housed in one maximum- and two medium-security Southern correctional facilities. Specifically, they examined demographic characteristics (race, education level, and residence while growing up), being convicted of a personal crime, the number of personal crimes for which the respondent had been convicted, and how those factors affected acts of bestiality. Of the 261 inmates, 16 (16.3%) indicated they had engaged in bestiality. There were no significant racial or residential differences between the 16 bestialics and the overall sample. Of those in the bestiality group, about one-third (31.3%) had less than an eighth-grade education relative to only 9.2% of the sample. Moreover, an additional 31.3% of inmates in the bestiality group completed high school compared to 39.6% of the sample. They also found that three-quarters of the bestiality group had been convicted of a personal crime compared with 47.9% of the non-bestialic sample. Finally, 31.4% of the bestialic group had been convicted of more than three personal crimes compared to only 5.4% of the rest of the sample. All three of these relative differences between bestialics and non-bestialics in the sample regarding formal education, conviction of a personal crime and its frequency were statistically significant. In the same study, they also found that inmates with less education and those who had been convicted of committing crimes against people on one or more occasions were more likely to have had sex with animals during their childhood or adolescence than those in the overall sample.

Four years later, Hensley et al. (2010) sought to replicate their previous study by surveying 180 inmates at a medium- and maximum-security prison in another Southern state. Their investigation also examined whether inmates who had engaged in childhood bestiality differed from those who did not in terms of race, childhood residence, education, commission of a personal crime, and the number of personal crimes committed. Similar to their earlier findings, there were no significant differences between the study sample and inmates who had engaged in bestiality with regard to race or residence while growing up. However, in this study, there were also no significant differences in the educational level between bestialics and the sample inmates. At the same time, as Hensley et al. found in their 2006 study, there were significant differences between the sample and inmates who had engaged in bestiality regarding their commission of a personal crime and the frequency with which they did so. In other words, inmates who had engaged in youthful bestiality were more likely to commit adult interpersonal crimes on two or more occasions as compared to non-bestialics in the sample (Hensley et al., 2010).

Theorizing about the Bestiality Link

The study of animal abuse, including bestiality, as a potential harbinger of later interpersonal violence provides us with an opportunity to develop a more conceptual understanding of this phenomenon. Previous studies about animal cruelty, including the sexual abuse of animals, have supported social learning theory and, in particular, two relatively opposing explanations: the graduation (or progression) hypothesis and the generalized deviance hypothesis. Studies of bestiality per se have also supported the sexually polymorphous theory.

Bestiality is one of several different forms of animal cruelty. As Beetz (2005) has noted, the data have shown that bestiality is found most often among violent offenders, sex offenders, and the sexually abused. At this point in the research on the link between animal cruelty (including bestiality) and interpersonal violence, researchers are divided over the specification of the time-ordered sequence of animal abuse and interpersonal violence. On the one hand, the graduation hypothesis posits that individuals who begin abusing animals during their youth move on or "graduate" to committing violent acts against humans. The studies by Hensley et al. (2006, 2010) demonstrated that inmates who reported committing bestiality as youths were more likely to be convicted of or to commit personal crimes as adults.

On the other the hand, according to the generalized deviance hypothesis, there is no specific time order to the sequence of violence committed against animals and people by deviant individuals such that personal crimes are no more likely to follow the abuse of animals than the reverse. A few studies have supported this hypothesis, such as the study by Arluke, Levin, Luke, and Ascione (1999) that compared the criminal records of 153 animal abusers with a matched control group of 153 nonabusers. Although animal abusers were five times more likely to have been convicted of violent crimes than nonabusers, generally there was no specific order to their crimes against animals relative to humans.

None of the studies that supported the generalized deviance hypothesis investigated the sexual abuse of animals, with the exception of an Australian study by Alys, Wilson, Clarke, and Toman (2009). Their study compared 20 incarcerated male sexual homicide offenders, 20 male sex offenders from an outpatient treatment program, and 20 male college students. While the results actually supported both hypotheses, of importance here is that the sexual murderers reported significantly more sexual abuse of animals than either the sex offenders or the controls. Moreover, none of the sex offenders reported abusing animals as youths while almost all of the sexual homicide offenders did.

As Flynn (2011) has noted, the youthful commission of animal abuse may not be a determinative risk factor for later adult interpersonal violence, but nor should it be disregarded. The findings from the foregoing studies suggest that perhaps when animal cruelty is refined in terms of the form it takes, then that risk may become more determinative. Bestiality as a form of animal abuse or, as Beirne (1997, 2009) has declared, as "interspecies sexual assault" is significant in the present discussion since the studies that have been conducted linking youthful bestiality and adult interpersonal violence also support the sexually polymorphous theory discussed by Merz-Perez and Heide (2004).

According to Merz-Perez and Heide (2004), the sexual abuse of animals (and humans for that matter) provides the perpetrator with a psychological and/or physiological "release" because for them sex and aggression have been learned together. Infantile sexuality can assume a number of different forms. In certain individuals, "perverse sexual activities" are violent ones that fall outside the parameters of acceptable behavioral norms. These activities, including bestiality, occur when "sexuality and aggression have become developmentally fused, and the two are mutually inclusive in the psyche of the offender" (Merz-Perez & Heide 2004, p. 66). These sex acts are acts of violence during which animals, like humans, are reduced to the status of objects to be manipulated, exploited, and controlled. It could be speculated that as children, these now adult perpetrators were exposed to adults engaging in violent sexual behaviors in the home or elsewhere. Clearly, the foregoing studies represent only a starting point for future research in this area because much is still unknown about those individuals who have had sexual encounters with animals and their propensity for interpersonal aggression.

Crush Videos

Research on the topic of animal crushing, however, is quite limited. Though laws and legislation have been enacted in Washington DC since the late 1990s, criminal justice scholars have yet to give the topic of crushing the attention it deserves. Even with the lack of academic research, internet sites such as stopcrush.com and peta.com are informative in educating and preventing the spread of animal crushing videos. As these incidents of animal cruelty begin to increase worldwide, there will be a need for further research in order to understand what causes this behavior and if it could possibly lead to interpersonal violence.

Crush videos graphically depict the beating, burning, cutting, stabbing, skinning and killing of small animals (The Mary T. and Frank L. Hoffman Family Foundation, 2008). These films serve as sexual gratification for those who can only be aroused by the torturing of animals. Crush films can be broken down into two categories, soft crush and hard crush (Humane Society of the United States, 2010). The most common form of crushing is soft crush; this is the torture of invertebrates, such as worms and spiders. Less common, but more horrific is the practice of hard crush. Hard crush is the act of inflicting pain on larger animals such as cats and dogs. Though the animals differ from film to film, most crushing films show females from the legs down physically dominating and brutally destroying small creatures with high-heeled shoes (The Mary T. and Frank L. Hoffman Family Foundation, 2008). The women in these films make anywhere from $25 to $1,000 per video, while viewers pay anywhere between $80 for one clip to $200 for three clips (Ahyong, 2011). To date, this viral commodity has proven to be as difficult to regulate as it is profitable (Humane Society of the United States, 2010).

Hard crush videos begin with a woman "teasing" the viewer by pinning the animal down with her stiletto heel and slashing its eyes and stomach with their other heel in a clear and torturous display of dominance over the animal (Brady, 2007). After the initial "teasing" is complete, the torturer takes the animal's life by crushing it between their stilettoes, buttocks, or breasts. With most individuals, this fetish usually begins with an interest in soft crush. Once viewers are no longer sexual aroused by watching the crushing of insects, they move on to larger animals such as frogs and mice. It is believed to be that once the viewer's sexual gratification runs its course with small insects and small animals, they begin to explore larger game which customarily consists of cats and dogs (Brady, 2007). Once known as a repulsive but rare fetish, the development of the internet and streaming video has allowed for crushing films to reach a larger and wider audience. Moreover, because these videos can be uploaded anonymously and perpetrators' faces are hidden from view, the detection and prosecution of those who produce and participate in them is almost impossible.

Even so, there are laws that ban crush films. In 1999, the first statute was enacted making it illegal to possess, create, and sell a depiction of animal cruelty (18 USC §48). However, in 2008, the United States Court of Appeals for the Third Circuit ruled that the ban on the sale and procession of such films was a violation of the Constitution under the 1st Amendment (*United States v. Stevens*, 2008). Due to the vagueness of the legislation that was enacted in 1999, the United States Supreme Court affirmed the decision made by the United States Court of Appeals for the Third Circuit (Liptak, 2010). In its creation, the initial legislation did not differentiate between animal cruelty and the art of hunting. It was not until President Barack Obama signed the Animal Crush Video Prohibition Act of 2010 that clarity was given to the previous law by making it illegal to create, sell, distribute, advertise, market, or exchange crush films (Animal Crush Video Prohibition Act of 2010, 2010).

In July 2012, Ashley Nicole Richards and Brent Wayne Justice from Houston, Texas were arrested for making, producing, and distributing crush videos. They were the first defendants to be charged under the 2010 federal statute. Ms. Richards used weapons including meat cleavers, knives, and high heels to torture and crush dogs and cats. Both defendants were charged with five counts of animal cruelty under the 2010 statute, which carried a maximum of 45 years in prison. In addition, prosecutors added two counts of obscenity independent of the crush statute. However, in April 2013, a U.S. District Court Judge threw out the crush video charges on First Amendment grounds and that animal crush videos were not obscene (Malisow, 2013). He argued that the Animal Crush Video Prohibition Act of 2010 was unconstitutional and too broad. On May 29, 2014, however, Ms. Richards pled guilty to three counts of animal cruelty and was sentenced to 10 years in prison while Mr. Justice remained in jail (ABC13, 2014).

On June 13, 2014, the U.S. Court of Appeals for the Fifth Circuit ruled that the 2010 law was constitutional because it prohibits obscenity not protected by the First Amendment and that Congress has an interest in preventing the violence depicted in those videos (Dunn, 2014). The Court reversed and remanded the case from the U.S. District Court in the Southern District of Texas, reinstating the charges against Ms. Richards and Mr. Justice.

Ultimately, both Justice and Richards were convicted and sentenced under the 2010 statute (Federal Bureau of Investigation, 2016; United States Department of Justice, 2016). During 2016, Justice, who was convicted in state court and sentenced to 50 years in prison in February, was found guilty on federal charges in May and sentenced a few months later to 57 months in federal prison. Richards, who pled guilty to the charges against her in state court, was sentenced to 10 years in prison in 2015. In federal court, prosecutors determined that Justice produced, advertised, and sold the crush videos, while Richards was the performer in front of the camera. According to a plea deal, she testified against Justice.

In an effort to further narrow the focus of prohibitions associated with the production of crush videos that depict the torture and slow suffering death of animals (mammals, birds, reptiles, and amphibians) for humans' sexual arousal and gratification, Congress enacted the Preventing Animal Cruelty and Torture Act in November 2019 (H.R. 724). This federal law, that had bipartisan support and was signed into law by President Trump, retains the existing prohibitions for knowingly making these videos and for their interstate distribution, but it also specifically prohibits the intentional crushing of animals and mandates punishment for such acts by fines and a seven-year maximum prison term. Exceptions are clarified as unintentional acts or those performed during medical or scientific procedures, euthanasia or in order to protect persons or their property, or both.

However, enacting new laws prohibiting the creation, distribution and sale of crush videos is just a beginning. Apprehending perpetrators and enforcing these laws is what actually stops this form of animal cruelty. Recently, the popularity of crush videos has spawned a counter movement among animal activists to become internet "sleuths" (Orecchio-Egresitz, 2020). For example, a network of animal activists determined to track down an Indiana woman who was making crush films gained national recognition for infiltrating her internet-based operation, gathering evidence and turning her over to state law enforcement. Another development in publicizing the dangers of crush videos for both animals and humans was the airing of the Netflix docuseries, "Don't F**k with Cats," showing how a would-be murderer's obsession with animal-torture videos led to the perpetrator's eventual act of homicide and how a grassroots effort by animal advocates led to his detection and capture. It is vitally important to raise public awareness and to apprehend these criminals, but for every case solved there are still many more in the making in what seems like a never-ending cycle.

Bestiality Laws

Currently, the federal government does not provide any criminal statutes against bestiality, with the exception of the Uniform Code of Military Justice (UCMJ). Interestingly, immediately prior to the passage of the National Defense Authorization Act for Fiscal Year 2012, Article 125 of the UCMJ was almost repealed (National Defense Authorization Act for Fiscal Year 2012, 2011). The language banning sodomy and bestiality was dropped from the original bill, only to be added after criticism from the People for the Ethical Treatment of Animals (PETA) and the Family Research Council, a conservative group (Morgenstern, 2011). In December 2013, a provision of the National Defense Authorization Act of 2014 repealed the ban on consensual sodomy found in Article 125 and added a provision that specifically bans bestiality (National Defense Authorization Act for Fiscal Year 2014, 2013). Specifically, Article 125 of the UCMJ states that any person who engages in "unnatural carnal copulation with an animal is guilty of bestiality and shall be punished as a court martial shall direct" (10 USC §925—Art 125). This provision applies to military personnel only.

Without any other such federal prohibitions of bestiality, banning sexual acts with an animal has been left to the states. Currently, 48 states have criminal laws making sexual activity between a human and an animal either a felony or misdemeanor (Wisch, 2021). Only New Mexico and West Virginia (and Washington DC) still do not have laws against bestiality. Most recently in 2021, Wyoming and Hawaii made a sexual act with an animal illegal. Beyond possible jail time and fines, some states require psychological or psychiatric treatment at the offender's expense and may also ban the offender from owning or being around animals for a stipulated time period following their release. Moreover, while court cases in Michigan and Kansas have not resulted in obligatory sex offender registration for convicted bestialics, in 2015, a California court upheld a contrary ruling for a repeat offender and in 2017, the Texas statute made sex offender registration mandatory (Wisch, 2021). It is possible that other states could eventually follow suit. Below is a brief review of those states that make bestiality a felony and those that deem it a misdemeanor.

Felony State Statutes

Of the 48 states that make bestiality a crime, 22 states now provide felony penalties for a first violation of bestiality statutes. Those states are: Arizona, Delaware, Georgia, Idaho, Illinois, Indiana, Kentucky, Louisiana, Massachusetts, Michigan, Mississippi, Montana, New Jersey, North Carolina, Oklahoma, Rhode Island, South Carolina, South Dakota, Tennessee, Texas, Virginia, and Washington (HSUS, 2021; Oil City News, 2021; Wisch, 2021, 2022).

In Arizona, anyone who engages in any sexual contact with a dead or live animal is punishable under a Class 6 felony, the same felony classification as used in South Dakota and Virginia (AZ ST §13-1411; SD ST §22-22-42; VA ST §18.2-361). People convicted under Arizona law may also be required to undergo a psychological assessment and pay for their own counseling. In addition, if the animal was taken to an animal shelter, the person convicted of bestiality may have to reimburse the animal shelter (AZ ST §13-1411). These same stipulations are also found in the Illinois, Tennessee, and Washington statutes on bestiality. All three of these states also require that people convicted of sex crimes against an animal relinquish any animals that currently reside in their residence and may prevent them from having animals in the future (IL ST CH 720 §5/12-35; TN ST §39-14-214; WA ST 16.52.205).

In Delaware, "a person is guilty of bestiality when the person intentionally engages in any sexual act involving sexual contact, penetration or intercourse with the genitalia of an animal or intentionally causes another person to engage in any such sexual act with an animal for purposes of sexual gratification." It is considered a class D felony in Delaware (DE ST TI 11 §775) and Indiana (IN ST 35-46-3-14).

The Georgia bestiality statute states, "a person commits the offense of bestiality when he performs or submits to any sexual act with an animal involving the sex organs of the one and the mouth, anus, penis, or vagina of the other" (GA ST §16-6-6). Anyone convicted of bestiality in Georgia has committed a felony punishable by no less than one year and no more than five years in prison. Anyone who violates the buggery statute in South Carolina faces a maximum of five years in prison or a fine of not less than $500 or both (SC ST §16-15-120). However, in Idaho, the minimum sentence for committing bestiality is no less than five years in prison (ID ST §18-6605) and in Rhode Island the minimum is seven years with a maximum of 20 years (RI ST §11-10-1).

In Mississippi, Montana, and Oklahoma, the maximum number of years for violating the state's crime against nature law is 10 years (MS ST §97-29-59; MCA 45-8-218; OK ST T. 21 §886). However, the Michigan statute sets a maximum of 15 years but further states that, "if such person was at the time of the said offense a sexually delinquent person, [the crime] may be punishable by imprisonment in the state prison for an indeterminate term, the minimum of which shall be 1 day and the maximum of which shall be life" (M.C.L.A. 750.158). The Massachusetts bestiality law states, "whoever commits the abominable and detestable crime against nature, either with mankind or with a beast, shall be punished by imprisonment in the state prison for not more than twenty years" (MA ST 272 §34).

Misdemeanor State Statutes

Twenty-six states also provide misdemeanor penalties for violating bestiality statutes. Those states are: Alabama, Alaska, Arkansas, California, Colorado, Connecticut, Florida, Hawaii, Iowa, Kansas, Maine, Maryland, Minnesota, Missouri, Nebraska, Nevada, New Hampshire, New York, North Dakota, Ohio, Oregon, Pennsylvania, Utah, Vermont, Wisconsin and Wyoming (HSUS, 2021; Oil City News, 2021; Wisch, 2022). In most of these states that allow for misdemeanor punishment for bestiality, the statutes are sparsely worded. However, in Iowa, a person convicted of bestiality is guilty of an aggravated misdemeanor and must submit to a psychological evaluation and treatment at that person's expense (IA ST § 717C.1). According to the Minnesota statute, "Whoever carnally knows a dead body or an animal or bird is guilty of bestiality, which is a misdemeanor. If knowingly done in the presence of another, the person may be sentenced to imprisonment for not more than one year or to payment of a fine of not more than $3,000 or both" (MN ST 609.294). Most recently, sex with an animal became a misdemeanor in Wyoming on July 1, 2021 punishable by a year in jail and a $1,000 maximum fine (WY ST 6-4-601). This was the result of a 2020 case after a man was caught on camera having sexual intercourse with a mare and a foal after hours at a stable in Sweetwater County, WY (Oil City News, 2021).

In Missouri, a person who commits unlawful sex with an animal once is guilty of a misdemeanor, but if that person has already been convicted of that crime, it is a Class D felony (MO ST 566.111). In Nevada, if the animal is seriously injured or killed, the gross misdemeanor act becomes a felony. The statute criminalizes sexual conduct with an animal, promoting the same activity for another person or making any video for the purpose of sexual gratification and is punishable by the usual fines and jail time along with psychological evaluation and treatment if recommended, forfeiture of animal ownership and being in an animal's presence and restitution costs of the animal's veterinary bills (Wisch, 2021). Most recently, in Hawaii, state legislators made second offense bestiality a Class C felony (five years in prison plus a $10,000 fine) and if committed in the presence of or forcing the participation of a minor, would be a Class B felony (10 years in prison and $25,000 fine). Moreover, the perpetrator could be mandated to receive psychological or psychiatric treatment at their own expense and be banned from owning, living or working with any animal after serving their term (Wisch, 2022). This legislation cited the finding that animal sexual violence is, in many instances, a precursor for other violent crimes against people, including child sexual abuse (HSUS, 2021).

Conclusion

During the past two decades, animal welfare has become an important social issue, particularly as companion animals are seen more and more as family members and less as "pets." At the same time, there is a growing public awareness that animals' welfare and rights are a reflection on the goodness of human society. Just in the past few years, several more states have enacted laws against bestiality bringing the total to 48, but two states and our own nation's capital lag behind. Among professionals in related fields and disciplines, there is a much greater recognition for the transspecies link between animal sexual abuse and human interpersonal violence. And although the body of research on animal sexual assault is growing, it is very slow and sparse.

We need much more research by willing and capable academics that is based on common definitions of terms, criteria and effective agreed upon measures of animal sexual assault. Otherwise, studies will not complement each other and our knowledge base will be too random to inform public policy and ameliorative programs (Maher & Pierpoint, 2020). Concurrently, we need to support and foster the continued education of law enforcement, probation officers, prosecutors, judges, and legislators. This underscores the need for a much more concerted effort of cross-reporting among medical and veterinary professionals, animal welfare agencies and volunteer groups, social service workers, and law enforcement to determine the dynamic connection between animal sexual assault and other forms of violence, including the sexual abuse of children and adults.

For example, beginning in 2016, the FBI's National Incident-Based Reporting System (NIBRS), had law enforcement report on all forms of animal cruelty, including bestiality, to log and track this information because of the growing recognition that those who engage in animal cruelty also commit violent crimes against people. But according to Edwards (2019), only about one-third of law enforcement agencies nationwide report these statistics to the FBI. Moreover, in a number of states veterinarians, animal control officers, and shelter workers are not required to report suspected animal abuse (Edwards, 2019; Wisch, 2020). Indeed, in approximately 14 states where there is no such requirement and no immunity laws, veterinarians may not report suspected animal abuse because they can be sued for libel or defamation by the animal's owner (Wisch, 2020).

In sum, a good deal of progress has been made toward protecting animals and punishing their abusers. At the same time animals' pain and suffering are still too often ignored or undetected. Clearly, much work remains to be done because it is our responsibility to give animals their voice as victims in a world dominated by humans.

References

ABC13. (2014) Houston woman sentenced for animal cruelty over "crush" videos. Retrieved from http://abc13.com/pets/woman-sentenced-for-animal-cruelty-over-crushvideos/83489/.

Abel, G. G., Becker, J., Cunningham-Rathner, J., & Rouleau, J. L. (1987). Self-reported sex crimes of 561 non-incarcerated paraphilias. *Journal of Interpersonal Violence*, 2, 3–25.

Abel, G. G., & Rouleau, J. L. (1990). The nature and extent of sexual assault. In W. L. Marshall, D. R. Laws, & H. E. Barbaree (Eds.), *Handbook of sexual assault: Issues, theories, and treatment of the offender* (pp. 9–12). Plenum Press.

Aggrawal, A. (2011). A new classification of zoophilia. *Journal of Forensic and Legal Medicine, 18*, 73–78.

Ahyong, V. (2011). Crush fetish video making couple to be charged for animal cruelty. Retrieved from http://www.environmentphilippines.com/2011/07/news-crush-fetish-video-making-couple.html.

Alvarez, W. A., & Freinhar, J. P. (1991). A prevalence study of bestiality (zoophilia) in psychiatric patients, medial in-patients, and psychiatric staff. *International Journal of Psychosomantics, 38*, 1–4.

Alys, L., Wilson, J. C., Clarke, J., & Toman, P. (2009). Developmental animal cruelty and its correlates in sexual homicide offenders and sex offenders. In A. Linzey (Ed.), *The link between animal abuse and human violence* (pp. 145–162). Sussex Academic Press.

American Psychiatric Association. (1952). *Diagnostic and statistical manual of mental disorders* (1st ed.). Author.

American Psychiatric Association. (1962). *Diagnostic and statistical manual of mental disorders* (2nd ed.). Author.

American Psychiatric Association. (1980). *Diagnostic and statistical manual of mental disorders* (3rd ed.). Author.

American Psychiatric Association. (1987). *Diagnostic and statistical manual of mental disorders* (3rd rev. ed.). Author.

American Psychiatric Association. (1994). *Diagnostic and statistical manual of mental disorders* (4th ed.). Author.

American Psychiatric Association. (2000). *Diagnostic and statistical manual of mental disorders* (4th ed., text revision). Author.

American Psychiatric Association (2013). *Diagnostic and statistical manual of mental disorders* (5th ed.). Author.

Animal Crush Video Prohibition Act of 2010, H.R.5566, 111th Congress, 1st Session. (2010).

Arluke, A., Levin, J., Luke, C., & Ascione, F. R. (1999). The relationship to animal abuse to violence and other forms of antisocial behavior. *Journal of Interpersonal Violence, 14*(9), 963–975.

Ascione, F. R. (1999). The abuse of animals and human interpersonal violence. In F. R. Ascione & P. Arkow (Eds.), *Child abuse, domestic violence, and animal abuse: Linking the circles of compassion for prevention and intervention* (pp. 50–61). Purdue University Press.

Beetz, A. M. (2002). *Love, violence, and sexuality in relationships between humans and animals*. Shaker Verlag.

Beetz, A. M. (2004). Bestiality and zoophilia: A scarcely investigated phenomenon between crime, paraphilia, and love. *Journal of Forensic Psychology Practice, 4*(2), 1–36.

Beetz, A. M. (2005). Bestiality and zoophilia: Associations with violence and sex offending. In A. M. Beetz & A. L. Podberscek (Eds.), *Bestiality and zoophilia: Sexual relations with animals* (p. 46–70). Purdue University Press.

Beirne, P. (1997). Rethinking bestiality: Towards a concept of interspecies sexual assault. *Theoretical Criminology, 1*(3), 317–340.

Beirne, P. (2001). Peter Singer's 'heavy petting' and the politics of animal sexual assault. *Critical Criminology, 10*, 43–55.

Beirne, P. (2009) *Confronting Animal Abuse: Law, Criminology and Human-Animal Relations*. Rowman & Littlefield.

Brady, L. (2007). Crush videos: Animal torture and murder as a fetish. Retrieved from http://voices.yahoo.com/crush-videos-animal-torture-murder-as-fetish-324553.html?cat=17.

Duffield, G., Hassiotis, A., & Vizard, E. (1998). Zoophilia in young sexual abusers. *The Journal of Forensic Psychiatry, 9*(2), 294–304.

Dunn, L. (2014). Fifth circuit rules that animal crush video law prohibits obscenity and Congress has significant interest in preventing animal cruelty. Retrieved from http://aldf.org/blog/fifth-circuit-rules-that-animal-crush-video-law-prohibits-obscenity-and-congress-has-significant-interst-in preventing-animal-cruelty/.

Edwards, M.J. (2019) Arrest and prosecution of animal sex abuse (bestiality) offenders in the United States, 1975–2015. *Journal of the American Academy of Psychiatry and the Law* online. 47(3):335–346.

Federal Bureau of Investigation. (2016). "Animal Cruelty: Houston 'Crush' Cases were First under Federal Statute." September 29. Retrieved from: https://www.fbi.gov/news/stories/houston-animal-crush-cases-were-first-under-federal-statute.

Fleming, W. M., Jory, B., & Burton, D. L. (2002). Characteristics of juvenile offenders admitting to sexual activity with nonhuman animals. *Society & Animals, 10*(1), 31–45.

Flynn, C. P. (1999). Animal abuse in childhood and later support for interpersonal violence in families. *Society & Animals, 7*(2), 161–172.

Flynn, C. P. (2011). Examining the links between animal abuse and human violence. *Crime Law and Social Change, 55*, 453–468.

Flynn, C. (2012) Understanding Animal Abuse: A Sociological Analysis. Lantern.

Humane Society of the United States. (2021). "Hawaiian legislature passes animal protection measures." Retrieved from: https://www.humanesociety.org/news/hawaiian-legislature-passes-animal-protection-measures.

Hensley, C., Tallichet, S. E., & Dutkiewicz, E. L. (2010). Childhood bestiality: A potential precursor to adult interpersonal violence. *Journal of Interpersonal Violence, 25*(3), 557–567.

Hensley, C., Tallichet, S. E., & Singer, S. D. (2006). Exploring the possible link between childhood and adolescent bestiality and interpersonal violence. *Journal of Interpersonal Violence, 21*(7), 910–923.

Hickey, E. W. (2010). *Serial murderers and their victims* (5th ed.). Wadsworth Cengage Learning.

Holoyda, B. (2017). Bestiality in forensically committed sexual offenders: a case series. *Journal of Forensic Science*. 62:541–4.

Holoyda, B., Ravipreet, G. and Welch, K. M. (2020). Bestiality among sexually violent predators. *Journal of American Psychiatry Law*. 48: 358–64.

H. R. 724. Preventing Animal Cruelty and Torture Act or the PACT Act. Public Law No: 116–72(11/25/2019). Retrieved from: https://www.congress.gov/bill/116th-congress/house-bill/724.

Humane Society of the United States. (2010). Animal crush videos: Senate committee testimony. Retrieved from: http://www.humanesociety.org/news/resources/animal_crush_video_senate.html.

Hunt, M. (1974). *Sexual behavior in the 1970s.* Playboy Press.

Kinsey, A. C., Pomeroy, B., & Martin, C. E. (1948). *Sexual behavior in the human male.* W. B. Saunders.

Kinsey, A. C., Pomeroy, W. B., Martin, C. E. & Gebhard, P. H. (1953). *Sexual behavior in the human female.* W. B. Saunders.

Levitt, L., Hoffer, T. and Loper, A. (2016). Criminal histories of a subsample of animal cruelty offenders. *Aggression and Violent Behavior*, 30:48–58.

Liptak, A. (2010). Justices reject ban on videos of animal cruelty. *New York Times.* Retrieved from http://www.nytimes.com/2010/04/21/us/21scotus.html?ref=dogfighting.

Maher, J. and Pierpoint, H. (2020). A violent interspecies relationship: The case of animal sexual assault. In Brisman, A. and South, N. (Eds.) International Handbook of Green Criminology, second edition (pp. 497–511). Routledge.

The Mary T. and Frank L. Hoffman Family Foundation (2008). About crush. Retrieved from http://www.stopcrush.org/?page_id=2.

Malisow, C. (2013). Open season: Do laws against animal crushing videos violate free speech? Retrieved from http://www.houstonpress.com/2013-05-16/news/ashley-nicole-richards/full/.

Merz-Perez, L., Heide, K. M., & Silverman, I. J. (2001). Childhood cruelty to animals and subsequent violence against humans. *International Journal of Offender Therapy and Comparative Criminology, 45*(5), 556–573.

Merz-Perez, L., & Heide, K. M. (2004). *Animal cruelty: Pathway to violence against people.* Rowman & Littlefield Publishers, Inc.

Miletski, H. (1999). *Bestiality—zoophilia: An exploratory study.* San Francisco: The Institute for the Advanced Study of Human Sexuality.

Miletski, H. (2000). Bestiality/zoophilia: An exploratory study. *Scandinavian Journal of Sexology, 3*, 149–150.

Miletski, H. (2001). Zoophilia—implications for therapy. *Journal of Sex Education and Therapy, 26*, 85–89.

Miletski, H. (2002). *Understanding bestiality and zoophilia.* East-West Publishing, LLC.

Miller, C. (2001). Childhood animal cruelty and interpersonal violence. *Clinical Psychology Review,* 21:735–749.

Morgenstern, M. (2011). Sodomy and bestiality bans will stay in military law books. *The Blaze*. Retrievedfromhttp://www.theblaze.com/stories/sodomy-bestiality-bans-will-stay-in-military-law-books/.

National Defense Authorization Act for Fiscal Year 2012, H1540CR.HSE, 112th Congress, 1st Session. (2011).

National Defense Authorization Act for Fiscal Year 2014, H3304CR.HSE, 113th Congress, 1st Session. (2013).

Orecchio-Egresitz, Haven. (2020). "The availability of 'animal crush' content has created a cat-and-mouse subculture of attention-seeking animal abusers and the web sleuths who suss them out." *Insider.* July 29. Retrieved from: https://www.insider.com/making-animal-crush-torture-videos-serial-killer-warning-sign-2020-7.

Peretti, P. O., & Rowan, M. (1982). Variables associated with male and female chronic zoophilia. *Social Behavior and Personality, 10*(1), 83–87.

Ressler, R. K., Burgess, A. W., Hartman, C. R., Douglas, J. E., & McCormack, A. (1986). Murderers who rape and mutilate. *Journal of Interpersonal Violence, 1,* 273–287.

Sandnabba, N. K., Santtila, P., Nordling, N., Beetz, A. M., & Alison, L. (2002). Characteristics of a sample of sadomasochistically-oriented males with recent experience of sexual contact with animals. *Deviant Behavior, 23,* 511–529.

United States Court of Appeals for the Third Circuit. (2008). *United States of America v. Robert J. Stevens.* Retrieved from http://randazza.wordpress.com/2008/07/20/united-states-v-stevens-protecting-animals-is-not-a-reason-to-amputate-part-of-the-first-amendment/.

United States Department of Justice. (2016). "Houston Man Sent to Federal Prison for Producing and Distributing Animal Crush Videos." United States Attorney's Office Southern District of Texas. August 18. Retrieved from: https://www.justice.gov/usao-sdtx/pr/houston-man-sent-federal-prison-producing-and-distributing-animal-crush-videos.

Wiegand, P., Schmidt, V., & Kleiber, M. (1999). German shepherd dog is suspected of sexually abusing a child. *International Journal of Legal Medicine, 112,* 324–325.

Wilcox, D. T., Foss, C. M., & Donathy, M. L. (2005). A case study of a male sex offender with zoosexual interests and behaviours. *Journal of Sexual Aggression, 11*(3), 305–317.

Wisch, R. F. (2020). Table of Veterinary Reporting Requirement and Immunity Laws. Retrieved from: https://www.animallaw.info/topic/table-veterinary-reporting-requirement-and-immunity-laws.

Wisch, R. F. (2021). Table of State Animal Sexual Assault Laws. Animal Legal & Historical Center. Retrieved from https://www.animallaw.info/topic/table-state-animal-sexual-assault-laws.

Wisch, R. F. (2022). Table of State Animal Sexual Assault Laws. Animal Legal & Historical Center. Retrieved from https://www.animallaw.info/topic/table-state-animal-sexual-assault-laws.

Wyoming bans bestiality; Hawaii move toward ban would leave only two states without law. (2021). Casper, WY — Oil City News. Retrieved from: https://oilcity.news/...g/legislature/2021/04/05/wyoming-bans-bestiality-hawaii-move-toward-ban-would-leave-only-two-states-without-law/.

Statutes

10 USC §925—Art. 125. Forcible sodomy; bestiality.

18 USC §48—Animal Crush Videos

18 USC §48—Revised. PL 116-72 Preventing Animal Cruelty and Torture Act

AZ ST §13-1411

DE ST TI 11 §775

GA ST §16-6-6

HI ST 711-1109.8

ID ST §18-6605

IA ST §717C.1

IL ST CH 720 §5/12-35

IN ST 35-46-3-14

KY ST KRS §525.137

MA ST 272 §34

MCA 45-8-218

M. C.L.A. 750.158

MN ST 609.294

MO ST 566.111

MS ST §97-29-59

NV ST N.R.S. 201.455

NH ST N.H. Rev. Stat. §644:8g

NJ ST N. J. S. A. 4:22-17

OH ST R.C. §959.21

OK ST T. 21 §886

RI ST §11-10-1

SC ST §16-15-120

SD ST §22-22-42

TN ST §39-14-214

TX ST V. T. C. A., Penal Code §21.09

VA ST §18.2-361

VT ST 13 V.S.A. §352

WA ST 16.52.205

WY ST 6-4-601

Section III

Animal Cruelty

Antecedents and Future Behavior

Chapter 12

Animal Cruelty and Delinquency, Criminality, and Youth Violence

Nik Taylor and Tania Signal

Nearly five decades ago, Margaret Mead (1964, p. 21) stated, "The worst thing that can happen to a child is for him (sic) to harm an animal and get away with it. Animal cruelty kills respect for life." In the intervening years, the concept of the "Link" (i.e., that engagement in deliberate harm of animals is related in some manner to propensity for violence more generally) has been explored from a number of perspectives including (but not limited to) criminology, psychology, sociology, and social work (see HSUS, 2007). Cruelty to animals (CTA) is recognized across these disciplines as being of major concern not only for the health and welfare of the animal victim (Benetato, Reisman, & McCobb, 2011; Taylor & Signal, 2008), but also for the psychological, physical and social well-being of the perpetrator (e.g., Currie, 2006), and for society generally (Hensley, Tallichet, & Dutkiewicz, 2009; McPhedran, 2009). Throughout this chapter, we bear all three groups in mind as we present an overview of the main research in the area of animal cruelty and its links to other delinquency and criminality.

Four Main Areas of Animal-Human Research

In 2004, Becker and French (p. 401) argued that there were four main areas of research into human-animal violence links, namely:

(1) *Animal abuse as part of the continuum of abuse within the family (see Chapter 13 in the current volume for a thorough review);*

(2) *Animal abuse as an indicator of child abuse;*

(3) *The therapeutic potential of animals in child development and within post-abuse work; and*

(4) *Animal abuse perpetrated by children who show later aggressive and deviant behaviour.*

Animal Abuse as Part of the Continuum of Abuse within the Family and Animal Abuse as an Indicator of Child Abuse

The argument here is that the established continuum of violence within familial relationships needs to be extended to include abuse of animal members of the family. This includes emotional, physical, and sexual abuse. This is supported by evidence which demonstrates that there is a link between interpersonal, familial human-directed violence, and deliberate animal cruelty. For example, Ascione, Weber, and Wood (1997) surveyed 38 women in the U.S. who were entering a refuge to escape violence. They found that of the 74% who had pets, 71% had experienced their partner either threatening to harm or actually harming their pet. A decade later, Volant, Johnson, Gullone, and Coleman (2008) reported very similar percentages within an Australian cohort of women. They surveyed 102 women with a history of family violence and a demographically-matched sample of 102 women without such a history. They found that 53% of the women who reported family violence experience also reported that their pets had been harmed and 17% of these reported that their pets had been killed. This contrasted with only 6% of the matched sample reporting (accidental) harm of animals and no pet deaths. More recently still, Febres et al. (2014) investigated animal abuse among 307 men arrested for domestic violence. They reported that 41% (n = 125) had indicated committing at least one act of animal abuse since the age of 18. For these men, physical abuse of an animal occurred with the highest frequency (80%, n = 100), followed by threats (71.2%, n = 89), followed by neglect (12%, n = 15).

Animal harm within a violent/abusive family dynamic may also be indicative of the level of danger presented by the abuser, as can be seen above with its closer linkage to physical violence as opposed to threatening behavior and/or neglect. Simmons and Lehmann (2007) interviewed 1,283 women seeking refuge from domestic violence in Texas (between 1998 and 2002). They concluded that abusers who were violent to their partners, and who also abused the family pet, utilized a greater range, and severity, of aggressive violence including emotional and sexual violence and stalking. They also reported that the men who abused animals as well as their partners engaged in more controlling behavior than did men who did not abuse animals. The tactics utilized by domestic violence perpetrators were even more pronounced among abusers who killed the pet.

A further example of the family violence dynamic can be found in the work of DeViney, Dickert, and Lockwood (1983) who investigated 57 families where physical child abuse had occurred. They found that 50 of these families had incidents whereby at least one family member had also abused the family pet. In the majority of cases, this animal abuse was performed by the abusive parent, but sometimes the abuse was committed by the child. In a retrospective study, utilizing psychiatric intake assessments where a single check box of 'cruelty to animals' had been ticked, Boat et al. (2011) compared frequency of aggressive behavior with abuse history for 55 children. They found that the cruelty group was 2.45 times more likely to have experienced problems with peers, 5.37 times more likely to have perpetrated bullying, and 2.81 times more likely to have experienced sexual abuse, when compared to a control group. The correlation between childhood cruelty to animals and family violence witnessed or experienced, and/or child maltreatment, is noted throughout the literature (e.g., Currie, 2006; DeGue & DiLillo, 2009; Duncan, Thomas & Miller, 2005; McEwan, Moffitt & Arseneault, 2014).

Adams (1995, p. 64), in her analysis of the "woman-animal abuse connections," argued that the pets of abused children were often used to maintain their silence. She also pointed out that child victims of sexual abuse often harmed animals themselves and, thus, child harm of animals should be taken as an indicator of some kind of family dysfunction. In a similar vein, Becker and French (2004) cite the findings from an analysis of case histories drawn from a national, UK-based, specialist service working with children who sexually abused other children and who committed other violent offenses. This analysis demonstrated that approximately one-fifth of the children had a history of sexually abusing animals.

Ascione and Arkow (1999) argued that children in dysfunctional families often have their trauma compounded by witnessing displays of animal abuse. Witnessing these displays alongside the abuse of their mothers may increase the children's later propensity for interpersonal violence as well as increasing the likelihood of their subsequent abuse of animals. This is substantiated by, for example, the findings of Volant et al. (2008) who reported that children were witness to the abuse within the family (both human- and animal-directed) in 29% of the cases. Ascione and Arkow (1999) suggest that domestic violence, animal abuse, and child maltreatment form interlocking circles of abuse. A recent study where children's engagement in animal cruelty (singular and persistent) was assessed bi-annually from age 5 to age 12 along with family risk factors (particularly adult domestic violence and physical maltreatment of the child) found that CTA was more common in children who had been maltreated. However, the strength of the predictive relationship was greater when other risk factors such as an impoverished environment and domestic violence were present (McEwan et al., 2014). (See Chapter 13 for more on animal cruelty and domestic violence.)

The Therapeutic Potential of Animals in Child Development and within Post-Abuse Work

As Becker and French (2004) highlight, the role that animals can play within therapy are numerous, including sources of comfort and support, the promotion of childhood resilience, the rebuilding of trusting relationships, and the promotion of healing following trauma. It is within this framework that Animal-Assisted Therapy is often used (e.g., Lockwood & Ascione, 1998), building on the pioneering work of Levinson and his dog Jingles with children diagnosed with autism (Levinson, 1978).

In a modern context, a distinction is drawn between Animal-Assisted Therapy (i.e., therapies which involve both the presence of, and interaction with, an animal) and

Humane-Education (i.e., curriculum-based presentations regarding animal well-being), although the two may well overlap in practice. Despite superficial differences, both forms of "intervention" are predicated upon the idea that empathy may well be a mediating factor within human-animal violence links (e.g., Hastings, Zahn-Waxler, Robinson, Usher, & Bridges, 2000; Warden & Mackinnon, 2003), thus, Humane Education has been posited as one particularly effective mechanism whereby a lack of human-directed empathy may be remedied by teaching animal-welfare appropriate attitudes (Ascione, 1992; Ascione & Weber, 1996; Barker, Best, Fredrickson, & Hunter, 2000). Based on similar principles, Animal-Assisted Therapy has been used successfully with a number of groups including incarcerated and institutionalized individuals, the elderly, and victims of trauma (see Beck & Katcher, 1996). Recently Animal-Assisted Therapy has been shown to be effective in not only addressing maladaptive (psychological) correlates of childhood abuse, but to also reduce the prevalence of animal harm by abused children (Taylor, Fraser, Signal & Prentice, 2014).

The final area that Becker and French (2004, p. 401) highlight as being one where particular (research and popular) attention has been paid to human-animal violence links is "animal abuse perpetrated by children who show later aggressive and deviant behaviour." It is to this that the remainder of the chapter now turns.

Animal Abuse Perpetrated by Children Who Show Later Aggressive and Deviant Behavior

The majority of studies in this area involve retrospective accounts of animal cruelty by males incarcerated at the time of the research for violent crimes. For example, Schiff, Louw, and Ascione (1999) documented the animal abuse histories of 117 males in a South African prison. They reported that of the 58 men who had committed aggressive crimes, 63.3 percent also documented cruelty to animals. This was in comparison to 10.5% of the non-aggressive inmates reporting instances of animal cruelty. O'Grady, Kinlock, and Hanlon (2007) examined the relationship of a range of developmental factors (e.g., drug abuse, family history, socio-economic status, engagement in animal abuse, etc.) with history of violent criminal activity in an incarcerated (drug-using) sample. Over 30% of the total sample reported engaging in deliberate animal harm. O'Grady et al. also reported that a history of torturing animals was strongly predictive of the most violent incarcerated individuals (murder or attempted murder).

Engaging in deliberate animal harm at a young age seems to be particularly predictive of a violent or anti-social trajectory. For example, Fleming, Jory, and Burton (2002), following an examination of the family characteristics, victimization histories, and number of offenses committed by young offenders, reported that 96% of those who had engaged in sexual activity with non-human animals had also committed sex offenses against humans. Those who had engaged in sexual activity with non-human animals also reported higher levels of emotional and physical abuse within their families of origin. Age of onset (see later for a discussion of this in relation to psychological diagnoses) has been found to be related to both the frequency of abuse and the type of animal targeted. For example, Tallichet, Hensley, O'Bryan, and Hassel (2005) reported that an earlier onset of cruel acts towards animals was predictive of engaging in multiple acts of animal cruelty within a sample of 261 incarcerated men. Of the men surveyed, 43% disclosed engaging in deliberate animal cruelty. Potentially of significant importance (at least for profilers and researchers) is the fact that those inmates who were younger (i.e., under 12 years of age) when first committing CTA tended to target cats almost exclusively.

Following increased interest in the animal abuse histories of serial killers, researchers have also linked a history of animal cruelty to killings and general violence perpetrated by school-age children (Ascione, 2001). For example, Khan and Cooke (2008) reported that engaging in animal abuse was predictive of serious violence directed at a sibling utilizing a weapon. CTA was also found to relate to "less serious" (i.e., without a weapon) sibling violence, but not as strongly. Other commonalities between bullying and animal abuse have been identified, in particular, an association with delinquency and other anti-social behaviors (e.g., Baldry & Farrington, 2000; Henry, 2004; Sanders et al., 2013, 2014). Looking outside the family, Henry and Sanders (2007) investigated reported experience of animal abuse (witnessing and committing) and bullying (both as a victim and as a perpetrator) as a child within a cohort of 185 male university students. They reported two main findings, firstly that there was a distinct difference between those who were involved in a single episode of animal abuse and those who had multiple experiences of animal abuse. Specifically one-time "abusers" were not statistically different on measures of bullying (victimization or perpetration) from non-abusers. Secondly, they reported a strong interaction between high levels of bullying (again experienced as a victim and/or the perpetrator) and high tolerance of animal cruelty—for those individuals who reported experiencing multiple instances of animal abuse. Henry and Sanders suggest that their findings (in tandem with similar findings from studies such as Baldry, 2003) support the "desensitization" hypothesis—that is, that acts of violence against animals (either witnessed or perpetrated) desensitize an individual to the effects of violence, potentially also reinforcing the use of violence as a means of social control. We return to a discussion of the desensitization hypothesis later in the chapter.

In a later study (Sanders et al., 2013), with 250 male students (enrolled on an Introductory Psychology course at a US institution) confirmed the association between animal abuser and the perpetration of bullying as well as a significant, positive relation between animal abuse and being a victim of bullying. Extending analyses beyond investigations of relations between bullying and animal abuse, Sanders et al., also investigated links with socio-emotional functioning using the Strengths and Difficulties Questionnaire. Bullies, victims and animal abuses all scored highly on the conduct problems and hyperactivity subscales, with hyperactivity being specifically linked to animal abuse perpetration. Animal abuse was more likely to correlate with conduct problems among victims, rather than perpetrators, of bullying and the authors note that despite complex patterns their research suggests that bullying, animal abuse and victimization tend to co-occur. They argue that "a clear picture is beginning to emerge, in which the maltreatment of animals is consistently associated with being both a perpetrator and a victim of bullying" (p. 234).

One of the limitations of Henry and Sanders' (2007) study, however, was the age of the participants (young adults) and the inherent retrospective nature of the data collected. In contrast, Gullone and Robertson (2008) assessed concurrent engagement in bullying behaviors and animal abuse within a sample of 249 adolescents (average age approximately 14 years) attending three secondary schools in Melbourne, Australia. Over 20% of the sample admitted to having engaged in animal abuse, with boys being significantly more likely than girls to engage in such behaviors. Thirty-seven percent of the sample reported witnessing animal abuse, which was most frequently paternally-perpetrated. Consistent with large-scale studies of childhood bullying in Australia, the authors report that nearly 18% of the children had engaged in bullying behaviors in the past year and nearly 30% had been the target of bullying, either on their own or as part of a group. Witnessing animal abuse was found to be a predictor for both engaging in, and being the victim of, bullying. Engagement in animal abuse was predicted by family of origin factors (e.g., violence/conflict). The authors concluded that their study provides further empirical evidence for the co-occurrence of aggressive and anti-social behaviors towards humans and non-humans.

In a more recent study, Knight et al. (2014) utilized data from a national, longitudinal, and multi-generational sample (n = 1614; data collected between 1990 and 2004) to investigate both inter- and intra-generational links between domestic violence (DV) and animal abuse. They found that (1) parental history of animal abuse was predictive of the parents' own later involvement in both the perpetration of, and the parents' likelihood of being victims of, DV; (2) a child's history of animal abuse can be predicted by their parents' perpetration of DV; and, (3) evidence for intergenerational continuity of animal abuse was lacking. Echoing conclusions by Henry and Sanders (2007) and Sanders et al. (2013), outlined above, Knight et al. (2014) argue that "the implications of these findings are that early animal abuse is not only a risk factor for later involvement in violent DV perpetration but also violent victimization" (p. 3027) and also call for further research into animal abuse and victimization, as well as perpetration.

From a psychological viewpoint, the *Diagnostic and Statistical Manual of Psychological Disorders* IV-TR contains deliberate animal abuse only as an indicator of Conduct Disorder (CD), with this disorder being posited as a preliminary to later adulthood antisocial behavior (e.g., Cohen & Strayer, 1996). Authors have suggested that approximately 25% of children meeting the criteria for CD engage in deliberate animal harm, and this behavior has been suggested as one of the earliest, observable, symptoms of anti-social behavior (Miller, 2001). Indeed, persistent behavioral (conduct) problems with an early onset are considered a marker of an increased likelihood of developing serious socio-emotional problems later in life (Luk, Staiger, Wong, & Mathai, 1999). For example, Luk et al. (1999) compared a sample of children referred to a mental health service for persistent behavioral issues (meeting at least one criteria other than CTA for Conduct Disorder, n = 141) to a community sample all aged between 5 and

12 years of age. Just under a third (28%) of the clinic-referred sample were reported by parents/caregivers to be "cruel to animals." In contrast only one of the non-referred children (n = 36) was reported to engage in CTA. Comparing the CTA to non-CTA referred children Luk et al. (1999), noted that the former group tended to be characterized by more severe conduct symptoms and poorer family functioning. Unexpectedly, older CTA children were found to have significantly elevated self-perception, with Luk et al. suggesting that this might be related to the "callous and unemotional" subtype of Conduct Disorder proposed by some researchers as a potential marker for childhood psychopathy and potentially serious adulthood psychopathology/criminality. (See Chapter 16 for further discussion of psychological theories.)

Simons, Wurtele, and Durham (2008) examined the differential, developmental, experiences of 269 convicted sexual offenders. Splitting the offenders into "Rapists" and "Child Abusers" (as defined by more than 80% of their disclosed victims being either an adult or a child), Simons et al. assessed a range of childhood experiences including frequency, severity and type of animal abuse (i.e., physical and sexual). The authors further investigated disclosures of animal abuse by animal type (domestic vs. stray) and ascertained motivations for the disclosed CTA although this was not reported within the publication. Child abusers (n = 132) were found to be significantly more likely to have engaged in bestiality as a child (38% vs. 11%), and at a younger age than rapists. In contrast, rapists were significantly more likely to have engaged in non-sexual acts of CTA (68% vs. 44%), with a higher frequency and younger age of onset than child abusers. Importantly, despite the difference in the typographies of animal cruelty and typology of sexual offending, CTA was found to precede human-directed sexual abuse by an average of two years for child abusers and six years for rapists. It must be acknowledged here that there were a number of other significant, differential, developmental experiences between the two "classes" of sexual offender, such as physical abuse and domestic violence in family of origin for rapists, sexual abuse, and early exposure to pornography for child abusers. However, there is a clear need for further research into the links between CTA and sexual offending. Importantly, Simons et al. note that these results and conclusions drawn from them can't be generalized to female perpetrators as their developmental paths and experiences have not been well-explored.

Gendered Experiences of CTA

As can be seen by the studies summarized above, the majority of the extant literature in this area examines the "Link" within male populations only. Research addressing female-perpetrated CTA remains comparatively rare. Felthous and Yudowitz (1977) compared the histories of 31 female offenders with those of 19 male offenders, finding a significant relation between cruelty to animals and violent criminal activity for female as well as male offenders. The first part of the study involved the comparison of the female offenders with the male offenders and results showed that while the men had a greater tendency to *kill* animals, the *torturing* of animals was of nearly equal prevalence in the two samples. The second part of the study consisted of a comparison between assaultive and non-assaultive female offenders and the results showed that cruelty to animals was the only childhood behavior that differentiated the two groups with statistical significance. Felthous and Yudowitz concluded that experience of deliberate animal harm was as significant for females as for males with equal frequency of perpetration across genders (however, male-perpetrated cruelty more often involved the death of the animal in question).

There has been an apparent increase in scholarly interest in women's experience of CTA, with an emphasis on assessing their direct engagement in CTA rather than as passive or unwilling witnesses to CTA. For example, Connelly (2007) compared the histories of 100 female inmates (41 characterized as aggressive and 59 as non-aggressive) to those of 104 male inmates (59 characterized as aggressive and 45 as non-aggressive). Connelly reported that female inmates were just as likely to have abused animals as were male inmates. Interestingly, aggressive female inmates disclosed more overall instances of animal cruelty (particularly in adolescence) and substantially higher rates of sexually abusing animals (including into adulthood) than male inmates. Febres et al. (2012) examined both the prevalence of adulthood animal abuse and its links with interpersonal violence perpetration in a sample of women arrested for domestic violence and referred to batterer intervention programs in the US. They found animal abuse to be over-represented in the sample with 17% of the 87 women reporting at least one instance of animal abuse since the age of 18, compared to a 0.28% prevalence rate among women in the general public. In contrast to assumptions about the gendered nature of neglect (see below) the majority of acts reported were of physical CTA with only one case of neglect mentioned. Importantly most of the women reported multiple acts of CTA (average 8–9) rather than singular experiences with the most commonly endorsed item on the Aggression Toward Animals Scale that concerning threatening behavior toward nonhuman animals (i.e., 'Did you threaten, scare, intimidate, or bully an animal on purpose?') followed by physically aggressive acts (i.e., 'Did you hit an animal with an object that could hurt?'). However, adulthood animal abuse proved to correlate only with severe physical, but not psychological, abuse (of humans). While researchers have shown that a history of specific types of CTA seem to relate to 'styles' of interpersonal violence in male perpetrators (e.g., Merz-Perez et al., 2001) the small sample size precludes similar analyses here. Sanders and Henry (2014) recently extended their examination of links between CTA and psychological variables to a retrospective study of 500 female undergraduates. They concluded that similar patterns of behavioral difficulties were present in female animal abusers as had previously been found with males. Given these two recent studies there is clearly a need to address the gendered nature of violence within larger, community-relevant, samples.

Indeed, despite these studies, there remains a focus on male acts of cruelty to animals within the literature, which reflects a gendered bias within criminology more broadly (e.g., Heidensohn, 2010). This is often reflected within the argument that men abuse whereas women neglect. This is itself a reflection of gendered ideology in that it is an extension of the belief that females are more passive and nurturing than are males. Within the human-animal violence literature, women are then taken to task for neglect as opposed to deliberate violence. Similarly, the assumption that males are violent, whereas females are not, is one which pervades criminology (e.g., Heidensohn, 2010) and human-animal scholars need to guard against reproducing these entrenched beliefs through the very design of their studies. There is, similarly, a heteronormative bias in extant literature regarding animal abuse and future research needs to investigate animal abuse perpetration, particularly within the context of domestic violence, within same sex and Lesbian, Gay, Bisexual, Transgender, Queer/Questioning, and Intersex (LGBTQI) relationships.

CTA and Generalized Deviance

Underpinning all ideas of the "Link" are two separate, but related, theses: the graduation thesis and the desensitization (sometimes called "generalization of deviance") thesis. The graduation thesis is based on the idea that those who deliberately harm animals will graduate to the deliberate harm of humans while the desensitization thesis is more concerned with the general levels of callous behavior which permeate modern life. This is seen to manifest itself in certain personality traits such as deliberate animal harm which can then be seen as a risk factor for the development of further anti-social behaviors, directed at humans (Beirne, 2004).

Arguably, much early research in the area of human-animal violence links prioritized the idea of graduation over desensitization. Following three plus decades of concerted research in the area, however, this is starting to change. In part due to the methodological problems inherent to studies which seek to determine causality between human- and animal-directed violence, more attention is now being paid to the idea of human-animal violence links with generalized deviant behavior (e.g., Arluke, Levin, Luke, & Ascione, 1999). The proposition here is that cruelty to animals is seen as one aspect of a range of maladaptive (antisocial) behaviors that heighten the risk for adulthood antisocial behavior (Dadds, Turner, & McAloon, 2002). For example, when Arluke et al. (1999) examined the criminal records of 153 individuals prosecuted for acts of animal cruelty and a matched sample of non-abusers (who also had criminal records), they found that those who had abused animals were significantly more likely to be involved in other criminal activity (including violent interpersonal behavior). Interestingly, instances of animal cruelty were found to be no more likely to precede, than follow, other criminal activity for this cohort. In a review of studies with incarcerated individuals, Ascione (2001) concluded that deliberate animal abuse may be typical of the developmental histories of between 25% and 66% of violent criminals. Recent research also suggests that simply witnessing animal abuse significantly increases both the likelihood of engaging in such abuse (Thomson & Gullone, 2006) and is a strong predictor for engaging in bullying behaviors (Gullone & Robertson, 2008).

In one of the few studies involving non-incarcerated participants, Henry (2004) asked students (Introductory Psychology, n = 169) to recall their past history of either witnessing or engaging in deliberate CTA, their general attitudes towards the treatment of animals, and instances of "delinquent" (i.e., antisocial) behavior. Overall, those who reported either witnessing (51%, n = 86) or engaging in animal cruelty (18%, n = 30) were more likely to report engaging in a variety of antisocial behaviors. The results of this study are particularly important for the desensitization hypothesis as it illustrates that CTA exists within a "matrix of antisocial behaviors" within a non-incarcerated population. Henry also comments on the interplay between gender and the effect of witnessing CTA (insufficient women reporting engaging in CTA to allow analyses), with women showing heightened sensitivity towards animals and men reduced sensitivity following such exposure. While suggesting that this pattern warrants further examination, Henry suggests that an individual's response to observing CTA may depend on the context within which the cruelty occurs, particularly whether the individual was a willing observer or coerced. Gender may be correlated strongly with this, with Henry suggesting that the observed, heightened sensitivity towards animal suffering may reflect the fact that women may be non-willing witnesses of animal cruelty.

There does exist, however, considerable disagreement regarding the specifics of both these theses, not to mention a lack of (uncontested) empirical data. For example, Tallichet and Hensley (2005) point out that those who harm "convenient" animals (i.e., their own or neighborhood companion animals) may be less at risk of developing serious anti-social behaviors than those who deliberately seek out a range of animals to harm, thus suggesting that even the desensitization thesis may be dependent upon a range of other factors. Other research has failed to find predictive utility in the graduation thesis at all (e.g., Dadds et al., 2006). For example, Taylor and Signal (2004), in an Australian community-based sample, found that links between aggression and animal attitude measures only existed on a correlational level, failing to reach predictive significance.

It must be acknowledged, however, that although a number of other studies have found similar patterns of increased criminality and/or elevated propensity for violence linked to experiences of animal abuse (e.g., Kellert & Felthous, 1985), other research has found less support for the link. Miller and Knutson (1997) for example, reported that types of violent criminals could not be differentiated simply by self-reported engagement in animal abuse.

Despite such problems, there is no lack of public interest in, and awareness of, "The Link." For example, in a study of approximately 1,200 Australians, Taylor and Signal (2006) found that 63% thought there was a link between family violence and deliberate animal harm. Animal protection agencies also utilize "The Link" in their various campaigns, for example, First Strike in Scotland and New Zealand and the Humane Society of the United States. A number of innovative projects have also been established, in response to recognition of human-animal violence links, to foster the companion animals of women entering refugees fleeing violence (e.g., DVConnect's Pets in Crisis, Queensland, Australia),[1] and, increasingly, there is a recognition of the need to

1. For a review of the first six months of this project, see Taylor, Signal, and Stark (2006).

provide services for those in violent situations who live with companion animals (see, e.g., Kreinert, Walsh, Matthews & McConkey, 2012). Furthermore, such ideas are now permeating the legal system with, for example, states in the U.S. such as California and Illinois recently enacting legislation that allows judicial discretion to include pets in domestic violence protection orders (see The National Link Coalition for more information, http://www.nationallinkcoalition.org/).

One problem with this, however, is that such campaigns often blur the boundaries between correlational concepts (i.e., that conceptually there is a link between the two forms of aggression) and causality (i.e., that children who are cruel to animals will necessarily go on to become serial killers or other harmers of humans). It remains the case that the empirical evidence for causality is, to date, ambiguous at best.

Despite the lack of clear causative evidence, deliberate CTA committed by children and young people has been (and remains) the focus of numerous research endeavours, both theoretical and empirical, all of which indicate the serious implications and/or correlates of this aberrant behavior (Becker & French, 2004). While acknowledged as a behavior that is challenging to define, isolate, explain, and rationalize (Ascione, 2001; Benetato et al., 2011; Gleyzer, Felthous & Holzer, 2002; Hensley et al., 2009), it is also seen as a behavioral anomaly that requires urgent recognition, prevention, and intervention (Arluke & Lockwood, 1997; Flynn, 2000; Lockwood & Hodge, 1986; Merz-Perez, Heide, & Silverman, 2001).

Indeed, Merz-Perez and Heide (2003) suggest that it is more important to understand the motivations behind acts of animal cruelty than the behaviors themselves. Arluke and Sanders (2009) support this, explaining that better knowledge of the motives behind animal cruelty will hopefully result in better prevention (and treatment for abusers), while acknowledging that research in the field has become somewhat preoccupied with the consequences of animal cruelty rather than what underlies it. In (arguably) one of the first studies to try and delineate the motives behind animal cruelty, Kellert and Felthous (1985) derived nine theoretical motivations for adult-perpetrated animal abuse, namely:

1. "Control" of the animal (often under the guise of "training");
2. Retaliation against an animal;
3. Prejudice against a certain species (e.g., cats);
4. Express aggression via animal (e.g., possession of a dog trained to fight);
5. Enhance own aggression (e.g., using an animal as target practice);
6. To shock others (for self-amusement);
7. Retaliate against another person (e.g., kill the neighbor's dog, girlfriend's rabbit);
8. Displaced hostility (abuse animal as harming person is too risky); and
9. Nonspecific sadism (i.e., enjoy the suffering in and of itself).

CTA: Social and Community Considerations

As Ascione (2001) points out, the role of family, social, and community factors should not be overlooked. Two particularly important animal-abuse related factors which have been gaining a lot of research attention are maladaptive family environment/abusive parental practices (e.g., Ascione, 2001; Hastings, Zahn-Waxler, Usher, Robinson & Bridges, 2000) and empathy (e.g., Taylor & Signal, 2005).

Many researchers have noted that not all children who abuse animals become juvenile offenders or adult criminals, and sometimes these children do not come from dysfunctional, violent families, and indeed appear to be "normal" or "typical" (e.g., Flynn, 2000; Flynn, 2001; Miller & Knutson, 1997; Randour, 2007). According to Dadds et al. (2002), certain features of childhood CTA have been suggested to be more meaningful when assessing the predictive utility of animal abuse, namely: direct involvement, impulsivity, lack of remorse, variety of cruel acts, the species targeted, and the motivations behind the cruelty. Ascione, Thompson, and Black (1997) derived 13 developmentally-related CTA motivations from case reports and interviews with children engaging in animal abuse. These motivations included curiosity/exploration, mood enhancement (i.e., relief of boredom), peer pressure, sexual gratification, abuse (and displaced hostility resulting from same), post-traumatic play, imitation, self-injury, and rehearsal for interpersonal violence. Based on these and experiences of animal protection professionals, Ascione (2001) proposed three general taxonomies for childhood animal abusers:

1. Exploratory/curious animal abuse
2. Pathological animal abuse
3. Delinquent animal abuse

Children in the exploratory/curious animal abuse category are generally very young (i.e., pre-school) and are typified by having little understanding of animal needs and being poorly supervised. It must be noted, however, that age alone is not sufficient for membership in this category as animal cruelty is often one of the first Conduct Disorder (CD) symptoms to be observed. Norris and Wilson (2003) mention a median reporting age (of onset of animal cruelty) of about 6.5 years—earlier than the median age for first report of bullying, cruelty to humans, vandalism or arson. Those with developmental delays may also fall within this exploratory/curious typology despite being older in age (Ascione, 2001). Ascione (2001) suggests that Humane Education interventions would be one way to reduce the prevalence of animal abuse perpetrated by children within this group.

In the second category (pathological), children are generally older (although see the caveats regarding age above) and CTA is indicative of some form of psychological disturbance (e.g., CD, empathy deficit). Researchers have suggested that CTA may be a marker for particularly severe CD with heightened risk for future violence, (e.g., Frick et al., 1993; Luk et al., 1999). In a review of the literature, McPhedran (2009) suggested that the presence of childhood CTA was a marker for a poorer prognosis particularly with a younger age of onset. Importantly, the CTA may also be a result of abuse; specifically, researchers report that children who abuse animals are often victims of sexual or physical abuse themselves (Adams & Donovan, 1995; Currie, 2006). It is with respect to this that childhood CTA should also be taken as a "red flag" warranting further attention/investigation if disclosed regardless of the any other presenting behaviors/indicators (e.g., DeGue & DiLillo, 2009; Lockwood & Hodge, 1986). Ascione (2001) suggests that professional, clinical intervention is needed to reduce animal abuse by those falling within this group.

Individuals in the third, delinquent, group are generally adolescent in age with animal abuse likely to be one of a range of antisocial behaviors they are engaging in (Ascione, 2001). Often animal abuse is carried out with peers and may form part of initiation rituals. Membership of this group is highly correlated with the risk for adulthood criminality (due to engaging in a range of anti-social behaviors not solely due to animal abuse) and interpersonal violence. Ascione (2001) suggests that judicial and clinical intervention is required in order to reduce animal abuse within this cohort. (See Chapters 15 and 16 in the current volume for a more detailed consideration of the motivational factors underlying animal abuse.)

A number of studies have been conducted in an effort to isolate circumstances that precede CTA. The earliest recorded study (Tapia, 1971) and follow-up study (Rigdon & Tapia, 1977) focused on investigating causative variables associated with episodes of childhood CTA. The researchers examined the case histories of 18 male children who were placed in psychiatric care (the average age of the sample was 9½ years), all of whom had presented with a history of CTA. The results indicated that the majority of the children had been raised in a less than ideal environment that included episodes of parental neglect, hostility, violence, and rejection. A follow-up study conducted six years later concluded that in order to reduce the CTA, the best course of action was to remove the child from the chaotic home environment or through treatment practices aimed at altering and improving familial relationships (Rigdon & Tapia, 1977).

Subsequent studies have isolated specific domestic features that present as precursors to childhood CTA. For example, Wax and Haddox (1974) established a positive relationship between childhood CTA and a disorganized household and irregular parental practices while DeViney et al. (1983) (as cited in Flynn, 2000), noted that the presence of child abuse and other practices of violence within the family may be a forerunner for childhood CTA. Ascione (1998) concluded from his research that episodes of domestic violence may increase the likelihood of childhood CTA and may therefore foster psychological instability in the witnessing children. This is likely to be particularly the case where children witness CTA within the violent relationship environment (e.g., Baldry, 2003; Flynn, 1999). Interestingly, in a large, epidemiologic study in the US (with over 30,000 participants) Vaughn et al., (2011) found that experience of childhood sexual, but not physical, abuse significantly increased the odds of individuals engaging in CTA. Lockwood and Hodge (1986) conclude that evidence of childhood CTA is a positive indication that there is something in the child's life that requires an immediate response. However, identifying CTA as an observer can be very challenging (McPhedran, 2009) for a number of reasons including the often solitary nature of CTA and embarrassment/shame of behalf of the witnessing parent/caregiver. Awareness and acknowledgement of childhood CTA, first and foremost, is the responsibility of those people in close proximity to the child (e.g., parents, neighbors, teachers) (Dadds et al., 2002). However, once the behavior has been recognized, the child needs to be referred to professional practitioners (Dadds et al., 2002).

Methodological Issues

In an attempt to explain the discrepancies in the literature with regard to the link, Felthous and Kellert (1987) have suggested that methodological differences such as the way in which animal abuse histories are derived (interviews vs. chart reviews), and whether researchers examine repeated patterns or single instances of violence, are important. Specifically, they suggest that those studies that have failed to find an association tend to rely on chart reviews rather than interviews and often examine single instances of abuse/violence rather than repeated patterns of violent or cruel behavior.

Research in this area is often marred by methodological issues. For instance, no clear agreement exists on the definition of animal abuse (e.g., Ascione, 2001, Becker & French, 2004, Beirne, 2004) or on whether deliberate neglect should be taken into account (Ascione, 2001). The majority of research utilizes either parental reports of children's animal abuse and/or child self-reports of abuse which often differ drastically in terms of estimated prevalence (Ascione, 2001; Miller, 2001). Additional methodological problems are to be found in the fact that much research rests upon retrospective reports drawn from (male) incarcerated offenders.

This signals a clear need to develop more specific and responsive instruments. For example, much of the work in this area involves the use of generalized instruments such as the Attitude towards the Treatment of Animals Scale (Herzog, Betchart, & Pitman, 1991; Taylor & Signal, 2006). While a robust and useful measure of general attitudes towards the treatment of animals, it may be that it is not specific enough for use within clinical populations where the aim is to test human-animal abuse theses for their predictive ability (nor should it be expected to be given that this was not its purpose by design). Evidence available to date seems to suggest that it is the deliberate cruel treatment of animals—as opposed to generalized attitudes towards them—which is important in predicting human-directed aggression, certainly within clinical/aggressive populations. Similarly, it may be that aggression across species, or animal category (e.g., "wild" animal vs. domesticated animal or vice versa), plays a more important part than general attitude towards animals in predicting those who will graduate from animal-directed to human-directed violence (e.g., Tallichet & Hensley, 2005). Research into human-animal abuse theses has tended to concentrate on, and prioritize, companion animal abuse, although more recent work in the field is beginning to analyze the importance of variables such as cross-species animal abuse and cross-animal category abuse (that is, abusing animals deemed as "pets" or "pests" for example) (Merz-Perez et al., 2001).

Conclusion: Condoned Animal Harm

Traditionally, animal cruelty has been defined as "... *socially unacceptable* behavior that intentionally causes unnecessary pain, suffering, or distress to and/or death of an animal" (Ascione, 1993, p. 228). Cazaux (1999, p. 120) points out that research in this area has focused on individual instances of cruelty and abuse against individual (usually companion) animals—at the expense of any other forms of animal cruelty and abuse. She refers to this inattention as selective indignation and posits that one explanation for this may be that such individual instances of animal cruelty are more readily amenable to control and thus more "susceptible to correction and enforcement" and therefore more easily taken up by the criminological community. While discussing criminological approaches to human-animal abuse in particular, Cazaux' point can be generalized to other disciplines; much of the extant research focuses on cruelty considered to be socially unacceptable. As a consequence, much institutionalized and/or *condoned* abuse and cruelty remains under-investigated and under-theorized. Cazaux argues that individual instances of animal abuse are tied to those animals that are deemed subjects (such as "pets") while the vast majority of animal abuse takes place with animals deemed as objects (such as farm animals). In a similar vein, Agnew (1998, p. 179) argues for a broad definition of animal abuse which does encompass these taken-for-granted forms of animal abuse and points out that a further advantage of such a broad perspective is that it would not be "tied to prevailing beliefs about animals ... [which] ... vary by time and place."

Following similar lines of argument, Beirne (1999a, p. 125) points out that when animals do enter criminological discourse, they "tend to be cast as creatures of anthropocentrism and anthropomorphism, as unproblematic objects that are only coincidentally present in some undesirable aspect of the complex web of human relationships." He further points out that certain existing criminological theories may have potential in extending the boundary of criminology to include animals. For example, Sutherland's argument (1949) that criminologists should study anything defined as socially harmful by any branch of law seems to offer one way forward, as do other forms of non-mainstream criminology, such as postmodern and critical criminologies. However, Beirne (1999a, p. 129) cautions us that we cannot adopt such theories wholesale as they all too often begin from a point of "human exceptionalism and speciesism." He points out that "animals ... remain without standing in a sort of legal and moral wilderness" (Beirne, 1999b, p. 10) and argues that this needs re-addressing in light of new ideas concerning the importance of animal abuse as a legitimate area of study.

The advantages of taking a broader view of animal cruelty and abuse can be seen in the following example which is of particular relevance to this chapter. A small, but growing, body of research points to problems endemic to communities where slaughterhouses and meatworks are located. In 2008, Dillard called for legal redress for "slaughterhouse workers" due to the psychological trauma caused by their daily experience of "large-scale violence and death" (p. 391) within an institutional culture that does little to reduce animal or human suffering. Authors have been quick to point out that the repetitive nature of slaughterhouse work coupled with a modern cultural sensibility which dictates a need to "render invisible what used to be a bloody spectacle" (Vialles, 2002, p. 66) leads to a "lack of identification with one's job" which elsewhere is often experienced as a distressing feature of production line work, yet in the slaughterhouse constitutes "a prerequisite for 'getting used to it'" (Vialles, 2002, p. 51).

Some have argued that it is not surprising, then, that this kind of human suffering gives rise to animal suffering. Indeed, Porcher (2011) argues that animals *and* humans share in physical and mental suffering as a result of modern intensive farming practices which include, but are not limited to, the slaughterhouse. Both Dillard (2008) and Grandin (1998) assert that abuse of animals at meat processing plants occurs frequently. For example, when Grandin (1998) undertook surveys of meat processing plant employees in the United States, she found that approximately 4% of employees directly involved with livestock had committed acts of deliberate animal cruelty in the course of their work. She further added that it appeared that these individuals took pleasure in observing the animals' suffering. Dillard (2008) suggests that employment within the animal production industry (specifically farmers and meatworkers) tends to lower "... employees' ability to empathize and identify with the pain suffered by the animals whose lives (and deaths) they are controlling" (p. 399). Dillard further explains that this type of distancing and compromised/poor attitude towards animals affects the way that workers treat the animals they interact with, specifically that this "disconnect" increases the likelihood of deliberate cruelty. She also suggests that this emotional distancing potentially affects male employees more strongly than female employees (based on findings from Porcher, Cousson-Gélie, & Dantzer, 2004).

While many of these issues obviously need to be addressed from the animal welfare perspective, research into the human-animal violence "Link" would suggest that this needs to be addressed from a human-welfare perspective, too. That is, as detailed above, research indicates that correlations exist between an individual's treatment of animals and his or her treatment of humans. Given that a reduction in empathy towards animals is a prerequisite for slaughterhouse work, and the increasing number of reported instances of cruelty that occurs within the job, as well as evidence that the mere presence of a slaughterhouse in a given community is indicative of higher levels of criminal and antisocial behavior, this is clearly an area in need of further research (e.g., Fitzgerald, 2010; Fitzgerald, Kalof, & Dietz, 2007).

Anecdotal evidence suggests that there may be higher incidences of familial violence as well as other crimes and social problems amongst populations of meatworkers (e.g., Artz, Orazem, & Otto, 2007; Dillard, 2008). For example, the establishment and/or presence of a (large) meat processing plant in a number of rural American towns has been reported to be connected to increases in homelessness, crime, familial violence, and child abuse within the community. Fitzgerald, Kalof, and Dietz (2007) summarized the existing literature (both popular and academic) on this issue, suggesting that three factors are often linked with the observed increase in criminal behavior. These are: (1) pressure on existing social infrastructures resulting in social disorganization, (2) the demographic characteristics of the workforce (e.g., young, male, and often immigrant), and (3) increased unemployment rates (due to high turnover of staff). However, as noted by Fitzgerald et al., none of these have been empirically tested. Indeed when Fitzgerald et al. examined arrest rates across a number of communities comparing situations where either a large animal-processing facility was present or a large-scale manufacturing plant (with similar sized workforce and demographic factors), they reported that the three factors did not, on their own or in combination, account for the increase in total arrest rates. Increases in arrests for violent crime, including rape and other sex offenses, were only observed in communities surrounding meat works. Fitzgerald et al., conclude that there is sufficient evidence to support the existence of the "Sinclair Effect" (i.e., that the unique and violent nature of the work involved has a deleterious effect on employees) (Fitzgerald et al., 2007) which in turn has deleterious effects on the surrounding neighborhoods. In a recent, questionnaire-based, study of the impact of occupation type (i.e., meatworkers and farmers benchmarked against a large community sample) on attitude towards animals and overall propensity for violence, Richards, Signal, and Taylor (2012) reported that meatworkers, but not farmers, showed significantly elevated levels of aggression compared to a community sample. Meatworkers' aggression scores were found to be similar to those reported in some incarcerated samples (e.g., Williams, Boyd, Cascardi, & Poythress, 1996). Richards et al. (2012) suggest that this provides support for assertions by Dillard (2008) regarding the psychological damage done to employees within meat processing plants. That is, that due to constant exposure to violence and the type of institutional climate present at slaughterhouses, workers are vulnerable psychologically. These conclusions also substantiate Fitzgerald et al.'s (2007) findings of a differential effect on violent crime rates by employment within a meat processing facility.

With its focus on individual instances of harm to individual animals deemed "worthy," criminology is currently at risk of ignoring this area as a focus of research. Perhaps because it is easier to research and police, there has been a general focus on interpersonal violence and companion animal abuse. However, this leaves a large area of social and public life unexplored by criminologists and other social scientists when it is actually the case that criminology has a great deal to contribute to this issue (see Taylor, 2011).

What is clear from the foregoing review and discussion of the literature is that this is an area of ongoing import and interest. There is clearly a need for further research into the factors that lead to CTA (e.g., family dynamics, underlying pathology, and gender) and the variables that link CTA with other antisocial, delinquent, and violent behavior. It would seem, from the review, that research attention is turning away from the "triad" (nocturnal enuresis, fire setting, and CTA) and the graduation thesis, with more and more studies depicting CTA as part of a general environment of violence and antisocial behavior (see Chapter 14). The evidence regarding the utility of the "desensitization" approach for predicting and controlling the negative sequelae of CTA at a young age is slowly accruing. For example, studies that show that CTA predates other forms of delinquency and sexual violence (e.g., Simons et al., 2008), in conjunction with those that illustrate the "red flag" nature of CTA for bullying propensity (e.g., Henry, 2004), make CTA a significant behavioral anomaly that warrants close attention. It is an unfortunate truth that the implied risk for future harm of other humans, rather than the harm to the animals themselves, is more likely to produce policy (e.g., cross-reporting; see e.g., Girardi & Pozzulo, 2012) and service provision (e.g., pet fostering for families entering domestic violence refuges) changes. However, we can hope that at least the increased attention, and concomitant earlier detection of CTA, will reduce the number of animals that suffer at the hands of children and adults, abusers and bullies.

References

Adams, C. (1995). Woman battering and harm to animals, in C. Adams & J. Donovan (Eds.) *Animals and women: Feminist theoretical explanations*. Durham and London: Duke University Press.

Adams, C., & Donovan, J. (1995). *Animals and women: Feminist theoretical explanations*. Durham and London: Duke University Press.

Agnew, R. (1998). The causes of animal abuse: A social-psychological analysis, *Theoretical Criminology*, *2*(2), 177–209.

Arluke, A., Levin, J., Luke, C., & Ascione, F. (1999). The relationship of animal abuse to violence and other forms of antisocial behavior, *Journal of Interpersonal Violence, 14*(9), 963–975.

Arluke, A., & Lockwood, R. (1997). Guest editors' introduction: Understanding cruelty to animals. *Society & Animals, 5*(3), 183–193.

Artz, G., Orazem, P., & Otto, D. (2007). Measuring the impact of meat packing and processing facilities in nonmetropolitan counties: A difference-in-differences approach, *American Journal of Agricultural Economics, 89*, 557–570.

Ascione, F. (1992). Enhancing children's attitudes about the humane treatment of animals: Generalisation to human-directed empathy, *Anthrozoös, 5*(3), 76–191.

Ascione, F. (1998). Battered women's reports of their partners and their children's cruelty to animals, *Journal of Emotional Abuse, 1*, 119–133.

Ascione, F. (2001). Animal abuse and youth violence, *OJJDP: Juvenile Justice Bulletin, September*, 1–15.

Ascione, F., & Arkow, P. (Eds.) (1999). *Child abuse, domestic violence, and animal abuse: Linking the circles of compassion for prevention and intervention*. Lafayette: Purdue University Press.

Ascione, F., & Weber, C. (1996). Children's attitudes about the humane treatment of animals and empathy: One-year follow-up of a school-based intervention, *Anthrozoos, 9*, 188–195.

Ascione, F., Weber, C., & Wood, D. (1997). The abuse of animals and domestic violence: A national survey of shelters for women who are battered, *Society & Animals, 5*(3), 205–218.

Ascione, F., Thompson, T., & Black, T. (1997). Childhood cruelty to animals: Assessing cruelty dimensions and motivations, *Anthrozoös, 10*(4), 170–182.

Baldry, A. (2003). Animal abuse and exposure to interparental violence in Italian youth. *Journal of Interpersonal Violence, 18*, 258–281.

Baldry, A. C., & Farrington, D. P. (2000). Bullies and delinquents: Personal characteristics and parental styles, *Journal of Community and Applied Social Psychology, 10*(1), 17–31.

Barker, S. B., Best, A. M., Fredrickson, M., & Hunter, G. (2000). Constraints in assessing the impact of animals in education, *Anthrozoös 13*(2): 74–79.

Beck, A., & Katcher, A. (1996). *Between pets and people: The importance of animal companionship*. Indiana: Purdue University Press.

Becker, F., & French, L. (2004). Making the links: Child abuse, animal cruelty and domestic violence, *Child Abuse Review, 13*, 399–414.

Beirne, P. (1999a). For a nonspeciesist criminology: Animal abuse as an object of study, *Criminology, 37*(1), 117–147.

Beirne, P. (1999b). Confronting Animal Abuse: Law, Criminology and Human-Animal Relationships. Maryland: Rowman and Littlefield.

Beirne, P. (2004). From animal abuse to interhuman violence? A critical review of the Progression Thesis, *Society & Animals, 1*(1), 39–65.

Benetato, M., Reisman, R., & McCobb, E. (2011). The veterinarian's role in animal cruelty cases. *Journal of the American Veterinary Medical Association, 238*, 31–34.

Boat, B., Pearl, E., Barned, J., Richet, L., Crouch, D., Barzman, D., & Putnam, F. (2011). Childhood cruelty to animals: Psychiatric and demographic correlates, *Journal of Aggression, Maltreatment & Trauma, 20*(7), 812–819.

Cazaux, G. (1999). Beauty and the beast: Animal abuse form a non-speciesist criminological perspective, *Crime, Law & Social Change, 31*(2), 105–126.

Cohen, D., & Strayer, J. (1996). Empathy in conduct-disordered and comparison youth, *Developmental Psychology, 32*(6), 988–998.

Connelly, H. J. (2007). *Animal abuse as an early predictor of violent crime later in life: A comparison of male and female inmates* (Unpublished doctoral dissertation), Alliant International University, California.

Currie, C. L. (2006). Animal cruelty by children exposed to domestic violence. *Child Abuse & Neglect, 30,* 425–435.

Dadds, M. R., Turner, C., & McAloon, J. (2002). Developmental links between cruelty to animals and human violence. *Australian and New Zealand Journal of Criminology, 35,* 363–382.

DeGue, S., & DiLillo, D. (2009). Is animal cruelty a "red flag" for family violence? Investigating co-occurring violence towards children, partners, and pets. *Journal of Interpersonal Violence, 24,* 1036–1056.

DeViney, E., Dickert, J., & Lockwood, R. (1983). The care of pets within child abusing families, *International Journal for the Study of Animal Problems, 4,* 321–329.

Dillard, J. (2008). Slaughterhouse nightmare: Psychological harm suffered by slaughterhouse employees and the possibility of redress through legal reform. *Georgetown Journal on Poverty Law and Policy, 15*(2), 391–408.

Duncan, A., Thomas, J., & Miller, C. (2005). Significance of family risk factors in development of childhood animal cruelty in adolescent boys with conduct problems, *Journal of Family Violence, 20,* 235–239.

Febres J., Shorey, R., Brasfield, H., Zucosky, H., Ninnemann, A., Elmquist, J., …, & Stuart, G. (2012). Adulthood animal abuse among women court-referred to batterer intervention programs, *Journal of Interpersonal Violence, 27*(15), 3115–3126.

Febres, J., Brasfield, H., Shorey, R., Elmquist, J., Ninnemann, A., Schonbrun, Y., …, & Strart, G. (2014). Adulthood animal abuse among men arrested for domestic violence, *Violence Against Women, 20*(9), 1059–1077.

Felthous, A. R., & Yudowitz, B. (1977). Approaching a comparative typology of assaultive female offenders. *Psychiatry, 40*(6), 270–276.

Fitzgerald, A. (2010). A social history of the slaughterhouse: From inception to contemporary implications. *Human Ecology Review, 17(1),* 58–69.

Fitzgerald, A. J., Kalof, L., & Dietz, T. (2007). Slaughterhouses and increased crime rates: An empirical analysis of the spillover from "The Jungle" into the surrounding community. *Organization & Environment, 22*(2), 158–184.

Fleming, W. M., Jory, B., & Burton, D. (2002). Characteristics of juvenile offenders admitting to sexual activity with nonhuman animals. *Society & Animals, 10*(1), 31–46.

Flynn, C. (2000). Battered women and their animal companions: Symbolic interaction between human and non-human animals, *Society & Animals, 8*(2), 99–127.

Flynn, C. (2001). Acknowledging the "zoological connection": A sociological analysis of animal cruelty, S*ociety & Animals, 9,* 71–87.

Flynn, C. P. (1999). Exploring the link between corporal punishment and children's cruelty to animals. *Journal of Marriage & the Family, 61*(4), 971–981.

Frick, P. J., Lahey, B. B., Loeber, R., Tannenbaum, L., Van Horn, Y., Christ, M. A. G., . . . , & Hanson, K. (1993). Oppositional defiant disorder and conduct disorder: A meta-analytic review of factor analyses and cross-validation in a clinic sample. *Clinical Psychology Review, 13*, 319–340.

Girardi, A., & Pozzulo, J. (2012). The significance of animal cruelty in child protection investigations, *Social Work Research, 36*(1), 53–60.

Gleyzer, R., Felthous, A. R., & Holzer, C. E. (2002). Animal cruelty and psychiatric disorders, *Journal of the American Academy of Psychiatry and Law, 30*, 257–265.

Grandin, T. (1998). Fast food chains audit animal handling practices. *Meat & Poultry*, December, 57.

Gullone, E., & Robertson, N. (2008). The relationship between bullying and animal abuse behaviors in adolescents: The importance of witnessing animal abuse. *Journal of Applied Developmental Psychology, 29*, 371–379.

Hastings, P. D., Zahn-Waxler, C., Robinson, J., Usher, B., & Bridges, D. (2000). The development of concern for others in children with behavior problems. *Developmental Psychology, 36*, 531–546.

Heidensohn, F. (2010). On Writing "The deviance of women": Observations and analysis, *The British Journal of Sociology, 61*, 127–132.

Henry, B. (2004). The relationship between animal cruelty, delinquency, and attitudes toward the treatment of animals. *Society & Animals, 12*(3), 185–207.

Henry, B., & Sanders, C. E. (2007). Bullying and animal abuse: Is there a connection? *Society & Animals, 15*, 107–126.

Hensley, C., Tallichet, S. E., & Dutkiewicz, E. L. (2009). Recurrent childhood animal cruelty: Is there a relationship to adult recurrent interpersonal violence? *Criminal Justice Review, 34*, 248–257.

Herzog, H., Betchart, N., & Pittman, R. (1991). Sex role identity and attitudes toward animals, *Anthrozoös, 4*(3), 184–192.

HSUS. (2007). *American Humane: Protecting children and animals*, Retrieved from: http://www.americanhumane.org/site/PageServer?pagename=lk_home&JServSessionIdr007=a2n8v9wra1.app25a.

Khan, R., & Cooke, D. J. (2008). Risk factors for severe inter-sibling violence: A preliminary study of a youth forensic sample. *Journal of Interpersonal Violence, 23*, 1513–1530.

Kellert, S. R., & Felthous, A. R. (1985). Childhood cruelty toward animals among criminals and non-criminals, *Human Relations, 38*, 1113–1129.

Knight, K., Ellis, C., & Simmons, S. (2014). Parental predictors of children's animal abuse: Findings from a national and intergenerational sample, *Journal of Interpersonal Violence, 29*(16), 3014–3034.

Kreinert, J., Walsh, J., Matthews, K., & McConkey, K. (2012). Examining the nexus between domestic violence and animal abuse in a national sample of service providers, *Violence and Victims, 27*(2), 280–295.

Levinson, B. (1978). Pets and personality development, *Psychological Reports, 42,* 1031–1038.

Lockwood, R., & Ascione, F. (Eds.). (1998). *Cruelty to animals and interpersonal violence.* Indiana: Purdue University Press.

Lockwood, R., & Hodge, G. (1986) The tangled web of animal abuse: the links between cruelty to animals and human violence, *Humane Society News*, Summer, 1–6.

Luk, E. S., Staiger, P. K., Wong, L., & Mathai, J. (1999). Children who are cruel to animals: A revisit. *Australia and New Zealand Journal of Psychiatry, 33*(1), 29–36.

McEwan, F., Moffitt, T., & Arseneault, L. (2014). Is childhood cruelty to animals a marker for physical maltreatment in a prospective cohort study of children? *Child Abuse & Neglect, 38,* 533–543.

McPhedran, S. (2009). Animal abuse, family violence, and child wellbeing. *Journal of Family Violence, 24,* 41–52.

Mead, M. (1964) Cultural factors in the cause of pathological homicide, *Bulletin of the Menninger Clinic, 2,* 11–22.

Merz-Perez, L., & Heide, K. M. (2003). *Animal cruelty: Pathway to violence against people.* Lanham, MD: Rowman & Littlefield.

Merz-Perez, L., Heide, K., & Silverman, I. J. (2001). Childhood cruelty to animals and subsequent violence against humans, *International Journal of Offender Therapy and Comparative Criminology, 45*(5), 556–573.

Miller, C. (2001). Childhood animal cruelty and interpersonal violence, *Clinical Psychology Review, 21*(5), 755–749.

Miller, K. S., & Knutson, J. F. (1997). Reports of severe physical punishment and exposure to animal cruelty by inmates convicted of felonies and by university students, *Child Abuse & Neglect 21*(1), 59–82.

Norris, G., & Wilson, P. (2003). Relationship of criminal behaviour and mental illness in young adults: Conduct Disorder, cruelty to animals and young adult serious violence. *Psychiatry, Psychology and the Law, 10*(1), 239–243.

O'Grady, K. E., Kinlock, T. W., & Hanlon, T. E. (2007). Prediction of violence history in substance-abusing inmates, *The Prison Journal, 87,* 416–433

Porcher, J. (2011). The relationship between workers and animals in the pork industry: A shared suffering, *Journal of Agricultural and Environmental Ethics, 24*(1), 3–17.

Porcher, J., Cousson-Gélie, F., & Dantzer, R. (2004). Affective components of the human-animal relationship in animal husbandry: Development and validation of a questionnaire, *Psychological Reports, 95*, 275–290.

Randour, M. L. (2007). Integrating animals into the family violence paradigm: Implications for policy and professional standards. *Journal of Emotional Abuse, 7*(3), 97–116.

Richards, E., Signal, T. D., & Taylor, N. (in press). A different cut? Occupation, attitude to animals and propensity for aggression. *Society & Animals.*

Rigdon, J. D., & Tapia, F. (1977). Children who are cruel to animals: A follow-up study. *Journal of Operational Psychiatry, 8*(1), 27–36.

Sanders, C. E., & Henry, B. C. (2014). Nonhuman animal cruelty, bullying and behavioral difficulties among women. *Society & Animals, Advance online,* doi: 10.1163/15685306-12341355.12341355.

Sanders, C., Henry, B., Giuliani, C., & Dimmer, L. (2013). Bullies, victims, and animal abusers: Do they exhibit similar behavioral difficulties? *Society & Animals, 21*, 225–239.

Schiff, K., Louw, D., & Ascione F. (1999). Animal relations in childhood and later violent behaviour against humans, *Acta Criminologica, 12*, 77–86.

Signal, T., & Taylor, N. (2006). Attitudes to animals: Demographics within a Community sample, *Society & Animals, 14*(2), 147–158.

Simmons, C. A., & Lehmann, P. (2007). Exploring the link between pet abuse and controlling behaviors in violent relationships. *Journal of Interpersonal Violence, 22*(9), 1211–1222.

Simons, D. A., Wurtele, S. K., & Durham, R. L. (2008). Developmental experiences of child sexual abusers and rapists. *Child Abuse & Neglect, 32*, 549–560.

Sutherland, E. (1949). *White collar crime*, New York: Holt, Rinehart & Winston.

Tallichet, S. E., & Hensley, C. (2005). Rural and urban differences in the commission of animal cruelty, *International Journal of Offender Therapy and Comparative Criminology, 49*(6), 711–726.

Tallichet, S. E., Hensley, C., O'Bryan, A., & Hassel, H. (2005). Targets for cruelty: Demographic and situational factors affecting the type of animal abused, *Criminal Justice Studies: A Critical Journal of Crime, Law & Society, 18*(2), 173–182.

Tapia, F. (1971). Children who are cruel to animals. *Child Psychiatry & Human Development, 2*(2), 70–77.

Taylor, N. (2011). Criminology and human-animal violence research: The contribution and the challenge, *Critical Criminology, 19*, 251–263.

Taylor, N., Fraser, H., Signal, T., & Prentice, K. (2014). Social Work, Animal Assisted Therapies and Ethical Considerations: A Case Example from Central Queensland. British Journal of Social Work, online first doi: 10.1093/bjsw/bcu115.

Taylor, N., & Signal, T. (2004). Attitudes to animals: An indicator of interpersonal violence? *Journal of the Home Economics Institute of Australia, Inc., 11*(3), 9–12.

Taylor, N., & Signal, T. (2005). Empathy and attitudes towards animals. *Anthrozoos, 18*(1), 18–27.

Taylor, N., & Signal, T. (2006). Community demographics and the propensity to report animal cruelty, *Journal of Applied Animal Welfare Science, 9*(3), 14–20.

Taylor, N., & Signal, T. (2008). Throwing the baby out with the bathwater: Towards a sociology of the human-animal abuse 'link.' *Sociological Research Online, 13*(1/2).

Taylor, N., Signal, T., & Stark, T. (2006). Domestic violence, child abuse and companion animal harm: Service provider perspectives. *Journal of the Home Economics Institute of Australia, 13*(1), 2–5.

Thompson, K., & Gullone, E. (2003). Promotion of empathy and prosocial behaviour in children, *Australian Psychologist, 38*(3), 175–182.

Thompson, K., & Gullone, E. (2006). An investigation into the association between the witnessing of animal abuse and adolescents' behavior toward animals. *Society & Animals, 14*, 223–243.

Vaughn, M. G., Fu, Q., Beaver, K. M., DeLisi, M., Perron, B. E. & Howard, M. O. (2011). Effects of childhood adversity on bullying and cruelty to animals in the United States: Findings from a national sample. Journal of Interpersonal Violence, 26(11), 3509–3525.

Vialles, N. (2002). *Animals to edible.* Cambridge: Cambridge University Press.

Volant, A. M., Johnson, J. A., Gullone, E., & Coleman, G. J. (2008). The relationship between domestic violence and animal abuse: An Australian study, *Journal of Interpersonal Violence, 23*(9), 1277–1295.

Warden, D., & Mackinnon, S. (2003). Prosocial children, bullies and victims: An investigation of their sociometric status, empathy and social problem-solving strategies, *British Journal of Developmental Psychology 21*, 367–385.

Wax, D. E., & Haddox, V. G. (1974). Enuresis, fire setting, and animal cruelty: A useful danger signal in predicting vulnerability of adolescent males to assaultive behavior, *Child Psychiatry and Human Development, 4,* 151–156.

Williams, T. Y., Boyd, J. C., Cascardi, M. A., & Poythress, N. (1996). Factor structure and convergent validity of the aggression questionnaire in an offender population. *Psychological Assessment, 8*(4), 398–403.

Chapter 13

Animal Cruelty and Family Violence

Aimée X. Delaney

Family Violence and Animal Cruelty

Animals are one of the innocent victims caught within family violence. Approaches to family violence tend to focus solely on human family members, with little consideration for familial animal companions (Flynn, 2000). This also appears to be reflected in the greater part of the research. In one of the most recent meta-analyses of family violence research, Chan et al. (2021) do not address either animal cruelty within family violence or exposure to familial animal cruelty. Instead, incidences of family violence have historically been examined as independent factors rather than co-occurring factors inclusive of animal cruelty (Chan et al., 2021). When examining family violence within the context of law, animal cruelty is not often considered either (Randour et al., 2021). Yet familial companion animals are often used as instruments to perpetrate family violence, occurring concurrently with violence perpetrated against human family members (Arkow, 2015; Ascione et al., 2007; Barrett, 2018; Barrett, 2020; Collins et al., 2018; Fitzgerald et al., 2020; Giesbrecht, 2021; Jordan & Lem, 2014; Krienert et al., 2012; Newberry, 2017; Stevenson et al., 2018).

Animal cruelty has been classified as part of a pattern of "dangerous behavior" to both animals and humans (Ascione et al., 2007; McDonald et al., 2015). Animal cruelty is not simply a warning sign of family violence, but involves an integral role within the dynamics of family violence. For example, perpetrators use animals as part of the emotional manipulation of victims—refusing food, veterinary care, or shelter for the familial animal companion. Perpetrators use threats against familial animal companions to ensure victims' compliance with their demands. There is also a correlation between severe animal cruelty and the severity of intimate partner violence (Randour et al., 2021). But familial animal companions are often neglected within the scope of family violence interventions (Flynn, 2000). Intervention professionals may not recognize the signs of animal cruelty. This chapter will outline the current research defining and explaining the animal cruelty-family violence relationship, and explore the current state of animal cruelty within family violence including current policies and laws. This chapter will also offer future directions and potential solutions for intervention professionals and researchers.

Definitions

The family involves a system of related entities, either biologically or legally, typically residing within the same household. Within modern society, families are socially constructed and these constructions may include non-human members such as companion animals (Buries, 2021) (see also Chapter 3 of this book). Across the familial life course, family interactions vary and these interactions may be impacted by the presence of familial companion animals (Buries, 2021). Thus, it is important to include familial animal companions within the definition of family when examining family violence. What do these terms mean: violence, family violence, and animal cruelty? This section offers basic definitions for the main terms used in this chapter.

Violence

Violence is "behavior expended to inflict harm on another" (Delaney, 2021b, p. 5). This includes actions towards others as well as exposure to violent behavior, as these actions inflict physical, psychological, or social harm. For example, adult human victims of animal cruelty within family violence tend to appear significantly more afraid and nervous in the presence of law-enforcement and have injuries and pain as a result of the abuse (Campbell et al., 2021). This encompasses all three of these dimensions of harm. For youth exposed to animal cruelty within family violence, this type of violence is harmful to their development and holds long-term consequences into adulthood (e.g., see Kennedy et al., 2010; Negriff, 2020; Petro, 2010). Animal cruelty within family violence is therefore a manifestation of violence.

Animal Cruelty

Animal cruelty is defined in Chapter 1 of this book. To expand upon this definition, when specifically considering animal cruelty within family violence, the definition also needs to include threats, neglect, physical abuse, and otherwise harming a familial animal companion (Barrett et al., 2020). It may also include sexual acts and torture towards familial animal companions. In extreme cases, killing a familial companion animal is also animal cruelty (Dale & Yeung, 2021) and is another tactic of family violence.

Family Violence

Family violence has many different definitions. But these definitions tend to focus on a variety of behaviors intended to exert control over other individuals, including psychological, physical, or sexual harm (Lindhorst & Tajima, 2008). Definitions of family violence also need to involve the harm caused by financial abuse. This is particularly important when we consider familial companion animals. Obtaining these animals, as well as maintaining their health, can be quite costly (American Veterinary Medical Association, 2022; The Hollard Insurance Company, 2021). Denying human victims money to provide care for their familial animal companions is part of the dynamics of family violence. Current definitions of family violence tend to be separated into either intimate partner violence (IPV) or child maltreatment.

Intimate partner violence. IPV is defined as violence occurring between partners involved in an intimate relationship. This violence can include physical acts, psychological behavior (e.g., words used to harm the victim), and sexual coercion or force (Krug et al., 2002). Just as important when considering definitions of IPV is a lack of action, commonly known as neglect. Neglect involves the omission of and otherwise ignoring the needs of dependent adult family members. For example, caregiver neglect can be considered a manifestation of elder abuse towards an intimate partner who is dependent on that family member. When considering the full scope of animal cruelty within family violence, neglecting the basic needs of a familial companion animal could be considered neglect within the family. This is particularly important when an adult family member is dependent on a familial animal companion, such as a service animal or emotional support.

Child maltreatment. Child maltreatment is defined similarly to IPV: violence occurring between an adult and a person identified as a minor within society. This violence also includes physical, psychological, and sexual abuse as well as neglect. Neglect is an important consideration within child maltreatment. Youth are in a precarious situation within the family, in that youth are dependent on adult family members for their care, safety, and overall welfare. When adult family members ignore the emotional needs of youth family members, this may be considered a manifestation of neglect. The human-animal bond is beneficial for overall social and emotional well-being (McConnell et al., 2019; Thielke et al., 2019). Neglect would therefore apply in the instances of animal cruelty within the family. When considering the full scope of family violence towards humans and animals, neglecting the basic needs of the youths' familial companion animal's needs is an act of child maltreatment: neglect for the youth's emotional state and violence within the family.

These definitions typically do not consider acts of family violence being conjoined and simultaneously incorporating animal cruelty. Family violence definitions seem to still separate instances of IPV, child maltreatment, and animal cruelty. As discussed in this section, modernized definitions of family violence must include animal cruelty.

Theoretical Explanations

There are many reasons why individuals or groups engage in the cruelty of animals. If we knew the definitive reasons for perpetrating animal cruelty, then this social problem would be solved. Since we do not, the best explanations are theories that explore the varying reasons based on specific circumstances. The focus of this section is to explore the specific circumstances of family violence and how this expression of violence can contribute to or exasperate animal cruelty, and offer some theories to help explain the animal cruelty-family violence link. A more general discussion of theories explaining animal cruelty can be located within Chapters 15 and 16 of this book.

Social Learning Theory

Learning theories serve to explain why people engage in violent behavior, with the argument of these theories suggesting people learn it (*cf.* Bandura, 1977). Under the premises of these theories, individuals learn animal cruelty by observing and mimicking family members repeatedly (Ormrod, 1999). Youth, in particular, may imitate their family members' violent behaviors on animals rather than other humans, as animal companions may be easier to physically control when testing out violent behaviors. Youth who mimic animal cruelty perpetrated by other family members are more likely to engage in cruelty towards animals themselves because they have learned through the family that violence is acceptable (Hensley et al., 2012; McEwen et al., 2014).

Cycle of Violence

The cycle of violence is a repetitive sequence of family violence and animal cruelty. Family violence fosters violent tendencies within youth. Youth who experience or witness family violence may act out that violence towards animals and this violent behavior gets repeated within their families as adults. Research supports this contention; children who engage in violence towards animals will eventually engage in violence towards other humans (Juliadilla & Noveni, 2021). Later within the life course, the now adult may engage in violence towards their intimate partners, children, other family members, and possibly familial animal companions. Thus, they have created a cycle of violence.

Norms of Violence

When families engage in violence, either through direct action, exposing other members, or indirectly by failing to make violence deviant, other members are inculcated into a normative environment of violence (Delaney, 2021c). The meaning of violence conveyed within the family is that violence is an acceptable behavior. This violence may spill over into the treatment of animals (*cf.* Delaney, 2021b), including acts of animal cruelty. Human family members are simply reproducing the norms of the family by engaging in violence towards familial animal companions. And familial animal cruelty may be covertly supported within the normative structure of society, where violence is a socially acceptable means of behavior towards others. The consistent reinforcement of violence encourages these norms of violence.

In summary, these theories share a common theme: families play an important role in instances of animal cruelty (Juliadilla & Noveni, 2021), shaping attitudes and behaviors towards animal welfare. Theoretically, companion animals must be included within any situation of family violence.

Familial Companion Animals

About half of all households in the United States have a familial companion animal, with estimates ranging from 49% up to 68% (Applebaum et al., 2020; Applebaum et al., 2021; Statista, 2021; United States Census Bureau, 2017). The statistics internationally are not well published. And, while familial animal companions appear to exist at higher rates within White non-Hispanic families in the United States compared to families of color (Applebaum et al., 2020), more research is needed to understand cultural connections between family diversity and familial animal companions within the United States. The majority of these familial animal companions are dogs, with cats closely following (American Veterinary Medical Association., 2022; Hollard Insurance Company, 2021; World Atlas, 2022). Internationally, estimate for dogs as familial companion animals are 471 million, with cats at 370 million (Statista, 2021; The Hollard Insurance Company, 2021).

Given the prevalence of familial animal companions, it is no surprise that many people consider companion animals to be part of the family. Animals have become an important aspect of family life (Applebaum et al., 2021). Estimates indicate that up to 90% of households having a companion animal consider those animals to be members of the family (Applebaum et al., 2021). This percentage is slightly higher among youth, with almost 93% reporting companion animals to be members of their family (Bures et al., 2019). In fact, youth may consider their companion animals to have a sibling type relationship with them (Power, 2008). Embedded within family relationships are the relationships with familial companion animals (Charles, 2014; Irvine & Celia, 2017).

The human-animal bond is an emotional relationship (Volsche, 2019). This emotional relationship with familial animal companions becomes stronger over time and throughout the life course of the family members, often offering a sense of social support (Applebaum et al., 2021; Giesbrecht, 2021). In fact, more than half of individuals report that their familial companion animals are a major source of emotional support (Campbell et al., 2021). Humans may form such a strong bond with their familial animal companions that these animals can serve as a steppingstone for childless couples in their decision on whether or not to have children (Buries, 2021; Laurent-Simpson, 2017b; Laurent-Simpson, 2017c). And for youth in the family, companion animals may serve as emotional support, like pseudo-siblings (Cassels et al., 2017; Laurent-Simpson, 2017a; Laurent-Simpson, 2017b; Laurent-Simpson, 2017; Volsche, 2019). But this bond with a familial companion animal may serve as another method to perpetrate family violence.

Current State of Animal Cruelty within Family Violence

There is a long history of research documenting the link between animal cruelty and family violence (e.g., see Ascione, 1998; Ascione et al., 1997; DeGue & DiLillo, 2009; DeViney et al., 1983; Hartman et al., 2018; Simmons & Lehmann, 2007; Walker,

1984). Instances of family violence, alone, are estimated to occur in between 1% and 71% of any given population (Cannon et al., 2010; Chan, 2017; Grossman & Lundy, 2003; Pritchard, 2007; Zink & Fisher, 2007), with animal cruelty co-occurring with family violence in about 25% to 100% of these cases (Ascione, 1997; Campbell et al., 2021; Faver & Strand, 2003; Flynn, 2000; McDonald, et al., 2015; Simmons & Lehmann, 2007). This wide range of estimates can be accounted for based on variation in definitions of family violence transnationally and the type of violence perpetrated.

Perpetrators of violence may use the pets as weapons to threaten their victims as well as exploit the emotional bond victims have with their companion animals (e.g., see Barrett et al., 2020; Collins et al., 2018; Fitzgerald et al., 2019) and intentionally target companion animals as a means to control or retaliate against family members (Collins et al., 2018). One human service provider shared the following story about a victim of animal cruelty within the family: "a client who saw her beloved dog shot was left very badly traumatized, she also said her abuser likes to kick and hurt the animal, just to upset her" (Geisbrcht, 2021, p. 11). Threatening or actually harming familial companion animals is a common method of psychological violence within the family (Campbell et al., 2021). In addition to the emotional bonding, familial companion animals assist family members with coping with trauma (Costab & Gomes, 2018; Mackin, et al., 2017; Schofield et al., 2016; Schaffer et al., 2014). Perpetrators may know this, and use the familial animal companion as means to execute their abuse within the family. Animals have been the quintessential weapon of family violence. And the most severe violence towards animal companions tends to co-occur with family violence (Simmons & Lehmann, 2007).

Animals are weaponized in many other ways. One way is to use the animal to harass a victim (Randour et al., 2021), such as exposing family youth to the violence perpetrated against animals. Research indicates that this occurs in up to 59% of family violence cases (Campbell et al., 2021). Another way is to actively involve family youth in the acts of animal cruelty. This may encompass forcing youth to physically harm or to engage in sexual acts with the familial companion animal. The perpetrator may, in these ways, cause emotional or psychological harm to other family members (in addition to victimizing the youth themself). Victims of family violence have legitimate fear of harm to their familial companion animals, occurring both while the family is intact and when the victim leaves the family. One of the reasons victims do not leave violent families is because they often must leave their familial animal companion. Adult family members may also choose to remain in the harmful relationship due to concerns over the safety and well-being of their familial companion animals (Bright et al., 2018; Haden et al., 2018) or delay seeking assistance for fear of being separated from their companion animals (Giesbrecht, 2021). In other instances, human victims who leave family violence situations may return to the family in order to ensure the safety and well-being of their familial companion animal (Giesbrecht, 2021).

This violence is known to intervention professionals. In one study, more than half of human service professionals (65%) agreed that animal cruelty occurred concurrently with family violence among the clients they serve (Giesbrecht, 2021). Other studies show that families in domestic violence shelters are more likely to report a family member engaging in familial animal cruelty, compared to other women in the community (Ascione, 2007), estimating this occurs in more than half of these families (Hartman et al., 2018). Although only a small percentage of victims report animal cruelty co-occurring within family violence to law-enforcement officers (Campbell et al., 2021), the low response may be accounted for by the officers' gathering of this data at the moment of impact for family violence. It may be possible that the perpetrator was still present, and the victim may have feared retaliation for their responses. Victims may also have feared losing their familial companion animals due to the perpetrator's abuse, fearing law enforcement officers removing either them or their companion animals from the family. A survey of human services and animal welfare professionals in Canada found that the majority of professionals (89%) believe the safety and safe keeping of familial companion animals impacted victims' decision-making processes about whether or not to remain in the violent family (Giesbrecht, 2021).

Companion animals are also victims of family violence. The animal is not being used solely as a purpose to harm the human victim, but rather the familial animal companion is also experiencing their own victimization. The risk of violence to the familial animal companion is only increased because of the emotional bond to the human victim. As succinctly put by one human service provider, "if one partner has an attachment or investment in an animal, that animal can potentially be just as at risk as the partner experiencing abuse or violence" (Geisbrcht, 2021, p. 12).

More accurate estimates of animal cruelty within family violence may not thoroughly be known. Most research has focused on reports from victims of intimate partner violence at domestic violence shelters (Ascione, 1998; Flynn, 2000; McDonald et al., 2017), while other studies have relied solely on reports to law enforcement responding to incidences of family violence (Campbell et al., 2021). Despite laws that protect animals from harm,[1] these laws often fail to include familial animal companions as a victim of family violence. Familial animal companions are still seen as property of the adults within the family. Veterinarians may be aware of or have witnessed harm to familial animal companions as a result of family violence, yet many of these professionals still do not report today (Applebaum et al., 2021; Dale & Yeung, 2021; Green & Gullipone, 2005; Jordan & Lem, 2014; Williams et al., 2008). Law enforcement reports tend to provide little to no information regarding the outcome for the familial animal companion, including the location, safekeeping, or sheltering of the animal that experienced familial animal cruelty (Campbell et al., 2021). Beyond these statistics, estimates transnationally are difficult given the lack of consistency with definitions of both animal cruelty and family violence across different nations. Overall, family victimization, including familial animal companions, may be significantly greater than what is reported in the current research (Chan et al., 2021).

1. See Chapters 3 and 4 for more information on laws protecting animals.

Animal Cruelty within the Family as Polyvictimization

Polyvictimization has been defined as multiple yet different victimization experiences occurring either simultaneous or sequential through the life course (Cuevas et al., 2010; Hahm et al., 2010; Finkelhor et al., 2011; Finkelhor et al., 2007; Hamby et al., 2010). These victimization experiences can be expanded into family violence, particularly given the family system traverses the life course. Familial polyvictimization is defined as "a co-occurrence of more than two different types of victimization" among "different members within a family" and perpetrated by a family member (Chan et al., 2021, p. 290). Families often co-experience IPV and child maltreatment (e.g., see Ascione, 1997; Ascione et al., 2007; Ascione et al., 1997; Barrett et al., 2020; Chan et al., 2021; DeGue & DiLillo, 2009; Fitzgerald et al., 2020; Fitzgerald et al., 2019; Haden et al., 2018; Jegatheesen et al., 2020; Krienert et al., 2012; Rauktis & Moser, 2021; Simmons & Lehmann, 2007). The emerging research shows animal cruelty often co-occurs within violent families (as discussed previously). Since the family includes companion animals, familial polyvictimization includes familial animal companions and cruelty perpetrated towards these animals (Chan, 2017; Randour et al., 2021). All these circumstances represent familial polyvictimization.

Families who engage in one type of violence to control behaviors of other family members may also engage in violent means in which to control the familial companion animal. This is a spill-over effect within the family system (*cf.* Delaney, 2021b). The dynamics of the family may be that violence is considered a normative means in which to control behavior. Familial companion animals are an instrument in which to perpetrate that violence as well as become the target of violence. For example, if a caregiver in the family cannot provide the care necessary for companion animals, these adults may also not be able to provide the care necessary for the youth in the household (Rauktis & Moser, 2021). This neglect may lead the perpetrator to engage in physical violence towards that caregiver, as retaliation, and the physical violence may be accompanied with psychological abuse (e.g., name-calling). Ultimately, the caregiver may not have been able to provide for the family youth and animal companion because the perpetrator controls the finances and does not provide the financial means to care for the family members (i.e., financial abuse). In this same scenario, the adult exposing the youth and familial animal companions to family violence creates a system of victimization towards youth, via neglect and exposure to violence towards other family members (Jegatheesan et al., 2020). This is an example of polyvictimization. Violence perpetrated by one member of the family may transcend to other members of the family and become the norm within the family—an accepted level of violence as control (i.e., norms of violence within the family [*cf.* Delaney, 2021b]). But more research is needed surrounding animal cruelty as a manifestation of familial polyvictimization and more specifically within family violence (Chan et al., 2021).

Impact of Animal Cruelty within Family Violence

The consequences of familial animal cruelty are severe. Intended abuse and neglect towards familial companion animals leads to psychological harm on the other family members (Ascione et al., 2007; Campbell et al., 2021; Collins et al., 2018; Fitzgerald et al., 2019; Lindhorst & Tajima, 2008; McDonald et al., 2018; McDonald et al., 2019; Newberry, 2017; Simmons & Lehmann, 2007), and experiences with chronic fear and guilt (Collins et al., 2018; McDonald et al., 2018). Familial animal companions may serve as a family member's only emotional support, due to the perpetrator's isolation of the human family member (McDonald et al., 2015), becoming one of the only means for the family member to manage their stress (Carter & Porges, 2016). This may be another reason for human family members to remain within the family despite potential grave harm (Collins et al., 2018; McDonald et al., 2018; McDonald et al., 2015; McDonald et al., 2016; Schaffer et al., 2014). One of the major dangers of family violence is that both humans and animals are at substantially higher risk of suffering severe or fatal injury, with about 80% of victims reporting concerns that they or their familial animal companions will eventually be killed by the alleged perpetrator (Campbell et al., 2021). Other research supports this contention: the severity and frequency of family violence increases when animal cruelty is also present (Ascione et al., 2007; Barrett et al., 2017).

Long-term outcomes for youth who are exposed to both familial animal cruelty and family violence include chronic stress (Campbell et al., 2021) and experiencing increased instances of child maltreatment (Campbell & Thompson, 2015). The family violence-animal cruelty link serves not only as victimization, but also a precursor for later perpetration (Becker et al., 2004; Browne et al., 2016; Campbell et al., 2021; Rauktis & Moser, 2021).[2] Violence, as a form of family dysfunction, increases the likelihood of behavioral disorders in youth (Juliadilla & Noveni, 2021). Youth family members may act out as part of a normative violent behavioral response (Gorman-Smith & Tolan, 1998), including engaging in animal cruelty (Spencer et al., 2018). Youth exposed to animal cruelty within family violence have been found to be more likely to engage in animal cruelty themselves (Applebaum et al., 2021; Ascione et al., 2007; McEwen et al., 2014; Juliadilla & Noveni, 2021). These violent acts towards animals may be performed as practice for engaging in violence against other humans (Juliadilla & Noveni, 2021). Youth may inculcate violence as an appropriate behavior to the shared meanings developed from the normative collective expectations of the family, and thus creates a victimizing effect on the youth (*cf.* Delaney, 2021a). In this sense, youth may fail to develop empathy towards animals (Juliadilla & Noveni, 2021) and recreate violence against other living beings. But again, more research is needed to understand the relationship between family youth and familial companion animals (Muldoon et al., 2019) rather than relying on theoretical premises.

2. See Chapter 12 in this book for more on juveniles and animal cruelty.

Preventative Measures for Cruelty to Familial Animal Companions

Families with animal companions experience many protective factors, including less depression (Peacock et al., 2012), less social isolation (Irvine, 2013), and increases in social competence, self-esteem, and prosocial behavior among youth (Van Houtte & Jarvis, 1995). Familial companion animals have been shown to increase positive social relationships (Carter & Porges, 2016), and may even counteract the harm caused by chronic stress (Carter & Porges, 2016; Stanić et al., 2017; Zheng et al., 2010). Family attachments also serve as a preventative function for violence, in that "parental support and control have been found to be critically important" in the parenting processes (Barnes et al., 2006, p. 1085), with one intention of the family serving to instill social control over the unaccepted behaviors of the family members (*cf.* Delaney, 2021b). As a society, we need to cultivate empathy for animals, including general animal welfare (Juliadilla & Noveni, 2021), in order to prevent future violence.

Laws and Policies

The National Council of Juvenile and Family Court Justices (2019) in the United States passed a resolution making animal cruelty a crime of violence. This action was taken to assist families experiencing violence in dealing with the co-occurrence of familial animal cruelty (National Council of Juvenile and Family Court Justices, 2019). Recently, in Australia, the government recognized the rights of familial companion animals by altering the definition of intimidation within IPV to include harm or threatened harm to familial animal companions (Prosperi-Porta & Pai, 2021). The result of this newly conceptualized definition provides law enforcement with the resources to charge perpetrators of familial animal cruelty with a domestic violence offense. At the same time, the penalties for animal cruelty significantly increased in Australia (Prosperi-Porta & Pai, 2021). And, protection orders in Australia now include language directing perpetrators to refrain from harming the familial animal companion (Prosperi-Porta & Pai, 2021). Laws for protection orders have also been implemented in the United States to help protect familial animal companions. Thirty-three states, plus the district of Columbia and Puerto Rico, include familial animal companions within protection laws for victims of family violence (Randour et al., 2021). Mandated reporting laws are another direction to help intervene in instances of animal cruelty within family violence. As of 2021, 37 states in the USA had mandated reporting laws requiring veterinarians to report instances of familial animal cruelty (Randour et al., 2021). However, without the necessary training, intervention professionals may not understand what constitutes familial animal cruelty, family violence, and the co-occurrence of these two forms of violence (Randour et al., 2021).

Advocates have called for laws that prevent discrimination against familial companion animals, such as in the availability of housing (Applebaum et al., 2021). This call was answered with Australian law that now explicitly prevents housing restrictions based solely on familial animal companions (Prosperi-Porta & Pai, 2021). This will assist victims leaving the family with being sheltered with their non-human animal family members (McDonald, 2021). But these laws need to be extended further within other nations to allow for familial companion animals to accompany family members to shelters, foster homes, and other residential facilities that support victims of family violence.

The possibility that these recent changes have a deterrent effect is unknown at this time because these changes are so recent. Some governments are at least starting to recognize the relationship between family violence and animal cruelty. The Australian government is so progressive with recognizing animal cruelty under the context of family violence that they have approved funding to provide for animal sheltering and safekeeping for victims (Prosperi-Porta & Pai, 2021). Policy efforts have been made by the Humane Society of the United States and the American Society of the Prevention of Cruelty to Animals to offer access to veterinary care within vulnerable communities (Applebaum et al., 2021), and support for human victims who do not leave due to lack of sheltering for familial animals. Other than procuring funding, there has not been much change within family violence policies to include familial companion animals.

Because in many nations family violence victims still cannot bring familial companion animals with them to shelters, few human service professionals ask these victims about familial animal cruelty. Yet, a high percentage of both human service and animal welfare professionals receive requests from human victims to house their familial companion animals when trying to leave a violent family household (Giesbrecht, 2021). A small percentage of these human service professionals (28%), and even smaller percentage of these animal welfare professionals (8%), believe there are sufficient community resources for housing victims of animal cruelty when trying to assist victims (Giesbrecht, 2021). This uncertain state for the sheltering of familial companion animals continues to be one of the many reasons why victims choose to stay in a family violence situation (Newberry, 2017). Because companion animals may serve as a protective buffer for stress, particularly among children (Buries, 2021), policies for law enforcement and human service professionals need to take into consideration the importance of the relationship between family violence victims and their familial companion animals.

Future Directions

Animal cruelty within family violence is a public health issue. Intervention professionals, including first responders, need to be aware of the signs of animal cruelty when investigating cases of family violence. An important part of evaluation for youth exposed to family violence is also examining their experiences with animals (McDonald et al., 2018). An indicator of family dysfunction may be having a large number of animals transitioning in and out of the home (Loar & Coleman, 2004). It is imperative that intervention workers cooperate when dealing with animal cruelty within family violence, both in recognizing signs of familial animal cruelty as well as responding to animal cruelty within family violence. This includes law enforcement, human services, and animal welfare professionals (Campbell et al., 2021).

Law Enforcement

One of the downfalls of law enforcement involvement in animal cruelty within family violence is that law enforcement officers are more likely to place victims within temporary housing, such as shelters, and be less likely to arrest the alleged perpetrator (Campbell et al., 2021). As mentioned previously, many shelters do not allow housing for familial companion animals, making the human victims more likely to return to the violent household where the perpetrator is still present. Training needs to be implemented for animal control officers/humane law enforcement officers to recognize risk factors for animal cruelty within family violence. Some of these risk factors include drug or alcohol use within the family, access to guns in the home, a history of attempting or threatening suicide, stalking human family members, the use of sexual force towards an intimate partner, strangulation of intimate partner, and death threats to both the intimate partner and youth in the family (Campbell et al., 2021). Law enforcement officers also need to provide resources to the victims to assist with familial companion animals remaining with the family (Randour et al., 2021).

Animal Welfare Professionals

Veterinary schools are now teaching students about animal cruelty within family violence. There have been emerging developments in the education of future veterinarians, including curriculum on animal cruelty and the link to family violence (Armitage-Chan, 2020; Dale & Yeung, 2021). A study of two cohorts of veterinary students in New Zealand found that the students overwhelmingly support (95% and 98%) the need for this curriculum (Dale & Yeung, 2021). In this same study, over 99% of these veterinary students supported legal and ethical obligations for veterinarians to report instances of animal cruelty to the authorities (Dale & Yeung, 2021). And while the research indicates veterinarians are aware of the connections between family health and animal welfare (Pinillos et al., 2016; Lockwood & Arkow, 2016), many veterinarians are still reluctant to become involved due either to a lack of confidence in dealing with the situation (Dale & Yeung, 2021; Green & Gullipone, 2005) or a lack of resources available for companion animals (Dale & Yeung, 2021; Green & Gullipone, 2005; Williams et al., 2008). Animal welfare professionals need similar training on animal cruelty, family violence, and the link between these two acts of violence similar to what is offered to law enforcement. More importantly, these professionals need training on mandatory reporting and intervention techniques when directly faced with animal cruelty within family violence.

Recommendations for Professionals

More collaboration is needed between the different types of intervention workers (Dale & Yeung, 2021). Intervention workers make many considerations when working with the co-occurrence of family violence and animal cruelty. Assessments need to include questions about familial companion animals (Loar, 2014), adult interactions and responses to familial companion animals (Rauktis & Moser, 2021), and the relationship between the familial companion animals and other members of the family

(Hodgson & Darling, 2011). Consideration is needed for the bond between youth and familial companion animals. When safety dictates that youth must be removed from the home, intervention workers need to assess the concern of the youth for familial animal companions (Rauktis & Moser, 2021) and offer some type of contact between these two family members as many placements for youth, including foster care and residential facilities, do not allow the placement of a youth's familial companion animal.

Solutions

A current option available for animal victims of family violence is animal foster care (Giesbrecht, 2021). However, oftentimes, when human victims are separated from their familial animal companions, these humans are not allowed visitation at the alternative placement (Giesbrecht, 2021). And, while the companion animal is safe, the support system for both human and animal victims has been lacerated even if temporarily. Another issue with the current option is the time limits placed on the ability to provide shelter for the animal victim (Giesbrecht, 2021), such as the limited hours of operation for professional organizations (even when the human victim can visit). Human victims may lose custody of their familial companion animal permanently if the animal is placed in a shelter that has time constraints on how long the animal may stay there. There is also the issue of an animal foster family not wanting the human victim in their home or the human family members to know the location of the foster home. The animal foster family may have concerns for their own safety. The current options for familial animal companions leaving circumstances of family violence remain restricted.

A solution to this issue is offering shelters specifically designed to accept all survivors of family violence, both humans and familial animal companions concurrently. There may also be a fostering system designed to provide placement for the animal victim of family violence that implements safeguards for human victims to visit without risk of victimization from the perpetrator towards the family members or the animal foster family. For example, visitation may occur at an animal welfare protection agency or area police department. However, like any social service, the ability to offer such programs hinges on funding. Funding for social service programs tends to be limited, and humans tend to be favored over animals in the hierarchal decision making of funding systems. Human service professionals have noted that funding for services to address animal victims, particularly the sheltering of these animal victims of family violence, is severely underfunded (Giesbrecht, 2021).

Human service professionals have expressed the need for providing victims with options that include consideration for both the human and their animal companion (Giesbrecht, 2021). Society can provide these options. To summarize from other sections of this chapter, there are several ways in which practitioners working directly with victims and survivors can improve the current state of animal cruelty within family violence that requires minimal effort. First, there can be more training offered to intervention professionals to better understand the dynamics involved with animal cruelty within family violence (Giesbrecht, 2021) and the resources available within communities to address the issues. Second, professional organizations and individual professionals can be mandated to screen for instances of animal cruelty when working with family members of all age levels. This may include simply asking questions about familial animal companions and their status within the family (Giesbrecht, 2021). Third, human service providers and animal welfare professionals can make active efforts to strengthen their partnerships (Giesbrecht, 2021) when working with both animal and human victims. Fourth, professionals can provide referrals to resources within the community if those resources are not directly available from the professionals and their organizations. And finally, services need to be implemented that include the sheltering and safekeeping of familial companion animals who experience family violence (Giesbrecht, 2021; Stevenson et al., 2018). These measures may be necessary in order to "make the safety of all family members a priority" (Stevenson et al., 2018, p. 14) and foster equitable justice within society for humans and their familial animal companions.

Summary

The link between animal cruelty and family violence has historically been overlooked (Flynn, 2000), both by intervention professionals and within research. Yet, the relationship between humans and their familial companion animals can indicate the health and safety of the family members (Hoffer et al., 2018), a benefit for intervention professionals in assessing the overall circumstances of family violence. More efforts need to be made to include companion animals as part of the family systems. This includes protection for familial companion animals when investigating instances of family violence, as well as options for these familial companion animals to travel with family members when circumstances warrant leaving a violent family household. More research is needed to understand why some perpetrators utilize animal cruelty within situations of family violence while other perpetrators do not (Applebaum et al., 2021).

There are changing views of familial animal companions among intervention professionals as more intervention professionals become aware of the association between animal cruelty and family violence. There is a call for familial animal companions to be recognized as having rights within the family. Legal scholars are arguing that cruelty to animals within the family needs to be considered family violence, and some courts have begun to recognize this (Randour et al., 2021). Animal safekeeping is an important issue to consider when working with family violence victims and survivors (Giesbrecht, 2021). The animal cruelty-family violence link needs to be implemented into all education and training for intervention professionals. This includes law enforcement, social services, and veterinary services. The importance of inclusion of familial companion animals within treatment for intimate partner violence and child maltreatment cannot be overstated.

References

American Veterinary Medical Association. (2022, January). *U.S. pet ownership statistics.* https://www.avma.org/resources-tools/reports-statistics/us-pet-ownership-statistics.

Applebaum, J. W., MacLean, E. L., & McDonald, S. E. (2021). Love, fear, and the human-animal bond: On adversity and multispecies relationships. *Comprehensive Psychoneuroendocrinology, 7*, 1–12. https://doi.org/10.1016/j.cpnec.2021.100071.

Applebaum, J. W., Peak, C. W., & Zsembik, B. A. (2020). Examining US pet ownership using the general social survey. *The Social Sciences Journal*, 1–10. https://doi.org/10.1080/03623319.2020.1728507.

Arkow, P. (2018, June 4). *A link across the lifespan: Animal abuse as a marker for traumatic experiences in child abuse, domestic violence and elder abuse.* Academy on violence and abuse. https://avahealthorg.presencehost.net/file_download/inline/b64aff80-5461-4d9b-9cdc-cf9b47f30174.

Armitage-Chan, E. (2020). Best practice and supporting professional identity formation: use of a professional reasoning framework. *Journal of Veterinary Medical Education, 47*(2), 125–136. https://doi.org/10.3138/jvme.0218-019r.

Ascione, F. R. (1997). Battered women's reports of their partners and their children's cruelty to animals. *Journal of Emotional Abuse, 1*, 119–133. https://doi.org/10.1300/J135v01n01_06.

Ascione, F. R., Weber, C. V., Thompson, T. M., Heath, J., Maruyama, M., & Hayashi, K. (2007). Battered pets and domestic violence: Animal abuse reported by woman experiencing intimate violence and by non-abused woman. *Violence Against Women, 13*(4), 354–373. https://doi.org/10.1177/1077801207299201.

Ascione, F. R., Weber, C. V., & Wood, D. S. (1997). The abuse of animals and domestic violence: A national survey of shelters for women who are battered. *Society & Animals, 5*(3, 205–218. https://doi.org/10.1163/156853097X00132.

Bandura, A. (1977). *Social learning theory.* General Learning Press.

Barrett, B. J., Fitzgerald, A., Peirone, A., Stevenson, R., & Cheung, C. H. (2018). Help-seeking among abused women with pets: Evidence from a Canadian sample. *Violence & Victims, 33*(4), 604–626. DOI: 10.1891/0886-6708.vv-d-17-00072.

Barrett, B. J., Fitzgerald, A., Stevenson, R., & Cheung, C. H. (2020). Animal maltreatment as a risk marker of more frequent and severe forms of intimate partner violence. *Journal of Interpersonal Violence, 35*(23–24), 5131–5156. DOI: 10.1177/0886260517719542.

Becker, O. G., Steuewig, J., Herrera, V. M., and McCloskey, L. A. (2004). A study of fire-setting and animal cruelty in children: Family influences and adolescent outcomes. *Journal of the American Academy of Child and Adolescent Psychiatry, 43*(7), 905–912. DOI: 10.1097/01.chi.0000128786.70992.9b.

Bright, M. A., Huq, M. S., Spencer, T. Applebaum, J. W., & Hardt, N. (2018). Animal cruelty as an indicator of family trauma: Using adverse childhood experiences to look beyond child abuse and domestic violence. *Child abuse & Neglect, 76*, 289–296. DOI: 10.1016/j.chiabu.2017.11.011.

Browne, J. A., Hensley, C., & McGuffee, K. M. (2016). Does witnessing animal cruelty and being abused during childhood predict the initial age and recurrence of committing childhood animal cruelty? *International Journal of Offender Therapy and Comparative Criminology, 61*(16), 1850–1865. https://doi.org/10.1177/0306624X16644806.

Bures, R. M. (2021). Integrating pets into the family life cycle. In R. M. Bures and N. R. Gee (Eds.), Well-being over the life course (pp.11–23). Springer. DOI: 10.1007/978-3-030-64085-9_2.

Bures, R. M., Mueller, M. K., & Gee, N. R. (2019). Measuring human-animal attachment in a large US survey: Two brief measures for children and their primary caregivers. Frontiers and Public Health, 7, 107. https://doi.org/10.3389/fpubh.2019.00107.

Campbell, A. M. & Thompson, S. L. (2015). The emotional treatment of children in domestically violent homes: Identifying gaps in education and addressing common misconceptions. *Child abuse & Neglect, 48*, 39–49. DOI: 10.1016/j.chiabu.2015.08.009.

Campbell, A. M., Thompson, S. L, Harris, C. L., & Wiehe, S. E. (2021). Intimate partner violence in pet abuse: responding law-enforcement officers' observations and victim reports from the scene. *Journal of Interpersonal Violence, 36*(5–6), 2353–2373. https://doi.org/10.1177/0886260518759653.

Cannon, E. A., Bonomi, A. E., Anderson, M. L., Rivara, F. P., & Thompson, R. S. (2010). Adult health and relationship outcomes among women with abuse experiences during childhood. *Violence and Victims, 25*, 291–305. DOI: 10.1891/0886-6708.25.3.291.

Carter, C. S., & Porges, S. W. (2016). Neural mechanisms underlying human-animal interaction: An evolutionary perspective. In L. S. Freund, S. McCune, L. Esposito, N. R. Gee, & P. McCardle (Eds.), *The social neuroscience of human-animal interaction* (pp. 89–105). American Psychological Association. https://doi.org/10.1037/14856-006.

Cassels, M. T., White, N., Gay, N., & Hughes, C. (2017). One of the family? Measuring early adolescence relationship with pets and siblings. *Journal of Applied Developmental Psychology, 49*, 12–20. https://doi.org/10.1016/j.appdev.2017.01.003.

Chan, K. L. (2017). Family poly-victimization and elevated levels of addiction and psychopathology among parents in a Chinese household sample. *Journal of Interpersonal Violence, 32*, 2433–2452. https://doi.org/10.1177/0886260515592617.

Chan, K. L., Chen, Q., & Chen, M. (2021). Prevalence and correlates of the co-occurrence of family violence: a meta-analysis on family polyvictimization. *Trauma, Violence, & Abuse, 22*(2), 289–305. https://doi.org/10.1177/1524838019841601.

Charles, N. (2014). 'Animals just love you as you are:' Experiencing kinship across the species barrier. *Sociology, 48*(4), 715–730. https://doi.org/10.1177/0038038513515353.

Collins, E. A., Cody, A. M., McDonald, S. E., Nicotera, N., Ascione, F. R., & Williams, J. H. (2018). A template analysis of intimate partner violence survivors' experiences of animal maltreatment: Implications for safety planning an intervention. *Violence Against Women, 24*(4), 452–476. https://doi.org/10.1177/1077801217697266.

Costa, E. C. V. & Gomes, S. C. (2018). Social support and self-esteem moderate the relation between intimate partner violence and depression and anxiety symptoms in Portuguese women. *Journal of Family Violence, 33*(5), 355–368. https://doi.org/10.1007/s10896-018-9962-7.

Cuevas, C. A., Finkelhor, D., Clifford, C., Ormrod, R. K., & Turner, H. A. (2010). Psychological distress as a risk factor for re-victimization in children. *Child Abuse & Neglect, 34*, 235–243. https://doi.org/10.1037/a0020099.

Dale, M. & Yeung, P. (2021). Animal abuse in family violence: Reflections from work shopping with veterinary students. *Aotearoa New Zealand social work, 33*(1), 99–107.

DeGue, S. & DiLillo, D. (2009). Is animal cruelty a "red flag" for family violence? Investigating the co-occurring violence toward children, partners, and pets. *Journal of Interpersonal Violence, 24*(6), 1036–1056. https://doi.org/10.1177/0886260508319362.

Delaney, A. X. (2021a). Intersections of childhood victimization experiences, gender, and power: The makings for sexual coercion? *International Criminal Justice Review, 31*(2), 106–121. https://doi.org/10.1177/1057567720982655.

Delaney, A. X. (2021b). *Norms of violence: Violent socialization processes and the spill over effect for youth crime*. Routledge.

Delaney, A. X. (2021c). The victimizing effect of violent socialization: Intimate partner use of coercive sexual practices transnationally. *International Journal of Offender Therapy and Comparative Criminology*. https://doi.org/10.1177/0306624X21994064.

DeViney, E., Dickert, J., & Lockwood, R. (1983). The care of pets within child abusing families. *International Journal for the Study of Animal Problems, 4*(4), 321–329.

Favar, C. A. & Strand, E. B. (2003). To leave or to stay? Battered women's concern for vulnerable pets. *Journal of Interpersonal Violence, 18*(12), 1367–1377. DOI: https://doi.org/10.1177/0886260503258028.

Finkelhor, D., Turner, H. A., Hamby, S. L., & Ormrod, R. (2011). Polyvictimization: Children's exposure to multiple types of violence, crime, and abuse. Washington, DC: U.S. Department of Justice, Office of Juvenile Justice and Delinquency Prevention.

Finkelhor, D., Ormrod, R. K., & Turner, H. (2007). Polyvictimization and trauma in a national longitudinal cohort. *Development & Psychopathology, 19*, 149–166. https://doi.org/10.1017/S0954579407070083.

Fitzgerald, A. J., Barrett, B. J., Gray, A., & Cheung, C. H. (2020). The connection between animal abuse, emotional abuse, and financial abuse and intimate relationships: Evidence from a nationally represented sample of the general public. *Journal of Interpersonal Violence, 35*(13–14). https://doi.org/10.1177/0886260520939197.

Fitzgerald, A. J., Barrett, B. J., Stevenson, R., & Cheung, C. H. (2019). Animal maltreatment in the context of intimate partner violence: A manifestation of power and control? *Violence Against Women, 25*(15), 1806–1828. https://doi.org/10.1177/1077801218824993.

Flynn, C. P. (2000a). Why family professionals can no longer ignore violence towards animals. *Family Relations, 49*(1), 87–95. https://doi.org/10.1111/j.1741-3729.2000.00087.x.

Flynn, C. P. (2000b). Woman's best friend. *Violence Against Women, 6*(2), 162–177. https://doi.org/10.1177/10778010022181778.

Giesbrecht, C. J. (2021). Animal safekeeping situations of intimate partner violence: Experiences of human service and animal welfare professionals. *Journal of Interpersonal Violence, 11–12*. https://doi.org/10.1177/08862605211025037.

Gorman-Smith, D. & Tolan, P. H. (1998). The role of exposure to community violence and developmental problems among inner-city youth. *Development and Psychology, 74*, 101–116.

Green, P. C. & Gullipone, E. (2005). Knowledge and attitude of Australian veterinarians to family animal abuse and human interpersonal violence. *Australian Veterinary Journal, 83*(10), 619–625. DOI: 10.1111/j.1751-08132005tb13275.x.

Grossman, S.F. & Lundy, M. (2003). Use of domestic violence services across race enough in the city by women age 55 and older: The Illinois experience. *Violence Against Women, 9*(12), 1442–1452.

Haden, S. C., McDonald, S. E., Booth, L. J., Ascione, F. R., & Blakelock, H. (2018). An exploratory study of domestic violence: Perpetrators reports of violence against animals. *Anthrozoös, 31*(3), 337–352. https://doi.org/10.1080/08927936.2018.1455459.

Hahm, H. C., Lee, Y., Ozonoff, A., & Van Wert, M. J. (2010). The impact of multiple types of child maltreatment on subsequent risk behaviors among women during the transition from adolescence to young adulthood. *Journal of Youth and Adolescence, 39*, 528–540. DOI: 10.1007/s10964-009-9490-0.

Hamby, S., Finkelhor, D., Turner, H., & Ormrod, R. (2010). The overlap of witnessing partner violence with child maltreatment and other forms of victimizations in a nationally representative survey of youth. *Child Abuse & Neglect, 34*, 734–741. https://doi.org/10.1007/978-3-319-40920-7_1.

Hartman, C. A., Hageman, T., Williams, J. H., & Ascione, F. R. (2018). Intimate partner violence in animal abuse and an immigrant-rich sample of mother-child dyad recruited from domestic violence programs. *Journal of Interpersonal Violence, 33*(6), 1030–1047. https://doi.org/10.1177/0886260515614281.

Hensley, C., Tallichet, S. E., & Dutkiewicz. (2012). Exploring the age of onset and recurrence of childhood animal cruelty: Can animal cruelty be learned from witnessing others commit it? *International Journal of Offender Therapy and Comparative Criminology, 56*(4), 614–626. https://doi.org/10.1177/0306624X11405480.

Hodgson, K. & Darling, M. (2011). Pets in the family: Practical approaches. *Journal of the American Animal Hospital Association, 47*(5), 299–305. https://doi.org/10.5326/JAAHA-MS-5695.

The Hollard Insurance Company. (2021). *A Guide to Worldwide Pet Ownership.* Pet Secure. https://www.petsecure.com.au/pet-care/a-guide-to-worldwide-pet-ownership/.

Irving, L. (2013). Animals as life changers and life savers: Pets in the redemption narratives of homeless people. *Journal Contemporary Ethnography, 42*, 3–30. https://doi.org/10.1177/0891241612456550.

Irvine, L. & Cilia, L. (2017). More-than-human families: Pets, people, and practices in multispecies household. *Sociology Compass, 11*(2), e12455. https://doi.org/10.1111/soc4.12455.

Jegatheesen, B., Enders-Slegers, M. J., Ormrod, E., & Boyden, P. (2020). Understanding the link between animal cruelty and family violence: The bioecological systems model. *International Journal of Environmental Research and Public Health, 17*(9), 3116–3159. https://doi.org/10.3390/ijerph17093116.

Jordan, Y. & Lem, M. (2014). One health, one welfare: Education and practice. Veterinary students' experiences with community veterinary outreach. *Canadian Veterinary Journal, 55*(12), 1203–1206.

Juliadillal R. & Novenie, NA. (2021). Are childhood cruelty to animals indicates as mental disorder? *Psychosophia, 3*(1), 56–72. https://doi.org/10.32923/psc.v3i1.1748.

Kennedy, T. D., Edmonds, W. A., Dann, K. T., & Burnett, K. F. (2010). The clinical and adaptive features of young offenders with histories of child-parent violence. *Journal of Family Violence, 25*(5), 509–520.

Krienert, J. J., Walsh, J. A., Matthews, K., & McConkey, K. (2012). Examining the nexus between domestic violence an animal abuse and a national sample of service providers. *Violence & Victims, 27*(2), 280–295. DOI: 10.1891/0886–6708.27.2.280.

Krug, E. G., Mercy, J. A., Dalhberg, L. L., & Zwi, A. B. (2002). World report on violence and health. *Lancet, 360*(9339), 1083–1088. https://doi.org/10.1016/S0140-6736(02)11133-0.

Laurent-Simpson, A. (2017a). "Phil's calling grandma": The role of external support and human—companion animal identity pairings. *Symbolic Interaction, 40*(2), 212–228. https://doi.org/10.1002/symb.281.

Laurent-Simpson, A. (2017b). "They make me not wanna have a child": Effects of companion animals on fertility intentions of the child free. *Sociological inquiry, 87*(4), 586–607. https://doi.org/10.1111/soin.12163.

Laurent-Simpson, A. (2017c). Considering alternate sources of role identity: Childless parents and their animal "kids." *Sociological Forum, 32*(3), 610–634. https://doi.org/10.1111/socf.12351.

Lindhorst, T. & Tajima, E. (2008). Reconceptualizing in operationalizing contacts and survey research on intimate partner violence. *Journal of Interpersonal Violence, 23*, 362–388. https://doi.org/10.1177/0886260507312293.

Loar, L. (2014). "How is Fido?": What the families companion animals can tell you about risk assessment and effective interventions—if only you would ask! In T. Ryan (Ed.), *Animals in Social Work: Why and how they matter* (pp. 13135–13150). Pallgrave-McMillian. DOI: 10.1057/9781137372291_9.

Loar, L. & Coleman, L. (2004). *Teaching empathy: Animal-assisted therapy programs for children and families exposed to violence.* Latham Foundation.

Lockwood, R. & Arkow, P. (2016). Animal abuse in interpersonal violence: The cruelty connection and its implications for veterinary pathology. *Veterinary Pathology, 53*(5), 910–918. https://doi.org/10.1177/0300985815626575.

Mackin, D. M., Perlman, G., Davila, J., Kotov, D. N., & Klein, D. N. (2017). Social support buffers the effect of interpersonal life stress and suicidal ideation and self-injury during adolescence. *Psychological Medicine, 47*(6), 1149–1161. DOI: 10.1017/S0033291716003275.

McConnell, A. R., Paige Lloyd, E., and Humphrey, B. T. (2019). We are family: Viewing pets as family members improves well-being. *Anthrozoös, 32*(4), 459–470. https://doi.org/10.1080/08927936.2019.1621516.

McDonald, S. C., Cody, A. M., Booth, L. J., Peirce, J. R., Luce, C. O. C., Williams, G. H., & Ascione, F. R. (2018). Animal cruelty among children and violent household: Children's explanation of their behavior. *Journal of Family Violence, 33*(7), 469–480.

McDonald, S. E., Cody, A. M., Collins, A. A., Stim, H. T., Nicotera, N., Ascione, F. R., & Williams, J. H. (2018). Concomitant exposure to animal maltreatment and social emotional adjustment among children exposed to intimate partner violence: A mixed method study. *Journal of Child & Adolescent Trauma, 11*(3), 353–365. DOI: 10.1007/s40653-017-0176-6.

McDonald, S. E., Collins, E.A., Maternick, A., Nicotera, N., Graham-Bermann, S., Ascione, F. R., & Williams, J. H. (2019). Intimate partner violence survivors' reports of their children's exposure to companion animal maltreatment: A qualitative study. *Journal of Interpersonal Violence, 13*, 2627–2652. https://doi.org/10.1177/0886260516689775.

McDonald, S. E., Collins, E. A., Nicotera, N., Hageman, T. O., Ascione, F. R., Williams, J. H., & Graham-Bermann, S. A. (2015). Children's experiences of companion animal maltreatment and household characterized by intimate partner violence. *Child Abuse & Neglect, 50*, 116–127. DOI: 10.1016/j.chiabu.2015.10.005.

McDonald, S. E., Graham-Bermann, S. A., Maternick, A., Ascione, F. R., & Williams, J. H. (2016). Patterns of adjustment among children exposed to intimate partner violence: A person centered approach. *Journal of Child & Adolescent Trauma, 9*(2), 137-152. DOI: 10.1007/s40653-016-0079-y.

McEwen, F. S., Moffitt, T. E., & Arseneault, L. (2014). Is childhood cruelty to animals a marker for physical maltreatment and a prospective cohort study of children? *Child Abuse & Neglect, 38*(3), 533–543. https://doi.org/10.1016/j.chiabu.2013.10.016.

Muldoon, J. C. C., Williams, G. M., & Curry, C. (2019). Differences in boys' and girls' attachments to pets in early-mid adolescence. *Journal of Applied Developmental Psychology, 62*, 50–58. https://doi.org/10.1016/j.appdev.2018.12.002.

National Council of Juvenile and Family Court Justices. (2019, August 09). The NCJFCJ releases resolution regarding animal cruelty and its link to violence. https://www.ncjfcj.org/news/the-ncjfcj-releases-resolution-regarding-animal-cruelty-and-its-link-to-violence/.

Negriff, S. (2020). ACEs are not equal: Examining the relative impact of household dysfunction versus childhood maltreatment on mental health in adolescence. *Social Science & Medicine, 245*(112696), 1–8. https://doi.org/10.1016/j.socscimed.2019.112696.

Newberry, M. (2017). Pets in danger: Exploring the link between domestic violence and animal abuse. *Aggression & Violent Behavior, 34*, 273–281. https://doi.org/10.1016/j.avb.2016.11.007.

Ormrod, J. E. (1999). *Human learning* (3rd ed.). Merrill, Prentice Hall Australia.

Peacock, J., Chur-Hanson, M. A., & Winefield, H. (2012). Mental health implications of human attachment companion animals. *Journal of Clinical Psychology, 68*(3), 292–303. DOI: 10.1002/jclp.20866.

Petro, J. (2010). Increasing collaboration and coordination of the child welfare and juvenile justice systems to better serve dual jurisdiction youth: A literature review. Washington, DC: Welfare League of America. Retrieved from: http://www.cwla.org/programs/juvenilejustice/jjlitreview.pdf.

Pinillos, R. G., Applebaum, M. C., Manteca, X., Scott-Park, F., Smith, C., & Velarde, A. (2016). One welfare—a platform for improving human and animal welfare. *The Veterinary Record, 179*(16), 412–413. DOI: 10.1136/vri5470.

Power, E. (2008). Furry families: Making a human-dog family through home. *Social & Cultural Geography, 9*(5), 535–555. https://doi.org/10.1080/14649360802217790.

Pritchard, J. (2007). Identifying and working with older male victims of abuse in England. *Journal of Elder Abuse & Neglect, 19*(1/2), 109–127. https://doi.org/10.1300/J084v19n01_08.

Prosperi-Porta, G. & Pai, R. (2021). Animal law update: Positive changes for animals in 2021. *LSJ: Law Society of NSW Journal, 77*, 86–87. DOI: 10.3316/informit.751188254435124.

Randour, M.L., Smith-Blackmoor, M., Delaney, N., Desousa, G., & Guyony, A. (2021). Animal abuse as a type of trauma: Lessons for human and animal service professionals. *Trauma, Violence, & Abuse, 22*(2), 277–288. https://doi.org/10.1177/1524838019843197.

Rauktis, M. E. & Moser, E. (2021). Child and animal maltreatment: Intersections, challenges and opportunities for intervening with melted and families. *APSAC Advisor, 33*(1), 10–15.

Schaffer, M. H., Morton, P. M., & Ferraro, K. F. (2014). Child maltreatment and adult health in a national sample: Heterogeneous relational contacts, divergent effects? *Child abuse & neglect, 38*(3), 395–406. https://doi.org/10.1016/j.chiabu.2013.08.003.

Schofield, T. J., Conger, R. E., Gonzales, G. A., & Merrick, M. D. (2016). Harsh parenting, physical health, and the protective role of positive parent-adolescent relationships. *Social Science & Medicine, 157*, 18–26. DOI: 10.1016/j.socscimed.2016.03.027.

Simmons, C. A. & Lehmann, P. (2007). Exploring the link between pet abuse and controlling behaviors and violent relationships. *Journal of Interpersonal Violence, 22*(9), 1211–1222. https://doi.org/10.1177/0886260507303734.

Spencer, T., Bright, M., Hardt, N., Applebaum, J. W., & Huq, M. S. (2018). Animal cruelty as an indicator of family trauma: Using adverse childhood experiences to look beyond child abuse and domestic violence. *Child Abuse & Neglect, 76*, 287–296. DOI: 10.1016/j.chiabu.2017.11.011.

Stanić, D., Plećaš,-Solarović, B., Mirković, D., Jovanivić, P., Dronjak, S., Marlović, B. Dordević, T., Ignjatović, S., & Pešić, V. (2017). Oxytocin and corticosterone—induced chronic stress model: Focus on adrenaline gland function. *Psychoneuroendocrinology, 80*, 137–146. https://doi.org/10.1016/j.psyneuen.2017.03.011.

Statista. (2021, August 18). *Pet ownership in the U.S.—statistics & facts*. https://www.statista.com/statistics/198095/pets-in-the-united-states-by-type-in-2008/.

Stevenson, R., Fitzgerald, A., & Barrett, B. J. (2018). Keeping pet safe in the contacts of intimate partner violence: Insights from domestic violence shelter staff in Canada. *Affilia: Journal of Women in Social Work, 33*(2), 236–252. https://doi.org/10.1177/0886109917747613.

United State Census Bureau. (2017, April 7). *Census Bureau Statistics on Pets*. https://www.census.gov/newsroom/press-releases/2017/cb17-tps30.html.

Van Houtte, B. & Jarvis, P.A. (1995). The role of pets in pre-adolescent psychosocial development. *Journal of Applied Developmental Psychology, 16*(3), 463–479. https://doi.org/10.1016/0193-3973(95)90030-6.

Volsche, S. (2019). Understanding cross-species parenting: A case for pets as children. In L. Kogan & C. Blazina (Eds.), *Clinical guide to treating companion animals' issues: Addressing human-animal interaction* (pp. 129–141). Elsevier. DOI: 10.1016/B978-0-12-812962-3.00008-3.

Walker, L. E. A. (1984). *The battered woman syndrome*. Springer Publishing Company.

Williams, V., Dale, A. R., Clarke, A. N., & Garrett, N. (2008). Animal abuse and family violence: Survey on the recognition of animal abuse by veterinarians in New Zealand and their understanding of the correlation between animal abuse and human violence. *New Zealand Veterinary Journal, 56*(1), 21–28. https://doi.org/10.1080/00480169.2008.36800.

World Atlas. (2022, January). *The most popular animals owned as pets in the US.* https://www.worldatlas.com/articles/the-most-popular-animals-owned-as-pets-in-the-us.html.

Wuerch, M. A., Giesbrecht, C. J., Price, J. A. B., Knutson, T. & Wach, F. (2020). Examining the relationship between intimate partner violence and concern for animal care and safekeeping. *Journal of Interpersonal Violence, 35*(9–10), 1866–1887. https://doi.org/10.1177/0886260517700618.

Zheng, J., Babygirijia, R., Bülbül, M., Cerjak, D., Ludwig, K., & Takahashi, T. (2010). Hypothalamic oxytocin mediate adaptation mechanisms against chronic stress and rats. *American Journal of Physiology-Gastrointestinal and Liver Physiology, 299*(4), 946–953. https://doi.org/10.1152/ajpgi.00483.2009.

Zink, T. & Fisher, B. S. (2007). The prevalence and incidence of intimate partner and interpersonal mistreatment and older woman in primary care offices. *Journal of Elder Abuse & Neglect, 18*(1), 83–105. https://doi.org/10.1300/J084v18n01_04.

Chapter 14

Animal Cruelty, Firesetting, and Homicide

Lindsey S. Davis and Louis B. Schlesinger

The search for predictors of homicide has been ongoing since the initial descriptive studies of offenders by the early alienists. For example, Goring (1913), Krafft-Ebing (1886), Kretchmer (1925), and Lombroso (1876/1911) all attempted to describe and understand the psychosocial backgrounds of individuals who committed murder and how these factors contributed to their criminal conduct. In the first half of the 20th Century, the study of homicide was essentially limited to case studies. By the second half of the century, attention was being given to homicide as an area of serious scientific inquiry, with some empirical support for clinical observations.

MacDonald (1963), for instance, studied 100 inpatients who had been admitted to a psychiatric hospital for evaluation because they had made homicidal threats. Only one patient committed an intentional homicide during the 15-month follow-up period. Thus, the probability of homicidal acting out would seem to be low, but the time period during which a future homicide may occur might be much longer than this follow-up period. MacDonald did find, however, that "in the very sadistic patients, the triad of childhood cruelty to animals, firesetting, and enuresis [bedwetting] was often encountered" (pp. 126–127). Thus, MacDonald believed this triad could be useful in predicting a particular type of offense—the sadistic homicide.

Hellman and Blackman (1966) later conducted a study that lent statistical support to MacDonald's belief that the childhood triad was correlated with violent behavior at a later age. They found that about three-fourths of those charged with violent crimes (not necessarily homicide) had exhibited a complete or partial triad, whereas only 28% of nonviolent subjects reported a history of these behaviors. Felthous and Bernard (1979) pointed out methodological weaknesses in Hellman and Blackman's study, but their research did offer some corroboration for MacDonald's early observations. Its simplicity, as well as some empirical support, contributed greatly to "the MacDonald triad" becoming commonly considered a robust and accepted predictor of homicide (Justice et al., 1974; Schechter & Everitt, 1996). However, this opinion was never really MacDonald's; as he clearly stated, his findings do not support the notion that "childhood firesetting, cruelty to animals, and enuresis to the age of five or beyond, is significantly higher in persons who have committed criminal homicide than in persons who have made homicidal threats" (MacDonald, 1968, p. 61).

A close look at the clinical and research literature since the 1960s reveals a complex relationship between MacDonald's triad and adult violent crime, particularly murder. The research has addressed the usefulness of (a) the complete triad, (b) a partial triad including animal cruelty and/or firesetting, and (c) other risk factors as being predictive of aggressive and homicidal behavior. But it is often forgotten, or not emphasized, that MacDonald's (1963) observations of the significance of the triad—if there is any significance—related only to "very sadistic" (p. 126) individuals. Therefore, the triad may be useful for examining particular types of violence, specifically, sadistic sexual aggression and sadistic sexual homicide.

Animal Cruelty and Firesetting: Research Findings

Animal Cruelty

The literature is highly inconsistent with respect to the relationship between a history of childhood animal cruelty and the commission of homicide. In fact, most studies (e.g., Hellman & Blackman, 1966) have been overly inclusive, examining the relationship of animal cruelty to adult violent crime, rather than to homicide. For instance, Langevin et al. (1983) conducted the only study of MacDonald's triad and its relationship specifically to homicide, and these researchers found little predictive value or significance for the triad. Wax and Haddox (1974) did find significance for the triad in a small number of violent (but not homicidal) male adolescents; they believe this finding confirms the usefulness of the triad to some extent. In 1978, Felthous and Keller reviewed the literature with respect to animal cruelty and aggression (but not homicide). They found the results of various studies to be inconsistent and contradictory, with several methodological problems.

Since then, Merz-Perez et al. (2001) have found a possible significant relationship between childhood cruelty to animals and later violence against humans. However, Gleyzer et al. (2002) reached a different conclusion. These researchers found that a history of substantial animal cruelty is associated with antisocial personality disorder, antisocial personality traits, and substance abuse. Their findings could not determine that a history of animal abuse is predictive of adult violent crime, because many offenders who committed adult violent crimes did not have such a history. This conclusion was echoed by Patterson-Kane and Piper (2009), who also found that animal abuse is not uncommon among violent offenders, but that the majority of violent offenders do not report a history of such abusive behavior.

Haden and Scarpa (2005) found that animal cruelty is not uncommon among children in general and may be associated with some adult criminal behavior, but this relationship is not strong. Similarly, in Levin and Arluke's (2009) sample of undergraduate students, 28% admitted to having abused an animal, a rate far higher than the likelihood of committing a homicide. One of the few studies to look more closely at method, severity, and frequency of animal abuse as possible predictors (Tallichet et al., 2005) found no link between childhood animal abuse and violence against humans in a sample of adult offenders. Also demonstrating the continuing inconsistency of the research is a study by Overton et al. (2011), who found that only *recurrent* animal cruelty was statistically significantly predictive of adult violence toward humans.

A graduation hypothesis has been posited, which suggests that the abuse of animals constitutes a lower rung on the ladder that leads to physical aggression against humans. A meta-analysis by Walters (2013) indicates that this hypothesis is supported in studies which compare violent and non-violent offenders, but only because of other confounding variables; in short, these offenders differ in many ways beyond their animal abuse histories. After adjusting the meta-analysis, Walters (2013) concluded that animal cruelty only predicts later violence towards humans in female subjects; in males, animal cruelty is not predictive of later violent offenses.

A small study (Verlinden et al., 2000) of eight school shootings reported that half of school shooters had committed prior acts of animal cruelty. In a slightly larger study of 23 school shootings (Arluke & Madfis, 2013), 43% of offenders had committed prior acts of animal cruelty. Of those who had committed prior acts of cruelty, 90% committed cruelty in a hands-on manner and 70% abused cats or dogs. Arluke and Madfis (2013) have suggested that it is this type of "up-close and personal method of abuse" that is most predictive of later acts of extreme violence (p. 12). Meanwhile, Dadds et al. (2002) have suggested that it is not the act of animal abuse, but the malice—or absence of malice—motivating the act that is predictive of later violent behavior.

It is clear that studying only the relationship between animal cruelty and adult violent behavior is much too broad and leads to inconsistent results depending on the sample, methodology, and operational definitions of all variables. Moreover, most violent behavior by adults is not even reported and rarely results in arrest, and a history of animal cruelty is often determined by retrospective self-report, which may or may not be accurate.

Case Study 1

A 12-year-old male (A.A.) and his family adopted a pet cat from a shelter. The pet was initially evaluated by a veterinarian and found to be in good health. Two months later, A.A.'s father brought the cat back to the veterinarian because the pet was limping and there was an odor coming from his paw. He was treated and returned to the family. The cat was brought back to the veterinarian two months later, who found that all 18 claws appeared to have been forcibly removed. The veterinarian said it would have taken a lot of time to do this, causing the pet tremendous pain and suffering ... "The cat must have suffered repeatedly." The veterinarian found only three of the cat's twelve incisor teeth to be present. She stated that she believed the pet suffered "excruciating pain and was restrained, held down, or knocked out" in order for the teeth to have been pulled out. In addition, the animal had a fractured tail due

> to manual injury or trauma, an ear infection, and all his whiskers were cut off. Her opinion was that the cat had been tortured routinely; she removed the cat from the family and the police and prosecutor's office were contacted.
>
> During the evaluation, two other veterinarians were consulted, and both supported the treating veterinarian's conclusions. They concluded, "These acts of abuse occurred repeatedly over an extended period of time … planning would have been necessary to commit this act of abuse." All three veterinarians held the opinion that the pain must have been so excruciating that the cat must have been anesthetized in some way.
>
> The 12-year-old offender had been in some form of counseling since the age of 9. He was reportedly teased by peers repeatedly because of his very small stature (for which he was now being evaluated by an endocrinologist). A.A.'s father knew his son committed the abuse and began crying at the veterinarian's office, stating, "I know my son did this. There's something wrong with him." However, A.A.'s mother said her son had nothing to do with the abuse and claimed all of the cat's injuries were present when they adopted him from the shelter.
>
> A.A. was being treated by a psychotherapist and a psychiatrist during the time of the abusive behavior. Both of the child's treatment providers were angry and offended that the authorities were called. The psychiatrist stated that it was "extremely unnecessary" and caused his patient more harm. His theory was that A.A. displaced his own "picking behavior" onto the cat and accidentally picked his claws too close. The psychiatrist claimed the A.A. was not capable of such abuse because "he is not a conduct disorder and he does not have antisocial traits."

This case illustrates the minimal exposure mental health professionals have with respect to the ominous significance of animal cruelty (Schlesinger, 2021). As Johnson (2018) also acknowledged, evidence of animal cruelty is often minimized or mishandled by clinicians. In this case, the psychiatrist's theory that A.A. displaced his emotions onto the cat is likely, but rather than displacing his anxiety or "picking behavior," he was more likely displacing anger—very likely pent up from repetitive peer ridicule. Such teasing and bullying often have a devastating emotional impact on children. In one study (Tanner at al., 2016), just over half (54.2%) of adolescents with histories of firesetting reported a history of being bullied, and 73.3% of adolescents with histories of both firesetting and self-harming behaviors reported being bullied.

The veterinarian's recorded statement to the authorities was detailed and very disturbing by any standard. She described cruel and sadistic behavior and, contrary to the treatment providers' opinions, children are quite capable of engaging in cruel and sadistic behavior, notwithstanding the absence of conduct disorder or antisocial traits. It is understandable that treatment providers want to be supportive and protective of their patients; however, neither provider found it necessary to observe the veterinarian's recorded statement. The first step in treatment must be recognition of the problem. In this case, the problem was much more than just displaced anxiety and picking behavior. The need to include an educational component regarding the significance of animal abuse in clinical training and continuing education is obvious.

Firesetting

Nonserious firesetting is a fairly common behavior for children and adolescents, particularly boys (Grolnick et al., 1990; Kafry, 1980; Lewis & Yarnell, 1951), but, in some individuals, firesetting becomes pathological. Pathological firesetting is psychologically driven, not motivated by material gain, and typically connotes repetitive or intentionally destructive behavior, as opposed to *fire play*, which is likely to reflect developmentally appropriate curiosity. *Pyromania*—which is rare in both children and adults—literally means "fire madness" and is classified as an impulse-control disorder in the *Diagnostic and Statistical Manual of Mental Disorders, 5th Edition* (American Psychiatric Association [APA], 2013). The diagnostic criteria for the disorders are:

1. Deliberate and purposeful fire setting on more than one occasion.
2. Tension or affective arousal before the act.
3. Fascination with, interest in, curiosity about, or attraction to fire and its situational contexts (e.g., paraphernalia, uses, consequences).
4. Pleasure, gratification, or relief when setting fires or when witnessing or participating in their aftermath.
5. The fire setting is not done for monetary gain, as an expression of sociopolitical ideology, to conceal criminal activity, to express anger or vengeance, to improve one's living circumstances, in response to a delusion or hallucination, or as a result of impaired judgment (e.g., major neurocognitive disorder, intellectual disability, substance intoxication).
6. The fire setting is not better explained by conduct disorder, a manic episode, or antisocial personality disorder (pp. 476–477).

Although there are logical motives for setting a fire (such as to collect insurance money on the destroyed property or to cover up another crime), the pathological firesetter sets fires irrationally—to express aggression or hostility, avenge a real or perceived wrong, gain attention or recognition, build self-worth, obtain sensual or sexual satisfaction, or respond to a delusional hallucination (Rider, 1980). Compulsive firesetting is not driven by a rational decision-making process but by an irresistible impulse (or compulsion) to set fires; the pyromaniacs studied by Lewis and Yarnell (1951), for example, "said they set their fires for no practical reason and received no material profit from the act, their only motive being to obtain some sort of sensual satisfaction" (p. 86).

Furthermore, setting fires provides a means of expressing anger and frustration and creating destruction while avoiding a direct confrontation with the source of those unpleasant emotions. Children who set fires commonly cite revenge and retaliation as their primary motives (Mavromatis, 2000); however, children and adolescents may be unable to identify and verbalize the underlying dynamics that guide their behavior. For example, Swaffer and Hollin (1995) interviewed 17 juvenile firesetters regarding the motives for their crimes. The most commonly reported motive—endorsed by 29.4% of the sample—was revenge, followed by peer pressure (17.6%), concealment of another crime (17.6%), self-harm (17.6%; all female), and fascination with fire (5.9%). Three of the juveniles denied having intentionally set any fires.

Lewis and Yarnell (1951) stated, "A persistently recurring motive given by these firesetters is that they were impelled to set a fire because they wanted to see a fire: logical but tautological, and it would seem that this 'motive' comes close to approximating pure instinctual impulse" (p. 398). Many researchers have concluded that this "irresistible impulse," coupled with the presence of mounting tension before and relief after the firesetting, indicates an underlying sexual element to these crimes. "They describe mounting tension, the restlessness, the urge for motion, the conversion symptoms such as headaches, palpitations, ringing in the ears, and the gradual merging of their identity into a state of unreality; then the fires are set" (Lewis & Yarnell, 1951, p. 87). As one 15-year-old boy explained: "When I light a fire, it's like eating. It's an urge and I get rid of it. After the urge is done with, I'm satisfied for a while" (as cited in Sakheim & Osborn, 1994, p. 27). An adult male in Lewis and Yarnell's (1951) study stated, "After the firesetting, it was a common practice for me to go home and to go to sleep; this argues a relief of tension. If tension was present when I went to bed, it would scarcely be possible for me to go to sleep" (p. 164).

Deviant sexual fantasy gets redirected into acting out in a variety of ways; in some individuals, urges are satiated through firesetting behavior. Most repetitive firesetting involves less obvious sexual dynamics; therefore, the sexual element in these crimes is often missed by law enforcement (Banay, 1969; Schlesinger & Revitch, 1997). In fact, the sexual motivation may not be elicited during a brief interview process but may rather be revealed only through an extensive therapeutic relationship. Based on his review of the literature, Fras (1983) concluded that "the sexually-motivated fire setter's goals are to achieve both instinctual gratification of the sexual need and the magic resolution of the interpsychic conflict—all of this in an individual who has started out with feelings of sexual inferiority and recently suffered social setbacks" (p. 200). Like other types of compulsive-repetitive offenders, this type of firesetter typically repeats the behavior until apprehended.

Some disagreement remains, however, about the sexual nature of firesetting. For example, Quinsey et al. (1989) observed no sexual arousal to fire stimuli in their sample of firesetters and interpreted their results as a lack of support for a sexual theory. Fras (1983) argued:

> [In juvenile firesetters, sexuality] seems to play no greater a part than any other aspect of their mental apparatus.... Most of these children and adolescents are psychosexually delayed and, in the case of the adolescents, sexually most disinterested. There is no indication that fire setting is a substitution for

> sexuality; rather, their lack of sexual interest and activity is one of the facets of severe maturational delay (p. 198).

Setting fires has been theorized by some to be a displacement of anger toward a rejecting or neglectful parent (Sakheim et al., 1985; Yarnell, 1940), and firesetters may be likely to have a history of sexual abuse (Martin et al., 2004). In a study of 205 juvenile firesetters referred for assessment and treatment (Root et al., 2008), 48% of the sample had experienced maltreatment. Maltreated children more frequently than children who were not maltreated reported setting fires out of anger and more frequently described setting fires immediately after a family-related stressor. Maltreated children were also more likely to engage in repeated firesetting, both in the number of fires and in the duration of firesetting behavior. It is believed that firesetting can provide a sense of agency that might otherwise be unavailable in the environments of these juveniles.

It is not surprising that firesetters display a wide range of psychopathology. For example, Moore et al. (1996) found those with a history of firesetting had more pathological MMPI-A profiles; Leong (1992) found most (70.3%) of a sample of firesetters had prior psychiatric hospitalizations, and more than half (51.7%) were psychotic at the time of their offense. Many firesetters appear to have learning delays or disabilities and/or deficits in executive functioning (Sakheim et al., 1985). Similarly, many in Yarnell's (1940) study exhibited learning disabilities, and Lewis and Yarnell (1951) described a group of "mental defective" firesetters who set fires predominantly to see a fire or to see fire engines. One such 21-year-old had set a fire in a factory and adjacent sheds with the hope of asphyxiating the townspeople and destroying the town. "Fire thrilled him more than anything else and he was mad at everybody, because all the children teased him. In early childhood, he had burned a rooster, and set a fire in the home when he was angry with his sister" (p. 131). Sakheim et al. (1985) characterized child firesetters as "emotionally complex youngsters whose capacity for deliberation, self-control, and direct verbal expression of inner impulses and feelings is quite limited. They are troubled children who resort to primitive behavioral mechanisms for the expression of confused inner needs, at times wreaking havoc and creating tragedy" (p. 468). Further research has found that depression, oppositional defiant disorder (ODD), and attention deficit hyperactivity disorder (ADHD) are all risk factors for firesetting (Becker et al., 2004).

In addition to various forms of psychopathology, firesetters also display a constellation of antisocial behaviors and violence. Firesetting juveniles have been reported to exhibit significantly more lying, stealing, destructive behavior, running away, sexual misbehavior, and other antisocial conduct than do children who do not set fires (Jacobson, 1985; Martin et al., 2004). "Has deliberately engaged in fire setting with the intention of causing serious damage" is listed among the DSM-5 diagnostic criteria for Conduct Disorder, a childhood behavior disorder characterized by persistent violation of age-appropriate norms and the rights of others (APA, 2013, p. 470), and research has consistently shown a relationship between firesetting and diagnoses of Conduct Disorder (e.g., Heath et al., 1985; Sakheim et al., 1985).

Thus, both Kolko et al. (1985) and Stickle and Blechman (2002) found that firesetting juveniles engage in more aggressive behavior than their peers. In a sample of nonclinical, outpatient, and inpatient children (Kolko & Kazdin, 1991), those who had engaged in firesetting in the previous 12 months showed higher levels of behavioral dysfunction, antisocial behavior, hostility, emotionality, and impulsivity than those who had not engaged in firesetting. Unsurprisingly, in Becker et al.'s (2004) longitudinal study of children who had set fires prior to their first interview in 1990, 40.6% had been referred to juvenile court for violent offenses by 2000, as compared with just 12% of the non-firesetting children.

More recently, a ten-year longitudinal study (Lambie et al., 2019) followed youth who completed the New Zealand Fire Service's Fire Awareness and Intervention Programme, an in-home educational intervention of two to four sessions conducted by a trained firefighter and supervised by a licensed psychologist. At follow-up, more than half (62%) of the program participants referred for firesetting went on to commit criminal offenses within the ten-year window, and more than a quarter (28%) had committed a violent offense; however, not one of the offenders in the sample went on to commit a murder during the follow-up period. Only 5% engaged in an arson offense during that time. Among those with a firesetting history, it appeared that having a history of pre-intervention offending or conduct problems; exposure to abuse, neglect, familial violence, or the child welfare system; and psychosocial/emotional problems were all risk factors for future offending. The data suggest that this intervention program may be effective in reducing future arson behaviors among firesetting youth but are not sufficient to address violent urges.

It is clear that firesetting and other dysfunctional behavioral patterns that begin during childhood and adolescence often become increasingly serious throughout the individual's lifetime, particularly if appropriate disciplinary measures are not taken to address the behavior early on and when additional stressors are present in the home environment. Wax and Haddox (1974), for example, cautioned that "in adolescents a lack of mastery over [enuresis, animal cruelty, and especially firesetting] must represent a clear failure in the development of various controls and therefore must be viewed as a warning signaling vulnerability to explosive impulse expression" (p. 155). In a study of psychiatric inpatients aged 15 to 30 (Felthous & Bernard, 1979), the presence of two or more elements of the predictive triad was extremely rare but was associated with the presence of two or more aggressive behaviors (i.e., homicidal threats, carrying a deadly weapon, physical assault). In a second study of 450 U.S. naval servicemen (Felthous & Bernard, 1979), those subjects exhibiting two-thirds of the triad were among the most aggressive in the sample.

Baglivio et al. (2017) and others have criticized the extant literature on co-occurring animal cruelty and firesetting for insufficient sample sizes. In response, Baglivio et al. (2017) investigated a sample of 292,649 juvenile offenders using data from their juvenile records and risk assessments. They found that animal cruelty and firesetting were extremely rare in this sample (0.59% and 1.56%, respectively); however, these behaviors co-occurred in 0.17% of the sample, a rate nearly twice as high as would be predicted by chance.

In offender samples, the rates of firesetting histories tend to be quite high. For example, in one study of adult offenders (Langevin et al., 1988), 50% of murderers and 18% of sex offenders had a history of firesetting. Meanwhile, in Leong's (1992) sample of adult arsonists, 31% had prior arrests for violent offenses.

Conclusion

The empirical research with respect to animal cruelty, firesetting, and their relationship specifically to homicide is inconsistent and insufficient. But to conclude that MacDonald's (1963) early observation of the triad has no importance is incorrect. Instead of asking a general question about the predictive significance of animal cruelty, firesetting, or both to homicide or interpersonal violence, a more specific question should be framed, keeping in mind that MacDonald's observations related not to all criminal offenders, but only to the "very sadistic" ones.

Motivational Spectrum in the Classification of Homicide

All murder is not alike. Revitch (1977), Revitch and Schlesinger (1981), and Schlesinger (2004) have argued that homicide must be classified in a rational manner in order to understand its psychopathology, psychodynamics, and prognostic factors. Thus, behavior such as animal cruelty or firesetting may have different predictive significance for different types of homicide. And, in keeping with MacDonald's observations, it would seem that sadistic murder is the type of homicide in which animal cruelty and firesetting are most relevant.

In search of a common denominator to be used as a basis for classification—and from which predictions could be derived—Revitch and Schlesinger (1978, 1981) and Schlesinger (2020) developed the concept of the motivational spectrum of homicide, which comes from an analysis of the dynamics of the antisocial act itself. These motivational stimuli are spectrally distributed with purely external (sociogenic) factors on one end of the continuum and purely internal (psychogenic) factors on the other end. From the external to the internal range of the continuum, five separate categories of homicide have been differentiated: (1) sociogenic or environmental, (2) situational, (3) impulsive, (4) catathymic, and (5) compulsive. In compulsive offenses, external factors play a minimal role, while internal (psychogenic) pressures are paramount. The reverse is true for the environmental/socially-stimulated offenses. The other categories of offenses have a mixture of external and internal factors, depending on their position on the continuum.

Separate from the motivational spectrum are homicides that are a direct outgrowth of a primary psychiatric disorder such as a psychosis, an organic condition, or a toxic state. In such cases, an individual responds to psychotic symptoms, the disinhibiting effects of various substances, or perhaps the weakening of controls caused by various organic disorders. An example is the case of a 29-year-old male who became overtly psychotic and believed his pet dog was communicating telepathically, making faces at him, and threatening him. He disemboweled the dog with a steak knife and buried her in the woods. This individual had no prior acts of aggression and no prior psychotic episodes.

Environmental/Sociogenic Homicides

Many crimes throughout history have been a result of external or social influences rather than psychological forces within the individual. Contract killing and terroristic murder are two examples of homicide derived from social-environmental factors, specifically cultural influences in the case of contract murder and religious/political influences in the case of terroristic murder. A history of animal cruelty would probably have little relevance in this type of homicide. And firesetting can occur during riots or wartime, for example, as a form of revenge (Revitch, 1977).

Situational Homicides

Situational homicides are essentially reactions to stressful circumstances (Schlesinger, 2004). They may be committed by individuals with little or minimal psychopathology; however, all types of personalities may be involved. The biblical Cain-Abel murder is the prototype of a situationally stimulated homicide: the murder occurred suddenly, as a result of an argument between family members, stemming in part from jealousy and anger. According to the Federal Bureau of Investigation's (FBI) Uniform Crime Reports (U.S. Department of Justice, 2010), about 60% of all homicides would fall in the situational category; they include domestic murders, felony murders, murders within romantic triangles, and the like. There may be some relevance of animal cruelty and firesetting to this type of homicide because these background behaviors indicate a predisposition to violent and aggressive reactions. For example, the research (e.g., Merz-Perez et al., 2001; Overton et al., 2011; Wax & Haddox, 1974) seems to suggest that animal cruelty has some relationship to or indicates a predisposition toward violence, as does firesetting (Mavromatis, 2000).

Impulsive Homicides

Impulsive individuals typically react to situations in a diffuse stimulus-response manner, with little ability to modulate emotion. Such individuals tend to drift in and out of behavioral difficulties, with a life pattern characterized by unpredictability and lack of direction. An illustrative case is that of a 25-year-old male who impulsively strangled a woman after intercourse in response to her threat of accusing him of rape. A history of minor antisocial acts, low average intelligence, and lack of direction were found in his background. In impulsive homicides, animal cruelty or firesetting may have some predictive relevance because they can serve as a marker for a general expression of hostility and anger (Revitch & Schlesinger, 1981).

Catathymic Homicides

The concept of catathymia was originally introduced in the field of criminal behavior by Wertham (1937) as an explanation for unprovoked, isolated episodes of severe violence without an organic basis. Wertham's original definition of catathymic crisis was "a transformation of the stream of thought, as the result of certain complexes of ideas, that are charged with a strong affect, usually a wish, a fear, or an ambivalent striving" (p. 975). Revitch and Schlesinger (1981) and Schlesinger (2020) updated the concept of catathymia; they considered it to be not a diagnostic entity (as did Wertham) but rather a psychodynamic or motivational process. Revitch (1977), Revitch and Schlesinger (1981), and Schlesinger (2007, 2020) differentiated two types of catathymic homicides, acute and chronic. The acute process is essentially a sudden, unprovoked murder or severe assault triggered by the eruption of an overwhelming emotion attached to internal ideas or conflicts—typically inadequacy extending to the sexual arena. An example of an acute catathymic homicide is that of an 18-year-old high school senior who strangled a woman to death after he was unable to effect an erection following her seductive advances and ridiculing remarks. The subject was able to recall the event, but initially believed it was a dream (Revitch & Schlesinger, 1978).

In the chronic catathymic process, depressed mood and obsessive rumination precede the violent act for weeks or many months. Here, the subject develops a fixed idea that the only way to free himself from the source of threat to his psychic stability and inner tension is through violence. The aggressive act itself seems ego-alien, with a dreamlike quality. The typical victim of a chronic catathymic homicide is usually a romantic partner, a no-longer-loved one, or sometimes a relative stranger with whom the subject has become obsessed and whom the subject has often stalked (Meloy, 1992). In some cases, the anger is turned inward and suicide or murder-suicide results.

Catathymic homicides of both acute and chronic types derive from a breakthrough of underlying sexual conflicts, typically deep feelings of sexual inadequacy with which the offender has been secretly struggling. Because catathymic homicides are a form of sexual homicide, both animal cruelty and firesetting in the offender's background have relevance. An account of a chronic catathymic arson was graphically described by Yukio Mishima (1956) in his novel *The Temple of the Golden Pavilion*. Mishima's main character sets fire to an iconic building and he has distinct sexual emotions and a feeling of relief while watching the structure burn.

Compulsive Homicides

Compulsive homicides are on the extreme end of the motivational spectrum and stem from internal psychogenic forces with little or no environmental influence. These offenses may be committed in a specific, repetitive-ritualistic manner (Meloy, 2000), or they may be of a diffuse nature. Fantasies usually precede the homicide by many years. Compulsive murders are also sexual murders, but they do not stem from underlying sexual conflicts as do catathymic homicides. Instead, killing the victim is itself sexually arousing and part of the offender's sexual-arousal pattern (Schlesinger, 2007, 2008, 2020). And the offender's behavior at the crime scene almost always involves ritualistic conduct—which is sexually gratifying—such as leaving the victim in a degrading position or with insertions of foreign objects (Schlesinger et al., 2010).

Once a murderer begins, the killing may be repeated frequently—in serial fashion—or at intervals with years in between. The murder is repeated because it is so sexually stimulating and gratifying. Numerous accounts in the literature tell of individuals who committed a homicide and served a lengthy prison term, only to repeat a similar homicide when released on parole (Guttmacher, 1963; Revitch, 1977). Compulsive-repetitive murder is the most relevant type for understanding the predictive significance of both animal cruelty and firesetting in the future offender's background (Schlesinger, 2001). In fact, a review of the research literature with respect to animal cruelty and firesetting shows that these behaviors are most significant in sexually-motivated cases. For example, Ressler et al. (1986) found that zoophilia and general cruelty to animals were prominent in the childhood histories of murderers who committed rape and mutilated their victims.

Petersen and Farrington (2007) also reported case histories of serial sexual killers and mass murderers who were cruel to animals during their childhoods. Hensley and Tallichet (2008) found that children who abuse an animal out of fun are significantly more likely to engage in interpersonal violence as an adult than are those who do not abuse animals. Hensley and Tallichet (2009) also concluded that drowning an animal and having sex with an animal were both predictive of adult interpersonal violence, and Ascione et al.(2003) found that animal cruelty and sexual contact with animals were positively associated with a history of sexual abuse. In addition, Hensley et al. (2010) found that childhood bestiality was a significant positive predictor of adult interpersonal violence.

Animal Cruelty, Firesetting, and Sexual Homicide

Animal Cruelty

The earliest descriptions of sexual murderers regularly noted a history of animal cruelty in their childhoods. For example, Krafft-Ebing (1886) discussed the case of Vincenz Verzeni, who was a sexual murderer and had a background of animal cruelty. "When he was twelve years old, he experienced a peculiar feeling of pleasure while wringing the necks of chickens. After this he often killed great numbers of them" (p. 67). Krafft-Ebing also reported the case of Sergeant Bertrand, who fantasized about having sex with dead animals, later engaged in such activities, and then progressed to disinterring human bodies and having sex with corpses. Krafft-Ebing reported many other cases of animal cruelty in the backgrounds of sexual murderers. He theorized that, as youngsters, such individuals are afraid of committing a criminal act with a human but engage in torture of animals "to stimulate or excite their lust" (p. 84).

In the 20th Century, Peter Kurten (Wilson & Pitman, 1962), who engaged in bestiality as an adolescent, became further involved with bestiality and progressed to serial sexual murder as an adult. Kurten befriended a dog catcher who taught him how to torture and masturbate animals. From ages 13 through 15, Kurten engaged in numerous sexual acts with pigs, sheep, and goats, sometimes stabbing the animals to death while having intercourse with them.

Guttmacher (1960) also found that sexual murderers frequently had a background of animal cruelty. He offered his theory for their conduct, which differed in some ways from Krafft-Ebing's view (1886):

> [Offenders] give vent to their hostile impulses through cruelty to animals. Their real hatred is not against animals but, of course, against their fellow man. Animals are mere substitutes, they serve as scapegoats. Furthermore, dumb brutes cannot file complaints with the police and in some quarters a certain degree of cruelty to animals is accepted as a sublimation of sadistic impulses. Certainly, this is true of hunting (p. 100).

Perhaps one of the most well-known contemporary cases illustrating the connection between animal cruelty and serial sexual murder is that of Jeffrey Dahmer (Schwartz, 1992). As a child, Dahmer was fascinated with roadkill, butchered and dissected small animals, nailed cats and frogs to trees behind his house, and once put a dog's head on a stick. Dahmer killed 17 men, most of whom he picked up in gay bars. He engaged in cannibalism and necrophilia and also attempted to make his victims zombies by injecting muriatic acid into their brains with a turkey baster. Eventually arrested, he pled guilty and was later killed in prison by a fellow inmate.

A number of studies have also demonstrated the ominous significance of animal cruelty in the backgrounds of sexual murderers and potential sexual murderers. Johnson and Becker (1997) found that 34% of their adolescent subjects who wanted to commit serial sexual murder reported severe animal cruelty. One child shot, drowned, stabbed, or set on fire numerous animals, sometimes injuring or killing 10 animals a day. Another of their adolescent subjects felt sexual arousal after dissecting animals once he killed them; he kept many of their skulls in his bedroom as trophies. Another subject killed dogs by snapping their necks while they were alive, and yet another killed snakes and rabbits and often searched for roadkill, cutting them open and examining their insides. Myers et al. (1998) similarly found that 28% of their sample of adolescents who had already committed one sexual murder also had a history of animal cruelty. In a sample of German sexual murderers (Stupperich, 2005 as cited in Stupperich & Strack, 2016), many who had histories of animal abuse indicated that they had fantasies of inflicting harm on human victims while they tortured animals, suggesting the animal abuse served as an intermediary step towards more severe violent offending.

Positive associations between psychopathy—a condition characterized by lack of remorse, impulsivity, and callousness—and the killing and torture of animals (e.g., Kavanagh et al., 2013) and between psychopathy and sexual sadism (e.g., Holt et al., 1999) suggest that psychopathic tendencies may underlie the connection between animal cruelty and sadistic violence. As Meloy (2000) stated, "virtually all" known perpetrators of sexual homicide present with psychopathic features (p. 7). Stupperich and Strack (2016) found in a small sample of German forensic patients that animal abuse was associated with the affective/interpersonal factors of psychopathy (which are more highly associated with sadistic criminal behavior) more so than antisocial/lifestyle factors of psychopathy. Furthermore, Trentham et al. (2018) emphasized the importance of *repeated* instances of animal abuse as predictive of later recurrent interpersonal violence, which holds significance for sexual homicide offenders because they are often compulsive, repeat offenders. Consistent with their findings, a study by Mesa (2012) indicated that serial sexual homicide offenders were more likely than non-serial homicide offenders to have histories of animal cruelty.

The Significance of Cats

Revitch (1978), Revitch and Schlesinger (1981, 1989), and Schlesinger and Revitch (1997) noted that cruelty to cats, in particular, was often found in the childhood backgrounds of individuals who went on to commit serial sexual homicides. Perhaps this pattern is found because cats are generally considered a female symbol, more than other animals such as dogs (Revitch, 1978). Cats arouse anger in the potential sex murderer, who is typically a male fantasizing about killing a female. Felthous (1980) concluded that "cats more than dogs seem to induce a child's sadistic projections and cruel behavior. [A number of subjects] who had tortured cats admitted an intense dislike of this animal, in particular, but disclosed no insight into the animosity" (p. 175). Revitch (1978) reported the case of an adolescent who set cats on fire and experienced a euphoric feeling while watching them burn. This offender compared cats to women, noting similarities in their looks and behavior. Tapia (1971) similarly found that out of 18 subjects with a history of severe violence, all but one had previously hurt a cat.

Ressler and Schachtman (1992) described two serial sexual murderers who had tortured cats when they were children. One individual attached cherry bombs to cats' legs and made "many cats in his neighborhood three-legged" (p. 96). In fact, Albert DeSalvo, commonly known as the Boston Strangler, tortured cats during his childhood and described his behavior:

> I don't like cats.... I used to shoot cats with a bow-and-arrow, put it right through their belly and sometimes they ran with the arrow right through them yowling, and I don't recall being too upset by that.... Sometimes when I would see them, before the shoot, I'd get such a feeling of anger that I think I could tear those cats apart with my bare hands. I don't understand this, but just that I hated them and they had done nothing to me" (as cited in Rae, 1967, p. 61).

In Ressler et al.'s (1988) study, carried out under the auspices of the Federal Bureau of Investigation (FBI), a nonrandom national sample of 36 incarcerated sexual murderers was extensively studied. These investigators found repetitive examples of childhood sadistic behavior toward animals, particularly cats. One of their subjects said: "I killed a cat once. I can't tell you why. I was just mad and the cat came at the wrong time and I strangled this cat" (p. 38). Another subject also described killing cats:

> One time I found a kitten and it was raining. The kitten was shivering and I brought it home. About two weeks later the house was full of fleas. From there I just started hating cats.... I don't know what happened. My father thought I did something to it, and I thought my father did something to it because I came home from school one day and the cat just wasn't there.... That's when I got to tying cherry bombs to cats' leg, light it, and watch the cat run down the street.... Made a lot of one-legged cats (p. 38).

The following two cases assessed by the co-author (Schlesinger) are additional examples of cat-killing in the backgrounds of serial sexual murderers.

Case Study 2

A 32-year-old male was arrested after he brutally attacked and almost killed a woman who came to his assistance after his car broke down on a highway. He smashed her in the nose and eyes multiple times, shoved his fingers up her rectum while strangling her and, at the same time, bit her on the chin and then bit her on her left breast. After the assault, the offender threw the victim out of his moving car and assumed that she had died. She miraculously lived, and the offender was arrested.

The distinct placement of the bite marks resulted in his being linked to a similar ritualistic sexual murder in a different state. In this murder, he met a woman who was walking home from a store on a busy highway. The offender grabbed her, dragged her inside a construction area, shoved his fingers up her rectum while strangling her, and bit her on the chin and her left breast. He said he wanted to look at the victim's eyes while killing her and watching her die slowly at his hands.

This offender's history included chronic behavior problems, school expulsion, and an allegation of being sexually abused. Interestingly, his friends had nicknamed him "Catman" because, as an adolescent, he was known to have killed many cats after engaging in some type of sexual activity with them.

Case Study 3

A 30-year-old male was convicted of the murder of a 26-year-old woman and her two young children. He also murdered two other women ages 62 and 40. The offender killed all the victims by manual strangulation after hogtying them, raping them anally and vaginally, and making small knife cuts all over their bodies to cause pain and suffering. All the crime scenes had an absence of physical evidence because the offender had shaved off all of his body hair and entered the homes naked, except for sneakers with several socks pulled over them. He poured alcohol in the vaginas and rectums of his victims because he believed alcohol would remove any trace of DNA. This offender said he got the idea of using alcohol from the well-known film *Presumed Innocent,* whose plot involved the use of a spermicide to eliminate semen. However, he did not know that alcohol does not eliminate DNA, but rather preserves it, which led to his arrest, conviction, and execution.

As a child, the future offender tortured and killed cats. In fact, his mother found a number of strangled cats hanging from her clothesline when he was 8 or 9 years old. He was sent for an evaluation, but there was never any follow-up.

Firesetting

Just as there are many notorious sexual murderers with a history of animal cruelty, there is no shortage of sexual murderers with a history of firesetting. Prolific serial murderer Peter Kurten not only abused animals but was also a serial arsonist as an adolescent (Wilson & Pitman, 1962). He derived pleasure from setting and watching fires and continued setting fires into adulthood, even setting on fire the body of one of his many victims. Jane Toppan, the psychopathic nurse who poisoned an unknown number of patients in the late 1800s, was also a pyromaniac who derived erotic pleasure from watching fires. After an entire household under her care turned up dead, Toppan was arrested and admitted that she had an irresistible sexual impulse to kill (Schechter, 2003). Thomas Piper, who raped and bludgeoned to death four victims, had a history of firesetting (Schechter & Everitt, 1996), as did Arthur Shawcross, who killed numerous prostitutes.

Case Study 4

Arthur Shawcross exhibited all three prongs of MacDonald's triad. As a child, he had frequent nightmares that caused him to wet the bed (Olsen, 1993). By adolescence, he had begun torturing animals and setting fires. Shawcross enjoyed burning barrels of trash and once set a brushfire that had to be extinguished by firefighters.

With his small stature and bizarre affectations, he was a natural target for bullies at school. His classmates called him "Oddie" and tormented him relentlessly (Berry-Dee, 2003). At home, he felt that he could never please his domineering mother (Olsen, 1993). From an early age, it was apparent that Shawcross escaped into a rich fantasy world, speaking aloud to imaginary friends, daydreaming often, and fantasizing about his sister, Jean. He claims to have engaged in sexual activity with her and also to have been molested by an adult man (Olsen, 1993). He was held back in school and eventually dropped out.

After a stint serving in the Vietnam War, Shawcross returned to setting fires, destroying a barn, a milk-bottling plant, and the paper factory where he was employed (Berry-Dee, 2003). He was apprehended while attempting to rob a gas station and sentenced to a 5-year prison term, of which he served only 22 months. After his release, Shawcross's criminal behavior escalated dramatically. He raped a 16-year-old girl. Then, he raped, killed, and mutilated a 10-year-old boy. Soon thereafter, he raped and strangled a 7-year-old girl, stuffing grass into her orifices and leaving her body in a sewage pipe. He was again imprisoned for these crimes and again conned his way into early parole.

Upon release, Shawcross began a string of murders. He seized upon vulnerable women, mainly drug addicts and prostitutes, strangling or beating them to death and leaving their bodies exposed to the elements to deteriorate (Berry-Dee, 2003). Shawcross' fantasies were expressed in his ritualistic treatment of the bodies; most bodies had vegetation inserted into their orifices, many showed signs of cannibalism (to which Shawcross has admitted), and the genitals were frequently mutilated or excised. Shawcross claims to have taken 53 lives in total (Berry-Dee, 2003).

Ressler et al. (1988) found that in their sample of 36 sexual murderers, 56% had set fires during childhood, 52% set had fires during adolescence, and 28% had set fires during adulthood. Langevin and his colleagues (1988) found a somewhat lower rate (33%) in their sample of sexual killers. In a sample of adolescent sexual murderers (Myers et al., 1998), 36% had a history of firesetting, often in conjunction with animal cruelty and fighting. One young man attempted to burn down his mother's home, set a van on fire, and set his aunt's bed on fire as a child, stating that he "wanted to see someone burn" (p. 324). He and a peer were responsible for raping and bludgeoning to death an adult woman in her home, allegedly to avenge an outstanding drug debt.

A social-learning theory of serial murder (Hale, 1993) suggests that such offenders endure humiliating experiences in youth and internalize them. Never able to retaliate directly, perhaps because the humiliator is a parent, the child cannot release his frustration and later vents his rage against a symbolic victim. Consistent with this theory, the childhoods of sexual murderers, like the childhoods of firesetters, often include parental alienation and unstable family life (Marshall, 1989; Ressler et al., 1988). Two-thirds of the serial killers reviewed by Stone (2001) indicated emotional abuse during youth in the form of parental humiliation, often in the context of sexuality.

Singer and Hensley (2004) investigated the histories of three notorious sexual murderers—Carl Panzram, Ottis Toole, and David Berkowitz—in order to test this social-learning theory of serial killing. The authors believe that early attempts to vent frustration through firesetting may be insufficient, leading to increasingly aggressive forms of expression, ultimately culminating in homicide. All three of these individuals experienced rejection and humiliation at the hands of a parent or parents, against whom they could not retaliate. A single fire was insufficient to alleviate the tension, leading to the setting of multiple fires. Eventually, this behavior escalated to murder.

Panzram, beaten and neglected by his parents, began setting fires in adolescence and killed random victims as an adult. Toole's father abandoned the family, and, during childhood, Toole's mother dressed him as a girl. He often burned vacant buildings and continued setting fires in response to stress throughout his adult life. And Berkowitz developed a generalized hatred for women—possibly as a result of an unresolved conflict surrounding his being abandoned by his biological mother—and was known as a loner. He recorded 1,488 fires in his diary before and during the time he committed a series of murders of female strangers. Ressler and Schachtman (1992) believed that Berkowitz's firesetting "were all a prelude to his moving into the arena in which he could exercise the ultimate control, homicide" (p. 80). The following case of Joseph "The Shoemaker" Kallinger illustrates the connection between sexual murder and a background of firesetting as an important factor in understanding the offender's conduct (Schreiber, 1983):

Case Study 5

Joseph Kallinger, born in 1936, was abandoned as an infant and was adopted by a couple who subjected him to severe physical and emotional abuse. The couple showed him no affection, hit him with a hammer, held his hand over a flame, told him that his penis was defective, and regularly threatened to send him back to the orphanage. As a child, he was molested at knifepoint by a group of older boys. He began engaging in antisocial behavior out of rage and frustration and heard voices instructing him to cut someone. By adolescence, Kallinger had developed sadistic fantasies, masturbating while stabbing at pornographic images with a knife.

At the age of 15, after the voice of God told Kallinger that it was his mission to heal people through their feet, he became ardently invested in shoemaking. In 1958, at age 22, a figure appeared to him, commanding that he burn down his house. Although this fire was set as a result of a hallucination and resulted in material gain from an insurance claim, a sexual element was quite clear. As he related to author Flora Schreiber (1983), having an orgasm as he spoke, "It was thrilling and the flames brought me a lot of joy. Fire gave me the same kind of sexual feeling I had from holding a knife in my left hand" (p. 118). He later set fire to his next home four times, and he once set fire to his place of work, a shoemaker's shop.

Kallinger was married twice and had six children. Three of Kallinger's children filed abuse charges against him in 1972; he was convicted, but served only a few months of his sentence. Soon thereafter, an invisible floating head named "Charlie" commanded him to castrate and murder young boys.

In 1974, Kallinger and his 13-year-old son, Michael, lured a 10-year-old boy into an abandoned factory, tortured him, sliced off his penis, and killed him. Three weeks later, Kallinger drowned his 12-year-old son, Joey, while Michael watched. In November 1974, Kallinger and his son began invading homes, holding the residents captive, sexually assaulting the women, and stealing their valuables. Their spree ended in January 1975, when Kallinger slit the throat of one of his eight captives in a home in New Jersey. Two weeks later, Kallinger and his son were arrested. Kallinger was sentenced to life in prison, where he died of a seizure in 1996, at the age of 59.

Discussion

Substantial evidence shows that animal cruelty and firesetting are behaviors indicative of severe emotional disturbance, but this disturbance may manifest itself in various ways and does not necessarily predict homicide. Although animal cruelty and firesetting appear to be more common in homicidal populations than in nonoffender samples, there is insufficient evidence that MacDonald's triad is a valid predictor of homicidal behavior, a conclusion at which MacDonald himself also arrived. Far more people exhibit the complete or partial triad than actually commit homicide, and the triad fails to reliably discriminate homicidal offenders from other types of offenders; however, the triad behaviors appear to be better predictors when they co-occur rather than appear independently.

As we observe in many of the reported cases, the triad typically appears amidst a wide array of maladaptive behaviors and traumatic or invalidating experiences. For instance, a child who has sexual encounters with relatives, is constantly bullied, performs poorly in school, and feels unable to please his parents might have significant behavioral troubles, even in the absence of animal cruelty, firesetting, or enuresis. But when significant acting out, such as hurting animals and setting fires, occurs, the likelihood of a good adjustment in adulthood is remote. The more severe the acting out in childhood is, the poorer the prognosis.

Unfortunately, the research is limited in quantity and suffers a variety of methodological problems. Much of the literature relies on case studies, and the available empirical studies often lack control groups (Sakheim et al., 1985). Even in the empirical studies, the data are often based solely on self-report, which renders their reliability questionable. Furthermore, because of the rarity of youth firesetting and animal cruelty—as well as the social stigma associated with being identified as a child who engages in these behaviors—most studies suffer from small sample sizes, which severely limit the statistical conclusions and generalizability of the findings. Stone's (2001) review of killers' biographies highlights the fact that information about childhood firesetting, animal cruelty, and enuresis is often not available; when looking into an offender's background, if information on these features is not available, we can conclude neither their presence nor their absence.

Lack of agreed-on operational definitions, particularly around firesetting behaviors, adds to the methodological problems. For example, terms such as *firesetting, fire play, pyromania, arson,* and *pyrophilia* are often used; however, each has a nuanced definition, and not all refer to a type of pathological firesetting that may have predictive value. In addition, many fires do not meet the legal definition of arson (Grant & Kim, 2007); therefore, any study of arsonists will systematically exclude a large portion of pathological firesetters, and effects observed in these samples may be diluted by the more logical profit-motivated and crime-concealment firesetters. Similarly, *animal cruelty* encompasses a wide range of behaviors, some of which may be predictive while others may not.

Flawed definitions and limited capacity for sampling contribute to sampling errors, a considerable source of error in this area of research, as arson studies and animal cruelty studies often sample only those who have been identified and apprehended. Essentially, we are studying only unsuccessful pathological firesetters and animal abusers (i.e., those who get caught), as we know little about those who have not been identified. The same dilemma plagues research on sexual homicide, in which the field of knowledge is confined to those killers who have been apprehended; at-large killers are necessarily beyond the purview of study. In both cases, one might expect some systematic differences between the type of offender who gets caught and the type of offender who does not.

Despite Hellman and Blackman's (1966) conclusion that the triad should be used as a prognostic indicator of aggressive behavior in adulthood, it seems that MacDonald's initial view that the triad is most relevant to sadistic criminal behavior is more valid. Intuitively, it would seem that a child who takes joy in drowning a kitten or electrocuting a dog might later get aroused by exacting cruelty on humans. Whereas most acts of homicide are committed in the context of a conflict between the offender and the victim, sexual homicide most often reflects the offender's enjoyment of dominating another human being in a sadistic manner. Future research on sadistic and sexually-motivated homicide offenders—using larger samples, appropriate case controls, and strict operational definitions of firesetting and animal cruelty—would be a logical next step toward supporting the usefulness of MacDonald's proposed triad.

References

American Psychiatric Association (2013). *Diagnostic and statistical manual of mental disorders* (5th ed.). https://doi.org/10.1176/appi.books.9780890425596.

Arluke, A., & Madfis, E. (2013). Animal abuse as a warning sign of school massacres: A critique and refinement. *Homicide Studies, 18*(1), 7–22.

Ascione, F. R., Friedrich, W. N., Heath, J., & Hayashi, K. (2003). Cruelty to animals in normative, sexually abused, and outpatient psychiatric samples of six to twelve year old children: Relations to maltreatment and exposure to domestic violence. *Anthrozoos, 16,* 194–212.

Baglivio, M. T., Wolff, K. T., Delisi, M., Vaughn, M. G., & Piquero, A. R. (2017). Juvenile animal cruelty and firesetting behaviour. *Criminal Behaviour and Mental Health, 27,* 484–500.

Banay, R. S. (1969). Unconscious sexual motivation in crime. *Medical Aspects of Human Sexuality, 3,* 91–102.

Becker, K. D., Stuewig, J., Herrera, V. M., & McCloskey, L. A. (2004). A study of firesetting and animal cruelty in children: Family influences and adolescent outcomes. *Journal of the American Academy of Child and Adolescent Psychiatry, 43*(7), 905–912.

Berry-Dee, C. (2003). *Talking with serial killers: The most evil people in the world tell their own stories.* Blake.

Dadds, M. R., Turner, C. M., & McAloon, J. (2002). Developmental links between cruelty to animals and human violence. *The Australian & New Zealand Journal of Criminology, 35,* 363–382.

Felthous, A. R. (1980). Aggression against cats, dogs, and people. *Clinical Psychiatry in Human Development, 10,* 169–177.

Felthous, A. R., & Bernard, H. (1979). Enuresis, firesetting, and cruelty to animals: The significance of two thirds of this triad. *Journal of Forensic Sciences, 24*(1), 240–246.

Felthous, A. R., & Keller, S. R. (1987). Childhood cruelty to animals and later aggression against people: A review. *American Journal of Psychiatry, 144,* 710–717.

Fras, I. (1983). Fire setting (pyromania) and its relationship to sexuality. In L. B. Schlesinger & E. Revitch (Eds.), *Sexual dynamics of antisocial behavior* (pp. 192–205). Thomas.

Gleyzer, R., Felthous, A. R., & Holzer, C. E. (2002). Animal cruelty and psychiatric disorders. *Journal of the American Academy of Psychiatry and Law, 30,* 257–265.

Goring, C. (1913). *The English convict.* Her Majesty's Stationary Office.

Grant, J. E., & Kim, S. W. (2007). Clinical characteristics and psychiatric comorbidity of pyromania. *Journal of Clinical Psychiatry, 68*(11), 1717–1722.

Grolnick, W. S., Cole, R. E., Laurenitis, L., & Schwartzman, P. (1990). Playing with fire: A developmental assessment of children's fire understanding and experience. *Journal of Clinical Child Psychology, 19*(2), 128–135.

Guttmacher, M. S. (1960). *The mind of the murderer*. Farrar, Straus, and Cudahy.

Guttmacher, M. S. (1963). Dangerous offenders. *Crime and Delinquency, 9*, 381–390.

Haden, S. C., & Scarpa, A. (2005). Childhood animal cruelty: A review of research, assessment, and therapeutic issues. *Forensic Examiner, 14*, 23–32.

Hale, R. L. (1993). The application of learning theory to serial murder or "You too can learn to be a serial killer." *American Journal of Criminal Justice, 17*(2), 37–45.

Heath, G. A., Hardesty, V. A., Goldfine, P. E., & Walker, A. M. (1985). Diagnosis and childhood fire-setting. *Journal of Clinical Psychology, 41*(4), 571–575.

Hellman, D. D., & Blackman, N. (1966). Enuresis, firesetting, and cruelty to animals: A triad predictive of adult crime. *American Journal of Psychiatry, 122*, 1431–1435.

Hensley, C., & Tallichet, S. E. (2008). The effects of inmate self-reported childhood and adolescent animal cruelty: Motivations and the number of convictions for adult violent interpersonal crimes. *International Journal of Offender Therapy and Comparative Criminology, 52*, 175–184.

Hensley, C., & Tallichet, S. E. (2009). Childhood and adolescent animal cruelty methods and their possible link to adult violent crimes. *Journal of Interpersonal Violence, 24*, 147–158.

Hensley, C., Tallichet, S. E., & Dutkiewicz, E. L. (2010). Childhood bestiality: A potential precursor to adult interpersonal violence. *Journal of Interpersonal Violence, 25*, 557–567.

Holt, S. E., Meloy, J. R. & Strack, S. (1999). Sadism and psychopathy in violent and sexually violent offenders. *Journal of the American Academy of Psychiatry and the Law, 27*(1), 23–32.

Jacobson, R. R. (1985). Child firesetters: A clinical investigation. *Journal of Child Psychology and Psychiatry, 26*(5), 759–768.

Johnson, B. R., & Becker, J. V. (1997). Natural born killers? The development of the sexually sadistic serial killer. *Journal of the American Academy of Psychiatry and Law, 25*, 335–348.

Johnson, S. A. (2018). Animal cruelty, pet abuse and violence: The missed dangerous connection. *Forensic Research & Criminology International Journal, 6*(6), 403–415.

Justice, B., Justice, R., & Kraft, I. (1974). Early-warning signs of violence: Is a triad enough? *American Journal of Psychiatry, 131*, 457–459.

Kafry, D. (1980). Playing with matches: Children and fire. In D. Canter (Ed.), *Fires and human behavior* (pp. 47–61). Wiley.

Kavanagh, P. S., Signal, T. D., & Taylor, N. (2013). The Dark Triad and animal cruelty: Dark personalities, dark attitudes, and dark behaviors. *Personality and Individual Differences, 55*(6), 666–670.

Kolko, D. J., & Kazdin, A. E. (1991). Aggression and psychopathology in matchplaying and firesetting children: A replication and extension. *Journal of Clinical Child Psychology, 20*(2), 191–201.

Kolko, D. J., & Kazdin, A. E. (1991). Motives of childhood firesetters: Firesetting characteristics and psychological correlates. *Journal of Child Psychology and Psychiatry, 32*(3), 535–550.

Kolko, D. J., Kazdin, A. E., & Meyer, E. C. (1985). Aggression and psychopathology in childhood firesetters: Parent and child reports. *Journal of Consulting and Clinical Psychology, 53*(3), 377–385.

Krafft-Ebing, R. von (1886). *Psychopathia sexualis* (C. G. Chaddock, Trans.). Davis.

Kretchmer, E. (1925). *Physique and character.* Kegan Paul.

Lambie, I., Randell, I., Krynen, A., Reed, P., & Ioane, J. (2019). Risk factors for future offending in child and adolescent firesetters following a fire service intervention program. *Criminal Justice and Behavior, 46*(6), 832–852.

Langevin, R., Ben-Aron, M. H., Wright, P., Marchese, V., & Handy, L. (1988). The sex killer. *Annals of Sex Research, 1*(2), 263–302.

Langevin, R., Paitich, D., Orchard, B., Hardy, L., & Russon, A. (1983). Childhood and family background of killers, seen for psychiatric assessment: A controlled study. *Bulletin of the American Academy of Psychiatry and Law, 11,* 331–341.

Leong, G. B. (1992). A psychiatric study of persons charged with arson. *Journal of Forensic Sciences, 37*(5), 1319–1326.

Lewis, N. D. C., & Yarnell, H. (1951). Pathological firesetting (Pyromania). In *Nervous and mental disease monograph no. 82.* Coolidge Foundation.

Lombroso, C. (1911). *Crime: Its causes and remedies* (H. P. Horton, Trans.). Boston: Little, Brown. (Original work published 1876)

MacDonald, J. M. (1963). The threat to kill. *American Journal of Psychiatry, 121,* 125–130.

MacDonald, J. M. (1968). *Homicidal threats.* Thomas.

Marshall, W. L. (1989). Intimacy, loneliness, and sexual offenders. Behavioral *Research and Therapy, 27,* 491–503.

Martin, G., Bergen, H. A., Richardson, A. S., Roeger, L., & Allison, S. (2004). Correlates of firesetting in a community sample of young adolescents. *Australian and New Zealand Journal of Psychiatry, 38*(3), 148–154.

Mavromatis, M. (2000). Serial arson: Repetitive firesetting and pyromania. In L.B. Schlesinger (Ed.), *Serial offenders* (pp. 67–102). CRC Press.

Meloy, J. R. (1992). *Violent attachments.* Aronson.

Meloy, J. R. (2000). The nature and dynamics of sexual homicide: An integrative review. *Aggression and Violent Behavior, 5*, 1–22.

Merz-Perez, L., Heide, K. M., & Silverman, I. J. (2001). Childhood cruelty to animals and subsequent violence against humans. *International Journal of Offender Therapy and Comparative Criminology, 45*, 556–573.

Mesa, V. B. (2012). *Criminal, antisocial, and temporal patterns in the histories of serial and non-serial sexual murderers.* City University of New York.

Mishima, Y. (1956). *The Temple of the Golden Pavilion* (I. Morris, Trans.). New York: Berkley.

Moore, J. M., Jr., Thompson-Pope, S. K., & Whited, R. M. (1996). MMPI-A profiles of adolescent boys with a history of firesetting. *Journal of Personality Assessment, 67*(1), 116–126.

Myers, W. C., Burgess, A., & Nelson, J. A. (1998). Criminal and behavioral aspects of juvenile sexual homicide. *Journal of Forensic Sciences, 43*, 321–328.

Olsen, J. (1993). *The misbegotten son: A serial killer and his victims.* Delacorte Press.

Overton, J. C., Hensley, C., & Tallichet, S. E. (2011). Examining the relationship between childhood animal cruelty motives and recurrent adult violent crimes towards humans. *Journal of Interpersonal Violence, 20*, 1–17.

Patterson-Kane, E. G., & Piper, H. (2009). Animal abuse as a sentinel for human violence: A critique. *Journal of Social Issues, 65*, 589–614.

Petersen, M. L., & Farrington, D. P. (2007). Cruelty to animals and violence to people. *Victims and Offenders, 2*, 21–43.

Quinsey, V. L., Chaplin, T. C., & Upfold, D. (1989). Arsonists and sexual arousal to fire setting: Correlation unsupported. *Journal of Behavior Therapy and Experimental Psychiatry, 20*(3), 203–209.

Rae, G. W. (1967). *Confessions of the Boston Strangler.* New York: Pyramid Press.

Ressler, R. K., Burgess, A. W., & Douglas, J. E. (1988). *Sexual homicide: Patterns and motives.* Free Press.

Ressler, R. K., Burgess, A. W., Hartman, C. R., & Douglas, J. E. (1986). Murderers who rape and mutilate. *Journal of Interpersonal Violence, 1*, 273–287.

Ressler, R. K., & Schachtman, T. (1992). *Whoever fights monsters.* St. Martin's Press.

Revitch, E. (1977). Classification of offenders for prognostic and dispositional evaluation. *Bulletin of the American Academy of Psychiatry and Law, 5*, 41–50.

Revitch, E. (1978). Sexually motivated burglaries. *Bulletin of the American Academy of Psychiatry and Law, 6*, 277–283.

Revitch, E., & Schlesinger, L. B. (1978). Murder: Evaluation, classification, and predicting. In I. L. Kutash, S. B. Kutash, & L. B. Schlesinger (Eds.), *Violence: Perspectives on murder and aggression* (pp. 138–164). Jossey-Bass.

Revitch, E., & Schlesinger, L. B. (1981). *Psychopathology of homicide.* Thomas.

Revitch, E., & Schlesinger, L. B. (1989). *Sex murder and sex aggression.* Thomas.

Rider, A. O. (1980). The firesetter: A psychological profile, Part II. *FBI Law Enforcement Bulletin, 49*(7), 7–17.

Root, C., MacKay, S., Henderson, J., Del Bove, G., & Warling, D. (2008). The link between maltreatment and juvenile firesetting: Correlates and underlying mechanisms. *Child Abuse & Neglect, 32,* 161–176.

Sakheim, G. A., & Osborn, E. (1994). *Firesetting children: Risk assessment and treatment.* Washington, DC: Child League of America.

Sakheim, G. A., Vigdor, M. G., Gordon, M., & Helprin, L. M. (1985). A psychological profile of juvenile firesetters in residential treatment. *Child Welfare, 64*(5), 453–476.

Schechter, H. (2003). *The serial killer files: The who, what, where, how, and why of the world's most terrifying murderers.* Ballantine.

Schechter, H., & Everitt, D. (1996). *The A–Z encyclopedia of serial killers.* Pocket Books.

Schlesinger, L. B. (2001). The potential sex murderer: Ominous signs, risk assessment. *Journal of Threat Assessment, 1,* 47–72.

Schlesinger, L. B. (2004). Classification of antisocial behavior for prognostic purposes: Study the motivation, not the crime. *Journal of Psychiatry and Law, 32,* 191–219.

Schlesinger, L. B. (2007). Sexual homicide: Differentiating catathymic and compulsive murders. *Aggression and Violent Behavior, 12,* 242–256.

Schlesinger, L. B. (2008). Compulsive-repetitive offenders: Behavioral patterns, motivational dynamics. In R. N. Kocsis (Ed.), *Serial murder and the psychology of violent crimes* (pp. 15–33). Humana Press.

Schlesinger, L. B. (2020). *Sexual murder: Catathymic and compulsive homicides.* CRC Press.

Schlesinger, L. B., Kassen. M., Mesa, V. B., & Pinizzotto, A. J. (2010). Ritual and signature in serial sexual homicide. *Journal of the American Academy of Psychiatry and Law, 38,* 239–246.

Schlesinger, L. B., & Revitch, E. (1997). Sexual dynamics in homicide and assault. In L. B. Schlesinger & E. Revitch (Eds.), *Sexual dynamics of antisocial behavior* (2nd ed.) (pp. 203–223). Thomas.

Schreiber, F. R. (1983). *The Shoemaker: The anatomy of a psychotic.* Signet.

Schwartz, A. D. (1992). *The man who could not kill enough.* Carol Press.

Singer, S. D., & Hensley, C. (2004). Applying social learning theory to childhood and adolescent firesetting: Can it lead to serial murder? *International Journal of Offender Therapy and Comparative Criminology, 48*(4), 461–476.

Stickle, T. R., & Blechman, E. A. (2002). Aggression and fire: Antisocial behavior in firesetting and nonfiresetting juvenile offenders. *Journal of Psychopathology and Behavioral Assessment, 24*(3), 177–193.

Stone, M. H. (2001). Serial sexual homicide: Biological, psychological, and sociological aspects. *Journal of Personality Disorders, 15*, 1–18.

Stupperich, A., & Strack, M. (2016). Among a German sample of forensic patients, previous animal abuse mediates between psychopathy and sadistic actions. *Journal of Forensic Sciences, 61*(3), 699–705.

Swaffer, T., & Hollin, C. R. (1995). Adolescent firesetting: Why do they say they do it? *Journal of Adolescence, 18*, 619–623.

Tallichet, S. E., Hensley, C., & Singer, S. D. (2005). Unraveling the methods of childhood and adolescent cruelty to nonhuman animals. *Society & Animals*, *13*(2), 91–108.

Tanner, A., Hasking, P., & Martin, G. (2016). Co-occurring non-suicidal self-injury and firesetting among at-risk adolescents: Experiences of negative life events, mental health problems, substance use, and suicidality. *Archives of Suicide Research, 20*, 233–249.

Tapia, F. (1971). Children who are cruel to animals. *Child Psychiatry and Human Development, 2*, 70–77.

Trentham, C. E., Hensley, C., & Policastro, C. (2018). Recurrent childhood animal cruelty and its link to recurrent adult interpersonal violence. *International Journal of Offender Therapy and Comparative Criminology, 61*(8), 2345–2356.

U.S. Department of Justice (2010). *Crime in the United States: FBI's uniform crime reports*. Washington, DC: U.S. Government Printing Office.

Verlinden, S., Hersen, M., & Thomas, J. (2000). Risk factors in school shootings. *Clinical Psychology Review*, *20*(1), 3–56.

Walters, G. D. (2013). Testing the specificity postulate of the violence graduation hypothesis: Meta-analyses of the animal cruelty-offending relationship. *Aggression and Violent Behavior, 18*(6), 797–802.

Wax, D. E., & Haddox, V. G. (1974). Enuresis, fire setting, and animal cruelty: A useful danger signal in predicting vulnerability of adolescent males to assaultive behavior. *Child Psychiatry and Human Development, 4*(3), 151–156.

Wertham, F. (1937). The catathymic crisis: A clinical entity. *Archives of Neurology and Psychiatry, 37*, 974–977.

Wilson, C., & Pitman, P. (1962). *Encyclopedia of murder.* Putnam.

Yarnell, H. (1940). Fire setting in children. *American Journal of Orthopsychiatry, 10*, 272–286.

Section IV

Theoretical Perspectives

Chapter 15

Examining Animal Abuse through a Sociological Lens: An Expanding and Evolving Theoretical Field

Rochelle Stevenson, Amy J. Fitzgerald, and Antonio R. Verbora

Introduction

The purpose of this chapter is to provide a survey of sociological theorizing of animal abuse and the studies that have begun to test these theories. The amount of theorizing and empirical research in this area has increased dramatically in the past two decades. Here, we isolate and discuss 10 theories that employ sociological (and often other disciplinary) insights to better understand animal abuse.

Sociology has a long history of questioning boundaries and taken-for-granted assumptions and this modus operandi can be usefully extended to examining animal abuse. Theoretical and empirical examinations of animal abuse have thus far tended to focus on intentional actions defined as illegal and unnecessary, primarily against companion animals (for critiques of this focus, see Agnew, 1998; Beirne 1999; Cazaux, 1999). Limiting the discussion in this way, however, renders invisible most of the harms animals are subjected to in our culture: harm through neglect, harm defined as legal, harm against species other than companion animals, and harms deemed necessary. We agree with Beirne's (2002, p. 385) position that we have "no legitimate warrant arbitrarily to restrict... inquiries into animal abuse to a notion of harm defined as such either by state authorities or by fickle public opinion," and therefore extend our analysis in this chapter beyond the boundaries of what has been socially and legally recognized as harmful.

In order to include harms against animals that are socially authorized in our analysis, we must employ a broad and encompassing definition of animal abuse. Consequently, we herein employ Agnew's (1998) definition. He defines animal abuse

> as any act that contributes to the pain or death of an animal or that otherwise threatens the welfare of an animal. Such abuse may be physical (including

> sexual) or mental, may involve active maltreatment or passive neglect, may be direct or indirect, intentional or unintentional, socially approved or condemned, and/or necessary or unnecessary (however defined) (p. 179).

We also adopt Beirne's (2014) use of the term theriocide to refer to the killing of animals by people. He recommends the use of this term as a parallel to the use of the term homicide to refer to the killing of one human by another, notably because if the killing of animals by humans is as harmful to them as homicides are to humans, then the proper naming of such deaths offers a respectful remedy, however small, to the extensive privileging of human lives over those of animals (Beirne, 2014, p. 62). If there is a drawback to such encompassing definitions of harming and killing animals, it is that theorizing can become somewhat more complicated. However, we consider this difficulty more desirable than somewhat arbitrarily truncating the scope of the discussion.

Our discussion of the theories we focus on here flows from the micro to the macro level of analysis and moves roughly from a focus on the etiology of socially disapproved harms against animals and theriocide, to analyses of the connections between the lethal and sub-lethal harms perpetrated against animals and those perpetrated against people (both socially approved and disapproved of). In each case, we provide an overview of the central tenets of the theory and explore how each one has been applied through empirical research. Due to the scope of this chapter and space limitations, we cannot provide an exhaustive overview of all sociological theories that might be brought to bear on the subject of animal abuse and theriocide, all of the research associated with each theory, or all of the potential limitations of each theory. We therefore focus our discussion here on the most commonly used applications of sociological theories to understand animal abuse (social learning, frustration and strain, differential coercion, violence graduation, generalization of deviance, social disorganization, feminist, masculinities, (eco)Marxist, and cultural spillover), a sample of the empirical applications of each, and the most significant limitations of each theory.

Social Learning Theory

The fundamental assumption of social learning theory is that we learn our behavior from important others (such as peers, family members, or even respected celebrities) and then repeat the behavior through imitation or modelling. In the literature on animal abuse, there are three primary ways that social learning is thought to occur: (1) witnessing animal abuse leads to the modelling of the behavior directly; (2) the experience of victimization leads to enacting the behavior against animals; and (3) the observation of violence against humans leads to modelling the behavior against animals.

The power of direct modeling in explaining animal abuse has been demonstrated empirically. For instance, Baldry (2003) surveyed Italian youth about their exposure to and commission of various kinds of violence, including animal abuse. About half of the 1,396 youth aged 9 to 17 who participated reported having committed animal abuse, with boys more likely than girls to have abused animals. The strongest predictor for committing acts of animal abuse was being exposed to animal abuse committed by peers, followed by exposure to parental abuse of an animal (Baldry, 2003). In short, seeing peers abuse animals, especially given the adolescent desire to fit in and be accepted, can lead to imitating the behavior. In situations of exposure to parental violence against animals, the reasons for imitating the behavior could be as simple as wanting to model the behavior of a respected parent, or as complex as needing to feel the power and control that the parent is perceived to hold. The behavior could also be imitated due to more general communication of attitudes about the appropriate treatment of animals, that "such behavior is acceptable or perhaps even admirable" (Henry, 2004a, p. 291).

Henry (2004a, 2004b) also explored the role that exposure to animal abuse had in relation to engaging in abusing animals but did not differentiate or limit the relationships of the individuals involved. Using questionnaires distributed to 206 undergraduate students, Henry (2004a) found that students who reported they had observed animal abuse prior to age 13 (i.e., prior to adolescence) were over three times more likely to report that they had subsequently engaged in animal abuse than those who had not observed any animal abuse. Again, using undergraduate students, Henry (2004b) found that the strength of the correlation between observation and commission of animal abuse increased with the frequency of observation. Students who had observed more than one act of animal cruelty were significantly more likely to engage in animal abuse than students who had never observed or only once observed animal abuse. Henry's (2004a, 2004b) results suggest that age of exposure to animal abuse, along with the frequency of exposure, have a fairly strong impact on the likelihood of the individual engaging in acts of animal cruelty, supporting a social learning theory of animal abuse.

Hensley and Tallichet (2005) examined both the observation of and participation in acts of animal cruelty in their sample of incarcerated male offenders. Witnessing a family member or a friend hurt or kill an animal was positively correlated with the number of times the respondents hurt or killed an animal. However, witnessing a neighbor commit animal cruelty was not correlated with the respondent's own acts of animal abuse. These findings provide a potentially important qualification of social learning theory for explaining animal abuse: the behavior of those who are not part of one's close social sphere may not be as consequential.

In addition to those studies demonstrating the role of social learning in the perpetration of animal abuse and theriocide, research on bystander behavior also indicates that social learning can contribute to non-engagement by bystanders. In an evaluation of bystander behavior, Arluke (2012; 2013) conducted interviews with undergraduate students who had witnessed abuse of animals, but who had not participated in the abuse themselves. He found that the degree of acceptance of the animal abuse by bystanders was rooted in peer relationships: the bystanders had learned the social group's definition of the animal's reaction to the abuse as amusing and that the abuse was to be kept from adults and those in authority in order to preserve the friendships.

Though Baldry (2003), Henry (2004a, 2004b), and Hensley and Tallichet (2005) focused on direct modeling of animal abuse (and Arluke's 2012 study explored the modeling of nonintervention), social learning can also occur through the observation of violence against people or through the experience of being a victim of violence. The intergenerational transmission (IGT) hypothesis focuses more specifically on intra-familial relationships, and applied to animal abuse, the IGT hypothesis illuminates the possibility of modeling through observation of violence against humans and animals, as well as experiences of victimization. There are two basic forms of modelling in this context: (1) specific modelling, where the specific behavior of the parent or important figure is imitated, often in a gendered or role-based way, and (2) general modelling, where the general patterns of violence and aggression observed or experienced are carried forward into relationships with others, including animals.

There is mixed evidence regarding the IGT hypothesis. Knight, Ellis, and Simmons (2014) found a positive correlation between parents' commission of intimate partner violence (IPV) and animal abuse by their children, but the parents' victimization had no significant bearing on subsequent animal abuse by the children. The study also looked at the potential of intergenerational continuity of animal abuse, meaning that animal abuse by the parent would be continued by the child, and found no support for the IGT in this regard. Like Knight et al. (2014), Bright and colleagues (2018) found that adverse childhood experiences, including household violence, physical abuse, emotional abuse, and physical neglect, increased the odds that the youth in their study would engage in animal cruelty. Bright et al. (2018) did not examine parental acts of animal cruelty, but the IGT is supported by their study in terms of the continuation of aggression and abuse. Drawn from a sample of mother-child pairs (n = 46) who had experienced IPV, McDonald et al. (2018) interviewed children directly about their own commission of animal cruelty and the motivations for their behavior and combined this with maternal reports. Seventy-two percent of the children in the sample engaged in animal cruelty, and 78% of these children also witnessed animal cruelty. Most of the acts of cruelty were attributed either by the child, the mother, or both, to imitating the abuser's treatment of or aggression towards the animals. McDonald et al.'s (2018) study shows strong support for the IGT; "in households where harm to animals is minimized, normalized ... and/or seen as necessary," the result is the transmission of these attitudes from adult to child (p. 476).

Other research has found a relationship between physical punishment by a parent and the perpetration of animal abuse by the subject of the punishment. For instance, in a sample of 256 undergraduate students, Flynn (1999) documents a significant positive relationship between the frequency of physical punishment and the commission of animal abuse, but this relationship differed based on gender. While there was no significant relationship for those who identified as female, almost 60 percent of male-identified students who had been physically punished had engaged in animal cruelty versus a 23 percent commission rate by male students who had not been corporally punished. Further, Flynn (1999) found that this relationship was only significant when the physical punishment came from the male parent. This suggests a blend of general and specific modelling in connection to animal abuse. The physical punishment was modelled in the generalized aggression against animal others, while the specific gendered role of dominance and aggression was modelled using animals as targets. Flynn (1999) proposes that this can be understood via social learning, as "the socialization experience for male children emphasizes dominance and aggression [and] cruelty to animals may provide some males with the opportunity to rehearse these skills" (p. 978). This research points to a specific way that the intergenerational transmission of violence can occur.

A significant proportion of the research looking at the IGT of animal abuse focuses on exposure to domestic violence more broadly and tends to support the general modelling context of IGT. The connection between children's exposure to domestic violence and their subsequent commission of animal abuse is well-documented. In an early study, Kellert and Felthous (1985) found that incarcerated men who reported experiencing domestic violence in childhood were more likely to report committing acts of animal cruelty. Nearly every youth in Baldry's (2003) study who engaged in animal abuse also reported that they had witnessed violence between their parents. In Ascione's (1998) research, women who attended a domestic violence shelter with their children were questioned about animal abuse. Based on maternal reports, 32 percent of children engaged in cruelty against the family pet (Ascione, 1998). Other studies (e.g., Ascione & Arkow, 1999; Ascione, Weber, & Wood, 1997; DeGue & DeLillo, 2009; Gullone, 2014; Quinlisk, 1999; Stevenson, 2009; Zilney, 2007) document similar patterns connecting exposure to violence in the family and abuse against animals.

Subsequent studies using control groups also offer strong support for the IGT hypothesis. Ascione et al. (2007), Currie (2006), and Volant, Johnson, Gullone, and Coleman (2008) all used samples drawn from domestic violence shelters, as well as control groups that had not experienced domestic violence, in order to explore the prevalence of animal abuse in families with violence. In her Canadian study, Currie (2006) found that children who had been exposed to domestic violence were nearly three times more likely to be cruel to animals than children who had not experienced violence in the home. In Australia, Volant et al. (2008) found that 29 percent of children in the domestic violence group had been exposed to animal abuse in the home versus none of the children in the control group. Additionally, and importantly for the IGT hypothesis, children who had experienced domestic violence and witnessed animal abuse were significantly more likely than children with no exposure to have engaged in animal abuse themselves. Ascione et al. (2007) discovered that the women in their sample drawn from a shelter for abused women who reported that their partners had committed animal abuse also reported that the children often witnessed the abuse of the pet. Further, between maternal reports and the children's self-disclosure, nearly 40 percent of children had engaged in abuse against the family pet. This would indicate support for the IGT of animal cruelty for a sizable proportion of the children. Perhaps the most interesting result of Ascione et al.'s (2007) study, however, was the revelation that nearly half of the children had actively placed themselves in harm's way to protect their pet from the abuse perpetrated against them. This would contradict social learning and IGT more specifically in that those children evidence the opposite attitude and behavior than what is being modelled in the home. This highlights one of the critiques of social learning theory and the related IGT hypothesis: there is difficulty explaining why only certain individuals, and not every person who witnesses violence in the home or against animals, model the behavior in the form of animal abuse. Further research is needed to better understand the trajectory of perpetrating animal abuse and to tease apart the significance of the three social learning routes to perpetration.

Frustration and Strain

A somewhat related explanation of animal abuse theorizes that it occurs as the result of frustration or strain. According to this perspective, individuals engage in animal abuse because they have learned that it is a suitable vehicle for reducing stress and strain, and abusive behavior may occur as more expressive aggression in response to frustration and strain. The frustration and strain theories were developed to explain aggression more generally, and both point to blocked goals as important precursors (Dollard, Doob, Miller, Mowrer, & Sears, 1939; Einstadter & Henry, 2010). According to the frustration theory, "aggression, rather than occurring spontaneously for no reason, is the response to the frustration of some goal-directed behavior by an outside source" (Linsely, 2006, p. 18). The general strain theory builds upon and goes beyond frustration related to blocked goal-directed behavior. According to early formulations of strain theory, criminality is the result of the failure to achieve conventional goals (Tibbetts & Hemmens, 2010). The revised, or more general strain theory, theorizes that criminal activity can also result from the removal of positive stimuli and from negative affective states, such as anger and frustration (Agnew, 2010, p. 202).

Agnew (1998) developed a specific theoretical model to explain animal abuse. His model integrates insights from several theories, including social learning, strain theory, and control theory to help explain why individuals abuse animals. Agnew's theory focuses on three factors related to the likelihood that an individual will harm animals. He argues that animal abuse will likely occur when individuals (1) are unaware of the consequences of their abusive actions; (2) believe the abuse is justified; and (3) perceive that the benefits of their actions outweigh the costs. Agnew (1998) further identifies five other factors that can interact with the three main factors: (1) individual traits (e.g., empathy); (2) socialization; (3) strain or stress; (4) degree of social control; and (5) the characteristics of the animal involved. Finally, all of these factors can be impacted by structural or demographic variables, such as gender, race/ethnicity, age, education, occupation, urban/rural location, and region. To summarize, according to his thorough model of animal abuse, individuals who experience frustration or strain (which can take many forms) may engage in animal abuse to manage their associated negative emotions (Agnew, 1998). However, this strain does not occur in a vacuum—it is related to other individual traits (e.g., socialization, social control) and structural variables—and the actions occur within the context of specific knowledge, beliefs, and attitudes related to animals, as well as in relation to the perceived costs and benefits of the action (Agnew, 1998).

Consistent with the theoretical work, empirical research has uncovered a wide variety of motivations for animal abuse among those who admit to being perpetrators, and this research indicates that stress and frustration can indeed play a role. For instance, in their research on men with histories of animal abuse, Kellert and Felthous (1985) identify nine reported motives. As listed previously in Chapter 12, the motivations include the following:

1. To control an animal.
2. To express aggression and frustration through an animal.
3. To retaliate against another person.
4. To retaliate against the animal.
5. To satisfy a prejudice against a species or breed.
6. To express one's own aggressiveness.
7. To shock people for amusement.
8. Displacement of hostility from a person to an animal.
9. Non-specific sadism.

Strain or frustration are most evident in the motivations they describe as expressing aggression and frustration through an animal (#2) and displacement of hostility from a person to an animal (#8), although they may be implicit in some of the other motivations, as animal abuse is often multidimensional and not caused by one single motivating factor (Gullone, 2009).

Strain and frustration can play an important role in animal abuse amongst adolescents. Using data from the 2006 Swiss National Self-Reported Delinquency Survey, Lucia and Killias (2011) explored cruelty toward animals among 3,600 pupils in 7th, 8th, and 9th grades (ages 13 to 16). Taking into account personal background, personality characteristics, and social context, their findings indicate that adolescents can engage in animal cruelty to avoid dealing with painful or aversive situations. For instance, an adolescent compelled to remain in a particular environment that is painful or aversive (e.g., family household or school) or enduring traumatic events (e.g., divorce or death) may experience strain and frustration as a result, which can contribute to delinquency, including animal abuse. In short, the incapacity to cope with strain, frustration, and anger can push an individual toward animal maltreatment. Research points to the same abusive trajectory amongst adults. For instance, through analysis of case studies of animal abuse, Howells, Watt, Hall, and Baldwin (1997) point to the contributory role of stress and frustration caused by breakdowns of several valued relationships, the deterioration of relationships with family, and problems at work. They also identify poor self-control and poor anger control as fundamental underlying problems (see also Lucia & Killias, 2011). The likelihood that stress and frustration exacerbated by poor self-control will result in animal abuse amongst adolescents and adults could be mitigated by empathy, as illustrated in Agnew's (1998) model. In the absence of empathy, however, animal abuse becomes more likely (Ascione, 1993).

Mowen and Boman IV (2020) explored Agnew's model using the US-based Pathways to Desistance dataset, comprised of longitudinal data from youth between 14 and 17 who had been convicted of a serious criminal offence. While they found that the variables related to strain were not significantly associated with animal abuse, they did find that the individual-level factors in the model (race, alcohol use, early life offending, inferiority, impulsivity) and socialization (suspensions from school) significantly increased the odds of committing animal abuse. On the other hand, higher scores on the moral beliefs variable related to the socialization factor, and bonds to school representing increased social control, were significantly associated with decreased odds that the youth would engage in animal cruelty. Mowen and Boman IV (2020) suggest the two measures of strain in the data, feeling happy with life and anxiety, may not have captured the subjective experience of strain. Like the findings in Lucia and Killias (2011), it could be argued that increased feelings of inferiority, impulsivity, early life offending, and suspensions from school, all of which are associated with increased odds of animal cruelty, are manifestations of either acting out against or internalizing frustration and strain. Furthermore, Mowen and Boman IV (2020) found that "Black respondents report significantly greater odds of animal abuse than White respondents" (p. 772). Though in Mowen and Boman IV's (2020) model, race was an individual trait, there is a strong connection with strain in other literature. Systemic racism results in social marginalization and racial disparities in income, employment, health, neighborhood resources, and education (American Psychological Association, 2017), all factors which contribute to frustration and strain.

Despite some limitations of the aforementioned studies (e.g., lack of adequate control or comparison groups), they do provide at least partial support for the stress and frustration theories. Support is found across various respondent groups (e.g., school-based youth and incarcerated adults) and data collection methods (e.g., self-reporting, third-party reports, and analysis of criminal records). However, additional research is necessary to determine the potential of strain and frustration in explaining animal abuse and theriocide across disparate contexts along the continuum of socially approved/disapproved harm. Agnew (1998) himself cautions that his theoretical model is based on limited empirical research. As Flynn (2010) points out, the applicability of each of the factors in Agnew's theory of animal abuse will likely vary depending upon the level of social permissibility of the action. Further, although Agnew (1998) points to some important structural and demographic variables that can be related to animal abuse (e.g., gender and age), there is a need to look at cultural forces even more broadly (examined later in this chapter). In particular, Flynn (2010) suggests examining the ways in which various social institutions, such as the economy and religion, facilitate animal abuse. Doing so will be necessary to develop a comprehensive understanding of animal harm and theriocide.

Differential Coercion

Not only can contexts of strain and frustration be conducive to animal abuse, so can contexts of coercion. The connection between coercion and crime was first made in the context of delinquency and the family dynamic (see Brown, Esbensen, & Geis, 2012). Subsequent research explored the coercive control patterns in workplaces, schools, and among peers and their connection to serious, chronic delinquency (Colvin, 2000). Borrowing insights from Lonnie Athens, John D. Hewitt, Robert Agnew, Travis Hirschi, and Michael R. Gottfredson, Mark Colvin (2000) developed an integrated theory of chronic criminality, which he termed "differential coercion." His theory ties together several distinct patterns of coercion and connects them to social-psychological states which are conducive to criminality. In terms of exploring the etiology of criminal activity, Colvin (2000) argues that

> Criminals are made, not born. They emerge from a developmental process that is punctuated by recurring erratic episodes of coercion. They become both the recipients and the perpetrators of coercion, entrapped in a dynamic that propels them along a pathway toward chronic criminality (p. 1).

This theory foregrounds the differential levels and forms of coercion to which people are exposed and points to two different sources of coercion: interpersonal and impersonal. Interpersonal coercion is direct; that is, it involves the use or threat of force as well as the intimidation from significant others (e.g., parents and peers). Impersonal coercion, on the other hand, is indirect. This type of coercion involves pressures beyond individual control (e.g., social and economic pressure), which can be directly linked to poverty and unemployment. In sum, according to this theory, being exposed to high levels of interpersonal and/or impersonal coercion likely triggers the development of social-psychological deficits (Colvin, 2000). These deficits increase the likelihood of engaging in criminal activity, such as animal abuse.

Recent research has addressed how aspects of differential coercion theory could be used to explain the behavior of those who mistreat animals. Animal abuse may be related to coercion in at least two ways: individuals subjected to a coercive environment may perpetrate animal abuse and the threat of perpetration of animal abuse may be used to coerce an individual into doing something against their will. In the context of the former pathway to animal abuse, Ascione (1993) argues that children raised by parents who rely on punitive or aversive control (e.g., harming a child's pet to foster compliance) may learn to generalize aversive control techniques to their companion animals. Loring and Bolden-Hines (2004) have explored the latter possibility, focusing specifically on how coercion in the form of threats to harm pets can play a role in the commission of other crimes. The authors studied a group of emotionally and physically abused women at a shelter for abused women. Participants reported several forms of coercion used by their abusive partners, such as threats or actual harm to their pets or children, to coerce them into committing illegal acts (e.g., fraud, robbery, and drug trafficking). One-third of Loring and Bolden-Hines' (2004) sample of women who had committed at least one illegal act and had a pet reported they had engaged in illegal act(s) to spare their pet from abuse.

Coercion can also be used to induce victims of IPV into engaging in animal abuse: a number of cases have been identified where abused women have been coerced into assisting their abuser in perpetrating animal cruelty in order to keep themselves and their children out of harm's way (Roguski, 2012; Tiplady, 2013). Hicks (2012) describes a specific case where a man coerced his girlfriend into holding their puppy so he could drill into their puppy's head. Police reportedly found 29 dog carcasses on the property, illegal guns, blood and hair covered tools, and a beagle dog's pelt and eyes in a jar. There are also instances where women may even end their pet's life so as to avoid further animal cruelty at the hands of their abusive partner (see Tiplady, 2013; Walker, 1984). One example involved a domestic violence victim who drowned her kittens, rather than allowing her husband to "take pot shots at them with his rifle" (Hunter, 2006, p. 188). Victims of IPV can also be coerced into performing sexually abusive acts with their companion animal(s) (Tiplady, 2013; see also Abrahams, 2007; Adams, 2004; and Flynn, 2010 on the role that coercion can play in animal abuse in the context of IPV).

More research is needed to uncover additional ways in which coercion may play a role in the perpetration of animal abuse and to provide insight into how much animal abuse and theriocide overall can actually be attributed to coercion. The focus of the application of this theory to animal abuse to date has been exclusively on individual, interpersonal coercion. It may be worth expanding the application of this theory by addressing the second source of coercion—impersonal coercion—and the role it may play in animal abuse. Doing so would necessitate unpacking and examining the forms of cultural coercion that can impact (and help to rationalize) the actions of individuals and groups.

Violence Graduation Hypothesis

The theories discussed up to this point have focused on the etiology of animal abuse. The subsequent theories we discuss shift the focus from pure etiology to also explore how animal abuse is related to the perpetration of harm against people. The violence graduation hypothesis (VGH), also called the progression thesis (Beirne, 2004), is likely the most well-known of these types of theories. Commonly referred to in reference to spree killers and serial murderers, the VGH states that perpetrators begin with violence against animals and it 'graduates' or 'progresses' to violence against humans (Ressler, Burgess, Hartman, Douglas, & McCormack, 1986; Wright & Hensley, 2003). There are two key elements of this theory: a temporal element where the animal abuse must precede the human-directed violence and a correlational element in which individuals who commit animal abuse are more likely than those who do not to engage in violence against humans.

The VGH is also one of the oldest theories about animal abuse. The British philosopher, John Locke, argued that youth should be watched for cruelty against animals as this could lead to further cruelty against others (Unti, 2008). The theory also appeared in art, the most famous being William Hogarth's 1750/1 The Four Stages of Cruelty, which graphically depicts the progression from animal cruelty in childhood to violence against humans in adulthood. Concern about the connection between animal abuse, and subsequent violence against people, continued into the twentieth century. The Macdonald Triad of fire-setting, enuresis (bedwetting), and animal cruelty, developed in 1961, was considered to be a predictor of later violence against humans (see Chapter 14); children were said to graduate from these unacceptable and destructive behaviors to violent behaviors in adulthood, including harming other people (Hellman & Blackman, 1966; Wax & Haddox, 1973). Anthropologist Margaret Mead (1964) also asserted that animal abuse was a warning sign for future delinquency and violence, and therefore needed to be addressed with punishment to discourage the behavior.

Studies analyzing the childhood and adolescent behavior of serial and spree murderers offered some support for the VGH. Wright and Hensley (2003) examined the histories of five serial murderers, including Jeffrey Dahmer and Henry Lee Lucas, all of whom had first engaged in or experimented with abuse or killing of animals before 'graduating' to violence against humans. In some cases, the methods used to abuse the animals were the same methods utilized in the later brutalization of their human victims. As noted in Chapter 14, Arluke and Madfis (2014) examined cases of school shooters to determine the value of using animal abuse as a predictor for future episodes of violence against humans. While they did find evidence of animal abuse in the histories of 43 percent of school shooters, Arluke and Madfis (2014) question the strength of the connection and the widely held belief in the veracity of the VGH. Case studies, while powerful examples, offer limited utility for supporting the VGH as they tend to be limited in number and restricted to rare incidents of extreme violence.

The most common method used in violence graduation research has been to identify convicted violent offenders in adulthood and then use retrospective reports of animal cruelty in childhood or adolescence to search for violence progression. For instance, Tallichet and Hensley (2004) used the number of convictions for murder, attempted murder, rape, attempted rape, and aggravated assault to measure interpersonal violence in an incarcerated sample of men. Previous acts of animal cruelty were measured by the question "how many times have you hurt or killed animals, other than for hunting?" (Tallichet & Hensley, 2004, p. 310). In their sample, committing animal cruelty was the most powerful predictor of committing repeated acts of interpersonal violence in adulthood, even stronger than race, age, or educational attainment. The respondents who had engaged in animal cruelty in childhood or adolescence had an average of 1.33 convictions for violent offenses in adulthood compared to the average of 0.56 violent offenses among those who had not committed animal abuse (Tallichet & Hensley, 2004). Replication studies with different incarcerated populations have returned nearly identical results. Hensley, Tallichet, and Dutkiewicz (2009) added simple assault and robbery to the list of violent offenses, and found that participants who had a higher number of convictions for violent offenses were more likely to have committed animal cruelty in childhood or adolescence. More recently, Trentham, Hensley and Policastro (2018) tested the relationship between animal cruelty (hurting or killing animals, age at which animal harm first occurred), demographic variables (race, high school completion, rural/urban residence in childhood), and commission of violent offences (murder, attempted murder, rape, attempted rape, assault, robbery) in a sample of 257 incarcerated men. Just under half of the sample (n = 126) reported engaging in animal cruelty before age 18, with multiple acts of animal harm reported. Trentham et al. (2018) found that the only significant relationship was between childhood animal cruelty and interpersonal violent offenses committed as adults. Other researchers, such as Kellert and Felthous (1985), Merz-Perez, Heide, and Silverman (2001), and Merz-Perez and Heide (2004), came to the same conclusion: aggressive or violent offenders are more likely to report committing animal cruelty in childhood.

Not all the work on the VGH has been with incarcerated populations. Knight, Ellis, and Simmons (2014) used a sample of the general population drawn from the National Youth Survey Family Study (NYSFS) in the Unites States, which offers longitudinal and multigenerational data. Knight, Ellis, and Simmons (2014) tested both intra- and intergenerational aspects of animal abuse. On an intragenerational level, respondents who reported engaging in animal abuse in childhood were over three times more likely to have committed IPV in adulthood, results which show strong support for the VGH.

These studies testing the VGH have important limitations worth noting (for a detailed overview see Beirne, 2009 and Marceau, 2019). First, retrospective reports can be limited, particularly in attempting to recall the temporal order of events (i.e., did the animal abuse precede violence against humans). The research by Knight et al. (2014) does partly address this, although the limitation of recall was still present in this study. Questions about animal abuse were only added in much later waves of the survey, meaning that adults were questioned about their commission of animal abuse during childhood and adolescence. Although the children (mean age 17.56) of the adults in the study were also questioned about their animal abuse, the issue of recall was still present as the youth were asked if they had ever committed animal abuse, as well as the age at which the act was committed. This allowed Knight et al. (2014) to calculate that the average recall range for the incident for the youth was seven years. Petersen and Farrington (2007) and Flynn (2011) both suggest that longitudinal research with waves beginning in childhood, and with questions about animal abuse, would help to mitigate the issues with memory and recall prevalent in the existing literature testing the VGH. Second, there is a flaw in using incarcerated male populations to test the VGH, which compose the majority of participants in VGH research. According to the principles of the VGH, the focus of the aggression shifts from or graduates to violence against humans, which implies a desistance from violence against animals in favor of violence against humans in adulthood. When the participants are incarcerated, in some cases serving life sentences, they do not have the ability to offend against humans or animals, and the presence or absence of animal abuse in adulthood cannot necessarily be measured.

Generalization of Deviance Hypothesis

The generalization of deviance hypothesis is typically presented as an alternative to the violence graduation hypothesis. This theory holds that animal abuse is part of a spectrum of antisocial and criminal behavior, and not specifically connected to violence against other humans. The generality of deviance hypothesis also does not have a temporal element, but treats animal abuse as one of many possible deviant behaviors that individuals of any age can engage in.

One of the few studies to specifically examine the generality thesis was conducted by Arluke, Levin, Luke, and Ascione (1999). Matching official records of the Massachusetts Society for the Prevention of Cruelty to Animals with the police records of offenders, the authors assessed the generality versus the specificity of the non-animal related offenses. Arluke et al. (1999) also used a control group of individuals selected from the same neighborhood and of the same age and gender as the abusive group. The results support the hypothesis: the abusive group was over three times more likely to have a criminal record, including violent, drug, and property related offenses than the control group. Arluke et al. (1999) acknowledge the possibility of graduation in forms of deviance, but propose that the graduation may not be simply temporal and there are other dimensions to consider. It could be that individuals may graduate from abusing more remote targets (stray animals or strangers) to more intimate targets (friends, partners, or pets).

A subsequent study conducted by the Chicago Police Department found similar results in that 86 percent of those who had been arrested for animal cruelty had convictions for a variety of other offences as well (Flynn, 2011). Like the study by Arluke et al. (1999), the Chicago Police Department evaluated criminal records. A focus on adult records does present a limitation, as juvenile offences are not likely to be noted in the records of adult offenders, so any potential graduation of violence is unknown to the researchers. This limitation could result in confirmation bias for the generalization of deviance hypothesis, rather than a true test of the theory.

Other researchers have focused on the potential generalization of aggression more specifically. Henry and Sanders (2007), for instance, looked at the concurrence of incidents of animal abuse and bullying behavior in both the victimization and perpetration spheres. They recruited male undergraduate students from a first-year psychology class and assessed the victimization and perpetration rates of both physical and verbal bullying as well as reported incidents of animal abuse. Most of the reported animal abuse took place in two age groups, 6 to 12 and 13 to 18, and the majority of bullying occurred during elementary and high school (matching the age groups for animal abuse). Henry and Sanders (2007) found that multiple acts of animal abuse were significantly associated with relatively high rates (33 percent of participants) of physical bullying, but not verbal bullying. Given the concurrent time frames, these data suggest some degree of generalized aggression when it comes to bullying behavior.

Gullone and Robertson (2008) and Parkes and Signal (2017) also examined the relationship between bullying and animal abuse, but both studies surveyed a younger population: secondary school students between the ages of 12 and 16 (Gullone and Robertson 2008), and between 14 and 18 (Parkes and Signal 2017). Examining the age group with the highest incidence of perpetrating animal abuse minimized the limitation of retrospective accounts and memory recall. Both studies found that witnessing animal abuse was significantly associated with bullying perpetration as well as committing animal abuse. Gullone and Robertson (2008) state that both bullying and animal abuse are relatively common during adolescence given the number of respondents who reported engaging in animal abuse "sometimes" (20 percent) and bullying behaviors in the past year (18 percent).

Further research, ideally studies using a longitudinal design and multiple sources of data and control groups, is needed to examine the multifaceted relationship between various forms of animal abuse and forms of deviance, including aggression. The bulk of the research conducted has thus far focused primarily on socially disapproved of harms against animals and the relationship to deviance and aggression (Flynn, 2002, is a noteworthy exception). There is little information available about the potential connection between socially approved forms of animal harm and deviance.

Social Disorganization

While Agnew (1998) did acknowledge the impact of community-level strain in his general theory of animal abuse, his focus was on the individual. First proposed by Shaw and McKay of the Chicago School, social disorganization theory shifts the focus from the individual to the community, looking at the structural factors that impede the ability of residents to form bonds with neighbors, which serve to decrease social control and increase community disorganization. Four structural factors contribute to social disorder, and thus higher rates of crime: "residential instability, economic disadvantage, high levels of ethnic heterogeneity, and family disruption" (Sampson & Grove, 1989; White & Quick, 2019, p. 930). Social disorganization theory has recently been proposed as a possible way to understand animal abuse.

Burchfield (2016) explored the connection between animal crime (abuse/neglect and fighting) and community-level factors using police, crime, and census data in Chicago. Burchfield (2016) composed a hardship index variable to reflect the level of social disorganization, which included the percent of the population without a high school diploma, percent of households below the poverty level, unemployment rates, income levels, and crowded housing. Communities were also divided into high animal crime (defined as "areas with mean number of animal crimes .5 standard deviations above the mean") and low animal crime areas (Burchfield, 2016, p. 374). Animal crime was mainly abuse or neglect, reflecting about 90% of animal crimes known to police. When comparing communities, Burchfield (2016) found that communities with high animal crime had significantly higher levels of hardship, as well as higher levels of violent and property crime. The author appropriately notes, however, that police presence and enforcement in disadvantaged communities tends to be higher, and thus animal and other crimes may be more likely to be detected and charged. Reese, Vertalka, and Richard (2020) also used police data from a large urban center, Detroit, in evaluating several theories of animal cruelty: links to domestic violence, generality of deviance, perpetrator traits, and social disorganization. They found the strongest support for social disorganization as a theory for animal cruelty, followed by generality of deviance. Socioeconomic neighborhood characteristics (high unemployment, high rent as a proportion of income, high levels of poverty) accounted for 81% of the variance in animal cruelty, whereas physical neighborhood characteristics (such as high building vacancy, few green/recreation spaces, higher crime) accounted for 72% of variance in animal cruelty. There was weak support for interpersonal violence as measured by domestic violence and no support for a perpetrator trait theory of animal cruelty (Reese et al., 2020). Given that official police statistics tend to vastly undercount domestic violence, it is not surprising that Reese et al (2020) found a weak relationship with animal cruelty. Research with survivors of domestic violence offers robust support for the connection with animal abuse (see research in this chapter).

White and Quick (2019) also investigated social disorganization and animal cruelty via official police statistics from Virginia Beach. They hypothesized that neighborhoods with higher social disorder (measured though offenses like public drunkenness, littering, trespass, and disturbing the peace) and disorganization (measured via economic disadvantage, residential instability, ethnic heterogeneity, and family disruption) would be correlated with higher animal cruelty offenses, and the results supported their hypotheses. White and Quick (2019) also found that animal cruelty offences were positively correlated with domestic assaults and negatively correlated with median household income. White and Quick (2019) posit that "where there is weak neighborhood organization, social control is weakened and residents are not effective in preventing the occurrence of disorderly behavior" (p. 936), including offenses against animals. While White and Quick (2019) focused on a much smaller suburban area than Burchfield (2016), their results support using social disorganization to understand animal cruelty.

Reese, et al. (2020) advise caution when using social disorganization to explain animal cruelty: "by employing demographic indicators to measure 'disorganization' such studies also run the risk of 'blaming the victims' whereby systemic inequalities are redefined as neighborhood problems as opposed to conditions that place both human and nonhuman animals at risk" (p. 4). Disorganized communities are more likely to receive increased police attention, which increases detection of minor offenses, which leads to higher crime rates. Residents living in close proximity to each other increase the likelihood that animal cruelty, typically a covert crime, will be witnessed. Poverty and low income reflect a lack of financial resources, which can contribute to (perhaps unintentional) animal neglect. While social disorganization offers a window into the social and structural conditions in which animal abuse may be more likely to occur, a deeper look into the nuances of the relationship between structural and community conditions and animal abuse and neglect is needed.

Feminist Theories

Feminist theorists have illuminated the cultural normalization of violence, particularly against women. They argue that this violence is symptomatic of a patriarchal culture that privileges masculinity while devaluing femininity, and that patriarchy legitimizes the use of violence to achieve power and control with the goal of maintaining the sexist status quo. Such theorizing shifts the level of analysis from the individual to the larger structures that facilitate violence. Feminist examinations of animal abuse have extended this analysis and argue that patriarchy and speciesism (the privileging of one's own species above others) are mutually reinforcing and both facilitate violence. Much of this theorizing has taken place under the banner of ecofeminism. It should be noted that some ecofeminist theorizing relies on simplistic, essentialized conceptions of gender differences, and theorizes a biological basis for the 'caring nature' of women (Dejmanee, 2013). Providing a detailed account of the problems associated with such a perspective is well beyond the scope of this chapter. Instead, we focus on more social constructionist-oriented threads of ecofeminism that do not necessarily share these limitations.

To explain why sexism and the exploitation of animals are related, social ecofeminists point to the similar ways in which women and animals have been constructed as the Other to privileged masculinity. These classes of Other have been relegated to the devalued side of many normative dualisms in patriarchal culture, including culture/nature, public/private, and mind/body (see Adams, 1990; Kheel, 1995; King, 1991; Noske, 1989). Noske (1989) explores the culture/nature dualism in detail and explains that, as a result of this particular dualism, humans consider themselves unique and vastly different from animals, and nature more generally. Humans are believed to belong to an entirely different order, the realm of culture, whereas other beings are regarded simply as nature. However, membership in the realm of the cultural has not been equally afforded to humans: hegemonic conceptions of masculinity (discussed in the next section) have been associated with culture, whereas women and subordinated masculinities have been largely identified with nature. As a result, nature, and those associated with it, have been constructed as the Other and of lesser value than those associated with culture.

Similarities in the mechanisms through which women and animals have been oppressed, the ways in which this oppression is obfuscated, how it is rationalized, and the language used to denigrate both groups are illustrative of how interconnected these forms of oppression actually are. Two examples from the literature are useful in illustrating this interconnection. The first is the argument that animals and women have been treated like natural resources. More specifically, the productive and reproductive capacities of women and animals are expropriated, and their contributions are simultaneously undervalued (Salleh, 1995). For women, this manifests itself in, among other things, attacks against their reproductive rights and the devaluation of their reproductive labor. There are countless examples of how animals are treated like natural resources. For instance, female "livestock" animals are bred to create more livestock animals. The products of their reproductive labor are taken from them and commodified (e.g., their offspring, milk, and eggs). This connection is also evidenced by similar trajectories of trafficking of women, children, and animals, through which the victims are commodified as resources (Sollund, 2013).

Another thread within the literature examines how animals and women have been constructed in such similar ways that a structure of absent referents exists whereby one group can stand in for the other. Adams (1990) has been at the forefront of this theorizing. She explains,

> Sexual violence and meat eating, which appear to be discrete forms of violence, find a point of intersection in the absent referent. Cultural images of sexual violence, and actual sexual violence, often rely on our knowledge of how animals are butchered and eaten (p. 68).

In her work, Adams elucidates the numerous ways in which actual animals have been obfuscated in the process of people consuming their flesh (e.g., through packaging and advertising). They are similarly bracketed out, or used as the absent referent, in the use of meat as a metaphor for women's oppression (e.g., references to women as pieces of meat).

Adams (1990) and Salleh (1995) therefore argue that not only are there similarities in the oppression of women and animals, but importantly these forms of oppression become mutually reinforcing. In addition to the conceptual connections between the oppression and abuse of women and animals, feminist theorists and researchers have also identified some more manifest relationships between these forms of oppression.

Patriarchal/speciesist culture goes beyond just devaluing nature and those associated with it. Adams (1994) argues that this culture is also characterized by a reverence for and promotion of dominance and control. The abuse of animals may be one mechanism through which one can accomplish this culturally prescribed pursuit of dominance and control. In fact, research indicates that the desire for control is a common motivator of animal abuse, particularly among serial animal abusers. A study of 112 inmates found that those who admitted to multiple acts of animal abuse were three times more likely to report being motivated by a desire to control the animal than those who admitted to few acts of animal abuse (Hensley & Tallichet, 2005). Research also indicates that animal abuse can be a vehicle for establishing dominance and control over people. This dynamic has been prominent in the research on IPV.

Using a national, longitudinal dataset, Knight et al. (2014) found that controlling for other predictive variables, an earlier history of engaging in animal abuse significantly predicts subsequent perpetration of violent IPV, such that an individual who was engaged in animal abuse when younger has a 3.61 greater likelihood of perpetrating violent IPV than those without histories of animal abuse perpetration. Fitzgerald, Barrett, Gray, and Cheung (2020) examined a nationally representative sample of Canadian adults, specifically looking at the connections between animal abuse and experiencing financial (e.g., preventing access to income, forced to give up possession or money) and emotional abuse (e.g., insults, limiting contact with others, threats) in the context of IPV. They found that both forms of IPV were significantly more likely when the respondents also reported animal abuse, and that those who report their partner abused their pet(s) are 25% more likely to report fearing for their lives (Fitzgerald, Barrett, & Gray, 2021).

This relationship between animal abuse and IPV has also been documented through accounts of abused women. Studies in Canada and the U.S. have found that anywhere from 25 percent (Simmons & Lehmann, 2007) to 89 percent (Fitzgerald, Barrett, Stevenson, & Cheung, 2019) of abused women with pets report that their pets were also mistreated by their abusers. Studies in other countries, including Ireland (Allen, Gallagher, & Jones, 2006), Australia (Volant et al., 2008), and the Bahamas (Fielding, 2010) have found similar rates of coexistence between animal abuse and IPV. In addition to finding significant overlap between these forms of abuse, the research indicates that animal abuse is most likely to be present in the more severe cases of IPV (e.g., Ascione et al., 2007; Barrett, Fitzgerald, Stevenson, & Cheung, 2020; DeGue & DiLillo, 2008; Simmons & Lehmann, 2007) and that batterers who abuse pets tend to use more forms of violence and exhibit more controlling behaviors (Simmons & Lehmann, 2007; Fitzgerald et al., 2019).

Interview-based and survey research with abused women indicates that the women believe that the abuse of their pets by their abusive partners did not originate from their partners' loss of control and uncontrollable aggression as many might assume; instead, they report the mistreatment of their pets was used as a tool to further abuse them and their children. The survivors surveyed by Fitzgerald et al. (2019) perceived that emotional abuse of the animals, as well as neglect and threats to harm the animals, were rooted in the perpetrators' desire to control them. Animal abuse can be a particularly useful tool because many of these women and children form very close relationships with their pets (Fitzgerald, 2005; Flynn, 2000). These relationships can be so close that some abused women refer to their pets as part of their "strategies for survival," and describe how their pets assisted them with depression and feelings of despair, to the point that, for some abused women, their pets are the one thing that keeps them from killing themselves (Fitzgerald, 2007). This research has corroborated Adams' (1995) earlier theorizing that the abuse of animals can be instrumentalized by batterers to achieve power and control over their partners and/or the children.

Feminist analyses of animal abuse, therefore, highlight both the conceptual and lived connections between the oppression of women and animals. This foregrounding of the ways in which forms of human oppression are connected with the oppression and abuse of animals is a notable strength of feminist analyses of animal abuse (Taylor, 2011). At the same time, however, we must guard against anthropocentric evaluations of animal abuse which problematize it solely on the grounds that it is connected conceptually, and sometimes practically, to the oppression and abuse of people (Beirne,

1999). Some feminist scholars have gone beyond simply using the connections between the oppression of women and animals as the basis for arguing against the (ab) use of animals, and additionally assert that women have a positive moral duty to care for animals, or to promote nonharm through carefulness (see Aristarkhova, 2012; Donovan & Adams, 2007). However, we must also be careful not to make women solely responsible for challenging harm to animals and for bearing the burden of their care (Dejmanee, 2013).

To summarize, according to feminist theorizing, women and animals have been relegated to the devalued, nature side of the culture/nature binary. This devaluation, along with the valorization of control and dominance within patriarchal culture, puts animals at risk of abuse. This combination places animals at risk of socially approved violence (e.g., being used as natural resources) and socially disapproved violence, where they can be abused to satisfy someone's desire to exert control and dominance over them or as a vehicle to establish control and dominance over a human victim. This pursuit of dominance and control is an important part of the hegemonic masculinity concept, a topic we turn to next.

Masculinities

Examinations problematizing the construction of masculinity emerged from feminist theorizing of gender. At the forefront of this endeavor, Connell (1987) explains that masculinity is not only socially constructed, but it "is always constructed in relation to various subordinated masculinities as well as in relation to women" (p. 183). A hegemonic form of masculinity emerges from these constructions. Simply put, this is the cultural ideal of masculinity. This ideal is connected to heteronormativity, economic success, dominance, and control, among other things (for a review of the concept and response to critiques see Connell & Messerschmidt, 2005). This form of masculinity is not static: it varies across space and time.

Messerschmidt (2004) has made an important contribution by applying this concept to understand crime. He describes how men who do not meet the lofty characteristics of the hegemonic ideal (e.g., wealthy, white, strong, aggressive, dominant, cisgender, and heterosexual) can use crime to accomplish masculinity. In other words, crime is structured action: "men construct masculinities in accord with their position in social structures and, therefore, their access to power and resources" (Messerschmidt, 2004, p. 3). Critical examinations of masculinity are particularly important in the context of understanding crime because the vast majority of perpetrators are men. For instance, men are responsible for approximately 90 percent of violent crimes (Chesney-Lind & Faith, 2001).

Such analyses can be usefully extended to analyzing animal abuse. As with violent crime in general, the majority of perpetrators of animal abuse are male. Data from a nationally representative sample in the U.S. indicate that 83.78 percent of those who report committing animal abuse identify as men (Vaughn et al., 2009). One of the strongest and most consistent predictors of perpetrating animal abuse and supporting animal exploitation is being male (Baldry, 2003; Herzog, 2007; Luke, 2007). A recent study using hypothetical animal abuse scenarios found that 20 percent of female versus 40 percent of male participants endorsed the harmful behavior taking place in the scenario (Alleyne, Tilston, Parfitt, & Butcher, 2015). This relationship between gender and animal abuse is strong across age categories (Gullone, 2014). Whereas men engage in more animal abuse, the reverse is true for women in the aggregate: they exhibit less aggressive, more positive, and less dominionistic attitudes towards animals (Herzog, 2007; Matthews & Herzog, 1997; Signal & Taylor, 2006). In general, the size of the influence of gender on attitudes towards animals has ranged rather dramatically in research, but it generally meets the threshold to be considered a moderate effect (Herzog, 2007; Kavanagh, Signal, & Taylor, 2013).

Some theorists (e.g., Agnew, 1998; Beirne, 1995) have noted that animal abuse might be a particularly useful mechanism for accomplishing masculinity; according to Agnew (1998), animal abuse can be particularly useful for accomplishing masculinity because the direct abuse of an animal displays aggression and dominance, and simultaneously requires emotional detachment, all qualities of hegemonic masculinity. Research has provided some indirect evidence for this proposition. In their early research on animal abuse, Kellert and Felthous (1985) identified nine main motivations reported by their (all male) participants (listed earlier). What is interesting is that the majority of motivations they identified could be connected to accomplishing masculinity. Animal abuse could be used as a resource for accomplishing masculinity by exerting and demonstrating control (motivation #1), to retaliate against perceived wrongs and perhaps more specific challenges to masculinity (motivations #2 and #7), to demonstrate and enhance aggression (motivations #4 and #5), and shocking the sensibilities of others (motivation #6).

Research on wildlife crime has drawn a more explicit link between masculinity and animal abuse. As a result of this research, a typology of wildlife regulation violators has been developed, and one of the four categories identified encompasses offenders who are "primarily motivated by power and notions of masculinity" (Nurse, 2013, p. 135). These types of offenders are most likely to engage in their harmful behavior with others, and these offenders are likely to derive pleasure from their actions. Further, these offenders are likely to argue that their actions are justified based on tradition and/or that the animals involved do not feel pain (Nurse, 2013).

Cross-cultural research on "blood sports" also highlights the role that masculinity plays in motivating participation (of mainly men). Ethnographic research has documented how men construct their own masculine identities through blood sports, such as dog, cock, and bull fighting (see Evans et al., 1998; Marvin, 1988). In a review of such studies, Iliopoulou and Rosenbaum (2013, pp. 134–135) conclude that

> violence, power, control, and aggression are common themes associated with masculinity for all three contexts [dog, cock, and bull fighting] and might

explain why animal cruelty associated with blood sport becomes 'legitimized' or 'normal' in an effort to achieve manhood.

This normalization of animal abuse, particularly in the context of 'doing masculinity' can contribute to a great deal of abuse being dismissed as simply "boys being boys." Arluke (2002) found in his research on histories of animal abuse among undergraduate students that a significant proportion of animal abuse is currently constructed as normative. He suggests that some forms of animal abuse are defined as a form of what Fine (1986) refers to as "dirty play." Building on Hughes' (1962) concept of "dirty work," Fine (1986) asserts that "dirty play" is part of the process of socializing boys into men. He reasons that actions by boys, such as aggressive pranks, use of sexualized language, and use of racist language, should be conceptualized as dirty play because they generally take place in the presence of friends, which he considers quite different from the perpetration of such actions while alone, which would be indicative of a "destructive impulse." There is research evidence indicating that a sizable proportion of young men do engage in animal abuse in the presence of others. For instance, 48 percent of abusers in a Massachusetts sample abused animals in the presence of others (Arluke & Luke, 1997) and 47 percent of a Swiss sample reported they engaged in animal abuse in the presence of others (Lucia & Killias, 2011). Further, a survey of 112 inmates, who admitted to animal abuse, found that 38 percent reported the abuse was perpetrated for fun (Hensley & Tallichet, 2005). Hensley, Tallichet, and Dutkiewicz (2012) found in their sample of inmates in a Southern state in the U.S. that only one type of animal abuse was consistently concealed: sexual animal abuse. These findings would appear to be conceptually consistent with motivation #6 delineated by Kellert and Felthous (1985): to shock people for amusement. In making sense of the seemingly normative character of some forms of animal abuse, Arluke (2002, p. 406) explains that "abusers may gain things from their acts that the larger society supports and defines as essential." Pagani and colleagues (2010) propose that what is gained from animal abuse is aggression, competition, and diminished empathy—all characteristics associated with hegemonic masculinity.

Boys and young men who lack power and resources as a result of their social positioning, particularly due to their age, may find animal abuse powerful as a vehicle for accomplishing masculinity, and they may also by extension become apathetic bystanders in the face of abuse. This argument is put forward by Evans, Gauthier, and Forsyth (1998) to explain the attraction of dog fighting for working class men in the Southern U.S. Moreover, McLoughlin (2018) points out how the hegemonic masculine norms of "emotional stoicism" (p. 330) and exercising power over weaker others (the animals who are killed) are valued in a slaughterhouse environment. This animal (ab)use is not only perpetrated in response to larger social structures, it can also serve to reinforce these structures. This way of "doing gender" perpetuates some of the most problematic aspects of masculinity, such as lack of empathy and aggression, as well as the speciesism that has normalized the instrumentalization of animals to serve humans ends. In more recent research on actions of bystanders in the presence of animal abuse, such as dog fighting, Arluke (2012) finds that one of the barriers to bystander intervention is the definition of much animal abuse as "dirty play," instead of as morally problematic or criminal.

Masculinity is also linked to animal harm in less direct ways. Adams (1990) argues there is a connection between masculinity and meat consumption in our culture. She describes how in historic times of crisis, the consumption of meat by men has been privileged. It was believed to provide them with the strength and aggressiveness required of masculinity. Today, meat and masculinity remain closely connected, and men who refrain from the consumption of meat risk having their masculinity questioned. A study of undergraduate students by Rothgerber (2012) empirically tests this connection between meat consumption and masculinity and finds not only do levels of meat consumption vary by gender, but justifications of meat consumption are also gendered. The self-identified male students in the study were significantly more likely to justify their meat consumption by denying that animals suffer, asserting that animals are lower than humans in the hierarchy of beings, utilizing religious or health justifications, and espousing the belief that humans are destined to consume animals. The female student participants, on the other hand, were more likely to use indirect methods to justify meat consumption, such as avoiding thinking about their consumption of animals and trying to dissociate the meat they consume from the animal it once was. Rothgerber (2012) also used a scale to measure masculinity among the participants and found that it was positively related to all of the justifications used most commonly by the male participants to justify meat consumption, and additionally, high levels of meat consumption were positively associated with the masculinity scale.

This connection between masculinity and the consumption of animals is illustrated in contemporary advertisements. Rogers (2008) documents numerous examples of companies using the perceived 'crisis in masculinity' to sell their product by framing said products as a way to restore the 'natural' gender balance. For instance, men whose masculinity has been 'challenged' (e.g., by successful women) are viewed in advertisements for fast food restaurants restoring the balance by purchasing and consuming hamburgers. Thus, the use and exploitation of animals can be used as an indirect mechanism for accomplishing masculinity.

As discussed above, the abuse and exploitation of animals may be a particularly useful mechanism for accomplishing masculinity because it requires the suppression of empathy and emotion, implicit or explicit aggression, and the expression of dominance and control. Luke (2007) further suggests that men may be more inclined to harm animals because they have fewer opportunities to create and sustain life, and many forms of animal exploitation are framed as generativity (e.g., hunting and animal agriculture creates food, vivisection creates scientific discoveries and saves lives). He reasons that women are less likely to support the institutions of animal exploitation because they do not gain a sense of purpose from them as men do. Luke (2007) suggests that this is not only important for understanding the perpetration of harm against animals, but also for those who seek to understand the successes of and challenges facing the animal rights movement. The two main areas of success in the movement have been the substantial reduction in the testing of cosmetics on animals and sustained campaigns against the purchase of fur products, yet these are not necessarily more harmful quantitatively and qualitatively than other uses of animals. Luke (2007) clarifies this point:

> Trapping, ranching, testing on animals—these are not inherently more pernicious than other forms of animal exploitation. But since their products are thought to result from women's demands, we are able to approach a societal consensus that they represent unacceptable levels of cruelty to animals. Killing animals for sport, for science, for a steak dinner, or a leather jacket—that is not excessive violence, that is men's violence (p.18).

The feminist and masculinities perspectives point to the larger structure of patriarchy as influencing who harms animals, and these perspectives partially address the question of why. In order to more fully address this question, however, we must also attend to the larger political economic structure. The vast majority of harm to which animals are exposed (e.g., through agriculture and entertainment) is at least partially related to commodification and the pursuit of profits and is largely institutionalized.

(Eco)Marxism

As discussed earlier, in his theoretical model of animal abuse, Agnew (1998) identifies the "perceived benefits of abuse outweigh[ing] the costs" as one of three factors that directly increases the likelihood of animal abuse. In many forms of harms against animals, the benefit is an economic one (see Benton, 1993; Boggs, 2007). To illustrate this point, Agnew (1998) quotes Alex Pacheco, co-director of the largest animal rights organization in the world, as saying "'the whole problem is a business problem. The reason animals are in the predicament they are in today is that it's a good business proposition" (p. 190). And the costs of animal exploitation, particularly in the form of regulatory and legal sanctions, are notoriously low.

Legally defined as property, animals are used as instruments in the production of capital (see Fitzgerald, 2015; Gunderson, 2011; Nibert, 2002; Torres, 2007). The animal agriculture industry is a good illustration of how this process works. "Livestock animals," a term which is demonstrative of their commodification, are kept alive using a calculation to maximize production. Inputs of protein-dense food make them bulk up quickly and medications are used to reduce 'product loss' through disease and death. Costs are kept to a minimum by housing as many animals in as little space as possible. Once they reach a plateau in their production (meat animals have bulked up as much as possible, dairy cows' production of milk begins to taper, egg production among chickens begins to drop off) they are slaughtered (for a more detailed description of this process see Fitzgerald, 2015; Foer, 2010; Mason & Finelli, 2006). Even the slaughtering process is designed to reduce costs. There is a highly specialized division of labor and the speed of the (dis)assembly line has been increased to maximize production to the point that worker injuries are common, as are improperly stunned animals (see Eisnitz, 1997; Fitzgerald, 2010; Schlosser, 2005). Although diagnoses of the problems associated with modern animal agriculture often point to technology and its intervention in animal lives, the root of the problem is capital's drive for profit maximization (Gunderson, 2011). Thus, the profit motive works against the best interests of the animals, and the animal welfare laws that are in place to prevent "abuses" of animals are based on the premise that some harm is necessary. It is the harms deemed economically unnecessary that are considered abusive.

Although some minor changes are afoot (such as increases in cage sizes for chickens and pigs in some jurisdictions), the size of the industry globally, and the number of animals subjected to harm within it, is expected to increase. Novek (2003) frames the increase in industrial animal agriculture in North America as part of an international treadmill of production (on the topic of expanding the conceptualization of the treadmill of production, see also Lynch, Long, Barrett, & Stretesky, 2013; Lynch, Stretesky, & Long, 2020). In the pursuit of profits, the industry must continually increase production and stimulate demand. The international demand for meat is growing, and the transition to a meat-based diet, especially in Asia, is expected to increase demand even further. Using the expansion of the hog industry in Manitoba as an example, Novek (2003) points to some of the outcomes of this treadmill of production:

> The expansion of the hog industry in Manitoba presents a useful case study of the global treadmill of production in agriculture. It has been characterized by the ascendancy of large-scale, specialized producers allied with meat processors, suppliers and other corporate interests. Smaller hog producers and more traditional mixed farmers have found themselves at a disadvantage compared to factory farms (p. 19).

Thus, the "factory farm" or Confined Animal Feeding Operation (CAFO) becomes hegemonic. This will subject greater numbers of animals to harm in the name of productivity and profit.

Just as some of the earlier theories discussed posit a relationship between the perpetration of harm against animals and that against people, those coming from an (eco) Marxist perspective also envision a connection between these forms of harm grounded in the capitalist economic system. Nibert (2002, 2013) argues that the exploitation of animals and human groups have similar historic origins and that these forms of oppression remain mutually reinforcing. In recognition of the similar historic trajectories of oppression, some have suggested looking to successful fights for human rights to develop strategies for institutionalizing more humane treatment of animals. Anderson (2011) recommends looking at the history of child labor law reform for strategies to agitate for improved living and dying conditions for animals. The speciesism that makes the commodification of animals possible, however, must also be addressed.

Boggs (2007) argues that the only way to overturn the economically-grounded exploitation of animals, which he refers to as 'institutionalized barbarism,' is "subversion of those hegemonic beliefs and attitudes which maintain speciesism in its multiple forms" (p. 33). He acknowledges that this is difficult to do in the face of the immense power wielded by corporations, which does not show signs of weakening any time soon. The power of these corporations vis-à-vis animal exploitation has been evidenced by their successful lobbying in some states (e.g., Iowa, Missouri, Utah) to get laws passed to criminalize taking pictures or videos inside animal agriculture facilities and misrepresenting one's intentions in gaining employment in such a facility (known colloquially as 'ag-gag' laws), essentially outlawing what has been a rather successful form of whistleblowing and repressing freedom of expression (Frye, 2014; Liebmann, 2014; Pitts, 2012). Such laws have expanded beyond US borders; three provinces in Canada have passed ag-gag legislation, Alberta in 2019, Ontario in 2020, and most recently Manitoba in 2021 (Lazare, forthcoming).

Economic factors not only contribute to the harm experienced by animals used as food, they also influence the use of animals as entertainment. For instance, many blood sports (e.g., dog fighting, cock fighting, bull fighting, fox hunting) originated with the affluent classes. It is suggested that these sports gained popularity historically because they offer an 'even playing field' between the classes, whereby lower status classes can use these practices as a means for attaining status otherwise not afforded to them. Even when privileged classes abandon a specific blood sport, it may nonetheless live on among the less affluent (Iliopoulou & Rosenbaum, 2013).

An industry has even been built around our culture's most beloved animals: companion or 'pet' animals. This industry commodifies animals, modifies their physiology to suit human tastes in some cases, and profits by selling these sentient 'products' to consumers (Sollund, 2011). Although they are the most beloved group of animals, they are also vulnerable to economic forces. For instance, the economic recession that began in 2007, and the accompanying foreclosure crisis, resulted in a dramatic increase in the number of animals surrendered at shelters and 'economic euthanasia' among those who could no longer afford to care for their pets (Nowicki, 2011). This is yet another example of the way that the suffering of human groups and animals can be intertwined, and a recent study by Morris (2013) shows that this is even apparent at the national level. His examination of the relationship between animal welfare, income, and income inequality across countries finds that nations with greater income equality tend to have higher levels of animal welfare (as measured by consumption of animal products, regulation of the most egregious abuses of farm animals, and the use of animals in experiments). Morris (2013) finds that nations characterized by greater income equality consume less meat and have more stringent regulations governing the most harmful forms of intensive animal agriculture. He concludes that it is quite possible that the relationship between better welfare and income equality is not causal but is related to some factor (like curtailment of corporate power) that improves both welfare and income inequality. Societies that promote income distribution may also generally be fairer societies that also promote better treatment of animals (Morris, 2013, p. 291).

The consequences of the economic factors described above are twofold. The first consequence is the most obvious: a growing number of animals are being subjected to harmful living (not to mention dying) conditions in the pursuit of profits. The second consequence is cultural. The endorsement of the use of animals as a means to an end, as property to be used to extract profit, by the political economic system sends a more general cultural message that the (ab)use of animals is acceptable, and even encouraged in certain contexts (see Verbora, 2015). This sentiment can spill over into our other relations with animals, perhaps even to our relations with other people. The (eco)Marxist perspective is not well-equipped to address this latter consequence. To do so, we turn to an emerging area of theorizing being applied to animal (ab)use: cultural spillover.

Cultural Spillover

This perspective is somewhat similar to the violence graduation hypothesis and the deviance generalization hypothesis discussed earlier. Whereas those hypotheses focus on disapproved forms of animal harm, the cultural spillover hypothesis proposes that socially approved violence can also be associated with unapproved of forms of violence and/or aggression. Beirne (2004) begins to articulate this possibility in relation to the human-animal relationship by suggesting that "[w]henever human-animal relationships are marked by authority and power, and thus by institutionalized social distance, there is an aggravated possibility of extra-institutional violence" (p. 54). Although in this context the focus is on human-animal relationships, this proposition parallels studies of other contexts where socially approved harm against people is said to spill over into unapproved harm against people, such as studies documenting extra-institutional violence among military personnel (e.g., Allen, 2000; Marshall, Panuzio, & Taft, 2005; Marshall & McShane, 2000; Mercier, 2000; Rosen, Kaminski, Parmley, Knudson, & Fancher, 2003) and prison guards (Black, 1982; Kauffman, 1988; Stack & Tsoudis, 1997).

There are a number of scenarios that are possible when applying this hypothesis to human-animal relationships. First, it is possible that socially approved of violence against people (such as in the contexts of the military or prisons) could spill over into disapproved of violence against animals (e.g., cruelty against companion animals). This would not be particularly surprising, given the above cited research indicating that socially approved violence against people can spill over into disapproved of violence against people. Research into this possibility is necessary.

Second, it is possible that authorized violence against animals could spill over into unauthorized violence against animals. Flynn (2001, p. 79) presents this possibility as follows: "The more we harm animals in ways that society deems acceptable, the more likely individuals may be to engage in animal cruelty and the less likely individuals and social institutions may be to seriously sanction it." Slade and Alleyne (2021) note the increasing number of online videos surfacing in the media showing evidence of animal abuse by some slaughterhouse workers. In 2008, for instance, two workers at a slaughterhouse in California were captured on undercover video kicking, shocking, and dragging 'downed' (i.e., injured or disabled) cattle. The president of the company that owned the facility attempted to assuage the public by depicting the abuse as the actions of two rogue individuals (Associated Press, 2008), implying that it was an individual-level and not a systemic problem. However, there is reason to think that this goes beyond the problematic actions of a couple of individuals, which have the full support of animal agriculture (Lazare, forthcoming). Such actions signal that the animal agriculture industry is aware of such violent behavior towards animals, but seeks to hide it from the public eye.

Gullone (2014, p. 74) warns more specifically that "given the pivotal roles for aggression learning played by witnessing cruelty, exposure to aggressive models, and media violence, concern is warranted also with regard to legalized aggressive behaviors such as hunting, attending rodeos, and fishing." For instance, research indicates that those who work in primary industries (such as animal agriculture) have more negative or utilitarian/dominionistic attitudes towards animals (Signal & Taylor, 2006). It is possible that such attitudes could spill over into harmful actions towards animals that are not socially approved. That is, being immersed in an environment where animals are used as instruments for socially approved ends might extend to using animals as instruments for socially disapproved of ends. Of course, that does not suggest that all people who use animals instrumentally would eventually engage in what is legally defined as animal abuse; however, it is possible that such an environment would facilitate such a boundary transgression, more than one in which animals are viewed as individual, sentient beings with inviolable interests and even rights. Research is needed to examine the likelihood and mechanisms behind such boundary transgressions.

Third, and finally, it is possible that socially approved violence against animals could spill over into aggression and violence against people. Research in this area is also just beginning. A study by Fitzgerald, Kalof, and Dietz (2009) was designed specifically to examine the potential spill over from the industrialized slaughter of animals used as food to violence against people in the broader community. This study was prompted by a number of community studies that found that crime rates increased dramatically in areas where large slaughterhouse facilities had opened (see, for instance, Stull & Broadway, 2004). The study by Fitzgerald and colleagues (2009) set out to examine whether crime rates and slaughterhouse employment levels were related across 581 counties in the U.S. Even when controlling for factors commonly associated with crime (e.g., population density, number of young men in the population, and income levels), they found that slaughterhouse employment levels are related at the county level to total arrest rates, arrests for violent crimes, rape, and other sex offenses. They also found that this relationship does not exist among other industries (in fact, several had negative relationships with these crime variables).

More recently, Jacques (2015) explored similar questions to Fitzgerald et al. (2009) in assessing the spillover of violence against animals in a slaughterhouse to violence against humans. Hypothesizing that the presence of an abattoir in a community is related to increased arrests, increased domestic violence, and increased assaults, Jacques (2015) examined the crime statistics in 2000 in nonurban communities in Iowa, Kansas, and Nebraska, states which at the time had the highest concentration of cattle slaughterhouses. Like Fitzgerald et al. (2009), Jacques (2015) found that a slaughterhouse in the community was associated with increased overall arrest rates (22%) as well as a substantial increase in arrests for rape (166%) and family related offences (90%). Interestingly, proximity to a slaughterhouse was not significantly related to arrests for aggravated assault or murder, and Jacques (2015) postulated that report rates (rather than arrest rates) may be a better measure to use for future studies in rural communities where rates of these crimes are relatively low. Notwithstanding limitations, together these two studies provide support for the cultural spillover of violence thesis.

Additional support is found in Slade and Alleyne's (2021) systematic review of the literature on slaughterhouse work and its impacts on social and mental health. Initially working with a sample of nearly 500 articles, after eliminating research focusing on physical effects, non-empirical studies, and articles not in English, 14 studies were included for analysis. Every study included reported poorer mental health and negative psychological effects related to slaughterhouse employment. For instance, Victor and Barnard (2016) looked at the well-being of slaughterhouse employees in South Africa, conducting 14 narrative interviews with employees responsible for the killing of the animals. Participants reported emotional trauma, alongside fear, sadness, and guilt over their actions, which faded to emotional detachment in order to cope with the day-to-day realities of their jobs. Importantly, participants stated that the stress of their employment spilled over into their personal relationships, as Victor and Barnard (2016) observe that "[s]laughterers seem to find an expression for their anger in incidents of fighting in and outside of the work ... [and] Anger is often directed at defenseless others and triggered by trivial reasons with little regard to the consequences thereof" (p. 9).

A study conducted in Turkey provides some exploratory data on the psychological effects of slaughterhouse work. The study compared the psychological well-being of 43 butchers working in slaughterhouses and 39 butchers working in supermarkets with a control group of office workers. Among their samples, the butchers report statistically greater experiences of somatization, obsessive-compulsiveness, interpersonal sensitivity, depression, anxiety, anger-hostility, phobic anxiety, paranoid ideation, and psychosis than the control group (Emhan, Yildiz, Bez, & Kingir, 2012). Importantly, however, it is unclear if these problems developed in the course of their work or if these problems predated their employment as butchers. Blaznik (2018) looked at butcher education in European Union Countries, noting that in several countries training begins in adolescence (ages 15 or 16). Education includes learning how to stun, slaughter, scald, dehair, and eviscerate cows and pigs, in both theory and on-the-job training. Blaznik (2018) raises important questions about the long-term psychological implications of such educational practices, pointing to the decrease in empathy and desensitization to violence at critical developmental moments for adolescents. "When society trains young people to kill and dismember animals, even at the cost of their own mental health, this behaviour is deemed acceptable and is promoted" (Blaznik, 2018, p. 210); yet this presents an inherent contradiction to the understanding of the negative impacts of unacceptable animal cruelty.

MacNair's (2002) work on perpetration-induced stress among soldiers, executioners, and law enforcement officers can help to theoretically contextualize the findings of these studies. MacNair argues that even the perpetration of socially approved violence can have significant negative psychological consequences for the perpetrators, even when they were just following orders in perpetrating the violence. Although slaughterhouse workers are not one of the groups MacNair studied, she suggests that they be examined for perpetration-induced traumatic stress. She asks the following worthwhile questions:

> Does the fact that these are merely animals prevent the psychological consequences that would accrue if people were to be treated in this way? Does the fact that this kind of violence is done in massive numbers make it more of a psychological problem than violence to one or a few animals would? (MacNair, 2002, p. 88).

Research examining the actions of those who witness animal abuse (i.e., bystanders) indicates that one of the barriers to action most commonly identified is that the abuse took place within a larger social context of normalized violence. In other words, the bystanders see the violence "as part of a broader pattern of inevitable, albeit unfortunate, everyday violence toward humans and animals" (Arluke, 2013, p. 11). Socially approved violence may not only spill over into harmful behavior against animals, it may also spill over and create a more general environment of apathy, where those who witness even extreme forms of abusive behavior are disinclined to intervene.

Although the studies described in this section cannot conclude that there is a causal spillover effect, through their use of time-series design, statistical controls, and use of comparison industries, they provide suggestive evidence. Further research is needed to examine this and other contexts where socially authorized animal harm may spill over into the unauthorized harming of animals and people. In his thorough review of the literature on the relationship between animal abuse and interpersonal violence, Flynn (2011) also recommends the pursuit of further research in this area in particular.

Conclusion

Several conclusions can be drawn from this overview of current sociological theorizing of animal abuse. First, although we have discussed each of the 10 theories addressed in this chapter separately, it should be clear from our review that there are some important points of convergence between many of the theories. For instance, gender recurs in several theories. It is most explicit in the feminist and masculinities perspectives, but also appears more subtly and intersects with the more micro-level theories discussed (particularly social learning). Such commonalities between these theories present particularly fertile ground for further development and potential theoretical integration.

Second, it should be apparent from our discussions here that there is a great deal of research that still needs to be done to better understand the explanatory potential of the sociological theories presented in this chapter. The testing of these theories through additional empirical research will no doubt lead to theoretical refinements and a greater understanding of places where theoretical integration may be useful.

Finally, we have argued throughout this chapter that theoretical and empirical attention should be paid to both harms to animals legally defined as abusive as well as harms to animals currently not prohibited and even socially accepted. However, doing so will require some theoretical dexterity. If we truly wish to understand the harmful treatment of animals in our culture, we must be willing to explore the spectrum of harmful treatment—from the socially prohibited, through the socially discouraged, to the socially accepted. The gradations along this spectrum will continue to shift over time, but the speciesism that grounds the entire continuum must be confronted.

References

Abrahams, H. (2007). *Supporting Women After Domestic Violence: loss, trauma and recovery*. Jessica Kingsley Publishers.

Adams, C. J. (1990). *The sexual politics of meat: A feminist-vegetarian critical theory*. Continuum.

Adams, C. J. (1994). Bringing peace home: A Feminist philosophical perspective on the abuse of women, children, and pet animals. *Hypatia: A Journal of Feminist Philosophy, 9*(2), 63–84. https://doi.org/10.1111/j.1527-2001.1994.tb00433.x.

Adams, C. J. (1995). Woman-battering and harm to animals. In C. J. Adams and J. Donovan (eds), *Animals & Women: Feminist Theoretical Explorations* (pp. 55–84). Duke University Press.

Agnew, R. (1998). The causes of animal abuse: A social-psychological analysis. *Theoretical Criminology*, *2*(2), 177–209. https://doi.org/10.1177/1362480698002002003.

Agnew, R. (2010). Pressured into crime: General strain theory. In F. Cullen & R. Agnew (Eds.), *Criminological theory: Past to present (Essential readings)*, (pp. 201–209). Roxbury Publishing.

Allen, L. C. (2000). The influence of military training and combat experience on domestic violence. In P. Mercier & J. Mercier (Eds.) *Battle cries on the homefront* (pp. 81–103), Charles C. Thomas.

Allen, M., Gallagher, B. & Jones, B. (2006). Domestic violence and the abuse of pets: Researching the link and its implications in Ireland. *Practice, 18*(3), 167–181. https://doi.org/10.1080/09503150600904060.

Alleyne, E., Tilston, L., Parfitt, C., Butcher, R. (2015). Adult-perpetrated animal abuse: Development of a proclivity scale. *Psychology, Crime & Law, 21*(6), 570–588. https://doi.org/10.1080/1068316X.2014.999064.

American Psychological Association (APA). (2017, July). *Ethnic and Racial Minorities & Socioeconomic Status*. https://www.apa.org/pi/ses/resources/publications/minorities.

Anderson, J. L. (2011). Protection for the powerless: Political economy history lessons for the animal welfare movement. *Stanford Journal of Animal Law and Policy*, 4, 1–63.

Aristarkhova, I. (2012). Thou shall not harm all living beings: Feminism, Jainism, and animals. *Hypatia, 27*(3), 636–650. https://doi.org/10.1111/j.1527-2001.2012.01281.x.

Arluke, A. (2002). Animal abuse as dirty play. *Symbolic Interactionism, 25*(4), 405–430. https://doi.org/10.1525/si.2002.25.4.405.

Arluke, A. (2012). Interpersonal barriers to stopping animal abuse: Exploring the role of adolescent friendship norms and breeches. *Journal of Interpersonal Violence, 27*(15), 2939–2958. https://doi.org/10.1177/0886260512441073.

Arluke, A. (2013). Bystander apathy in animal abuse cases: Exploring barriers to child and adolescent intervention. *Anthrozoos, 25*(1), 5–23. https://doi.org/10.2752/175303712X13240472427753.

Arluke, A., Levin, J., Luke, C., & Ascione, F. R. (1999). The relationship of animal abuse to violence and other forms of antisocial behavior. *Journal of Interpersonal Violence, 14*(9), 963–975. https://doi.org/10.1177/088626099014009004.

Arluke. A., & Luke, C. (1997). Physical cruelty toward animals in Massachusetts, 1975–1996. *Society & Animals*, *5*(3), 195–204. https://doi.org/10.1163/156853097X00123.

Arluke, A., & Madfis, E. (2014). Animal abuse as a warning sign of school massacres: A critique and refinement. *Homicide Studies, 18*(1), 7–22. https://doi.org/10.1177/1088767913511459.

Ascione, F. R. (1993). Children who are cruel to animals: A review of research and implications for developmental psychology. *Anthrozoös*, *6*(4), 226–247. https://doi.org/10.2752/089279393787002105.

Ascione, F. R. (1998). Battered women's reports of their partners' and their children's cruelty to animals. *Journal of Emotional Abuse, 1*(1), 119–133. https://doi.org/10.1300/J135v01n01_06.

Ascione, F. R., & Arkow, P. (Eds.). (1999). *Child abuse, domestic violence, and animal abuse: Linking the circles of compassion for prevention and intervention*. Purdue University Press.

Ascione, F. R., Weber, C. V., & Wood, D. S. (1997). The abuse of animals and domestic violence: A national survey of shelters for women who are battered. *Society & Animals, 5*(3), 205–218. https://doi.org/10.1163/156853097X00132.

Ascione, F. R., Weber, C. V., Thompson, T. M., Heath, J., Maruyama, M., & Hayashi, K. (2007). Battered pets and domestic violence: Animal abuse reported by women experiencing intimate violence and by nonabused women. *Violence Against Women, 13*(4), 354–373. https://doi.org/10.1177/1077801207299201.

Associated Press. (2008, February 17). Two slaughterhouse workers charged with abuse. *USA Today*. Retrieved from http://usatoday30.usatoday.com/money/industries/food/2008-02-15-slaughterhouse-charges_N.htm.

Baldry, A. C. (2003). Animal abuse and exposure to interparental violence in Italian youth. *Journal of Interpersonal Violence, 18*(3), 258–281. https://doi.org/10.1177/0886260502250081.

Barrett, B. J., Fitzgerald, A., Stevenson, R., & Cheung, C. H. (2020). Animal maltreatment as a risk marker of more frequent and severe forms of intimate partner violence. *Journal of Interpersonal Violence, 35*(23–24), 5131–5156. https://doi.org/10.1177/0886260517719542.

Beirne, P. (1995). The use and abuse of animals in criminology: A brief history and current review. *Social Justice, 22*(1), 5–31.

Beirne, P. (1999). For a nonspeciesist criminology: Animal abuse as an object of study. *Criminology, 37*(1), 117–147. https://doi.org/10.1111/j.1745-9125.1999.tb00481.x.

Beirne, P. (2002). Criminology and animal studies: A sociological view. *Society & Animals, 10*(4), 381–386. https://doi.org/10.1163/156853002320936845.

Beirne, P. (2004). From animal abuse to interhuman violence? A critical review of the progression thesis. *Society & Animals, 12*(1), 39–65 https://doi.org/10.1163/156853004323029531.

Beirne, P. (2007). Animal rights, animal abuse and green criminology. In P. Beirne, & N. South (Eds.), *Issues in green criminology* (pp. 55–83). Willan.

Beirne, P. (2009). *Confronting animal abuse: Law, criminology, and human-animal relationships*. Rowman & Littlefield.

Beirne, P. (2014). Theriocide: Naming animal killing. *International Journal for Crime, Justice and Social Democracy, 3*(2), 49–66. https://doi.org/10.5204/ijcjsd.v3i2.174.

Benton, T. (1993). *Natural relations: Ecology, animal rights & social justice.* New York: Verso.

Black, R. (1982). Stress and the correctional officer. *Police Stress, 5*, 10–16.

Blaznik, M. (2018). Training young killers: How butcher education might be damaging young people. *Journal of Animal Ethics, 8*(2), 199–215. https://doi.org/10.5406/janimalethics.8.2.0199.

Boggs, C. (2007). Corporate power, ecological crisis, and animal rights. *Fast Capitalism, 2*(2), 31–47. https://doi.org/10.32855/fcapital.200701.002.

Brown, S. E., Esbensen, F. A., & Geis, G. (2012). *Criminology: Explaining crime and its context.* Routledge.

Bright, M. A., Huq, M. S., Spencer, T., Applebaum, J. W., & Hardt, N. (2018). Animal cruelty as an indicator of family trauma: Using adverse childhood experiences to look beyond child abuse and domestic violence. *Child Abuse & Neglect, 76*, 287–296. https://doi.org/10.1016/j.chiabu.2017.11.011.

Burchfield, K. B. (2016). The sociology of animal crime: An examination of incidents and arrests in Chicago. *Deviant Behavior, 37*(4), 368–384. https://doi.org/10.1080/01639625.2015.1026769.

Cazaux, G. (1999). Beauty and the beast: Animal abuse from a non-speciesist criminological perspective. *Crime, Law and Social Change, 31*(2), 105–126. https://doi.org/10.1023/A:1008347609286.

Chesney-Lind, M., & Faith, K. (2001). What about feminism? Engendering theory-making in criminology. In R. Paternoster & R. Bachman (Eds.), *Explaining crime and criminals* (pp. 287–302). Roxbury.

Colvin, M. (2000). *Crime and coercion: An integrated theory of chronic criminality*. Palgrave Macmillan.

Connell, R. W. (1987). *Gender and power*. Stanford University Press.

Connell, R. W., & Messerschmidt, J. W. (2005). Hegemonic masculinity: Rethinking the concept. *Gender & Society, 19*(6), 829–859. https://doi.org/10.1177/0891243205278639.

Currie, C. L. (2006). Animal cruelty by children exposed to domestic violence. *Child Abuse & Neglect, 30*(4), 425–435.

DeGue, S., & DiLillo, D. (2009). Is animal cruelty a "red flag" for family violence? Investigating co-occurring violence toward children, partners, and pets. *Journal of Interpersonal Violence, 24*(6), 1036–1056. https://doi.org/10.1177/0886260508319362.

Dejmanee, T. (2013). The burdens of caring: A postfeminist perspective on PETA's animal protection campaigns. *Australian Feminist Studies, 28*(77), 311–322. https://doi.org/10.1080/08164649.2013.821726.

Dollard, J., Doob, L., Miller, N., Mowrer, O., & Sears, R. (1939). *Frustration and aggression*. Yale University Press.

Donovan, J. and Adams, C. (eds.) (2007). *The feminist care tradition in animal ethics*. Columbia University Press.

Einstadter, W. J., & Henry, S. (2006). *Criminological theory: An analysis of its underlying assumptions*. Rowman and Littlefield.

Emhan, A.,Yildiz, A., Bez, Y., & Kingir, S. (2012). Psychological symptom profile of butchers working in slaughterhouse and retail meat packing business: A comparative study. *Kafkas Universitesi Veteriner Fakültesi Dergisi, 18*, 319–22. https://doi.org/10.9775/kvfd.2011.5494.

Eisnitz, G. (1997). *Slaughterhouse: The shocking story of greed, neglect, and inhumane treatment inside the U.S. meat industry*. Prometheus.

Evans, R., Gauthier, D. K., and Forsyth, C. J. (1998). Dogfighting: Symbolic expression and validation of masculinity. *Sex Roles, 39*(11–12), 825–837. https://doi.org/10.1023/A:1018872404355.

Fielding, W. (2010). Domestic violence and dog care in New Providence, the Bahamas. *Society & Animals, 18*(2), 183–203. https://doi.org/10.1163/156853010x492024.

Fine, G. A. (1986). The dirty play of little boys. *Society, 24*(1), 63–67.

Fitzgerald, A. J. (2005). *Animal abuse and family violence: Researching the interrelationships of abusive power*. Edwin Mellen.

Fitzgerald, A. J. (2007). 'They gave me a reason to live': The protective effects of companion animals on the suicidality of abused women. *Humanity & Society, 31,* 355–378. https://doi.org/10.1177/016059760703100405.

Fitzgerald, A. J. (2010). A social history of the slaughterhouse: From inception to contemporary implications. *Human Ecology Review, 17*(1), 58–69.

Fitzgerald, A.J. (2015). *Animals as food: (Re)connecting production, processing, consumption, and impacts*. Michigan State University Press.

Fitzgerald, A. J., Barrett, B. J., & Gray, A. (2021). The co-occurrence of animal abuse and intimate partner violence among a nationally representative sample: Evidence of "The Link" in the general population. *Violence and Victims, 36*(6), 770–792. https://doi.org/10.1891/VV-D-19-00047.

Fitzgerald, A. J., Barrett, B. J., Gray, A., & Cheung, C. H. (2020). The connection between animal abuse, emotional abuse, and financial abuse in intimate relationships: Evidence from a nationally representative sample of the general public. *Journal of Interpersonal Violence*. https://doi.org/10.1177/0886260520939197.

Fitzgerald, A. J., Barrett, B. J., Stevenson, R., & Cheung, C. H. (2019). Animal maltreatment in the context of intimate partner violence: A manifestation of power and control? *Violence Against Women, 25*(15), 1806–1828. https://doi.org/10.1177/1077801218824993.

Fitzgerald, A. J., Kalof, L., & Dietz, T. (2009). Slaughterhouses and increased crime rates: An empirical analysis of spillover from 'The jungle" into the surrounding community. *Organization & Environment, 22*(2), 158–184 https://doi.org/10.1177/1086026609338164.

Flynn, C. P. (1999). Exploring the link between corporal punishment and children's cruelty to animals. *Journal of Marriage and the Family, 61*(4), 971–981. https://doi.org/10.2307/354017.

Flynn, C. P. (2000). Battered women and their animal companions: Symbolic interaction between human and nonhuman animals. *Society & Animals, 8*(2), 99–127. https://doi.org/10.1163/156853000511032.

Flynn, C. P. (2001). Acknowledging the "zoological connection": A sociological analysis of animal cruelty. *Society & Animals, 9*(1), 71–87. https://doi.org/10.1163/156853001300109008.

Flynn, C. P. (2002). Hunting and illegal violence against humans and other animals: Exploring the relationship. *Society & Animals, 10,* 137–154. https://doi.org/10.1163/156853002320292291.

Flynn, C. P. (2010). A sociological analysis of animal abuse. In F. Ascione (Ed.), *The international handbook of animal abuse and cruelty: Theory, research, and application* (pp. 155–174), Purdue University Press.

Flynn, C. P. (2011). Examining the links between animal abuse and human violence. *Crime, Law, and Social Change, 55,* 453–468. https://doi.org/10.1007/s10611-011-9297-2.

Foer, J. S. (2010). *Eating animals.* Back Bay Books.

Frye, J. (2014). Big ag gags the freedom of expression. *First Amendment Studies, 48*(1), 27–43. https://doi.org/10.1080/21689725.2014.888859.

Gullone, E. (2009). A lifespan perspective on human aggression and animal abuse. In A. Linzey (Ed.), *The link between animal abuse and human violence* (pp. 38–60). Sussex Academic Press.

Gullone, E. (2014). Risk factors for the development of animal cruelty. *Journal of Animal Ethics, 4*(2), 61–79. https://doi.org/10.5406/janimalethics.4.2.0061.

Gullone, E., & Robertson, N. (2008). The relationship between bullying and animal abuse in adolescents: The importance of witnessing animal abuse. *Journal of Applied Developmental Psychology, 29,* 371–379. https://doi.org/10.1016/j.appdev.2008.06.004.

Gunderson, R. (2011). From cattle to capital: Exchange value, animal commodification, and barbarism. *Critical Sociology, 39*(2), 259–275. https://doi.org/10.1177/0896920511421031.

Hellman, D. S., & Blackman, N. (1966). Enuresis, firesetting and cruelty to animals: A triad predictive of adult crime. *American Journal of Psychiatry, 122,* 1431–1435.

Henry, B. C. (2004a). Exposure to animal abuse and group context: Two factors affecting participation in animal abuse. *Anthrozoös, 17*(4), 290–305. https://doi.org/10.2752/089279304785643195.

Henry, B. C. (2004b). The relationship between animal cruelty, delinquency, and attitudes toward the treatment of animals. *Society & Animals, 12*(4), 185–207. https://doi.org/10.1163/1568530042880677.

Henry, B. C., & Sanders, C. E. (2007). Bullying and animal abuse: Is there a connection? *Society & Animals, 15*(2), 107–126. https://doi.org/10.1163/156853007x187081.

Hensley, C., & Tallichet, S. E. (2005). Learning to be cruel?: Exploring the onset and frequency of animal cruelty. *International Journal of Offender Therapy and Comparative Criminology, 49*(1), 37–47. https://doi.org/10.1177/0306624X04266680.

Hensley, C., Tallichet, S. E., & Dutkiewicz, E. L. (2009). Recurrent childhood animal cruelty: Is there a relationship to adult recurrent interpersonal violence? *Criminal Justice Review, 34*(2), 248–257. https://doi.org/10.1177/0734016808325062.

Hensely, C., Tallichet, S. E., & Dutkiewicz, E. L. (2012). The predictive value of childhood animal cruelty methods on later adult violence: Examining demographic and situational correlates. *International Journal of Offender Therapy and Comparative Criminology, 56*(2), 281–295. https://doi.org/10.1177/0306624X10397120.

Herzog, H. (2007). Gender differences in human-animal interactions: A review. *Anthrozoos, 20*(1), 7–21. https://doi.org/10.2752/089279307780216687.

Hicks, I. (2012, April 5). Guilty in dog torture case. *The Intelligencer*. Retrieved from http://theintelligencer.net/page/content.detail/id/568137/Guilty-In-Dog-Torture-Case.html.

Howells, K., Watt, B., Hall, G., & Baldwin, S. (1997). Developing programs for violent offenders. *Legal and Criminological Psychology, 2*(1), 117–128. https://doi.org/10.1111/j.2044-8333.1997.tb00337.x.

Hunter, R. (2006). *Point Last Seen*. Debut Publishing.

Iliopoulou, M. A. & Rosenbaum, R. P. (2013). Understanding blood sports. *Journal of Animal and Natural Resource Law, 9,* 125–140.

Jacques, J. R. (2015). The slaughterhouse, social disorganization, and violent crime in rural communities, *Society & Animals, 23*(6), 594–612. https://doi.org/10.1163/15685306-12341380.

Kauffman, K. (1988). *Prison officers and their world.* Harvard University Press.

Kavanagh, P., Signal, T., Taylor, N. (2013). The Dark Triad and animal cruelty: Dark personalities, dark attitudes, and dark behaviors. *Personality and Individual Differences, 55*, 666–670. https://doi.org/10.1016/j.paid.2013.05.019.

Kellert, S. R., & Felthous, A. R. (1985). Childhood cruelty toward animals among criminals and noncriminals. *Human Relations, 38*(12), 1113–1129.

Kheel, M. (1995). License to kill: An ecofeminist critique of hunters' discourse. In C. J. Adams, & J. Donovan (Eds.), *Animals and women: Feminist theoretical explorations* (pp. 85–125). Duke University Press.

King, R. J. H. (1991). Environmental Ethics and the Case for Hunting. *Environmental Ethics, 13*, 59–85. https://doi.org/10.5840/enviroethics199113117.

Knight, K. E., Ellis, C., Simmons, B. (2014). Parental predictors of children's animal abuse: Findings from a national and intergenerational sample. *Journal of Interpersonal Violence, 29*(16), 3014–3034. https://doi.org/10.1177/0886260514527825.

Lazare, J. (forthcoming, 2022). Animal rights activism and the Constitution: Are ag-gag laws justifiable limits? *Osgoode Hall Law Journal.*

Liebmann, L. (2014). Fraud and First Amendment protections of false speech: How United States v. Alvarez impacts constitutional challenges to ag-gag laws. *Pace Environmental Law Review, 31*(2), 566–593.

Linsely, P. (2006). *Violence and aggression in the workplace: A practical guide for all healthcare staff.* Radcliffee Publishing.

Loring, M. T., & Bolden-Hines, T. A. (2004). Pet abuse by batterers as a means of coercing battered women into committing illegal behaviour. *Journal of Emotional Abuse, 4*(1), 27–37. https://doi.org/10.1300/J135v04n01_02.

Lucia, S. and Killias, M. (2011). Is animal cruelty a marker of interpersonal violence and delinquency? Results of a Swiss national self-report study. *Psychology of Violence, 1*(2), 93–105. https://doi.org/10.1037/a0022986.

Luke, B. (2007). *Brutal: Manhood and the exploitation of animals.* University of Illinois Press.

Lynch, M. J., Long, M. A., Barrett, K. L., and Stretesky, P. B. (2013). Is it a crime to produce ecological disorganization? Why green criminology and political economy matter in the analysis of global ecological harms. *British Journal of Criminology, 53,* 997–1016. https://doi.org/10.1093/bjc/azt051.

Lynch, M., Stretesky, P., & Long, M. (2020). The Treadmill of Production and the Treadmill of Law: Propositions for Analyzing Law, Ecological Disorganization and Crime. *Capitalism, Nature, Socialism, 31*(1), 107–122. https://doi.org/10.1080/10455752.2018.1545241.

MacNair, R. (2002). *Perpetration-induced traumatic stress: The psychological consequences of killing.* Praeger.

Marceau, J. (2019). *Beyond Cages: Animal Law and Criminal Punishment.* Cambridge University Press.

Marshall, A. D., Panuzio, J., & Taft, C. T. (2005). Intimate partner violence among military veterans and active duty servicemen. *Clinical Psychology Review, 25,* 862–876. https://doi.org/10.1016/j.cpr.2005.05.009.

Marshall, D., & McShane, M. (2000). First to fight: Domestic violence and the subculture of the Marine Corps. In P. Mercier & J. Mercier (Eds.), *Battle cries on the homefront: Violence in the military family* (pp. 15–29). Charles C. Thomas.

Marvin, G. (1988). *Bullfight.* Blackwell.

Mason, J. & Finelli, M. (2006). Brave new farm? In P. Singer (Ed.) *In defense of animals: The second wave* (pp. 104–122). Blackwell Publishing.

Matthews, S. & Herzog, H. (1997). Personality and attitudes toward the treatment of animals. *Society & Animals, 5*(2), 169–175. https://doi.org/10.1163/156853097X00060.

McDonald, S.E., Cody, A.M., Booth, L.J., Peers, J.R., Luce, C.O, Williams, J.H., & Ascione, F.R. (2018). Animal cruelty among children in violent households: Children's explanations of their behavior. *Journal of Family Violence, 33*, 469–480. https://doi.org/10.1007/s10896-018-9970-7.

McLoughlin, E. (2018). Knowing cows: Transformative mobilizations of human and non-human bodies in an emotionography of the slaughterhouse. *Gender, Work & Organization, 26*(3), 322–342. https://doi.org/10.1111/gwao.12247.

Mead, M. (1964). Cultural factors in the cause and prevention of pathological homicide. *Bulletin in the Menninger Clinic, 28*, 11–22.

Mercier, P. J. (2000). Violence in the military family. In P. Mercier & J. Mercier (Eds.), *Battle cries on the homefront: Violence in the military family* (pp. 3–11). Charles C. Thomas.

Merz-Perez, L., & Heide, K. M. (2004). *Animal cruelty: Pathway to violence against people*. Altamira.

Merz-Perez, L., Heide, K. M., & Silverman, I. J. (2001). Childhood cruelty to animals and subsequent violence against humans. *International Journal of Offender Therapy and Comparative Criminology, 45*(5), 556–573. https://doi.org/10.1177/0306624X01455003.

Messerschmidt, J. (2004). Varieties of 'real men'. In M. Kimmel & M. Messner (Eds.), *Men's lives* (6th ed.) (pp. 3–20). Pearson.

Morris, M. C. (2013). Improved nonhuman animal welfare is related more to income equality than it is to income. *Journal of Applied Animal Welfare Science, 16*, 272–293. https://doi.org/10.1080/10888705.2013.768921.

Mowen, T.J., & Boman IV, J.H. (2020). Animal abuse among high-risk youth: A test of Agnew's theory. *Deviant Behavior, 41*(6), 765–778. https://doi.org/10.1080/01639625.2019.1595373.

Nibert, D. A. (2002). *Animal rights/human rights: Entanglements of oppression and liberation*. Rowman & Littlefield.

Nibert, D. A. (2013). *Animal oppression and human violence: Domesecration, capitalism, and global conflict*. Columbia University Press.

Noske, B. (1989). *Humans and other animals: Beyond the boundaries of anthropology*. Pluto Press.

Novek, J. (2003). Intensive hog farming in Manitoba: Transnational treadmills and local conflicts. *The Canadian Review of Sociology and Anthropology, 40*(1), 3–26.

Nowicki, S. A. (2011). Give me shelter: The foreclosure crisis and its effects on America's animals. *Stanford Journal of Animal Law and Policy, 4*, 97–121.

Nurse, A. (2013). Perspectives on criminality in wildlife. In R. Walters, D. S. Westerhuis, & T. Wyatt (Eds.) *Emerging issues in green criminology: Exploring power, justice, and harm* (pp. 127–143). Palgrave Macmillan.

Quinlisk, J. A. (1999). Animal abuse and family violence. In F. R. Ascione, & P. Arkow (Eds.), *Child abuse, domestic violence, and animal abuse: Linking the circles of compassion for prevention and intervention* (pp. 168–175). Purdue University Press.

Pagani, C., Robustelli, F., & Ascione, F. R. (2010). Investigating animal abuse: Some theoretical and methodological issues. *Anthrozoos, 23*(3), 259–276. https://doi.org/10.2752/175303710X12750451259011.

Peterson, M. L., & Farrington, D. P. (2007). Cruelty to animals and violence to people. *Victims & Offenders, 2*(1), 21–43. https://doi.org/10.1080/15564880600934187.

Pitts, J. (2012). 'Ag-gag' legislation and public choice theory: Maintaining a diffuse public by limiting information. *American Journal of Criminal Law, 40*, 95–110.

Reese, L.A., Vertalka, J. J., & Richard, C. (2020). Animal cruelty and neighborhood conditions. *Animals, 10*(11), 2095. https://doi.org/10.3390/ani10112095.

Ressler, R. K., Burgess, A. W., Hartman, C. R., Douglas, J. E., & McCormack, A. (1986). Murderers who rape and mutilate. *Journal of Interpersonal Violence, 1*(3), 273–287. https://doi.org/10.1177/088626086001003002.

Rogers, R. (2008). Beasts, burgers and Hummers: The crisis of masculinity in contemporary television. *Environmental Communication, 2*(3), 281–301. https://doi.org/10.1080/17524030802390250.

Roguski, M. (2012). *Pets as Pawns: The Co-existence of Animal Cruelty and Family Violence.* Royal New Zealand Society for the Prevention of Cruelty to Animals and The National Collective of Independent Women's Refuges, Auckland, New Zealand. https://nationallinkcoalition.org/wp-content/uploads/2013/01/DV-PetsAsPawnsNZ.pdf.

Rosen, L. N., Kaminski, R. J., Parmley, A. M., Knudson, K. H., & Fancher, P. (2003). The effects of peer group climate on intimate partner violence among married male U.S. army soldiers. *Violence against Women, 9*, 1045–1071. https://doi.org/10.1177/1077801203255504.

Rothgerber, H. (2012). Real men don't eat (vegetable) quiche: Masculinity and the justification of meat consumption. *Psychology of Men and Masculinity, 14*(4), 363–375. https://doi.org/10.1037/a0030379.

Salleh, A. (1995) Nature, woman, labor, capital: Living the deepest contradiction. *Capitalism, Nature, Socialism, 6*(1), 106–124. https://doi.org/10.1080/10455759509358619

Schlosser, E. (2005). *Fast food nation: The dark side of the all-American meal.* Houghton Mifflin.

Signal, T. D., & Taylor, N. (2006). Attitudes to animals: Demographics within a community sample. *Society & Animals, 14*(2), 147–157. https://doi.org/10.1163/156853006776778743.

Simmons, C. A., & Lehmann, P. (2007). Exploring the link between pet abuse and controlling behaviors in violent relationships. *Journal of Interpersonal Violence, 22*(9), 1211–1222. https://doi.org/10.1177/0886260507303734.

Slade, J., & Alleyne, E. (2021). The Psychological Impact of Slaughterhouse Employment: A Systematic Literature Review. *Trauma, Violence, & Abuse*. https://doi.org/10.1177/15248380211030243.

Sollund, R. (2011). Expressions of speciesism: The effects of keeping companion animals on animal abuse, animal trafficking and species decline. *Crime, Law, and Social Change, 55*, 437–451. https://doi.org/10.1007/s10611-011-9296-3.

Sollund, R. (2013). The victimization of women, children and non-human species through trafficking and trade: Crimes understood through an ecofeminist perspective. In N. South and A. Brisman (eds.), *Routledge international handbook of green criminology* (pp. 317–330). Routledge.

Stack, S. J., & Tsoudis, O. (1997). Suicide risk among correctional officers: A logistic regression analysis. *Archives of Suicide Research, 3,* 183–186. https://doi.org/10.1023/A:1009677102357.

Stevenson, R. (2009). *Violence affects all members of the family: Safe pet programs in western Canada.* (Unpublished BA (Honors)). Simon Fraser University, Burnaby, BC.

Stull, D., & Broadway, M. (2004). *Slaughterhouse blues: The meat and poultry industry in North America*. Wadsworth.

Tallichet, S. E., & Hensley, C. (2004). Exploring the link between recurrent acts of childhood and adolescent animal cruelty and subsequent violent crime. *Criminal Justice Review, 29*(2), 304–316. https://doi.org/10.1177/073401680402900203.

Taylor, N. (2011). Criminology and human-animal violence research: The contribution and the challenge. *Critical Criminology, 19*(3), 251–263. https://doi.org/10.1007/s10612-010-9124-6.

Torres, B. (2007). *Making a killing: The political economy of animal rights*. Oakland, CA: AK Press.

Tibbetts, S. G., & Hemmens, C. (2010). *Criminological Theory: A Text/Reader*. Thousand Oaks, CA: SAGE Publications, Inc.

Tiplady, C. (2013). *Animal abuse: Helping animals and people.* CABI Publishing.

Trentham, C. E., Hensley, C., & Policastro, C. (2018). Recurrent childhood animal cruelty and its link to recurrent adult interpersonal violence. *International Journal of Offender Therapy and Comparative Criminology, 62*(8), 2345–2356. doi:10.1177/0306624X17720175.

Unti, B. (2008). Cruelty indivisible: Historical perspectives on the link between cruelty to animals and interpersonal violence. In F. R. Ascione (Ed.), *The international handbook of animal abuse and cruelty: Theory, research, and application* (pp. 7–30). Purdue University Press.

Vaughn, M. G., Fu, Q., DeLisi, M., Beaver, K. M., Perron, B. E., Terrell, K., & Howard, M. O. (2009). Correlates of cruelty to animals in the United States: Results from the national epidemiologic survey on alcohol and related conditions. *Journal of Psychiatric Research, 43*(15), 1213–1218. https://doi.org/10.1016/j.jpsychires.2009.04.011.

Verbora, A. (2015). The political landscape surrounding anti-cruelty legislation in Canada. *Society & Animals, 23*(1), 45–67. https://doi.org/10.1163/15685306-12341353.

Victor, K., & Barnard, A. (2016). Slaughtering for a living: A hermeneutic phenomenological perspective on the well-being of slaughterhouse employees. *International Journal of Qualitative Studies on Health and Well-being, 11*, 30266. https://doi.org/10.3402/qhw.v11.30266.

Volant, A. M., Johnson, J. A., Gullone, E., & Coleman, G. J. (2008). The relationship between domestic violence and animal abuse: An Australian study. *Journal of Interpersonal Violence, 23*(9), 1277–1295. https://doi.org/10.1177/0886260508314309.

Walker, L. E. (1984). *The Battered Woman Syndrome*. Springer Publishing.

Wax, D. E., & Haddox, V. G. (1973). Sexual aberrance in male adolescents manifesting a behavioral triad considered predictive of extreme violence: Some clinical observations. *Journal of Forensic Sciences, 19*(1), 102–108.

White, G., & Quick, L. (2019) Animal cruelty, domestic violence, and social disorganization in a suburban setting. *Deviant Behavior, 40*(8), 930–941. https://doi.org/10.1080/01639625.2018.1445442.

Wright, J., & Hensley, C. (2003). From animal cruelty to serial murder: Applying the graduation hypothesis. *International Journal of Offender Therapy and Comparative Criminology, 47*(1), 71–88. https://doi.org/10.1177/0306624X02239276.

Zilney, L. A. (2007). *Linking animal cruelty and family violence*. Cambria Press.

Chapter 16

Psychological Theories of Animal Cruelty

Mary Lou Randour and Maya Gupta

Introduction

The purpose of this chapter is to offer an approach to understanding the psychological theories underlying cruelty to animals. Just as there could be no one psychological theory for all forms of human-directed harm and violence, the same is true for animal-directed harm and violence. Both forms of maltreatment encompass many different types of behaviors, attitudes, and practices. For example, depending on legal and scholarly definitions, animal cruelty may refer to neglect, physical abuse, sexual abuse, emotional abuse, animal hoarding, organized animal fighting, or other acts. (See Chapters 1, 8, 9, 10, and 11.) In addition, some might argue that there are practices that—although legal and falling within societal and professional norms—are cruel toward animals, such as factory farming (see Chapters 4 and 9) and laboratory animal research. The viewpoint that some socially acceptable practices also amount to cruelty toward animals, in the moral if not legal sense, is worthy of more discussion and debate than it usually receives.

For the purposes of this discussion, we will be guided by two definitions of animal cruelty. The first is proposed by Ascione (2001, p. 2) who offered the following: "socially unacceptable behavior that intentionally causes unnecessary pain, suffering, or distress to and/or death of an animal." The second definition, which is comparable to the one proposed by Ascione, was developed by the Uniform Crime Reporting Program of the Federal Bureau of Investigation when it added the category of animal cruelty to the National Incident Based Reporting System (NIBRS) in 2014:

> Intentionally, knowingly, or recklessly taking an action that mistreats or kills any animal without just cause, such as torturing, tormenting, mutilation, maiming, poisoning, or abandonment. Included are instances of failure of duty to provide care, e.g., shelter, food, water, care if sick or injured; transporting or confining an animal in a manner likely to cause injury or death; causing an animal to fight with another; inflicting excessive or repeated unnecessary pain or suffering (e.g., uses objects to beat or injure an animal).

This definition does not include proper maintenance of animals for show or sport, use of animals for food, or lawful hunting, fishing or trapping. It is also important to consider definitions of animal cruelty under the law, which vary considerably among countries and U.S. states.

In brief, our exploration into the psychologies of animal cruelty will discuss how a particular psychological theory or conceptual framework may be used to better understand one aspect or type of animal cruelty versus another. Our intention is to illustrate that animal cruelty is a heterogeneous behavior and that examining its etiology and function on a case-by-case basis may offer greater insights into prevention and intervention than simply painting all animal cruelty with a single brush.

Before reviewing the psychological theories and frameworks that may be applicable to animal cruelty, it is helpful to lay out the empirical basis with the following short review of the existing literature on the causes and correlates of animal cruelty.

Causes and Correlates of Animal Cruelty

The accumulating research that links animal cruelty behavior to other forms of violence, as well as to antisocial behavior more generally, motivates the desire among researchers, policymakers, and program developers to better understand the psychologies of animal cruelty as well as the underlying biological, social, and emotional mechanisms that influence behavior and attitudes toward animals. Other writers in this volume have offered a detailed and comprehensive discussion of the empirical evidence for associations between animal cruelty and other types of crime. For example, researchers have found significant associations between animal cruelty and other crimes, including interpersonal violence, illegal possession of drugs and guns, and property destruction (Arluke et al., 1999; Burchfield, 2017; Hoffer et al., 2018; Levitt et al., 2016; Vaughn et al., 2009). Moreover, participation in recurrent animal cruelty in childhood may serve as a marker for the development of aggressive and antisocial behavior (Longobardi & Barnes-Rivera, 2019). Victims of domestic violence also appear to experience cruelty toward their animals, or threats thereof, by their partners at higher rates than non-victims (Ascione et al., 2007; Walton-Moss et al., 2005), and severity of animal cruelty within the relationship has been linked to severity of domestic violence (Barrett et al., 2020; Febres et al., 2014; Simmons & Lehmann, 2007).

In 1987, the mental health profession acknowledged the significance of animal cruelty with its inclusion of physical aggression toward animals as a criterion for a diagnosis of conduct disorder in the revised third edition of the *Diagnostic and Statistical Manual of Mental Disorders* by the American Psychiatric Association. In a meta-analytic review of the symptoms of conduct disorder (Frick et al., 1993), cruelty to animals was among the earlier-reported symptoms, appearing at 6.75 years of age. In addition, children who are cruel to animals exhibit more severe conduct disorder problems than other children (Luk et al., 1999).

The question of whether children who have themselves been mistreated are more likely to abuse animals has somewhat mixed findings. On the one hand, there are studies which have found that children who were cruel to animals were more likely to have been maltreated (McEwen et al., 2014) and that parental involvement in interpersonal violence was associated with children's involvement in animal cruelty (Knight et al., 2014). Another study that examined childhood adversity in relation to both bullying and cruelty to animals, however, concluded that "the cumulative burden of childhood adversities had strong effects on the increased likelihood of bullying but not cruelty to animals" (Vaughn et al., 2011, p. 3509). One possible explanation for the disparity in these findings is that the study by Vaughn et al. (2011) used a national sample, but only asked one question about animal cruelty. The study by McEwen et al. (2014) was longitudinal, so mothers were asked at four different points if their children were cruel to animals (ages 5, 7, 10, and 12). The data are richer if there are multiple times at which information can be obtained about a studied variable, such as animal cruelty. (Any data set would also be more robust if data were collected from a number of different sources about a studied variable, as was the case in the studies by Loeber and his colleagues (2003, 2006), which were both longitudinal and used multiple sources.)

Although research into the causes and correlates of animal cruelty has seen a substantial increase in the last twenty-five years, it is also the case that a number of these studies have been limited by relying on retrospective or other self-report data, the use of convenience samples, varying operational definitions of cruelty, and a lack of experimental controls or other methods to enhance the scientific rigor of the research. At the same time, while any one study may have limitations, the body of evidence supports the overall idea of associations between animal cruelty and the commission of other aggressive and/or antisocial acts, in particular domestic violence.

Psychological Theories for Understanding Animal Cruelty

The theories and approaches considered here to understand cruelty toward animals include the following: instinct and drive theories, theories of social learning, ecological systems theory, conceptual frameworks of bimodal types of aggression, and neurobiological influences. Additionally, the literature on cognitive models, developmental pathways of antisocial behavior, and theories of attachment and empathy development will be reviewed for their relevance in understanding animal cruelty.

Instinct and Drive Theories

Instinct theory, as represented by Freud and Lorenz, proposed that human beings were animated by an aggressive energy that requires expression, which is biological in nature. The concept, drawn from popular culture, is that anger is an emotion that is stored inside and needs to be "released" in order to prevent an uncontrolled explosion. Research demonstrates that this is not the case. For more than 40 years, studies have revealed that encouraging the expression of anger directly toward another person or indirectly (such as toward an object) actually increases aggression. The discharge of "excess energy" toward safe targets will not decrease aggression. In fact, it will increase it (Lohr et al., 2007; Travis, 1982). Drive theories, also mentioned by Pepler and Slaby (1994), focus not on instincts but on internal drives that are vulnerable to external stimuli. The frustration-aggression theory (Dollard et al., 1939), proposes that the existence of frustration inevitably leads to aggression. Frustration, however, is only one of many potential instigators of aggressive behavior. Moreover, rather than frustration, Berkowitz (1993) suggested that the aversive experiences themselves led to aggression. Reliance on either instinct or drive theory alone may not be useful for trying to understand animal cruelty. Thinking by scholars in the field of ethology suggests that most learning is based on general processes; however, it also is "customized through the operation of natural selection in context- and specifies specific ways to solve particular problems" (Gould, 2002, p. 239).

Social Learning Theory

Social learning theory is considered both a sociological and psychological theory (see Chapter 15). Bandura (1973) posited that individuals can learn behaviors not only through experiencing the consequences of their own actions, but also through observing the actions of others and their consequences. In the "Bobo doll" experiments (Bandura et al., 1961), children who observed an adult behaving violently toward a doll subsequently behaved more aggressively when given the opportunity to play with the doll and other toys. Although these studies are not without criticisms, Bandura's model may provide a useful framework for examining the potential for observational learning of animal cruelty. Can observing someone harming an animal teach someone to engage in animal cruelty?

Agnew (1998) draws upon social learning theory in his integrated theory of the causes of animal cruelty, considering both socially unacceptable and socially accepted forms of harm to animals. In Agnew's integrated theory, social learning underlies the view that animal cruelty is likely when an individual perceives that the benefits of the cruelty outweigh the costs; this theory posits that that animal cruelty is further driven by general socialization. Agnew notes that if children observe parents mistreating animals, they may imitate the cruelty; similarly, parents who demonstrate kindness toward animals may serve as models for appropriate interactions. Traditional behavior theory suggests that children's imitative behavior may then be reinforced by their parents' response: directly rewarding the act (e.g., praising the child), rewarding the child through attention (whether positive or negative), or tolerating the behavior and failing to correct or punish the child. Social learning theory adds that the child may experience intrinsic reinforcement for the behavior, such as satisfaction.

Several studies have documented a connection between witnessing violence toward animals and engaging in animal cruelty. Baldry (2003) found that witnessing animal cruelty by peers and/or by mothers was the strongest predictor (beyond gender) for children perpetrating animal cruelty themselves. Thompson and Gullone (2006) also noted an association between witnessing and perpetrating animal cruelty, with higher frequency of witnessing and greater closeness of relationship to the abuser (stranger vs. family member/friend) playing a particular role. DeGue and DiLillo (2009) found that individuals who had witnessed animal cruelty were eight times more likely than those who had not witnessed animal cruelty to perpetrate animal cruelty themselves. While not indicative of causality, one possible interpretation of the findings of these studies is that they are at least broadly consistent with a social learning model.

Can individuals learn to abuse animals if they are either the direct victims of violence or have witnessed violence against people, as opposed to witnessing violence against animals? Ascione (1993) has suggested such a generalization, as well as Flynn (1999) who observed an association between corporal punishment and perpetrating animal cruelty. Offering additional support for this idea are studies by McEwen et al. (2014) and Bright et al. (2018) that children who are cruel to animals were more likely to have been mistreated than other children.

There are other studies, however, that do not support the idea that experiencing or witnessing family violence puts an individual at greater risk for abusing an animal. In a study (Baldry, 2003) that examined, among other factors, interparental violence and animal cruelty perpetration, no association was found. There was, however, a finding that for children who had both witnessed domestic violence and been cruel themselves, maternal violence against the father was also a significant predictor of children's cruelty toward animals. Dadds et al. (2006) demonstrated no relationship between abusive or high conflict family environments and children's perpetration of animal cruelty. In the absence of this association, the authors suggested a dispositional model of animal cruelty based on callous-unemotional personality traits (described later in this chapter). As described previously, DeGue and DeLillo (2009) found that only exposure to animal cruelty, and not exposure to family violence or family conflict, predicted later animal cruelty.

Yet another study, by Gullone and Robertson (2008), found that both family conflict and witnessing animal cruelty predicted animal cruelty perpetration in adolescents. Dadds et al. (2006) suggest that one possible reason for these mixed findings on the presence or absence of a relationship between witnessing or being the victim of family violence and perpetrating animal cruelty may be sampling differences: the association may be stronger in clinical samples where family violence tends to be more severe. Similarly, work by Currie (2005) indicating that children exposed to domestic violence were more likely to abuse animals employed a sample screened in for male-to-female domestic violence, in which the females had received counseling concerning the violence. That study also suggested that differences in age of participants across studies may be salient, particularly in combination with exposure to violence: children exposed to domestic violence who become cruel to animals may be reflecting the influence of that exposure over time ["pathological animal cruelty" in Ascione's (2001) typology], as distinct from children not exposed to domestic violence who abuse animals for other reasons and who may thus be younger as a whole.

Bullying has also been considered as a potential social learning model for the development of animal cruelty, albeit with mixed findings: Baldry (2005) found that bullying victimization was predictive of animal cruelty only among boys, whereas Gullone and Robertson (2008) saw no association between bullying victimization and animal cruelty, but did not conduct separate analyses by gender. Frequency of animal cruelty may also be relevant. For example, Henry and Sanders (2007) found that whereas neither a history of bullying victimization nor bullying perpetration differentiated college males who reported engaging in no animal cruelty from those who reported abusing animals only once, bullying victimization and perpetration were uniquely associated with those who engaged in multiple acts of animal cruelty as opposed to one or no acts. As noted earlier, studies that collect information at multiple points and/or from multiple sources may provide clearer and more compelling findings.

Future research on the applicability of social learning theory to animal cruelty may shed light on some of these finer-grained aspects. For example, since social learning theory holds that witnessing the consequences of a behavior observed in others can also influence whether the behavior is learned and imitated, it would be worthwhile to investigate whether children whose peer or adult models were punished for abusing animals are less likely to engage in animal cruelty themselves than those whose models were reinforced for the behavior (for example, receiving approval from others) or who simply got away with it. Further, social learning based on direct observation may be less readily apparent as an explanation for situations where a child is cruel toward animals despite family members and peers consistently modeling positive interactions with animals. In some of these cases, there may simply be an unknown external person modeling animal cruelty for the child. However, it is also possible that other forms of social learning may be operating in such situations: verbal instruction (hearing a description of a behavior and how to engage in it, rather than directly observing it) or symbolic learning (e.g., reading about a real or fictional character engaging in the behavior). These forms of learning may be relevant to "copycat" crimes of animal cruelty, particularly in our media-saturated age.

Ecological Systems Theory

When social learning theory does not fully explain a behavior, it is possible that the more expansive and inclusive bioecological systems model of Bronfenbrenner (1992) could provide additional insights. In this model, there are four systems: microsystem, mesosytem, exoesystem, and macrosystem. The microsystem involves face-to-face interactions of an individual; the mesosystem contains the interactions between microsystems, e.g., home and school; the exosystem involves the interconnections between two or more systems in which the individual may not be present in one setting, e.g., for the child, the relationship between school and parents; and the macrosystem includes cultural, economic, social, and governmental factors that influence the microsystem. Jegatheesan et al. (2020) explored this model as a framework for understanding associations between animal cruelty and other forms of violence, focusing on the interactions between systems and levels that influence the learning and behavior of the humans and animals at the model's center.

Bimodal Theories of Aggression

Both the literature on children's aggression and that on adult aggression have broadly converged on a bimodal classification, using such terms as predatory/proactive/premeditated/instrumental to describe one general mode of aggression and affective/reactive/impulsive/expressive to describe the other (Berkowitz, 1993; Campbell et al., 1999; Crick & Dodge, 1996; Meloy, 1988; Weinshenker & Siegel, 2002). Babcock et al. (2014) caution that the two primary terminology schemes, impulsive/premeditated and reactive/proactive aggression, may not be as interchangeable as previously thought and may actually measure somewhat separate constructs. For the purpose of this discussion, however, we use the terms "reactive" and "proactive" to denote a general distinction between the two major modes of aggression.

Reactive aggression typically occurs in response to a perceived threat or provocation. Meloy (1988, 2002) sees this as "garden variety" violence that typically is preceded by an intense autonomic arousal and a subjective experience of conscious emotion, typically anger or fear. A threat is perceived, it is time-limited, and the goal of the violence is to "return to normal." This contrasts with predatory, or proactive, aggression in which minimal emotion is present and, when present, tends to be positive due to a sense of exhilaration and enhanced self-esteem.

Raine et al. (1998) hypothesized that affectively (reactively) violent offenders would have lower prefrontal activity, higher subcortical activity, and reduced prefrontal/subcortical ratios relative to control subjects, while predatory violent offenders would show relatively normal brain functioning. They studied 15 predatory murderers and nine affective murderers in the left and right hemisphere prefrontal (medial and lateral) and subcortical (amygdala, midbrain, hippocampus, and thalamus) regions, comparing them to 41 "normal" subjects. Glucose metabolism was assessed using positron emission tomography in 41 comparison subjects and the 24 violent offender subjects. Unplanned and impulsive acts of murder were the result of the subject having less ability to regulate and control aggressive impulses due to deficient prefrontal regulation. The authors hypothesized that affective aggression is associated with the development of a lack of control mechanisms identified with prefrontal functioning in the brain, while predatory murderers do not lack this ability.

Other research on reactive violence that may be relevant for understanding the psychology of animal cruelty offenders includes that of Tweed and Dutton (1998), who noted that individuals who exhibit affective or reactive styles may be more likely to engage in interpersonal violence because of a loss of self-control, or because they lack any other coping strategies. The work of Downey and colleagues (Downey et al., 2000a) on rejection sensitivity may also be useful: individuals who are highly rejection sensitive tend to defensively expect, readily perceive, and overreact to perceived rejection by others. In combination with high investment in dating relationships, rejection sensitivity predicts dating violence in college men (Downey et al., 2000b).

Seeking to apply previous work on reactive and proactive violence to the study of animal cruelty, Gupta (2008) examined college students' self-reports of animal cruelty and intimate partner violence. She found strong associations between rejection sensitivity and expressive (reactive) representations of aggression, and between callousness and instrumental (proactive) representations of aggression. For males, callousness directly predicted both intimate partner violence (IPV) and animal cruelty. For females, the pattern appeared more complex. Similar to males, callousness was strongly associated with instrumental, but not expressive representations, and rejection sensitivity was associated with expressive but not instrumental representations. However, unlike with males, for females, instrumental representations were associated with animal cruelty, but not with intimate partner violence.

More recently, Walters and Noon (2015) also attempted to examine reactive vs. proactive aggression in its potential link to animal cruelty. Their results suggested that animal cruelty is associated primarily with tendencies toward proactive behavior and "earns its reputation as a predictor of future criminality by virtue of its association with behaviors that center on instrumental criminality and premeditated violence" (p. 1381). Direct comparison between this finding and those of Gupta (2008) is difficult, however, due to differences in the populations studied: Walters and Noon's sample was predominantly male, and consisted of delinquent youth rather than college students.

To the extent that callousness may be linked to proactive aggression, several studies that have examined associations between callousness and animal cruelty warrant mention here. A connection between callousness and violent and/or generally antisocial behavior is already fairly well established: Frick et al., (2005) found that the presence of callous-unemotional (CU) traits in antisocial youth may designate an especially severe, aggressive, and chronic type of psychopathic disturbance. Directly relating callousness to animal cruelty, Dadds et al. (2006) studied the associations among cruelty to animals, family conflict, and psychopathic traits in childhood. They found that, for both male and female genders, CU traits were associated strongly with animal cruelty. The authors conclude:

> These results suggest that cruelty to animals may be an early manifestation of the subgroup of children developing conduct problems associated with traits of low empathy and callous disregard rather than the more common pathway of externalizing problems and parenting problems (p.411).

Similarly, Vaughn et al. (2011) conclude that "individuals who are cruel to animals are more likely to possess a liability toward callous, unemotional traits that are highly inheritable and less likely to be modified by the environmental input than are bullying behaviors" (p. 3509). Supporting this conclusion, in their prison study cited earlier, Hensley and Tallichet (2008) found that abusing animals "for fun" was closely linked to committing interpersonal violence as an adult. While callousness was not measured directly, participants' indication that they engaged in animal cruelty for amusement points to a strong possibility of callousness among these individuals.

Further study of reactive and proactive styles of aggression, and their relative associations with such traits as rejection sensitivity and callousness, could hold promise for validating a typology of animal abuse motivations that provides stronger models for prevention, prediction, and intervention. For example, Cavell (2000) notes that treatments that teach self-control could benefit the reactive aggressive child more than the proactively aggressive child. Walters et al. (2007) also suggest that different therapy approaches, both cognitive and psychotropic, may be warranted for adults who engage in either proactive or reactive violence. In the treatment of animal cruelty, it could be similarly helpful to know the chosen aggression modality of a perpetrator of animal cruelty because of the potential to develop tailored treatments for both children and adults.

Neurobiological Theories

Understanding the role that genetics and biology might play in the development of aggressive and antisocial behavior and, in particular, intentional cruelty toward animals could be a fruitful line of investigation. Any such discussion should acknowledge that genetic and biological factors are not solely determinative of behavior but have a complex influence on it. Biology is not destiny, however, biological and genetic factors may make individuals more or less vulnerable to other factors such as family dysfunction, early trauma, poor nutrition, inadequate education, lack of social resources, and economic inequality. Numerous factors contribute to the development of childhood aggression, including animal cruelty; however, they can be classified into two major factors: biological and psychosocial (Jianghong, 2004). Moreover, because research suggests that intentional animal cruelty begins at an early age (Loeber et al., 2003; Patterson et al., 1998), it is reasonable to speculate that some forms of early onset animal cruelty may be influenced by the interplay of neurobiological predispositions and the environment.

> In general, the line of research that examines biological underpinnings suggests that ... hyperaggressive youngsters appear to live in a state of chronic central nervous system underarousal.... (I)t is possible that low arousal might indicate an impaired sense of fear or anxiety, which in turn might make it more difficult for the hyper-aggressive youth to learn from punishment (Moeller, 2001, p. 91).

A selected and targeted review of the neuroimaging literature on psychopathic tendencies and antisocial behavior sought to explore the extent to which this literature supports recent cognitive neuro-scientific models of psychopathy and antisocial behavior. Neuroimaging research reveals that individuals who present with a tendency for reactive, but not instrumental, aggression show increased amygdala response to emotionally evocative stimuli. In contrast, individuals with psychopathic tendencies exhibit decreased amygdala and orbitofrontal cortex responses to emotionally provocative stimuli or during emotional learning paradigms (Blair, 2010). Neurobiological weaknesses, as demonstrated by the decreased amygdala response, do not mean that these individuals only have a reduced ability to understand the emotion of others. Instead, evidence suggests that individuals who show little arousal to the distress of others also will exhibit decreased physiological arousal to their own distress (Shirtcliff et al., 2009).

Individuals who commit intentional acts of animal cruelty may exhibit different degrees of biological influences. Those individuals who act because they lack control mechanisms in their brain theoretically need a different type of intervention and would have a different prognosis. For example, a 24-year-old man convicted by a Texas court of aggravated animal cruelty displayed signs of predatory aggression. He was convicted of the torture and death of a cat whom he had taken from her front porch. Over a period of several hours and in several locations, he tortured her in various ways until she died. This is contrasted with other criminal conviction of a young man from Maryland who was convicted of the death of an animal. Enraged at his pit bull puppy, he beat him to death and discarded his body on the street. His act was impulsive and not planned.

Neurobiological approaches also can be useful for understanding animal hoarding, another form of animal cruelty. Dementia and other types of cognitive decline and impairment, including deficits in the areas of attention, memory, decision-making, and categorization, have been associated with hoarding in general (Grisham et al., 2007; Grisham et al., 2010). However, the diagnostic category of Hoarding Disorder in the Fifth Edition of the *Diagnostic and Statistical Manual of Psychiatric Disorders* (American Psychiatric Association, 2013) specifies that the disorder is not diagnosed if the hoarding behavior results directly from degenerative neurocognitive impairment. In Chapter 10 of this book, "Animal Hoarding," the authors detail the characteristics, causes, and interventions for animal hoarding.

Cognitive Theories

There has been considerable research on the relationship between intelligence and other forms of aggressive behavior. The research on the effect of measured IQ on subsequent antisocial behavior coalesces around the following findings: antisocial youth score 8 to 10 points below the mean on IQ; the non-verbal intelligence of antisocial youth is lower; neuropsychological measures indicate that aggressive children also display verbal deficits; and differences in IQ are not explained by socioeconomic status or racial difference, or a greater likelihood of being arrested. Low IQ is both linked to youthful antisocial behavior and later antisocial behavior (Farrington, 2005; Moeller, 2001).

In general, cognitive impairment, or low intelligence, is defined as having low-level verbal intelligence as well as difficulty in manipulating non-verbal concepts and poor reasoning skills (Farrington, 2005). In discussing these cognitive factors, Prior and Paris (2005, p. 17) note, "All of these factors are seen as significant in terms of the development and consolidation of cognitive impairment ..." Determining the cognitive ability of a child, youth, or adult who engages in any form of animal cruelty seems an important factor to consider in designing an intervention. However, as Moeller notes, the research findings are correlative and not causal; "low IQ alone does not seem responsible for children's aggression, and low IQ might only characterize a certain portion of hyper-aggressive children" (2001, p. 188).

Contrasted to level of intelligence are theories of cognitive development, such as that of Piaget. The focus is on stages of development in the thinking process, not on general intelligence. In this construction, there are four stages of cognitive development: the sensorimotor, preoperational, concrete operational and formal operational. Each individual must acquire the skills in one stage before entering the next stage of development. In the sensorimotor stage, one of the major accomplishments is object permanence (i.e., an object continues to exist when out of sight). At the preoperational stage, it is difficult for the child to take another person's viewpoint. By the concrete operational stage, thinking becomes more logical and less egocentric, but only in the formal operational stage is it possible to entertain multiple potential solutions to problems. When advancing through stages, it is not simply that the child has more information about the world, but that the child fundamentally has a different approach to how the world is understood (Evans, 1973).

Some forms of animal cruelty, especially the neglect of an animal, may be partly explained by the possibility that the individual has not progressed beyond a concrete operational stage of thinking to a formal operational style. Especially in the early stages of concrete thinking, it is difficult to understand another's viewpoint. In this situation, an individual's assessment of an animal on a chain without proper nutrition may not be the same as an individual who had gained a higher degree of cognitive development. The remediation in this case would be an educational approach that focused on the person's ability to take another's perspective or feeling state.

Also relevant to the development of aggression is the concept of hostile attributional bias. Aggressive children tend to attribute hostile intentions to others and view these others as enemies who require a forceful response. Cognitive-behavior based treatment is one of the treatments of choice for children with conduct disorder (Kazdin, 1994). For example, a child with tendencies toward hostile attributional bias may be more likely to assume that the reason his dog upset his water bowl was to "get even" with him for not taking him for a walk. He could respond by beating the dog, who in turn becomes more wary of the child, leading the child to assume that the dog is punishing him.

In addition to the specific case of attributional bias as a cognitive miscue that can lead to poor decision-making, other cognitive factors include models of problem solving, notions of information processing, formulations of social skills, and concepts of social scripts (Pepler & Slaby, 1994).

The implication of applying cognitive theories to any form of animal cruelty, whether neglect or intentional, animal fighting or animal hoarding, is that there is an assumption that cognitions can be altered. For example, the ways in which children use social information processing skills influences their choice of behavior. Reactive-aggressive children demonstrate a hostile bias, leading to reactive anger. Other aggressive children evaluate aggression and its consequences as relatively useful in achieving desired outcomes, and some social information processing leads children to select instrumental goals in a situation rather than relational goals (Crick & Dodge, 1996). Interventions should target these cognitions, challenge them, and offer alternatives that produce more desirable outcomes.

Developmental Pathways of Aggression

The literature on developmental pathways, rather than seeking to create typologies of violent behavior such as predatory and affective, focuses more on trying to understand how this behavior develops and maintains itself, or is extinguished, over a lifetime. Some of the literature on developmental pathways focuses on trying to identify "onset" and then tracking which factors are associated with the continuation of antisocial behavior into adolescence and adulthood and which may "protect" an individual from such a trajectory. There is consistent agreement in the field of developmental pathways of aggression that early aggression is "a behavioral problem that is a major risk factor for later juvenile delinquency, adult crime, and violence (Farrington, 1995; Moffitt et al., 1996). Underscoring the importance of early onset, DeLisi et al. (2013, p. 12) somewhat ironically noted, "The broader significance of early onset delinquency is never trite."

In the following section, we will examine the literature on developmental pathways of aggressive behavior in general and then look at research which provides evidence for the notion that the appearance of animal cruelty is a significant indicator in the developmental pathways of aggressive behavior.

Models for aggression in general. Reviewing the research on child delinquency, Loeber et al. (2003) make the following points:

- Years of criminology research strongly support the notion that the best predictor of future behavior is past behavior.
- The antisocial careers of male juvenile offenders start, on average, at age 7.
- The preschool years are critical times to identify, and intervene, to prevent disruptive behavior.

The authors also list the factors that could have the most influence on the development of anti- and pro-social behavior during preschool and beyond: language, temperamental characteristics (which would include neurobiological factors), and low attachment to caregivers. We discuss the influences of neurobiological factors and ability to attach in other sections of this chapter.

Key findings from longitudinal data analyzed by Tremblay et al. (2003) confirm some of the points made by Loeber et al. (2006). These findings include: 1) that kindergarten disruptive behavior predicts delinquency during the transition from childhood to early adolescence, and 2) kindergarten personality predicts delinquency during the transition from childhood to adolescence. Regarding personality, high impulsive and low anxious low reward dependent subjects were the most at risk for antisocial behavior.

Considering the early onset of aggressive behaviors, Tremblay et al. (2003) wondered, "When does it begin? The question is significant because if animal cruelty is one of the manifestations of deviant behavior than it is critical to identify and understand it, and develop appropriate responses to it." Equally important is the question of how to determine when an individual no longer engages in antisocial behavior. Three ways to characterize this variable have been outlined: recidivism, termination, and desistance. Recidivism and termination refer to a point in time when an individual either re-commits a crime (recidivism) or ceases all criminal activity (termination). A greater focus on desistance has predominated in the criminal justice field in recent years. In a study conducted for the National Institute of Justice, desistance from crime "... is regarded as a process rather than an event" (Kazemian, 2021). Using the framework of desistance as a process bears implications for how to evaluate the success or failure of treatment programs for animal cruelty and other anti-social behaviors. Others propose that desistance is well-suited for a biosocial perspective and can be understood as a process that occurs naturally over time or can be encouraged by well-designed intervention efforts (Boisvert, 2021).

One of the challenges in understanding the development of animal cruelty has been that very few studies on the development of aggression have included questions about animal cruelty. However, one significant longitudinal study, the "Pittsburgh study," did so. The researchers (Loeber et al., 2006) used a model that stresses the interaction among risk and protective factors thought to influence tendencies to engage in antisocial acts and to commit offenses. They assumed that individual development occurs in the context of different social environments that exert different influences on the child. In addition to looking at predictors and trajectories of the development of antisocial, aggressive behavior, factors associated with persistence, and desistence, in antisocial behavior were examined. Of interest to current purposes, one of the four factors associated with persistence in antisocial, aggressive behavior from early childhood to adulthood was physical aggression toward people and animals. (R. Loeber, personal communication, June 24, 2004).

Animal Cruelty and Developmental Pathways of Aggression

As mentioned earlier, many of the studies on the causes and correlates of animal cruelty have been limited by their design (e.g., use of convenience samples, lack of a control group). Integrating the literature on the developmental pathways of aggression with the literature on the etiology of animal cruelty could be a productive effort. The research findings from the extensive research on developmental pathways is robust and can support and explicate the research that has focused on the significance of animal cruelty as an early marker of deviant behavior.

Trying to understand the etiology and maintenance of aggression, including animal cruelty, is a complicated endeavor. Few would contend that there is *one* individual representation of aggression or antisocial behavior that would offer a direct causal link to later aggression, whether it is animal cruelty, low verbal skills, or an impulsive temperament. Human behavior is complex, representing multiple influences. Rather, research—whether examining aggression in general or animal cruelty in particular—points to the significance of animal cruelty as *one* of the complex set of psychosocial factors to consider in understanding developmental pathways of aggression.

Central to underlying theories of animal cruelty in its possible connections to other aggression has been the debate contrasting the so-named graduation/progression hypothesis (animal cruelty preceding interpersonal violence) and the deviance generalization hypothesis (animal cruelty occurring in association with other criminal and socially deviant acts, without implication of temporal sequencing). In their systematic review of 32 studies examining associations between animal cruelty and violence among children and adolescents, Longobardi and Badenes-Ribera (2019) found some support for both hypotheses, with those findings fitting the graduation hypothesis generally involving recurrent, as opposed to isolated, acts of animal cruelty. It is possible that graduation and deviance generalization represent different groups of individuals with different underlying mechanisms for their aggression.

Attachment Theory

The "father" of attachment theory was John Bowlby, who established the core of attachment theory with his three volumes, Attachment (1969), Separation (1973) and Loss (1980). Drawing upon concepts from ethology, cybernetics, information processing, developmental psychology, and psychoanalysis, the basic premise of attachment theory is that there is a primary attachment between a child and her or his caregiver that is "hard wired" for evolutionary purposes, and that anxiety is experienced when that attachment is threatened. Additionally, grief is experienced when there is a loss. If Bowlby was the "father" of attachment theory, then Mary Ainsworth was the "mother," or perhaps the "big sister," by expanding and validating his theory with the innovative methodology referred to as the "Strange Situation." This situation tested types of attachment children had to their caregivers. In this test situation, an infant and the infant's caregiver would be brought into a room with an adult stranger, and the mother would leave. The reaction of the infant when the caregiver left and then returned was noted. Since Bowlby and Ainsworth, there have been scores of researchers examining various facets of attachment and its importance to development, well-being, and its relationship to violent behavior.

Ainsworth (1978) and her colleagues identified three styles of attachment. Secure attachment was characterized by infants who competently expressed their needs and accepted maternal care. The other two were pathological: avoidant, represented by infants who appeared minimally distressed when the caregiver left and avoided her when she returned, and ambivalent/resistant, characterized by infants who had great difficulty with separating and also could not find comfort from their caregivers upon their return.

Bartholomew (1990, 1994, 1997) expanded on the Bowlby/Ainsworth work to develop models of adult attachment. In the adult model, three pathological types of attachment are considered: 1) preoccupied individuals who have a negative perception of self and a positive perception of others, and are very dependent on the other's approval and acceptance; 2) fearful individuals who have a negative perception of self and others and avoid close contact, fearing rejection; 3) dismissing individuals who have a positive perception of self and a negative perception of others. A fourth type of adult attachment pathology not included in the Bartholomew model is the disorganized individual, which may be associated with severely disturbed individuals (Fonagy, 1996).

Meloy (2003) observed the potential of attachment theory and pathological attachment for understanding criminal behavior, asserting the following:

- Insecure attachment is a risk factor for violent criminality.
- Secure attachment is likely a protective factor, particularly when the child is raised in a deprived environment.
- The capacity to reflect, or take another's perspective, may be an important mediating variable for affective violence.
- Dismissing pathologies of attachment may be associated with constitutional, or temperamental, characteristics and disorganized attachment may be associated with trauma.

This assessment has since been supported by ongoing research indicating that insecure attachment may be strongly associated with many types of criminality (Ogilvie et al., 2014). The construct of psychopathy is prominent in such models. For example, Khetrapal (2009) notes that individuals exhibiting psychopathy also exhibit a form of disorganized attachment. He continues, "The erratic style of attachment not only negatively affects psychosocial adjustment but also has a negative influence on the neurobiological systems ... that are responsible for functions like emotional processing and social adjustment" (p. 9). Referencing the Psychopathy Checklist—Revised (PCL-R; Hare, 2003), Van den Berg and Oei (2009) explain:

> Dismissed and disorganized/unresolved attachment representations can fairly easily be identified in PCL-R items: factors 1 and 2, the interpersonal and affective factors, provide insights into how psychopathic patients avoid reciprocal relationships; factor 4, the antisocial lifestyle factor, corresponds to disorganized attachment representations, recognizable by impulsive and irresponsible behavior (p. 49).

Other studies of attachment representations of juvenile and incarcerated adult offenders support the idea that psychopathy, in part, is influenced by impairments in attachment, and is a developmental process (Frodi et al., 2001; Saltaris, 2002). In a Swedish study, 24 adult psychopathic criminal offenders incarcerated in either a psychiatric hospital or a medium security prison were assessed with Hare's PCL-R, then interviewed with the Adult Attachment Interview, and completed a self-report questionnaire about parent rearing techniques. There was an extensive over-representation of individuals who were dismissive of attachment and attachment-related experiences. Also, there was an association between a higher psychopathy score and family constellation of a rejecting father and an emotionally very warm, idealized mother (Frodi et al., 2001).

Attachment also has been proposed as an important factor in the psychology of hoarding (Patronek & Nathanson, 2009; see Chapter 10). It is proposed that avoidance and insecure attachment are central to many animal hoarding cases, and suggest that the compulsive caregiving and self-reparative relationships described in the literature on disordered attachment styles may lend themselves to the accumulation of animals perceived to be in need. While this chapter separates hoarding from other forms of cruelty, it appears that attachment and attachment problems may form a useful framework for examining the full spectrum of animal cruelty to the extent that we conceptualize cruelty as "the human-animal bond gone awry."

In general, the interesting research findings from the field of attachment and violence provide support for the careful examination of how attachment styles may influence the etiology and typologies of animal cruelty offenders and how interventions could be tailored to take this into account.

Empathy Development

Prior to this point, we have focused on the data that link callousness to the etiology and manifestation of violent behavior, including animal cruelty. However, as Shirtcliff et al. (2009) note, there is a "counterpart" to callousness. Many researchers have suggested that the counterpart is the trait of empathy, and some have suggested that callousness is a disorder of empathy (Soderstrom, 2003).

Numerous studies have documented that empathy plays a central role in moral reasoning, motivates prosocial behaviors, and inhibits aggression toward others (Decety & Lamm, 2006). Empathy involves neural processes and social learning. Decety and Lamm conclude that empathy relies "both on bottom-up information processing (shared neural systems between first-hand emotional experiences and the perception or imagination of the other's experience) as well as top-down information processing that allows modulation and self-regulation" (p. 1160). Some of the latest research on how to understand empathy and its development also focuses on mapping neural pathways (Interlandi, 2015). The interest in finding neural pathways to the development of empathy in no way implies that this learning is fixed. Rather, it appears that the development and alternation of neural pathways can, to some extent, be influenced by behavioral and social interventions. While acknowledging the interplay of brain structure, hormonal processing, and social and psychological learning in the development of empathy, Randour (2005) reviewed the research on the development and teaching of empathy and proposed that empathy is a skill that can be taught and learned. Noting that empathy plays an important role in a child's success at school and in their social and personal lives, she linked empathy development to the role that animals play in its creation and development.

Recognizing the development of empathy may be especially appropriate for treating certain types of offenders who exhibit little concern for others (i.e., callousness). Burke (2001) identified the development of empathy as a part of the treatment for adolescent sex offenders. Another study employed the use of rescued shelter animals to teach a message of anti-violence and to convey principles of prosocial behavior to children in elementary and middle school (Sprinkle, 2008). Using student self-report, disciplinary, and teacher observational data to measure violent and aggressive behaviors, beliefs about aggression, and level of empathy, the study found the programs significantly altered students' normative beliefs about aggression, levels of empathy, and the students participating also showed a decrease in aggressive behaviors.

Conclusion

This chapter proposed that there are many different psychological theories that can aid our understanding of the psychology of animal cruelty. As cruelty toward animals may occur in many different forms, and for many different reasons, it follows that any single theory is likely insufficient to encompass such heterogeneous behavior. Moreover, there is often more than one theory that can explicate a given form of animal cruelty. Further, even within a single form of animal cruelty, and even between two apparently similar acts (for example, two ten-year-old children, each referred to a psychologist after kicking the family dog), individual presentations and motivations may differ greatly, requiring different approaches to understand each case.

Taken both individually and together, the theories reviewed in this chapter—with origins in understanding human-directed aggression—offer potentially useful starting points for the understanding of animal-directed maltreatment. Owing to the comparative paucity of scholarship on animal-related topics, further research is greatly needed to more clearly establish the validity of these theories in their application to animal cruelty—not only in general, but for which individuals and behaviors under which circumstances.

References

Agnew, R. (1998). The causes of animal abuse: A social-psychological analysis. *Theoretical Criminology*, *22*, 177–209.

Ainsworth, M. D. S., Blehar, M. C., Waters, E., & Wall, S. (1978). *Patterns of attachment: A psychological study of the strange situation*. Lawrence Erlbaum Associates.

American Psychiatric Association. (2013). *Diagnostic and statistical manual of mental disorders* (5th ed.). https://doi.org/10.1176/appi.books.9780890425596.

Arluke, A., Levin, J., Luke, C. & Ascione, F. (1999). The relationship of animal abuse to violence and other forms of antisocial behavior. *Journal of Interpersonal Violence, 14,* 963–975.

Ascione, F. R. (1993). Children who are cruel to animals: A review of research and implications for developmental psychopathology. *Anthrozoös, 6,* 226–247.

Ascione, F. R. (2001). Animal abuse and youth violence. *Juvenile Justice Bulletin.* U.S. Department of Justice.

Ascione, F. R., Friedrich, W. N., Heath, J, & Hayashi, K. (2003). Cruelty to animals in normative, sexually abused, and outpatient psychiatric samples of 6- to 12-year-old children: Relations to maltreatment and exposure to domestic violence. *Anthrozoös, 16,* 194–210.

Ascione, F. R., Weber, C. V., Thompson, T. M., Heath, J., Maruyama, M., & Hayashi, K. (2007). Battered pets and domestic violence: Animal abuse reported by women experiencing intimate violence and by non-abused women. *Violence Against Women, 13,* 354–373.

Babcock, J. C., Tharp, A. L. T., Sharp, C., Heppner, W., & Stanford, M. S. (2014). Similarities and differences in impulsive/premeditated and reactive/proactive bimodal classifications of aggression. *Aggression and Violent Behavior, 19,* 251–262.

Baldry, A. C. (2003). Animal abuse and exposure to interparental violence in Italian youth. *Journal of Interpersonal Violence, 18,* 258–281.

Baldry, A. C. (2005). Animal abuse among preadolescents directly and indirectly victimized at school and at home. *Criminal Behavior and Mental Health, 15,* 97–110.

Bandura, A., Ross, D. & Ross, S. A. (1961). Transmission of aggression through imitation of aggressive models. *Journal of Abnormal and Social Psychology, 63,* 575–82.

Bandura, A. (1973). *Aggression: A social learning analysis.* Prentice Hall.

Barrett, B. J., Fitzgerald, A., Stevenson, R., & Cheung, C. H. (2020). Animal maltreatment as a risk marker of more frequent and severe forms of intimate partner violence. *Journal of Interpersonal Violence, 35(23–24),* 5131–5156.

Bartholomew, K. (1990). Avoidance of intimacy: An attachment perspective. *Journal of Social and Personal Relationships, 7,* 147–178.

Bartholomew, K. (1994). The assessment of individual differences in adult attachment. *Psychological Inquiry, 5,* 23–17.

Bartholomew, K. (1997). Adult attachment processes: Individual and couple perspectives. British *Journal of Medical Psychology, 70,* 249–263.

Becker, K. K., Stuwig, J., Herrera, V. M., & McCloskey, L. A. (2004). A study of firesettting and animal cruelty in children: Family influences and adolescent outcomes. *Journal of the American Academy of Child & Adolescent Psychiatry, 43,* 905–912.

Berkowitz, L. (1993). *Aggression: Its causes, consequences, and control.* McGraw-Hill.

Blair, R. J. (2010). Neuroimaging of psychopathy and antisocial behavior: A targeted review. *Current Psychiatry Reports, 12,* 76–82.

Boisvert, D. L., (2021). Biosocial factors and their influence on desistance. NCJ301499, in *Desistance from crime: Implications for research, policy, and practice.* U.S. Department of Justice, National Institute of Justice, NCJ301497.

Bowlby, J. (1969*). Attachment & loss: Vol. 1: Attachment* (2nd ed.). Basic Books.

Bowlby, J. (1973). *Attachment and loss: Vol. 2. Separation.* Basic Books.

Bowlby, J. (1980). *Attachment & loss. Vol. 3. Loss, sadness, and depression.* Basic Books.

Bright, M. A., Huq, M. S., Spencer, T., Applebaum, J. W., & Hardt, N. (2018). Animal cruelty as an indicator of family trauma: Using adverse childhood experiences to look beyond child abuse and domestic violence. *Child Abuse and Neglect, 76,* 287–296.

Bronfenbrenner, U. (1992). *Ecological systems theory.* Jessica Kingsley Publishers.

Burchfield, K. B. (2018). The nature of animal crime: Scope and severity in Chicago. *Crime & Delinquency, 64,* 1904–1924.

Burke, D. M. (2001). Empathy in sexually offending and non-offending adolescent males. *Journal of Interpersonal Violence, 16,* 222–233.

Campbell, A., Muncer, S., McManus, I. C., & Woodhouse, D. (1999). Instrumental and expressive representations of aggression: One scale or two? *Aggressive Behavior, 25,* 435–444.

Cavell, T. A. (2000*). Working with parents of aggressive children: A practitioner's guide.* American Psychological Association.

Crick, N. R. & Dodge, K. A. (1996). Social information processing mechanisms in reactive and proactive aggression. *Child Development, 67,* 993–1002.

Currie, C. L. (2006). Animal cruelty by children exposed to domestic violence. *Child Cruelty & Neglect, 30,* 425–435.

Dadds, M. R., Whiting, C., & Hawes, D. J. (2006). Associations among cruelty to animals, family conflict, and psychopathic traits in childhood. *Journal of Interpersonal Violence, 3,* 411–429.

Dadds, M. R. Jambrak, J., Pasalich, D., Hawes, D. J., & Brennan, J. (2011) Impaired attention to the eyes of attachment figures and the developmental origins of psychopathy. *Journal of Child Psychology and Psychiatry, 52,* 238–245.

Decety, J., & Lamm, C. (2006), Human empathy through the lens of social neuroscience. *The Scientific Journal, 6,* 1146–1163.

DeGue, S., & DiLillo, D. (2009). Is animal cruelty a "red flag" for family violence? Investigating co-occurring violence toward children, partners, and pets. *Journal of Interpersonal Violence, 24,* 1036–1056.

DeLisi, M., Neppl, T. K., Lohman, B. J., Vaughn, M. G., & Shook, J. J. (2013). Early starters: Which type of criminal onset matters most for delinquent careers? *Journal of Criminal Justice, 41,* 12–17.

Dollard, J., Doob, L. W., Miller, N. E., Mowrer, O. H., & Sears, R. R. (1939). *Frustration and aggression.* Yale University Press.

Downey, G., Feldman, S. & Ayduk, O. (2000a) Rejection sensitivity for intimate relationships. *Journal of Science and Personality Psychology, 70*, 1327–1343.

Downey, G., Feldman, S. & Ayduk, O. (2000b) Rejection sensitivity and male violence in romantic relationships. *Personal Relationships, 7*, 45–61.

Evans, R. (1973). *Jean Piaget: The Man and His Ideas*. E. P. Dutton & Co., Inc.

Farrington, D. P. (1995). The development of offending and anti-social behavior from childhood: *Child Psychology and Psychiatry, 36*, 929–964.

Farrington, D. P. (2005). Childhood origins of antisocial behavior. Special issue. *Forensic Psychology, 12*, 177–190.

Febres, J., Brasfield, H., Shorey, R. C., Elmquist, J., Ninnemann, A., Schonrum, Y. C. Stuart, G. (2014). Adulthood animal abuse among men arrested for domestic violence. *Violence Against Women, 20*, 1059–1077.

Flynn, C. P. (1999). Animal abuse in childhood and later support for interpersonal violence in families. *Society & Animals, 8*, 99–127.

Fonagy, P. (1996). Male perpetrators of violence against women: An attachment theory perspective. *Journal of Applied Psychoanalytic Studies, 1*, 7–27.

Frick, P. J., Lahey, B. B., Loeber, R., Tannenbaum, L., Van Horn, Y., Christ, M. A. G., & Hanson, K. (1993). Oppositional defiant disorder and conduct disorder: A meta-analytic review of factor analyses and cross-validation in a clinic sample. *Clinical Psychology Review, 13*(4), 319–340.

Frick, P. J., Stickle, T. R., Dandreaux, D. M., Farrell, J. J., & Kimonis, E. R. (2005). Traits in predicting the severity and stability of conduct disorder and delinquency. *Journal of Abnormal Psychology, 33*, 471–487.

Frodi, A., Dernevik, M., Sepa, A., Philipson, J., & Bragesjo, M. (2001). Current attachment representations of incarcerated offenders varying in degree of psychopathy. *Attachment and human development, 3*(2), 269–283.

Gould, J. L. 2002. Learning instincts. In C. R. Gallistel (Ed.), *Stevens' handbook of experimental psychology* (3rd ed.) (pp. 239–257). John Wiley and Sons.

Grisham, J. R., Brown, T. A., Savage, C. R., Steketee, G., & Barlow, D. H. (2007). Neuropsychological impairment associated with compulsive hoarding. *Behavioral Research Therapy, 45*, 1471–1483.

Grisham, J. R., Norberg, M. M., Wiliam, A. D., Certoma, S. P. & Kadib, R. (2010). Categorization and cognitive deficits in compulsive hoarding. *Behavior Research Therapy. 48*, 866–872.

Gullone, E., & Robertson, N. (2008). The relationship between bullying and animal abuse behaviors in adolescents: The importance of witnessing animal abuse. *Journal of Applied Developmental Psychology, 29*, 371–379.

Gullone E., An evaluative review of theories related to animal cruelty, *Journal of Animal Ethics, 4*, 37–57.

Gupta, M. (2008). Functional links between intimate partner violence and animal abuse: Personality features and representations of aggression. *Society & Animals, 16*, 223–242.

Hare, R. D. (2003). *The Hare Psychopathy Checklist—Revised* (2nd ed.). Multi-Health Systems.

Hensley, C., & Tallichet, S. E. (2008). The effect of inmates' self-reported childhood and adolescent animal cruelty: Motivations on the number of convictions for adult violent interpersonal crimes. *International Journal of Offender Therapy and Comparative Criminology, 52*, 175–184.

Henderson, B. B., Hensley, C., & Tallichet, S. E. (2011). Childhood animal cruelty methods and their link to adult interpersonal violence. *Journal of Interpersonal Violence, 26*, 2211–2227.

Henry, B. C., & Sanders, C. E. (2007). Bullying and animal abuse: Is there a connection? *Society & Animals, 15*, 107–126.

Hensley, C. & Tallichet, S. E. (2008). The effect of inmates' self-reported childhood and adolescent animal cruelty motivations on the number of convictions for adult violent interpersonal crimes. *Journal of Offender Therapy and Comparative Criminology, 52*, 175–184.

Hensley, C., Tallichet, S. & Dutkiewicz, E. (2008). Recurrent animal cruelty: Is there a relationship to adult recurrent interpersonal violence? *Criminal Justice Review, 34*, 248–257.

Hoffer, T., Hargreaves-Cormany, Muirhood, Y., & Meloy, J. R. (2018). *Violence in animal cruelty offenders*. Springer.

Interlandi, J. (2015, March 22). The empathy gap. *New York Times Magazine*. MM50.

Jegatheesan, B., Enders-Siegers, M., Omerod, E., & Boyden, P. (2020). Understanding the link between animal cruelty and family violence: The bioecological systems model. International Journal of Research in Public Health, 17, 3116

Jianghong, L. (2004). Childhood externalizing behavior: theory and implications. *Journal of Child and Adolescent Psychiatric Nursing, 17*, 93–103.

Kazdin, A. E. (1994). Intervention for aggressive and antisocial children. In L. D. Eron, J. H, Gentry & P. Schegel (Eds.), *Reason to hope: A psychosocial perspective on violence & youth* (pp. 341–382). American Psychological Association.

Kazemian, L. (2021). Pathways to desistance from crime among juveniles and adults: Applications to criminal justice policy and practice. NCJ301503, in *Desistance from crime: Implications for research, policy and practice.* U.S. Department of Justice, National Institute of Justice, 2021), NCJ 301497.

Khetrapal, N. (2009). The early attachment experiences are the roots of psychopathy. *Interpersona: An International Journal of Personal Relationships, 3*, 1–13.

Knight, K. E., Ellis, C. & Simmons, S. B. (2014). Parental predictors of children's animal abuse: Findings from a national and intergenerational sample. *Journal of Interpersonal Violence,* 1–21.

Levitt, L., Hoffer, T. A., & Loper, A. B. (2016). Criminal histories of a subsample of animal cruelty offenders. *Aggression and Violent Behavior, 30,* 45–58.

Loeber, R., Farrington, D. P., Petechuck, D. (2003). Child delinquency: Early intervention and prevention. *Bulletin.* Washington, DC: U.S. Department of Justice, Office of Juvenile Justice and Delinquency Prevention.

Loeber, R., Slot, N. W. & Stouthamer-Loeber, M. (2006). A three-dimensional, cumulative developmental model of serious delinquency. In P. O. H. Wilstroom & R. Sampson (Eds.), *The explanation of crime: Contexts and mechanisms* (pp.153–194). Cambridge University Press.

Lohr, J. M., Olatunji, B. O., Baumeister, R. F., & Bushman, B. J. (2007). The psychology of anger venting and empirically supported alternatives that do no harm. *Scientific Review of Mental Health Practice, 5,* 53–64.

Longobardi, C., & Badenes-Ribera, L. (2019). The relationship between animal cruelty in children and adolescent and interpersonal violence: A systematic review. *Aggression and Violent Behavior, 46,* 201–211.

Luk, E. S. L., Staiger, P. K., Wong, L. & Mathai, J. (1999). Children who are cruel to animals: A revisit. *Australian and New Zealand Journal of Psychiatry, 33,* 29–36.

McEwen, F. S., Moffitt, T. E., Arseneault, L. (2014). Is childhood cruelty to animals a marker for physical maltreatment in a prospective cohort study of children? *Child Cruelty & Neglect, 28,* 533–543.

Meloy, R. J. (1988). *The psychopathic mind: Origins, dynamics, and treatment.* Jason Aronson.

Meloy, R. J. (2003). Pathologies of attachment, violence, and criminality. In A. Goldstein (Ed.), *Handbook of psychology* (Vol. 11, pp. 509–526). Wiley.

Moeller, T. G. (2001). *Youth aggression and violence: A psychological approach.* Lawrence Erlbaum Associates.

Moffitt, T. E., Caspi, A., Dickson, N., Silva, P., & Stanton, W. (1996). Childhood-onset versus adolescent-onset antisocial conduct problems in males: Natural history from ages 3 to 18 years. *Development and Psychopathology, 1,* 104–118.

Ogilvie, C.A., Newman, E., Todd, L., & Peck, D. (2014). Attachment & violent offending: A meta-analysis. *Aggression and Violent Behavior, 19,* 322–339.

Patronek, G. J., & Nathanson, J. N. (2009). A theoretical perspective to inform assessment and treatment strategies for animal hoarders. *Clinical Psychology Review, 29,* 274–281.

Patterson, G. R., Forgatch, M. S., Yoerger, K. L., & Stoolmiller, M. (1998). Variables that initiate and maintain an early-onset trajectory for juvenile offending. *Development and Psychopathology, 10*, 531–547.

Pepler, D. J. & Slaby, R. G. (1994). Theoretical and developmental perspectives on youth and violence. In L. D. Eron, J. H. Gentry & P. Schegel (Eds.), *Reason to hope: A psychosocial perspective on violence & youth* (pp. 27–58). American Psychological Association.

Prior, D. & Paris, A. (2005). Preventing children's involvement in crime and anti-social behavior: A literature review. National Evaluation of the Children's Fund. Research Report. No. 623. University of Birmingham.

Raine, A., Meloy, J. R., Bihrle, S. Stoddard, J., Lacasse, L. & Buchsbaum, M. S. (1998). Reduced prefrontal and increased subcortical brain functioning assessed using positron emission tomography to predatory and affective murderers. *Behavioral Science & the Law, 16,* 319–332.

Randour, M. L. (2005). *The empathy connection*. Doris Day Animal Foundation.

Saltaris, C. (2002). Psychopathy in juvenile offenders: Can temperament and attachment be considered as robust developmental precursors? *Clinical Psychology Review, 22,* 729–752.

Shirtcliff, E. A., Vitacco, M. J., Graf, S. R., Gostisha, A. J., Merz, J. L., & Zahn-Waxler, C. (2009) Neurobiology of empathy and callousness: implications for the development of antisocial behavior. *Behavioral Science & the Law*, 27(2), 137–71.

Simmons, C. A. & Lehmann, P. (2007). Exploring the link between pet abuse and controlling behaviors in violent relationships. *Journal of Interpersonal Violence, 22,* 1211–1222.

Soderstrom, H. (2003). Psychopathy as a disorder of empathy. *European Child Adolescence Psychiatry, 12,* 249–252.

Sprinkle, J. E. (2008). Animals, empathy, and violence: Can animals be used to convey principles of prosocial behavior to children? *Youth Violence and Juvenile Justice, 6, 47–58.*

Thompson, K. L., & Gullone, E. (2006). An investigation into the association between the witnessing of animal abuse and adolescents' behavior toward animals. *Society & Animals, 14,* 221–243.

Tavris, C. (1982). *Anger: The misunderstood emotion.* Simon & Schuster.

Tremblay, R. E., Vitaro, F., Nagin, D., Pagani, L. & Seguin, J. R. (2003). The Montreal longitudinal and experimental study: Rediscovering the power of descriptions. In T. P. Thornberry & M. D. Krohn (Eds.), *Taking stock of delinquency: An overview of findings from contemporary longitudinal studies* (pp. 205–254). Kluwer Academic.

Tweed, R. G. & Dutton, D. G. (1998). A comparison of impulsive and instrumental subgroups of batterers. *Violence and Victims, 13,* 217–230.

Van den Berg, A. & Oei, T. L. (2009). Attachment and psychopathy in forensic patients. *Mental Health Review Journal, 14,* 40–51.

Vaughn, M. G., Fu, W., DeLisi, M., Beaver, K. M., & Perron, B. E. (2009). Correlates of cruelty to animals in the United States: Results from the National Epidemiologic Survey on Alcohol and Related Conditions. *Journal of Psychiatric Research, 43,* 1213–1218.

Vaughn, M. G., Fu, Q., Beaver, K. M., DeLisi, M., Perron, B. E., & Howard, M. O. (2011). Effects of childhood adversity on bullying and cruelty to animals in the United States: Findings from a national sample. *Journal of Interpersonal Violence, 26,* 3509–3525.

Walters, G. D. (2013). Testing the specificity postulate of the violence graduation hypothesis: Meta-analyses of the animal cruelty-offending relationship. *Aggression and Violent Behavior, 187,* 97–802.

Walters, G. D., Frederick, A. A., & Schlauch, C. (2007). Postdicting arrests for proactive and reactive aggression with the PICTS Proactive and Reactive Composite Scales. *Journal of Interpersonal Violence, 22,* 1415–1430.

Walters, G. D. & Noon, A. (2015). Family context and externalizing correlates of childhood animal cruelty in adjudicated delinquents. *Journal of Interpersonal Violence, 30,* 1369–1386.

Walton-Moss, B. J., Manganello, J., Frye, V., & Campbell, J. D. (2005). Risk factors for intimate partner violence and associated injury among urban women. *Journal of Community Health, 30,* 377–389.

Weinshenker, N. J., & Siegel, A. (2002). Bimodal classification of aggression: Affective defense and predatory attack. *Aggression and Violent Behavior, 7,* 237–250.

Section V

Current and Controversial Topics

Chapter 17

Animal Cruelty in the Age of Social Media

Patricia Grove

Introduction

Within the past ten years, platforms like Instagram, Facebook, Twitter, and YouTube have exploded with activity and new users. Social media has become an integral part of society; it allows for constant communication and engagement on a plethora of shared beliefs. This somewhat recent invention has both its benefits and its downfalls; information is more readily available, yet misinformation tends to thrive on these platforms. In terms of animals, many users love to share pictures and videos of their beloved furry friends. Pet influencers, a new phenomenon, garner hundreds of thousands of followers and tend to be extremely popular. Still, the intersection of animal content and social media is not always positive. Recently, there have been claims of mass circulation of animal cruelty content: content that involves purposefully hurting or neglecting a variety of animals for a variety of reasons. User agreements and community guidelines tend to gloss over instances of animal abuse, allowing for animal cruelty content to fall through the cracks of review. There is much to be learned about how animal cruelty content thrives on social media and whether it thrives at all.

There is much to examine when viewing the intersection of animal cruelty and social media. On a grander scale, there are many unanswered questions about the aspects of social media that attract animal cruelty content creators and animal rights activists alike. The usage and gains from social media for these content creators remains unclear. Considering that social media is still a relatively new phenomenon, little information exists on its influence on animal cruelty. For the purpose of simplicity, this chapter aims to analyze general factors associated with animal cruelty and social media: the current literature, types of prevalent cruelty, current policies and regulations, activism, and legal issues associated with social media. It would be negligent to fail to mention news media and reality TV, as they are major forms of media that frequently intersect with animal cruelty. Therefore, two sections will be dedicated to a brief review of news media and reality TV.

The Current Literature

Despite claims of mass circulation of animal cruelty images and videos on social media, the empirical research surrounding the topic is scarce. Research on animal cruelty in media typically focuses on news media, reporting, and public perceptions. Findings regarding cruelty on social media are few and far between. However, one major study was conducted in 2021. The Asia for Animals Coalition (AfA), a network of animal rights groups, conducted a large-scale study with the aim of finding reoccurring themes within animal cruelty posts on social media. The study covers a large range of topics, including types of animal cruelty content, platforms and monetization, legalities, social impacts, and future suggestions. The AfA defined animal cruelty as "a range of human behaviours, performed intentionally or unintentionally, that cause animals harm or suffering which may be immediate or long-term, physical, emotional or psychological" (Social Media Animal Cruelty Coalition [SMACC], 2021). The AfA studied three main platforms: YouTube, Tik Tok, and Facebook. Of these three platforms, an overwhelming majority (89.2%) of the animal cruelty videos were found on YouTube (SMACC, 2021). Findings do not suggest that YouTube hosts the most animal cruelty content; rather, animal cruelty content is easiest to find on that platform. Over the span of thirteen months, AfA documented a total of 5,480 individual videos of animal cruelty (SMACC, 2021). The types of cruelty documented range from obvious and intentional to obvious and unintentional, with obvious and intentional (77.5%) being the most documented form of cruelty (SMACC, 2021). The top five types of animal species featured in these videos were birds, dogs/cats, wildlife, reptiles, and primates, in that order (SMACC, 2021).

The AfA also analyzed how perpetrators of online animal cruelty operate. Findings indicate that perpetrators typically are active on more than one platform (SMACC, 2021). Users will reupload/share/post previously deleted content to new accounts. Perpetrators, using their "celebrity-like status" (SMACC, 2021), are then able to get their followers to engage with their cruelty content on new platforms. Additionally, perpetrators are often misleading in their locations. Videos listed as produced in one location are often created in a different location. The AfA reasons that this is done to monetize videos, as eligibility for monetization is not present in all countries (SMACC, 2021).

In terms of monetization, Lady Freethinker, a member of the AfA, investigated the monetization of animal cruelty content on YouTube. Between April and May of 2020, roughly 2,000 videos depicting animal cruelty garnered over one billion views (Lady Freethinker, 2020). In terms of profit, it is estimated that YouTubers posting cruelty content could earn nearly $15 million total (Lady Freethinker, 2020). Even more concerning is the estimate that YouTube itself could earn "over $12 million in ad revenue alone" (Lady Freethinker, 2020). In their study, Lady Freethinker defined animal cruelty as "content in which non-human animals are deliberately harmed for entertainment or shown to be under severe psychological distress, physical pain, or dead ..." and provided a list of specific animal abuse content (Lady Freethinker, 2020). Videos matching this criterion were separated into three major categories: wildlife, companion animals, and farmed animals. Wildlife videos garnered the most attention, with a total of 1,804 videos attracting 1.1 billion views and over 30 thousand subscribers (Lady Freethinker, 2020). Companion animal videos totaled at 670 videos with 120 million views and 4.2 million subscribers (Lady Freethinker, 2020). Lastly, farmed animal videos totaled at 67 videos, 12.6 million views, and 99,491 subscribers (Lady Freethinker, 2020). Many subcategories of videos exist, including animal fighting, eating animals alive, monkey torture, fake animal rescues, hunting animals with animals, and fox-hound hunting (Lady Freethinker, 2020). Of these subcategories, hunting animals with other animals was the most prevalent. Some states in the US have outlawed hunting with dogs, therefore some of the videos viewed potentially break the law (Lady Freethinker, 2020). Despite these videos violating YouTube's terms of service, 91% of the examined videos were still live at the end of the investigation (Lady Freethinker, 2020).

On a smaller scale, research shows that social media can be used as a tool to promote more specific forms of animal cruelty. Montrose et al. (2021) reviewed YouTube, Facebook, and Instagram for evidence of organized dog fighting. A total of 58 videos were identified, with the most content available on YouTube (n = 27) (Montrose et al., 2021). Over half (63%) of the analyzed YouTube videos showed dog fights involving physical contact (Montrose et al., 2021). All videos found on Facebook and Instagram showed physical fights. In terms of breed, dogs were most often described as pit bulls (Montrose et al., 2021). Montrose et al.'s (2021) research indicates a need for more intense monitoring of content available on these platforms.

There is a need for further research on social media and its impact on animal cruelty. It is unclear whether the use of social media has increased rates of animal cruelty, or if instances of cruelty are simply more visible. In order to fight cruelty online, more research should be conducted on the types of perpetrators and the material goods they obtain from committing such acts. The motivations of posting animal cruelty content is not entirely clear; Although it can be lucrative, not every animal cruelty content creator makes a large sum of money online. Finally, more research needs to be conducted in the realm of online cruelty and the law. It is uncertain how often animal cruelty content creators are found and prosecuted for their crimes. There is still much to be learned about the intersection of social media and animal cruelty.

Types of Animal Cruelty on Social Media

As the Asia for Animals Coalition found, there are many different forms of animal cruelty to be seen on social media. One of the most pertinent forms of cruelty are faked animal rescue videos. These videos typically depict "an attacking animal and a victim in a muddy hole surrounded by vegetation" (Maron, 2021). All videos follow the same formula: they are usually five minutes in length, with an "attacking animal" being thwarted by a purported human savior. (Maron, 2021). The victim animals are typically not the natural prey the of the attacking animals. For example, one video depicted an eagle attacking a snake. Eagles, however, do not typically hunt snakes. Rather, their diet consists of small mammals, waterfowl, prairie dogs, raccoons, and rabbits (National Eagle Center, n.d.). There are many examples of unnatural interactions between the animals that are clearly forced by humans. The example used by National Geographic is that of a gibbon slowly being squeezed to death by a python (Maron, 2021). Mark Auliya, a herpetologist at the Zoological Research Museum Alexander Koenig, points out that pythons bite first, then begin constricting around their prey. This was not evident in the video, showing clear signs of human intervention (Maron, 2021).

World Animal Protection, a worldwide animal rescue group, conducted a review on the rise of fake animal rescue YouTube videos. Between October of 2018 and May of 2021, World Animal Protection found a total of 181 fake animal rescue videos on YouTube. They reported that "the 50 most viewed videos alone had collectively been viewed 133.5 million times and secured 13 million subscribers to their channels" (World Animal Protection, 2021). This result is highly concerning; it shows that fake animal rescue videos can gain massive traction online. Fake animal rescue videos pose a major threat to the physical and psychological wellbeing of the animals involved. World Animal Protection warns that "depending on the species involved, [these videos] can also raise conservation concerns and severe public health risks" (World Animal Protection, 2021).

A variety of "prey" animals were seen in the 10 most viewed fake rescue videos. These species included dogs, chickens, ducks, geese, rabbits, lizards, snakes, and more. Of the species seen as prey, chickens and dogs were the most prevalent (World Animal Protection, 2021). There were five major categories of predator animals in the ten most viewed videos, four of which were different species of snake. The fifth species was the short-toed snake eagle (World Animal Protection, 2021). Results from World Animal Protection's review show that snakes are the most often used predator animal and chickens are the most commonly used prey animal. As mentioned previously, fake animal rescue videos can pose a threat to conservation efforts. Two species used in these videos, the elongated tortoise and the Siamese crocodile, are critically endangered (World Animal Protection, 2021).

Beyond the issue of endangerment, fake animal rescue videos circulate misinformation about the activities of many misunderstood species. With a total audience of 13 million subscribers, this misinformation can create dangerous misunderstandings of animal behavior. Additionally, these videos are typically titled using the words "primitive man," which creates a dangerous racial connotation (Maron, 2021).

Another major theme of animal cruelty in social media is the use of animals as entertainers. Though there is a long history of using animals as entertainment, the expansion of social media has proliferated the practice. The AfA cautions that "images of wild animals in human environments, dressed in human clothing and/or interacting with humans perpetuates the idea that they can thrive under such conditions" when the natural needs of these animals cannot be met in captivity (SMACC, n.d.). Examples of the use of animals as entertainment can be seen in many videos on social media; the videos of monkeys on unicycles or doing tricks may seem innocuous to the average viewer, but the animals involved are often mistreated and abused by their handlers.

One of the dangers of this form of cruelty is that it is usually seen as an innocent practice. One viral video from 2019 depicts a chimpanzee scrolling through Instagram. Many users who viewed the video found it endearing, though the truth behind the video was far less palatable. Primatologist experts who viewed the video reported that it was likely the chimpanzee was living in a domestic home. This is a problem, as the biological needs of chimpanzees are impossible to meet in that setting (Cole & Emerson, 2019). Experts caution the consumption of videos depicting animals as entertainment (Cole & Emerson, 2019). These videos create a misunderstanding that wild animals such as monkeys, elephants, and big cats can be successfully domesticated.

The danger of using animals as entertainment does not only lie in the misunderstandings it can cause. Animals used in entertainment are typically physically abused during their "training." People for the Ethical Treatment of Animals (PETA) reports that "trainers use bullhooks, whips, tight collars, muzzles, electric prods, and other painful tools of the trade" to achieve the physical feats done by animals in circuses (People for the Ethical Treatment of Animals (PETA, n.d.). The same techniques are used to train the animals seen in entertainment videos on social media; monkeys do not have the natural propensity to ride a bike or do tricks.

A third and lesser known form of online cruelty is shown in videos where content creators will eat animals alive. In their review, Lady Freethinker listed eating animals alive as one of the major subcategories of animal cruelty found on YouTube (Lady Freethinker, 2020). Lady Freethinker found a total of 15 channels and 80 videos amassing over 374 million views and 17.3 million subscribers (Lady Freethinker, 2020). While eating live animals is found in many cultures, it is still largely considered a form of animal cruelty.

Current Policies

Each social media platform has its own policy on what content can be shared. However, not every platform defines animal abuse in the same way, and some do not list animal abuse as a reportable offense. In both its terms of service and community guidelines, Instagram does not address animal cruelty specifically. It does, however, prohibit "the sale of live animals between private individuals" (Instagram, n.d. a). The coordination of poaching and selling of endangered animals is also prohibited in Instagram's community guidelines (Instagram, n.d. a). When making a report, Instagram lists "animal cruelty" as an offense in the "violence or dangerous organizations" category.

Instagram has made strides to address animal cruelty on its platform. In 2017, Instagram instated a program that would notify its users when they searched a hashtag associated with animal abuse (Daly, 2017). This program targeted a "range of wildlife hashtags" (Daly, 2017). A page in the Help Center was created to educate Instagram users on wildlife exploitation. Instagram warns users to "consider whether an animal has been smuggled, poached or abused for the sake of tourism" (Instagram, n.d. b). With the apparent boom in shared animal cruelty content, however, it is unclear if this program has truly had an effect on discouraging wildlife exploitation.

Much like Instagram, Facebook does not address animal cruelty in its general terms of service or general community guidelines. However, Facebook does address animal cruelty in its Facebook Community Standards section. Rules on animal cruelty content can be found under the "violent and graphic content" section. This section details what violent content cannot be posted and content that will be allowed on the platform but labelled with a warning screen. Animal cruelty content falls in the latter category; it is not specifically against the community guidelines to post. Facebook acknowledges that "people value the ability to discuss important issues ..." therefore it does not fully ban animal cruelty content (Facebook, n.d.). Instead, Facebook provides a warning screen and only allows users over the age of 18 to view the post (Facebook, n.d.) Facebook does not state how it vets cruelty content that is "important" to advocacy and conversation. The current policy would seem to allow for the sharing of all forms of animal cruelty, regardless of the intent of the poster.

As stated by the AfA, YouTube was found to have the most cruelty content in the SMACC's review. YouTube prohibits animal cruelty content under the "violence or graphic content" section of its community guidelines (YouTube, n.d.). YouTube specifically outlines two forms of animal cruelty: animal fights and fake animal rescues. (YouTube, n.d.) However, YouTube does not specifically prohibit eating animals alive. Instead, it states that "content that includes a human maliciously causing an animal to experience suffering when not for traditional or standard purposes such as hunting or food preparation" is prohibited (YouTube, n.d.). This loophole allows for eating animals live content to thrive.

When a YouTube video violates community guidelines, the platform dictates that it will remove the content and send an email to the user. After three strikes, the user is at risk of having their channel deleted (YouTube, n.d.). However, as reported by both Lady Thinker and the AfA, many cruelty videos on YouTube remained live for a long period of time. This indicates that YouTube's community guidelines may allow cruelty content to fall through the cracks of review.

Tik Tok, a social media app that gained attention in 2019, is a platform that hosts short videos. Of the three previously discussed platforms, Tik Tok has the least descriptive animal cruelty policy. Tik Tok's animal cruelty policy can be found under the "violent and graphic content" section of its community guidelines page (Tik Tok, n.d.) Tik Tok prohibits content that depicts "the slaughter or other non-natural death of animals; dismembered, mutilated, charred, or burned animal remains, and animal cruelty and gore" (Tik Tok, n.d.). While Tik Tok prohibits "animal cruelty" in general, it is unclear what forms of animal cruelty may not be considered against community guidelines.

Instagram, Facebook, YouTube, and Tik Tok all have some form of policy regarding cruelty content. However, these policies vary. The variation between policies could allow for animal cruelty content creators to engage with one platform more than the other. Instead of being driven off the internet, these creators could simply move to a platform with lest strict guidelines. Additionally, it is unclear how these policies truly prevent animal cruelty content online. Reported videos still need to be reviewed, and sometimes videos can remain live for long periods of time.

Case Study: Alinity

While there are many videos of animal cruelty content online, some creators have garnered attention through the treatment of their animals on social media. In 2019, Twitch streamer Natalia Mogollon, known as *Alinity*, came under fire for two different instances of alleged animal abuse while streaming. The first incident occurred when Mogollon allowed her cat to drink vodka (De La Rosa, 2019). Though the amount of alcohol Mogollon's cat ingested is unclear, even the smallest amount of vodka is highly toxic to cats. The Pet Poison Helpline reports that "ingestion of alcohol can cause dangerous drops in blood sugar, blood pressure, and body temperature" as well as "seizures and respiratory failure" (Pet Poison Helpline, n.d.). The second incident occurred during an *Apex Legends* stream, when Mogollon threw her cat over her shoulder (Juarez, 2019). Both incidents sparked outrage online and many community members demanded that Mogollon be banned from Twitch. In fact, a Change.org petition calling for Mogollon's banishment has since garnered 60,174 signatures (Samuels, n.d.)

In response to online outrage, Mogollon invited the SPCA to inspect her home (Juarez, 2019). The Saskatoon SPCA determined that there was no malintent behind Mogollon's actions and that all animals were in healthy condition (Juarez, 2019). Mogollon is still massively popular on Twitch and has faced little repercussions aside from public disapproval. Twitch's community guidelines never specifically address any forms of animal cruelty. Rather, it delineates that users must comply with local laws (Twitch, n.d.).

The Mogollon situation highlights many issues with instances of online animal cruelty. Though many community members may be outraged by actions of cruelty, there seems to be little repercussion for major streamers. Twitch enforces violations of its community guidelines through warnings and suspensions. Considering that animal cruelty is not specifically prohibited in the community guidelines, some forms of cruelty may slip through the cracks. While Mogollon's action of tossing her cat could be disputed, feeding her cat alcohol was incredibly dangerous and could have resulted in serious injury to the animal. An issue with online cruelty is that younger individuals may engage with this type of content and see the treatment as a joke. Uneducated individuals may feed their own pets alcohol without knowing the dangers of alcohol poisoning. With well over 1,000,000 subscribers, it can be argued that Mogollon, as well as other major streamers, have some sort of responsibility to educate their viewers on their mistakes.

Activism on Social Media

While social media can be a tool to produce and share animal cruelty content, animal rights activists can use social media to engage with the public and spread their message. Katarzyna Szpargala of the Institute of Social Research and Cultural Studies at the National Yang Ming Chiao Tung University in Taiwan argues that "social media has influenced society and affected sociocultural and political changes" (Szpargala, 2021). The question is, as Szpargala asks, "to what extent?" Determining the extent of influence is difficult and complex. Animal rights activist may be very active on social media, but that does not mean they influence the offline action of their followers. A major question to ask is what the goals of online activism are.

Szpargala points out that "the animal movement is not homogenous; various groups have different agendas, goals, and philosophies toward animal rights and welfare" (Szpargala, 2021). This would lead to different activist groups using both the internet and social media in different ways. Animal shelters, for example, "often promote their animals and events, which increases adoption" (Szpargala, 2021). For the sake of simplicity, this chapter will refer to groups focused on animal welfare and activism as "animal rights groups" and individuals as "animal rights activists."

Angga Prawadika Aji's research on social media examined the effect of social media activity on the three main components of a social movement: collective identity, actual mobilization, and network organization (Aji, 2019). Aji identifies collective identity as one of the most important components of a social movement; without similar beliefs and goals, a social movement would never get off the ground (Aji, 2019). Animal rights groups in Indonesia used social media to form collective identity (Aji, 2019). Social media allowed these groups to engage with more people and therefore bring more attention to the movement. Additionally social media "[shortened] the path of participant involvement to join and [provided] a variety of channels to engage in micro actions," thus allowing for actual mobilization (Aji, 2019). At the very least, these animal rights groups were able to get followers to participate in discussions and share photos of their own pets (Aji, 2019). Simple communication, however, is not inherently beneficial to animal rights groups.

Frequently, social media is rife with misunderstandings and misinterpretations. Therefore, attention on social media is not always a good thing. In 2014, animal rights activists and indigenous rights activists clashed over a simple hashtag on twitter: the #sealfie (Knezevic et al., 2018). Popular talk show host Ellen DeGeneres had taken a selfie at the Oscars; The selfie had been a "covert fundraising effort for the Humane Society of the United States" (Knezevic et al., 2018). The Humane Society has historically been a staunch opponent of seal hunting, known as "sealing" (Knezevic et al., 2018). While animal rights activists called for the end to seal hunting, indigenous people voiced the importance of seal hunting in their survival and culture. Rodney Mercer, a Newfoundland artist, protested DeGeneres's support of the Humane Society by creating a portrait of the talk show host from seal skin (Knezevic et al., 2018). Thus, the #sealfie was born.

The issue highlighted by the #sealfie debacle is that social media is not the place for meaningful debate. While the #sealfie amplified Inuit voices, there was little engagement from animal rights groups (Knezevic et al., 2018). Twitter's 140-character limit does not allow for proper discussion. While Inuit people were given a platform to share their opinions, they were "not heard by those who wield a great deal of power in political discussions of sealing" (Knezevic et al., 2018). This indicates that having a platform does not "imply political influence" (Knezevic et al., 2018). Animal activists who did engage with indigenous activists were acting as individuals; no animal rights group engaged with the hashtag (Knezevic et al., 2018). Additionally, social media can act as an echo chamber. The algorithm feeds users content that it believes they would like, leading to a lack of diverse opinions. If the goal of online activism is to simply connect like-minded people, then social media is a good resource for animal rights groups to use. However, if the goal is to enact real-world change through social media, the results are less clear.

Social media has also opened the door for unconventional forms of activism. Richard Watts, a UK-based animal rights advocate, publishes four panel comics about veganism (Jeffries, 2020). Watt's comics are unlike typical forms of activism: the drawing method is crude, with many of the images lacking text bubbles (Jeffries, 2020). Watt's goal is to highlight the "logical incoherence of the non-vegan position" to get non-vegans to question their own thinking (Jeffries, 2020). Watt believes his comics are a "niche" form of activism (Jeffries, 2020). The rebuttals in his comics give vegans a framework to use when debating with non-vegans. Watt believes that activism fails to address the core problem of the debate: that "most individuals enter such conversations from a deeply entrenched position and would rather 'win' the debate ... than 'lose' it" (Jeffries, 2020). Therefore, Watt's "comic book activism" gives readers an understanding of the mechanisms that protect the non-vegan worldview (Jeffries, 2020).

Whether it be comics, blogs, infographics, or adoption posts, animal rights groups have been using social media as an outlet to connect with old and new members. Still, the extent of the influence of these posts are not clear. Social media activism has both its benefits and its downfalls. Most importantly, it is highly unlikely that activism on social media leads to real world action from the general public.

Animal Cruelty, Social Media, and the Law

Different countries have different laws regarding animal cruelty. In the United States, each state has its own provision on what constitutes animal cruelty. The variation in language can make prosecution of online acts of cruelty difficult. Additionally, it may be difficult to determine the jurisdiction of online animal abuse cases. As reported by the AfA, many animal cruelty content creators will lie about the location in which the content was shot and uploaded (SMACC, 2021). This makes the identification of these perpetrators even more difficult.

Beyond the simple identification of animal cruelty perpetrators, frequently there are issues with the intersection of social media and the law itself. *The Washington Post* reports that the prosecution of online acts of cruelty is complicated (Beachum, 2019). Lifestyle YouTuber Brooke Houst's treatment of her Doberman in a viral "prank" video sparked outrage and controversy on the internet (Beachum, 2019). Houst was physically violent with her dog in the now removed video. She slapped, pushed, and spit on her Doberman (Beachum, 2019). Online outrage prompted the Los Angeles Police Department (LAPD) Animal Cruelty Task Force to examine the case; However, as *The Washington Post* reports, the LAPD determined that "it didn't rise to the level of animal cruelty" (Beachum, 2019). Though Houst's actions are viewed as cruel, they aren't necessarily illegal.

California Penal Code 597 PC describes animal cruelty as "maliciously killing, harming, maiming, or torturing a living animal" (Shouselaw, n.d.). Under California law, animal cruelty can be charged as either a misdemeanor or felony. As it stands, California law allows for a degree of physical violence to be used against animals without it being considered criminal. This is highlighted by Houst's actions, as she was physically violent with her pet, yet no charges were filed against her. This begs the question of what actions constitute a "cruel beating," "needless suffering," and "unnecessary cruelty," all of which are prohibited under California law. It would seem that in the context of Houst's case, kicking, spitting, and pushing an animal is not considered "unnecessary cruelty." In addition, it is often difficult to prove the mental state of actors in animal cruelty cases. In the case of California, a "malicious intent" is necessary (Shouselaw, n.d.)

Much like in the Mogollon case, actions that are deemed inappropriate by the public are not inherently illegal. The online outrage highlights what Jessica Rubin, a professor at the University of Connecticut's animal law clinic, calls a need for current animal cruelty laws to reflect a modern relationship with animals as pets (Beachum, 2019). In terms of current statutes, frequently abuse is only considered if the skin of the animal is broken or bruised (Beachum, 2019). Despite online outrage, Houst's treatment of her dog was not violent enough to be considered animal cruelty.

News Media and Animal Cruelty

Animal cruelty in news media is portrayed differently from cases seen on social media. This is likely attributed to differing goals between social media and news media; social media is a content sharing platform allowing anyone to post nearly anything they want. News media is focused on sharing information to large amounts of people. While social media tends to be rife with misinformation, news media is typically seen as "one of the primary sources for factual crime information for the general public" (Grugan, 2019). Thus, cruelty in news media is often focused on factual reporting, rather than content creation for lucrative gain. Still, there are identifiable themes in animal cruelty reports on the news. It can be argued that news media has a larger influence on public opinion than social media, therefore it is important to understand how the news portrays different forms of animal cruelty. A 2019 content analysis identified seven themes typically found in news media animal cruelty content: "neutrality, condemnation, sympathy for the animal, drama, advocacy, humor, and sympathy for the offender" (Grugan, 2019). Neutral news articles (42.1%) were seen most frequently of the seven themes. These articles articulated a simple description of the incident (Grugan, 2019). This highlights the main difference between cruelty content shared on social media and cruelty content reported by news media. Much of the cruelty content shared on social media is either shared for the purpose of entertainment or education. Animal cruelty reports in news media are shared for the purpose of informing the public of a crime. Therefore, news media focuses more on the criminogenic aspect of animal cruelty by identifying perpetrators, crime scene details, and investigator actions.

Naturally, the second most prevalent theme identified was condemnation (25.4%) (Grugan, 2019). Language used in these articles are typically derogatory towards both the offender and the act committed (Grugan, 2019). These articles can be compared to social media posts that intend to "educate" users on the horrors of animal cruelty. Though not entirely the same, these two share a common theme: disgust with the perpetrator and his/her actions. These articles arguably influence perceptions on different forms of animal cruelty. When a prosecutor reports the actions of an individual are deplorable and inhumane for a certain kind of crime, that crime may be seen as more serious compared to other forms of cruelty (Grugan, 2019). A danger arises from this presumption; some cases of cruelty may not receive the same attention or treatment because they are seen as "lesser" or not as severe.

News media clearly has themes in its reporting of animal cruelty. However, these themes are not the only concepts that influence public perception of cruelty. Though news media is often the only source for reliable information, many have criticized the frequent practice of sensationalizing stories. Cohen and Richardson (2002), in their article *Pit Bull Panic,* point to the frequent demonization of the American Bull Terrier (Cohen & Richardson, 2002). Pit bulls have often been characterized as violent, uncontrollable, and simply evil (Cohen & Richardson, 2002). Sensationalized stories of pit bull violence have led to real world consequences. Some places ban pit bull ownership outright, and many insurance companies refuse homeowners insurance to those with pit bulls (Cohen & Ricardson, 2002). Pit bulls have been notoriously used in dog fights, solidifying the public's misinformed belief that this breed is simply more violent than other dog breeds (Cohen & Richardson, 2002). Cohen and Richardson (2002) report that *The New York Times* published 72 stories on pit bulls from 1987 to 2000, over one third of which involved pit bull attacks (Cohen & Richardson, 2002). Pit bull supporters do concede that the dogs do have risks; most prominent is that a bite from a pit bull can lead to much more damage compared from a bite from other dog breeds (Cohen & Richardson, 2002). However, this risk is present in many large dog breeds. The news media plays a large role in controlling how the public perceives certain dog breeds, especially the pit bull.

The clear demonization of pit bulls in the past can lead to adverse consequences. First, cruelty against pit bulls may not be taken as seriously; their "violent" nature may be seen as deserving of violent punishment. Second, pit bulls will continue to be used in dog fights as long as they keep their undeserved title as the most violent breed. Though not entirely attributable to the influence of news media, the continued use of pit bulls in dog fights is influenced by public perception brought forth by misinformation on the breed.

Exposure to animal cruelty cases in the news influence consumers in many ways, one of which is damaging to mental health. Some news coverage of cruelty cases includes graphic footage obtained from "undercover filming" (Tiplady et al., 2015). Though some criticize the use of such vulgar videos, others assert that showing the violent truth is the only way to inform the public of horrific animal cruelty (Tiplady et al., 2015). In their article, Tiplady et al. (2015) detail that there is a "need to balance exposure with an ethical responsibility to present the images in a way that provides enough information to inform without unnecessarily traumatizing viewers" (Tiplady et al., 2015). Participants in the study initially report that an animal cruelty exposé made them feel "horror" and "disgust" (Tiplady et al., 2015). These feelings persisted between one week and twelve months of the initial exposé (Tiplady et al., 2015). Some participants reported internalizing their feelings of disgust (Tiplady et al., 2015). Still, a majority of participants reported that they would be likely to view animal cruelty stories in the news in the future (Tiplady et al., 2015).

In 2012, Tiplady et al. (2012) conducted a similar study on how the public responds to an exposé of animal cruelty. The study analyzed public responses after a report of cruelty to cattle from Indonesian abattoirs. Despite reports of sadness, disgust, and horror, few people made an effort to enact real change. The most common reaction reported was pity for the abused animal (85%), followed by sadness (72%) and anger (68%) (Tiplady et al., 2012). Initially, 26% of respondents asserted that they would take action to stop live export (Tiplady et al. 2012). Women reported feeling sadness and anger than men (Tiplady et al., 2012). Yet, women were also more likely to "be more concerned about a lack of cultural sensitivity to Indonesians" (Tiplady et al., 2012). When examining which respondents took action after the event, it was found that women were more likely than men to discuss the media coverage or to take action (Tiplady et al., 2012). Those in a younger age bracket (18–29) were more likely to engage in discussion, stop eating meat, and make a donation to an animal rights non-profit (Tiplady et al., 2012).

Despite causing intense negative emotion, it would seem that coverage of animal cruelty cases in the news does not necessarily influence the behavior of the public. Though, this is likely not an issue, as the purpose of news media is often to report on topics, not provide a call to action. One thing to be learned from the reporting of animal cruelty in news media is that the language used in articles can influence public perception on cruelty. Though viewers may see animal cruelty is horrific and abhorrent, they still may not take action.

Reality TV and Animal Cruelty

Reality TV provides an entirely different type of content than news media and social media. Using Reiss's 16 basic desires and values as a theoretical framework, Reiss and Wiltz (2004) posit that people enjoy watching reality TV for two possible reasons. First, "viewers feel they are more important (have higher status) than the ordinary people portrayed on reality television shows," and second, reality TV implies that the lives of "ordinary" individuals are interesting and worth watching (Reiss & Wiltz, 2004). Both ideas relate to the fact that those in the study who enjoyed watching reality TV were mostly status-oriented people (meaning that they have an above average need to feel important) (Reiss & Wiltz, 2004). Still, viewers could consume reality TV content because of how ridiculous, unrealistic, or funny the show may be. Reality TV is often exaggerated and staged, yet viewers continue to enjoy the screaming matches on *Keeping Up with the Kardashians* or *Housewives of Orange County*.

There are many forms of reality TV, from Jersey *Shore* (2009), which followed the eventful lives of a group of young adults living in Seaside heights, to *Survivor* (2000), which followed a competition of two teams living in the wilderness. Beyond the funny, dramatic, and entertaining reality TV shows, there is a sect of more serious and graphic reality TV content: cop shows. These shows typically follow a police department on their rounds and depict investigations and arrests. In this version of reality TV lies a more specific genre of cop shows: shows that follow officers in an animal cruelty division. A major animal cruelty reality TV show was *Animal Cops* (2002). *Animal Cops* refers to several reality TV shows starting in Detroit in 2002. Typically airing on Animal Planet, these shows followed officers on their rounds while investigating cases of animal cruelty. *Animal Cops* took place in many different jurisdictions, including Houston, Philadelphia, San Francisco, South Africa, Phoenix, and Miami. These shows sometimes depict graphic instances of animal cruelty, and often use language like "shocked," "desperate," and "alarming," to hook viewers into watching.

Similarly, a show called *Animal Precinct* (2001) followed the same story line. This show, which predates *Animal cops*, tracked the Humane Law Enforcement Division of the American Society for the Prevention of Cruelty to Animals (ASPCA) in New York City. Again, this show depicted graphic instances of animal cruelty and left many viewers grimacing. There are many reasons the popularity of these shows may flourish. It could be speculated that people engage with this type of reality TV simply because it's interesting. These shows engross viewers with morally black and white content that shows obvious "good guys" and "bad guys." Morally ambiguous content is sometimes difficult to consume and can leave viewers with uncomfortable questions about themselves and the world around them. With clear victims and aggressors, content becomes more easily palatable. In these shows, the abused animals are clear victims that viewers can sympathize with.

Reality TV mirrors social media in the purpose of its depiction of animal cruelty. Both versions of media show animal cruelty as a form of entertainment, though for differing reasons. In the case of reality TV, animal cruelty is presented in a "realistic" manner. These shows depict real cases of abuse, malnourishment, and neglect. The pull of these shows is that the innocent animal victims are eventually rescued by human heroes. The entertainment lies not in the actual abuse of the animals; rather, it is gathered from the heroic actions of the police officers. Comparatively, it cannot be argued the entertainment surrounding animal cruelty on social media comes from saving animals from deplorable conditions. It is unclear why people consume animal cruelty content on social media, though it can be speculated that people find these cases interesting, if not entertaining.

Conclusion

Social media presents a host of issues involving animal cruelty. First, it is unclear how often animal cruelty content is produced and uploaded, and whether the content is caught by current system of review. A lack of empirical literature on the subject leaves more questions than answers. It would seem that animal cruelty content remains live for long periods of time, especially on YouTube (SMACC, 2021). This begs the question of whether the content is reviewed and remains live or if it is not reviewed at all. It is unclear how often this content is reported, if at all. Additionally, reporting animal cruelty content may not be the best course of action. If the content is reported and removed, there is little chance the perpetrator could be caught and prosecuted. Beyond that, the perpetrator may simply upload the same content to a different social media platform with less stringent community guidelines.

Animal cruelty is sometimes thought to be shared on the dark web, out of the view of the general public and law enforcement. Naturally, some of this may be true for the more gruesome acts of cruelty; however, it has been shown that cruelty is shared in "broad daylight," so to speak. Especially in the cases of faked animal rescue videos, this content is often easily accessible and is not confined to private accounts or communities. Again, this questions the efficacy of current social media community guidelines and terms of service. Without any substantial data, it is hard to say that these policies are effective in deterring uploads of animal cruelty content.

Even more concerning is the fact that animal cruelty content creation can be lucrative. Again, YouTube seems to be the largest perpetrator, whether intentionally or unintentionally. With ad revenue, both content creators and YouTube can accrue a large sum of money from unethical and immoral content (Lady Freethinker, 2021). With the chances of monetary gain, it is unlikely that YouTube, or other social media platforms, would ever fully ban animal cruelty content. Knowing what forms of animal cruelty content are the most popular would aid in finding out what kind of content brings in the most money. While Facebook allows cruelty content for the purpose of education, it is unclear how it determines what content is educational and what content is created for the purpose of entertainment (Facebook, n.d.).

On the note of entertainment, further research should be conducted on the motivations for creation and consumption of animal cruelty content. Naturally monetary gain is one reason, but there could be others that are less clear. Knowing motivations could aid in identifying perpetrators. The motivation for consumption of this content is nearly as important as the motivation for creating it; without viewers, there would be no monetary gain.

Activism on social media seems to be less fruitful when the goal is to produce real world action from consumers. However, social media allows for similar minded activists to congregate or stay up to date on the actions of certain non-profits. While social media can create a sense of togetherness between activists, it is unlikely that online activism will produce offline action. Online activism allows for different forms of activism to thrive, such as Watt's vegan comics. It would seem that online cruelty thrives as much as online activism, if not more.

Social media offers different issues for animal cruelty than news media and reality TV, likely because of the differing purposes of sharing cruelty cases. As mentioned previously, news media typically focuses on sharing factual elements of a crime, mostly in a neutral and detached manner (Grugan, 2019). Sometimes other themes are present, like condemnation and sympathy for the animal (Grugan, 2019), but typically news articles are meant to inform. Issues with news media arise when stories are sensationalized, as in the case of stories about pit bulls (Cohen & Richardson, 2002). Reality TV differs in that its purpose is simply to entertain, oftentimes at the expense of dramatizing real world events. Cop shows tend to be popular, likely because of the gritty portrayal of criminal violence.

The public views animal cruelty in a host of different ways; whether it be used as entertainment on social media or reality TV, or seen as a report on the news, people continue to engage with animal cruelty content. Thus, the importance of understanding the intersection of social media and animal cruelty content remains evident.

References

Aji, A. (2019). The role of social media in shaping the animal protection movement in Indonesia. *Jurnal Studi Komunikasi, 3*(3), 389–401. https://doi.org/10.25139/jsk.v3i3.1666.

Beachum, L. (2019, September 17). *They're accused of abusing their pets in viral videos. But laws don't always consider it cruelty*. Washingtonpost.com. https://www.washingtonpost.com/science/2019/09/17/they-abused-their-pets-viral-videos-laws-dont-always-consider-it-cruelty/.

Cohen, J., & Richardson, J. (2002). Pit bull panic. *Journal of Popular Culture, 36*(2), 285–317. https://doi.org/10.1111/1540-5931.00007.

Cole, S., & Emerson, S. (2019) *That viral video of a chimp scrolling Instagram is bad, actually*. Vice.com. https://www.vice.com/en/article/8xzn7z/viral-video-of-a-chimp-scrolling-instagram-is-bad.

Daly, N. (2017) *Exclusive: Instagram fights animal abuse with new alert system*. Nationalgeographic.com. https://www.nationalgeographic.com/animals/article/wildlife-watch-instagram-selfie-tourism-animal-welfare-crime.

De La Rosa, A. (2019, July 19). *Popular Twitch streamer Alinity spits vodka in her cat's mouth/abuses it on stream* [Video]. Youtube.com. https://www.youtube.com/watch?v=-vxW8o-w9EY.

Facebook. (n.d.). *Violent and graphic content*. Facebook.com.

Grugan, S. T. (2019). Capturing cruelty: A content analysis of companion animal cruelty in the news media. *Society & Animals, 27*(1), 92–108. https://doi.org/10.1163/15685306-12341530.

Instagram. (n.d. a) *Community Guidelines*. Instagram.com. https://help.instagram.com/477434105621119?ref=igtos.

Instagram. (n.d. b) *How do I learn more about wildlife exploitation?* Instagram.com. https://help.instagram.com/859615207549041.

Jeffries, D. (2020). "Bacon Tho": Richard Watts' vegan sidekick comics as social media activism. *Inks: The Journal of the Comics Studies Society, 4*(3), 266–287.

Juarez, S. (2019, July 27). *SPCA closes investigation into Alinity Divine for throwing her cat*. Dailydot.com. https://www.dailydot.com/upstream/spca-investigation-alinity-divine/.

Knezevic, I., Pasho, J., & Dobson, K. (2018). Seal hunts in Canada and on Twitter: Exploring the tensions between indigenous rights and animal rights with #Sealfie. *Canadian Journal of Communication, 43*(3), 421–439. https://doi.org/10.22230/cjc.2019v44n3a3376.

Lady Freethinker. (2020) *YOUTUBE: Profiting from animal abuse. Investigation by Lady Freethinker*. Ladyfreethinker.org. https://ladyfreethinker.org/wp-content/uploads/2020/12/Lady-Freethinker-Report-YouTube-Profits-From-Animal-Abuse.pdf.

Maron, D. (2021) *How fake animal rescue videos have become a new frontier for animal abuse*. NationalGeographic.co.uk. https://www.nationalgeographic.co.uk/animals/2021/07/how-fake-animal-rescue-videos-have-become-a-new-frontier-for-animal-abuse.

Montrose, T., Kogan, L., & Oxley, J. (2021). The role of social media in promoting organized dog fighting. *The Veterinary Nurse, 12*(8). https://doi.org/10.12968/vetn.2021.12.8.386.

National Eagle Center (n.d.). *What does a bald eagle eat?*. Nationaleaglecenter.org. https://www.nationaleaglecenter.org/eagle-diet feeding/#:~:text=Their%20prey%20items%20include%20waterfowl,birds)%20or%20scavenge%20on%20carrion.

People for the Ethical Treatment of Animals. (n.d.). *Animals used for entertainment.* Peta.org. https://www.peta.org/issues/animals-in-entertainment/.

Pet Poison Helpline. (n.d.). *Alcohol.* Petpoisonhelpline.com. https://www.petpoisonhelpline.com/poison/alcohol/.

Reiss, S., & Wiltz, J. (2004). Why people watch reality TV. *Media Psychology, 6,* 363–378.

Samuels, C. (n.d.). *Ban Alinity on Twitch.* Change.org. https://www.change.org/p/twitch-ban-alinity-on-twitch?redirect=false.

Shouselaw. (n.d.). *Penal Code 597 PC—California animal abuse & animal cruelty laws.* Shouselaw.com. https://www.shouselaw.com/ca/defense/penal-code/597/.

Social Media Animal Cruelty Coalition. (2021) *Making money from misery: How social media giants profit from animal abuse.* Asiaforanimals.com. https://www.asiaforanimals.com/_files/ugd/63e9f4_7a5711baf32e4e2e9dea11d0b23b954c.pdf.

Social Media Animal Cruelty Coalition. (n.d.). *Social Media Animal Cruelty Coalition (SMACC).* Asiaforanimals.com. https://www.asiaforanimals.com/smacc.

Szpargala, K. (2021). *Animal welfare and social media—Is the internet an ally of animals?* Cdjproject.web.nctu.ed.tw. https://cjdproject.web.nctu.edu.tw/2021/08/30/animal-welfare-and-social-media-is-the-internet-an-ally-of-animals/#:~:text=Social%20media%20contributes%20to%20raising,which%20users%20may%20unintentionally%20support.

Tik Tok. (n.d.). *Community Guidelines.* Tiktok.com. https://www.tiktok.com/community-guidelines?lang=en.

Tiplady, C. M., Walsh. D. B., & Phillips, C. J. C. (2012). Public response to media coverage of animal cruelty. *Journal of Agricultural and Environmental Ethics, 26,* 869–885.

Tiplady, C. M., Walsh. D. B., & Phillips, C. J. C. (2015) Ethical issues concerning the public viewing of media broadcasts of animal cruelty. *Journal of Agricultural and Environmental Ethics, 28,* 635–645.

Twitch. (n.d.). *Community Guidelines.* Twitch.com. https://safety.twitch.tv/s/article/Community-Guidelines?language=en_US.

World Animal Protection. (2021). *Views that abuse: The rise of fake "animal rescue" videos on YouTube.* Worldanimalprotection.us. https://dkt6rvnu67rqj.cloudfront.net/cdn/ff/qDu4rED0vYiYhJ6E8m-kUwGOqfzulIEao54AFb-uQeo/1625065255/public/media/Views_that_Abuse_YouTube_Report_World_Animal_Protection_Canada.pdf.

YouTube. (n.d.). *Violent or graphic content policies.* Youtube.com. https://support.google.com/youtube/answer/2802008?hl=en&ref_topic=9282436.

Chapter 18

Emerging Issues and Future Directions in the Area of Animal Cruelty

Shannon T. Grugan and Mary P. Brewster

Introduction

Earlier chapters in this text have addressed the past and current status of anti-cruelty legislation, public perceptions of cruelty, media portrayal of animal cruelty, the prevalence and incidence of cruelty, types of animal cruelty, links between animal cruelty and other criminality, and theoretical approaches to understanding the phenomenon. In this chapter, we will explore emerging issues related to animal cruelty and discuss future directions in the nature, legislation, public perception, and study and documentation of this behavior.

Advocacy and Activism

Journalist Will Potter (2009, p. 671) once wrote that as "going green has gone mainstream in the United States, ... there has been growing public concern for animal-welfare issues." This concern has resulted in ever-increasing levels of advocacy and activism. Some have described this as a "social movement" (Haile et al., 2021; Jacobsson, 2016). Advocacy is defined as "the act or process of supporting a cause or proposal" (Merriam-Webster, 2022b). Activism, on the other hand, is defined as "a doctrine or practice that emphasizes direct vigorous action especially in support of or opposition to one side of a controversial issue" (Merriam-Webster, 2022a). There are currently 46,000 "animal-focused non-profit organizations in the United States" (Cause IQ, 2022). Some animal rights organizations that are typically considered to be activist groups include People for the Ethical Treatment of Animals (PETA) and the Animal Liberation Front (ALF). In the past, members of these organizations have been known to take extreme and sometimes violent action to get their messages across. Included in these activities were such incidents as that of the assassination of Dutch politician Pim Fortuyn in 2002 by vegan animal rights activist Volkert van der Graaf. The murder presumably occurred because van der Graaf was angered by Fortuyn's supportive stance regarding intensive farming and fur farming (Munro, 2005). Another example of extreme activist violence was the Animal Liberation Front's bombing of two meat-transport trucks in Switzerland in 2007 (Flükiger, 2008). Media coverage of the Dutch and Swiss cases and other extreme actions taken by self-proclaimed activists in the U.S., U.K., and Australia has helped to create and perpetuate the image of activists as irrational and violent. Sensationalistic coverage by the news media of these types of relatively infrequent, though extreme and destructive, incidents may undermine the efforts of nonviolent activists as they seek change in the treatment of animals.

> The public view of animal rights activists is often colored by media coverage of violent forms of protest. Legislative reactions to these types of incidents have included the passage of the Serious and Organized Crime and Police Act in the U.K. in 2005 and the 2008 Animal Enterprise Terrorism Act (AETA) in the U.S. The U.K. Act "allow[s] stiff sentences to be imposed on those who intimidate companies and individuals that contract with animal-testing labs" and the U.S. Act is intended "to combat property damage and threats that produce 'a reasonable fear' of death and injury for researchers or their relatives" (Cressey, 2011, p. 452). While the U.K. law has resulted in convictions of violent activists, the application of the U.S. law "has been challenged in the courts" (Cressey, 2011, p. 452). Rather than prosecuting violent "ecoterrorists," the U.S. law has targeted animal advocates who have engaged in nonviolent protests. AETA and other "ag gag" (agricultural gag) legislation continue to exist in many jurisdictions, restricting some of protestors' activities. For example, some jurisdictions have legislation that "prohibit[s] activities such as trespass onto agricultural animal operations, gaining entry onto farms using false pretences, and interfering with the transport of farmed animals to slaughter" (Lazare, 2020, p. 86). AETA has reportedly been used to prosecute offenses such as filming the mistreatment of farm animals from a public roadway and then sharing the footage with others (Potter, 2018).

There has been some evidence that the criminalization of conventional and nonviolent protest activity is spreading to other countries (e.g., Lazare, 2020; Yates, 2011) and that legislation and prosecution has been modeled after the AETA (Potter, 2018). Despite some legal protections, some still fear animal activists. Recently, members of the University of Washington's Animal Care and Use Committee filed a lawsuit to prevent the university from releasing their names to People for the Ethical Treatment of Animals (PETA) due to safety concerns (Grimm, 2022).

Due to historical highly-publicized cases of violent extremist actions by some animal activists, there is often a misconception that activist groups are not interested in effecting change through more peaceful efforts. However, from 2016–2020, there had been only one terroristic attack or plot by animal rights "extremists" in the United States (Hwang, 2021). Despite the seriousness of the occasional use of incendiary devices, activist groups tend to target businesses rather than individuals and so, fortunately, no fatalities have occurred during these incidents (Hwang, 2021). Violent animal activism is the exception in the U.S., not the rule. In fact, most activist groups during the past 20 years have used and continue to use a wide array of nonviolent strategies, and believe that "violence is . . . counterproductive to the movement's goal in promoting the compassionate treatment of nonhuman animals" (Doherty, 2002, p. 90). Some of the less-violent tactics used by activists include demonstrations, gatherings to protest animals being transported to slaughterhouses, surreptitiously video recording and subsequently publicizing videos of mistreatment of animals in the animal food industry, occupations of animal farms, lobbying, pamphleteering, and pursuing animal protection litigation (Lazare, 2020; Tauber, 2010). Protests and occupations of working farms within the farming community have been reported, and there have been conflicts between some animal rights activist groups and farmers (Ceccato et al., 2022). Although some might describe extreme actions by activists as "ethically vigilante" (Allen & von Essen, 2018), use of alternatives to violence gives "protestors a moral advantage" (Munro, 2005, p. 80). Additionally, modern-day access to the mass media enhances the ability of activists to spread the word about their protests and the mistreatment of animals (Aji, 2019; Munro, 2005).

While the distinction between the terms *advocacy* and *activism* may appear to be slight, some advocates do not want to be "confused" with activists due to the misperception of activists as violent extremists. In fact, the passage of a federal eco-terrorism law and the framing by the media of activism/activists as violent terrorism/terrorists have further added to this perception held by the general public and by many advocates themselves. One study of volunteers in the purebred rescue movement illustrated advocates' concerns regarding being labeled as activists. Qualitative interviews with 26 rescue workers, most of whom had either a college degree or graduate degree, overwhelmingly viewed themselves as advocates, rather than activists, due to the nature of their work not involving "picketing, protesting, being political, [or] being 'in-your-face'" (Greenebaum, 2009, p. 295). Moreover, the rescue workers were concerned that they might be "associated with activism . . . and the radical and extreme" PETA. According to Greenebaum (2009), the rescuers had more of an "animal welfare perspective" than an "animal rights stance;" that is, they thought that animals had "intrinsic value," but only "*limited* rights" such as the right to a quality life (p. 297).

In addition to planned protests and other activities by organized activist groups, there continue to be impromptu acts of vigilantism. For example, a group of citizens in Hollywood, CA responded violently to a case of a man dragging and kicking a small dog on a leash that allegedly belonged to his mother (Klemack, 2022). Even after the dog was taken from the alleged abuser and was safe from further harm, a group of men continued to assault the abuser. Similarly, there have been many reported cases of violent attacks, and sometimes even murder, committed against dog thieves in Vietnam (e.g., Cuong, 2016; "Hanoi man," 2022; Winn, n.d.). These extreme cases of vigilantism are risky and dangerous, and should legally be handled by law enforcement.

More recent non-violent advocacy and activism has attempted to increase efficacy in the prosecution of perpetrators of animal cruelty. One such approach is Connecticut's attempt to reduce the number of nolle prossed and dismissed animal cruelty cases by appointing law school students and volunteer attorneys as legal advocates for justice in these cases (Rubin, 2018; 2021). These court-appointed advocates can engage in work ranging from investigative interviewing to writing briefs to "making recommendations to the judge" (Winkler, 2019, p. 247). Along similar lines, while it does not call for court-appointed advocates, Ohio law allows for specially-appointed prosecutors in cases of animal cruelty (Winkler, 2019). These prosecuting attorneys are employed by various humane societies in Ohio, and can prosecute cases on their own or alongside elected prosecutors or ADAs (Winkler, 2019).

Research on Animal Advocates and Activists

Within the realm of study related to animal cruelty, most research focusing on humans has involved studying the perpetrators of the abuse (e.g., hoarders, those committing intentional harm to animals, etc.). While not a new area of research, another important body of literature focuses on animal advocates and animal activists. It is likely to be this group that influences public perceptions of the issue of animal cruelty, and with that, effects cultural and legislative change.

The research on animal activism thus far suggests that, whether the result of biology, social learning, or "identif[ication] with the oppressed status of animals" (Gaarder, 2011), the majority of animal activists are women (see e.g., Carmona, 2012; Park & Valentino, 2019), and women are stronger proponents of animal rights than are men (Glanville et al., 2021; Kruse, 1999). Initial involvement in activism may be due to any number of reasons. One study found that while "attitudes [related to] caring for one's own animal" do not vary by gender, women tend to have higher levels of concern and affection for mistreated animals (Glanville et al., 2021, p. 12). Similar gender differences have been found among Spanish citizens' attitudes toward animal welfare in bullfighting (María et al., 2017) and Australian citizens' attitudes towards horseracing (Wilson et al., 2021). Results from another study also showed the same types of gender differences in terms of views about animal rights, awareness of animal cruelty, and the sentience of animals (Balieva & Lazarova, 2020).

Other research on animal advocacy has focused on how awareness of animal cruelty creates attitudinal and behavioral changes. For example, a survey of vegan animal activists in Spain revealed that exposure to information about animal cruelty was a common reason provided for the conversion to veganism and animal rights activism (Carmona, 2012). Education through the school system and mass media, then, may be key to increasing public awareness and concern for animals, and the public's involvement as advocates and activists in anti-cruelty efforts. This increased awareness among the general public, as well as among law enforcement officers, social service providers, and mental health professionals, may help to mitigate the impact of animal cruelty. A smaller scale approach to education (i.e., pamphleting) was not found to be as effective (Haile et al., 2021), so mass and social media may be the more effective means through which to create change.

In Chapter 17 of this text, Grove highlights some aspects of the media's role in disseminating information related to cruelty. Coverage of certain high-profile cases in the mainstream *news* media may even more effectively serve to heighten public awareness about animal cruelty, as occurred in the Michael Vick dogfighting case Jarvie et al. (2021) make the case that "online platforms enable animal activism on a networked scale, with unprecedented immediacy" (p. 354). Some call for a multi-strategy approach that includes highlighting the environmental impact of factory farming to sway the public's view of the exploitation of animals in the agribusiness industry (Almiron, 2019). In addition to the news media as influential in reaching potential activists, the dissemination of information about animal protection can also take place in the school setting. Thomas and Beirne (2002) argued for the inclusion of humane education in character education among youth for the "cultivation of empathy" (p. 190). They claimed that there was an absence of humane education at the middle and high school levels, and that teenagers were "ripe for activism" (Thomas & Beirne, 2002, p. 195). Unfortunately, despite continued interest in educating various populations about animal cruelty in an effort to change attitudes and behavior (e.g., Haile et al., 2021; Tallberg et al., 2022), not every strategy designed for this purpose have shown great effect (e.g., Haile et al., 2021).

Effectiveness of Activism

Animal activism appears to have been effective in several cases throughout the world. For example, beginning in the late nineteenth century, a group of biologists became active in an attempt to fend off the extinction of the American alligator. Eventually (in the middle of the 20th century), they joined forces with others wildlife advocates and with policymakers in the creation of the American Alligator Council (Barrow, 2009). The results of their work included both research on the species as well as the passage of local, state, and federal laws to protect the American alligator. In 1987, the U.S. Fish and Wildlife Service removed the American alligator from its endangered species list due to a "complete recovery of the species" (National Parks Conservation Association, n.d.). Another example of effective activism is the significant role played by the Humane Society of the United States (HSUS) in the creation and passage of felony anti-cruelty laws (Allen, 2005, p. 443). Legislation will be discussed in greater detail below, but as a result of the push for felony legislation, currently all 50 U.S. states have felony anti-cruelty statutes (Berry, 2014).

Dillard (2002) argued that activists could be persuasive when using civil disobedience that is "nonviolent/non-threatening ... and when participants demonstrate not only a willingness to suffer for their beliefs but also an interest in communicating that suffering to onlookers" (p. 47). This was illustrated by the protests organized by the Fund for Animals against the annual Fred Coleman Memorial Shoot. The event, which was colloquially known as the Hegins pigeon shoot, was the largest event of its kind in the United States. Event organizers purchased over 5,000 pigeons from breeders and caged them for days or weeks leading up to the Labor Day event. Up to 250 shooters participated in taking aim at the pigeons that were released one at a time from their cages. Fewer than one-third of the birds were estimated to have died instantly from gunshot wounds. Often, the birds were merely wounded and dropped to the field. Young "trapper boys" were assigned the task of retrieving the injured birds from the field and decapitating them "over the rim of a barrel or with their bare hands" (Dillard, 2002, p. 50). The dead birds were later disposed of as trash.

Early protests at the event were disorganized and tense and did not garner the public support desired by the protestors. In 1996, the Fund for Animals sent only a small contingent of protestors whose sole purpose was to help the pigeons without engaging in name calling, insults, threats, shoving, etc. A dozen protestors engaged in civil disobedience by lying on the killing field and delaying the start of the event by two hours. The remaining activists later assisted in rescuing injured pigeons from the field. Interviews with event observers revealed that the impact of the activists was much more positive and emphasized the suffering of the pigeons rather than the conflict between the activists and pigeon shoot participants. The result was more positive press coverage and perceptions by observers (Dillard, 2002). Following the event in 1998, the Hegins Township Labor Day Committee decided to end the 65-year-old fundraising tradition allegedly because they were "exhausted from 12 years of battling animal rights activists who relentlessly sued them" (Latty, 2000). Live pigeon shoots are still legal in Pennsylvania and have continued to take place at private gun clubs. There have been multiple attempts to pass laws to prohibit these events in recent years. As of this writing, a bill (S.B. 702) sponsored by Senator Patrick Browne (R-Lehigh) to ban these shoots in the state of Pennsylvania is currently pending. Some have argued that the National Rifle Association's political clout is preventing the passage of the bill (Humane Society Legislative Fund, 2012).

Due in large part to the efforts of advocates and activists, in December 2021,

> the Humane Cosmetics Act was reintroduced in the House and Senate by a bipartisan group of legislators including Senators as well as 70 other house co-sponsors. The bill would end the use of animal-based testing for cosmetics in the U.S. and prohibit the sale of any cosmetic product that has been tested on animals after the date of enactment (Humane Cosmetics Act, 2022, p. 166).

The bipartisan support for the bill as well as reported overwhelming public support for banning the use of animals in cosmetic testing ("Humane Cosmetics Act," 2022) is indicative of a trend of increased inclusivity in animal protection that may eventually extend to factory farming, the use of non-human animals in scientific research, etc. Other successfully-passed legislation following pressure from advocates and activists has been discussed in earlier chapters in this volume (e.g., Chapter 5) and will also be addressed later in this chapter.

Another example of effective activism is that which led to Ringling Bros. and Barnum & Bailey Circus shutting down in 2017 after more than 145 years of performances that included animal acts. A series of lawsuits filed by activists alleging abuse of animal performers led to the demise of the renowned circus (Greenwood, 2017a). Lawsuits continue to be filed against other circuses and others profiting from animal performances (Greenwood, 2017a).

While there are a great variety of actions taken by animal advocates and activists, Broad (2018) proposes that "effective altruism" should be based upon a scientific approach whereby the greatest and most cost-effective impact can be realized. Effective altruism proponent William MacAskill (2016) aptly titled his book on the subject *Doing Good Better.* Effective altruism entails networking that will encourage "the use of private resources to produce public benefits" (Broad, 2018, p. 779), and will most effectively reduce non-human animal suffering. In particular, Broad (2018) notes that this approach will be used in "anti-factory farm advocacy and in promotion of animal food replacement technologies" (p. 787).

Continued research on advocacy and activism may help to further efforts in animal protection. Specifically, research focused on gaining a better understanding of how activists are "created," public perceptions of and responses to activism, and the impact of activism on legislative change, may help to encourage more effective strategies in anti-cruelty efforts. Research on violent activism and resultant legislation that restricts activities of activists might also further our understanding of the legislative process.

Media and Public Awareness of Animal Cruelty

The actions of both animal advocates and activists have played a part in increasing public awareness of cruelty to animals, but a more popular source of information has, not surprisingly, been the media. As mentioned previously, extreme cases of animal abuse that have been picked up by the media can bring to the public's attention the problem of animal cruelty. For example, beginning in the early 1990s in southern England, a series of horse assaults ("maimings") occurred and media coverage of the events led to a moral panic—one of the first moral panics (if not *the* first moral panic) involving victims that were nonhuman animals (Yates et al., 2001). Interestingly, though, there had historically been relatively little press coverage of the cruelty inflicted upon over 200 racehorses annually in Britain (Yates et al., 2001). Without media coverage, little public pressure for change exists. Once "picked up" by the media, however, news of animal cruelty spreads quickly.

The impact of the news media on animal cruelty cannot be overstated. Mass media coverage of animal cruelty has been found to impact meat demand (Tonsor & Olynk, 2011) and support altering farming and research practices (Bayvel, 2005). Dissemination of information has shown the potential for garnering public support for banning inhumane practices in farming (Tuyttens et al., 2011). A number of "activist documentaries" such as "*Dominion,*" "*The Cove,*" "*Mine,*" and "*Food, INC.*" have raised public awareness and "advocate[d] for change, whether in regard to mass wild animal kills, companion animals in natural disasters, or the modern food industry" (Woodson,

2011, p. 200; see also Tallberg et al., 2022). Similarly, shocking footage of animal cruelty that has been posted online and/or circulated by means of social media can have an impact on public views of animals and their treatment. For example, in 2008, PETA posted online video recordings of severe abuses against pigs at a factory farm (PETA, n.d.). This case of "shock advocacy" appeared to effectively raise the public's consciousness (Scutter & Mills, 2009), and led to charges being filed against, and the subsequent convictions of, the perpetrators of the cruelty (PETA, 2009). Even farmers who have their *own* web presence are more likely to be harassed and victimized by those who oppose their animal production work (Ceccato et al., 2021). Exposure throughout various forms of media removes the "cloak of concealment" within which much institutionalized animal abuse occurs (Petković, 2021).

As the media increase coverage of animal cruelty as sport, it is likely that public outrage will increase to the point at which citizens will pressure legislators to pass new laws to prohibit or at least control the conditions surrounding these activities. Long-standing cultural and institutionalized cruelty towards animals in "sport" will likely become increasingly scrutinized as has been seen in the case of bullfighting (e.g., Beilin, 2012; María, 2017) and whip use during Thoroughbred racing (e.g., Evans & McGreevy, 2011). For example, Evans and McGreevy (2011) analyzed the usefulness of whip use during horse racing and found that there was no statistical association between frequency of whip use and velocity, deeming this cruel behavior unnecessary and ineffective in accomplishing its intended purpose. Increasing public awareness of cruel practices in animal-related "sports" can alter public perception and ultimately lead to changes in practice. For example, in Barcelona, one former 20,000-seat bullring has been repurposed and transformed into a thriving "retail and entertainment complex" with a multiplex movie theater, a gym, and museum, and retail stores (Brown, 2012). The bullring transformation was not purely due to a change in morals. In fact, as is often the case, the decision was largely a financial one; with greater public concern for animal protection came a loss of interest in attending bullfights and thus reduced profits. One might expect similar changes to occur in Thoroughbred horse and greyhound racing, as well as in rodeos.

Mass media has proven to be a double-edged sword. While it has provided important information to the public about the abuses of animals in various industries throughout the world, it has also sometimes created moral panic. Such was the case in the U.K. following a 1990 fatal attack on an 11-year-old boy by two Rottweilers and two 1991 non-fatal attacks by pit bulls. Very soon after the dog attacks, the *Dangerous Dogs Act* (1991) was passed in the U.K., which criminalized the owning, breeding, and sale of pit bulls as well as three other dog breeds. Within five years of the passage of the Act, over 1,000 dogs deemed "weapon dogs" or "dangerous dogs" were seized from their owners and subsequently killed (Hallsworth, 2011). As mass media continues to expand, so too will its potential to both help and harm animals.

Other examples of the mass media's ability to undermine efforts to protect animals include the proliferation of online puppy mills, web-based trade of exotic animals, and the availability of crush videos on the internet. The nature of the electronic dissemination of information and constitutional protections in the United States make legislation of the industries particularly challenging. (See Chapter 9.) In 1999, federal legislation (18 U.S.C. §48) was passed to prevent "crush videos," but was deemed unconstitutional (due to overbreadth) by the U.S. Supreme Court ruled in 2010 (United States v. Stevens, 2010). The law was written in such a way that it would subject to "up to five years in prison, anyone who 'knowingly creates, sells, or possesses a depiction of animal cruelty with the intention of placing that depiction in interstate or foreign commerce for commercial gain" (Zimmerman, 2010, p. 17). Despite its presence on the books for over a decade, the law was never actually used to prosecute creators or distributors of crush videos during its first 15 years of existence. It was, however, applied to a few cases of the distribution of images of animal fighting. Immediately after the Supreme Court's decision to strike the law, a new federal bill was introduced and passed into law—H.R. 5566, the Animal Crush Video Prohibition Act of 2010. This law had bipartisan support and is worded more specifically to prohibit "videos where an animal is 'tortured, maimed, or mutilated,' and also specifically does not apply to depictions of hunting" (Zimmerman, 2010, p. 18). Following the first prosecution of two Texas individuals under this legislation, the law was deemed unconstitutional by a district court. However, the United States Court of Appeals for the Fifth Circuit reversed the district court's judgment and upheld the constitutionality of the Act, holding that "on its face §48 is limited to unprotected obscenity and therefore facially constitutional" (United States v. Ashley Nicole Richards; Brent Justice, 2014). In 2015 and 2016, the crush video legislation finally resulted in convictions of Nicole Richards and Brent Justice, respectively, with Justice sentenced to 57 months of incarceration followed by three years of probation (United States Department of Justice, 2016).

Changing Views of Animals and of Cruelty

A survey of 1,031 U.S. households conducted by Edge Research in 2004 revealed that animal protection was important to respondents. When asked "How important is it to you that animals are protected from cruelty and abuse?", two-thirds of respondents reported that it was "very important" (Lockwood, 2006, p. 9). Similarly, a Gallup poll found that 62% of Americans believed that nonhuman "animals deserve some protection but can still be used for the benefit of humans" and 32% thought that animals should be afforded the same rights as humans (Riffkin, 2015). Interestingly, another Gallup poll indicated that only 5% of Americans are vegetarian and 3% are vegan (Reinhart, 2018). Despite the increase in the reported desire for animal protection, most people are not necessarily ready to afford non-human animals the same rights afforded to humans. In one study comparing responses to animal (cat/dog) versus human (baby/girlfriend) abuse cases, Burke et al. (2021) found an equal level of moral outrage, but less punitive views of animal abuse than human abuse.

The treatment of nonhuman animals has focused on "[t]he level of sentience and consciousness in other species" (Burghardt, 2009, p. 499) or "level of awareness or consciousness of ill treatment" (p. 499). Many have suggested that anthropomorphism is a key element in determining views of animals (e.g., Herzog & Galvin, 1997; Hills, 1995). That is, the greater the attribution of human (emotional and intellectual) characteristics to an animal, the greater one's concern for a given species' welfare (see Chapter 7). However, humans may not portray all species of animals equally. The idea of the phylogenetic continuum was first introduced by Aristotle; the higher an animal on the phylogenetic scale, the more complex the animal and the greater the number of human-like attributes possessed by the animal. Species, then, can be viewed along a continuum; people would presumably be less anthropomorphic in their perceptions of a frog or a fish than of a dog or a chimpanzee (see e.g., Knight et al., 2009).[1] In a study of punishment recommendations for animal abusers, Allen and colleagues (2002) found that the greater the perceived similarity between abused animals and humans, the more harshly the research subjects believed the perpetrators should be punished.

Considering the results of the Edge Survey and Gallup poll, it is somewhat surprising that humans are able to behave in ways that may contribute to cruelty towards nonhuman animals. For example, the vast majority of people eat the meat of animals bred on factory farms and use products tested on animals or made from animal parts. These same people may be opposed to the use of cats, dogs, and chimpanzees in scientific research. How is it, then, that people hold seemingly contradictory views of animals? It may be due, in part, to ignorance regarding the ways in which animals are treated in factory farm and scientific lab settings. It may also "be due to the belief in the mentality of different species, as well as ... affection for particular kinds of animals" (Knight et al., 2009, p 467).

Research on the varying human attitudes towards nonhuman animal use and abuse has been relatively scant. One study examined the attitudes and beliefs of scientists, animal welfarists, and laypeople towards the use of animals for medical research, dissection in biology class, entertainment (i.e., hunting and "keeping animals in zoos"), and personal decoration ("clothing made from animal products, cosmetics testing") (Knight et al., 2009, 476). Other variables included on the survey included perceptions of choice (i.e., "the existence of alternatives to using animals"), views of humans as superior to animals, and "belief in animal mind" (p. 467). While the attitudes of animal welfarists were largely consistent across types of animals and the purpose of animal use, scientists' attitudes were "multidimensional;" they "did not support the use of animals for dissection, personal decoration, and entertainment," although they were proponents of the use of animals in research (Knight et al., 2009, p. 476). The polarized views of scientists and animal welfarists towards the use of animals in scientific

1. Burghardt (2009) points out that extant research literature provides information regarding "the similarities and differences between human and non-human animals and their relevance for decisions about our treatment of other species" (p. 515), but that this anthropocentric approach is not necessarily that useful. Burghardt questions whether "consciousness and sentience [are] overvalued as markers on the ethical ruler" and suggests that perhaps "our moral philosophy" should be balanced by "an ecological vision" (p. 516) and a new ethics of "environmental survival" (p. 517).

research could be explained by their conflicting views of the availability of alternatives; scientists typically justified their support of animal use in research by arguing that there were no suitable alternatives.

The more educated that people become about factory farming, the use of animals for testing purposes in laboratories, etc., the greater the cognitive dissonance and resultant discomfort and anxiety that people experience. When there is a disconnect between one's actions and moral standards, social and psychological processes can help to mitigate the anxiety caused by one's behavior. Those who are aware of their actions may use various techniques of neutralization to downplay the harm to the animal victims (Sykes & Matza, 1957). Similarly, Bandura created the concept of moral disengagement to explain how a person can act in an inhumane way despite contradictions with one's standards (Bandura, 1999). Both techniques of neutralization and mechanisms of moral disengagement involve cognitively reframing the nature of one's actions in order to make them appear justifiable. This can be accomplished through the marginalization of one's victims, the denial of harm to victims, and other minimizations of one's harm to animals. There has been some evidence to support the validity of both techniques of neutralization and moral disengagement among deer poachers (Eliason & Dodder, 1999), blood sport participants (see Chapter 9), and hunters (Presser & Taylor, 2011). Some have even noted the applicability of moral disengagement in terms of people's unwillingness to punish perpetrators of animal cruelty (Vollum et al., 2004). One study assessed the moral persuasion of college students to reduce meat consumption through distributing animal advocacy pamphlets. Results revealed very little lasting impact on students' behavior (Haile et al., 2021). Inconsistency between morals and behavior is not limited to laypersons; in one study, 40% of animal activists were reportedly meat eaters (Herzog & Golden, 2009).

Shooster (2015) argues that "animal rights is a social justice issue" since social justice values include "(1) an opposition to arbitrary discrimination, (2) support of the marginalized, and (3) a respect for autonomy and individual rights" (p. 40). He points out that speciesism is similar to racism, sexism, and classism in its arbitrary justification of "violence and inequality"; that "nonhuman animals are marginalized on a scale and to a degree that is incomprehensible" (p. 42) and that "social justice means opposition to ... human domination over the lives of nonhuman animals" (Shooster, 2015, p. 43). Shooster (2015) takes aim predominately at the animal food production industry, focusing on the injustices of eating animals. Interestingly, while there has been an increase in the U.S. public's concerns about animal cruelty and interest in animal rights over recent decades, the increase in self-identified vegetarians since the 1990s has not been dramatic (Šimčikas, 2018). Even while there has been an increase in the number of vegetarian restaurants and increased interest in plant-based foods (Šimčikas, 2018), global demand for meat products has continued to remain high in recent years (Food and Agricultural Organization of the United Nations, 2022). Tallberg et al. (2022) describe an animal activism approach that they have used in teaching their business students. The approach included exposing students to the often-hidden realities of animal food production as they hoped to "create a business society which takes on a fiercely compassionate engagement with social justice topics" (Tallberg et al., 2022, p. 71).

Some animal advocates are calling for the expansion of the application of animal cruelty statutes to all sentient beings. While there is general agreement over protection of cats and dogs, there is less consensus regarding other non-human animals (Greenwood, 2017b). The U.S. is behind some other developed nations in its recognition of chicken and poultry as sentient beings (Park, 2021). Some legal advocates call for more inclusive protections for non-human animals (Kotzmann & Nip, 2020). Kotzmann and Nip (2020) argue that animal cruelty laws should apply to cases involving all sentient animals, although the inclusion of fish might have to wait "until the public are sufficiently educated to understand that fish are also capable of experiencing pain and suffering" (p. 317).

The validation of animal cruelty as a serious crime has, in recent years, also finally been reflected by the inclusion of these types of offenses in the FBI's National Incident-Based Reporting System (NIBRS). The maintenance by a government agency of statistics related to this type of crime reflects the importance of recognizing non-human animal victims by our society at large. Chapter 8 in this volume provides detailed information about the measurement of animal cruelty as well as current statistics.

Current Application and Future Trends in Anti-Cruelty Legislation

Legislative evolution often reflects (or is the result of) the evolution of social consciousness. As humans become aware of animal cruelty, through mass or social media and other means, resultant change in cultural norms, values, and politically important public opinion, become reflected in legislation. While the shifts in awareness of animal cruelty and perceptions of animals have facilitated improvement in the protections outlined in current anti-cruelty legislation in the United States, there are still many issues and obstacles to overcome in establishing consistency in defining animals, prohibited behaviors, and appropriate sanctions.

Although every state currently has laws that prohibit some form of animal cruelty, legislators across the United States are continuing to grapple with specification of the actions that constitute improper treatment of animals (including how to handle the issue of intent), the types of animals that should be included under protective laws, the penalties for engaging in prohibited behavior, and the best ways to regulate cruelty going forward. Similarly, the legal status of animals as property continues to be challenged in the court system. However, as it will be discussed below, defining the status of animals is as contentious, and at times contradictory, as defining cruelty. Recently enacted pieces of state legislation, pending state and federal legislation, and recent court decisions are good examples of this disjointed patchwork and indicate that lawmakers and judicial representatives are far from achieving consensus on many issues pertaining to animal cruelty. While the specific topical issues may change, it is likely that legislators will continue to produce these mismatched and contradictory laws that add to the existing assortment of animal cruelty legislation the United States for the foreseeable future.

Recent Laws, Judicial Action, and Pending Legislation

A recent sign that collective awareness and concern about animal welfare issues in the United States has increased substantially came in 2019 with passage of the Preventing Animal Cruelty and Torture Act (PACT Act). This federal law shored up existing laws about crushing videos to include the prohibition of specific acts of cruelty usually but only associated with these videos, including burning, drowning, suffocating, impalement, and other forms of severe harm (H.R. 724, 2019–2020). This law does not fully centralize prohibitions against animal cruelty at the federal level, but those who have been advocating for this sort of centralization view this as a step in the right direction.

Centralization of cruelty and protective laws for animals has become a highly discussed topic in recent years. Some have likened the trajectory of animal cruelty and protective laws in the United States to that of environmental protection in the late 1960s and early 1970s (Senatori & Frasch, 2010). Early environmental protection began with disjointed state laws and lack of public understanding and support. Over time, the environmental protection movement began building momentum, gaining the attention of the federal government, and increasing the public's level of understanding and support until a number of important federal laws were passed and the Environmental Protection Agency (EPA) was created to provide oversight and enforcement support. Senatori and Frasch (2010) argue that just like environmental regulation in the 1970s, animal cruelty regulation could ultimately be centralized, with oversight given to a federal agency that they theoretically dub the "Animal Protection Agency," or APA. Of course, federal oversight has not and likely will not be a panacea that eradicates or even appropriately deals with acts of animal cruelty. In fact, if extending the analogy between environmental protection and animal welfare, the creation of the EPA has not been a cure-all for the environmental ills that plague the environment, simply because, like many of the social problems that have demanded centralized regulation under the federal government, there is no feasible way of eradicating the sources of the problems. What centralized agency regulation can do is just that—regulate the problem at hand so that it is manageable and handled in a consistent uniform manner throughout the country. Additionally, given the current world economic climate and increasing international political tensions, it is likely that policymakers at a federal level would argue that there are more pressing anthropocentric concerns on the federal agenda than a newly formed agency for animals that would cost time, money, and manpower. Furthermore, opponents of centralization/federalization, argue that animal cruelty and protection laws should be left to the states and that laws like the PACT Act of 2019 are merely symbolic of shifts in society's views of animal welfare and protection and could be more harmful than beneficial in the long run (Stegman, 2020). However, from an animal rights perspective, the argument can be made that centralized federal oversight could transform what is currently a mess of disjointed, jumbled, and disorganized state level laws into a streamlined and comprehensive scheme of centralized federal regulation. Whether or not centralization is effective or politically popular, largescale, systematic, and sweeping regulation of animal cruelty and animal protection at the federal level is not the current reality of animal cruelty law in the United States. Most of the laws that govern animal protection in the United States remain the purview of individual states.

For every state that passes a law expanding definitions of certain types of cruelty, increasing the power of regulatory agencies, or increasing penalties, there is another that vetoes similar legislation or passes laws that limit the definition of cruelty, associated penalties, or requirements. By 2014, all 50 states had identified some form of animal cruelty as a felony level offense. South Dakota was the last state to enact a felony level provision for acts of cruelty in 2014 (Berry, 2014). During 2021 alone, the HSUS reported that 102 new laws were passed at the state and local level that enhanced the protection of a variety of different animals (Block, 2022). With so many, they cannot all be discussed at length. Some representative examples of recently enacted legislation that have expanded provisions related to cruelty at the state level include:

- In Illinois, pets sold in pet stores can now only come from rescues, shelters, and animal control facilities, not puppy mills or breeders (Block & Amudson, 2022).
- The states of Maryland, Virginia, Hawaii, and Maine banned sales of cosmetics tested on animals (Block, 2021).
- New Mexico banned trapping, snaring, and poisoning of animals on public lands (Associated Press, 2022).
- Nevada became one of the latest states to ban the sale of eggs from hens kept in cages (Wilkins, 2021).

In addition to the creation of new protection laws, there have been some promising developments in relation to stopping problematic laws that could continue to contribute to cruelty to animals. For example, according to the Animal Legal Defense Fund (2022) in 2022, a controversial "Ag-Gag" law in Iowa, discussed elsewhere in this chapter, was struck down by the U.S. District Court as unconstitutional and a violation of the First Amendment.

While the above laws and legal decisions indicate promising expansions of animal cruelty protections, there have also been a number of recently enacted laws that do just the opposite. In many instances, the rollback of provisions and penalties for animal-based regulation is due to intense lobbying by those with legitimate financial interests as stake, such as commercial breeders, pet store owners, and livestock farmers. Breeders and puppy mill owners have put intense pressure on regulation of breeding that has resulted in laws being modified or outright repealed. For example, in 2011

Missouri repealed a proposition that was voted into law by the Missouri public earlier that year requiring commercial breeders to limit the number of breeding dogs to 50 and provide rest periods for breeding females between breeding cycles (Animal Law Coalition, 2012a; Associated Press, 2011). Similarly, McNutt (2012) reports that a law passed in Oklahoma in 2012 relaxed existing regulation of commercial pet breeding and transferred inspection and oversight of breeding from an independent board to the state's Department of Agriculture. Many believe that the transfer of oversight to the existing agency will decrease the standard of care provided by commercial breeders (Animal Law Coalition, 2012b; McNutt, 2012). More recently, in 2015 lawmakers in Alabama have refused to review a piece of legislation calling for increased standards of care for breeders with 10 or more breeding dogs (Edgemon, 2015) Additionally, according to the Animal Law Coalition, horse slaughter has become a particularly active arena for animal legislation—for both opposition and support of slaughter—due largely to the lifting of the federal ban on the practice in late 2011 and its subsequent reinstatement in 2014. Even before the ban was lifted in 2011, many states had laws banning slaughter of horses for meat for a very long time. New Jersey led the charge to keep the transportation/slaughter of horses for meat illegal in the wake of the federal ban, while a number of states, including Idaho, Wyoming, North Dakota, Nebraska, and Montana, had enacted laws allowing horse slaughter and the sale of horse meat (Animal Law Coalition, 2012). In terms of lobbying, many of the state laws allowing horse slaughter or transportation for slaughter were symbolic gestures that were actually passed prior to the lift of the federal ban to show support for the practice. According to Massey (2014), by 2013, plans were in place to open active horse slaughterhouses in New Mexico, Missouri, and Iowa. However, none of these plants was ever opened due to potential violations of environmental and food production laws unrelated to cruelty (Massey, 2014). With the reinstatement of the ban, slaughter or horses for meat on U.S. soil has been stopped for the time being; however, transportation of horses from the U.S. to places like Mexico and Canada for slaughter remains a legal, though contentious issue. The Save America's Forgotten Equines (SAFE) Act (2021–2022) is a piece of pending legislation that, if passed, would prohibit transport and sales of horses in the U.S. for the purpose of slaughter for horse meat (H.R. 3355, 2021–2022).

In terms of the courts, state judiciaries do not make direct changes to policy in regard to animal cruelty but in recent cases, the status of animals as property has been questioned in the courtroom. Recent court decisions, while perhaps precedent setting, have also been contradictory. Many court cases addressing issues of cruelty have grappled with the rights of animals, or lack thereof. For example, in 2012, the New Jersey State Supreme Court effectively reinforced the long-held notion that animals are property when it ruled that a dog owner was entitled to damages, but not payment, for emotional stress for a killed pet (Newcomer, 2012). Within days of the ruling in New Jersey, the Oregon State Supreme Court ruled that animals are not just property, arguing that animals can be considered victims of a crime when cruelty occurs. According to the court, their "primary concern was to protect individual animals as sentient beings, rather than to vindicate a more generalized public interest in their welfare" (Wright, 2012). In a rather unusual and high-profile case in 2021, the offspring of hippopotamuses owned by Columbian drug kingpin Pablo Escobar that now roam parts of Columbia as an invasive species were granted personhood in the form of classification of the hippos as "interested persons" by a U.S. court (Cheng, 2021). This designation was sought to identify the rights of these hippos as the debate about what to do with them as an invasive species is ongoing and is the first decision by a U.S. court of its kind.

While recently enacted state legislation and court decisions are indicative of a contradictory patchwork of current regulatory practices, pending federal legislation and state legislation paint a slightly more consistent picture of potential enhancement of enumerated protections for animals. However, since the below are pending, it is possible that many will never come to pass. Some notable pending legislation includes:

- Animal Cruelty Enforcement Act of 2021, a federal act that would establish a new section in the DOJ's Environmental and Natural Resources Division to enforce federal animal cruelty laws (H.R. 1016, 2021–2022)
- Child and Animal Abuse Detection and Reporting Act of 2021, a federal act that would require additional federal reporting on animal cruelty that may be cooccurring with child abuse (H.R. 763, 2021–2022)
- Humane Cosmetics Act of 2021, a federal act that would effectively outlaw testing of cosmetics on animals at a national level (S. 3357, 2021–2022)
- Victoria's Law, proposed legislation in Pennsylvania that would pet stores selling animals from puppy mills and breeders (S.B. 234, 2021)

Recent and pending legislation like that above indicate that, at the very least, lawmakers are taking animal cruelty issues seriously and are devoting an ever-increasing amount of attention to the phenomenon. However, even with an upward trend in regulations that are intended to afford additional protections, the creation of laws regarding animal abuse remain piecemeal and inconsistent. Additionally, some of these laws can be ineffective and difficult to successfully prosecute. This is especially the case when looking at interstate transport activities where certain actions may be prohibited in one state but not another. The distant future may include resolution to these problems in the form of more action and oversight from the federal government.

Important Emerging Legislative Issues

Horsemeat production and puppy mills are not the only hot button issues to be handled by lawmakers in recent sessions. Other issues of animal cruelty currently in the forefront of new legislative acts that are currently being developed at both the state and federal levels include shark-finning and the use of hidden cameras at factory farming facilities. According to the Humane Society International (2012), shark-finning is a form of wildlife cruelty that involves capture of sharks for the purpose of removing their fins, which are sought after for the purpose of making soup. The sharks are then released back into the sea finless, leaving them incapable of swimming properly. The sharks will usually die shortly after being released as a result of blood loss, suffocation, or attack from other predators. Millions of sharks are killed as a result of finning each year (Humane Society International, 2012). While boats and vessels registered to the U.S. have been prohibited by federal law from engaging in shark-finning since passage of the Shark Finning Protection Act of 2000, shark hunting (i.e., killing the shark and taking the entire carcass) and possession of shark fins currently remain legal at the federal level (H.R. 5461, 2000). While federal government regulation has been lax, state legislators are beginning to address the issues of shark hunting and shark-finning by targeting the shark fin market For example, the Humane Society of the United States (HSUS) reports that in 2011, Hawaii became the first state to ban the sale and distribution of shark fin products, including shark fin soup (HSUS, 2011). Illinois, California, Hawaii, Oregon, Washington, Maryland, Delaware, and New York have passed laws joining Hawaii in this ban (HSUS, 2012d; Shark Stewards, 2015). As of 2021, there is a pending federal act to ban all sales of shark fin products in the United States (H.R. 2811, 2021–2022).

While shark-finning legislation continues to build momentum, another emerging trend in anti-cruelty legislation also indicates that animal rights issues are continuing to be prioritized over corporate concerns. Legislation criminalizing the use of hidden cameras by investigative journalists, activists, and whistleblowing employees and/or requiring pre-screening of potential employees of factory farms to ensure they are not affiliated with a news organization, humane organization, or activist group—so called, "ag-gag" laws mentioned previously in this chapter—are controversial and have been seen by many as a troubling development in humane legislation in the last decade (HSUS, 2012a). Proponents of the ag-gag laws (most of whom are industry insiders) argue, weakly, that prohibiting hidden cameras "protect[s] the nation's food supply" (Rasmussen, 2012, p. 4). Opponents of the legislation argue that hidden camera footage has been an important source for investigative journalists providing information on factory farming to the public and has served as compelling evidence in investigations when recorded by whistleblowers and undercover activists (HSUS 2012a; Rasmussen, 2012). Since 2012, 24 states have attempted to pass some form of ag-gag legislation, but passage has only been successful in six states, including Iowa, Utah, Kansas, Missouri, Montana, and North Dakota. However, since Kansas has had the law in place since 1990, many are more concerned about the precedent sent by the 2012 passage of the first recent ag-gag statute in Iowa and the subsequent passage in the additional states listed here (American Society for the Prevention of Cruelty to Animals, 2015; Animal Law Coalition, 2012; Rasmussen, 2012;). However, again perhaps because of increasing awareness about the realities of factory farming and the true purpose of ag-gag laws within society in recent years, the ag-gag laws in Iowa, Utah, and Kansas have since been challenged successfully in court by various advocacy groups (Animal Legal Defense Fund, 2022). The tide may be turning when it comes to preventing whistleblowing on factory farming operations as a result.

The Future of Anti-Cruelty Legislation

While the United States has made notable strides in provisions for animal welfare and the prevention of cruelty over the last 150 years, legislation is far from perfect and there is still much work to be done. There is a pressing need to standardize definitions of cruelty, the legal status of animals, and the proper way of handling offenders. It is unlikely that national consensus on these issues will come in the form of state-based legislation but the future of centralized federal oversight, while a novel idea, is only hypothetical at the current time. For the time being, it appears that most forms of animal protection will primarily be state issues and that these concerns will in turn have to be addressed at the state level.

Any legislative body in the United States, state or federal, would benefit from looking to the European Union (EU) as an example. According to the European Commission on Health and Consumers, the EU has formally recognized in the Treaty of Lisbon, which was entered in 2009, that "animals are sentient beings" capable of suffering and feeling pain, with various EU laws reflecting this view ("The EU and animal welfare," n.d.). While there are movements to reinforce the rights that are inherent in sentience, the United States generally still holds a 19th century view of animals as property. This has impeded expansion of appropriate legal protections. The bottom line is that animal cruelty legislation in the United States, while uneven and lacking in uniformity on a national scale, is moving in the right direction in regards to some types of cruelty and may be moving in the wrong direction in others. Hopefully, someday, animals may be afforded legal uniform protections appropriate to their status at both the state and federal level.

Improvement in the Investigation and Prosecution of Animal Cruelty Cases

Due to increases in legislative provisions, education and training of investigative professionals and prosecutors, and public awareness, there have been numerous improvements made in the handling of animal cruelty cases as criminal events in recent years. These improvements span the entire enforcement life cycle, with many resources available for training and a move towards cooperation, information-sharing, and knowledge-sharing between animal cruelty investigators, police, prosecutors, and other law enforcement agencies. These improvements are ongoing and new to many jurisdictions, but as these improvements continue to develop, it is likely that enforcement of anti-cruelty laws in the United States, in the form of efficient investigations and prosecutions, will continue to improve as well.

Numerous training programs and instructional tools have been developed in recent times to assist police officers, animal investors, and other law enforcement personnel with issues related to proper investigation of animal cruelty. A number of schools and educational vendors have begun to provide certification and training for animal cruelty investigators and police officers. For example, the University of Missouri Law Enforcement Training Institute houses the National Animal Cruelty Investigations School, which provides training on animal law, proper levels of care for various species, recognition of cruelty and dangers in the field, and other issues relevant to police and veterinary personnel throughout the United States (National Animal Cruelty Investigations School, n.d.). In addition to training courses, many organizations have created standalone training materials and guidance documentation that provide information on how to determine if cruelty is occurring or has occurred. For example, the Humane Society of the United States (HSUS) has made available a "Q and A" packet entitled "Making the Connection: What Law Enforcers Need to Know" that contains information regarding the definition of animal abuse and tips for enforcement. The packet describes how both humane investigators and police officers are responsible for the enforcement of anti-cruelty laws (HSUS, n.d.). There are similar texts at the state level, for example, the New York State Humane Society has a guidance document entitled "How to Investigate Animal Cruelty in New York State—A Manual of Procedures." This document includes step-by-step instructions on preparations that should be made prior to even receiving animal cruelty complaints or tips as well as procedures to follow during investigations and prosecution. This manual has been lauded by judges, police officers, other emergency responders, and even the HSUS as a comprehensive guide to investigating animal cruelty for New York and beyond (New York State Humane Association, n.d.).

In addition to the focus on better training for field investigators, there have also recent advances in the use of veterinary forensics and as a result, development of better training for veterinarians involved in animal cruelty investigations. Collection, identification, and analysis of evidence by forensic veterinarians have begun to strengthen investigations and resulting enforcement actions levied against animal cruelty perpetrators. For example, in 2011, a case of animal cruelty involving two cats that were tortured and killed was the first case successfully resolved based upon analyses of animals' DNA. One cat's DNA evidence was found on the couch on which he was set on fire, and the other's DNA was found on part of an umbrella used to beat and kill her (Baldwin, 2011; Newman, 2011). In recognition of the fact that forensic analysis can be useful in cases of animal cruelty, there has been a surge in creation of tools and a movement towards better training for forensics-based veterinary medicine. In terms of forensic tools, the American Society for the Prevention of Cruelty to Animals (ASPCA) has created its own mobile crime scene unit which provides equipment for forensic evaluation as well as on-site medical response for wounded animals. This vehicle "includes a fully equipped surgical suite, medical supplies, a digital microscope, exhumation apparatus, an entomology kit, blood-testing equipment, and evidence collection supplies" and was paid for by an anonymous donor so that forensic veterinarian Dr. Melinda Merck could further her work (which included assistance in the Michael Vick dogfighting case) in gathering evidence to help prosecute people involved in dogfighting, puppy mills, and extreme cases of hoarding ("ASPCA unleashes animal CSI unit," 2008). In terms of education and training, the ASPCA and the University of Florida partnered to begin the ASPCA Veterinary Forensic Science program in 2009. This program provides general forensics-based training courses for both law enforcement personnel and veterinarians as well as a graduate certificate program in forensic science for veterinarians (University of Florida, n.d.). Well-trained investigators and the emergence of forensic evidence as an important investigative tool are likely to improve the overall quality of animal cruelty investigations and may result in an increase in the number of successful prosecutions in the future (see also Chapter 6 of this text).

With the above in mind, successful prosecution of animal cruelty rests upon three related elements: (1) improvements in investigation and the scientific advances discussed above, (2) procedures, definitions, and prohibited actions specified in anti-cruelty legislation discussed previously in this chapter and throughout the text, and (3) the prosecutor's knowledge of animal law and animal cruelty. In regard to this third element, Lockwood (2006) argues that the "successful prosecution of crimes against animals requires specialized knowledge of not only relevant laws, but also of veterinary medicine, veterinary forensics, animal care, and the practices used in organized crimes against animals, such as dog and cockfighting" (p. 3). Training, guidance documents, and tools similar to those for investigators exist to provide understanding of these issues to prosecutors. For example, the National District Attorneys Association, in partnership with the ASPCA and the Animal Legal Defense League (ALDF), has created the National Center for Prosecution of Animal Abuse (NCPAA) with the mission of educating prosecutors and others with roles that are important to the outcome of cases (like veterinarians and investigators) on effective ways of handling cruelty cases (National District Attorneys Association, n.d.).

All of the above improvements in enforcement point to the practices of cooperation, information sharing, and collaboration among investigators, medical professionals, and prosecuting attorneys. While these practices are fundamental to increasing effectiveness of any enforcement endeavor, this is especially true of animal cruelty crimes because historically, these have not been the typical day-to-day crimes encountered by police or prosecutors. In this regard, Hughes and Lawson (2011) argue that there is a plurality in the policing of animal cruelty, because the responsibility of investigating animal cruelty "from initial inquiry to prosecution and back again to prevention" falls to both private humane organizations (such as local SPCAs and other organizations that provide humane law enforcement) as well as government-run police departments and prosecutors' offices (p. 378). Therefore, sharing of information and strategies between agencies is of particular importance for prevention of cruelty, as well as identification and ultimately, the appropriate disposition of cruelty cases. In fact, the HSUS suggests in its aforementioned training materials for police officers that police should "get to know local humane investigators who may be aware of potentially violent situations that have not come to the attention of the police" (HSUS, n.d.). Additionally, the ASPCA has been instrumental in leading the charge for better sharing of best practices by partnering with law enforcement agencies to create resources for the various stakeholders in animal cruelty enforcement cases. For example, the U.S. Department of Justice, Office of Community Oriented Policing Services (COPS), and the ASPCA collaborated to create the Dogfighting Toolkit for Law Enforcement—a manual to help police, other investigators, prosecutors and veterinarians who encounter dog fighting rings or signs of dog fighting (ASPCAPro, n.d.a) The ASPCA also has a repository of templates for the various forms and legal documentation that are likely to be required in cruelty cases, including forms for voluntary surrender of animals and a number of forms related to the cataloging of evidence and tracking of forensic information. The documents in this repository are available for public use by any law enforcement agency or veterinarian (ASPCAPro, n.d.b).

Beyond sharing information and practices, actual cooperation within investigations has started to appear in the form of state and local animal cruelty task forces. The makeup of these task forces varies from place to place but they generally include police officers, humane law officers/animal control officers, and representatives from local prosecutors' offices. For example, according to the Los Angeles Animal Services Office (n.d.), the city's Animal Cruelty Task Force (ACTF) includes two animal control officers and five police officers from the Los Angeles Police Department (LAPD), including two detectives and three patrol officers, who work collaboratively with veterinarians as well as a group of prosecutors specifically trained to handle animal cruelty crimes. In 2006, the year in which the task force was established, the ACTF successfully investigated 290 complaints, resulting in numerous citations and removal of many animals from dangerous conditions as well as 51 arrests and 15 felony prosecutions (L.A. Animal Services Office, n.d.). According to Zilney and Zilney (2005), in a slightly different example of agency investigatory cooperation in Canada, Ontario's Family and Child Services (FCS) and the Ontario Humane Society engaged in a yearlong pilot program of referrals for suspected cases of animal and domestic abuse, respectively. This reciprocation resulted in FCS referring 20% of their home visits to the Humane Society for concerns about animal welfare and likewise, the Humane Society referred almost 5% of its cases to FCS for potential family abuse situations that would likely have gone undiscovered otherwise (Zilney & Zilney, 2005). This indicates that agency cooperation can result in better investigations of animal cruelty crimes as well as other types of co-occurring crimes. Another example of collaboration occurs during hearings or trial, with investigators providing testimony and specific details of their evidence and veterinarians and forensic scientists serving as expert witnesses. According to Lockwood (2006), veterinarians are crucial to a prosecution's case in provision of information including the physical condition of all animals involved and their response to treatment, the actions that could have prevented the injuries, illness, death, or other harm done to the animals, and the time and cause of death for animals that are killed as a result of the cruelty.

The way forward for investigation and prosecution of animal crimes is one of increasing education, training, and collaboration. Emergence of these elements can already be seen to have increased the efficacy of animal cruelty cases in the examples discussed above. As these investigators, veterinarians, prosecutors, and other professionals involved in animal cruelty enforcement initiatives continue to increase their knowledge, skills, and levels of cooperation with one another, it is likely that enforcement of anti-cruelty laws in the United States will continue on to improve in regard to efficient identification and proper investigation and prosecution of cruelty cases.

Increased Legitimacy as a Social Phenomenon

The study of animal cruelty has sometimes been considered a pseudo-intellectual endeavor; the topic has historically been on the fringes of the mainstream social sciences. As illustrated throughout earlier chapters of this book, there is, cumulatively, a broad body of literature from a variety of disciplines including law, philosophy, ethics, veterinary sciences, biology, sociology, psychology, and criminology. Despite this, the study of animal abuse and animal rights has traditionally been viewed as a less-than-credible niche rather than a legitimate topic of rigorous and legitimate research and theoretical endeavors. This has especially been the case within the social sciences. Although Bryant (1979) called for the sociological study of "zoological crime" more than three decades ago, relatively little empirical response ensued (Flynn, 2001). It was a bit of a breakthrough, then, when in 1998 Nigel South and Piers Beirne edited a special issue of the journal, *Theoretical Criminology*, that focused on "a green criminology" and included essays related to the moral and legal standing of animals (Benton, 1998) and the need for expansion of the definition of animal abuse (Agnew, 1998). Over a decade later, Beirne coedited a special issue of *Crime, Law and Social Change* that focused specifically on animal abuse. Beirne described the volume as "the first issue in any criminology journal to be devoted entirely to the study of animal abuse" (Beirne, 2011, p. 355). In his introduction to the volume, Beirne (2011) described a symposium that he attended in Wales a year earlier, entitled "Situating Animal Abuse in Criminology." The meeting was attended by "20 or so criminologists and scholar activists ... in order to encourage the study of animal abuse in criminology" (Beirne, 2011, p. 549). While the conference was not as well-attended as the more mainstream gatherings in the field of criminology, the international group of scholars from England, Wales, Ireland, Norway, and the United States shared ideas in the form of discussion and formal paper presentations.

What has criminology to say about human-animal relationships and about animal abuse,

> in particular? From a discipline much of whose focus is provided by concepts of harm, pain, suffering, inequality, social exclusion and identity fractures, the brief answer to this question is: very little indeed (Beirne, 2011, p. 353).

This is surprising considering that

> the study of animal abuse lies squarely within criminology's moral and intellectual compass.... [A]t this moment, the prospects for a pro-animal research programme in the sociology and criminology of animal abuse are quite bright

> [and there have been] many scholarly studies of animal abuse ... published in the last two or three years (Beirne, 2011, p. 353).

Several arguments have been made to support the legitimacy and importance of studying animal abuse (Beirne, 1999; Calley, 2011). Many of these have been supported, at least to some extent, by content within this text. First, as described in Chapters 12 and 13 in this volume, there is some evidence to suggest that animal abuse is linked to other aggression, delinquency, and criminality. While additional research is needed, the mere possibility of this link calls for attention to animal cruelty. As described in Chapters 2, 3, 4, and 5, a body of legislation exists prohibiting various acts of cruelty to animals. Beirne (1999) points out Edwin Sutherland's suggestion "that criminologists ... study anything defined as *socially harmful* by any branch of law" (p. 129), as well as Jeremy Bentham's argument for the humane treatment of animals in his utilitarian calculus (see Chapters 1 and 2). One of the strongest arguments for the legitimacy and importance of studying animal abuse is that animal abuse is a violation of the animals' rights as "moral patients;" that is, animals have "the right not to be harmed" (Beirne, 1999, p.134). "[A]s an act of violence against innocent nonhuman victims," animal abuse is ripe for further "empirical investigation, theory development, and the practical application of research findings to social policy" (Flynn, 2011, p. 466). Finally, as described in Chapter 15, animal abuse is "one of several forms of oppression identified by feminists as an interconnected whole" (Beirne, 1999, p. 140).

The Status of Empirical Study of Animal Violence

Because of the long-standing view of animal cruelty as something either outside of the realm of the social sciences or as niche topic, there is still much work to be done in assessing animal cruelty from a criminological perspective. There has been very little theory development and even less empirical testing. Animal cruelty is a somewhat unusual topic of study in criminology due to the fact that the victims in these crimes are non-human and criminology is generally considered to be anthropocentric and concerned with human interactions, human criminal behavior, and human victims (Beirne, 1999). Although willfully causing harm to animals is generally thought of as deviant behavior and many forms of cruelty have been formally criminalized in the eyes of the law, scholarly study of animal abuse as a crime phenomenon in its own right has been very limited. In a statement that mirrors the legal treatment of animals in the United States as property, Taylor (2011) acknowledges that "animals only enter the realm of criminology currently as 'objects' and never as 'subjects'" (p. 252). And indeed, as described elsewhere in this text, existing animal cruelty research is dominated by identification of correlations between an individual's violent acts towards animals and violent acts towards humans, such as animal violence as a component of the psychopathic triad or as a correlate of domestic violence (e.g., Arluke et al., 1999; DeGue & Dilillo, 2009; Flynn, 2011).

There is a need to clarify the relationship between animal cruelty and other forms of violence, but the future of this research is discussed at length elsewhere in this book in Chapters 12 and 13. Less attention has been paid to animal cruelty as a topic of criminological study in its own right. There are many questions to be answered including: What causes a person to engage in animal violence? Is violence towards animals different from violence towards humans? Is violence towards animals always indicative of violence towards humans? What is the impact of this violence on the whole of society?

"Sui generis" Study of Animal Cruelty

There has been an initiative over the last decade to view animal abuse as an object of criminological study under the broader guise of human-animal interaction and not solely as a signifier of additional criminality perpetrated against human victims. This came out as part of the realization there is much to be gained from examining animal abuse "sui generis," meaning that it can stand alone as a legitimate and important topic of theory development and study in the field, separate from solely focusing on implications for human criminality and/or human victimization (Beirne, 1999, p 117). Beirne (1999) has been the most prolific proponent of this initiative and justifies the importance of criminological research of animal violence based on:

> the status of animal abuse as (1) a signifier of actual or potential interhuman conflict [as outlined in detail in the studies discussed within other chapters of this book], (2) an existing object of criminal law, (3) an item in the utilitarian calculus on the avoidance of pain and suffering,[2] (4) a violation of rights, and (5) [as previously mentioned] one of several oppressions identified by feminism as an interconnected whole (p. 117).

So far, this expansion of animal abuse has been comprised of scant literature that is more philosophical and theoretical than it is empirical. This is likely because animal abuse study for the sake of animals goes against the grain of the more mainstream anthropocentric paradigm of criminology. It has even been argued that criminology is currently ill-equipped to engage in study of animal violence and that new and innovative methodological frameworks need to first be developed before "sui generis" study of animal crime can begin (Taylor, 2011).

Agnew's (1998) Integrative Model of Animal Violence

Agnew (1998) has developed one of the only proposed theoretical frameworks for causation of animal violence. In it, he applies aspects of social control, social learning, and general strain theory, arguing that animal violence generally occurs when various aspects of these theories[3] coincide or manifest within individuals who are "unaware of

---

2. Beirne (1999) expounds on this later by saying "animals are sentient beings who can suffer and feel pain ... they have an interest in avoiding pain ... [therefore] humans are obliged not to inflict it on them" (p. 131).

3. For example, preexisting weak attachments to peers and family (social control), having previously witnessed animal violence (social learning), or experiencing some type of stress then coping by engaging in violence towards animals (general strain theory).

the abusive consequences of their behavior for animals ..., do not think their abusive behavior is wrong, and ... believe they benefit from their abusive behavior" (Agnew, 1998, p. 182). Perceptions of animals are an important implied piece of Agnew's framework. The general idea is that background characteristics, traits, and experiences can together or separately shape an individual's attitudes and beliefs about animals. In cases where an individual's beliefs are negative, they may be more likely to abuse or neglect a pet or could be more easily triggered to do so due to frustration or strains that trigger abusive outbursts. There have been many studies of people's perception of animals. However, since criminology has consistently ignored animal violence, these studies have occurred outside the realm of criminology. The general finding of existing studies is that while most people believe that there is a moral obligation to do no harm to animals, there are those who take the amoral approach, seeing animals as non-feeling or inferior, or as nothing more than objects or property to do with as they please (Kellert, 1988). Research outside of criminology has shown that characteristics like age, gender, race, and level of education can directly affect attitudes and beliefs about animals (Kellert, 1988; Pifer, 1996).

Likewise, early socialization and certain personality traits may also influence an individual's perception of animals. In terms of socialization, Gottfredson and Hirschi (1990) argue that while level of self-control remains essentially stable over the life-course, it is not a set trait in an individual until about eight years of age. So, in this case, experiences in early childhood can impact the level of self-control one will have later in life. When looking at the direct influence of socialization on attitudes about animals, it has previously been discussed in this text that experiencing and observing abuse—of humans or animals—as a child is correlated with later abuse of animals. When looking at resulting personality traits, low self-control and lack of empathy are specifically mentioned in Agnew's (1998) theoretical construct. According to Agnew (1998), in regard to those with low self-control, as specified by Gottfredson and Hirschi (1990, p. 194),

> it seems reasonable to suppose that such an individual would be less aware of the abusive consequence of their actions for the animal, less willing to grant animals moral consideration and less aware and concerned about the negative personal consequences of their actions.

This theory was ignored in criminological research for several years. However, a recent test of Agnew's theory by Mowen and Boman (2020), indicated some support for aspects of the theory, specifically individual characteristics and traits like early history of other types of offending, alcohol use, impulsivity, and inferiority/low self-esteem.

From a criminological standpoint, animal cruelty and animal violence are much more complex than it would initially appear. There is more to animal violence as crime than merely the relationships of animal violence and psychopathy or animal violence and domestic violence. From a less anthropocentric orientation, criminological research could and should contribute a great deal to the understanding of human-animal interaction and in turn, will enhance the field's overall understanding of the nature of crime. As issues of animal cruelty become more prominent in the realm of criminal justice, the hope is that criminologists will follow Agnew's (1998) example and will begin to see violence perpetrated against animals as legitimate crimes and that these actions should be probed, investigated, and analyzed in the same way as other criminal behaviors. A reorientation of the perceptions of crime, violence, and victimization, and the framework for studying them, appears to be taking shape and will be necessary for animal violence to take its rightful place in the study of crime and crime causation.

Other Recent Research on Animal Cruelty and the Future of Animal Cruelty Research

There is evidence that animal cruelty is emerging as a recognized and legitimate area of study. As an area of study becomes deemed worthwhile and legitimate, there is often a corresponding surge in the proliferation of related educational programs, scholarly publications, and organizations. We are beginning to see this occur in the area of human-animal studies. According to the Animals and Society Institute, there are currently more than three dozen university-level programs in human-animal studies in the U.S., Canada, U.K., Germany, Switzerland, Israel, and Netherlands, in addition to nine such programs in veterinary schools in the U.S. and Canada and six U.S. animal law programs (Animals and Society Institute, 2011).

National professional organizations in the fields of psychology and sociology have created special sections on humans and animals; the American Psychological Association has a section on animal-human interaction (American Psychological Association, 2012), and the American Sociological Association began a section on animals and society (American Sociological Association, 2012). The American Bar Association has formed an Animal Committee "to address all issues concerning the intersection of animals and the law to create a paradigm shift resulting in a just world for all" (American Bar Association, n.d.). About 40 organizations and research institutes related to animals and society and at least 15 scholarly journals devoted to this subject matter (Animals and Society Institute, 2011). Animal cruelty, ethical treatment of animals, and animal welfare are emphasized by these programs, organizations, and journals.

One university program related to animal protection and animal cruelty is notable due its being offered through the Humane Society of the United States (HSUS). In the fall of 2009, the HSUS became "the first animal welfare organization to receive [the] authority and distinction of receiv[ing] a license as a higher education degree-granting institution by the District of Columbia Education Licensure Commission" (Humane Society of the United States, 2009). The University offers baccalaureate degrees and graduate certificates in "animal studies, animal policy and advocacy, and humane leadership." Additionally, according to the Animals and Society Institute (n.d.), there are currently 50 colleges and universities in the United States and abroad that offer degrees and certifications in animal advocacy, humane education, animal protection, and related topics.

Perhaps because of all of the above and the path blazed by criminologists like Agnew and Beirne in recent years to call for and begin exploring animal cruelty as a topic of criminological study and analysis, more and more research on animal cruelty has begun to appear. This involves not only testing of theory like that discussed in the previous section, but also research on additional aspects of animal cruelty including correlates with other forms of crime, analysis of situational factors that may lead to cruelty incidents, and analysis of the effectiveness of the sentencing and punishment of cruelty offenders.

The focus of recent animal cruelty research in criminology continues to be examination of cruelty in relation to other forms of violence, either looking at acts of animal cruelty as precursors for violence against humans later in life (Longobardi & Badenes-Ribera, 2019) or animal cruelty in relation to domestic violence (Taylor & Fraser, 2019). However, recent studies have also expanded to look at other factors related to animal cruelty including neighborhood context (Reese et al., 2020) and situational factors (Grugan, 2018). All of this indicates that the scientific study of animal cruelty as criminal behavior is a small, but growing endeavor.

Conclusion/Future Directions

The overarching theme of this text has been the recognition of animal cruelty as a problem as reflected in legislation, research, and theoretical development. Among the topics related to animal cruelty that are truly emerging and likely to be predictive of future directions are growth in the involvement in and impact of animal advocacy and nonviolent animal rights activism; increased public awareness of the nature and extent of various types of animal cruelty, largely due to the expansion of the role of the media in covering some of the most extreme cases; the continued evolution of animal protection and anti-cruelty legislation; the further growth of degree-granting programs and animal welfare curricula in institutions of higher learning; a slow, but steady, increase in animal cruelty research; and increased legitimacy of the study of animal cruelty (victims and perpetrators) in its own right. If the recent past is any indication of the future, we can, unfortunately, also expect to see the continuation and growth of some less desirable trends and activities (e.g., crush films, online puppy mills, etc.).

References

Agnew, R. (1998). The causes of animal abuse: A social-psychological analysis. *Theoretical Criminology. 2*(2), 177–209.

Aji, A. (2019). The role of social media in shaping the animal protection movement in Indonesia. *Jurnal Studi Komunikasi, 3*(3), 389–401. https://doi.org/10.25139/jsk.v3i3.1666.

Allen, M. & von Essen, E. (2018). Is the radical animal rights movement ethically vigilante? *Between the Species: An Electronic Journal for the Study of Philosophy & Animals, 22*(1), 260–285.

Allen, M. D. (2005). Laying down the law? Interest group influences on state adoption of animal cruelty felony laws. *Policy Studies Journal, 33*(3), 443–457.

Allen, M. W., Hunstone, M., Waerstad, J., Foy, E., Hobbins, T., Wikner, B., & Wirrel, J. (2002). Human-to-animal similarity and participant mood influence punishment recommendations for animal abusers. *Society & Animals, 10*(3), 267–284.

Almiron, N. (2019). Greening animal defense? Examining whether appealing to climate change and the environment is an effective advocacy strategy to reduce oppression of nonhumans. *American Behavioral Scientist, 63*(8), 1101–1119.

American Bar Association. (n.d.). Animal law. Retrieved from http://apps.americanbar.org/dch/committee.cfm?com=IL201050.

American Psychological Association. (2012). *Human-animal interaction*. Retrieved August 9, 2012, from http://www.apa.org/divisions/div17/sections/sec13/Home.html.

American Sociological Association (2012). *Animals and society*. Retrieved August 9, 2012, from http://www2.asanet.org/sectionanimals/.

American Society for the Prevention of Cruelty to Animals. (2015). Ag-gag bills at the state level. Retrieved May 21, 2015, from https://www.aspca.org/fight-cruelty/advocacy-center/ag-gag-whistleblower-suppression-legislation/ag-gag-bills-state-level.

American Veterinary Medical Association. (2014). State laws governing elective surgery procedures. Retrieved May 21, 2015, from https://www.avma.org/Advocacy/StateAndLocal/Pages/sr-elective-procedures.aspx.

Animal Law Coalition. (2012a). *Pending animal bills.* Retrieved August 1, 2012, from http://www.animallawcoalition.com/bills.

AnimalLawCoalition(2012b).*Govsignsweakenedokbreederbillintolaw*.RetrievedAugust 1, 2012, from http://www.animallawcoalition.com/companion-animal-breeding/article/1207.

Animal Legal Defense Fund. (2022). Ag-Gag Laws. Retrieved on April 9, 2022 from https://aldf.org/issue/ag-gag/?gclid=CjwKCAjwopWSBhB6EiwAjxmqDXPfx81hPkB7mcRrU4iIytNWWT_qhH7TEX5nlsbd9WgMnrDXKWNEohoCbowQAvD_BwE.

Animal Legal and Historical Center. (2015). Table of state law amendments from 2014. Retrieved May 20, 2015, from https://www.animallaw.info/topic/table-2014-amendments-statelaws.

Animals and Society Institute. (2011). *Human-Animal Studies.* Retrieved August 9, 2012, from http://www.animalsandsociety.org/pages/human-animal-studies.

Animals and Society Institute. (n.d.). *HAS certificate and degree programs.* Retrieved September 5, 2012, from http://www.animalsandsociety.org/degreeprograms.

Animal Welfare Institute (2014). New Jersey, New York pass laws to ban trade in ivory and rhino horns. Retrieved May 20, 2015, from https://awionline.org/awi-quarterly/2014-fall/new-jersey-new-york-pass-laws-ban-trade-ivory-and-rhino-horns.

ASPCAPro. (n.d.a). *Training: Dogfighting toolkit for law enforcement.* Retrieved August 14, 2012, from http://www.aspcapro.org/dogfighting-toolkit-for-law-enforcement.php.

ASPCAPro. (n.d.b). *Sample forms: Legal forms & veterinary forms.* Retrieved August 14, 2012, from http://www.aspcapro.org/sample-forms.php.

Arluke, A., Levin, J., Luke, C., & Ascione, F. (1999). The relationship of animal abuse to violence and other forms of antisocial behavior. *Journal of Interpersonal Violence, 14*(9): 963–975.

ASPCA unleashes animal CSI unit. (2008). *Law Enforcement Technology*, July, 80.

Associated Press. (2011). Missouri legislators undo puppy mill law. *The Washington Times Online.* Retrieved August 4, 2012, from http://www.washingtontimes.com/news/2011/apr/14/missouri-legislators-undo-puppy-mill-law/.

Associated Press. (2022). Trapping ban to take effect on public lands in New Mexico. *U.S. News and World Report.* Retrieved on April 6, 2022 from https://www.usnews.com/news/best-states/new-mexico/articles/2022-03-31/trapping-ban-to-take-effect-on-public-lands-in-newmexico#:~:text=It%20will%20be%20illegal%20to,ban%20that%20takes%20effect%20Friday.&text=March%2031%2C%202022%2C%20at%203%3A31%20p.m.&text=ALBUQUERQUE%2C%20N.M.,ban%20that%20takes%20effect%20Friday.

Bandura, A. (1999). Moral disengagement in the perpetration of inhumanities. *Personality and Social Psychology Review, 3*(3), 193–209.

Baldwin, C. (2011). Animal abusers put in jail thanks to DNA evidence. *Metro New York Online.* Retrieved August 16, 2012, from http://www.metro.us/newyork/local/article/811736-animal-abusers-put-in-jail-thanks-to-dna-evidence.

Balieva, G. N. & Lazarova, I. (2020). Factors that influence personal perceptions and reactions to animal cruelty. *Veterinarija ir Zootechnika, 78(100),* 90–96.

Barrow, M. (2009). Dragon in distress: Naturalists as bioactivists in the campaign to save the American alligator. *Journal of the History of Biology, 42*(2), 267–288.

Bayvel, A. C. D. (2005). Animals in science and agriculture—A global perspective. *Animal Welfare, 52*(6), 339–344.

Beilin, K. O. (2012). Bullfighting and the War on Terror: Debates on culture and torture in Spain, 2004–11. *International Journal of Iberian Studies, 25*(1), 61–72.

Beirne, P. (2011). Animal abuse and criminology: Introduction to a special issue. *Crime, Law and Social Change, 55*, 349–357.

Beirne, P. (1999). For a nonspeciest criminology: Animal abuse as an object of study. *Criminology, 27*(1), 117–147.

Benton, T. (1998). Rights and justice on a shared planet: More rights or new relations. *Theoretical Criminology, 2*(2), 149–175.

Berry, C. (2014). All 50 states now have felony animal cruelty provisions. Animal Legal Defense Fund. Retrieved May 20, 2015, from http://aldf.org/blog/50-states-now-have-felony-animal-cruelty-provisions/.

Block, K. (2021). Victory! These US states just made great progress for animals. A Humane World, The Humane Society of the United States. Retrieved on April 6, 2022 from https://blog.humanesociety.org/2021/07/these-us-states-just-made-great-progress-for-animals.html.

Block, K. & Amundson, S. (2022). Good news to start 2022: These new laws are now in place to protect animals. Humane Society Legislative Fund. Retrieved on April 6, 2022 from https://hslf.org/blog/2022/01/good-news-start-2022-these-new-laws-are-now-place-protect-animals.

Broad, G. M. (2018). Effective animal advocacy: Effective altruism, the social economy, and the animal protection movement. *Agriculture and Human Values, 35*, 777–789.

Brown, J. L. (2012). Bull market. *Civil Engineering, 81*(1), 62–69.

Bryant, C. (1979). The zoological connection: Animal-related human behavior. *Social Forces, 58*, 399–421.

Burghardt, G. M. (2009). Ethics and animal consciousness: How rubber the ethical ruler? *Journal of Social Issues, 65*(3), 499–521.

Burke, K.C. (2021). Harming cats and dogs: People are as morally outraged, but not as punitive, in animal versus human abuse case. *Humanist Psychologist,* [advanced online publication], https://doi.org/10.1037/hum0000247.

Calley, D. (2011). Developing a common law of animal welfare: Offences against animals and offences against persons compared. *Crime, Law and Social Change, 55*(5), 513–525.

Carlson, C. (2012) The ag gag laws: Hiding factory farm abuses from public scrutiny. *The Atlantic* Online. Retrieved August 17, 2012, from http://www.theatlantic.com/health/archive/2012/03/the-ag-gag-laws-hiding-factory-farm-abuses-from-public-scrutiny/254674/.

Carmona, E. D. (2012). Perfil del vegano/a de liberación animal en España. Revista Española de Investigaciones Sociológicas, *139*, 175–188.

Cause IQ (2022). Animal-focused nonprofit organizations. Retrieved on April 20, 2022 from https://www.causeiq.com/directory/animal-organizations-list/#:~:text=There%20are%2045%2C836%20animal%20organizations%20in%20the%20United%20States.

Ceccato, V., Lundqvist, P., Abraham, J., Goransson, E. & Svennefelt, C. A. (2022). Farmers, victimization, and animal rights activism in Sweden. *Professional Geographer, 72*(2), 350–363.

Cheng, A. (2021) Pablo Escobar's 'cocaine hippos' are legally people, U.S. court rules. The Washington Post. Retrieved on April l9, 2022 from https://www.washingtonpost.com/world/2021/10/26/pablo-escobar-cocaine-hippos-colombia/.

Cressey, D. (2011). Battle scars. *Nature, 470*(February 24), 452–453.

Cuong, M. (2016). 5 Vietnamese arrested for beating dog theft suspect to death. Retrieved on April 20, 2022 from https://e.vnexpress.net/news/news/5-vietnamese-arrested-for-beating-dog-theft-suspect-to-dead-3474741.html.

DeGue, S., & DiLillo, D. (2009). Is animal cruelty a "red flag" for family violence? *Journal of Interpersonal Violence, 24*(6), 1036–1056.

Dillard, C. L. (2002). Civil disobedience: A case study in factors of effectiveness. *Society and Animals, 10*(1), 47–62.

Doherty, B. (2002). *Ideas and actions in the Green Movement*. Routledge.

The EU and animal welfare: policy objectives (n.d.). *Animal Welfare and Health*. Retrieved August 4, 2012, from http://ec.europa.eu/food/animal/welfare/policy/index_en.htm.

Edgemon, E. (2015). Alabama lawmaker blocks legislation restricting puppy mills. AL.com. Retrieved May 20, 2015, from http://www.al.com/news/index.ssf/2015/05/alabama_ lawmaker_refuses_to_le.html.

ElephantsDC (2015). Why ban ivory sales? The facts. Retrieved May 20, 2015, from http://www.elephantsdc.org/the-facts2.html.

Eliason, S. L., & Dodder, R. A. (1999). Techniques of neutralization used by deer poachers in the western United States: A research note. *Deviant Behavior: An Interdisciplinary Journal, 20*, 233–252.

Enman-Beech, J. (2017). Conexion: A note on praxis for animal advocates. *Dalhousie Law Journal, 40(2)*, 545–578.

Evans, D., & McGreevy, P. (2011). An investigation of racing performances and whip use by jockeys in Thoroughbred races. *PLoS ONE, 6*(1), 1–5.

Flynn, C. (2011). Examining the links between animal abuse and human violence. *Crime, Law and Social Change, 55*, 453–468.

Flynn, C. P. (2001). Acknowledging the "zoological connection": A sociological analysis of animal cruelty. *Society & Animals, 9*(1), 71–87.

Flükiger, J. (2008). An appraisal of the Radical Animal Liberation Movement in Switzerland: 2003 to March 2007. *Studies in Conflict and Terrorism, 31*, 145–157.

Food and Agricultural Organization of the United Nations (FAO) (2022). Retrieved on April 10, 2022 from https://www.fao.org/faostat/en/#data/QCL.

Gaarder, E. (2011). Where the boys aren't: The predominance of women in animal rights activism. *Feminist Formations, 23*(2), 54–76.

Glanville, C., Ford, J., Cook, R., & Coleman, G.J. (2021). *Frontiers in Veterinary Science, 8:* 666727. Doi: 10.3389/fvets.2021.666727.

Gottfredson, M., & Hirschi, T. (1990). *A general theory of crime.* Palo Alto, CA: Stanford University Press.

Greenebaum, J. (2009). "I'm not an activist!": Animal rights vs. animal welfare in the purebred dog rescue movement. *Society & Animals, 17,* 289–304.

Greenwood, A. (2017a). Not the last act: The closing of Ringling Bros. hasn't stopped advocates from trying to ban performing animals at other circuses. *ABA Journal, 103*(8), 16–18.

Greenwood, A. (2017b). Animal advocacy: Lawmakers are strengthening animal cruelty measures across the country. *ABA Journal, 103*(1), 18–19.

Grimm, D. (2022). Animal care committee sues own university. *Science, 375*(6586), 1213–1214.

Grugan, S. (2018). The companions we keep: A situational analysis and proposed typology of companion animal cruelty offenses. *Deviant Behavior*, 39(6):1153–1169.

Haile, M., Jalil, A., Tasoff, J., & Bustamante, A.V. (2021). Changing hearts and plates: The effect of animal-advocacy pamphlets on meat consumption. *Frontiers in Psychology,12: 668674.* https://doi.org/10.3389/fpsyg.2021.668674.

Hallsworth, S. (2011). Then they came for the dogs! *Crime, Law, and Social Change, 55*, 391–403.

Herzog, H. A., & Galvin, S. (1997). Common sense and the mental lives of animals. An empirical approach. In R. W. Mitchell (Ed.), *Anthropomorphism, anecdotes and animals* (pp. 237–253), State University of New York Press.

Herzog, H. A., & Golden, L. L. (2009). Moral emotions and social activism: The case of animal rights. *Journal of Social Issues, 65*(3), 485–498.

Hills, A. M. (1995). Empathy and belief in the mental experiences of animals. Reviews and Research Reports. *Anthrozoös, 8*, 132–142.

H.R. 724—116th Congress: Preventing Animal Cruelty and Torture (PACT) Act (2019). In Congress.gov Retrieved on April 6, 2022 from https://www.congress.gov/bill/116th-congress/house-bill/724.

H.R. 1016—117th Congress: Animal Cruelty Enforcement Act (2021). In Congress.gov. Retrieved April 6, 2022 from https://www.congress.gov/bill/117th-congress/house-bill/1016?q=%7B%22search%22%3A%5B%22animal+cruelty%22%2C%22animal%22%2C%22cruelty%22%5D%7D&s=1&r=1.

H.R. 5461—106th Congress: Shark Finning Prohibition Act. (2000). In GovTrack.us. Retrieved August 17, 2012, from http://www.govtrack.us/congress/bills/106/hr5.

H.R. 3355—117th Congress: Save America's Forgotten Equines (SAFE) Act. (2021). In Congress.gov. Retrieved on April 27, 2022 from https://www.congress.gov/bill/117th-congress/house-bill/3355?q=%7B22search%22%3A%5B%22hr3355%22%2C%22hr3355%22%5D%7D&s=1&r=1)%20and%20S.%202732%20(https://

www.congress.gov/bill/117th-congress/senate-bill/2732?q=%7B%22search%22%3A%5B%22S2732%22%2C%22S2732%22%5D%7D&s=2&r=1.

H.R. 366—113th Congress: Animal Fighting Spectator Act of 2013. (2013). Retrieved May 20, 2015, from https://www.congress.gov/bill/113th-congress/house-bill/366.

H.R. 763—117th Congress: Child and Animal Abuse Detection and Reporting Act (2021–2022). Retrieved on April 9, 2022 from https://www.congress.gov/bill/117th-congress/house-bill/763?q=%7B%22search%22%3A%5B%22animal+cruelty%22%2C%22animal%22%2C%22cruelty%22%5D%7D&s=1&r=4.

"Hanoi man, neighbor arrested for beating dog thief to death" (2022). https://e.vnexpress.net/news/news/5-vietnamese-arrested-for-beating-dog-theft-suspect-to-dead-3474741.html.

Hughes, G., & Lawson, C. (2011). RSPCA and the criminology of social control. *Crime, Law and Social Changes, 55*, 375–389.

"Humane Cosmetics Act reintroduced in the U.S." (2022). *ALTEX, 391*(1), 166.

Humane Society International. (2012). *Shark Finning in Focus: What HSI is doing to save sharks from a brutal practice.* Retrieved August 17, 2012, from http://www.hsi.org/news/news/2012/06/shark_finning_in_focus_061512.html.

Humane Society Legislative Fund. (2012). Ayes and nays. *Humane Activist,* March/April, 8.

Humane Society of the United States. (2009). *Humane Society University to offer college degrees in animal protection studies.* Retrieved on August 1, 2012, from http://www.humanesociety.org/news/press_releases/2009/06/humane_society_university_degrees_animal_protection_studies_061809.html.

Humane Society of the United States. (2011). *Hawaii's shark fin product ban takes effect July 1.* Retrieved August 17, 2012, from http://www.humanesociety.org/news/press_releases/2011/06/hawaii_shark_fin_ban_062811.html.

Humane Society of the United States. (2012a). *Ag-gag bills and whistleblower suppression.* Retrieved August 17, 2012, from http://www.humanesociety.org/issues/campaigns/factory_farming/fact-sheets/ag_gag.html.

Humane Society of the United States. (2012c). *The HSUS urges Pennsylvania lawmakers to protect sharks from the fin trade.* Retrieved August 17, 2012, from http://www.humanesociety.org/news/press_releases/2012/08/pennsylvania_shark_finning_081712.html.

Humane Society of the United States. (2012d). *Illinois becomes fifth state to ban shark fin trade.* Retrieved August 17, 2012, http://www.humanesociety.org/news/press_releases/2012/07/illinois_bans_shark_fin_trade_070112.html.

Humane Society Veterinary Medical Association. (2012). HSVMA opposes "ag-gag" laws in order to preserve public scrutiny of food safety, animal health and handling on industrial farms. Retrieved May 20, 2015, from http://www.hsvma.org/ag-gag_law_opposition_041112#.VV5i4flViko.

Humane Society of the United States. (n.d.). *Making the connection: What law enforcers need to know*. Brochure.

Hwang, G. (2021). *Examining extremism: Violent animal rights extremists*. Retrieved April 16, 2022, from https://www.csis.org/blogs/examining-extremism/examining-extremism-violent-animal-rights-extremists.

Jacobsson, K. (2016). *Animal rights activism*. Amsterdam University Press.

Jarvie, K., Evans, J., & McKemmish, S. (2021). Radical appraisal in support of archival autonomy for animal rights activism. *Archival Science, 21*, 353–372.

Keiper, L. (2010). Dogs and cats have a voice under new Massachusetts law. *Reuters Online*. Retrieved August 1, 2012, from http://www.reuters.com/article/2010/07/20/us-usa-pets-devocalization-idUSTRE66J3Z220100720.

Kellert, S. R. (1988). Human-animal interactions: A review of American attitudes to wild and domestic animals in the twentieth century, in A. N. Rowan (Ed.) *Animals and people sharing the world,* (pp. 137–175). University Press of New England.

Klemack, J.C. (2022). Witnesses say they saw man beat dog before group attacks him. Retrieved on April 20, 2022 from https://www.nbclosangeles.com/news/local/actress-jena-malone-among-those-who-say-they-saw-man-beat-dog-before-good-samaritans-come-to-rescue/2863758/.

Knight, S., Vrij, A., Bard, K., & Brandon, D. (2009). Science versus human welfare? Understanding attitudes towards animal use. *Journal of Social Work Issues, 65*(3), 463–483.

Kotzmann, J. & Nip, G. (2020). Bringing animal protection legislation into line with its purported purposes: A proposal for equality amongst non-human animals. *Pace Environmental Law Review, 37,* 247–317.

Kruse, C. R. (1999). Gender, views of nature, and support for animal rights. *Society and Animals, 7*(3), 179–198.

Latty, Y. (2000). Hegins, Pa. ends annual pigeon shoot. Daily News, Feb. 1, 2000. Retrieved August 30, 2012, from http://articles.philly.com/2000-02-01/news/25575515_1_robert-tobash labor-day-committee-hegins-park.

Lazare, J. (2020). Ag-gag laws, animal rights activism, and the Constitution: What is protected speech? *Alberta Law Review, 58*(1), 83–106.

Lockwood, R. (2006). *Animal cruelty prosecution. Opportunities for early response to crime and interpersonal violence*. APRI.

Longobardi, C. & Badenes-Ribera, L. (2019). The relationship between animal cruelty and adolescent and interpersonal violence: A systematic review. *Aggression and Violent Behavior*, 46, 201–211.

Los Angeles Animal Service Office. (n.d.). *Animal Cruelty Task Force*. Retrieved August 12, 2012, from http://www.laanimalservices.com/about_us/ACTF.htm.

MacAskill, W. (2016). *Doing Good Better: How Effective Altruism can Help you Help Others, Do Work that Matters, and Make Smarter Choices about Giving Back.* Random House.

Manning, S. (2014). FBI makes animal cruelty a top-tier felony to help track abuse. *Huffington Post,* online. Retrieved May 20, 2015, from http://www.huffingtonpost.com/2014/10/01/fbi-animal-cruelty-felony_n_5913364.html.

María, G. A., Mazas, B., Zarza, F. J., & Miranda de la Lama, G. C. (2017). Animal welfare, national identity and social change: Attitudes and opinions or Spanish citizens towards bullfighting. *Journal of Agricultural and Environmental Ethics, 30, 809–826.*

Massey, B. (2014). Horse slaughter blocked by federal law. *USA Today.* Retrieved May 21, 2015, from http://www.usatoday.com/story/money/business/2014/01/17/horse-slaughter-blocked-by-federal-law/4604929/.

McNutt, M. (2012). Oklahoma pet breeders board not fighting legislation that could eliminate it. NewsOK, March 28. Retrieved from http://newsok.com/oklahoma-pet-breeders-board-not-fighting-legislation-that-could-eliminate-it/article/3661423.

Merriam-Webster Dictionary (2022a). "Activism." Retrieved February 13, 2022 from http://www.merriam-webster.com/dictionary/activism.

Merriam-Webster Dictionary (2022b). "Advocacy." Retrieved February 13, 2022 from http://www.merriam-webster.com/dictionary/activism.

Mowen, T. J. & Boman, J. H. (2020). Animal abuse among high-risk youth: A test of Agnew's theory. *Deviant Behavior* 41(6): 765–778.

Munro, L. (2005). Strategies, action repertoires and DIY activism in the animal rights movement. *Social Movement Studies*, *4*(1), 75–94.

National Animal Cruelty Investigations School. (n.d.). *University of Missouri Law Enforcement Training Institute.* Retrieved August 14, 2012, from http://leti.missouri.edu/animal-cruelty.aspx.

National District Attorneys Association. (n.d.). National Center for Prosecution of Animal Abuse. Retrieved August 14, 2012, from http://www.ndaa.org/animal_abuse_home.html.

National Parks Conservation Association. (n.d.). American alligator. Retrieved June 15, 2015, from http://www.npca.org/protecting-our-parks/wildlife_facts/alligator.html.

Newcomer, E. (2012). New Jersey's highest court bars distress claims in death of pets. *New York Times Online.* Retrieved June 15, 2015, from http://www.nytimes.com/2012/08/02/nyregion/new-jersey-supreme-court-bars-claims-of-distress-in-pet-deaths.html.

Newman, A. (2011, March 23). Animals' DNA is used to win convictions of abusers. *New York Times*, p. 24.

New York State Humane Society (n.d.). *How to investigate animal cruelty in NY State—A manual of procedures*. Retrieved August 12, 2012, from http://www.nyshumane.org/manual/manual.htm.

Pacelle, W. (2015). States make strides in passing animal protection laws. A humane nation. Retrieved May 20, 2015, from http://blog.humanesociety.org/wayne/2015/01/state-legislative-rankings.html.

Park, J. (2021). Yes, chickens have feelings too. The recognition of animal sentience will address outdated animal protection laws for chickens and other poultry in the United States. *San Diego International Law Journal, 22*(2), 335–364.

Park, Y. S. & Valentino, B. (2019). Who supports animal rights? Here's what we found. Washington Post, Retrieved on June 5, 2022, from https://www.washingtonpost.com/politics/2019/07/26/who-supports-animal-rights-heres-what-we-found/.

PA H.B. 164—2015 Session. Retrieved May 21, 2015, from http://www.legis.state.pa.us/CFDOCS/Legis/PN/Public/btCheck.cfm?txtType=HTM&sessYr=2015&sessInd=0&billBody=H&billTyp=B&billNbr=0164&pn=0664.

PETA. (n.d.). Mother pigs and piglets abused by Hormel supplier. Retrieved June 15, 2015, from https://secure.peta.org/site/Advocacy?cmd=display&page=UserAction&id=1131.

PETA. (2009, June 24). Four more Iowa pig factory farm workers admit guilt! Retrieved June 15, 2015, from http://www.peta.org/b/thepetafiles/archive/2009/06/24/four-more-former-iowa-pig-factory-farm-workers-admit-guilt.aspx.

Petković, D. (2021). "I believe a cage is a cage and no one deserves to be put in one": Animal liberation in contemporary film. *AM Journal, 25,* 143–155.

Pifer, L. (1996). Exploring the gender gap in young adults' attitudes about animal research. *Society & Animals, 4,* 37–52.

Potter, W. (2018). Sentinel species: The criminalization of animal rights activists as terrorists, and what it means for the civil liberties in Trump's America. *Denver Law Review, 95*(4), 877–907.

Potter, W. (2009). The green scare. *Vermont Law Review, 36,* 671–687.

Presser, L., & Taylor, W. V. (2011). An autoethnography of hunting. *Crime, Law and Social Change, 55,* 483–494.

Rasmussen, K. (2012). Efforts to restrict recordings of animal abuse could impede newsgathering. *News Media & the Law.* Spring, 4–8.

Reese, L. A., Vertalka, J. J., & Richard, C. (2020). Animal cruelty and neighborhood conditions. *Animals, 10*(11),1–12.

Reinhart, RJ (2018). Snapshot: Few Americans vegetarian or vegan. *Wellbeing, August 1, 2018.* Retrieved on April 3, 2022 from https://news.gallup.com/poll/238328/snapshot-few-americans-vegetarian-vegan.aspx.

Riffkin, R. (2015). In U.S., more say animals should have same rights as people. *Social & Policy Issues, May 18, 2015.* Retrieved on April 3, 2022 from https://news.gallup.com/poll/183275/say-animals-rights-people.aspx.

Rubin, J. (2018). Desmond's Law: A novel approach to animal advocacy. *Animal Law, 24*(2), 243–275.

Rubin, J. (2021). Desmond's Law: Early impressions of Connecticut's court advocate program for animal cruelty cases. *Harvard Law Review, 134,* 263–275.

S.3357—117th Congress Humane Cosmetics Act. In Congress.gov Retrieved on April 6, 2022 from https://www.congress.gov/bill/117th-congress/senate-bill/3357?q=%7B%22search%22%3A%5B%223357%22%2C%223357%22%5D%7D&s=3&r=2.

S.B. 234—Pet Retail Sale (Victoria's Law). Pennsylvania General Assembly. 2022. Retrieved on April 9, 2022 from https://www.legis.state.pa.us/CFDOCS/billInfo/billInfo.cfm?syear=2021&sInd=0&body=S&type=B&bn=234.

Scutter, J. N., & Mills, C. B. (2009). The credibility of shock advocacy: Animal rights attack messages. *Public Relations Review, 35*(2), 162–164.

Senatori, M., & Frasch, P. (2010). The future of animal law: Moving beyond preaching to the choir. *Journal of Legal Education, 60*(2), 209–236.

Shark Stewards (2015). U.S. states with shark fin trade regulations and penalties. Retrieved May 20, 2015, from http://sharkstewards.org/fin-free-tool/us-states-with-shark-fin-trade-regulations-penalties/.

Shooster, J. (2015). Justice for all: Including animal rights in social justice activism. *Harbinger, 40*(39), 39–44.

Šimčikas, Saulius (2018). Is the percentage of vegetarians and vegans in the U.S. increasing? Retrieved on April 8, 2022 from https://animalcharityevaluators.org/blog/is-the-percentage-of-vegetarians-and-vegans-in-the-u-s-increasing/#fn1-10-23521.

South, N., & Beirne, P. (Eds.). (1998). Editors' introduction. *Theoretical Criminology. Special Issue: For a Green Criminology, 2*(2), 147–278.

Sykes, G. M., & Matza, D. (1957). Techniques of neutralization: A theory of delinquency. *American Sociological Review, 22,* 664–670.

Stegman, L. S. (2020). Do we need to make a federal case out of it? The Preventing Animal Cruelty and Torture Act as over-federalization of criminal law. *American Criminal Law Review*, 57(4), 135–148.

Tallberg, L., Välikangas, L., & Hamilton, L. (2022). Animal activism in the business school: Using fierce compassion for teaching critical and positive perspectives. *Management Learning, 53*(1), 55–75.

Tauber, S. (2010). The influence of animal advocacy groups in state courts of last resort. *Society & Animals, 18,* 58–74.

Taylor, N. (2011). Criminology and human-animal violence research: The contribution and the challenge. *Critical Criminology, 19,* 251–263.

Taylor, N., & Fraser, H. (2019). *Companion animals and domestic violence.* Palgrave Macmillan.

Thomas, S. C., & Beirne, P. (2002). Humane education and humanistic philosophy: Toward a new curriculum. *Journal of Humanistic Counseling, Education and Development, 41*(Fall), 190–199.

Tonsor, G. T., & Olynk, N. J. (2011). Impacts of animal well-being and welfare media on meat demand. *Journal of Agricultural Economics, 62*(1), 59–72.

Tuyttens, F. A. M., Vanhonacker, F., Langendries, K., Aluwe, M, Millet, S. Bekaert, K., & Verbeke, W. (2011). Effect of information provisioning on attitude toward surgical castration of male piglets and alternative strategies for avoiding boar taint. *Research in Veterinary Science, 91*(2), 327–332.

United States Department of Justice. U.S. Attorney's Office. Southern District of Texas. (2016). Houston man sent to federal prison for producing and distributing animal crush videos. Retrieved on April 2, 2022 from https://www.justice.gov/usao-sdtx/pr/houston-man-sent-federal-prison-producing-and-distributing-animal-crush-videos.

United States v. Ashley Nicole Richards; Brent Justice, No. 13-20265 5th Cir. (2014).

United States v. Stevens, 130 S.Ct. L. Ed., 15777 (2010).

University of Florida (n.d.). *About: The ASPCA Veterinary Forensic Sciences Program.* Retrieved August 14, 2012 from http://forensics.med.ufl.edu/about/.

Vollum, S., Buffington-Vollum, J., & Longmire, D. R. (2004). Moral disengagement and attitudes about violence towards animals. *Society & Animals, 12*(3), 209–235.

Wilkins, T. (2021). Sisolak signs bill that will ban the sale of eggs coming from caged chicken in Nevada. Reno Gazette Journal. Retrieved on April 6, 2022 from: https://www.rgj.com/story/news/2021/06/11/new-nevada-law-ban-sale-eggs-caged-chickens/7625208002/.

Wilson, B. J., Thompson, K. R., McGreevy, P. D. (2021). *PLOS ONE, 16(3)*: e0248945. https://doi.org/10.1371/journal.pone.0248945.

Winkler, T. (2019). Protecting our pets: Courtroom advocate or special prosecutor? A critical comparison between two approaches to providing animals better protection in the courtroom. *St. Thomas Law Review, 31*(2), 245–269.

Winn, P. (n.d.). Dog thief down: Pet lovers turned vigilantes in Vietnam. Retrieved on April 20, 2022 from https://theworld.org/stories/dog-thief-down-pet-lovers-turned-vigilantes-vietnam-video.

Woodson, M. B. (2011). Three cases of advocacy: The Cove, Mine, and Food, INC. *Society & Animals, 18*, 200–204.

Worden, A. (2014). NRA claims 11th hour victory in battle over live pigeon shoots. *Philadelphia Inquirer.* Retrieved May 20, 2015, from http://www.philly.com/philly/blogs/pets/House-battle-over-live-pigeon-shoots-goes-down-to-the-wire-NRA-prevails.html?c=r.

Wright, P. (2012). Ore. court rules animals aren't just property. *San Francisco Chronicle Online.* Retrieved on August 2, 2012, from http://www.sfgate.com/news/article/Ore-court-rules-animals-aren-t-just-property-3757952.php.

Yates, R. (2011). Criminalizing protests about animal abuse. Recent Irish experience in global context. *Crime, Law and Social Change, 55,* 469–482.

Yates, R., Powell, C., & Beirne, P. (2001). Horse maiming in the English countryside: Moral panic, human deviance, and the social construction of victimhood. *Society & Animals, 9*(1), 1–23.

Zilney, L., & Zilney, M. (2005). Reunification of child and animal welfare agencies: Cross-reporting of abuse in Wellington County, Ontario. *Child Welfare, 84*(1), 47–66.

Zimmerman, M. (2010). Justices toss law banning videos of animal cruelty. *News Media and the Law, 34*(2), 17–18.

Appendix

Compilation of Animal Protection Agencies and Organizations

The following is a compilation of animal protection agencies and organizations. Below each agency/organization name and Website Uniform Resource Locator (URL) is a quote describing the agency/organization in its own words. Please note that this list merely provides a sample of agencies and is by no means exhaustive, nor does it imply that organizations omitted from the list have not made substantial contributions to the area of animal protection.

Alley Cat Allies
http://www.alleycat.org

"Alley Cat Allies is the global engine of change for cats. We protect and improve cats' lives through our innovative, cutting-edge programs. We are seen around the world as a champion for the humane treatment of all cats. We work toward a world where every cat is valued and protected and every community and shelter has policies and programs to save their lives ... When it comes to cat advocacy, Alley Cat Allies is working in communities to champion low-cost spay and neuter policies and programs, as well as lifesaving Trap-Neuter-Return (TNR) and Shelter-Neuter-Return (SNR). Once viewed as radical new concepts, these humane cat protocols are now mainstream. But we still have a lot of work to do to ensure policies and programs in every community serve the best interests of cats. We are a resource for tens of thousands of dedicated cat caregivers, advocates, nonprofit groups, and volunteers driving change and accelerating protection for millions of cats worldwide."

American Humane Association
http://www.americanhumane.org/

"Founded in 1877 as the country's first national humane organization, American Humane is committed to ensuring the safety, welfare and well-being of animals. For nearly a century and a half, our innovative, science-based leadership programs have been First to Serve in promoting and nurturing the bonds between animals and humans."

American Society for the Prevention of Cruelty to Animals (ASPCA)
http://www.aspca.org/

"The American Society for the Prevention of Cruelty to Animals® (ASPCA®) was the first humane society to be established in North America and is, today, one of the largest in the world. Our organization was founded on the belief that animals are entitled to kind and respectful treatment at the hands of humans and must be protected under the law. Headquartered in New York City, the ASPCA maintains a strong local presence, and with programs that extend our anti-cruelty mission across the country, we are recognized as a national animal welfare organization. We are a privately funded 501(c)(3) not-for-profit corporation, and are proud to boast more than 2 million supporters across the country. The ASPCA's mission, as stated by founder Henry Bergh in 1866, is 'to provide effective means for the prevention of cruelty to animals throughout the United States.'"

Animal Defenders International
https://www.ad-international.org/adi_home/

"Animal Defenders International (ADI) was founded in 1990. With offices in Los Angeles, London and Bogota, ADI educates and campaigns across the globe on animals in entertainment and other industries. We create public awareness of animal suffering and combine this with scientific and economic research. We provide technical briefings to legislators and governments. ADI has a worldwide reputation for providing video and photographic evidence exposing the behind-the-scenes suffering in industry and supporting this evidence with scientific research. ADI rescues animals all over the world and educates the public on animals and environmental issues. ADI in the UK is a registered non-profit membership guarantee company. ADI in the United States is a 501(c)(3) non-profit organization. ADI takes a unique holistic, self-sufficient approach to achieving long-term protection for animals. We work at all levels, from start to finish of a campaign—from investigations and gathering empirical evidence to scientific and economic research, publication of technical reports, through to public education and assisting with law enforcement and legal protection for animals."

Animal Farm Foundation, Inc.
https://animalfarmfoundation.org/

"As an organization that evolves to meet the needs of people and pets, Animal Farm Foundation (AFF) is currently focused on ending dog breed restrictions, whether they exist in policies or laws. These restrictions, which on their surface appear to exclude dogs based on how they look, are ultimately about excluding the people who own the dogs, often based on owner race or class. AFF provides law and policymakers with the science-backed information they need to create laws and policies that consider dogs and people as individuals and improve public safety. The organization works within the legal system to give dog owners skilled legal representation to end breed-specific legislation, keeping dogs and people together. Additionally, AFF grants funds to organizations who share its ethics and goals, plus consults with and offers free resources to advocates, so that communities can move forward."

Animal Legal Defense Fund
http://www.aldf.org/

"The Animal Legal Defense Fund files high-impact lawsuits to protect animals from harm, provides free legal assistance and training to prosecutors in their fight against animal cruelty, supports animal protection legislation, and provides resources and opportunities to law students and professionals to advance the field of animal law."

Animal Protection and Rescue League
https://www.aprl.org/

"APRL is a 501(c)(3) nonprofit organization with a mission to protect the rights and habitats of all animals. Since forming in 2003, APRL has influenced animal protection legislation, conducted numerous animal rescues, and educated hundreds of thousands of people about humane eating. APRL is based in San Diego, California with a second chapter in Orange County, California."

Animal Protection Institute (Born Free USA)
http://www.bornfreeusa.org/

"As a leading wildlife charity, we oppose the exploitation of wild animals in captivity and campaign to keep them where they belong—in the wild. We promote Compassionate Conservation to enhance the survival of threatened species in the wild and protect natural habitats while respecting the needs and safeguarding the welfare of individual animals. We seek to have a positive impact on animals in the wild and protect their ecosystems in perpetuity, for their own intrinsic value and for the critical roles they play within the natural world."

Animal Rescue Corps
https://animalrescuecorps.org/

"Animal Rescue Corps (ARC) is a 501(c)(3) national nonprofit animal protection organization founded in 2010 that takes direct action in three ways. First, we conduct emergency rescues of animals who fall victim to abuse and disaster. Second, we offer interventions to move high-risk and at-need animals from low-adoption shelters into high-adoption regions and offer other critical assistance to in-need shelters and communities. Third, we raise public awareness of animal suffering, and we offer training for animal shelters, professionals, civilians, and volunteers."

Animalearn
http://www.animalearn.org/

"Established in 1990, Animalearn, the educational division of the American Anti-Vivisection Society (AAVS), works to end the harmful use of animals in education. We strive to build awareness about animal use in the classroom and help to nurture a respect for all creatures. Animalearn helps both educators and students find the most effective non-animal methods to teach and study science."

Animals and Society Institute
http://www.animalsandsociety.org/

"The Animals & Society Institute (ASI) a nonprofit human-animal relationship think tank that is devoted to advancing human knowledge to improve animal lives. We are dedicated to improving the lives of animals and people through research and analysis that leads to more humane and compassionate communities. We believe our programs and research will promote the long-term societal changes needed to realize our vision which is to live in a compassionate world where animals flourish."

Animal Welfare Institute
http://www.awionline.org/

"Since 1951, the Animal Welfare Institute has been alleviating suffering inflicted on animals by humans. In the early years, AWI founder Christine Stevens sought to end the cruel treatment of animals in experimental laboratories. Inevitably, her work expanded to take on other animal welfare causes."

Anti-Fur Society
http://www.antifursociety.org

"The Anti-Fur Society is a group of dedicated, committed and caring volunteers working around the world to better the lives of fur-bearing animals. [Y]our contributions—100% of which will go toward helping fur-bearing animals regardless of their geographical location."

A Tail to Tell, Inc.
https://www.atailtotell.com/

"A Tail to Tell is a group of dedicated and committed volunteers. The volunteers in this group work tirelessly to raise money to rescue, rehabilitate, and provide outstanding veterinary care to any dog that is rescued from a puppy mill. This group was formed over 10 years ago when a small group of people saw the need for a rescue group in Pennsylvania to rescue dogs living in substandard conditions in the puppy mills. Since its inception the group has grown but the primary goal of this group has remained the same—to rescue, rehabilitate, and provide outstanding veterinary care to any dog rescued from a puppy mill."

Best Friends Animal Society
http://www.bestfriends.org/

"Back in 1984, a scrappy group of friends from far corners of the globe settled in a remote area of Utah's high desert ... and took the first steps to forever changing the future for pets in shelters. It's the story of Best Friends, but it's much more than the history of a spot on the map. This group of ordinary but passionate people believed that every pet has a story, too, each one worth saving, each life individual and important. Today, nearly four decades after they broke ground for a sanctuary in a remote region of the Southwest, achieving no-kill across the entire country is within reach."

Big Cat Rescue

https://bigcatrescue.org/

"Big Cat Rescue, one of the world's most influential sanctuaries for exotic cats, is a leading advocate for ending the abuse of captive big cats and saving wild cats from extinction. We are the most hated, feared and lied about by circuses, backyard breeders, roadside zoos, cub petting pimps and pseudo-sanctuaries because we are the most effective at ending the abuse of big cats. We wear that as a badge of honor."

Chimpanzee Sanctuary Northwest

https://chimpsnw.org/

"Chimpanzee Sanctuary Northwest (CSNW) is located on 90 acres of farm and forested land in the Cascade mountains, 90 miles east of Seattle. We would like to acknowledge that the sanctuary is located on the traditional land of the Kittitas band of the Yakama Tribe. The native Kittitas people referred to what we now call the Cle Elum River near the sanctuary as Tle-el-Lum, meaning Swift Water … CSNW is one of only a handful of sanctuaries in the country that cares for chimpanzees. CSNW was founded in 2003 to provide sanctuary for chimpanzees discarded from the entertainment and biomedical testing industries. On June 13, 2008, Annie, Burrito, Foxie, Jamie, Jody, Missy, and Negra arrived from a private biomedical facility in Pennsylvania. Some of the chimpanzees were kept as pets and used in entertainment when they were young. Some of them were captured in Africa as infants. All of them were used by the biomedical research industry to test hepatitis vaccines. Most of the females were also used as breeders during their years in labs and their babies were taken from them shortly after birth."

Chipangali Wildlife Orphanage

http://www.chipangali.com/

"Chipangali Wildlife Orphanage is a not-for-profit organisation dedicated to the rescue and care of orphaned, injured, abandoned, abused or wild animals in southern Africa."

Compassion Over Killing

https://animaloutlook.org/home/

"Compassion Over Killing is a national nonprofit animal protection organization based in Washington, DC with a second office in Los Angeles. Working to end animal abuse since 1995, Compassion Over Killing relies on a variety of strategies to expose cruelty to farmed animals and promote vegetarian eating as a way to build a kinder world for all animals."

Darwin Animal Doctors
http://darwinanimaldoctors.org/

"It all started in the Domincan [sic] Republic, with a three legged dog named Piggy. A tiny puppy who was injured but had no access to life-saving services. We brought him home to the USA where he blossomed and now changes the world. Piggy's strength, determination, and love of life inspired us! We realized that countless others around the world, who may also lack the opportunity to fulfill their potential, given the chance can change the world. Thus, we created DAD to lift up and empower others, and work with the to change the world for better."

Defenders of Wildlife
http://www.defenders.org/

"Founded in 1947, Defenders of Wildlife is the premier U.S.-based national conservation organization dedicated to the protection and restoration of imperiled species and their habitats in North America. Defenders' approach is direct and straightforward—We protect and restore imperiled species throughout North America by transforming policies and institutions and by promoting innovative solutions. We speak with one voice informed by scientific, legal and policy expertise, hands-on wildlife management experience and effective advocacy."

Dogs Deserve Better
https://dogsdeservebetter.org/

"Dogs Deserve Better is a 501(c)3 nonprofit organization dedicated to freeing the chained or penned dog as well as helping the dog who is abused, neglected, homeless and abandoned. Our goal is to rescue, rehabilitate and help the dog find a home where they can live inside with a loving and caring family."

Doris Day Animal League
https://www.dorisdayanimalfoundation.org/

"The Doris Day Animal Foundation (DDAF) is a national, nonprofit 501(c)(3) Public Charity founded in 1978 as the Doris Day Pet Foundation by legendary performer, Doris Day, with a straightforward mission that continues to this day: to help animals and the people who love them. As a grant-giving charity, DDAF funds other 501(c)(3) organizations across the United States that directly care for and protect animals."

Farm Sanctuary
http://www.farmsanctuary.org/

"Farm Sanctuary was founded in 1986 to combat the abuses of factory farming, advocate for institutional reforms, and encourage a new awareness and understanding of farm animals and the benefits of cruelty-free, plant-based living. In recent years, science has confirmed the inhumane and destructive impact of animal agriculture—a food system based on interrelated oppression and injustice. As the founding farm animal Sanctuary in the U.S., Farm Sanctuary has rescued and provided refuge for countless survivors of the animal agriculture system. Today, at Farm Sanctuary's Los Angeles, CA and Watkins Glen, NY Sanctuaries you will find nearly 1,000 rescued animals—each with an individual story to tell. These survivors are ambassadors, representing the billions of farm animals currently in the system. They, and others like them, have changed the hearts and minds of a generation."

Finding Shelter Animal Rescue
https://www.findingshelter.org/

Finding Shelter provides the most loving care for animals who need their help finding a permanent home. We are an organization based on love and respect for animals, supported by an incredible group of volunteers who work together to give these animals a quality life and the best chance for adoption.

Friends of Animals
http://www.friendsofanimals.org/

"Friends of Animals (FoA) is a non-profit, international animal advocacy organization incorporated in the state of New York since 1957. Friends of Animals advocates for the rights of nonhuman animals, free-living and domestic. Our goal is to free animals from cruelty and institutionalized exploitation around the world."

Global Federation of Animal Sanctuaries
https://www.sanctuaryfederation.org/

"Every day, the world over, wild and domestic animals are abandoned, displaced, or injured by humans and natural causes. The sole purpose of The Global Federation of Animal Sanctuaries (GFAS) is to ensure that these animals receive the highest standards of care during rescue, rehabilitation, and the rest of their life. We are the only globally recognized organization for certifying that a facility meets the GFAS Standards of Excellence and recognizes those as a true "sanctuary." As such, facilities around the world, large and small, come to GFAS for guidance and support in achieving and maintaining GFAS-accredited status."

The Humane League
https://thehumaneleague.org/

"What began as a tiny grassroots organization in 2005—protesting foie gras on bitterly cold nights at local restaurants in Philadelphia—has since grown into an effective and global nonprofit organization. Yet, one thing has stayed the same. We are, and always have been, for the animals. We started by focusing on institutional change—holding companies to account. In partnership with activists across the northeast, we ran dozens of campaigns, from Baltimore to Boston, winning cage-free commitments at every stop. Restaurant by restaurant, and campus by campus, working our way up to the biggest national corporations."

The Humane Society of the United States (HSUS)
http://www.humanesociety.org/

"Together with millions of supporters, the Humane Society of the United States takes on puppy mills, factory farms, the fur trade, trophy hunting, animal cosmetics testing and other cruel industries. Through our rescue, response and sanctuary work, as well as other hands-on animal care services, we help thousands of animals every year. We fight all forms of animal cruelty to achieve the vision behind our name: a humane society."

Humane Society International
https://www.hsi.org/

"Humane Society International works around the globe to promote the human-animal bond, rescue and protect dogs and cats, improve farm animal welfare, protect wildlife, promote animal-free testing and research, respond to natural disasters and confront cruelty to animals in all of its forms."

Humane Society Legislative Fund
https://hslf.org

"At the Humane Society Legislative Fund, our mission is to Get Political for Animals by working to pass animal protection laws at the state and federal levels, to educate the public about animal protection issues, and to support humane candidates for office."

Humane Society Veterinary Medical Association
http://www.hsvma.org/

"The Humane Society Veterinary Medical Association (HSVMA) was formed as a home for veterinary professionals who want to engage in direct care programs for animals in need and educate the public and others in the profession about animal welfare issues."

Institute for Humane Education
https://humaneeducation.org/

"The Institute for Humane Education (IHE) offers graduate programs, training, and resources for teachers and changemakers looking to create a more just, humane, and sustainable future by educating about the interconnected issues of human rights, environmental sustainability, and animal protection and building a society of solutionaries … IHE educates people to create a world in which all humans, animals, and nature can thrive."

International Fund for Animal Welfare
http://www.ifaw.org/united-states/

"IFAW (International Fund for Animal Welfare) is a global non-profit helping animals and people thrive together. We are experts and everyday people, working across seas, oceans, and in more than 40 countries around the world. We rescue, rehabilitate, and release animals, and we restore and protect their natural habitats. The problems we're up against are urgent and complicated. To solve them, we match fresh thinking with bold action. We partner with local communities, governments, non-governmental organizations, and businesses. Together, we pioneer new and innovative ways to help all species flourish."

International Primate Protection League
https://ippl.org/

"IPPL is a grassroots nonprofit organization dedicated to protecting the world's remaining primates, great and small. Since 1973 we have worked to expose primate abuse and battled international traffickers. We also operate a sanctuary for gibbons (the smallest of the apes) in South Carolina and support primate rescue efforts worldwide, especially in countries where primates are native. Our goal is to keep these uniquely threatened animals safe from human cruelty, negligence, and exploitation, envisioning a world where all primates can thrive in their native habitats."

The Latham Foundation
http://www.latham.org/

"Founded in 1918 by Edith and Milton Latham, The Latham Foundation for the Promotion of Humane Education is unique among the many organizations that exist today. It is helpful to know as much as possible about Milton and Edith Latham's purpose for the Foundation, because their intentions guide and inspire our operations today. Their mandate includes:

> To foster a deeper understanding of and sympathy with man's relations—the animals—who cannot speak for themselves,
>
> To inculcate the higher principles of humaneness upon which the unity and happiness of the world depend,
>
> To emphasize the spiritual fundamentals that lead to world friendship, and
>
> To promote the child's character through an understanding of universal kinship."

League Against Cruel Sports
http://www.league.org.uk/

"Standing on the side of animals, our aim is to make cruel sports a thing of the past. United we can end hunting, shooting and animal fighting. Driven by compassion and empowered by knowledge, we protect animals on our sanctuaries, carry out investigations to expose law-breaking and cruelty to animals, and campaign for stronger animal protection laws."

Leaping Bunny
https://www.leapingbunny.org/

"By 1996, 'cruelty-free' shopping had become popular, but it was also confusing, sometimes misleading, and ultimately frustrating. Companies had begun designing their own bunny logos, abiding by their own definition of 'cruelty-free' or 'animal friendly' without the participation of animal protection groups. In response, eight national animal protection groups banded together to form the Coalition for Consumer Information on Cosmetics (CCIC). The CCIC promotes a single comprehensive standard and an internationally recognized Leaping Bunny Logo. We work with companies to help make shopping for animal-friendly products easier and more trustworthy."

Marine Mammal Stranding Center
https://mmsc.org/

"The Marine Mammal Stranding Center (MMSC) is a 501(c)(3) organization. Formed in 1978, MMSC's mission is the rescue, rehabilitation and release of marine mammals and sea turtles. The Marine Mammal Stranding Center is the only Federally-authorized animal hospital in the State of New Jersey that responds to these animals in distress and provides medical treatment."

Mercy for Animals
https://mercyforanimals.org/

"Our mission is to construct a compassionate food system by reducing suffering and ending the exploitation of animals for food. Imagine a world free of cruelty, a world in which we nurture our bodies, minds, and spirits with wholesome, healthy food that is kind to animals and sustainable for our planet. Mercy [f]or Animals believes that world is possible. In fact, it is inevitable if we work together to elevate humanity to its fullest potential."

National Canine Research Council
https://nationalcanineresearchcouncil.com/

"National Canine Research Council is a non-profit canine behavior science and policy think tank. Our mission is to underwrite, conduct and disseminate academically rigorous research that studies dogs in the context of human society. We advocate innovative and practical canine policy."

Nonhuman Rights Project
https://www.nonhumanrights.org/

"The NhRP's work is designed to take the debate about nonhuman animals' legal status to the next level and free as many animals from captivity as possible. We're also committed to raising awareness of the importance of nonhuman rights, sharing our research and legal documents on our website, and building a strong community of nonhuman rights advocates. Through litigation, legislation, and education, we are changing the way people view nonhuman animals and paving the way for their fundamental rights."

Pennsylvania Society for the Prevention of Cruelty to Animals
http://www.pspca.org/

"What's in a name? Well, it turns out—a lot! It is surprising to many that the Pennsylvania SPCA is not associated with the ASPCA or any other SPCAs throughout the state or country. The ASPCA does not serve as a governing body, and though we are all partnering at times to improve animal welfare, we are not formally attached to one another. We are all our own nonprofit with individual missions. The PSPCA's mission is to protect animals, prevent cruelty and to improve the health and quality of life throughout Pennsylvania. We do this through our four physical locations—North Philadelphia, Danville, Lancaster and Main Line Animal Rescue, as well as through our Humane Law Enforcement Department which covers 18 counties throughout the state."

People for the Ethical Treatment of Animals
http://www.peta.org/

"People for the Ethical Treatment of Animals (PETA) is the largest animal rights organization in the world, and PETA entities have more than 9 million members and supporters globally. PETA opposes speciesism, a human-supremacist worldview, and focuses its attention on the four areas in which the largest numbers of animals suffer the most intensely for the longest periods of time: in laboratories, in the food industry, in the clothing trade, and in the entertainment business. We also work on a variety of other issues, including the cruel killing of rodents, birds, and other animals who are often considered "pests" as well as cruelty to domesticated animals. PETA works through public education, investigative newsgathering and reporting, research, animal rescue, legislation, special events, celebrity involvement, and protest campaigns."

Progressive Animal Welfare Society
http://www.paws.org/

"PAWS is people helping cats, dogs and wild animals go home and thrive—whether home is the family room or the forest. We do this by rehabilitating orphaned and injured wildlife, sheltering and adopting homeless cats and dogs, and educating the community to inspire compassionate action for animals. Since 1967, PAWS has united more than 130,000 cats and dogs with loving families, cared for more than 140,000 sick, injured and orphaned wild animals, and made the world a better place for countless others through outreach, education and advocacy."

Showing Animals Respect and Kindness
http://www.sharkonline.org/

"Showing Animals Respect and Kindness (SHARK) was founded in 1993 by former hunter Steve Hindi. As a 'sportsman,' Steve hunted many species of animals both on land and in the sea. He killed for thirty years until the life-shattering day when, en route to shark hunting in the Atlantic Ocean, Steve attended the infamous Hegins pigeon shoot in Pennsylvania ... SHARK is a non-profit organization with supporters around the US and beyond. SHARK receives no government funding and completely relies on donations and grants to work on issues ranging in scope from local to worldwide. With a small core of volunteers, and a staff of five, SHARK battles tirelessly against rodeos, bullfighting, pigeon shoots, turkey shoots, canned hunts (and all hunting), circuses, zoos, and marine parks ... any issue that involves violation of the innate rights of living creatures. SHARK also conducts animal rescues and education projects. Steve Hindi has an open invitation to debate 'the opposition.' Because of his domination of past debates with animal abusers, however, it has been years since the opposition has taken him on."

South Florida Wildlife Center
https://www.southfloridawildlifecenter.org/

"South Florida's wildlife is being displaced by a growing population and encroaching development, which results in injured and orphaned animals coming to our hospital in terrible distress. We save wildlife through rescue, clinic triage, state-of-the-art diagnostics and expert veterinary treatment. We are saving lives 365 days a year ... Saving the life of an animal begins the rehabilitation process for injured and orphaned wildlife. Our staff provides specialized therapy and treatment to support an animal's full recovery in preparation for release back to natural habitat. Our nursery team provides neonatal-like care for orphaned animals, and our habitats are designed to facilitate conditioning so that upon release, our wild patients leave in the healthiest condition possible ... Our goal is to release rehabilitated wild animals back to their natural habitats. SFWC is committed to doing what is right for every individual animal who enters our hospital. Our release work includes the re-nesting of baby animals back with their parents and facilitating releases back home for animals once they have fully recovered from their injuries ... Ninety percent of the animals who come into our center suffer from injuries that are the result of negative interactions with people. We work to educate the community about wildlife and how each of us can peacefully co-exist with our wild neighbors. In addition, SFWC is a teaching hospital that provides an intern/extern program for veterinary students, future rehabilitators and others looking to pursue a career in any of the life sciences."

Tigers in America
https://tigersinamerica.org/

"We rescue captive tigers from abusive and vulnerable environments. From discovery to sanctuary, we ensure every tiger receives lifetime care in a safe home. They have not lost their ability to fascinate and we should not lose our ability to care."

United Poultry Concerns
https://www.upc-online.org/

"United Poultry Concerns is a nonprofit organization dedicated to the compassionate and respectful treatment of chickens, turkeys, ducks and other domestic fowl. We hold that the treatment of these birds in the areas of food production, science, education, entertainment, and humane companionship situations has a significant effect upon human, animal, and environmental welfare. We seek to make the public aware of the ways in which poultry are used, and to promote the benefits of a vegan diet and lifestyle. We provide information through our quarterly magazine Poultry Press, our Website at www.upc-online.org, and our sanctuary in Machipongo, Virginia on the Eastern Shore."

Wildlife Alliance
https://www.wildlifealliance.org/

"Since 1995, Wildlife Alliance has implemented cutting-edge conservation programs in Southeast Asia, Russia, South America, and the Western Pacific … We are a team of 220 experts with a mission to keep global temperature below 2°C by the year 2030. We increase vegetation cover by planting new forests and we assist in creating and strengthening parks and reserves on land and sea. We protect the world's endangered wildlife species. Our current intervention is in the forests of the tropical belt because of their vital importance in regulating global climate … Wildlife Alliance is the leader in managing Protected Areas and creating Mobile Intervention Units."

World Animal Protection (formally the World Society for the Protection of Animals)
https://www.worldanimalprotection.org/change

"Our mission is to create a better world for animals. We end the needless suffering of animals. We influence decision makers to put animals on the global agenda. We help the world see how important animals are to all of us. We inspire people to change animals' lives for the better. We move the world to protect animals"

World Wildlife Fund
http://www.wwf.org/

"For 60 years, WWF has worked to help people and nature thrive. As the world's leading conservation organization, WWF works in nearly 100 countries. At every level, we collaborate with people around the world to develop and deliver innovated solutions that protect communities, wildlife, and the places in which they live."

Author Biographies

Phil Arkow (Chapter 1) is the coordinator of the National Link Coalition and a consultant for the American Society for the Prevention of Cruelty to Animals. He chairs the Latham Foundation's Animal Abuse and Family Violence Prevention Project. He co-founded the National Link Coalition, the National Animal Control Association, the Animal Welfare Federation of New Jersey, and the Colorado Federation of Animal Welfare Agencies. He trains internationally on a variety of human-animal bond and anti-cruelty topics. He is an adjunct faculty member at Harcum College where he teaches certificate courses in animal-assisted therapy, and at the University of Florida where he co-wrote and teaches the course on animal abuse and interpersonal violence. A former newspaper reporter and foundation communications officer, Arkow is a prolific writer. He has also served with the American Veterinary Medical Association, the Delta Society, the American Humane Association, the Academy on Violence and Abuse, the National Coalition on Violence Against Animals, and the American Association of Human-Animal Bond Veterinarians.

Arnie Arluke, Ph.D. (Chapter 10), is a Professor of Sociology and Anthropology at Northeastern University, Vice President and Director of Research at Forensic Veterinary Investigations, and a Visiting Scholar at the International Fund for Animal Welfare. His research examines conflicts and contradictions in human-animal relationships. He has published over 100 articles and twelve books, including *Regarding Animals, Brute Force*, *Just a Dog*, *The Sacrifice*, *Between the Species*, *The Photographed Cat*, and *Beauty and the Beast*. His research has received awards from the American Sociological Association, the Society for the Study of Symbolic Interaction, the International Association for Human-Animal Interaction Organizations, and the Massachusetts Society for the Prevention of Cruelty to Animals. He also co-edits the Animals, Culture, and Society series for Temple University Press.

Mary P. Brewster, Ph.D. (Co-Editor, Chapter 18), is a Professor of Criminal Justice and Graduate Program Coordinator at West Chester University of Pennsylvania. Her research interests include victimology and domestic violence, and she was principal investigator of a National Institute of Justice-sponsored project on former intimate stalking. She has published numerous articles and book chapters on various topics, including the media and the Michael Vick dogfighting case, stalking, domestic violence, specialized courts, crime victims, and sex offender registries. Dr. Brewster has served as editor of two other books (*Stalking: Psychology, Risk Factors, Interventions,* *and Law* and *Pennsylvania's Criminal Justice System*), contributing editor of *Criminal Justice Research Reports*, and associate editor of the *Encyclopedia of Criminology & Criminal Justice*.

Lindsey S. Davis, M.A. (Chapter 14), is a doctoral student in clinical forensic psychology at John Jay College of Criminal Justice in New York, NY. She received her B.A. in psychological and brain sciences from Dartmouth College in 2005 and her M.A. in forensic psychology from John Jay College in 2011. Lindsey conducts research on sexual homicide and other extraordinary crimes under the advisement of Dr. Louis Schlesinger in conjunction with the FBI's Behavioral Science Unit.

Aimée X. Delaney, Ph.D. (Chapter 13), is an Associate Professor of Criminal Justice at Worcester State University. She conducts research on family and community violence, focusing on risk factors associated with youth victimization and offending both within the United States and globally, family and intimate partner violence, and the impact of youth violence and victimization on the justice systems and communities. Her book, *Norms of Violence: Violent Socialization Processes and the Spillover Effect for Youth Crime*, discusses the victimization-crime paradox from the normalization of violence to control youth behavior. Dr. Delaney has published in peer reviewed journals, such as *Criminal Justice Review, Contemporary Perspectives in Family Violence, International Criminal Justice Review*, and *International Journal of Offender Therapy and Comparative Criminology*, along with other publications related to her grant-based work as the primary evaluator for non-profit youth coalitions working to prevent youth substance use/misuse/abuse. She has made more than 40 research presentations and invited talks at conferences and professional societies. Prior to working in academia, she was employed for many years in the American criminal/juvenile justice systems, including work in child protection, special investigations (internal affairs), and juvenile diversion.

Yolanda Eisenstein, J.D. (Chapter 3), is an animal law attorney in Santa Fe, New Mexico. She is a former adjunct professor of animal law and wildlife law at SMU Dedman School of Law and the University of New Mexico School of Law. Eisenstein is past chair of the American Bar Association TIPS Animal Law Committee and in 2018 received their "Excellence in Animal Law" Award in recognition of her work to advance the humane treatment of animals through the law. She currently serves on the board of the State Bar of New Mexico Animal Law Section and Animal Protection Voters of New Mexico. She has a master's degree in philosophy and juris doctor from SMU Dedman School of Law. Her books include *Careers in Animal Law, The ABA Legal Guide to Dog Laws*, and *Wildlife Law and Ethics*, on which she served as co-editor.

David Favre (Chapter 2) is a Professor of Law at Michigan State University College of Law. Over the past twenty years Professor Favre has written several articles and books dealing with animal issues including such topics as animal cruelty, wildlife law, the use of animals for scientific research, and international control of animal trade. His books include the case book *Animal Law: Welfare, Interest, and Rights* (3rd ed.), as well as *The Future of Animal Law* and *Respecting Animals*. He also has presented to international audiences on these topics. He created and is editor-in-chief of the largest animal legal web resource, www.animallaw.info. Now residing on a farm in lower Michigan, Professor Favre shares his space with sheep, chickens and the usual assortment of dogs and cats.

Amy J. Fitzgerald (Chapter 15) is a Professor of Criminology in the Department of Sociology and Criminology at the University of Windsor in Ontario, Canada. She also holds a hybrid appointment with the Great Lakes Institute for Environmental Research at the University of Windsor. Her research focuses on the intersection of harms (criminal and otherwise) perpetrated against people, non-human animals, and the environment. She has published several peer-reviewed articles, chapters, and books, and is currently working on three grant-funded projects. Fitzgerald is a founding member of the University of Windsor's Animal and Interpersonal Abuse Research Group, the recipient of a Distinguished Scholarship Award from the Animals and Society section of the American Sociological Association, the Mid-Career Outstanding Faculty Research Award from the University of Windsor, and was a visiting research fellow in the Animal Law and Policy Program at Harvard University in 2020.

Egan K. Green (Chapter 9) is a professor at Radford University in Radford, Virginia. He grew up in the mountains of western North Carolina where he was indoctrinated into rural lifestyles and norms. He carried this background into his studies as he completed his Bachelor of Science degree at Appalachian State University before completing his Master of Arts in Criminology at East Tennessee State University and his Ph.D. in Criminology at Indiana University of Pennsylvania. His master's thesis as well as his doctoral dissertation addresses wildlife crime and law enforcement issues. He has presented papers at national and regional conferences on rural criminal justice issues including conservation crime and law enforcement as well as illicit alcohol production, use and distribution. He has also published journal articles and book chapters on natural resource crimes as well as criminal justice ethics issues. Dr. Green is the lead author on a police management textbook.

Patricia Grove (Chapter 17) is a graduate student at West Chester University of Pennsylvania studying criminal justice. She received her B.S. in criminal justice in December 2021. Patricia received the Outstanding Student Award in the spring of 2020. With field experience at the Delaware County District Attorney's Office and the Bucks County Bar Association, Patricia has aspirations of attending law school in the future.

Shannon Grugan, Ph.D. (Chapter 18), earned her Ph.D. in criminal justice from Rutgers University and is currently an Associate Professor at West Chester University. Her research interests include environmental crime, animal cruelty, crime and justice on college campuses, and situational analysis and prevention of crime events.

Maya Gupta, Ph.D. (Chapter 16), earned her M.S. and Ph.D. in clinical psychology from the University of Georgia. She has worked extensively on the development of programs addressing intersections between domestic violence and animal cruelty, and secondarily on approaches to assessment and intervention with cruelty offenders. More broadly, her interests extend to the application of social science and human service approaches to promoting animal welfare and the human-animal bond. She is currently Senior Director of Research at the ASPCA, overseeing the development and dissemination of applied animal welfare research. She previously served as Executive Director of Ahimsa House (a statewide animal safehouse program for victims of domestic violence) and subsequently as Executive Director of the Animals & Society Institute. She is also an instructor in the University of Florida's Veterinary Forensic Sciences program, an adjunct professor in the Anthrozoology program at Canisius College, an instructor for the Veterinary Social Work and Veterinary Human Support programs at the University of Tennessee, a founding and ongoing steering committee member of both the National Link Coalition and the Section on Human-Animal Interaction in the American Psychological Association, and a member of the animal cruelty advisory committee of the Association of Prosecuting Attorneys.

Christopher Hensley (Chapter 11) is a full Professor of Criminal Justice in the Department of Criminal Justice at the University of Tennessee at Chattanooga. He received his doctorate in sociology from Mississippi State University. His most recent publications appear in the *International Journal of Offender Therapy and Comparative Criminology* and the *Journal of Interpersonal Violence*. His research interests include the link between childhood animal cruelty and later violence toward humans, prison sexuality, and attitudes toward correctional issues.

Orlando Hernandez (Chapter 8) earned a bachelor's degree in criminal justice with a minor in psychology from West Chester University of Pennsylvania. He subsequently earned a master's degree from the same university. Hernandez's recent research explores the relationship between animal cruelty data, as reported in the FBI's NIBRS report, socioeconomic factors, and geographic region within the United States.

Dr. Randall Lockwood (Chapters 1 and 6) is Senior Vice President for Forensic Sciences and Anti-Cruelty Projects with the ASPCA. For over thirty years Dr. Lockwood has worked with law-enforcement agencies serving as an expert on the interactions between people and animals. He has testified in dozens of trials involving cruelty to animals or the treatment of animals in the context of other crimes, including dogfighting, child abuse, domestic violence and homicide. His efforts to increase awareness of the connection between animal abuse and other forms of violence were profiled in an award-winning 1999 Arts & Entertainment Network documentary entitled *The Cruelty Connection*, and in 2008 he received a Public Service Award from the United States' Attorney's Office for his assistance in the Michael Vick dogfighting case.

Dr. Lockwood is a member of the American Academy of Forensic Sciences, a founding member of the International Veterinary Forensic Sciences Association, and a member of the Advisory Board of the National Center for the Prosecution of Animal Abuse and the Association of Prosecuting Attorneys. He is a Fellow of the Oxford Center for Animal Ethics and the Denver University Center for Human-Animal Interaction and Affiliate Assistant Professor, Small Animal Clinical Sciences, at the University of Florida College of Veterinary Medicine.

John Navarro (Chapter 9) is a doctoral student in the criminal justice department at the University of Louisville. He graduated with a Bachelor of Arts in psychology with a minor in criminal justice sciences from Illinois State University in 2011, and subsequently a Master's of Science in criminal justice sciences in 2014. Navarro was the recipient of the Fisher Award for Outstanding Thesis for the College of Applied Sciences and Technology in 2015. His current research interests include sexual deviance, identity theft, crime mapping, and mental illness.

Gary Patronek, VMD, Ph.D. (Chapter 10), is a veterinarian and an epidemiologist. Now partly retired, he remains affiliated with Tufts University as an Adjunct Professor at the Cummings School of Veterinary Medicine, where he held the position of Director of the Center for Animals and Public Policy from 1998–2003. His interest in animal hoarding stems from his experience as a shelter director supervising and participating in the investigation of reports of animal cruelty, especially cases of what was then called 'animal collecting' by the animal welfare community. A major portion of his research at Tufts involved a long-term collaboration with an interdisciplinary research group, the Hoarding of Animals Research Consortium (HARC), which he founded. Their body of work over more than a decade became instrumental in the mention of animal hoarding under the new [object] hoarding disorder first listed in DSM-5 in 2013. He has published numerous papers and textbook chapters and lectured internationally on the subject of animal hoarding. More recently, he was one of three editors, as well as a contributor, to the first book about the forensic evaluation of animal maltreatment offenders. He currently works as an independent researcher and consultant.

Elizabeth B. Perkins (Chapter 11) is a professor of criminology & criminal justice in the Department of Sociology, Social Work, and Criminology at Morehead State University. She received her doctorate in sociology from the University of Kentucky in 2010. Her most recent publications appear in *Criminology and Public Policy*, *International Journal of Offender Therapy & Comparative Criminology*, *The International Journal of Mental Health and Addiction*, *Journal of Psychoactive Drugs*, *The Journal of Social Service Research*, *Journal of Offender Rehabilitation*, *Police Forum*, and *Journal of Addiction Medicine*. Her research interests include policing, compassion fatigue, animal-human relations, terrorism, substance abuse, criminal justice organizations, and qualitative research methods.

Dr. Bethanie A. Poe, LMSW (Chapter 7), is the Veterinary Social Work Certificate Programs Coordinator and the Middle Tennessee HABIT Coordinator at the University of Tennessee, Knoxville. She has over a decade of experience in the field of interpersonal violence including working in domestic violence shelter, child protection, and with batterers' intervention programs, as well as in mental health education. Her areas of interest include cross-reporting, animal assisted interventions, and mental health education and communication.

Jacqueline Privett (Chapter 9) has a bachelor's degree in biology-zoology from Illinois State University. She is currently enrolled in a master's program from Miami University of Ohio, called Project Dragonfly's Advanced Inquiry Program. She is passionate about wildlife conservation and sustainability and hopes to work alongside animals in the future. After taking a course in eco-justice and completing an independent research paper and poster on the illegal trade and wildlife trafficking of elephants, Jacqueline dreams of working against that illegal trading to protect wildlife.

Dr. Mary Lou Randour (Chapter 16), a psychologist, is Senior Advisor, Animal Cruelty Programs and Training for the Animal Welfare Institute. In that role, she identifies programs, policy, and research projects—and builds coalitions to support them—on the topic of animal abuse and human violence. She was a practicing clinician for 17 years, and received post-graduate training at the Cambridge Hospital at Harvard Medical School and the Washington Psychoanalytic Institute. She is the organizer and past chair of the Section on Human Animal Interaction, Society of Counseling Psychology, American Psychological Association. Dr. Randour initiated the successful effort to have the Federal Bureau of Investigation add animal cruelty crimes as a separate category to the National Incident Based Reporting System, the agency's national database of crime statistics. Since then she has authored published papers on the analysis of NIBRS data as well as other topics related to the link between animal cruelty crimes and interpersonal violence.

Cassandra L. Reyes, Ph.D. (Co-Editor, Chapter 8), is an Associate Professor of Criminal Justice at West Chester University of Pennsylvania. She received her doctorate in criminology at Indiana University of Pennsylvania and her dissertation was entitled, "Of fists and fangs: An exploration of the degree to which the Graduation Hypothesis predicts future adolescent delinquency and aggression," which focused on childhood animal cruelty and later delinquency. Her main teaching and research areas of interest are on the relationship between animal cruelty and other forms of delinquency and criminality, and more recently how it correlates with socioeconomic issues via the usage of the Federal Bureau of Investigation's National Incident-Based Reporting System, US Census Bureau data, and Geographic Information Systems. She has presented numerous papers on animal cruelty at local, regional, and national criminology, criminal justice, and sociology conferences. She has also authored, co-authored, and co-edited several publications on animal cruelty. In addition, she spent nearly a decade working in law enforcement as a probation officer-bilingual and a parole officer-bilingual in Camden, NJ, where she had her first encounter with dogs being trained for dog fighting. Her combined law enforcement experience and passion about animal cruelty led her to create an animal cruelty and criminal justice elective course at West Chester University for the spring 2010 semester, which she now teaches every semester. Additionally, she is a Humane Society of the United States (HSUS) Humane Policy Volunteer Leader, through which she has enhanced her animal cruelty course by incorporating priority HSUS and other anti-animal cruelty legislation to provide an opportunity for her students to learn about lobbying and meeting with their elected legislators regarding those bills. Moreover, she has provided local, regional, and national trainings for practitioners on the link between animal cruelty and the criminal justice system.

Finally, she worked as a kennel nurse for a short time at a veterinary hospital in southern New Jersey. She currently resides with her husband and their three cats who they consider their "furry kids."

Dr. Christina Risley-Curtiss (Chapter 7), an Associate Professor Emeritus of Social Work at Arizona State University, has 50+ years of practice/teaching and research experience in public health, child welfare, and animal-human relations. Her areas of research and publications are in animal-human relationships. She developed, implemented and directed the only assessment and intervention program of its kind in the country for children who are abusing animals. She was a Fellow at the Oxford Centre on Animal Ethics, a member of the National Link Coalition steering committee and the Arizona Professional Animal Cruelty Task Force. She currently is a member of the European Humane Link Coalition She has presented at numerous conferences internationally/nationally on the positive role of animals in our lives; the co-occurrence of animal and human violence and intervening with children who are abusing animals. She does hands-on rescue work including having volunteered to help animals during the Katrina rescue and continues this work in her retirement rescuing and fostering animals. She also actively advocates in her local, national and international community for the humane treatment of all animals (e.g. local TNR programs and better animal abuse laws; the Ukrainian efforts to save animals during the Russian invasion). She continues to live in a trans-species cultural space with a number of rescue cats, a rescued greyhound and a variety of wildlife.

Joan E. Schaffner, J.D. (Chapter 4), Associate Professor of Law, George Washington University Law School, B.S. mechanical engineering, J.D., University of Southern California, M.S. mechanical engineering, Massachusetts Institute of Technology. Professor Schaffner teaches Civil Procedure, Legislation and Regulation, and Sexuality and the Law. Ze has authored *Introduction to Animals and the Law* and the chapters, "Valuing Nature in Environmental Law: Lessons for Animal Law and the Valuation of Animals" in *What Can Animal Law Learn from Environmental Law?*, "Value, wild animals and law" in *Animal Welfare and International Environmental Law: From Conservation to Compassion*, and "Laws and Policy to Address the Link of Family Violence" in *The Link Between Animal Abuse and Humane Violence*. She is a co-author and editor of *A Lawyer's Guide to Dangerous Dog Issues and Litigating Animal Law Disputes: A Complete Guide for Lawyers*. Professor Schaffner is Past Chair and Newsletter Editor, ABA TIPS Animal Law Committee; Co-Chair, ABA ILS International Animal Law Committee, Founding Chair and 2015 Chair, AALS Section on Animal Law; and Fellow, Oxford Centre for Animal Ethics. She is the recipient of the ABA TIPS Andrew C. Hecker Memorial Award, the AALS Excellence in Animal Law Award: Scholarship-Teaching-Service, and the ABA TIPS Excellence in the Advancement of Animal Law Award.

Louis B. Schlesinger, Ph.D. (Chapter 14), is a Professor of Forensic Psychology, John Jay College of Criminal Justice, Diplomate in Forensic Psychology of the American Board of Professional Psychology, and Distinguished Practitioner in the National Academies of Practice. He is co-principal investigator of a major research project on extraordinary crime with the FBI Behavioral Science Unit and a regular lecturer at the FBI Behavioral Analysis Unit in Quantico. Past President of the New Jersey Psychological Association, Dr. Schlesinger was also a recipient of the American Psychological Association's Karl F. Heiser Presidential Award.

Jacqueline L. Schneider, Ph.D. (Chapter 9), is the Chair and Professor in the Department of Criminal Justice Sciences at Illinois State University, Normal, IL. She earned her doctorate from the University of Cincinnati and a master's degree in public administration from The Ohio State University. She taught and conducted research in England where her work on stolen goods has been put forward as best practice and has attracted interest by policy makers in Chilé. In addition to her many other grants, Schneider was the first recipient of the Home Office's Innovative Research Challenge Grant (UK), and she received an outstanding teaching award in the United States. Her published works include several academic papers and chapters in book. Her main research areas include stolen goods markets and the illegal trade in endangered species. Her book *Sold into Extinction: The Global Trade in Endangered Species* was named the American Society of Criminology, Division of International Criminology's Distinguished Book Award, 2012.

Dr. Tania Signal (Chapter 12) is an Associate Professor-Senior Lecturer in Psychology at Central Queensland University, Rockhampton. She is originally from New Zealand and received her PhD from the University of Waikato in 2002. Her interest in the psychological underpinning of the human-animal dynamic has resulted in over 30 peer-reviewed journal articles, several book chapters and a co-edited book (with Associate Professor Taylor). She is part of the editorial panel for a number of human-animal studies journals such as Society & Animals and Human-Animal Interaction Bulletin and regularly reviews for a number of other journals. She is also an Animals and Society Institute Charter Scholar Member and part of the Animal Ethics Education Reference Group in Queensland.

Sarah Speed Gabel (Chapter 5) is Leadership Executive Director and Senior Policy Liaison for the House Democratic Policy Committee in the Pennsylvania House of Representatives. She is also the Executive Director of the Pennsylvania Animal Response Team, a statewide nonprofit emergency response agency embedded within the Pennsylvania Emergency Management Agency. Previously, Sarah has served at the Executive Director of the Judiciary Committees of both the Pennsylvania House and Senate and as the first Pennsylvania State Director for the Humane Society of the United States.

Emily Spivak (Chapter 5) is the Senior Specialist of Federal Policy Volunteer Engagement & Recruitment with the Humane Society of the United States. She graduated with a bachelor's degree in political science and a minor in civic and community engagement at Pennsylvania State University. She selected her major because of her drive to implement humane policies for all animals through the legislative process. During her college career, she interned for two PA State Senators and a federal U.S. Senator. She co-founded the Humane Society of the United States District Leader

Volunteer program in 2014, which has evolved into the Humane Policy Volunteer Leader program; this esteemed program actively engages volunteer leaders across the nation to advance federal, state and local animal protection legislation and policies.

Rochelle Stevenson, Ph.D. (Chapter 15), is an Associate Professor in Sociology at Thompson Rivers University, co-chair of CSA's Animals in Society research cluster, and faculty member with the Animal and Interpersonal Abuse Research Group (AIPARG). Coming from an academic background in criminology, the majority of her research is centered at the intersection of interpersonal violence and violence against animals. Her research includes examining the avenues available to women who want to leave an abusive relationship but do not want to leave their companion animal in a situation of potential harm, to national surveys of both residents of domestic violence shelters and shelter staff on the issue of animal abuse and mistreatment. Her research projects have also approached the issue of interpersonal violence from a different perspective: that of men who had committed abuse against their partner. Her work maintains an intersectional and anti-oppression foundation, that violence in any form needs to be named, understood, and stopped.

Rev. Dr. Elizabeth B. Strand (Chapter 7) is a Clinical Associate Professor and the Founding Director of Veterinary Social Work (VSW) at the University of Tennessee College of Veterinary Medicine and College of Social Work. She is a licensed clinical social worker, experienced family therapist, grief recovery specialist, and a mindfulness-based stress reduction teacher. She also is trained as a Rule 31 mediator, Anicare animal abuse treatment counselor and trainer, a compassion fatigue specialist and holds a Ph.D. in social work. She is also an ordained Interfaith Minister. Her interest-areas include the link between human and animal violence, animals in family systems, communication skills, conflict resolution and stress management in animal welfare environments, and the scholarly and practice development of veterinary social work. Her personal and professional mission is to encourage the humane treatment of both people and animals.

Suzanne E. Tallichet (Chapter 11) is a Professor of Sociology and Graduate Program Coordinator in the Department of Sociology, Social Work, and Criminology at Morehead State University. She received her doctorate in rural sociology from the Pennsylvania State University in 1991. Her publications about human-animal relations, particularly the link between animal abuse and human violence, appear in the *International Journal of Offender Therapy and Comparative Criminology, Journal of Interpersonal Violence, Criminal Justice Studies, Criminal Justice Review and Society & Animals*. Her research interests broadly include animals and society, environmental sociology, and regional studies with specific interest in compassion fatigue among shelter workers and human-wildlife encounters.

Associate Professor Nik Taylor (Chapter 12) is a sociologist who has been researching human-animal relations for over 15 years. She has published 4 books and over 40 journal articles and book chapters on the human-pet bond; treatment of animals and animal welfare; links between human aggression and animal cruelty; slaughterhouses;

meat-eating; and animal shelter work. Her most recent books include *The Rise of Critical Animal Studies* (ed., with Richard Twine, Routledge, 2014), *Humans, Animals and Society* (Lantern Books, 2013) and *Animals at Work* (with Lindsay Hamilton, Brill Academic, 2013). She is the managing editor of *Society & Animals*; a charter scholar of the Animals and Society Institute, a member of the ASI's Human-Animal Studies Executive Committee and sits on the Board of the International Society for Anthrozoology.

Rachel Touroo, DVM (Chapter 6), joined the ASPCA in March 2012 as the director of its Veterinary Forensics program and is currently the Senior Director of Veterinary Forensics. In this role she oversees the ASPCA Veterinary Forensic Science Center, assists law enforcement with animal cruelty cases throughout the United States, develops and carries out novel research in the area of veterinary forensics, and teaches Veterinary Forensic Medicine at the University of Florida, College of Veterinary Medicine and Veterinary Medicolegal Investigations for Florida International University, where she holds courtesy faculty appointments. Dr. Touroo has assisted with hundreds of animal cruelty cases throughout the U.S. and has been qualified as an expert witness on dozens of occasions in a variety of states, as well as in federal court. She is a Past President of the International Veterinary Forensic Sciences Association, a member of the ASB Crime Scene Investigations Consensus Body and active affiliate member of the Organization of Scientific Area Committees for Forensic Science, Crime Scene Investigations subcommittee. Dr. Touroo is an associate editor for *Forensic Science International: Animals and Environments*.

Caleb Trentham (Chapter 11) received his B.S. in criminal justice from the University of Tennessee at Chattanooga (UTC). He is currently working on his M.S.C.J. at UTC. He served in the U.S. Marine Corps.

Kristen Tullo (Chapter 5) is the Pennsylvania State Director with the Humane Society of the United States. She graduated with a master's degree in community psychology at Pennsylvania State University focusing her attention on animal welfare initiatives. She was an active participation in the campaign to secure passage of House Bill 1238, which incorporated Libre's Law, and was instrumental in the formation of Pennsylvania's bipartisan and bicameral Animal Protection Caucus.

Antonio R. Verbora (Chapter 15) is an instructor in the Department of Sociology and Criminology at the University of Windsor in Ontario, Canada. His graduate thesis examined the politics of animal anti-cruelty legislation in Canada. Using official transcripts of Canadian parliamentary debates, his study analyzed fifteen bills introduced to the House and Senate from 1999 to 2012. Among other things, the findings indicated that while there has been modest progress in the form of numerous attempts to improve the legal protections afforded to animals in Canada, political resistance from the Conservative Party and animal-use industries has been, and will likely continue to be, significant enough to circumvent real legal changes to the status of animals in Canada. He has published articles in education, green criminology, environmental criminology, and cybercrime and teaches courses in policing and security in Canada.

Index

Page numbers followed by an "f" indicate a figure; those by a "t," a table.

B

E

F

G

H

I

J

N

O

P

T

U

V

W